THE NEW INTERNATIONAL
WEBSTER'S
STANDARD
SPANISH

TRIDENT REFERENCE PUBLISHING

2006 EDITION

THE NEW INTERNATIONAL
WEBSTER'S STANDARD SPANISH

▲

Published by

TRIDENT REFERENCE PUBLISHING

SPANISH PRONUNCIATION

The Spanish alphabet has twenty–eight letters. Note that ch, ll, and ñ are considered to be separate single letters and are so treated in the alphabetization of Spanish words. While rr is considered to be a distinct sign for a particular sound, it is not included in the alphabet and except in syllabification (notably for the division of words at the end of a line) is not treated as a separate letter, perhaps because words never begin with it.

Letter	Name	Sound
a	a	Like **a** in English **father**, e.g. **casa**, **fácil**.
b	be	When initial or preceded by **m**, like **b** in English **book**, e.g., **boca**, **combate**. When standing between two vowels and when preceded by a vowel and followed by **l** or **r**, like **b** in English **voodoo** except that it is formed with both lips, e.g., **saber**, **hablar**, **sobre**. It is generally silent before **s** plus a consonant and often dropped in spelling, e.g., **oscure** for **obscuro**.
c	ce	When followed by **e** or **i**, like **th** in English **think** in Castilian, and like **c** in English **cent** in American Spanish, e.g., **acento**, **cinco**. When followed by **a**, **o**, **u**, or a consonant, like c in English **come**, e.g., **cantar**, **como**, **cubo**, **acto**, **creer**.
ch	che	Like **ch** in English **much**, e.g., **escuchar**
d	de	Generally, like **d** in English **dog**, e.g., **diente**, **rendir**. When standing between two vowels, when preceded by a vowel and followed by **r**, and when final, like **th** in English **this**, e.g., **miedo**, **piedra**, **libertad**.
e	e	At the end of a syllable, like **a** in English **fate**, but without the glide the English sound sometimes has, e.g., **beso**, **menos**. When followed by a consonant in the same syllable, like **e** in English **met**, e.g., **perla**, **selva**.
f	efe	Like **f** in English **five**, e.g., **flor**, **efecto**.

Letter	Name	Sound
g	ge	When followed by **e** or **i**, like **h** in English home, e.g., **gente**, **giro**. When followed by **a**, **o**, **u**, or a consonant, like **g** in English **go**, e.g., **gato**, **gota**, **agudo**, **grande**.
h	hache	Always silent, e.g., **hombre**, **alcohol**.
i	i	Like **i** in English machine, e.g., **comain**, **ida**. When preceded or followed by another vowel, it has the sound of English **y**, e.g., **tierra**, **reina**.
j	jota	Like **h** in English **home**, e.g., **jardín**, **junto**.
k	ka	Like English **k**, e.g., **kilociclo**.
l	ele	Like **l** in English **laugh**, e.g., **lado**, **ala**.
ll	elle	Somewhat like **lli** in William in Castilian and like **y** in English **yes** in American Spanish, e.g., **silla**, **llamar**.
m	eme	Like **m** in English man, e.g. **mesa**, **amar**.
n	ene	Generally, like **n** in English **name**, e.g., **andar**, **nube**. Before **v**, like **m** in English **man**, e.g., **invierno**, **enviar**. Before **c** (k) and **g** (g), like **n** in English **drink**, e.g., **finca**, **manga**.
ñ	eñe	Somewhat like **ni** in English **onion**, e.g., **año**, **enseñar**.
o	o	At the end of a syllable, like **o** in English **note**, but without the glide the English sound sometimes has, e.g., **boca**, **como**. When followed by a consonant in the same syllable, like **o** in English **organ**, e.g., **poste**, **norte**.
p	pe	Like **p** in English **pen**, e.g., **poco**, **aplicar**. It is often silent in **septiembre** and **séptimo**.
q	cu	Like **c** in English **come**. It is always followed by **ue** or **ui**, in which the **u** is silent, e.g., **querer**, **quitar**. The sound of English **qu** is represented in Spanish by **cu**, e.g., **frecuente**.

Letter	Name	Sound
r	ere	Strongly trilled when initial and when preceded by **l**, **n**, or **s**, e.g., **rico**, **alrededor**, **honra**, **israelí**. Pronounced with a single tap of the tongue in all other positions, e.g., **caro**, **grande**, **amar**.
rr	erre	Strongly trilled, e.g., **carro**, **tierra**.
s	ese	Generally, like **s** in English **say**, e.g., **servir**, **casa**, **este**. Before a voiced consonant (**b**, **d**, **g** (g), **l**, **r**, **m**, **n**), like **z** in English **zero**, e.g., **esbelto**, **desde**, **rasgar**, **eslabón**, **mismo**, **asno**.
t	te	Like **t** in English **stamp**, e.g., **tiempo**, **matar**.
u	u	Like **u** in English **rude**, e.g., **mudo**, **puño**. It is silent in **gue**, **gui**, **que**, and **qui**, but not in **güe**, and **güi**, e.g., **guerra**, **guisa**, **querer**, **quitar**, but **agüero**, **lingüistico**. When preceded or followed by another vowel, it has the sound of English **w**, e.g., **fuego**, **deuda**.
v	ve *or* uve	Like Spanish in all positions, e.g., **vengo**, **invierno**, **uva**, **huevo**.
x	equis	When followed by a consonant, like **s** in English **say**, e.g., **expresar**, **sexto**. Between two vowels, pronounced like **gs**, e.g., **examen**, **existencia**, **exótico**; and in some words, like **s** in **say**, e.g., **auxilio**, **exacto**. In **México** (for **Méjico**), like Spanish **j**.
y	ye *or* i griega	In the conjunction **y**, like **i** in English **machine**. When standing next to a vowel or between two vowels, like **y** in English **yes**, e.g., **yo**, **hoy**, **vaya**.
z	zeda *or* zeta	Like **th** in English **think** in Castilian and like **c** in English **cent** in American Spanish, e.g., **zapato**, **zona**.

Diphthong	Sound
ai, ay	Like **i** in English **might**, e.g., **baile**, **hay**
au	Like **ou** in English **pound**, e.g., **causa**
ei, ey	Like **ey** in English **they**, e.g., **reina**, **ley**
eu	Like **ayw** in English **hayward**, e.g., **deuda**
oi, oy	Like **oy** in English **boy**, e.g., **estoy**

SPANISH GRAMMAR

Stress, Punctuation, Capitalization

All Spanish words, except compound words and adverbs ending in **mente**, have only one stress. The position of this stress is always shown by the spelling in accordance with the following rules:

(a) Words ending in a vowel sound or in **n** or **s** are stressed on the syllable next to the last, e.g., **ca´sa**, **a´gua**, **se´rio**, **ha´blan**, **co´sas**.

(b) Words ending in a consonant except **n** or **s** are stressed on the last syllable, e.g., **se-ñor´**, **pa-pel´**, **fe-liz´**, **U-ra-guay´**, **es-toy´**.

(c) If the stress does not fall in accordance with either of the above rules, it is indicated by an acute accent placed above the stressed vowel, e.g., **ca-fé**, **a-pren-dí**, **na-ción**, **lá-piz**, **fá-cil**, **re-pú-bli-ca**. The acute accent is also used to distinguish between words spelled alike but having different meanings or parts of speech, e.g. **aun** (even) and **aún** (still, yet), **donde** (conj.) and **dónde** (adv.), **el** (def. art.) and **él** (pron.).

Question marks and exclamation points are placed both before and after a word or sentence, and the first is inverted, e.g. **¿Que tal?** (How's everything?), **¡Que lástima!** (What a pity!).

Capital letters are used less in Spanish than in English, e.g., **un inglés** (an Englishman), **el idioma español** (the Spanish language), **domingo** (Sunday), **enero** (January).

Gender of Nouns

A noun is either masculine or feminine. With few exceptions, nouns ending in **o** are masculine, e.g., **el libro** (the book); and nouns ending in **a**, **d**, and **ez** are feminine, e.g., **la ventana** (the window), **la ciudad** (the town), **la nuez** (the nut). There are no definitive rules for nouns that end in letters other than **o**, **a**, **d**, or **ez**.

Plural of Nouns

The plural of a noun is formed by adding **s** to those ending in an unstressed vowel or a stressed **é**; and **es** to those ending in a consonant. Nouns that end in **es** or representing a family name remain unchanged from the singular.

Definite Articles

The definite article corresponds to the gender of the noun it specifies.

The singulars of the definite article are **el** (masculine) and **la** (feminine). Plurals are **los** (masculine) and **las** (feminine).

The definite article is omitted before nouns in apposition, e.g., **Madrid, capital de España** (Madrid, the capital of Spain), and in the numbered names of rulers and popes, e.g., **Luis catorce** (Louis the Fourteenth).

Indefinite Articles

The singulars of the indefinite article are **un** (masculine) and **una** (feminine); the plurals are **unos** (masculine) and **unas** (feminine), e.g. **un mes** (a month), **unos meses** (some months); **una calle** (a street), **unas calles** (some streets).

The form **un** is also commonly used before feminine singular nouns beginning with a stressed **a** or **ha**, e.g., **un arma** (a weapon).

The plural forms **unos** and **unas** when followed by a cardinal number, mean *about*, e.g., **unos cinco años** (about five years).

The indefinite article is not used before a noun of nationality, religion, occupation, and the like, e.g., **Mi amigo es abogado** (My friend is a lawyer). If the noun is modified, the indefinite article is generally used, e.g., **Mi hermano es un abogado excelente** (My brother is an excellent lawyer). The indefinite article is omitted before **otro**, which therefore means both *other* and *another*, e.g., **Quiero otro libro** (I want another book).

Gender of Adjectives

Adjectives agree in gender and number with the noun they modify.

Adjectives ending in **o** become feminine by changing **o** to **a**, e.g., **alto** and **alta** (high). Adjectives ending in any other letter have the same form in the masculine and the feminine, e.g., **constante** (constant), **fácil** (easy), **belga** (Belgian), except adjectives of nationality ending in **l**, **s**, or **z** and adjectives ending in **or**, **án** and **ón**, which add **a** to form the feminine, e.g.,

español and **española** (Spanish), **inglés** and **inglesa** (English), **conservador** and **conservadora** (preservative), **barrigón** and **barrigona** (big–bellied).

Comparatives ending in **or** have the same form in the masculine and the feminine, e.g., **mejor** (better), **superior** (upper, superior).

Plural of Adjectives

Adjectives ending in a vowel form their plurals by adding **s**, e.g., **alto** and **altos**, **alta** and **altas** (high), **constante** and **constantes** (constant).

Adjective ending in a consonant form their plurals by adding **es**, e.g., **fácil** and **fáciles** (easy), **barrigón** and **barrigones** (big–bellied). Those ending in **z** change the **z** to **c** and add **es**, e.g., **feliz** and **felices** (happy).

The acute accent found on the last syllable of the masculine singular of some adjectives ending in **n** and **s** is omitted in the feminine singular and in the plural, e.g., **inglés** and **inglesa**, *pl.* **ingleses** (English).

Position of Adjectives

Adjectives generally follow the nouns they modify, e.g., **vino italiano** (Italian wine). However, they precede the noun they modify when used in a figurative, derived or unemphatic sense, e.g., **pobre hombre** (poor or pitiable man), but **un hombre pobre** (a poor man), **cierta ciudad** (a certain city), but **cosa cierta** (sure thing).

Shortening of Adjectives

When **bueno** (good), **malo** (bad), **primero** (first), **tercero** (third), **alguno** (some, any), and **ninguno** (none, no) are used before a masculine singular noun, they drop their final **o**, e.g., **buen libro** (good book), **mal olor** (bad odor), **primer capítulo** (first chapter), **algun muchacho** (some boy), **ningun soldado** (no soldier).

When **grande** (large, great) is used before a masculine or feminine singular noun, it drops **de**, e.g., **gran nación** (great nation). If the noun begins with a vowel or **h**, either **gran** or **grande** may be used, e.g., **grande amigo** or **gran amigo** (great friend).

Ciento (hundred) drops **to** before a noun, e.g., **cien años** (a hundred years), **cien dólares** (a hundred dollars).

The masculine **santo** (saint) becomes **san** before all names of saints except **Domingo** and **Tomás**, e.g., **San Francisco** (Saint Francis). Before common nouns it is not shortened, e.g., **el santo papa** (the Holy Father).

Formation of Adverbs

Adverbs are formed from adjectives by adding **mente** to the feminine form, e.g., **perfecto** (perfect), **perfectamente** (perfectly); **fácil** (easy), **fácilmente** (easily); **constante** (constant), **constantemente** (constantly). With two or more such adverbs in a series, **mente** is added only to the last one, e.g., **Escribe clara y correctamente** (He writes clearly and correctly).

Comparison of Adverbs

As with adjectives, the comparative and superlative of an adverb is formed by placing **más** (more) or **menos** (less) before the adverb, e.g., **despacio** (slowly), **más despacio** (more slowly).

The following adverbs have irregular comparatives and superlatives:

Positive	Comparative and Superlative
bien (well)	**mejor** (better, best)
mal (bad, badly)	**peor** (worse, worst)
mucho (much)	**más** (more, most)
poco (little)	**menos** (less, least)

Subject Pronouns

	Singular	Plural
1st person	**yo** (I)	**nosotros**, **nosotras** (we)
2nd person (familiar)	**tu** (thou, you)	**vosotros**, **vosotras** (you)
2nd person (formal)	**usted** (you)	**ustedes** (you)
3rd person masculine	**él** (he, it)	**ellos** (they)
3rd person feminine	**ella** (she, it)	**ellas** (they)
3rd person neuter	**ello** (it)	

With the exception of **usted** and **ustedes**, which are regularly expressed, these pronouns are used only for emphasis, for contrast, or to avoid ambiguity, and when no verb is expressed, e.g., **Yo trabajo mucho** (*I* work hard), **Él es aplicado pero ella es perezosa** (He is diligent, but she is lazy), **¿Quién llama? Yo** (Who is calling? I or me).

When the 3rd person subject is not a person, it is rarely expressed by a pronoun, e.g., **es larga** ((it) is long) and it is never expressed with impersonal verbs, e.g., **llueve** ((it is) raining).

The adjective **mismo**, *fem.* **misma** (self) is used with the subject pronouns to form the intensive subject pronoun, e.g., **yo mismo**, **yo misma** (I myself); **tú** (or **usted**) **mismo**, **tú** (or **usted**) **misma** (you yourself); **él mismo** (he himself), **ella misma** (she herself), **nosotros mismos**, **nosotros mismas** (we ourselves), **vosotros mismos**, **vosotros mismas** (you yourselves), **ellos mismos**, *fem.* **ellas mismas** (they themselves), **ustedes mismos**, **ustedes mismas** (you yourselves).

Prepositional Pronouns

	Singular	Plural
1st person	**mí** (me)	**nosotros**, **nosotras** (us)
2nd person (familiar)	**ti** (thee, you)	**vosotros**, **vosotras** (you)
2nd person (formal)	**usted** (you)	**ustedes** (you)
3rd person masculine	**él** (him, it)	**ellos** (them)
3rd person feminine	**ella** (her, it)	**ellas** (them)
3rd person neuter	**ello** (it)	
3rd person reflexive	**sí** (himself, herself, itself)	**sí** (themselves, yourselves, yourself)

These pronouns are used as objects of prepositions, e.g., **Compró un libro para mi** (He bought a book for me), **Compró un libro para sí** (He bought a book for himself), **Vd. compró un libro para sí** (You bought a book for yourself).

Relative Pronouns

The form **que**, meaning *that, which, who, whom*, is the most frequent relative pronoun and is invariable. It is used as both subject and object of the verb and refers to persons and things. For example, **El hombre que me conoce**... (The man *who* knows me...), **El hombre que conozco**... (The man *whom* I know...), **El libro que lee**... (The book *that* he is reading...), **El trabajo a que dedico mi tiempo**... (The work to *which* I devote my time...).

The form **quien**, *pl.* **quenes** (who, whom) is inflected for number, refers only to persons, and takes the personal **a** as direct object, e.g. **El amigo con quien viajé por España**... (The friend with *whom* I traveled in Spain...), **La señora a quien ví en la estación**... (The lady *whom* I saw at the station), **Los señores para quienes he traido estos libros**... (The gentlemen for *whom* I brought these books...).

The forms **el que** (*fem.* **la que**, *pl.* **los que**, **las que**) and **el cual** (*fem.* **la cual**, *pl.* **los cuales**, **las cuales**), both meaning *who, which, that*, agree in gender and number with their antecedent and are therefore used to replace **que** where the reference might be ambiguous, e.g., **El hijo de aquella señora, el cual vive en Nueva York**... (the son of that lady who (i.e., the son) lives in New York).

The forms **lo que** and **lo cual**, both meaning *what, which*, are invariable and refer to a previous statement, e.g., **No entiendo lo que él dice** (I don't understand what he is saying), **Llegó a medianoche, lo que indicaba que habia trabajado mucho** (He arrived at midnight, which indicated that he had worked hard.

The form **cuanto** (*fem.* **cuanta**, *pl.* **cuantos**, **cuantas**) contains its own antecedent and it means *all that which, all those which, all those who* or *whom, as much as, as many as.* For example, **Eso es cuanto quiero decir** (This is all that I want to say), **Dijo algo a cuantas personas se hallaban alli** (He said something to all the people who were there).

Regular Verbs

Spanish verbs are classified into three conjugations: those ending in **ar**, those ending in **er**, and those ending in **ir**, e.g., **hablar, comer, vivir**

First Conjugation	Second Conjugation	Third Conjugation
	Infinitive:	
hablar to speak	**comer** to eat	**vivir** to live
	Gerund:	
hablando speaking	**comiendo** eating	**viviendo** living
	Past Participle:	
hablado spoken	**comido** eaten	**vivido** lived
	Indicative:	
Present:		
hablo I speak	**como** I eat	**vivo** I live
hablas	**comes**	**vives**
habla	**come**	**vive**
hablamos	**comemos**	**vivimos**
habláis	**coméis**	**vivís**
hablan	**comen**	**viven**

First Conjugation	Second Conjugation	Third Conjugation
Imperfect:		
hablaba I was speaking	**comía** I was eating	**vivía** I was living
hablabas	**comías**	**vivías**
hablaba	**comía**	**vivía**
hablábamos	**comíamos**	**vivíamos**
hablabals	**comíais**	**vivíais**
hablaban	**comían**	**vivían**
Preterit:		
hablé I spoke	**comí** I ate	**viví** I lived
hablaste	**comiste**	**viviste**
habló	**comió**	**vivió**
hablamos	**comimos**	**vivimos**
hablasteis	**comisteis**	**vivisteis**
hablaron	**comieron**	**vivieron**
Future:		
hablaré I shall speak	**comeré** I shall eat	**viviré** I shall live
hablarás	**comerás**	**vivirás**
hablará	**comerá**	**vivirá**
hablaremos	**comeremos**	**viviremos**
hablaréis	**comeréis**	**viviréis**
hablarán	**comerán**	**vivirán**
Conditional:		
hablaría I should speak	**comería** I should eat	**viviría** I should live
hablarías	**comerías**	**vivirías**
hablaría	**comería**	**viviría**
hablaríamos	**comeríamos**	**viviríamos**
hablaríais	**comeríais**	**viviríais**
hablarían	**comerían**	**vivirían**

Irregular Verbs

All simple tenses are shown in these tables if they contain one irregular form or more, except the conditional, and the imperfect and future subjunctive.

The letters (a) to (h) identify the tenses as follows:

(a) gerund   (e) present subjunctive
(b) past participle   (f) imperfect indicative
(c) imperative   (g) future indicative
(d) present indicative   (h) preterit indicative

abolir: defective verb used only in forms whose endings contain the vowel **i**.

acertar
(c) **acierta**, acertad
(d) **acierto**, **aciertas**, **acierta**, acertamos, acertáis, **aciertan**
(e) **acierte**, **aciertes**, **acierte**, acertemos, acertéis, **acierten**

agorar
(c) **agüera**, agorad
(d) **agüero**, **agüeras**, **agüera**, agoramos, agoráis, **agüeran**
(e) **agüere**, **agüeres**, **agüere**, agoremos, agoréis, **agüeren**

airar
(c) **aíra**, airad
(d) **aíro**, **aíras**, **aíra**, airamos, airáis, **aíran**
(e) **aíre**, **aíres**, **aíre**, airemos, airéis, **aíren**

andar
(h) **anduve, anduviste, anduvo, anduvimos, anduvisteis, anduvieron**

argüir
(a) **arguyendo**
(b) **argüido**
(c) **arguye**, argüid
(d) **arguyo**, **arguyes**, **arguye**, argüimos, argüis, **arguyen**
(e) **arguya**, **arguyas**, **arguya**, arguyamos, arguyáis, **arguyan**
(h) **argüí**, **argüiste**, **arguyó**, argüimos, argüisteis, **arguyeron**

asir
(d) **asgo**, ases, ase, asimos, asis, asen
(e) **asga**, **asgas**, **asga**, **asgamos**, **asgáis**, **asgan**

aunar
(c) **aúna**, aunad
(d) **aúno**, **aúnas**, aunamos, aunáis, **aúnan**
(e) **aúne**, **aúnes**, aunemos, aunéis, **aúnen**

avongonzar
- (c) **avergüenza**, avergonzad
- (d) **avergüenzo**, **avergüenzas**, **avergüenza**, avergonzamos, avergonzáis, **avergüenzan**
- (e) **avergüence**, **avergüences**, **avergüence**, **avergoncemos**, **avergoncéis**, **avergüencen**
- (h) **avergonce**, avergonzaste, avergonzó, avergonzamos, avergonzasteis, avergonzaron

averiguar
- (e) **averigüe**, **averigües**, **averigüe**, **averigüeis**, **averigüen**
- (h) **averigüé**, averiguaste, averiguó, averiguamos, averiguasteis, averiguaron

bendecir
- (a) **bendiciendo**
- (c) **bendice**, bendecid
- (d) **bendigo**, **bendices**, **bendice**, bendecimos, bendecís, **bendicen**
- (e) **bendiga**, **bendigas**, **bendiga**, **bendigamos**, bendígáis, **bendigan**
- (h) **bendije**, **bendijiste**, **bendijo**, **bendijimos**, **bendijisteis**, **bendijeron**

bruñir
- (a) **bruñendo**
- (h) **bruñí**, **bruñiste**, **bruñó**, bruñimos, bruñisteis, **bruñeron**

bullir
- (a) **bullendo**
- (h) **bullí**, **bulliste**, **bulló**, bullimos, bullisteis, **bulleron**

caber
- (d) **quepo**, cabes, cabe, cabemos, cabéis, caben
- (e) **quepa**, **quepas**, **quepa**, **quepamos**, **quepáis**, **quepan**
- (g) **cabré**, **cabrás**, **cabrá**, **cabremos**, **cabréis**, **cabrán**
- (h) **cupe**, **cupiste**, **cupo**, **cupimos**, **cupisteis**, **cupieron**

caer
- (a) **cayendo**
- (b) **caido**
- (d) **caigo**, caes, cae, caemos, caéis, caen
- (e) **caiga**, **caigas**, **caiga**, **caigamos**, **caigáis**, **caigan**
- (h) caí, **caíste**, **cayó**, **caímos**, **caísteis**, **cayeron**

cocer
- (c) **cuece**, coced
- (d) **cuezo**, **cueces**, **cuece**, cocemos, cocéis, **cuecen**
- (e) **cueza**, **cuezas**, **cueza**, **cozamos**, **cozáis**, **cuezan**

coger
- (d) **cojo**, coges, coge, cogemos, cogéis, cogen
- (e) **coja, cojas, coja, cojamos, cojáis, cojan**

comenzar
- (c) **comienza**, comenzad
- (d) **comienzo, comienzas, comienza**, comenzamos, comenzáis, **comienzan**
- (e) **comience, comiences, comience, comencemos, comencéis, comiencen**
- (h) **comencé**, comenzaste, comenzó, comenzamos, comenzasteis, comenzaron

conducir
- (d) **conduzco**, conduces, conduce, conducimos, conducis, conducen
- (e) **conduzca, conduzcas, conduzca, conduzcamos, conduzcáis, conduzcan**
- (h) **conduje, condujiste, condujo, condujimos, condujisteis, condujeron**

construir
- (a) **construyendo**
- (b) **construído**
- (c) **construye**, construid
- (d) **construyo, construyes, construye**, construimos, construis, **construyen**
- (e) **construya, construyas, construya, construyamos, construyáis, construyan**
- (h) construi, construiste, **construyó**, construimos, construisteis, **construyeron**

continuar
- (c) **continúa**, continuad
- (d) **continúo, continúas, continúa**, continuamos, continuáis, **continúan**
- (e) **continúe, continúes, continúe**, continuemos, continuéis, **continúen**

crecer
- (d) **crezco**, creces, crece, crecemos, crecéis, crecen
- (e) **crezca, crezcas, crezca, crezcamos, crezcáis, crezcan**

dar
- (d) **doy**, das, da, damos, dais, dan
- (e) **dé**, des, **dé**, demos, deis, den
- (h) **dí, diste, dio, dimos, disteis, dieron**

decir
- (a) **diciendo**
- (b) **dicho**
- (c) **di**, decid
- (d) **digo**, **dices**, **dice**, decimos, decís, **dicen**
- (e) **diga**, **digas**, **diga**, **digamos**, **digáis**, **digan**
- (g) **diré**, **dirás**, **dirá**, **diremos**, **diréis**, **dirán**
- (h) **dije**, **dijiste,dijo**, **dijimos**, **dijisteis**, **dijeron**

delinquir
- (d) **delinco**, delinques, delinque, delinquimos, delinquis, delinquen
- (e) **delinca**, **delincas**, **delinca**, **delincamos**, **delincáis**, **delincan**

desosar
- (c) **deshuesa**, desosad
- (d) **deshueso**, **deshuesas**, **deshuesa**, desosamos, desosáis, **deshuesan**
- (e) **deshuese**, **deshueses**, **deshuese**, desosemos, desoséis, **deshuesen**

dirigir
- (d) **dirijo**, diriges, dirige, dirigimos, dirigis, dirigen
- (e) **dirija**, **dirijas**, **dirija**, **dirijamos**, **dirijáis**, **dirijan**

discernir
- (c) **discierne**, discernid
- (d) **discierno**, **disciernes**, **discierne**, discernimos, discernís, **disciernen**
- (e) **discierna**, **disciernas**, **discierna**, **discernamos**, **discernáis**, **distingan**

distinguir
- (d) **distingo**, distingues, distingue, distinguimos, distinguis, distinguen
- (e) **distinga**, **distingas**, **distinga**, **distingamos**, **distingáis**, **distingan**

dormir
- (a) **durmiendo**
- (c) **duerme**, dormid
- (d) **duermo**, **duermes**, **duerme**, dormimos, dormis, **duermen**
- (e) **duerma**, **duermas**, **duerma**, **durmamos**, **durmáis**, **duerman**
- (h) dormi, dormiste, **durmió**, dormimos, dormisteis, **durmieron**

empeller
- (a) **empellendo**
- (h) empellí, empelliste, **empelló**, empellimos, empellisteis, **empelleron**

enraizar
- (c) **enraíza**, enraizad
- (d) **enraízo**, **enraízas**, **enraíza**, enraizamos, enraizáis, **enraízan**
- (e) **enraíce**, **enraíces**, **enraíce**, **enraicemos**, **enraicéis**, **enraícen**
- (h) **enraicé**, enraizaste, enraizó, enraizamos, enraizasteis, enraizaron

erguir
- (a) **irguiendo**
- (c) **irgue** or **yergue**, erguid
- (d) **irgo**, **irgues**, **irgue**, **yergo**, **hergues**, **yergue** } erguimos, erguis { **irguen** **yerguen**
- (e) **irga**, **irgas**, **irga**, **yerga**, **yergas**, **yerga**, } **erguimos**, **erguis** { **irgan** **yergan**
- (h) erguí, erguiste, **irguió**, erguimos, erguisteis, **irguleron**

errar
- (c) **yerra**, errad
- (d) **yerro**, **yerras**, **yerra**, erramos, erráis, **yerran**
- (e) **yerre**, **yerres**, **yerre**, erremos, erréis, **yerren**

esforzar
- (c) **esfuerza**, esforzad
- (d) **esfuerzo**, **esfuerzas**, **esfuerza**, esforzamos, esforzáis, **esfuerzan**
- (e) **esfuerce**, **esfuerces**, **esfuerce**, **esforcemos**, **esforcéis**, **esfuercen**
- (h) **esforcé**, esforzaste, esforzó, esforzamos, esforzasteis, esforzaron

esparcir
- (d) **esparzo**, esparces, esparce, esparcimos, esparcís, esparcen
- (e) **esparza**, **esparzas**, **esparza**, **esparzamos**, **esparzáis**, **esparzan**

estar
- (c) **está**, estad
- (d) **estoy**, **estás**, **está**, estamos, estáis, **están**
- (e) **esté**, **estés**, **esté**, estemos, estéis, **estén**
- (h) **estuve**, **estuviste**, **estuvo**, **estuvimos**, **estuvisteis**, **estuvieron**

haber
- (c) **hé**, habed
- (d) **he, has, ha, hemos**, habéis, **han** (v. impers.), **hay**
- (e) **haya, hayas, haya, hayamos, hayáis, hayan**
- (g) **habré, habrás, habrá, habremos, habréis, habrán**
- (h) **hube, hubiste, hubo, hubimos, hubisteis, hubieron**

hacer
- (b) **hecho**
- (c) **haz**, haced
- (d) **hago**, haces, hace, hacemos, hacéis, hacen
- (e) **haga, hagas, haga, hagamos, hagáis, hagan**
- (g) **haré, harás, hará, haremos, haréis, harán**
- (h) **hice, hiciste, hizo, hicimos, hicisteis, hicieron**

inquirir
- (c) **inquiere**, inquirid
- (d) **inquiero, inquieres, inquiere**, inquirimos, inquiris, **inquieren**
- (e) **inquiera, inquieras, inquiera**, inquiramos, inquiráis, **inquieran**

ir
- (a) **yendo**
- (c) **vé, vamos**, id
- (d) **voy, vas, va, vamos, vais, van**
- (e) **vaya, vayas, vaya, vayamos, vayáis, vayan**
- (f) **iba, ibas, iba, íbamos, ibais, iban**
- (h) **fui, fuiste, fue, fuimos, fuisteis, fueron**

jugar
- (c) **juega**, jugad
- (d) **juego, juegas, juega**, jugamos, jugáis **juegan**
- (e) **juegue, juegues, juegue, juguemos, juguéis, jueguen**
- (h) **jugué**, jugaste, jugó, jugamos, jugasteis, jugaron

leer
- (a) **leyendo**
- (b) **leído**
- (h) leí, **leíste, layó, leímos, leísteis, leyeron**

ligar
- (e) **ligue, ligues, ligue, liguemos, liguéis, liguen**
- (h) **ligué**, ligaste, ligó, ligamos, ligasteis, ligaron

lucir
- (d) **luzco**, luces, luce, lucimos, lucís, lucen
- (e) **luzca, luzcas, luzca, luzcamos, luzcáis, luzcan**

mecer
(d) **mezo**, meces, mece, mecemos, mecéis, mecen
(e) **meza, mezas, meza, mezamos, mezáix, mezan**

mover
(c) **mueve**, moved
(d) **muevo, mueves, mueve**, movemos, movéis, **mueven**
(e) **mueva, muevas, mueva**, movamos, mováis, **muevan**

oir
(a) **oyendo**
(b) **oído**
(c) **oye, oíd**
(d) **oigo, oyes, oye, oímos**, oís, **oyen**
(e) **oiga, oigas, oiga, oigamos, oigáis, oigan**
(h) oí, **oíste, oyó, oímos, oísteis, oyeron**

oler
(c) **huele**, oled
(d) **huelo, hueles, huele**, olemos, oléis, **huelen**
(e) **huela, huelas, huela**, olamos, oláis, **huelan**

pedir
(a) **pidiendo**
(c) **pide**, pedid
(d) **pido, pides, pide**, pedimos, pedís, **piden**
(e) **pida, pidas, pida, pidamos, pidáis, pidan**
(h) pedí, pediste, **pidió**, pedimos, pedisteis, **pedeiron**

perder
(c) **pierde**, perded
(d) **pierdo, pierdes, pierde**, perdemos, perdéis, **pierden**
(e) **pierda, pierdas, pierda**, perdamos, perdáis, **pierdan**

placer
(d) **plazco**, places, place, placemos, placeis, placen
(e) **plazca, plazcas, plazca, plazcamos, plazcáis, plazcan**
(h) plací, placiste, plació (or **plugo**), placimos, placisteis, placieron

poder
(a) **pudiendo**
(c) (**puede**, poded)
(d) **puedo, puedes, puede**, podemos, podéis, **pueden**
(e) **pueda, puedas, pueda**, podamos, podáis, **puedan**
(g) **podré, podrás, podrá, podremos, podréis, podrán**
(h) **pude, pudiste, pudo, pudimos, pudisteis, pudieron**

poner
- (b) **puesto**
- (c) **pon**, poned
- (d) **pongo**, pones, pone, ponemos, ponéis, ponen
- (e) **ponga, pongas, ponga, pongamos, pongáis, pongan**
- (g) **pondré, pondrás, pondrá, pondremos, pondréis, pondrán**
- (h) **puse, pusiste, puso, pusimos, pusisteis, pusieron**

querer
- (c) **quiere**, quered
- (d) **quiero, quieres, quiere**, queremos, queréis, **quieren**
- (e) **quiera, quieras, quiera**, queramos, queráis, **quieran**
- (g) **querré, querrás, querrá, querremos, querréis, querrán**
- (h) **quise, quisiste, quiso, quisimos, quisisteis, quisieron**

raer
- (a) **rayendo**
- (b) **raído**
- (d) **raigo** (or **rayo**), raes, rae, raemos, raéis, raen
- (e) **raiga** (or **raya**), **raigas, raiga, raigamos, raigáis, raigan**
- (h) **raí, raíste, rayó, raímos, raísteis, rayeron**

regir
- (a) **rigiendo**
- (c) **rige**, regid
- (d) **rijo, riges, rige**, regimos, regís, **rigen**
- (e) **rija, rijas, rija, rijamos, rijáis, rijan**
- (h) regí, registe, **regió**, regimos, registeis, **rigieron**

reír
- (a) **riendo**
- (b) **reído**
- (c) **ríe, reíd**
- (d) **río, ríes, ríe, reímos**, reís, **ríen**
- (e) **ría, rías, ría, ríamos, riáis, rían**
- (h) reí, **reíste, rió, reímos, reísteis, rieron**

reunir
- (c) **reúne**, reunid
- (d) **reúno, reúnes, reúne**, reunimos, reunís, **reúnen**
- (e) **reúna, reúnas, reúna**, reunamos, reunáis, **reúnan**

rezar
- (e) **rece, reces, rece, recemos, recéis, recen**
- (h) **recé**, rezaste, rezó, rezamos, rezasteis, rezaron

rodar
  (c) **rueda**, rodad
  (d) **ruedo**, **ruedas**, **rueda**, rodamos, rodáis, **ruedan**
  (e) **ruede**, **ruedes**, **ruede**, rodemos, rodéis, **rueden**

roer
  (a) **royendo**
  (b) **roído**
  (d) **roo** (**roigo**, or **royo**), roes, roe, roemos, roéis, roen
  (e) **roa** (**roiga**, or **roya**), roas, roa, roamos, roáis, roan
  (h) roí, **roíste**, **royó**, **roímos**, **roísteis**, **royeron**

rogar
  (c) **ruega**, rogad
  (d) **ruego**, **ruegas**, **ruega**, rogamos, rogáis, **ruegan**
  (e) **ruegue**, **ruegues**, **ruegue**, **roguemos**, **roguéis**, **rueguen**
  (h) **rogué**, rogaste, rogó, rogamos, rogasteis, rogaron

saber
  (d) **sé**, sabes, sabe, sabemos, sabéis, saben
  (e) **sepa**, **sepas**, **sepa**, **sepamos**, **sepáis**, **sepan**
  (g) **sabré**, **sabrás**, **sabrá**, **sabremos**, **sabréis**, **sabrán**
  (h) **supe**, **supiste**, **supo**, **supimos**, **supisteis**, **supieron**

salir
  (c) **sal**, salid
  (d) **salgo**, sales, sale, salimos, salís, salen
  (e) **salga**, **salgas**, **salga**, **salgamos**, **salgáis**, **salgan**
  (g) **saldré**, **saldrás**, **saldrá**, **saldremos**, **saldréis**, **saldrán**

segar
  (c) **siega**, segad
  (d) **siego**, **siegas**, **siega**, segamos, segáis, **siegan**
  (e) **siegue**, **siegues**, **siegue**, **seguemos**, **seguéis**, **sieguen**
  (h) **segué**, segaste, segó, segamos, segasteis, segaron

seguir
  (a) **siguiendo**
  (c) **sigue**, seguid
  (d) **sigo**, **siegues**, **sigue**, seguimos, seguís, **siguen**
  (e) **siga**, **sigas**, **siga**, **sigamos**, **sigáis**, **sigan**
  (h) seguí, seguiste, **siguió**, seguimos, seguisteis, **siguieron**

sentir
  (a) **sintiendo**
  (c) **siente**, sentid
  (d) **siento**, **sientes**, **siente**, sentimos, sentís, **sienten**
  (e) **sienta**, **sientas**, **sienta**, sentamos, sentáis, **sientan**
  (h) sentí, sentiste, **sintió**, sentimos, sentisteis, **sintieron**

ser
  (c) **sé**, sed
  (d) **soy, eres, es, somos, sois, son**
  (e) **sea, seas, sea, seamos, seáis, sean**
  (f) **era, eras, era, éramos, erais, eran**
  (h) **fui, fuiste, fue, fuimos, fuisteis, fueron**

tañer
  (a) **tañendo**
  (h) tañí, tañiste, **tañó**, tañimos, tañisteis, **tañeron**

tener
  (c) **ten**, tened
  (d) **tengo, tienes, tiene**, tenemos, tenéis, **tienen**
  (e) **tenga, tengas, tenga, tengamos, tengáis, tengan**
  (g) **tendré, tendrás, tendrá, tendremos, tendréis, tendrán**
  (h) **tuve, tuviste, tuvo, tuvimos, tuvisteis, tuvieron**

teñir
  (a) **tiñendo**
  (c) **tiñe**, teñid
  (d) **tiño, tiñes, tiñe**, teñimos, teñis, **tiñen**
  (e) **tiña, tiñas, tiña, tiñamos, tiñáis, tiñan**
  (h) teñi, teñiste, **tiñó**, teñimos, teñisteis, **tiñeron**

tocar
  (e) **toque, toques, toque, toquemos, toquéis, toquen**
  (h) **toqué**, tocaste, tocó, tocamos, tocasteis, tocaron

torcer
  (c) **tuerce**, torced
  (d) **tuerzo, tuerces, tuerce**, torcemos, torcéis, **tuercen**
  (e) **tuerza, tuerzas, tuerza, torzamos, torzáis, tuerzan**

traer
  (a) **trayendo**
  (b) **traído**
  (d) **traigo**, traes, trae, traemos, traéis, traen
  (e) **traiga, traigas, traiga, traigamos, traigáis, traigan**
  (h) **traje, trajiste, trajo, trajimos, trajisteis, trajeron**

valer
  (d) **valgo**, vales, vale, valemos, valéis, valen
  (e) **valga, valgas, valga, valgamos, valgáis, valgan**
  (g) **valdré, valdrás, valdrá, valdremos, valdréis, valdrán**

variar
  (c) **varía**, variad
  (d) **varío, varías, varía**, variamos, variáis, **varían**
  (e) **varíe, varíes, varíe**, variemos, variéis, **varíen**

vencer
  (d) **venzo**, vences, vence, vencemos, vencéis, vencen
  (e) **venza, venzas, venza, venzamos, venzáis, venzan**

venir
  (a) **viniendo**
  (c) **ven**, venid
  (d) **vengo, vienes, viene**, venimos, venís, **vienen**
  (e) **venga, vengas, venga, vengamos, vengáis, vengan**
  (g) **vendré, vendrás, vendrá, vendremos, vendréis, vendrán**
  (h) **vine, viniste, vino, vinimos, vinisteis, vinieron**

ver
  (b) **visto**
  (d) **veo**, ves, ve, vemos, veis, ven
  (e) **vea, veas, vea, veamos, veáis, vean**
  (f) **veía, veías, veía, veíamos, veíais, veían**

volcar
  (c) **vuelca**, volcad
  (d) **vuelco, vuelcas, vuelca**, volcamos, volcáis, **vuelcan**
  (e) **vuelque, vuelques, vuelque, volquemos, volquéis,
      vuelquen**
  (h) **volqué**, volcaste, volcó, volcamos, volcasteis, volcaron

yacer
  (c) **yaz** (or yace), yaced
  (d) **yazco** (**yazgo**, or **yago**), yaces, yace, yacemos, yacéis,
      yacen
  (e) **yazca** (**yazga**, or **yaga**), **yazcas, yazca, yazcamos,
      yazcáis, yazcan**

The following verbs, some of which are included in the foregoing
table, and their compounds have irregular past participles:

abrir	cubierto	proveer	puesto
cubrir	dicho	pudrir	provisto
decir	escrito	romper	podrido
escribir	frito	solver	roto
freír	hecho	ver	suelto
hacer	impreso	volver	visto
imprimir	morir	muerto	vuelto
abierto	poner		

Notes

A

a, *prep.* to, at
abadía, *f.* abbey; abbacy
abajo, *adv.* under, below; downstairs
abanderado, *m.* (mil.) ensign; standard bearer
abandonar, *va.* to abandon
abandono, *m.* abandonment; carelessness
abanicar, *va.* to fan
abanico, *m.* fan; derrick
abarcar, *va.* to comprise
abarrotes, *m. pl.* groceries
abastecer, *va.* to supply
abatimiento, *m.* low spirits, depression
abdicar, *va.* to abdicate
abdomen, *m.* abdomen
abecé, *m.* alphabet
abecedario, *m.* alphabet
abedul, *m.* birch tree
abeja, *f.* bee
abejarrón or **abejorro,** *m.* bumblebee
abejón, *m.* drone; hornet
abertura, *f.* cleft, opening
abierto, *adj.* open; sincere
abismo, *m.* chasm, abyss
ablandar, *va., vn.* to soften
abnegar, *va.* to renounce
abochornar, *va., vr.* to shame, be embarrassed
abofetear, *va.* to slap one's face
abogacía, *f.* profession of law
abogado, *m.* lawyer; advocate
abogar, *vn.* to advocate; intercede
abolengo, *m.* ancestry
abolir, *va. def.* to abolish
abominable, *adj.* abominable
abominar, *va.* to detest
abonar, *va.* to manure; to credit with; to pay on an account; **abonarse,** to subscribe to
abono, *m.* fertilizer; payment; season ticket
abordar, *va.* to board a ship; approach (a subject)
aborrecer, *va.* to hate, abhor
abortar, *vn.* to miscarry, abort
aborto, *m.* abortion; mon-strosity
abotonar, *va.* to button
abr., abreviatura, abbr, abbreviation
abrasar, *va.* to burn; to scorch
abrazar, *va.* to embrace
abrazo, *m.* embrace, hug
abrelatas, *m.* can opener
abreviar, *va.* to abbreviate
abrevistura, *f.* abbreviation
abridor, *m.* opener; **abridor de latas,** can opener
abrigar, *va.* to shelter; **abrigarse,** to wrap, cover up
abrigo, *m.* shelter; wrap, over-coat
abril, *m.* April
abrir, *va., vr.* to open
abrochar, *va.* to hook, clasp on
abrumar, *va.* to overwhelm
absceso, *m.* abscess
absorto, *adj.* absorbed; amazed
abstemio, *adj.* abstemious; *m.* teetotaler
abstenerse, *vr.* to abstain
abstinencia, *f.* abstinence
abstracto, *adj.* abstract
abstraer, *va.* to abstract; **abstraerse,** to be lost in thought
absuelto, *adj.* absolved, ac-quitted
absurdo, *adj.* absurd; *m.* ab-surdity
abuela, *f.* grandmother
abuelo, *m.* grandfather; **abue-los,** *pl.* ancestors
abundancia, *f.* abundance
abundar, *vn.* to abound
aburrido, *adj.* bored; bore-some
aburrir, *va.* to bore; **aburrirse,** to be bored
abusar, *va., vn.* to abuse; to impose upon
abuso, *m.* abuse, misuse
a/c, a cuenta, on account, in part payment; **a cargo,** drawn on; in care of
A.C. or **A. de C., Anio de Cristo,** A.D. in the year of Our Lord
acá, *adv.* here, hither

acabar, *va., vn.* to finish, complete; to die

academia, *f.* academy

académico, *adj.* academic

acalorar, *va.* to heat; **acalorars**, to get excited, to become warm

acamper, *va.* to camp

acantonar, *va.* to quarter troops

acaparar, *va.* to monopolize

acariciar, *va.* to caress

acarrear, *va.* to transport; to occasion, cause

acarreo, *m.* cartage

acaso, *m.* chance, haphazard; **por si acaso**, just in case

acatar, *va.* to respect, obey (orders)

acatarrarse, *vr.* to catch cold

acaudalado, *adj.* rich, wealthy

acceder, *vn.* to accede, agree

accesible, *adj.* accessible

acceso, *m.* access, approach

accesorio, *adj.* accessory

accidental, *adj.* accidental

accidente *m.* accident

acción, *f.* act, action; share, stock

accionar, *vn.* to gesticulate

accionista, *m., f.* stockholder

aceitar, *va.* to oil

aceite, *m.* oil

aceituna, *f.* olive

acelerador, *m.* accelerator

acelerar, *va.* to accelerate

acento, *m.* accent

acentuar, *va.* to accentuate; to emphasize

acepción, *f.* meaning

aceptable, *adj.* acceptable

aceptación, *f.* acceptance

aceptar, *va.* to accept; to admit

acera, *f.* sidewalk

acerca de, *prep.* about

acercar, *va., vr.* to bring together; to approach

acérrimo, *adj.* very vigorous; **enemigo acérrimo**, bitter enemy

acertado, *adj.* accurate

acertar, *va.* to conjecture right

acertijo, *m.* riddle, conundrum

acicalarse, *vr.* to dress meticulously; to paint one's face

ácido, *m.* acid; *adj.* acid, sour

acierto, *m.* accuracy; ability

aclamación, acclamation

aclamar, *va.* to applaud

aclaración, *f.* explanation

aclarar, *va.* to clarify; **aclararse**, to clear up

aclimatar, *va.* to acclimatize

acne, *m.* (med.) acne

acogedor, *adj.* cozy, inviting

acoger, *va.* to receive; to protect; **acogerse**, to resort to

acogida, *f.* reception; welcome

acólito, *m.* acolyte; assistant

acometida, *f.* attack, assault

acomodado, *adj.* wealthy

acomodador, *m.* usher

acomodar, *va.* to accomodate, arrange; *vn.* to fit, suit

acompañamiento, *m.* accompaniment

acompañante, *m.* companion; accompanist

acompañar, *va.* to accompany

acongojarse, *vr.* to become sad

aconsejable, *adj.* advisable

aconsejar, *va.* to advise

acontecer, *vn. def.* to happen

acontecimiento, *m.* event, incident

acopiar, *va.* to gather, to store up

acorazado, *m.* battleship

acordar, *va.* to resolve; *vn.* to agree; **acordarse**, to remember

acorde, *m.* accord; chord

acortar, *va.* to abridge, shorten

acosar, *va.* to molest, harass

acostar, *va.* to put to bed; **acostarse**, to lie down; go to bed

acostumbrar, *va., vn.* to accustom; to be accustomed

acre, *adj.* acid; *m.* acre

acreditado, *adj.* accredited

acreditar, *va.* to assure, authorize; to credit; to accredit

acreedor, *m.* creditor; *adj.* worthy; **saldo acreedor**, credit balance

acrílico, *adj.* acrylic
acta, *f.* minutes of proceeding; **acta de venta,** bill of sale
ACTH, (med.) ACTH
actitud, *f.* attitude, posture
activar, *va.* to activate
actividad, *f.* activity; liveliness
activo *adj.* active, diligent; *m.* (com.) assets
acto, *m.* act; action
actuación, *f.* performance
actual, *adj.* actual, present
actualidad, actuality, current event
actuar, *vn.* to act
acuario, *m.* aquarium
acuático, *adj.* aquatic
acudir, *vn.* to assist, to be present; **acudir a,** to resort to
acueducto, *m.* aqueduct
acuerdo, *m.* agreement; resolution
acumulador, *m.* battery
acumular, *va.* to accumulate
acurrucarse, *vr.* to huddle
acusación, *f.* accusation
acusar, *va.* to accuse; to reproach; **acusar recibo de,** acknowledge receipt of
acusativo, *m.* accusative
acústica, *f.* acoustics
achacar, *va.* to impute, blame
achaque, *m.* ailment
achicar, *va.* to diminish; to bail a boat
adaptable, *adj.* adaptable
adaptar, *va.* to adapt
A. de J.C., antes de Jesucristo, B.C. Before Christ
adefesio, *m.* ridiculous attire
adelantado, *adj.* anticipated; **por adelantadodo,** in advance
adelantar, *va.,* *vn.* to advance; **adelantarse,** to take the lead
adelanto, *m.* progress, advance
adelgazarse, *vr.* to lose weight
ademán, *m.* gesture; attitude
además, *adv.* moreover, also; **además de,** besides
adentro, *adv.* within; inwardly
adepto, *adj.* adept; *m.* follower
adeudar, *va.* to owe

adherencia, *f.* adhesion, adherence
adherir, *vn.,* *vr.* to adhere
adhesión, *f.* adherence
adición, *f.* addition
adicto, *m.* addict; *adj.* addicted
adiós, *interj.* good-by, adieu
adivinanza, *f.* riddle
adivinar, *va.* to guess
adj., adjetivo, *adj.* adjective
adjetivo, *m.* adjective
adjuntar, *va.* to enclose, attach
administración, *f.* administration
administrar, *va.* to administer
admirable, *adj.* admirable
admiración, *f.* admiration; wonder; (gram.) exclamation point
admirar, *va.* to admire; **admirarse,** to be surprised
admisión, *f.* admission
admitir, *va.* to admit
adobar, *va.* to stew
adobo, *m.* stew
adolescencia, *f.* adolescence, youth
adolescente, *adj.,* *m.,* *f.* adolescent; bobby soxer
adonde, *adv.* whither, where
adopción, *f.* adoption
adoptar, *va.* to adopt
adoptivo, *adj.* adoptive; adopted
adormecer, *va.* to put to sleep
adornar, *va.* to embellish
adquirir, *va.* to acquire
adrede, *adv.* purposely
aduana, *f.* customhouse
adular, *va.* to flatter; to fawn
adulterar, *va.* to adulterate
adulto, *adj.* adult
adv., adverbio, *adv.* adverb
ad val., ad valórem, en proporción al valor, ad val. ad valorem, in proportion to the value
adverbio, *m.* adverb
adversario, *m.* adversary
adversidad, *f.* adversity
adverso, *adj.* adverse
advertencia, *f.* warning
advertir. *va.* to warn

aéreo, *adj.* air, aerial
aerógrafo, *m.* air brush
aeronáutica, *f.* aeronautics
aeroplano, *m.* airplane
aeropuerto, *m.* airport
afable, *adj.* affable
afamado, *adj.* famous
afán, *m.* anxiety, worry
afanarse, *vr.* to toil, labor
afección, *f.* disease
afectación, *t.* affectation
afectar, *va.* to affect
afectísimo, *adj.* devoted; yours truly
afecto, *m.* affection, love
afectuoso, *adj.* affectionate
afeitar, *va., vr.* to shave
afeminado, *adj.* effeminate
aferrado, *adj.* stubborn
afianzar, *va.* to bail, guarantee; to prop, fix
afición, *f.* preference; hobby
aficionado, **aficionada**, n. amateur
afilar, *va.* to sharpen
afiliado, *adj.* affiliated
afinar, *va.* to tune (musical instruments); to refine
afirmar, *va.* to secure, fasten; to affirm
afirmativo, *adj.* affirmative
aflicción, *f.* affliction, grief
afligirse, *vr.* to grieve
aflojar, *va.* to loosen
afmo. or **af.**mo, **afectísimo**, idiomatic expression for "Cordially yours,' etc.
afortunadamente, *adv.* fortunately, luckily
afortunado, adj. fortunate
afrenta, *f.* outrage; insult
afro, *adj.* Afro
afrontar, *va.* to confront
aftosa, *adj.* (vet.) hoof-and-mouth disease
afuera, *adv.* out, outside
afueras, *f. pl.* outskirts
ágape, *m.* banquet; testimonial dinner
agarrar, *va.* to grasp
agasajar, *va.* to entertain
agente, *m.* agent
agitado, *adj.* excited
agitar, *va.* to shake; **agitarse**, to become excited

aglomerar, *va., vr.* to conglomerate
agobiar, *va., vr.* to oppress, burden
agonía, *t.* agony, anguish
agonizar, *vn.* to be dying
agosto, *m.* August (month); harvest time
agotado, *adj.* sold out; exhausted
agotar, *va.* to exhaust; **agotarse**, to run out of
agraciado, *adj.* graceful; gifted
agradable, *adj.* pleasant
agradar, *va.* to please, gratify
agradecer, *va.* to appreciate (a favor)
agradecido, *adj.* grateful
agradecimiento, *m.* gratitude, gratefulness
agrandar, *va.* to enlarge
agrario, *adj.* agrarian
agravar, *va.* to aggravate
agraviar, *va.* to wrong; **agraviarse**, to take offense
agregar, *va.* to add
agresión, *f.* aggression
agresivo, *adj.* aggressive
agriar, *va., vr.* to sour
agrícola, *adj.* agricultural
agricultor, *m.* agriculturist, farmer
agricultura, *f.* agriculture
agridulce, *adj.* bittersweet
agrietarse, *vr.* to crack
agrimensor, *m.* land surveyor
agrio, *adj.* sour; rude
agrónomo, *m.* agronomist
agrupar, *va., vr.* to group (in a picture); to crowd
agto. or **ag.**to, **agosto**, Aug. August
agua, *f.* water, liquid; rain
aguacate, *m.* avocado, alligator pear
aguacerol, *m.* shower of rain
aguado, *adj.* watery
aguafuerte, *f.* etching
aguantar, *va.* to endure, bear
aguar, *va., vr.* to thin out with water; to spoil (a party, etc.)
aguardar, *va.* to expect, wait for
aguardiente, *m.* distilled liquor

aguarrás, *m.* turpentine

agudo, *adj.* acute; sharp-pointed

aguijón, *m.* sting of a bee, wasp, etc.; stimulation

águila, *f.* eagle

aguileño, *adj.* aquiline

aguinaldo, *m.* Christmas gift

aguja, *f.* needle; switch; **aguja de coser,** sewing needle

agujero, *m.* hole

aguzar, *va.* to whet; to stimulate

ahí, *adv.* there; **de ahí (que),** for this reason; **por ahí,** that way, more or less

ahijada, *f.* goddaughter

ahijado, *m.* godson

ahinco, *m.* zeal, earnestness

ahogar, *va., vr.* to drown; to suffocate

ahondar, *va.* to deepen; *vn.* to penetrate

ahora, *adv.* now, at present; *conj.* whether, or

ahorcar, *va., vr.* to kill by hanging

ahorita, *adv.* (Sp. Am.) just now, in just a minute

ahorrar, *va.* to save, economize

ahorro, *m.* saving, thrift

ahumar, *va.* to cure in smoke

ahuyentar, *va.* to put to flight

aire, *m.* air, wind

airear, *va.* to air, ventilate

airoso, *adj.* airy; graceful; successful

aislado, *adj.* insulated, isolated

aislador, *m.* (elec.) insulator

aislamiento, *m.* isolation; insulation; (fig.) solitude

aislar, *va.* to isolate; to insulate

ajar, *va.* to crumple

ajedrez, *m.* chess (game)

ajeno, *adj.* another's; contrary to

ají, *m.* chili pepper, chili

ajo, *m.* garlic; **¡ajo!** *interj.* darn!

ajustar, *va.* to regulate; to adjust; to tighten

ajuste, *m.* adjustment

al, contraction for **a el; al fin,** at last

ala, *f.* wing; brim of the hat

alabanza, *f.* praise, applause

alabar, *va.* to praise, extol

alabastro, *m.* alabaster; gypsum

alacena, *f.* cupboard

alacrán, *m.* scorpion

alambrado, *m.* wire fence

alambre, *m.* wire, copper wire; **alambre de púas,** barbed wire

alameda, *f.* poplar grove; tree-lined promenade

álamo, *m.* poplar, poplar tree; cottonwood tree

alarde, *m.* display; **hacer alarde,** to boast

alardear, *vn.* to brag, boast

alargar, *va.* to lengthen; to extend

alarido, *m.* outcry, howl

alarma, *f.* alarm

alarmante, *adj.* alarming

alarmar, *va., vr.* to alarm

a la v/, a la vista, (com.) at sight

alba, *f.* daybreak

albacea, *m.* executor; *f.* executrix

albañil, *m.* mason, bricklayer

albaricoque, *m.* apricot

albedrío, *m.* free will

alberca, *f.* reservoir; swimming pool

albergar, *va.* to lodge, house, harbor; **albergarse,** to take shelter

albergue, *m.* shelter

albóndiga, *f.* meat ball

alborada, *f.* early dawn; (mil.) morning watch

alborotar, *va.* to make a disturbance, stir

¡albricias! *interj.* good news!

álbum, *m.* album

albumen, *m.,* **albúmina,** *f.* albumen

alcachofa, *f.* artichoke

alcaide, *m.* jailer, warden

alcalde, *m.* mayor

alcaldía, *f.* mayor's office

alcance, *m.* reach, scope

alcancía, *f.* money box; sav-

ings bank
alcanfor, *m.* camphor
alcantarillado, *m.* sewage system
alcanzar, *va.* to overtake, to reach
alcaparra, *f.* caper
alcoba, *f.* alcove; bedroom
aidaba, *f.* knocker, door latch
aldea, *f.* village
aldeano, *m.* peasant
alegar, *va.* to allege, affirm
alegato, *m.* (law) allegation, pleading; (Sp. Am.) quarrel
alegrar, *va.* to gladden; **alegrarse,** to rejoice
alegría, *f.* mirth, cheer
alejamiento, *m.* distance, remoteness; aloofness
alejar, *va.* to remove to a greater distance; to separate; **alejarse,** to withdraw, move away
alemán, alemana, *adj., n.* German
Alemania, *f.* Germany
alentador, *adj.* encouraging
alentar, *va.* to animate; to cheer, encourage
alergeno, *m.* allergen
alergia, *f.* allergy
alerta, *adv.* vigilantly, **estar alerta,** to be alert
alerto, *adj.* alert, vigilant
aletear, *vn.* to flutter
alevosía, *f.* treachery
alfabético, *adj.* alphabetical
alfabeto, *m.* alphabet
alfiler, *m.* pin; **alfiler imperdible,** safety pin
alfiletero, *m.* pincushion
alfombra, *f.* carpet; rug
alfombrilla, (med.) measles
algarabía, *f.* clamor, din
álgebra, *f.* algebra
algo, *pron.* some, something; anything; *adv.* a little, rather
algodón, *m.* cotton
algodonero, *m.* cotton plant
alguno (algún), alguna, *pron.* somebody, someone, anyone; *adj.* some, any
alhaja, *f.* jewel, gem
aliado, *adj.* allied; *n.* ally
alianza, *f.* alliance, league

alias, *adv.* alias; otherwise
aliciente, *m.* attraction, incitement, inducement
aliento, *m.* breath; encouragement
aligerar, *va.* to lighten; to hasten
alimentación, *f.* food, nourishment, meals
alimentar, *va.* to feed, nourish
alimenticio, *adj.* nutritious
alimento, *m.* nourishment, food
alinear, *va.* to align
alistar, *va., vr.* to enlist; to get ready, make ready
aliviar, *va.* to lighten; to ease
alma, *f.* soul; heart
almacén, *m.* department store; warehouse
almacenar, *va.* to store, lay up
almanaque, *m.* almanac
almeja, *f.* clam
almendra, *f.* almond
almíbar, *m.* syrup
almidón, *m.* starch
almidonar, *va.* to starch
almirante, *m.* admiral
almohada, *f.* pillow
almohadón, *m.* large cushion
almorranas, *f. pl.* hemorrhoids, piles
almorzar, *vn.* to breakfast; to eat lunch
almuerzo, *m.* breakfast; lunch
alocado, *adj.* crack-brained
alojamiento, *m.* lodging accommodation
alojar, *va., vr.* to lodge
alondra, *f.* lark
Alpes, *m. pl.* Alps
alpiste, *m.* canary seed
alquilar, *va.* to let, hire, rent
alquiler, *m.* hire; house rent
alquitrán, *m.* tar
alrededor, *adv.* around
alrededores, *m. pl.* environs; neighborhood
alt., altitud, alt., altitude; **altura,** ht., height
alta, *f.* new member
altanero, *adj.* haughty
altar, *m.* altar
altavoz, *m.* loudspeaker
alterar, *va.* to alter, change; to

disturb; **alterarse,** to become angry

altercar, *va.* to dispute, quarrel

alternar, *va., vn.* to alternate

altiplano, *m.* high plateau

altísimo, *adj.* extremely high; **el Altísimo,** *m.* the Most High, God

altisonante, *adj.* high-sounding, pompous

altitud, *f.* altitude

altivo, *adj.* haughty, proud

alto, *adj.* high, elevated; loud; tall; *m.* height; story, floor; highland; (mil.) halt; (mus.) tenor

altoparlante, *m.* loudspeaker

altruismo, *m.* altruism

altura, *f.* height; highness; altitude; **alturas,** *pl.* the heavens

aludido, *adj.* referred to

aludir, *vn.* to allude, refer

alumbrado, *adj.* illuminated; *m.* lighting; **alumbrado fluorescente,** fluorescent lighting

alumbramiento, *m.* illumination; childbirth

alumbrar, *va.* to illuminate

alumbre, *m.* alum

aluminio, *m.* aluminum

alumno, disciple pupil

alusión, *f.* allusion, hint

alverjas, *f. pl.* peas

alza, *f.* advance in price; lift

alzar, *va.* to raise, lift up; to build; **aizarse,** to rise in rebellion

allá, *adv.* there; thither; **mas allá,** beyond

allanar, *va.* to level, flatten; to overcome (difficu lties)

allegado, *adj.* near; related; *n.* follower, ally

allí, *adv.* there, in that place

A.M., antemeridiano, A.M. or a.m., before noon

ama *f.* mistress; **ama de casa,** housewife; **ama de llaves,** housekeeper

amable, *adj.* amiable, kind

amado, n. beloved, darling

amaestrar, *va.* to teach, to train

amamantar, *va.* to suckle, nurse

amanecer, *m.* dawn, daybreak; *vn.* to dawn; to appear at daybreak

amanerado, *adj.* affected, overrefined

amansar, *va.* to tame, domesticate; to soften, pacify

amante, *m., f.* lover

amañarse, *vr.* to adapt oneself

amapola, *f.* (bot.) poppy

amar, *va.* to love

amargar, *va.* to make bitter; *vn., vr.* to be bitter

amargo, *adj.* bitter, acrid; painful

amargura, *f.* bitterness

amarillo, *adj.* yellow

amarrar, *va.* to tie, fasten

amasar, *va.* to knead

amatista, amethyst

amazona, amazon, masculine woman

ámbar, *m.* amber

Amberes, *f.* Antwerp

ambición, *f.* ambition

ambicioso, *adj.* ambitious

ambiental, *adj.* environmental; **contaminación ambiental,** environmental pollution

ambiente, *m.* environment

ambiguo, *adj.* ambiguous

ambos, *adj. pl.* both

ambulancia, *f.* ambulance

ambulante, *adj.* ambulatory; roving; **vendedor ambulante,** *adj.* peddler

amedrentar, *va.* to intimidate

amén, *m.* amen; acquiescence; **amén de,** besides; except.

amenaza, *f.* threat, menace

amenazar, *va.* to threaten

amenizar, *va.* to render pleasant; to adorn (a speech)

ameno, *adj.* pleasant, entertaining.

América del Norte, *f.* North America.

Amiérica del Sur, *f.* South America.

América Latina, *f.* Latin America.

americanismo, *m.* Americanism; an expression or word used in the Spanish of Spanish America

americano, americana, *n.,* *adj.* American

amiga, *f.* female friend

amigable, *adj.* friendly

amígdala, *f.* tonsil

amigo, amiga, n. friend.

aminoácido, *m.* amino acid.

amistad, *f.* friendship

amistoso, *adj.* friendly

amo, *m.* master, proprietor

amolar, *va.* to grind, sharpen

amoldar, *va., vr.* to mold; to adjust

amonestación, *f.* admonition; publication of marriage bans

amonestar, *va.* to admonish.

amontonar, *va.* to heap together; to accumulate

amor, *m.* love; the object of love; **por amor de,** for the sake of; **amor propio,** pride

amoroso, *adj.* affectionate

amortiguador, *m.* shock absorber

amortiguar, *va.* to mitigate; to deaden, absorb

amortizar, *va.* to amortize

amotinarse, *vr.* to mutiny

amparar, *va.* to shelter, favor, protect; **ampararse,** to claim protection

amparo, *m.* protection, help, support; refuge, asylum

amperio, *m.* (elec.) ampere

ampliación, *f.* amplification, enlargement

ampliar, *va.* to amplify; expand, increase

amplificador, *m.* amplifier

amplio, *adj.* ample

ampolla, *f.* blister; vial

amputar, *va.* to amputate

amueblar, *va.* to furnish

anales, *m. pl.* annals

analfabetismo, *m.* illiteracy

analfabeto, analfabeta, *n.* illiterate person

análisis, *m.* or *f.* analysis

analizar, *va.* to analyze

análogo, *adj.* analogous

anaquel, *m.* shelf in a bookcase

anaranjado, *adj.* orange colored

anatomía, *f.* anatomy

anatómico, *adj.* anatomical

anca, *f.* buttock; hindquarters (of a horse)

anciano, *adj.* aged, old; ancient.

ancla, *f.* anchor

anclar, *vn.* to anchor

ancho, *adj.* broad, wide; *m.* breadth, width

anchoa, *f.* anchovy

anchura, *f.* width, breadth

andamiaje, *m.* scaffolding

andamio, *m.* scaffold

andante, *adj.* walking, errant; (mus.) andante

andar, *vn.* to go, walk; to fare; to proceed; to function, (as a machine)

andén, *m.* (rail.) platform

andrajoso, *adj.* ragged

anécdota, *f.* anecdote

anegar, *va.* to inundate; **anegarse,** to be flooded

anémico, *adj.* anemic

anestesia, *f.* (med.) anesthesia

anestésico, *m., adj.* anesthetic

anexo, *adj.* annexed; *m.* attachment on a letter

anfitrión, *m.* host

ángel, *m.* angel

anglosajón, anglosajona, *n.,* *adj.* Anglo-Saxon

angosto, *adj.* narrow, close

anguila, *f.* (zool.) eel

angular, *adj.* angular; **piedra angular,** cornerstone

angustia, *f.* anguish

anhelo, *m.* longing

anillo, *m.* ring, small circle

ánima, *f.* soul

animación, *f.* animation, liveliness

animado, *adj.* lively; animated

animal, *m., adj.* animal brute

animar, *va., vr.* to animate, enliven; to encourage

ánimo, *m.* soul, spirit; courage; mind; intention

animoso, *adj.* courageous, spirited

aniquilar, *va., vr.* to annihilate, destroy

aniversario, m. anniversary
ano, m. anus
anoche, adv. last night
anochecer, vn. to grow dark
anónimo, adj. anonymous
anormal, adj. abnormal
anotación, f. annotation, note
anotar, va. to comment, note
ansia, f. anxiety, eagerness, yearning; worry
ansiar, va. to long for
ansioso, adj. anxious eager
antagonista, m., f. antagonist
antaño, adv. long ago; yore
antártico, adj. Antarctic
anteayer, adv. day before yesterday
antecesor, antecesora, n. predecessor; forefather
antedicho, adj. aforesaid
antemano, de antemano, adv. beforehand, in advance
antemeridiano, adj. in the forenoon
antena, f. feeler; antenna, aerial
antenoche, adv. night before last
anteojo, m. spyglass, eyeglass; **anteojos,** pl. eyeglasses
antepasado, adj. elapsed; **semana antepasada,** week before last; **antepasados,** m. pl. ancestors
anterior, adj. anterior, fore; previous
anterioridad, f. priority; preference
antes, adv. first; formerly; before; rather
antibiótico, m. antibiotic
anticipación, f. anticipation; **con anticipación,** in advance
anticipado, adj. in advance
anticipar, va. to anticipate, to forestall
anticuado, adj. antiquated; obsolete
antidetonante, m., adj. antiknock
antídoto, m. antidote
antier, adv. (contraction) day before yesterday
antiguamente, adv. formerly

antigüedad, f. antiquity; ancient times; **antigüedades,** f. pl. antiques
antigum, adj. antique, old
antihigiénico, adj. unsanitary
antihistamina, f. antihistamine
antílope, m. antelope
antimateria, f. antimatter
antipatía, f. antipathy
antipático, adj. disagreeable, displeasing
antiséptico, adj. antiseptic
antojarse, vr. to have a yen for
antojo, m. whim; longing
antorcha, f. torch, taper
anual, adj. annual
anualidad, f. anuity
anuario, m. annual; yearbook.
anular, va. to annul; adj. annular; **dedo anular,** ring finger
anunciador, m. announcer
anunciante, m. advertiser
anunciar, va. to announce; to advertise
anzuelo, m. fishhook; allurement
añadir, va. to add; to join
añejo, adj. old, age(wines)
añicos, m. pl. bits; **hacer añicos,** to break into bits
añil, m. indigo; bluing
año, m. year; **año bisiesto,** leap year; **cumplir años,** to have a birthday; **tener . . . años,** to be . . . years old.
apaciguar, va., vr. to appease, pacify, calm down
apachurrar, va. to crush, flatten.
apagado, adj. low, muffled
apañar, va. to grasp; to catch
aparador, m. buffet, sideboard; window, showcase
aparato, m. apparatus, appliance; ostentation, show
aparatoso, adj. pompous, showy
aparecer, vn. to appear
aparentar, va. to pretend, deceive
aparente, adj. apparent; suitable; evident
apariencia, f. appearance,

looks

apartado, *m.* post-office box

apartamento, or **apartamien-to,** *m.* apartment

apartar, *va.* to separate; to remove; **apartarse,** to withdraw

aparte, *m.* new paragraph; *adv.* apart, separately

apasionado, *adj.* passionate; impulsive; fond of

apasionarse, *vr.* to be prejudiced (about)

apatía, *f.* apathy, indifference

apego, *m.* attachment, fondness.

apelación, *f.* appeal; court appeal.

apellido, *m.* surname

apenarse, *vr.* to grieve; become embarrassed

apenas, *adv.* scarcely, hardly.

apéndice, *m.* appendix; supplement.

apendicitis, *f.* appendicitis

aperitivo, *m.* appetizer

apertura, *f.* opening, cleft

apestar, *vn.* to stink

apetito, *m.* appetite

apetitoso, *adj.* appetizing

ápice, *m.* summit point

apiñar, *va.* to press things close together; **apiñarse,** to clog, crowd

apisonadora, *f.* steam roller

aplacar, *va.* to placate

aplanar, *va.* to level, smooth

aplaudir, *va.* to applaud

aplauso, *m.* applause, praise

aplazar, *va.* to defer, postpone

aplicado, *adj.* studious, industrious

aplicar, *va.* to apply; to attribute

aplomo, *m.* poise, composure

apócope, *m.* shortening, cutting off

apoderado, *adj.* authorized, empowered; *m.* (law) proxy, attorney in fact

apoderar, *va.* to empower; to grant power of attorney; **apoderarse,** to take possession

apodo, *m.* nickname

apoplejía, *f.* apoplexy

aportar, *va.* to bring, contribute

aposento, *m.* room, abode

aposición, *f.* (gram.) apposition

apostar, *va.* to bet

apóstol, *m.* apostle

apoyar, *va.* to favor; to support; **apoyarse,** to lean upon

apoyo, *m.* prop, support; protection

apreciable, *adj.* appreciable, valuable, respectable; (com.) **su apreciable,** your favor (letter)

apreciar, *va.* to appreciate, value

aprecio, *m.* appreciation, esteem, regard

apremiar, *va.* to press, compel; to hurry

aprender, *va.* to learn

aprendiz, aprendiza, *n.* apprentice

aprensión, *f.* apprehension, fear, misgiving

apresurado, *adj.* hasty

apresurar, *va.* to accelerate, expedite; **apresurarse,** to hurry, hasten

apretado, *adj.* tight

apretar, *va.* to compress, tighten, squeeze; to pinch (of shoes)

apretón, *m.* sudden pressure; **apretón de manos** handshake.

aprieto, *m.* predicament

aprisa, *adv.* in a hurry

aprobación, *f.* approval

aprobar, *va.* to approve

apropiación, *f.* appropriation

apropiado, *adj.* appropriate, adequate

apropiar, *va.* to appropriate; **apropiarse,** take possession of

aprovechable, *adj.* available, usable

aprovechar, *va.* to avail, make use of; *vn.* to progress in studies,art, etc.; **aprovecharse de,** to take advantage of

aproximar, *va., vr.* to approach; to move near, approximate

aptitud, *f.* aptitude, fitness, ability; talent

apto, *adj.* apt, fit, able

apuesta, *f.* bet, wager

apuesto, *adj.* elegant

apuntador, *m.* observer; prompter; (naut.) gunner

apuntar, *va.* to aim; to level, point out; to note; to write down; (theat.) to prompt

apunte, *m.* annotation; note, sketch

apurado, *adj.* poor, destitute; to be in a hurry

apurar, *va.* to rush, hurry; **apurarse,** to hurry; to worry

apuro, *m.* want, indigence; embarrassment; **salir de un apuro,** to get out of a difficulty.

aquel, aquella, *adj.* and **aquél, aquélla,** *pron.* that

aquello, *pron.* that, the former

aquí, *adv.* here, in this place

aquietar, *va.* to quiet, appease, lull; **aquietarse,** to become calm

árabe, *n., adj.* Arabic, the Arabic language; an Arab

arado, *m.* plow.

arancel, *m.* tariff

arañar, *va.* to scratch; to scrape.

arar, *va.* to plow the land

arbitraje, *m.* arbitration

arbitrar, *va.* to arbitrate

arbitrario, *adj.* arbitrary

árbol, *m.* tree; shaft; (naut.) mast

arca, *f.* chest, wooden box

arcángel, *m.* archangel

arce, *m.* maple tree

arcilla, *f.* argil, clay

arco, *m.* arc; arch; fiddle bow; hoop; **arco iris,** rainbow

arcón, *m.* large chest; bin

archipiélago, *m.* archipelago

archivar, *va.* to file, place in archives

archivo, *m.* archives, file

arder, *vn.* to burn, blaze

ardid, *m.* stratagem, trick

ardiente, *adj.* ardent, intense

ardilla, *f.* squirrel

ardor, *m.* great heat; fervor, zeal

arduo, *adj.* arduous

área, *f.* area

arenoso, *adj.* sandy

arenque, *m.* herring

aretes, *m. pl.* earrings

argentino, *adj.* silvery; Argentine

argolla, *f.* large iron ring

argüir, *vn.* to argue

argumento, *m.* argument; plot of a play

aria, *f.* (mus.) aria, air

árido, *adj.* arid; barren

arisco, *adj.* fierce, surly

aristocracia, *f.* aristocracy

aristócrata, *m., f.* aristocrat

aristocrático, *adj.* aristocratic

aritmética, *f.* arithmetic

arma, *f.* weapon, arm

armamento, *m.* armament

armar, *va.* to furnish with arms; to man; to arm, fit up; to assemble

armario, *m.* clothes closet; cupboard; bookcase

armazón, framework, skeleton; *m.* skeleton of the body.

armiño, *m.* ermine

armisticio, *m.* armistice

armonía, *f.* harmony

armonioso, *adj.* harmonious

armonizar, *va.* to harmonize

aro, *m.* hoop

aroma, *m.* aroma, fragrance

arpa, *f.* (mus.) harp

arqueado, *adj.* arched, bent

arqueología, *f.* archaeology

arquitecto, *m.* architect

arquitectura, *f.* architecture

arraigar *vn.* to take root; to become deep-seated

arrancar, *va.* to pull up by the roots; to wrest; *vn.* to start out

arranque, *m.* sudden start; extirpation; tantrum; (auto.) ignition, starter

arrasar *va.* to demolish, destroy

arrastrado, *adj.* dragged along; miserable, destitute.

arrear, *va.* to drive horses, mules, etc.; to urge on

arrebatado, *adj.* impetuous, rash, inconsiderate

arrebatar, *va.* to carry off, snatch; to enrapture

arrebato, *m.* sudden attack, rage, fit; rapture

arreciar, *vn.* to increase in intensity

arrecife, *m.* reef

arreglado, *adj.* moderate; neat

arreglar, *va.* to regulate; to adjust; to arrange; **arreglarse,** to dress; to manage

arreglo, *m.* arrangement, settlement

arrendamiento, *m.* leasing; rental

arrendar, *va.* to rent, lease

arreos, *m. pl.* appurtenances, accessories

arrepentimiento, *m.* remorse

arrepentirse, *vr.* to repent

arrestar, *va.* to arrest

arriba, *adv.* above, over, up, high, overhead, upstairs

arribo, *m.* arrival

arriendo, *m.* lease, farm rent

arriesgado, *adj.* risky, dangerous

arriesgar, *va., vr.* to risk, hazard.

arrimar, *va.* to approach, draw near; **arrimarse a,** to lean against, seek shelter under; to join

arroba, *f.* weight of twenty-five pounds; measure (thirty-two pints)

arrodillarse, *vr.* to kneel

arrogancia, *f.* arrogance

arrogante, *adj.* haughty, proud

arrojado, *adj.* rash, bold

arrojar, *va.* to dart, fling; to dash; to shed (a fragrance); to emit (light); to throw out; **arrojar un saldo,** to show a balance

arrojo, *m.* boldness; fearlessness

arrollar, *va.* to wind, coil

arropar, *va.* to clothe, dress; to cover (with blankets, etc.)

arroyo, *m.* gully, creek

arroz, *m.* rice

arruga, *f.* wrinkle; rumple

arrugar, *va.* to wrinkle; to rumple, fold; **arrugar el ceño,** to frown; **arrugarse,** to shrivel

arruinar, *va.* to demolish; to ruin; **arruinarse,** to lose one's fortune

arte, *m., f.* art; skill; **bellas artes,** fine arts

arteria, *f.* artery

arterial, *adj.* arterial; **tensión arterial,** blood pressure

artesano, *m.* artisan, workman.

ártico, *adj.* arctic

articular, *va.* to articulate.

artificial, *adj.* artificial

artillería, *f.* gunnery; artillery

artimaña, *f.* stratagem, deception

artista, *m.f.* artist

artisticó, *adj.* artistic

artritis, *f.* (med.) arthritis

arveja, *f.* (bot.) vetch; (Sp. Am.) green pea

arzobispo, *m.* archbishop

as, *m.* ace

asa, *f.* handle, haft, hold

asado, *adj.* roasted; *m.* roast

asaltar, *va.* to attack; to assail

asalto, *m.* assault

asamblea, *f.* assembly, meeting

asar, *va.* to roast

asbesto, *m.* asbestos

ascendencia, *f.* ancestry; line of ancestors

ascendente, *adj.* ascending

ascender, *va., vn.* to ascend, climb; to be promoted; to amount to

ascendiente, *m.* ascendant, forefather; influence

ascenso, *m.* ascent; promotion

ascensor, *m.* elevator, lift

asco, *m.* nausea; loathing

aseado, *adj.* clean, neat

asear, *va.* to clean, make neat

asediar, *va.* to besiege

asegurado, *adj.* assured, secured, insured; *n.* policyholder

asegurar, *va.* to secure, insure; to assure; to affirm

asemejarse, *vr.* to resemble
asentimiento, *m.* assent
asentir, *vn.* to acquiesce, concede
aseo, *m.* cleanliness
aserción, *f.* assertion
aserrar, *va.* to saw
asesinar, *va.* to assassinate
asesinato, *m.* assassination
asesino, *m.* assassin
asesorar, *va.* to give legal advice to; **asesorarse**, to employ counsel; to take advice
asfalto, *m.* asphalt
asfixiar, *va., vr.* to asphyxiate, suffocate
así, *adv.* so, thus, in this manner; therefore, so that
asiático, asiática, *n., adj.* Asiatic
asiento, *m.* chair, stool; seat; entry
asignar, *vt.* to allocate, apportion, assign
asignatura, *f.* subject of a school course
asilo, *m.* asylum, refuge
asimismo, *adv.* similarly; likewise
asistencia, *f.* actual presence; attendance; assistance; help
asistir, *vn.* to be present; to attend; *va.* assist
asma, *f.* asthma
asno, *m.* ass; stupid fellow
asociado, asociada, *n.* associate
asociar, *va., vr.* to associate
asolar, *va.* to destroy, devastate
asolear, *va., vr.* to expose to the sun
asomar, *vn.* to begin to appear; to peep; to show; **asomarse**, to lean out
asombrar, *va.* to frighten, amaze; to astonish
asombroso, *adj.* astonishing, marvelous
aspecto, *m.* appearance; aspect
áspero, *adj.* rough, rugged; austere, gruff
aspiración, *f.* aspiration; ambition

aspiradora, *f.* vacuum sweeper
aspirar, *va.* to inhale; to aspire
aspirina, *f.* aspirin
asqueroso, *adj.* loathsome; dirty
asta, *f.* staff, pole
asterisco, *m.* asterisk
astilla, *f.* chip; splinter
astillero, *m.* dockyard
astringente, *adj., m.* astringent
astro, *m.* star
astrólogo, *m.* astrologer
astronave, *f.* space ship
astronomía, *f.* astronomy
astrónomo, *m.* astronomer
asueto, *m.* holiday, vacation
asumir, *va.* to assume
asunto, *m.* subject; matter; affair, business
asustar, *va., vr.* to frighten
atacar, *va.* to attack, ram
atajo, *m.* by-path; short cut
ataque, *m.* attack
atar, *va.* to tie, fasten
atarantado, *adj.* dazed
atareado, *adj.* busy
atarearse, *vr.* to work hard on a task
atascarse, *vr.* to become bogged
ataúd, *m.* coffin
atavío, *m.* dress, ornament
Atenas, *f.* Athens
atender, *vn.* to be attentive; to heed; *va.* to look after
atenerse, *vr.* to depend or rely (on)
atentado, *m.* attempt, transgression; attack, assault
atentar, *va.* to try; to attempt crime
atento, *adj.* attentive; mindful; courteous
atenuar, *va.* to diminish
ateo, atea, *n., adj.* atheist, atheistic
aterrar, *va., vr.* to terrify
aterrizaje, *m.* (avi.) landing
aterrizar, *vn.* (avi.) to land
atesorar, *va.* to treasure or hoard up riches
atestar, *va.* to attest, witness; to cram, crowd; **atestarse de**, to stuff oneself with

atestiguar, *va.* to witness, attest

atinar, *va.*, *vn.* to touch the mark; to conjecture rightly

atisbar, *va.* to pry

Atlántico, *n.*, *adj.* Atlantic

atlas, *m.* atlas

atleta, *m.*, *f.* athlete

atlético, *adj.* athletic

atmósfera, *f.* atmosphere

atmosférico, *adj.* atmospheric

atole, *m.* corn-flour gruel

atolondrar, *va.*, *vr.* to stun, daze

atollar, *vn.* to fall in the mud

atómico, *adj.* atomic

atomo, *m.* atom

atónito, *adj.* astonish

atontar, *va.*, *vr.* to stun, stupefy

atorar, *va.* to obstruct; **atorarse,** *vr.* to choke; to be stalled in the mud

atormentar, *va.* to torment

atornillar, *va.* to screw

atracar, *va.* to overhaul a ship; to glut; *vn.* (naut.) to make shore

atracción, *f.* attraction

atractivo, *adj.* attractive; *m.* charm, grace

atraer, *va.* to attract

atrapar, *va.* to trap; to overtake; to deceive

atrás, *adv.* backwards; behind; past

atrasado, *adj.* backward, behind the times; tardy; in arrears

atrasar, *va.* to postpone; to delay; **atrasarse,** to be in arrears

atraso, *m.* delay, backwardness; arrears

atravesar, *va.* to cross; to pass over; **atravesarse,** to get in the way; to thwart one's purpose

atreverse, *vr.* to dare, venture

atrevido, *adj.* bold, daring; impudent

atrevimiento, *m.* audacity

atribuir, *va.* to attribute, ascribe; to impute; **atribuirse,** to assume

atribular, *va.* to vex, afflict

atributo, *m.* attribute

atrio, *m.* porch; portico

atrocidad, *f.* atrocity

atropellar, *va.* to trample; to run over; **atropellarse,** to hurry, flurry

atropello, *m.* trampling; outrage, insult; **atropello de automóvil,** automobile collision

attmo. or **att.**mo, **atentísimo,** very kind, very courteous

atto. or **att.**° **atento,** kind, courteous

atuendo, *m.* attire, garb; pomp, ostentation

atun, *m.* tunny fish, tuna

aturdir, *va.* to bewilder, confuse; to stupefy

audacia, *f.* audacity, boldness

audición, *f.* broadcasting; audition

audiencia, *f.* audience; hearing; a high court

audífono, *m.* earphone

audio-visual, *adj.* audio-visual

auditorio, *m.* assembly; audience.

auge, *m.* the pinnacle of power

augurar, *va.* to predict

aula, *f.* classroom

aullar, *vn.* to howl

aumentar, *va.*, *vn.* to augment, increase

aumento, *m.* increase, growth

aun, *adv.* still, even; **aún,** *adv.* yet

aunque, *conj.* though, notwithstanding

aurora, *f.* first dawn of day

ausencia, *f.* absense

ausente, *adj.* absent

austero, *adj.* austere, severe

australiano, australiana, *n.*, *adj.* Australian

austriaco, austriaca, *n.*, *adj.* Austrian

autentico, *adj.* authentic

auto, *m.* judicial sentence; edict; auto, automobile

autobús, *m.* motorbus

autógrafo, *m.* autograph

autómata, *m.* automation; robot

automático, *adj.* automatic
automatización, *f.* automation
automatizar, *va.* to automate
automóvil, *m.* automobile
autonomía, *f.* autonomy
autónomo, *adj.* autonomous
autopista, *f.* expressway, superhighway
autor, *m.* author; maker
autoridad, *f.* authority
autorización, *f.* authorization
autorizado, *adj.* competent, reliable
autorizar, *va.* to authorize
auxiliar, *va.* to aid, help, assist; *adj.* auxiliary
auxilio, *m.* aid, help, assistance; **primeros auxilios,** first aid
a/v., a la vista, (com.) at sight
avaluar, *va.* to estimate, evaluate, appraise
avanzada, *f.* (mil.) vanguard
avanzar, *va., vn.* to advance
avaricia, *f.* avarice
avaro, *adj.* avaricious; *m.* miser
ave, *f.* bird; **ave de corral,** fowl
avellana, *f.* filbert, hazelnut
avemaría, *f.* Ave Maria, salutation to the Virgin Mary
avena, *f.* oats; oatmeal
avenida, *f.* avenue, boulevard
avenir, *va., vr.* to reconcile; to adapt (to circumstances)
aventajar, *va.* to have the advantage
aventar, *va.* to fan; to expel; to scatter; **aventarse,** to be puffed up
aventura, *f.* adventure
aventurar, *va.* to venture, risk
aventurero, *adj.* adventurous; *m.* adventurer
avergonzar, *va., vr.* to shame; be ashamed
aversion, *f.* aversion, dislike
avestruz, *m.* ostrich
aviación, *f.* aviation
aviador, *n.* aviator
aviar, *va.* to provision, equip
avión, *m.* airplane
avisar, *va.* to inform, give notice

aviso, *m.* information; notice; advertisement; warning
avispa, *f.* wasp
axila, *f.* armpit
¡ay! *interj.* alas!
aya, *f.* governess
ayer, *adv.* yesterday; lately
ayuda, *f.* help, aid
ayudante, *m.* assistant
ayudar, *va.* to help, assist
ayunar, *vn.* to fast
ayunas, en ayunas, *adv.* fasting, without food; ignorant (of an affair)
ayuntamiento, *m.* town council; city hall
azabache, *m.* jet
azada, *f.* spade, hoe
azadón, *m.* pickax; hoe
azafrán, *m.* saffron
azahar, *m.* orange blossom
azar, *m.* hazard; unforeseen disaster; **al azar,** at random
azogue, *m.* mercury
azorar, *va., vr.* to frighten, terrify
azote, *m.* whip, lash; scourge
azotea, *f.* roof garden
azteca, *n.* Aztec
azúcar, *m.* or *f.* sugar
azucarera, *f.* sugar bowl
azucena, *f.* white lily
azufre, *m.* sulphur, brimstone
azul, *adj.* blue
azulejo, *m.* tile; bluebird

B

baba, *f.* drivel; drool
babel, *m.* babel, confusion
babero, *m.* bib
baboso, *adj.* driveling, silly; *n.* (Sp. Am.) fool, idiot
bacalao, *m.* codfish
bacinica or **bacinilla,** *f.* chamber pot
bacteria, *f.* bacteria
bacteriólogo, *m.* bacteriologist
bachiller, *m.* bachelor (degree); a college graduate
bachillerato, *m.* bachelor's degree
bahía, *f.* bay
bailar, *vn.* to dance
bailarin, bailarina, *n.* dancer,

ballerina
baile, *m.* dance, ball
baja, *f.* fall, diminution; fall in prices; loss in membership
bajada, *f.* descent; downgrade
bajar, *va.* to lower; to decrease (the price); *vn.* to descend
bajeza, *f.* meanness; lowliness
bajo, *adj.* low; under; short; despicable; (mus.) bass
bala, *f.* bullet; bale of paper
balada, f. ballad
balance, *m.* fluctuation; rolling of a ship; balance; balance of accounts
balancear, *va., vn.* to balance; to roll; **balancearse,** to rock, to sway
balanza, *f.* scale; comparative estimate
balazo, *m.* shot; bullet wound
balboa, *m.* a coin of Panama
balbucear, *va., vn.* to stammer
balcón, *m.* balcony
baldar, *va.* to cripple
balde, *m.* bucket, pail; **de balde,** gratis; **en balde,** in vain
balistico, balistica, *adj.* ballistic
balneario, *m.* bathing resort
balon, *m.* ball; bale
baloncesto, *m.* basketball
balonvolea, *m.* volleyball
balsa, *f.* raft, float; ferry
bálsamo, *m.* balsam, balm
ballena, *f.* whale; whalebone
bambolear, *vn., vr.* to reel, sway
bambú *m.* bamboo
banano, *m.* banana plant or fruit
bancario, *adj.* banking
bancarrota, *f.* bankruptcy
banco, *m.* bench; bank; **banco de sangre,** blood bank
banda, *f.* sash; band; gang; border
bandeja, *f.* tray
banderera, *f.* banner, flag
bandido, *m.* bandit, robber
bando, *m.* faction, team
banquero, banquera, *n.* banker
banqueta, *f.* sidewalk; three-legged stool

banquete, *m.* banquet; feast
bañar, *va.* to bathe; to water; to dip; **bañarse,** to take a bath.
bañera, *f.* bathtub
baño, *m.* bath; bathtub, bathroom; varnish; coat (of paint)
baraja, *f.* playing card; pack of cards; game of cards
baranda, *f.* banister, railing
barandal, *m.* railing
baratillo, *m.* bargain counter
barato, *adj.* cheap, lowpriced
barbacoa, *f.* barbecue
barbaridad, *f.* barbarity; rudeness; (coll.) ridiculous act; **una barbaridad,** a piece of nonsense; an "awful" lot; **¡que barbaridad!** how terrible!
bárbaro, *adj.* barbarous, savage; rash, daring; rude
barbería, *f.* barbershop
barbero, *m.* barber
barca, *f.* boat; barge
baritono, *m.* (mus.) baritone
barniz, *m.* varnish
barnizar, *va.* to varnish
barómetro, *m.* barometer
barón, *m.* baron
baronesa, *f.* baroness
barquillo, *m.* cone-shaped wafer
barra, *f.* crowbar, lever
barraca, *f.* barrack; hut
barranca, *f.* cliff; gorge
barranco, *m.* ravine; gorge
barrera, *f.* clay pit; barrier
barriga, *f.* abdomen, belly
barril, *m.* barrel; cask; jug
barrio, *m.* district or section of a town; quarter; **barrios bajos,** slums
basar, *va.* to base
báscula, *f.* platform scale
base, *f.* base, basis
básico, *adj.* basic
basílica, *f.* basilica (cathedral)
basketbol, *m.* basketball
basta, *f.* basting; **¡basta!** *interj.* enough!
bastante, *adj.* sufficient; quite, considerable; *adv.* enough; rather
bastar, *vn.* to suffice

bastardilla, *f.* italic
bastardo, *adj., m.* bastard
bastidor, *m.* embroidery frame; **bastidores,** *pl.* stage scenery; wings; **tras bastidores,** backstage
bastilla, *f.* hem
bastón, *m.* cane, stick
bastos, *m. pl.* clubs (suit in cards)
basura, *f.* sweepings; garbage
basurero, *n.* dustpan; dunghill
bata, *f.* dressing gown
batalla, *f.* battle, combat
batallar, *vn.* to battle, dispute
batallón, *m.* (mil.) battalion
batata, *f.* sweet potato
batea, *f.* round wooden tray
batería, *f.* battery; (mus.) percussion section
batidor, *m.* beater
batir, *va., vn.* to beat
batista, *f.* batiste, cambric
batuta, *f.* baton; **llevar la batuta,** to lead, to preside
baúl, *m.* trunk, chest
bautismo, *m.* baptism
bautizar, *va.* to baptize, christen
bautizo, *m.* baptism
baya, *f.* berry
bayo, *adj.* bay (of a horse)
bayoneta, *f.* bayonet
bazar, *m.* bazaar
beata, *f.* overly pious woman; hypocrite
beato, *adj.* devout
bebedor, bebedora, *n.* drunkard, drinker
beber, *va., vn.* to drink; *m.* drinking
bebida, *f.* drink, beverage; **bebida alcohólica,** intoxicant
beca, *f.* scholarship, fellowship
becerro, *m.* calf; calfskin
beldad, *f.* beauty
Belén, *m.* Bethlehem; **estar en Belén,** to be absentminded
belga, *adj., n.* Belgian.
Bélgica, *f.* Belgium
bélico, *adj.* warlike, martial
beligerante, *n., adj.* belligerent
belleza, *f.* beauty
bello, *adj.* beautiful, hand-

some; **bellas artes,** fine arts
bemol, *m.* (mus.) flat
bencina, *f.* (chem.) benzine
bendecir, *va.* to bless
bendición, *f.* benediction; blessing
bendito, *adj.* sainted, blessed; simple
benefactor, *m.* benefactor
beneficencia, *f.* beneficence, charity
beneficiado, beneficiada, *n.* beneficiary
beneficiar, *va.* to profit; to benefit
beneficiario, *m.* beneficiary
beneficio, *m.* benefit; profit
benemérito, *adj.* worthy
benévolo, *adj.* benevolent
berenjena, *f.* eggplant
berrear, *vn.* to low, bellow
berrinche, *m.* fit of anger; sulkiness
besar, *va.* to kiss
beso, *m.* kiss
bestia, *f.* beast; animal; dunce, idiot.
bestial, *adj.* bestial, brutal
betabel, *m.* (Mex.) beet
betarraga or **betarrata,** (bot.) beet
betatrón, *m.* betatron
bevatrón, *m.* bevatron
biberón, *m.* nursing bottle
Biblia, *f.* Bible
bíblico, *adj.* Biblical
bibliografía, *f.* bibliography
biblioteca, *f.* library
bibliotecario, bibliotecaria, *n.* librarian
bicarbonato, *m.* bicarbonate
biceps, *m.* (anat.) biceps
bicicleta, *f.* bicycle
bicho, *m.* vermin; insect
bien, *m.* good; benefit;
bienes, *pl.* property, riches; land; *adv.* well; right; all right; **¡bienes!** *interj.* fine! all right!
bienal, *adj.* biennial
bienaventurado, *adj.* blessed, happy, fortunate
bienestar, *m.* well-being
bienhechor, *m.* benefactor
bienio, *m.* space of two years

bienvenida, *f.* welcome
bienvenido, *adj.* welcome
bifocal, *adj.* bifocal
biftec, *m.* beefsteak
bigamo, bigama, *n.* bigamist
bigote, *m.* mustache
bilingüe, *adj.* bilingual
bilis, *f.* bile
billar, *m.* billiards
billete, *m.* ticket; billet, label; note, short letter; love letter; banknote bill
billetera, *f.* billfold
billetero, billetera, *n.* (Sp. Am.) vendor of lottery tickets
billón, *m.* billion
billonario, billonaria, *n.* billionaire
bimestral, *adj.* bimonthly
bimestre, *m.* space of two months; bimonthly rent, salary, etc.
bimotor, *adj.* two-motored
binóculo, *m.* opera glass
bioastronáutica, *f.* bioastronautics
biografia, *f.* biography
biologia, *f.* biology
biombo, *m.* screen
biopsia, *f.* biopsy
bioquímico, *adj.* biochemical; *m.* biochemist
biosfera, *f.* biosphere
bisabuela, *f.* great-grandmother
bisabuelo, *m.* great-grandfather.
bisagra, *f.* hinge
bisel, *m.* bevel
bisemanal, *adj.* semiweekly.
bisonte, *m.* bison
bisoño, *adj.* inexperienced; *n.* novice
bistec, *m.* beefsteak
bizcocho, *m.* cake, ladyfinger
biznieta, *f.* great-granddaughter
biznieto, *m.* great-grandson
blanco, *adj.* white, blank; *m.* blank; target
blancura, *f.* whiteness
blando, *adj.* soft, smooth; mellow; mild, gentle
blanquear, *va., vn.* to bleach; to whitewash

blasfemia, *f.* blasphemy; oath
bledo, *m.* (bot.) wild amaranth; **no me importa un bledo,** I don't give a rap, I don't care
bloc, *m.* bloc, political group; pad (of paper)
bloqueo, *m.* blockade
blusa, *f.* blouse
boa, *f.* (zool.) boa
bobería, *f.* folly, foolishness
bobina, *f.* bobbin; coil; spool; (elec.) coil; **bobina de reacción (nuclear),** reactor (nuclear)
bobo, boba, *n.* dunce, fool; *adj.* stupid; silly
boca, *f.* mouth; entrance, opening; mouth of a river
bocacalle, *f.* street intersection or opening
bocamanga, *f.* armhole
boceto, *m.* sketch
bocina, *f.* bugle horn; speaking trumpet; automobile horn
bocio, *m.* goiter
bochornoso, *adj.* shameful; sultry (weather)
boda, *f.* wedding; **bodas de plata** or **de oro,** silver or golden anniversary
bodega, *f.* wine cellar; warehouse
bofetada, *f.* slap on the face
bofetón, *m.* box on the ear
boga, *f.* vogue, fad, popularity
bogar, *vn.* to row, paddle
boicotear, *va., vn.* to boycott
boina, *f.* beret
bola, *f.* ball; globe; marble; (coll.) lie, fib; disturbance
bolear, *vn.* to knock the balls about (billiards); (Mex.) to shine shoes
bolero, *m.* Spanish dancer; Andalusian dance; (Mex.) top hat; bootblack
boletín, *m.* bulletin
boleto, *m.* ticket; **boletode ida y vuelta,** round-trip ticket; **boleto sencillo,** one-way ticket
boliche, *m.* bowling
bolillo, *m.* (Mex.) kind of bread roll

boliviano, boliviana, *adj., n.* Bolivian; *m.* a Bolivian coin

bolo, *m.* bowling pin; bolo (knife); **bolos,** *pl.* bowling

bolsa, *f.* purse, pouch; case; money exchange; stock exchange

bolsillo, *m.* pocket

bomba, *f.* pump; bomb; **bomba atómica,** atomic bomb; **bomba de aerosol,** aerosol bomb; **bomba de hidrógeno,** hydrogen bomb; **bomba de neutrón,** neutron bomb

bombardeo, *m.* bombardment

bombear, *va.* to pump (water)

bombero, *m.* fireman

bombilla, *f.* light bulb; (Sp. Am.) a tube to sip maté

bombón, *m.* bonbon, candy

bonanza, f. bonanza

bondad, *f.* kindness

bondadoso, *adj.* kind

bonito, *adj.* pretty

bono, *m.* (com.) bond, certificate

boquiabierto, *adj.* open-mouthed

boquilla, *f.* mouthpiece

borbotón, *m.* bubbling, **hablar a borbotones,** to speak in torrents, babble

bordado, *m.* embroidery

bordar, *va.* to embroider

bordo, *m.* board; the side of a ship; (naut.) **a bordo,** on board; **franco a bordo,** free on board (f.o.b.)

borinqueño, borinqueña, *n., adj.* Puerto Rican

borrachera, *f.* drunkenness

borracho, *adj.* intoxicated

borrador, *m.* eraser; rough draft

borrar, *va.* to erase

borrasca, *f.* storm, squall

borrego, borrega, *n.* yearling lamb

borrico, *m.* ass; blockhead

borrón, *m.* ink blot, splotch

borronear, *va.* to sketch, scribble

borroso, *adj.* blurred

bosque, *m.* forest, woods

bosquejo, *m.* outline, sketch

bostezar, *vn.* to yawn; to gape

bostezo, *m.* yawn, yawning

bota, *f.* cask; boot

botánica, *f.* botany

botar, *va.* to cast, throw; to launch

botarate, *m., f.* fool

bote, *m.* small boat, rowboat; jar, bottle; **bote de salvamento,** lifeboat

botella, *f.* bottle, flask

botica, *f.* drugstore, pharmacy

boticario, *m.* druggist

botiquín, *m.* first-aid kit

botón, *m.* button; bud

bóveda, *f.* arch; vault

bovino, *adj.* bovine

boxeador, *m.* boxer, pugilist

boxear, *vn.* to box

boxeo, *m.* boxing, pugilism

boya, *f.* buoy

bozal, *m.* muzzle

bracero, *m.* day laborer

bragazas, *m.* milksop

bragueta, *f.* trousers fly

brama, *f.* rut, mating time

bramar, *vn.* to roar, bellow

brasa, *f.* live coal

brasero, *m.* brazier, hearth.

Brasil, *m.* Brazil

brasileño, brasileña, *n., adj.* Brazilian

brasilero, *adj.* (Sp. Am.) Brazilian

bravío, *adj.* savage, wild

bravo, *adj.* brave, valiant; fierce; excellent, fine; ¡bravo! *interj.* bravo!

bravura, *f.* bravery; courage; bravado, boast

brazalete, *m.* bracelet

brazo, *m.* arm; **brazos,** *pl.* hands, man power

brea, *f.* pitch, tar

brecha, *f.* breach; gap

bregar, *vn.* to contend, struggle

Bretaña, *f.* Brittany; **Gran Bretaña,** Great Britain

breve, *adj.* brief, short; **en breve,** shortly

brevedad, *f.* brevity

bribón, bribóna, *adj.* rascally; *n.* rogue

brida, *f.* bridle; check, curb

brigada, *f.* brigade
brillante, *adj.* bright, shining; *m.* brilliant, diamond
brincar, *vn.* to leap, jump
brinco, *m.* leap, jump, **dar brincos,** to leap
brindar, *vn.* to drink one's health, toast; *va.* to offer
brindis, *m.* health, toast
brío, *m.* strength, vigor
brioso, *adj.* vigorous, fiery
brisa, *f.* breeze
británico, británica, *adj., n.* British, Britisher
brocado, *m.* brocade
brocha, *f.* painter's brush
broche, *m.* clasp; brooch
broma, *f.* joke, jest
bromear, *vn.* to jest, joke
bromuro, *m.* bromide
bronce, *m.* bronze, brass
bronco, *adj.* rough, coarse
bronquio, *m.* bronchial tube
bronquitis, *f.* bronchitis
brotar, *vn.* to bud, germinate, to break out, appear (said of a disease)
bruja, *f.* witch, hag; *adj.* (coll.) broke, short of funds
brujo, *m.* sorcerer
brújula, *f.* compass; magnetic needle
bruma, *f.* mist, haze
brumoso, *adj.* misty, hazy
brusco, *adj.* rude, gruff
Bruselas, *f.* Brussels
brutal, *adj.* brutal, brutish
bruto, *m.* brute, blockhead; **bruto, bruta,** *adj.* brutal, stupid; crude (ore, oil, etc.); gross (profits, etc.); **en bruto,** in a raw (unmanufactured) state
bucear, *vn.* to dive
bucle, *m.* curl
buche, *m.* craw, crop; mouthful
buen, *adj.* good; **hacer buen tiempo,** to be good weather
buenaventura, *f.* fortune, good luck.
bueno, *adj.* good, perfect; proper; healthy; useful
buey, *m.* ox, bullock
búfalo, *m.* buffalo

bufanda, *f.* scarf
bufete, *m.* desk, lawyer's office
bufo, *m.* buffoon; **bufo, bufa,** *adj.* comic
bufón, *m.* buffoon; jester; *adj.* funny, comical
buho, *m.* owl
buitre, *m.* vulture
bujía, *f.* spark plug; candle
bulbo, *m.* (bot.) bulb
bulevar, *m.* boulevard
bulla, *f.* clatter; crowd
bullicio, *m.* bustle; uproar
buque, *m.* boat, ship, vessel
burdo, *adj.* coarse (of cloth); ordinary
burla, *f.* scoff, sneer; hoax
burlar, *va.* to mock, deceive; to frustrate; **burlar se de,** to make fun of
buró, *m.* bureau, chest of drawers
burocracia, *f.* bureaucracy
busca, *f.* search
busto, *m.* bust
buzo, *m.* diver
buzón, *m.* mailbox, letter drop

C

C., centigrado, C. Centigrade
c/, cargo, (com.) cargo, charge
C.A., corriente alterna, A.C. alternating current
cabal, *adj.* just, exact; complete, accomplished
caballería, *f.* cavalry; knighthood
caballeriza, *f.* stable
caballero, *m.* knight; gentleman
caballete, *m.* easel
caballo, *m.* horse; knight (in chess); **a caballo,** on horseback
cabaña, *f.* hut, shack; cottage, cabin; cabana
cabaret, *m.* cabaret, night club
cabecear, *vn.* to nod with sleep
cabecera, *f.* upper end; head (of a bed or a table); headwaters; **médico de cabecera,** attending physician

cabecilla, *m.* ringleader
cabellera, *f.* head of hair
cabello, *m.* hair of the head
cabelludo, *adj.* hairy; **cuero cabelludo**, scalp
caber, *va., vn.* to contain, include; to fit; to be possible
cabeza, *f.* head; top; leader
cabezudo, *adj.* headstrong, obstinate
cabida, *f.* content, capacity
cabildo, *m.* town council
cabina, *f.* (avi.) cockpit
cabizbajo, *adj.* pensive
cable, *m.* cable; rope
cablegrafiar, *va.* to cable
cablegráfico, *adj.* cable; **dirección cablegráfica**, cable address
cablegrama, *m.* cablegram
cabo, *m.* extremity cape, headland; end, tip; (mil.) corporal
Cabo de Buena Esperanza, Cape of Good Hope
Cabo de Hornos, Cape Horn
cabra, *f.* goat
cabria, *f.* hoist
cabritilla, *f.* kidskin
cabrito, *m.* kid
cacahuate or **cacahuete**, *m.* peanut
cacao, *m.* (bot.) cacao, cocoa seed
cacerola, *f.* casserole, pan
cacto, *m.* cactus
cacha, *f.* knife handle
cachete, *m.* cheek
cachorro, cachorra, *n.* cub (of any animal)
cachucha, *f.* man's cap
cada, *adj.* each, every;
cada uno, everyone; each
cadena, *f.* chain; series; network
cadencia, *f.* cadence
cadera, *f.* hip
cadete, *m.* (mil.) cadet
caducar, *vn.* to dote; to lapse (of a legacy, etc.)
C.A.E., cóbrese al entregar, C.O.D. or c.o.d. cash or collect on delivery
caer, *vn.* to fall; to befall, happen
café, *m.* coffee; café

cafetera, *f.* coffee pot; (Arg.) a noisy motorcycle; a jalopy
cafetería, *f.* coffee store; coffeehouse
cafeto, *m.* coffee tree
caída, *f.* fall, falling
caído, *adj.* fallen
caimán, *m.* caiman; (fig.) fox, sly individual
cajero, cajera, *n.* cashier
cajeta, *f.* (Mex.) confection made of goat's milk
cajón, *m.* drawer; locker; coffin; **ser de cajón**, (coll.) to be customary
cal, *f.* lime (mineral)
calabaza, *f.* pumpkin, gourd; **dar calabazas**, to jilt; to flunk.
calabozo, *m.* dungeon; jail
calamar, *m.* squid
calambre, *m.* cramp
calamidad, *f.* misfortune
calar, *va.* to penetrate, pierce
calavera, *f.* skull; madcap
calcetín, *m.* sock
calcio, *m.* calcium
calculador, *adj.* calculating; **calculador electrónico**, electronic computer
calculadora, *f.* adding machine
calcular, *va.* to calculate
cálculo, *m.* calculation; **cálculo bilario**, gallstone
caldera, *f.* caldron, kettle, boiler
calefacción, *f.* heating
calendario, *m.* almanac, calendar
calentador, *m.* heater
calentar, *va.* to warm, heat; **calentarse**, to grow hot; to dispute warmly
calentura, *f.* fever
calibre, *m.* caliber, gauge; (fig.) sort, kind
calicanto, *m.* stone masonry
cálido, *adj.* hot, warm
caliente, *adj.* hot; fiery
calificación, *f.* qualification; mark (in school)
calificar, *va.* to qualify; to rate
calisténica, *f.* calisthenics
cáliz, *m.* chalice; goblet

calma, *f.* calm; calmness

calmante, *m.* (med.) sedative

calmar, *va., vr.* to calm, quiet, pacify

calor, *m.* heat, ardor; **hacer** or **tener calor,** to be warm

calorífero, *m.* heater; **calorífero de aire caliente,** hot air heater

calumnia, *f.* slander

caluroso, *adj.* warm, hot

calva, *f.* bald spot

calvo, *adj.* bald

calzada, *f.* roadway, street

calzado, *m.* footwear

calzar, *va.* to put on, to block with a wedge

calzoncillos, *m. pl.* shorts

calzones, *m. pl.* trousers

callado, *adj.* silent; quiet

callar, *vn.* to be silent; to hush

calle, *f.* street

callejero, *adj.* fond of loitering in streets

callejón, *m.* alley, narrow pass

callo, *m.* corn; callus

cama, *f.* bed, couch; litter

cámara, *f.* hall; chamber; camera; cockpit; chamber of a firearm

camarada, *n.* comrade, companion

camarera, *f.* waitress; chambermaid

camarero, *m.* waiter; steward

camarilla, *f.* clique

camarón, *m.* (zool.) shrimp

camarote, *m.* berth, cabin

cambiar, *va.* to barter, exchange; to change; to alter; to make change (money)

cambio, *m.* exchange, barter; change

camelia, *f.* camellia

camilla, *f.* pallet, stretcher

caminante, *m.* traveler, walker

caminar, *vn.* to walk; travel

camino, *m.* road, way

camión, *m.* truck, bus

camioneta, *f.* station wagon, small truck

camisa, *f.* shirt

camiseta, *f.* undershirt

camisón, *m.* nightgown

camote, *m.* (Sp. Am.) sweet potato

campamento, *m.* (mil.) encampment, camp

campana, *f.* bell

campanada, sound of a bell

campanario, *m.* belfry, steeple

campanilla, *f.* hand bell; (anat.) uvula

campaña, *f.* campaign, expedition

campechano, *adj.* frank; hearty

campeón, *m.* champion

campeonato, *m.* championship

campesino, *adj.* rural; *n.* peasant

campestre, *adj.* rural, rustic

campo, *m.* country; countryside; field; camp; ground

cana, *f.* gray hair

Canadá, *m.* Canada

canadiense, *n., adj.* Canadian

canal, *m.* channel, canal; gutter

Canal de la Mancha, *m.* English Channel

canalla, *f.* mob, rabble, populace; *m.* scoundrel

canallada, despicable act

canario, *m.* canary bird

canasta, *f.* basket, hamper; canasta (card game)

canastilla, *f.* small basket; layette

cancelar, *va.* to cancel, erase

cáncer, *m.* (med.) cancer

canceroso, *adj.* cancerous

canciller, *m.* chancellor; consular assistant

candado, *m.* padlock

candela, *f.* fire; light

candelabro, *m.* candelabrum

candelero, *m.* candlestick

candidato, candidata, *n.* candidate

cándido, *adj.* candid

candor, *m.* candor, frankness

cangrejo, *m.* crawfish, crab

canguro, *m.* kangaroo

caníbal, *m.* cannibal

canilla, *f.* shinbone

canjear, *va.* to exchange

cano, *adj.* gray-headed

canoa, *f.* canoe

canoso, *adj.* white-haired

cansado, *adj.* tired; tiresome

cansancio, *m.* weariness

cantaleta, *f.* singsong

cantante, *m., f.* singer

cantar, *va., vn.* to sing

cántaro, *m.* pitcher; **llover a cántaros,** to rain heavily

cantera, *f.* quarry

cantidad, *f.* quantity, number

cantina, *f.* canteen; barroom

cantinero, *m.* bartender

canto, *m.* song; singing; stone; edge

cantor, cantora, *n.* singer

caña, *f.* cane, reed; sugar cane; stalk

cáñamo, *m.* hemp; hempen cloth

cañaveral, *m.* sugar-cane field

cañería, *f.* pipe line

caño, *m.* tube; pipe line

cañón, *m.* pipe; canyon; cannon; gun barrel; **cañón antiaéreo,** antiaircraft gun; **cañón anticarro** or **antitanque,** antitank gun

caoba, *f.* mahogany

caos, *m.* chaos; confusion

capa, *f.* cloak; layer, coating

capacidad, *f.* capacity

capacitar, *va., vr.* to enable, qualify; to delegate

capataz, *m.* overseer; foreman

capellán, *m.* chaplain, minister

caperuza, *f.* hood; **Caperucita Roja,** Little Red Riding Hood

capilla, *f.* hood; chapel

capital, *m.* capital, stock; *f.* capital, metropolis; *adj.* capital; principal

capitalismo, *m.* capitalism

capitalista, *n., adj.* capitalist

capitán, *m.* captain

capitolio, *m.* capitol

capítulo, *m.* chapter (of a book)

caporal, *m.* chief, ringleader

capota, *f.* cape; top (of vehicles)

capote, *m.* cape, cloak; raincoat; **decir para su capote,** to say to oneself

capricho, *m.* caprice, whimsical; obstinate

capturer, *va.* to capture

capullo, *m.* pod of silkworm; bud

caqui, *m., adj.* khaki

cara, *f.* face, front; surface

carabina, *f.* carbine; **ser como la carabina de Ambrosio** to be good for nothing, to be worthless

¡caracoles! *interj.* Blazes! Confound it!

carácter, *m.* character, nature, disposition

característica, *f.* trait, characteristic

característico, *adj.* characteristic

¡caramba! *interj.* Heavens!

carambola, *f.* carom (in billiards); trick; **por carambola,** indirectly, by chance

carátula, *f.* mask; title page

caravana, *f.* caravan; (Mex.) bow, curtsy

carbónico, *adj.* carbonic

carbono, *m.* (chem.) carbon

carbunclo, *m.* carbuncle

carburador, *m.* carburetor

cárcel, *f.* prison; jail

carcomido, *adj.* wormeaten

cardán, *m.* universal joint

cardenal, *m.* cardinal

cardiaco, *m.* cardiac

cardinal, *adj.* cardinal (point); principal, fundamental

cardo, *m.* thistle

carecer, *vn.* to want, lack

carencia, *f.* lack; scarcity

carestía, *f.* scarcity, want; famine; high price

careta, *f.* mask

carey, *m.* tortoise, shell turtle; tortoise shell

carga, *f.* load, burden; freight; cargo; load (of a firearm)

cargado, *adj.* loaded, full

cargador, *m.* freighter; loader

cargamento, *m.* load, cargo

cargar, *va.* to load, carry; to freight; to attack; to load a gun; to charge (on account)

cargo, *m.* debit; office; charge; care; accusation

caribe, *adj.* Caribbean

caricia, *f.* caress
caridad, *f.* charity
caries, *f.* (med.) caries, decay
cariño, *m.* fondness, love
cariñoso, *adj.* affectionate
carmesí, *m.* crimson
carnada, *f.* bait, lure
carnal, *adj.* related by blood;
  primo carnal, first cousin
carnaval, *m.* carnival
carne, *f.* flesh, meat; pulp of
  fruit
carnero, *m.* sheep, mutton
carnicería, *f.* meat market;
  slaughter
carnicero, *m.* butcher; *adj.*
  carnivorous
carnívoro, *adj.* carnivorous
caro, *adj.* expensive; dear
carpa, *f.* carp (fish); (Sp. Am.)
  a camping tent
carpeta, *f.* table cover; portfo-
  lio
carpintería, *f.* carpentry; carpenter's shop
carpintero, *m.* carpenter
carraspera, *f.* hoarseness
carrera, *f.* running; career;
  race; course, **carrera de relevos,** relay race; **carrera de
  vallas,** hurdles
carreta, *f.* cart; wagon
carretada, *f.* wagonload
carretaje, *m.* cartage
carretera, *f.* highway
carro, *m.* cart, freight car, car;
  wagon
carruaje, *m.* carriage, vehicle
carta, *f.* letter; charter
cartel, *m.* placard; handbill
cartera, *f.* brief case, letter
  case; pocketbook
cartero, postman
cartílago, *m.* cartilage
cartucho, *m.* cartridge
cartulina, *f.* Bristol board, fine
  cardboard
casa, *f.* house; concern; home
casamiento, *m.* marriage,
  wedding
casar, *va., vr.* to marry
cascabel, *m.* rattle; sleigh bell;
  (zool.) rattlesnake
cascajo, *m.* gravel
cascanueces, *m.* nutcracker

cascar, *va., vr.* to crack, break
  into pieces
cáscara, *f.* rind, peel, husk
casco, *m.* skull, cranium; helmet; hulk (of a ship); crown
  (of a hat); hoof
casero, casera, *n.* landlord or
  landlady; *adj.* domestic, familiar; homemade
casi, *adv.* almost, nearly
casilla, *f.* hut, booth, cabin;
  ticket office; **casilla de correos,** P.O. Box
casimir, *m.* cashmere
caso, *m.* case; event; occasion;
  (gram.) case
casta, *f.* caste, race, lineage;
  breed; kind, quality
castaña, *f.* chestnut
castaño, *m.* chestnut tree; *adj.*
  hazel; brown
castañuela, *f.* castanet
castellano, castellana, *n.,* *adj.*
  Castilian; Spanish language
castidad, *f.* chastity
castigar, *va.* to punish
castigo, *m.* punishment
Castilla, *f.* Castile
castillo, *m.* castle; fortress
castizo, *adj.* pure, correct (as
  to language)
casto, *adj.* pure, chaste
castrar, *va.* to geld, castrate
casual, *adj.* casual, accidental
casualidad, *f.* casualty, accident; chance, coincidence;
  por casualidad, by chance
catalán, catalana, *n.,* *adj.*
  Catalan, Catalonian
catálogo, *m.* catalogue; list
cataplasma, *f.* poultice, plaster
catar, *va.* to taste; to judge
catarata, *f.* cataract, waterfall;
  (med.) cataract
catarro, *m.* catarrh, cold
catástrofe, *f.* catastrophe, disaster
cátedra, *f.* professorship, subject taught by a professor
catedral, *adj., f.* cathedral
catedrático, *m.* professor of a
  university
categoría, *f.* category; rank
caterva, *f.* mob, throng

catolicismo, *m.* Catholicism
católico, *adj.*, *n.* Catholic
catorce, *m.*, *adj.* fourteen
catre, *m.* cot
cauce, *m.* trench, ditch, drain; bed of a river
caucho, *m.* rubber
caudal, *m.* property, wealth; abundance, plenty
caudaloso, *adj.* carrying much water (of rivers)
caudillo, *m.* chief, leader, dictator
causa, *f.* cause; occasion; motive, case, lawsuit; **a causa de,** on account of
causar, *va.* to cause, occasion
cautela, *f.* caution
cauterizar, *va.* to cauterize
cautivar, *va.* to captivate, charm, attract
cautivo, cautiva, *n.* captive, prisoner
caverna, *f.* cavern, cave
cavidad, *f.* cavity, hollow
cayo, *m.* cay, key
caza, *f.* game; hunting; *m.* (avi.) fighter plane
cazador, *m.* hunter, huntsman
cazar, *va.* to chase, hunt
cazuela, *f.* stewing pan; crock
C.C., corriente continua, D.C. or d.c., direct current
cebada, *f.* barley
cebo, *m.* food; bait, lure; priming
cebolla, *f.* onion
cebra, *f.* zebra
ceder, *va.* to grant, yield; *vn.* to submit, comply
cédula, *f.* charter, patent; ticket; permit, license; **cédulas hipotecarias,** mortgage, bank stock
céfiro, *m.* zephyr, breeze
cegar, *vn.* to become blind; *va.* to deprive of sight
ceguera, *f.* blindness
ceja, *f.* eyebrow
celda, *f.* cell
celebración, *f.* celebration
celebrar, *va.* to celebrate
celeste, *adj.* celestial, sky blue
celestial, *adj.* celestial; heavenly; perfect
célibe, *m.* unmarried person; bachelor
celo, *m.* zeal; rut (in animals); **celos,** *pl.* jealousy; **tener celos de,** to be jealous of
celosía, *f.* lattice of a window; Venetian blind
celoso, *adj.* jealous, zealous
célula, *f.* cell
cementar, *va.* to cement
cementerio, *m.* cemetery
cemento, *m.* cement; putty
cena, *f.* supper
cenagal, *m.* slough; swamp
cenar, *vn.* to have supper
cenicero, *m.* ash tray
ceniciento, *adj.* ash-colored; **Cenicienta,** *f.* Cinderella
cenit, *m.* zenith
censo, *m.* census
censor, *m.* censor, critic
censura, *f.* critical review censure, blame
censurar, *va.* to to censure, blame
centavo, *m.* a cent
centena, *f.* hundred
centenar, *m.* hundred
centenario, *adj.* centenary; *m.* centennial
centeno, *m.* (bot.) rye
centésimo, *adj.* centesimal, hundredth
centígrado, *adj.*, *m.* centigrade
centigramo, *m.* centigram
centímetro, *m.* centimeter
céntimo, *m.* centime; cent
central, *adj.* central, centric; *f.* central or main station; powerhouse; (Sp. Am.) sugar mill
centralizar, *va.* to centralize
céntrico, *adj.* central
centro, *m.* center
Centroamérica, *f.* Central America
cénts., céntimos, ¢ or c., cents
ceño, *m.* frown
cepillo, *m.* brush; **cepillo de dientes,** toothbrush; **cepillo de carpintero,** plane
cera, *f.* wax; wax taper
cerámica, *f.* ceramics

cerca, *f.* enclosure, fence; *adv.* near, close by

cercanía, *f.* proximity

cercano, *adj., adv.* near, close by

cercar, *va.* to inclose; to fence

cerciorar, *va., vr.* to ascertain, affirm

cerdo, *m.* hog, pig

cereal, *m.* cereal; grain

cerebral, *adj.* cerebral

cerebro, *m.* brain

ceremonia, *f.* ceremony

cerezo, *m.* cherry tree

cerillo, *m.* (Mex.) wax match

cernir, *va.* to sift, strain

cero, *m.* zero

cerrado, *adj.* closed; stupid, dense

cerradura, *f.* lock

cerrajero, *m.* locksmith

cerrar, *va., vn.* to close, shut; to lock; cerrarse, to be obstinate

cerro, *m.* hill

cerrojo, *m.* latch (of a door)

certeza, *f.* certainty, assurance

certidumbre, *f.* certainty, conviction

certificado, *m.* certificate; *adj.* certified, registered (as a letter)

certificar, *va.* to certify, affirm; to register (a letter)

cerveza, *f.* beer, ale, lager

cesante, *adj.* jobless

cesáreo, *adj.* Caesarian

cesión, *f.* cession, transfer; concession

cesionario, cesionaria, *n.* assignee, indorsee (of negotiable instrument)

césped, *m.* sod, lawn

cesta, *f.* basket

cesto, *m.* hand basket

cetro, *m.* scepter

cf, costo de flete, freight cost; caballo de fuerza, h.p. horsepower; confesor, confessor

cg., centigramo, cg. centigram

cia, or C.ia: Compañía, Co. or co. Company; Soc., Society

cicatriz, *f.* scar

ciclista, *m., f.* cyclist

ciclo, *m.* cycle

cielón, *m.* cyclone

ciclotrón, *m.* cyclotron

cidra, *f.* citron

ciego, *adj.* blind; *n.* blind person

cielo, *m.* sky, heaven

ciempiés, *m.* centipede

cien, *adj.* one hundred (used before a noun)

ciencia, *f.* science

cieno, *m.* mud, mire

científico, *adj.* scientific

ciento, *adj.* one hundred; *m.* a hundred

cierto, *adj.* certain, true

ciervo, *m.* deer, hart, stag

c.i.f., costo, seguro y flete, c.i.f., (com.) cost, insurance and freight

cifra, *f.* cipher, number

cigarra, *f.* katydid, cricket

cigarrera, *f.* cigarette case

cigarrillo, *m.* cigarette

cigarro, *m.* cigar; cigarette

cigüeña, *f.* (orn.) stork; (mech.) crank

cigüeñal, *m.* crankshaft

cilíndrico, *adj.* cylindrical

cilindro, *m.* cylinder; barrel

cima, *f.* summit, peak

cimentar, *va.* to lay a foundation, to establish fundamental principles

cimiento, *m.* groundwork of a building; basis, origin

cinc, *m.* zinc

cincel, *m.* chisel

cincelar, *va.* to chisel, engrave

cinco, *adj., m.* five

cincuenta, *m., adj.* fifty

cincha, *f.* girth, cinch

cine, cinema, cinematógrafo, *m.* moving-picture play or show

cinta, *f.* ribbon, tape, band

cintura, *f.* waistline

cinturón, *m.* belt; cinturón de asiento, cinturón de seguridad, seat belt, safety belt; cinturón salvavidas, life belt

ciprés, *m.* cypress tree

circo, *m.* circus

circuito, *m.* circuit
circulación, *f.* circulation
circular, *adj.* circular; *vn.* to circulate
círculo, *m.* circle; circumference; district; orb; club
circundar, *va.* to surround, encircle
circunferencia, *f.* circumference
circunspecto, *adj.* circumspect, cautious
circunstancia, *f.* circumstance, incident
ciruela, *f.* plum; **ciruela pasa,** prune
ciruelo, *m.* plum tree
cirugía, *f.* surgery
cirujano, *m.* surgeon
cisne, *m.* swan
cisterna, *f.* cistern; reservoir.
cita, *f.* citation, quotation; appointment, date
citación, *f.* quotation; summons,
citar, *va.* to make an appointment to meet a person; to convoke; to cite; to quote; to summon
cítrico, *adj.* (chem.) citric
ciudad, *f.* city
ciudadanía, *f.* citizenship; citizens
ciudadano, ciudadana, *n.* citizen
cívico, *adj.* civic
civil *adj.* civil, polite
civilización, *f.* civilization culture
civilizar, *va.* to civilize
civismo, *m.* patriotism
cizalla, *f.* metal shears
clamor, *m.* clamor, outcry
clamoroso, *adj.* clamorous; **exito clamoroso,** howling success
clandestino, *adj.* clandestine
clara, *f.* egg white
claraboya, *f.* skylight
claridad, *f.* light, brightness, clearness
clarificar, *va.* to brighten; to clarify
clarín, *m.* horn, bugle; trumpet; trumpeter

clarinete, *m.* clarinet; clarinet player
claro, *adj.* clear, bright; intelligible; light, evident, manifest; ¡**claroro!** *interj.* of course!
clase, *f.* class, rank; kind
clásico, *adj.* classical, classic
clasificar, *va.* to classify, class
clausura, *f.* closing; ad- journment
clausurar, *va.* to close; to adjourn
clave, *f.* key, code; (mus.) clef; *m.* harpsichord, clavichord
clavel, *m.* (bot.) pink, carnation
clavícula, *f.* clavicle, collarbone
clavija, *f.* pin, peg; plug, key
clavo, *m.* nail; **clavo de especia,** clove; **clavo de rosca,** screw
clemencia, *f.* clemency, mercy
clérigo, *m.* clergyman
clero, *m.* clergy
clima, *m.* climate.
clínica, *f.* clinic.
clínico, *adj.* clinical
clisé, *m.* plate, mat, cut
cloaca, *f.* sewer
cloro, *m.* (chem.) chlorine
clorofila, *f.* chlorophyll
cloroformo, *m.* chloroform
cloruro, *m.* (chem.) chloride
club, *m.* club, association
clueca, *adj.* clucking (of a hen)
clueco, *adj.* decrepit; (Sp. Am.) presumptuous, vain
cm. or **c/m, centímetro,** cm., centimeter
Co., Compañía, Co., Company; Soc., Society
c/o, a cargo de, c/o or c.o., in care of
coagular, *va., vr.* to coagulate, curd
coartar, *va.* to limit, restrain
cobarde, *adj.* cowardly, timid; *m.* coward
cobardía, *f.* cowardice
cobertizo, *m.* small shed
cobija, *f.* bed cover, blanket
cobijar, *va.* to cover; to shelter
cobra, *f.* (zool.) cobra
cobrador, *m.* collector; street-

car or train conductor

cobrar, *va.* to collect; to recover; to receive; to charge (price, fee)

cobre, *m.* copper

cóbrese al entregar, cash on delivery, C.O.D.

cobro, *m.* collection; payment

cocaína, *f.* cocaine

cocer, *va.* to boil, cook; *vn.* to boil; to ferment

cocido, *adj.* cooked, boiled; *m.* kind of beef stew

cociente, *m.* quotient

cocina, *f.* kitchen, cuisine; **cocina económica,** cooking range

cocinar, *va., vn.* to cook

cocinero, cocinera, *n.* cook

coco, *m.* coconut, coconut tree; bogey, bugaboo

cocodrilo, *m.* crocodile; faithless person

cocuyo or **cucuyo,** *m.* firefly

coche, *m.* coach; carriage; car; **coche de alquiler,** cab

cochino, *adj.* dirty, nasty; *m.* pig

coctelera, *f.* cocktail shaker

codicia, *f.* lust, greed

codicioso, *adj.* covetous

código, *m.* code of laws

codorniz, *f.* (orn.) quail

coerción, *f.* coercion

cofre, *m.* trunk; box, chest; hood (of an automobile)

coger, *va.* to catch; to surprise

cohecho, *m.* bribery

coherente, *adj.* coherent, cohesive

cohesión, *f.* cohesion

cohete, *m.* skyrocket; **cohete especial de combustible sólido,** solid-fuel space rocket

cohibir, *va.* to restrain

coincidencia, *f.* coincidence

coincidir, *vn.* to coincide

cojear, *vn.* to limp, hobble

cojera, *f.* lameness, limp

cojín. *m.* cushion

cojinete, *m.* bearing (of an axle, etc.)

cojo, *adj.* lame, cripple

col, *f.* cabbage

cola, *f.* tail; train (of a gown); line; glue; **hacer cola,** to stand in line

colaboración, *f.* collaboration

colaborar, *vn.* to collaborate

colador, *m.* colander, strainer

colapso, *m.* prostration, collapse

colar, *va., vn.* to strain, filter; **colarse,** (coll.) to squeeze (into a party) uninvited

colchón, *m.* mattress

colección, *f.* collection; set

colecta, *f.* collection of offerings

colectividad, *f.* collectivity; community

colectivización, *f.* collectivization

colectivizar, *va.* collectivize

colectivo, *adj.* collective; **contrato colectivo,** closed shop

colector, *m.* collector, gatherer

colegial, *m.* collegian; *adj.* collegiate

colegio, *m.* school; boarding school; college

cólera, *f.* anger, rage, fury; *m.* (med.) cholera

colérico, *adj.* enraged

colgante, *adj.* pendulous, hanging; **puente colgante,** suspension bridge

colgar, *va.* to hang; *vn.* to be suspended

colibrí, *m.* hummingbird

coliflor, *f.* cauliflower

colina, *f.* hill, hillock

colinabo, *m.* turnip

coliseo, *m.* opera house, theater

colmar, *va.* to heap up, fill up; **colmarse,** to reach the limit

colmena, *f.* hive, beehive

colmillo, *m.* eyetooth; long tusk

colmo, *m.* heap; completion; fill; limit

colocación, *f.* employment; situation, place; allocation

colocar, *va.* to arrange; to lay, place; to give employment to

colon, *m.* (anat.) colon

Colón, Columbus

colón, *m.* monetary unit of Costa Rica

colonia, *f.* colony; (Cuba) sugar-cane plantation; (Mex.) urban subdivision

colonial, *adj.* colonial

colonizar, *va.* to colonize

color, *m.* color, hue, dye; pretext

colorado, *adj.* ruddy, red

colorear, *va.* to color; to palliate, excuse; *vn.* to grow red

colorido, *m.* color; coloring

colorín, *m.* (orn.) linnet; vivid color; (Chile) a redheaded person

colosal, *adj.* colossal, great

coloso, *m.* colossus

columna, *f.* column; **columna vertebral,** spinal column

columpio, *m.* swing

collar, *m.* necklace

coma, *f.* comma (punctuation mark); (med.) coma

comadre, *f.* midwife; title given godmother of one's child; intimate woman friend, pal

comadrona, *f.* midwife

comandante, *m.* commander, chief; warden

comandita, *f.* (com.) silent partnership

comarca, *f.* territory, district; boundary, limit

combate, *m.* combat

combatiente, *m.* combatant

combatir, *va., vn.* to combat, fight; to attack; to contradict

combinar, *va., vr.* to combine

combustible, *adj.* combustible; *m.* fuel

comedia, *f.* comedy, play

comediante, *m., f.* actor, comedian

comedido, *adj.* eager to help

comedor, *m.* dining room

comején, *m.* white ant, termite

comentador, comentadora, *n.* commentator

comentar, *va.* to comment; to remark; to expound

comentario, *m.* comment, commentary

comer, *va.* to eat, chew; to dine; to take a piece in chess

comercial, *adj.* commercial

comerciante, *m.* trader, merchant, businessman

comerciar, *va.* to trade, have business intercourse with; **comerciar en,** to deal in

comercio, *m.* trade, commerce, business; communication, intercourse

comestable, *adj.* edible; **comestables,** *m. pl.* provisions, groceries

cometer, *va.* to commit

cometido, *m.* task, mission

comezón, *f.* itch

comicios, *m. pl.* elections; polls

cómico, *adj.* comic, comical; **cómico, cómica,** *n.* actor, actress

comida, *f.* food; dinner; meal

comienzo, *m.* beginning

comilón, comilona, *n., adj.* glutton

comillas, *f. pl.* quotation marks

comino, *m.* cumin (plant or seed); **no valer un comino,** to be worthless

comisario, *m.* commissary; deputy

comisión, *f.* trust, commission; committee

comisionado, *m.* commissioner

comisionar, *va.* to commission, depute

comité, *m.* committee

comitiva, *f.* retinue

como, *adv.* (interrogative, **cómo**) how, in what manner; as; like; **¿a cómo estamos?** what is the date?

cómoda, *f.* chest of drawers

comodidad, *f.* comfort; convenience

cómodo, *adj.* convenient, commodious; comfortable

compacto, *adj.* compact

compadecer, *va., vr.* to pity, sympathize with

compadre, *m.* godfather of one's child; friend, old pal

compañero, compañera, *n.* companion, comrade, friend, partner; pal

compañía, *f.* company, society; partnership

comparación, *f.* comparison

comparar, *va.* to compare

compartir, *va.* to share

compás, *m.* compass; (mus.) measure, time; beat

compasión, *f.* compassion, pity

compasivo, *adj.* compassionate

compatible, *adj.* compatible

compatriota, *m., f.* countryman; countrywoman; fellow citizen

compeler, *va.* to compel, constrain

compendio, *m.* summary

compensación, *f.* compensation

compensar, *va., vn.* to compensate

competencia, *f.* competition, rivalry; competence

competente, *adj.* competent

competidor, competidora, *n.* competitor

compilar, *va.* to compile

complacer, *va.* to please another; **complacerse,** to be pleased with

complaciente, *adj.* pleasing; accommodating

complejo, *m.* complex; **complejo, compleja,** *adj.* complex, intricate

complementario, *adj.* complementary

complemento, *m.* complement; (gram.) object

completar, *va.* to complete

completo, *adj.* complete

complexión, *f.* constitution, physique

complicación, *f.* complication

complicar, *va.* to complicate

cómplice, *m., f.* accomplice

complot, *m.* plot, conspiracy

componer, *va.* to compose; to repair; to settle; **componerse,** to arrange one's hair, clothes, etc., **componerse**

de, to be composed of

comportarse, *vr.* to comport oneself

compositor, compositora, *n.* composer; compositor

compostura, *f.* composition; mending, repairing; composure

compota, *f.* preserves

compra, purchase

comprar, *va.* to buy, purchase

comprender, *va.* to include, comprise; to understand

comprensible, *adj.* comprehensible

comprensión, *f.* understanding

comprensivo, *adj.* understanding

compresión, *f.* compression

compresor, *m.* compressor

comprimir, *va.* to compress; to condense; to repress

comprobante, *m.* voucher

comprobar, *va.* to verify, check; to confirm

comprometer, *va.* to compromise; to put in danger; **comprometerse,** to commit oneself; to become engaged

comprometido, *adj.* betrothed

compromiso, *m.* compromise; commitment; engagement

compuerta, *f.* lock, floodgate

compuesto, *m.* compound; *adj.* composed; repaired

compulsorio, *adj.* compulsory

computar, *va.* to compute

cómputo, *m.* computation

comulgar, *vn.* to take communion

común, *adj.* common, usual; *m.* watercloset

comunicación, *f.* communication

comunicar, *va.* to communicate

comunidad, community

comunión, communion; fellowship; common possession

comunismo, *m.* communism

comunista, *m., f.* communist

con, *prep.* with; by

conato, *m.* endeavor; crime attempted but not executed

concebir, *va., vn.* to conceive
conceder, *va.* to concede
concejal, *m.* councilman
concejo, *m.* town hall
concentración, *f.* concentration
concentrar, *va., vr.* to concentrate
concepción, *f.* conception
concepto, *m.* conception, concept; opinion
concerniente, *adj.* concerning
concernir, *v. imp.* to concern
concertar, *va.* to settle; *vn.* to agree, accord
concertista, *m., f.* concert performer or manager
concesión, *f.* concession, grant
conciencia, *f.* conscience
concienzudo, *adj.* conscientious
conciliación, *f.* conciliation
conciliar, *va.* to conciliate, reconcile
concilio, *m.* council
conciso, *adj.* concise, brief
conciudadano, conciudadana, *n.* fellow citizen; countryman
concluir, *va.* to conclude, complete; to infer
conclusión, *f.* conclusion; consequence
concluyente, *adj.* conclusive
concordancia, *f.* concordance, concord; harmony
concordar, *va.* to accord; *vn.* to agree
concordia, *f.* conformity, union, harmony
concretar, *va.* to combine, unite; to limit; to sum up
concreto, *adj.* concrete
concubina, *f.* concubine, mistress
concurrencia, *f.* audience
concurrentes, *m. pl.* attendants, guests
concurrido, *adj.* crowded, well-attended
concurrir, *vn.* to concur, agree; to attend
concurso, *m.* competition, contest

concusión, *f.* concussion
concha, *f.* shell; tortoise shell
condado, *m.* county
conde, *m.* earl, count
condecorar, *va.* to confer a decoration on
condensación, *f.* condensation
condensar, *va., vr.* to condense
condesa, *f.* countess
condescendencia, *f.* condescension, compliance
condescender, *vn.* to condescend
condición, *f.* condition, quality; stipulation
condimentar, *va.* to season (food)
condimento, *m.* condiment
condiscípulo, condiscípula, *n.* fellow-student
condolerse, *vr.* to condole, to sympathize
cóndor, *m.* (orn.) condor
conducente, *adj.* conducive
conducta, *f.* conduct; behavior
conducto, *m.* conduit; channel; **por conducto de,** through (agent)
conductor, *m.* conductor, guide
conectar, *va.* to connect
conejo, coneja, *n.* rabbit
conejillo, *m.* small rabbit; **conejillo de Indias,** guinea pig
conexión, *f.* connection
confección, *f.* (med.) compound; confection
confeccionar, *va.* to make, put together
confederación, *f.* confederacy, confederation
confederado, confederada, *n., adj.* confederate
conferenciante, *m., f.* public lecturer
conferenciar, *vn.* to hold a conference; to consult together
conferencista, *m., f.* lecturer, speaker
conferir, *va.* to confer, grant
confesar, *va.* to confess

confesión, *f.* confession
confesor, *m.* confessor
confiado, *adj.* confident; arrogant, forward
confianza, *f.* confidence, boldness; assurance; intimacy; trust; **digno de confianza,** reliable, trustworthy
confiar, *va., vn.* to confide, trust in; to hope, count on
confidencia, *f.* confidence
confidencial, *adj.* confidential
confidente, *m., f.* confidant
confín, *m.* limit, boundary
confinar, *va., vn.* to confine, limit; to border upon
confirmación, *f.* confirmation
confirmr, *va.* to confirm
confiscar, *va.* to confiscate
confite, *m.* candy, bonbon
conflicto, *m.* conflict
conformar, *va.* to conform; *vn.* to suit, fit; **conformarse,** to resign oneself
conforme, *adj.* conformable, suitable; **estar conforme,** to be in agreement; *adv.* according to
conformidad, *f.* conformity; patience, resignation
confort, *m.* comfort
confortante, *adj.* comforting; *m.* sedative
confortar, *va.* to comfort
confraternidad, *f.* confraternity, brotherhood
confrontar, *va.* to confront; to compare
confundir, *va., vr.* to confound; to perplex
confusión, *f.* confusion, disorder; perplexity
confuso, *adj.* confused; perplexed
conga, *f.* conga
congelación, *f.* freezing
congelador, *m.* freezer
congeladora, *f.* deep freezer
congelar, *va., vr.* to freeze, congeal
congeniar, *vn.* to be congenial
congénito, *adj.* congenital
conglomeración, *f.* conglomeration
congoja, *f.* anguish, grief

congratular, *va.* to congratulate
congregar, *va.* to assemble, meet
congreso, *m.* congress
congruencia, *f.* congruency
cónico, *adj.* conical
conjetura, *f.* conjecture
conjugar, *va.* to conjugate
conjunción, *f.* conjunction
conjunto, *adj.* united, conjunct; *m.* the whole, the ensemble
conjurar, *va., vn.* to conjure; to cospire
conmemoración, *f.* commemoration
conmemorar, *va.* to commemorate
conmemorativo, *adj.* memorial
conmigo, *pron.* with me, with myself
conmiseración, *f.* commiseration, pity
conmovedor, *adj.* affecting, moving, touching
conmover, *va., vr.* to disturb, move, stir
conmutador, *m.* electric switch
connivencia, *f.* connivance
conocedor, conocedora, *n.* expert; connoisseur
conocer, *va.* to know, to be acquainted; to understand
conocido, conocida, *n.* acquaintance
conocimiento, *m.* knowledge, understanding; consciousness; (com.) bill of lading; **poner en conocimiento,** to inform, to advise
conque, *conj.* so then
conquista, *f.* conquest
conquistador, *m.* conqueror
conquistar, *va.* to conquer
consagrar, *va.* to consecrate, dedicate
consciente, *adj.* conscious, aware
consecución, *f.* attainment
consecuencia, *f.* consequence; result
consecuente, *adj.* conse-

quent, logical

consecutivo, *adj.* consecutive

conseguir, *va.* to attain, get

consejero, *m.* counselor; councilor; advisor

consejo, *m.* counsel, advice; council; advisory board

consentido *adj.* pampered

consentimiento, *m.* consent, assent

consentir, *va.* to consent, to agree; to comply, acquiesce; to coddle

conserje, *m.* concierge, janitor

conserva, *f.* conserve, preserve; **conservas,** canned goods

conservador, *adj.* conservative

conservar, *va.* to conserve; to keep, maintain

conservatorio, *m.* conservatory

considerable, *adj.* considerable

consideración, *f.* consideration, regard

considerado, *adj.* prudent, considerate; esteemed

considerando, *conj.* whereas

considerar, *va.* to consider, think over; to respect

consigna, (mil.) watchword

consignación, *f.* consignation; consignment

consignar, *va.* to consign

consignatario, *m.* trustee; consignee

consigo, *pron.* with oneself

consiguiente, *adj.* consequent, consecutive; *m.* consequence, effect; **por consiguiente,** consequently

consistencia, *f.* consistence

consistente, *adj.* consistent; firm, solid

consistir, *vn.* to consist

consocio, *m.* partner, fellow member

consolación, *f.* consolation

consolar, *va.* to console, to cheer

consolidar, *va., vr.* to consolidate, strengthen

consorte, *m., f.* consort, companion

conspicuo, *adj.* conspicuous; prominent

conspiración, *f.* conspiracy, plot

conspirar, *vn.* to conspire, plot

constancia, *f.* constancy

constante, *adj.* constant, firm

constar, *v. imp.* to be evident or certain; to be composed of, consist of; **hacer constar,** to state; **me consta,** I know positively

constelación, *f.* constellation

consternar, *va.* to confound, dismay

constipación, *f.* cold; constipation

constipado, *m.* cold in the head

constitución, *f.* constitution

constitucional, *adj.* constitutional

constituir, *va., vr.* to constitute

construcción, *f.* construction

constructor, constructora, *n.* builder

construir, *va.* to build, construct; to construe

consuelo, *m.* consolation, comfort

cónsul, *m.* consul

consulado, *m.* consulate

consulta, *f.* consultation

consultar, *va.* to consult

consultivo, *adj.* advisory

consultor, consultora, *n.* adviser, counselor; *adj.* advisory, consulting

consultorio, *m.* doctor's office; clinic

consumar, *va.* to consummate, finish, perfect

consumidor, consumidora, *n.* consumer; *adj.* consuming

consumir, *va.* to consume; **consumirse,** to languish

consumo, *m.* consumption of provisions; demand (for merchandise)

consunción, (med.) consumption

contabilidad, *f.* accounting, bookkeeping

contacto, *m.* contact, touch
contado, *adj.* scarce, rare; **al contado**, cash, ready money
contador, *m.* accountant; counter; **contador de agua**, water meter; **contador Geiger**, Geiger counter
contagiar, *va.* to infect
contagio, *m.* contagion
contagioso, *adj.* contagious
contaminar, *va.* to contaminate
contante, *adj.* fit to be counted; **dinero contante y sonante**, ready cash
contar, *va.* to count, calculate; to relate
contemplar, *va.* to contemplate, to coddle
contender, *vn.* to contend; to contest
contendiente, *m., f.* competitor; contender
contener, *va.* to contain, comprise; **contenerse**, to repress
contenido, *m.* contents
contentar, *va., vr.* to content
contento, *adj.* glad; pleased; content; *m.* contentment
conteo, *m.* countdown
contestación, *f.* answer, reply
contestar, *va.* to answer
contienda, *f.* contest, dispute
contigo, *pron.* with you (sing.)
continental, *adj.* continental
continente, *m.* continent, mainland
contingente, *adj.* accidental; *m.* contingent; share
continuación, *f.* continuation, continuance, continuity
continuamente, *adv.* continuously, continually
continuar, *va., vn.* to continue
continuidad, *f.* continuity
continuo, *adj.* continuous, continual
contorno, *m.* environs; contour, outline
contrabajo, *m.* bass viol
contrabandista, *m.* smuggler
contracción, *f.* contraction
contradecir, *va.* to contradict
contradicción, *f.* contradiction
contradictorio, *adj.* contradictory
contraer, *va., vn.* to contract; to reduce; **contraerse**, to shrink up
contrahecho, *adj.* deformed
contralor, *m.* controller
contralto, *m., f.* contralto
contraorden, *f.* countermand
contrapeso, *m.* counterweight; (Chile) uneasiness; **hacer contrapeso a**, to counterbalance
contrapunto, *m.* (mus.) counterpoint, harmony
contrariar, *va.* to contradict, oppose; to vex
contrariedad, *f.* opposition; disappointment
contrario, contraria, *n.* opponent, antagonist; *adj.* contrary, opposite; hostile; **al contrario**, on the contrary
contrarrestar, *va.* to counteract
contraseña, *f.* countersign; (mil.) watchword, password
contrastar, *va.* to contrast; to assay metals
contraste, *m.* contrast; opposition
contratar, *va.* to engage, hire; to contract
contratiempo, *m.* disappointment; mishap
contratista, *m.* contractor
contrato, *m.* contract, pact
contraveneno, *m.* antidote
contribuir, *va.* to contribute
contribuyente, *m., f.* contributor; taxpayer
contrincante, *m.* competitor
contrito, *adj.* contrite
control, *m.* control, check
contusión, *f.* contusion
convalecencia, *f.* convalescence
convalecer, *vn.* to convalesce
convencer, *va.* to convince
convencimiento, *m.* conviction
convención, *f.* convention
convencional, *adj.* conventional

convenido, *adj.* agreed
conveniencia, *f.* utility, profit; convenience; ease; desirability
conveniente, *adj.* convenient, advantageous; desirable
convenio, *m.* pact
convener, *vn.* to agree, coincide; to compromise; to fit, suit
convento, *m.* convent
conversación, *f.* conversation
conversar, *vn.* to converse, talk
converso, *m.* convert
convertir, *va.* to transform, convert; to reform; **convertirse,** to become
convicción, *f.* conviction
convidado, *adj.* invited; **convidado, convidada,** *n.* invited guest
convidar, *va.* to invite
convincente, *adj.* convincing
convocar, *va.* to convoke, assemble
convoy, *m.* convoy, escort
convulsión, *f.* convulsion
conyugal, *adj.* conjugal
cónyuges, *m. pl.* married couple, husband and wife
coñac, *m.* cognac, brandy
cooperación, *f.* cooperation
cooperar, *vn.* to cooperate
cooperativo, *adj.* cooperative; **cooperativa,** cooperative society
coordinación, *f.* coordination
coordinar, *va.* to coordinate
copa, *f.* cup; goblet; top of a tree; crown of a hat; **copas,** *pl.* hearts (at cards)
Copenhague, *f.* Copenhagen
copete, *m.* toupee; pompadour; top, summit
copia, *f.* copy, transcript; imitation
copiar, *va.* to copy; to imitate
copioso, *adj.* abundant
copla, *f.* couplet; popular ballad, folksong
coqueta, *f.* coquette, flirt
coquetear, *vn.* to flirt
coquetería, *f.* coquetry, flirtation

coquetón, coquetona, *adj.* flirtatious
coraje, *m.* anger
corajudo, *adj.* ill-tempered
coral, *m.* coral; *adj.* choral
coraza, *f.* cuirass; armor plate; shell of a turtle
corazón, *m.* heart; core; benevolence; center
corazonada, *f.* sudden inspiration; presentiment, hunch
corbata, *f.* necktie
corcovado, *adj.* humpbacked, crooked
corcho, *m.* cork
cordel, *m.* cord, rope
cordero, *m.* lamb; meek, gentle man
cordial, *adj.* cordial, affectionate; *m.* cordial
cordialidad, *f.* cordiality
cordillera, range of mountains
cordón, *m.* cord, string; military cordon
cordura, *f.* prudence, sanity, good judgment
corista, *m.* chorister; *f.* chorus girl
cornada, *f.* thrust with horns
córnea, cornea
corneta, *f.* cornet; *m.* bugler
coro, *m.* choir, chorus
corona, *f.* crown; coronet; top of the head; crown (English silver coin); monarchy; halo
coronar, *va.* to crown; to complete, perfect
coronel, *m.* (mil.) colonel
coronilla, *f.* crown of the head
corporación, *f.* corporation
corporal, *adj.* corporal, bodily
corpulento, *adj.* corpulent
Corpus, *m.* Corpus Christi (religious festival)
corral, *m.* poultry yard; **aves de corral,** poultry
correa, *f.* leather strap, belt; **tener correa,** to bear teasing good-humoredly
corrección, *f.* correction; proper demeanor
correcto, *adj.* correct
corredor, *m.* runner; corridor, broker
corregidor, *m.* corregidor

(Spanish magistrate)

corregir, *va.* to correct, amend; to reprehand

correo, *m.* mail; mailman; post office

correoso, *adj.* leathery

correr, *vn.* to run; to race; to flow; to blow (applied to the wind); to pass away (applied to time); *va.* to race (an animal); **correrse**, to become disconcerted

correría, *f.* excursion, incursion; **correrías**, youthful escapades

correspondencia, *f.* correspondence; proportion

corresponder, *va.* to reciprocate; to correspond; to agree

correspondiente, *adj.* corresponding; suitable

corresponsal *m.* correspondent

corretear, *vn.* to run around (as children)

corrida, *f.* course, race; **corrida de toros**, bullfight

corrido, *m.* (mus.) a special rhythm

corriente, *f.* current (of water, electricity, etc.); stream; **tener al corriente**, to keep advised; *adj.* current; ordinary

corromper, *va., vr.* to corrupt

corrupción, *f.* corruption

cortapapel, *m.* paper knife

cortaplumas, *m.* penknife

corte, *m.* cutting; cut; felling of trees; cut goods to make a garment; *f.* (royal) court, the court of chancery; retinue; courtship, flattery; **hacer la corte**, to woo; **Cortes**, *f. pl.* Cortes, Spanish Parliament

cortejar, *va.* to make love, court

cortejo, *m.* cortege, procession

cortés, *adj.* courteous, polite

cortesano, *m.* courtier; **cortesana**, *f.* courtesan

cortesía, *f.* courtesy

cortina, *f.* curtain

corto, *adj.* short; shy

cortocircuito, *m.* short circuit

corva, *f.* bend of the knee

cosa, *f.* thing; matter

cosecha, *f.* harvest; crop

cosechar, *va.* to crop, reap

coser, *va.* to sew; **máquina de coser**, sewing machine

cosmético, *m.* cosmetic

cosmopolita, *n., adj.* cosmopolite, cosmopolitan

cosquillas, *f. pl.* tickling; **hacer cosquillas**, to tickle

costa, *f.* cost, price; expense; coast, shore

costado, *m.* side; (mil.) flank

costal, *m.* sack, large bag

costar, *vn.* to cost

coste, *m.* cost, expense

costear, *va.* to pay the cost; *vn.* to sail along the coast

costero, *adj.* coastal

costilla, *f.* rib; (coll.) wife

costo, *m.* cost, price

costoso, *adj.* costly, expensive

costra, *f.* crust

costura, *f.* seam; needlework; sewing

costurera, *f.* seamstress

cotidiano, *adj.* daily

cotización, *f.* (com.) quotation

cotizar, *va.* to quote (a price)

coto, *m.* (med.) goiter

cotorra, *f.* magpie; (coll.) talkative woman

coyote, *m.* coyote

coyuntura, *f.* joint, articulation

C.P.T., Contador Público Titulado, C.P.A. Certified Public Accountant

cráneo, *m.* skull, cranium

cráter *m.* crater

creación, *f.* creation

Creador, *m.* the Creator, God

creador, *adj.* creative

crear, *va.* to create, make; to establish

crecer, *vn.* to grow; to increase; to swell

creces, *f. pl.* increase; **pagar con creces**, to pay back generously

creciente, *f.* swell; leaven; crescent (of the moon); (naut.) flood tide; *adj.* growing, increasing; crescent

(moon)

crecimiento, *m.* growth

credencial, *f.* credential

crédito, *m.* credit; reputation

crédulo, *adj.* credulous

creer, *va.* to believe; to think; **¡ya lo creo!** you bet! of course!

crema, *f.* cream

cremallera, *f.* (mech.) rack; zipper

crepúsculo, *m.* twilight

crespo, *adj.* crisp; curly; *m.* (Sp. Am.) a curl

crespón, *m.* crepe

cresta, *f.* cockscomb; crest of some birds; top, summit of a mountain; (Col.) a thing one loves; love

cría, *f.* breed or brood of animals; hatch; (coll.) child reared by a nurse

criada, *f.* maid servant

criadilla, *f.* testicle; small loaf; truffle

criado, *m.* servant

criador, *m.* creator; breeder

crianza, *f.* breeding, education

criar, *va.* to create, produce; to breed; to nurse; to suckle; to bring up

crimen, *m.* crime

criminal, *adj., n.* criminal

crin, *f.* mane, horsehair

criollo, criolla, *n.* born in Latin America of European parents; peasant; *adj.* native, typical of the region

crisis, *f.* crisis

crisma, *f.* (coll.) head

crisol, *m.* crucible; melting pot

cristal, *m.* crystal; crystal glass; **cristal tallado,** cut crystal

cristalería, *f.* glassware

cristalino, *adj.* crystalline, clear

cristalizar, *va.* to crystallize

cristianismo, *m.* Christianism

cristiano, cristiana, *n., adj.* Christian

Cristo, *m.* Christ

Cristóbal Colón, Christopher Columbus

criterio *m.* criterion, judgment

crítica, *f.* criticism

criticar, *va.* to criticize

crítico, *m.* critic, censurer; *adj.* critical

cromo, *m.* chromium, chrome

crónico, *adj.* chronic

cronista, *m., f.* chronicler; reporter

croqueta, *f.* croquette

cruce, *m.* crossing; crossroads

crucificar, *va.* to crucify; to torment

crucifijo, *m.* crucifix

crucigrama, *m.* crossword puzzle

crudo, *adj.* raw, crude; green unripe; rude, cruel

cruel, *adj.* cruel

crueldad, *f.* cruelty

crujido, *m.* crack, creak

crujir, *vn.* to crackle, rustle; **crujir los dientes,** to grind the teeth

cruz, *f.* cross

cruzada, *f.* crusade

cruzado, *adj.* crossed; of crossed breed, etc.

cruzar, *va.* to cross

c.s.f.; costo, seguro y flete, c.i.f.; cost, insurance, and freight

cta. or **c.ᵗᵃ , cuenta,** (com.) a/c or acc., account

cta., cte. or **cta., corr.ᵗᵉ , cuenta corriente,** (com.) current account

cte. or **corr.ᵗᵉ, corriente,** current, usual, common

c/u, cada uno, each one, every one

cuaderno, *m.* memorandum book

cuadra, *f.* block of houses

cuadrado, *adj.* square; (Cuba) rude and stupid; *m.* square

cuadragésimo, *adj.* fortieth

cuadrángulo, *m.* quadrangle

cuadrilátero, *adj.* quadrilateral

cuadrilla, *f.* gang, crew, troop; matador and his assistants

cuadro, *m.* square; picture; picture frame

cuadrúpedo, *adj.* quadruped

cuajar, *va.* to coagulate; *vn.* to

succeed; to please; **cuajarse,** to coagulate

cual, *pron., adj.* which; such as; *adv.* as; how; like; **¿cuál?** *interr.* which (one)?

cualidad *f.* quality

cualquiera, *adj., pron.* any; anyone, anybody, somebody

cuan, *adv.* how, as (used only before adj. or adv.); **cuán,** *adv.* how, what

cuando (*interr.* **cuándo**), *adv.* when; in case that; if; although; even; sometimes

cuanto, *adj.* as many as, as much as; **¿cuánto?** how much?; **¿cuántos?** how many?; *adv.* as; the more; **cuanto antes,** at once; **en cuanto a,** with regard to

cuarenta, *adj.* forty

cuarentena, *f.* quarantine

cuaresma, *f.* Lent

cuartel, *m.* barracks; **cuartel general,** headquarters

cuarteto, *m.* quartet

cuarto, *m.* fourth part, quarter; dwelling, room; *adj.* fourth

cuate, *m., adj.* (Mex.) twin; (coll.) pal

cuatro, *adj.* four; *m.* figure four; (mus.) quartet ; **las cuatro,** *f. pl.* four o'clock

cubano, cubana, *adj., n.* Cuban

cúbico, *adj.* cubic

cubierta, *f.* cover; envelope; wrapping; deck of a ship; (auto.) hood

cubierto, *m.* place for one at the table; regular dinner

cubil, *m.* lair of wild beasts

cubo, *m.* cube; pail; hub (of a wheel)

cubrir, *va.* to cover; to disguise; to cover a mare; **cubrirse,** to put on one's hat

cucaracha, *f.* cockroach

cucurucho, *m.* paper cone

cuchara, *f.* spoon

cucharada, *f.* spoonful

cucharita, *f.* teaspoon

cucharón, *m.* ladle, dipper, large spoon; scoop

cuchicheo, *m.* whispering, murmur

cuchillo, *m.* knife

cuello, *m.* neck; neck of a bottle; collar of a garment; **cuello de estrangulación,** bottleneck

cuenca, *f.* valley, basin of a river; (anat.) eye socket

cuento, *m.* story, tale, narrative; **cuento de hadas,** fairy tale

cuerda, *f.* cord; string for musical instruments; spring of a watch or clock; **bajo cuerda,** underhandedly; **dar cuerda,** to wind

cuerdo, *adj.* prudent, judicious; in his senses

cuerno, *m.* horn; corn, callosity; **cuerno de abundancia** horn of plenty

cuerpo, *m.* body; cadaver, corpse; staff, corps

cuervo, *m.* (orn.) crow, raven

cuesta, *f.* hill; **cuesta arriba,** uphill; with great trouble and difficulty

cuestión, *f.* question; dispute; problem; matter

cuestionario, *m.* questionnaire

cueva, *f.* cave, grotto, den

cuidado, *m.* care, attention; solicitude, anxiety; accuracy; **tener cuidado,** to be careful; **¡cuidado!** *interj.* watch out!

cuidadoso, *adj.* careful

cuidar, *va.* to heed, care; to mind, look after; **cuidarse,** to be careful of one's health

cuita, *f.* grief, affliction

culata, *f.* breech of a gun; butt

culebra, *f.* snake; **culebra de cascabel,** rattlesnake

culo, *m.* breech, backside; anus; bottom

culpa, *f.* misdemeanor; sin; guilt; **tener la culpa,** to be at fault

culpable, *adj.* guilty

culpar, *va.* to accuse, blame

cultivar, *va.* to cultivate

cultivo, *m.* cultivation; farming; culture (of bacteria)

culto, *adj.* elegant, correct; polished; civilized; culture; worship, cult, religion; homage

cultura, *f.* culture

cumbre, *f.* top, summit

cumpleaños, *m.* birthday

cumplido, *adj.* polished, polite; *m.* compliment

cumplimiento, *m.* compliment; accomplishment; fulfillment; expiration (of credit, etc.)

cumplir, *va.* to execute, carry out; to fulfil; **cumplir años,** to have a birthday; *vn.* to fall due

cúmulo, *m.* heap, pile

cuna, *f.* cradle; native country; lineage; origin

cuñado, cuñada, *n.* brother- or sister-in-law

cuociente, *m.* quotient

cuota, *f.* quota, fixed share; fee

cupé, *m.* coupé; cab

cupo, *m.* quota, share

cupón, *m.* coupon

cúpula, *f.* cupola, dome

cura, *m.* priest, parson; *f.* healing, cure, remedy

curandero, *m.* quack, medicaster

curar, *va.* to cure, heal

curiosidad, *f.* curiosity; neatness; rarity

curioso, *adj.* curious, strange; neat; diligent

cursar, *va.* to study (a course)

curtir, *va.* to tan leather; to sunburn; to inure to hardships

curva, *f.* curve, bend, curved line; **curva cerrada,** sharp bend; **curva doble,** s-curve

curvo, *adj.* curved, bent

cúspide, *f.* apex, peak

custodia, *f.* custody, keeping, hold; guard, escort; (rel.) monstrance

custodiar, *va.* to guard, watch

cutícula, *f.* cuticle

cuyo, cuya, *pron.* of which, of whom, whose, whereof

czar, *m.* czar

Ch

ch/, cheque, check

chabacano, *adj.* coarse, awkward; *m.* (Mex.) apricot

chacarero, *m.* (Arg. Urug.) farmer on small scale

chacra, *f.* (Arg. Urug.) small size farm

chal, *m.* shawl

chalán, *m.* hawker, huckster; (Mex.) **chalán de río,** river ferry

chaleco, *m.* waistcoat, vest

chalina, *f.* scarf

chalupa, *f.* (Mex.) small canoe

chamaco, chamaca, *n.* (Mex.) small boy or girl

chamarra, *f.* mackinaw coat

chambón, chambona, *adj.* awkward, bungling; *n.* bungler

champaña, *m.* champagne

champú, *m.* shampoo

chamuscar, *va.* to singe, scorch

chancear, *vn., vr.* to joke, jest

chancla, *f.* old shoe

chanza, *f.* joke, jest, fun

chapa, *f.* thin metal plate flush on cheek; veneer

chaparro, *adj.* (Mex.) small or short (of a person)

chaparrón, *m.* violent shower of rain

chapulín, *m.* grasshopper

chaqueta, *f.* jacket, coat

charada, *f.* charade

charca, *f.* pool of water, pond

charco, *m.* pool of standing water

charla, *f.* idle chitchat, prattle, talk

charlatán, charlatana, *n.* idle talker; quack

charol, *m.* varnish; lacquer; enamel; patent leather

charro, *m.* churl; Mexican cowboy; *adj.* gaudy

chasco, *m.* joke, jest; disappointment; **llevarse chasco,** to be disappointed

chasis, *m.* chassis

chasquido, *m.* crack of a whip

chato, *adj.* flat, flattish; flatnosed

chaveta, *f.* bolt, pin, pivot; **perder la chaveta**, to become rattled

chelín, *m.* shilling

cheque, *m.* (com.) check

chicle, *m.* chewing gum

chico, *adj.* little, small; *n.* little boy or girl

chícharo, *m.* pea

chicharrón, *m.* crackling, pork rind or fat cooked until crisp

chichón, *m.* lump on the head occasioned by a blow

chiflar, *vn.* to whistle; **chiflarse**, (coll.) to become mentally unbalanced; to act silly

chile, *m.* (bot.) chili, red pepper

chileno, chilena, *n., adj.* Chilean

chillido, *m.* squeak, shriek

chimenea, *f.* chimney; smokestack; (naut.) funnel

chimpancé, *m.* chimpanzee

china, *f.* porcelain; pebble; (Cuba and P.R.) thin-skinned orange; **China**, China

chinche, *f.* bedbug; thumbtack

chinchilla, *f.* chinchilla

chinela, *f.* house slipper

chino, china, *n., adj.* Chinese; *m.* Chinese language

chiquillo, chiquilla, *n.* child, youngster

chiquito, chiquita, *adj.* little, small; *n.* little boy or girl

chiripa, *f.* fluke (in billiards); (coll.) fortunate chance; **de chiripa**, by mere chance

chisme, *m.* misreport; gossip

chismear, *va., vn.* to tattle, gossip

chismoso, *adj.* tattling, talebearing

chispa, *f.* spark; very small diamond; small particle; **¡chispas!** *interj.* blazes! **echar chispas**, to rave

chiste, *m.* joke, jest

chistoso, *adj.* funny, comical

chivo, chiva, *n.* kid, goat

chocante, *adj.* repugnant

chocolate, *m.* chocolate

chochear, *vn.* to dote

chochera, *f.* second childhood

chofer or **chófer**, *m.* chauffeur, driver

choque, *m.* shock; collision, crash, clash

chorizo, *m.* pork sausage

chorrear, *vn.* to drip from a spout, gush, drip; trickle

chorro, *m.* gush; **a chorros**, abundantly

chotear, *va.* to rib, kid, poke fun at

choza, *f.* hut, cabin

chuleta, *f.* chop; **chuleta de puerco**, pork chop

chulo, chula, *n.* jester, clown; *adj.* (Sp. Am.) pretty, darling

chusco, *adj.* pleasant, droll

chuzo, *m.* spear or pike; **llover a chuzos**, to rain heavily

D

D., Dn. or **D.ⁿ, Don**, Don, title equivalent to Mr., but used before given name

Da. or **D.ª, Doña**, Donna, title equivalent to Mrs. or Miss but used before given name

dádiva, *f.* gift, present; handout

dado, *m.* die (*pl.* dice); (*p.p.* of **dar**) **dado que** or **dado caso que**, in case that, provided that, since

daga, dagger

dalia, (bot.) dahlia

dama, lady, mistress; king (in checkers (theat. leading lady; **damas**, *pl.* checkers

danés, danesa, *n., adj.* Danish

Danubio, *m.* Danube

danza, *f.* dance

danzar, *vn.* to dance

dañar, *va.* to damage; to injure; to spoil

dañino, *adj.* harmful

daño, *m.* damage, injury

dar, *va., vn.* to give; to supply, **dar a conocer**, to make known; **dar prestado**, to lend; **darse por vencido**, to give up; **darse cuenta de**, to realize: **darse prisa,** to hurry

data, *f.* date; item in an account

datar, *va.* to date

dátil, *m.* (bot.) date

dato, *m.* datum; **datos,** *pl.* data

D. de J.C., después de Jesucristo, A.D. After Christ

DDT, DDT (insecticide)

de, *prep.* of; from; for

debajo, *adv.* under, underneath, below

debate, *m.* debate, contest

debe, *m.* (com.) debit; **debe y haber,** debit and credit

deber, *m.* obligation, duty; debt; *va.* to owe; to be obliged

debido, debida, *adj.* due; proper

débil, *adj.* feeble, weak

débito, *m.* debt; duty

debutar, *vn.* to make one's debut

década, *f.* decade

decadencia, *f.* decay, decline

decaer, *vn.* to decay, decline

decaído, *adj.* crestfallen

decano, *m.* senior, dean

decencia, *f.* decency

decente, *adj.* decent, honest

decididamente, *adv.* decidedly

decigramo, *m.* decigram

decimal, *adj.* decimal

décimo, *adj.* tenth
  va. to say, tell, speak; **querer decir,** to mean; *m.* familiar saying

decisión, *f.* decision, determination

decisivo, *adj.* decisive

declamar, *vn.* to harangue, recite

declaración, *f.* declaration, statement, explation; (law) deposition; railroad bill of lading

declarar, *va.* to declare, state; (law) to depose upon oath; **declararse,** to declare one's opinion; (coll.) to declare one's love

declinación, *f.* decline; (gram.) declension

declinar, *vn.* to decline; *va.* (gram.) to decline

declive, *m.* declivity, slope

decomisar, *va.* to confiscate

decoración, *f.* decoration, ornament; stage scenery

decorado, *m.* decoration, stage scenery

decorar, *va.* to decorate; to adorn; to illustrate

decoroso, *adj.* decorous, decent

decretar, *va.* to decree, decide; to determine

decreto, *m.* decree

dedal, *m.* thimble

dedicación, *f.* dedication; consecration

dedicado, *adj.* dedicated; destined

dedicar, *va.* to dedicate, devote, consecrate; **dedicarse,** to apply oneself to

dedicatoria, *f.* dedication

dedillo, *m.* little finger; **saber una cora al dedillo,** to know a thing perfectly

dedo, *m.* finger; toe; **dedo meñique,** little finger; **dedo pulgar,** thumb; **dedo del corazon,** middle finger; **dedo anular,** ring finger

deducción, *f.* deduction

deducir, *va.* to deduce, to subtract, deduct

defectivo, *adj.* defective

defectuoso, *adj.* defective

defender, *va.* to defend, uphold

defensa, *f.* defense, justification; apology; shelter, protection

defensiva, *f.* defensive

defensor, defensora, *n.* defender, supporter; lawyer

deferencia, *f.* deference

deficiencia, *f.* deficiency

deficiente, *adj.* deficient

déficit, *m.* deficit

definición, *f.* definition

definido, *adj.* definite

definir, *va.* to define, describe

definitivo, definitiva, *adj.* definitive, final; **en definiti-**

va, in short, definitely

deformado, *adj.* deformed

deformar, *va., vr.* to deform, disfigure

deforme, *adj.* deformed, ugly

deformidad, *f.* deformity

defraudar, *va.* to defraud

defunción, *f.* death

degenerar, *vn.* to degenerate

degollar, *va.* to behead

degradación, *f.* degradation

degradar, *va., vr.* to degrade

deidad, *f.* deity, divinity

dejado, *adj.* slovenly, indolent

dejar, *va.* to leave, let; to omit; to permit, allow; to forsake; to bequeath; **dejarse,** to abandon oneself (to)

del, of the (contraction of **de el**)

delantal, *m.* apron

delante, *adv.* ahead; **delante de,** *prep.* in front of

delantero, *adj.* foremost, first; **delantera,** *f.* forepart; lead, advantage; **tomar la delantero,** to take the lead

delatar, *va.* to accuse, denounce

delegación, *f.* delegation

delegado, delegada, *n.* delegate, deputy

delegar, *va.* to delegate, substitute

deleitar, *va.* to delight

deleite, *m.* pleasure, delight

deletrear, *va., vn.* to spell

delgado, *adj.* thin

deliberación, *f.* deliberation

deliberar, *vn.* to deliberate

delicadeza, *f.* delicacy, subtlety

delicado, *adj.* delicate, tender; fastidious; dainty

delicia, *f.* delight, pleasure

delicioso, *adj.* delicious, delightful

delincuencia, *f.* delinquency

delincuente, *m., f.* delinquent

delinquir, *vn.* to transgress the law

delirante, *adj.* delirious

delirar, *vn.* to be delirious

delirio, *m.* delirium; nonsense

delito, *m.* crime

delta, *f.* delta

demanda, *f.* demand, claim; lawsuit; request; **oferta y demanda,** supply and demand

demandado, demandada, *n.* defendant

demandar, *va.* to demand, petition, claim; to sue

demás, *adj.* other; **los** or **las demás,** the rest, the others; *adv.* besides; **y demás,** and so on; **por demás,** in vain, to no purpose

demasía, *f.* excess in the price; abundance, plenty

demasiado, *adj.* excessive, overmuch; *adv.* too much, excessively

demente, *adj.* mad, insane

democracia, *f.* democracy

demoler, *va.* to demolish

demonio, *m.* devil, demon; ¡**demonio!** *interj.* the deuce!

demora, *f.* delay

demorar, *vn.* to delay, tarry

demostración, *f.* demonstration

demostrar, *va.* to prove, demonstrate, show

demostrativo, *adj.* demonstrative

denigrar, *va.* to blacken; to calumniate

denominación, *f.* denomination

denominador, *m.* (math.) denominator

denominar, *va.* to call, give a name to

denso, *adj.* dense, thick

dentadura, *f.* set of teeth

dental, *adj.* dental

dentición, *f.* dentition, teething

dentífrico, *m.* dentifrice; *adj.* for tooth cleaning

dentista, *m.* dentist

dentistería, *f.* dentistry

denuncia, *f.* denunciation

denunciar, *va.* to denounce

departamento, *m.* department; section, bureau; apartment; (rail.) compartment

dependencia, *f.* dependency; relation, affinity

depender, *vn.* to depend, be dependent on; **depender de,**

to count on

dependiente, _m._ dependent; subordinate; clerk

deplorable, _adj._ deplorable

deplorar, _va._ to deplore, regret

deponer, _va._ to depose, declare; to displace; _vn._ to evacuate the bowels

deportar, _va._ to deport, banish

deporte, _m._ sport, amusement

deportive, _adj._ sport, athletic

deposición, _f._ deposition; assertion, affirmation; evacuation of the bowels

depositar, _va._ to deposit

depósito, _m._ deposit; warehouse

depraver, _va._ to deprave, corrupt

depresión, _f._ depression

deprimir, _va._ to depress

derecha, _f._ right hand, right side; right wing (in politics)

derecho, _adj._ right, straight; _m._ right; law; just claim; tax duty; fee; **dar derecho** to entitle

derivado, _m._ by-product; (gram.) derivative; _adj._ derived

derivar, _va., vn._ to derive; (naut.) to deflect from the course

derogar, _va._ to derogate, abolish

derramar, _va._ to drain off water; to spread; to spill; to shed; **derramarse,** to spill; to become scattered

derrame, _m._ leakage

derredor, _m._ circumference, circuit; **al derredor** or **en derredor,** about, around

derretir, _va., vr._ to melt

derribar, _va._ to demolish; to overthrow

derrocar, _va._ to overthrow; to demolish

derrochar, _va._ to squander

derrota, _f._ defeat, rout (of an army, etc.)

derrotar, _va._ to cause (a ship) to fall off her course; to defeat

derrotero, _m._ ship's course; (fig.) course, way

derrumbar, _va._ to demolish; **derrumbarse,** to crumble

derrumbe, _m._ landslide

desabotonar, _va._ to unbutton

desabrido, _adj._ tasteless, insipid

desabrigar, _va._ to uncover, to deprive of clothes or shelter

desabrochar, _va._ to unclasp, unbutton, unfasten

desacierto, _m._ error, blunder

desacomodar, _va._ to incommode, inconvenience; **desacomodarse,** to lose one's place

desacreditar, _va._ to discredit

desacuerdo, _m._ disagreement

desafiar, _va._ to challenge; to defy

desafinar, _vn., vr._ get out of tune

desafortunado, _adj._ unfortunate

desagradable, _adj._ disagreeable, unpleasant

desagradar, _va._ to displease, offend

desagradecido, _adj._ ungrateful; _n._ ingrate

desagrado, _m._ displeasure

desagüe, _m._ drain outlet

desahogado, _adj._ in comfortable circumstances

desahogar, _va._ to relieve; **desahogarse,** to unbosom

desahogo, _m._ ease, relief; unbosoming

desahuciar, _va._ to declare (a patient) incurable

desaire, _m._ disdain; slight

desalentar, _va._ to discourage; **desalentarse,** to lose hope, be discouraged

desaliento, _m._ dismay, discouragement, dejection

desaliñado, _adj._ slipshod

desalojar, _va._ to dislodge, evict; to displace

desamarrar, _va._ to untie

desamparar, _va._ to forsake

desanimado, _adj._ downhearted

desanimar, _va., vr._ to discourage

desapacible, _adj._ disagreeable, unpleasant

desaparecer, _vn._ to disappear

desaparición, _f._ disappearance

desapercibido, _adj._ unprepared, unguarded

desaplicado, _adj._ indolent, careless

desaprovechar, _va._ to misspend

desarmador, _m._ screwdriver

desarmar, *va.* to disarm; to disassemble; (fig.) to pacify

desarme, *m.* disarmament

desarreglado, *adj.* immoderate in eating, drinking, etc.; disarranged; slovenly

desarreglar, *va.* to disarrange

desarrollar, *va., vr.* to develop, unfold

desarrollo, *m.* development; evolution; developing of a photo

desarropar, *va.* to take off covers or blankets

desaseo, *m.* uncleanliness

desastrado, *adj.* wretched, miserable; ragged

desastre, *m.* disaster

desastroso, *adj.* disastrous

desatar, *va.* to untie, separate; **desatarse,** to lose all reserve

desatender, *va.* to pay no attention; to disregard, neglect

desatento, *adj.* inattentive, rude, uncivil

desatinado, *adj.* extravagant; tactless

desatino, *m.* extravagance, folly; nonsense, blunder

desavenencia, *f.* discord, disagreement

desayunarse, *vr.* to breakfast

desayuno, *m.* breakfast

desbandarse, *vr.* to disband

desbaratar, *va.* to destroy; to dissipate; **desbaratarse,** to break to pieces

desbocado, *adj.* wild (applied to a horse); foul-mouthed, indecent

desbordar, *vn., vr.* to overflow; to give vent to one's temper or feelings

desbordamiento, *m.* overflowing

descabellado, *adj.* disorderly; wild, unrestrained

descalabro, *m.* calamity, considerable loss

descalificar, *va.* to disqualify

descalzo, *adj.* barefooted

descansado, *adj.* rested, refreshed; quiet

descansar, *vn.* to rest; to repose, sleep

descanso, *m.* rest, repose

descarado, *adj.* bold, impudent

descaro, *m.* impudence

descarriar, *va.* to lead astray; **descarriarse,** to go astray; to deviate from justice or reason

descarrilar, *vn., vr.* (rail.) to jump the track; *va.* to derail

descartar, *va.* to discard; to dismiss

descendencia, *f.* descent, offspring

descender, *vn.* to descend; to be derived from

descendiente, *adj., m.* descending; descendant

descifrar, *va.* to decipher; to decode

descolgar, *va.* to unhang, take down

descolorido, *adj.* pale, colorless, faded

descollar, *vn.* to stand out; to excel, to surpass

descomponer, *va.* to spoil; to set at odds, disconcert; (chem.) to decompose; *vn.* to be indisposed; to change for the worse (of the weather); **descomponerse,** to get out of order; to become spoiled

descompuesto, *adj.* slovenly; out of order; spoiled (applied to food)

desconcertado, *adj.* baffled

desconcertar, *va., vr.* to disturb; to confound; to embarrass, disconcert

desconectar, *va., vr.* to disconnect

desconfiado, *adj.* suspicious, mistrustful

desconfianza, *f.* distrust, lack of confidence

desconfiar, *vn.* to mistrust, suspect

desconforme, *adj.* discordant; unlike; unsatisfied

desconocer, *va.* to disown, to disavow; to be ignorant of a thing; not to know a person; not to acknowledge (a favor)

desconocido, *adj.* unknown, unrecognizable; *n.* stranger

desconsiderado, *adj.* inconsiderate, imprudent

desconsolado, *adj.* disconsolate, dejected

desconsolador, *adj.* lamentable; disconsolate; disconcerting

desconsuelo, *m.* affliction; dejection, grief

descontar, *va.* to discount; to deduct

descontento, *m.* discontent, disgust; *adj.* unhappy, discontented

descontinuar, *va.* to discontinue

descorazonado, *adj.* depressed (in spirit)

descortés, *adj.* impolite

descortesía, *f.* discourtesy

descotado, *adj.* décolleté, low cut

descote, *m.* exposure of neck and shoulders

descrédito, *m.* discredit

describir, *va.* to describe

descripelón, *f.* description

descriptivo, *adj.* descriptive

descrito, *adj.* described

descuartizar, *va.* to quarter to divide the body into four parts); to carve

descubierto, *adj.* uncovered; bareheaded

descubrimiento, *m.* discovery, disclosure

descubrir, *va.* to discover, disclose; to uncover; to reveal; **descubrirse,** to take off one's hat

descuento, *m.* discount; decrease, rebate

descuidado, *adj.* careless, negligent

descuidar, *va., vn.* to neglect; **descuidarse,** to become negligent

descuido, *m.* indolence, negligence, forgetfulness

desde, *prep.* since, after, from; **desde luego,** of course

desdecirse, *vr.* to retract

desdén, *m.* disdain, scorn, contempt

desdeñar, *va.* to disdain

desdicha, *f.* misfortune

desdichado, *adj.* unfortunate, miserable

deseable, *adj.* desirable

desear, *va.* to desire, wish

desecar, *va.* to dry; to desiccate

desechar, *va.* to reject, refuse; to exclude

desembarcar, *va., vn.* to disembark

desembarque, *m.* landing

desembocar, *vn.* to flow into (as a river)

desembolso, *m.* disbursement, expenditure

desembuchar, *va.* to disgorge; (coll.) to unbosom

desempacar, *va.* to unpack

desempeñar, *va.* to perform (a duty); to discharge (any office)

desempeño, *m.* performance of an obligation

desempleo, *m.* unemployment

desencanto, *m.* disillusion

desenfrenado, *adj.* licentious, wanton

desenfrenar, *va.* to unbridle; **desenfrenarse,** to give full play to one's desires; to fly into a rage

desenfreno, *m.* licentiousness; unruliness

desengañar, *va., vr.* to disillusion, disappoint; to set right

desengaño, *m.* disillusion, disappointment

desenlace, *m.* denouement, outcome, conclusion

desenlazar, *va.* to unravel (a plot)

desenredar, *va.* to disentangle; **desenredarse,** to extricate oneself

desenterrar, *va.* to disinter, to dig up

desenvoltura, *f.* poise

desenvolver, *va.* to unwrap; to unroll; to develop; **desenvolverse,** to get along with assurance

desenvuelto, *adj.* poised

deseo, *m.* desire, wish

deseoso, *adj.* desirous

desequilibrio, *m.* unsteadiness, lack of balance

deserción, *f.* desertion

desertar, *va.* to desert; (law) to abandon a cause

desertor, *m.* deserter, fugitive

desesperación, *f.* despair, desperation; anger, fury

desesperadamente, *adv.* desperately

desesperado, *adj.* desperate, hopeless

desesperar, *vn., vr.* to despair; vex; *va.* to make desperate

desfalco, *m.* ebezzlement

desfallecer, *vn.* to pine, fall away, weaken

desfallecido, *adj.* faint, languid

desfallecimiento, *m.* languor, fainting, swoon

desfavorable, *adj.* unfavorable

desfigurar, *va.* to disfigure, deform; **desfigurarse,** to become disfigured or distorted

desfigurado, *adj.* deformed

desfile, *m.* parade

desganado, *adj.* having no appetite

desgano, *m.* lack of appetite; reluctance

desgarbado, *adj.* ungraceful, uncouth, gawky

desgarrado, *adj.* ripped, torn

desgarrador, *adj.* piercing; heartrending

desgarrar, *va.* to rend, tear

desgaste, *m.* wearing out, wastage

desgonzar, *va.* to separate; to unhinge; to disjoint

desgracia, *f.* misfortune, grief; disgrace; unpleasantness; **por desgracia,** unfortunately

desgraciado, *adj.* unfortunate, unhappy

desgreñar, *va.* to dishevel the hair

deshabitado, *adj.* deserted, desolate

deshecho, *adj.* undone, destroyed, wasted; melted; in pieces

deshelar, *va., vr.* to thaw

deshilachar, *va.* to ravel

deshilar, *va.* to ravel

deshojar, *va.* to strip off the leaves

deshonor, *m.* dishonor; insult

deshonra, *f.* dishonor; seduction of a woman

deshonroso, *adj.* dishonorable, indecent

deshuesar, *va.* to bone; to stone (fruit)

desidia, *f.* idleness, indolence

desidioso, *adj.* indolent, lazy, idle

desierto, *adj.* deserted, solitary; *m.* desert, wilderness

designación, *f.* designation

designar, *va.* to appoint; to name; to designate

designio, *m.* design, purpose

desigual, *adj.* unequal, unlike; uneven

desigualdad, *f.* inequality, dissimilitude; unevenness

desilusión, *f.* disillusion

desilusionar, *va., vr.* to disillusion

desinfectante, *m.* disinfectant

desinflamar, *va.* to cure an inflammation

desintegración, *f.* disintegration; fission

desintegrar, *vt., vi.* to disintegrate

desinterés, *m.* disinterestedness, unselfishness

desinteresado, *adj.* disinterested, unselfish

desistir, *vn.* to desist, cease, stop

deslave, *m.* washout

desleal, *adj.* disloyal; perfidious

deslealtad, *f.* disloyalty

desleír, *va.* to dilute, dissolve

deslenguado, *adj.* foulmouthed

desligar, *va.* to loosen, unbind, to extricate

desliz, *m.* slip, sliding; (fig.) slip, false step

deslizar, *vn., vr.* to slip, slide; to speak carelessly

deslucido, *adj.* unadorned; gawky; useless

deslumbrador, *adj.* dazzling

deslumbrar, *va.* to dazzle

desmantelado, *adj.* dismantled, stripped

desmañado, *adj.* clumsy, awkward

desmayar, *vn.* to be dispirited or fainthearted; **desmayarse,** to faint

desmayo, *m.* swoon; dismay, discouragement

desmedido, *adj.* out of proportion; excessive

desmejorar, *va.* to debase, make worse

desmembrar, *va.* to dismember; to curtail; to separate

desmemoriado, *adj.* forgetful

desmentir, *va.* to contradict

desmenuzar, *va.* to crumble, chip, to fritter; to examine minutely

desmerecer, *va., vn.* to become undeserving of; to compare unfavorably

desmesurado, *adj.* excessive; huge; immeasurable

desmoralizar, *va., vr.* to demoralize

desmoronar, *va.* to destroy little by little; **desmoronarse,** to decay, crumble

desnatar, *va.* to skim milk

desnivel, *m.* unevenness of the ground

desnudar, *va.* to denude, strip of clothes; to discover, reveal; **desnudarse,** to undress

desnudo, *adj.* naked, bare

desnutrición, *f.* malnutrition

desnutrido, *adj.* undernourished

desobedecer, *va.* to disobey

desobediencia, *f.* disobedience

desobediente, *adj.* disobedient

desocupar, *va.* to quit, empty; **desocuparse,** to quit an occupation

desodorante, *m.* deodorant

desolación, *f.* destruction; affliction

desolado, *adj.* desolate; lonely

desorden, *m.* disorder, confusion

desordenado, *adj.* disorderly, unruly

desordenar, *va., vr.* to disorder, disarrange

desorganización, *f.* disorganization

desorganizar, *va.* to disorganize

desorientado, *adj.* confused, having lost one's bearings

despacio, *adv.* slowly, leisurely

despacito, *adv.* gently, leisurely

despachar, *va.* to dispatch; to expedite; to dismiss

despacho, *m.* dispatch, expedition; cabinet; office

desparejar, *va.* to make unequal or uneven

desparpajo, *m.* pertness of speech or action

desparramar, *va.* to disseminate; to scatter, overspread; to squander

despavorido, *adj.* frightened, terrified

despecho, *m.* indignation, displeasure; despite, spite; **a despecho de,** in spite of

despedazar, *va.* to tear into pieces, cut asunder; to mangle

despedida, *f.* farewell, dismissal, leavetaking; close (of letter)

despedir, *va.* to discharge, dismiss from office; **despedirse,** to take leave

despegar, *va.* to unglue, detach; (avi.) to take off

despego, *m.* lack of love, coolness

despeinar, *va.* to entangle the hair

despejado, *adj.* sprightly, vivacious; clear, cloudless

despejar, *va.* to clear away obstructions; **despejarse,** to cheer up; to become clear weather

despejo, *m.* sprightliness; grace

despellejar, *va.* to skin

despensa, *f.* pantry, larder; provisions

despepitar, *va.* to remove the seeds from; **despepitarse,** to give vent to one's tongue

desperdiciar, *va.* to squander; not to avail oneself of

desperdicio, *m.* prodigality, profusion; remains; refuse

despertador, *m.* alarm clock

despierto, *adj.* awake; vigilant; brisk, sprightly

despilfarrar, *va.* to squander

despilfarro, *m.* slovenliness; waste

desplante, *m.* arrogant attitude

desplazado, *adj.* displaced

desplegar, *va.* to unfold, display; to explain, elucidate; to unfurl

desplomar, *va.* to make a wall bulge out; **desplomarse,** to bulge out; to collapse

desplome, *m.* downfall, collapse, tumbling down

despoblado, *m.* desert, uninhabited place; *adj.* depopulated

despoblar, *va., vr.* to deponulate; to desolate

despojar, *va.* to despoil; to deprive of, to strip; **despojarse,** to undress

despojos, *m. pl.* remains; debris, waste

desposado, *adj.* newly married; handcuffed

déspota, *m., f.* despot, tyrant

despótico, *adj.* despotic

despreciable, *adj.* contemptible, despicable, worthless

despreciar, *va.* to despise; to reject

desprecio, *m.* scorn, contempt

desprender, *va.* to unfasten, loosen, to separate; **desprenderse,** to give way, fall down; to extricate oneself; to be inferred

desprendimiento, *m.* alienation; unselfishness

despreocupado, *adj.* unconcerned, unconventional

desprestigio, *m.* loss of prestige

desprevenido, *adj.* unprepared

desproporción, *f.* disproportion

despropósito, *m.* absurdity, nonsense

desprovisto, *adj.* unprovided; devoid

después, *adv.* after, afterward, later; then; **después de J.C.** A.D., after Christ

desquitar, *va.* to retrieve a loss; **desquitarse,** to recoup; to retaliate, take revenge

desquite, *m.* revenge, retaliation

destacamento, *m.* (mil.) detachment

destacar, *va.* to build up, highlight; (mil.) to detach (a body of troops); **destacarse,** to stand out, be conspicuous

destapar, *va., vr.* to uncover

destartalado, *adj.* shabby; jumbled

destello, *m.* trickle; sparkle, gleam

destemplado, *adj.* inharmonious, out of tune; intemperate

destemplar, *va.* to distemper, alter, disconcert; to untune; **destemplarse,** to be ruffled; to be out of tune

desteñir, *va., vr.* to discolor, fade

desterrado, desterrada, *n.* exile; *adj.* exiled, banished

desterrar, *va.* to banish, exile

destierro, *m.* exile, banishment

destinar, *va.* to destine for, intend for

destinatario, destinataria, *n.* addressee, assignee

destino, *m.* destiny; fate, doom; destination; **con destino a,** bound for

destitución, *f.* destitution, abandonment

destituir, *va.* to deprive; to dismiss from office

destornillador, *m.* screwdriver

destornillar, *va.* to unscrew

destronar, *va.* to dethrone, to

depose

destrozado, *adj.* tattered, torn

destrozar, *va.* to destroy

destrucción, *f.* destruction, ruin

destructivo, *adj.* destructive

destruir, *va.* to destroy, ruin

desunir, *va.* to separate, to disunite

desuso, *m.* disuse; obsoleteness

desvalido, *adj.* helpless, destitute

desvanecer, *va.* to cause to vanish; to remove; *vn., vr.* to faint ; to become insipid; to vanish

desvarío, *m.* delirium, raving; giddiness; extravagance

desvelar, *va.* to keep awake; **desvelarse,** to be watchful, spend a sleepless night

desvelo, *m.* lack of sleep; watchfulness; care

desventaja, *f.* disadvantage

desventura, *f.* misfortune, calamity

deoventurado, *adj.* unfortunate

desvergonzado, *adj.* impudent, shameless

desvergüenza, *f.* shame; impudence

desvestir, vt. to undress

desviar, *va., vr.* to deviate; to dissuade

detallar, *va.* to detail, relate minutely; to itemize

detalle, *m.* detail; retail

detallista, *m.* retailer

detención, *f.* detention, delay

detener, *va.* to stop, detain; to arrest; to withhold; **detener,** to tarry; to stop

detenido, *adj.* under arrest

deteriorar, *va., vr.* to deteriorate

deterioro, *m.* deterioration

determinación, *f.* determination; boldness

determinado, *adj.* determinate; specific; resolute

determinar, *va., vr.* to determine; to resolve

detestable, *adj.* detestable

detester, *va.* to detest, hate

detonador, *m.* detonator, fuse, blasting cap

detrás, *adv.* behind; behind one's back

detrimento, *m.* detriment, damage, loss

deuda, *f.* debt

deudor, deudora, *n.* debtor

devastar, *va.* to desolate, lay waste

devengar, *va.* to earn or draw (as salary, interest, etc.)

devoción, *f.* devotion, piety; strong affection

devolución, *f.* (law) devolution; restitution, return

devolutivo, *adj.* returnable

devolver, *va.* to return; to restore; to refund, repay; (coll.) to vomit

devoto, *adj.* devout, pious; devoted

D. F., Distrito Federal, Federal District

día, *m.* day, daylight; **al día,** up to date

diabetes, *f.* diabetes

diabético, *adj.* diabetic

diablo, *m.* devil, Satan

diablura, devilishness

diabólico, *adj.* diabolical, devilish

diadema, diadem

diagnóstico, *m.* diagnosis

diagonal, *adj.* diagonal

diagrama, *m.* diagram

dialecto, *m.* dialect

diamante, *m.* diamond

diámetro, *m.* diameter

diana, *f.* (mil.) reveille

diantre, *m.* deuce, devil

diapasón, *m.* (mus.) diapason, octave; tuning fork

diario, *m.* journal, diary; daily newspaper; daily expense; *adj.* daily

diarrea , diarrhea

dibujante, *m.* draftsman; one who draws

dibujar, *va.* to draw, design

dibujo, *m.* drawing, sketch, draft

dicción, *f.* diction

diccionario, *m.* dictionary
diciembre, *m.* December
dictado, *m.* dictate; dictation
dictador, *m.* dictator
dictadura, *f.* dictatorship
dictáfono, *m.* dictaphone
dictamen, *m.* opinion, notion; suggestion
dictar, *va.* to dictate
dicha, *f.* happiness, good fortune; **por dicha,** by chance, luckily
dicho, *m.* saying, sentence, proverb; declaration; *adj.* said; **dejar dicho,** to leave word
dichoso, *adj.* happy, prosperous, lucky
diecinueve or **diez y nueve,** *m., adj.* nineteen
dieciocho or **diez y ocho,** *m., adj.* eighteen
dieciseis or **diez y seis,** *m., adj.* sixteen
diecisiete or **diez y siete,** *m., adj.* seventeen
Diego, *m.* James
diente, *m.* tooth, fang, tusk, jag; **dientes postizos,** false teeth; **hablar** or **decir entre dientes,** to mumble, mutter
diestra, *f.* right hand
diestro, *adj.* clever, handy
dieta, *f.* diet, regimen
dietética, *f.* dietetics
diez, *adj., m.* ten
difamar, *va.* to defame, libel
diferencia, *f.* difference; **diferencias,** *pl.* controversies, disputes
diferencial, *adj.* differential, different; *m.* (auto.) differential
diferenciar, *va., vr.* to differ, differentiate
diferente, *adj.* different, unlike
diferir, *va.* to defer, put off; to differ
difícil, *adj.* difficult
dificultad, *f.* difficulty
dificultar, *va.* to raise difficulties; to render difficult
difteria, *f.* diphtheria
difundir, *va.* to diffuse, outspread; to divulge
difunto, *adj.* dead, deceased; late; **difunta,** *n.* deceased person
difusión, diffusion, extension
difusora, (rad.) broadcasting station
digerible, *adj.* digestible
digerir, *va.* to digest; to think over, to examine carefully
digestión, *f.* digestion
digestivo, *adj.* digestive
digital, *f.* (bot.) digitalis, foxglove; *adj.* pertaining to the fingers; **impresiones** or **huellas digitales,** fingerprints
dignarse, *vr.* to condescend, deign
dignidad, *f.* dignity, rank
digno, *adj.* meritorious, worthy, deserving; **digno de confianza,** trustworthy, reliable
dije, *m.* charm, amulet; jewel
dilación, *f.* delay
dilatado, *adj.* large, extended; long delayed
dilatar, *va.* to dilate, expand; to spread out; to defer, to protract; **dilatarse,** to dilate; to delay
dilecto, *adj.* loved, beloved
diligencia, *f.* diligence; industriousness; errand; stagecoach
diligente, *adj.* diligent, industrious
dilucidar, *va.* to elucidate
diluvio, *m.* deluge
dimanar, *vn.* to spring from; to originate; to flow
dimensión, *f.* dimension
dimes, *m. pl.* **andar en dimes y diretes,** (coll.) to contend, to argue back and forth
diminutivo, *m., adj.* diminutive
diminuto, *adj.* tiny, minute
dimitir, *va.* to resign; to abdicate
Dinamarca, *f.* Denmark
dinámica, *f.* dynamics
dinámico, *adj.* dynamic
dinamita, *f.* dynamite
dínamo, *f.* dynamo
dinastía, *f.* dynasty

dineral, *m.* large sum of money

dinero, *m.* coin, money, currency

dintel, *m.* doorframe

Dios, *m.* God; **Dios mediante,** God willing; **Dios quiera, Dios lo permita,** God grant

dios, diosa, *m., f.* god, goddess

diploma, *m.* diploma

diplomacia, *f.* diplomacy

diplomarse, *vr.* to be graduated

diplomático, *adj.* diplomatic; *m.* diplomat

diputado, *m.* delegate, representative

diputar, *va.* to depute

dique, *m.* dike, dam

dirección, *f.* direction; guidance, administration; management; manager's office; address, addressing

directivo, *adj.* managing; **directiva,** *f.* governing body

directo, *adj.* direct, straight, nonstop; apparent, evident

director, *m.* director; conductor; editor (of a publication); manager

directora, *f.* directress; principal (of a school)

directorio, *m.* directory; board of directors

dirigente, *adj.* directing, ruling

dirigible, *m.* airship, dirigible

dirigir, *va.* to direct; to conduct; to govern; **dirigir la palabra,** to address (someone); **dirigirse,** to turn, to go; to address; **dirigirse a,** to speak to, to turn to

discernir, *va.* to discern, to distinguish

disciplina, *f.* discipline

disciplinar, *va.* to discipline

discípulo, discípula, *n.* disciple, scholar, pupil

díscolo, *adj.* ungovernable; peevish

discordancia, *f.* disagreement, discord

discordante, *adj.* dissonant, discordant

discoteca, *f.* discotheque; record shop or library

discreción, *f.* discretion

disculpa, *f.* apology, excuse

disculpar, *va., vr.* to excuse, acquit, absolve

discurrir, *vn.* to discourse upon a subject; to discuss; *va.* to invent, to contrive

discurso, *m.* speech

discusión, *f.* discussion

discutir, *va., vn.* to discuss, argue

disección, *f.* dissection, anatomy

diseminar, *va.* to scatter as seed; to disseminate, propagate

disensión, *f.* dissension, strife

disentería, *f.* dysentery

diseñar, *va.* to draw, design

diseño, *m.* design, draft

disertar, *vn.* to discourse, debate

disfraz, *m.* mask, disguise; masquerade

disfrazar, *va., vr.* to disguise, conceal; to mask

disfrutar, *va.* to enjoy

disgustar, *va.* to displease; to offend; **disgustarse,** to be displeased, to be worried

disgusto, *m.* sorrow, grief; aversion

disimular, *va.* to dissemble; to pretend; to tolerate

disimulo, *m.* dissimulation; pretence

disipación, *f.* dissipation

disipar, *va., vr.* to dissipate

dislocación, *f.* dislocation

disminuir, *va.* to diminish

disoluto, *adj.* dissolute

disolver, *va.* to loosen, untie; to dissolve; to melt, liquefy; **disolverse,** to dissolve, to break up

disonante, *adj.* dissonant, inharmonious; (fig.) discordant

disparar, *va., vn.* to shoot

disparate, *m.* nonsense, absurdity; blunder

disparejo, *adj.* unequal, uneven

disparidad, *f.* disparity

disparo, *m.* shot, discharge, explosion

dispenser, *va.* to dispense; to excuse, absolve; to grant

dispensario, *m.* dispensary of drugs; clinic

dispersar, *va., vr.* to scatter

displicente, *adj.* disagreeable, peevish

disponer, *va., vn.* to arrange; to dispose, prepare; to dispose of; to resolve

disposición, *f.* disposition, arrangement; resolution; disposal, command

dispuesto, *adj.* disposed, fit, ready; **bien dispuesto,** favorably inclined; **mal dispuesto,** unfavorably disposed

disputar, *va., vn.* to dispute, question; to argue

distancia, *f.* distance

distante, *adj.* distant, far off

distinción, *f.* distinction; difference; prerogative

distinguido, *adj.* distinguished, prominent, conspicuous

distinguir, *va.* to distinguish; to show regard for; **distinguirse,** to distinguish oneself; to excel

distintivo, *m.* insignia

distinto, *adj.* distinct, different; clear

distracción, *f.* distraction; amusement, pastime

distraer, *va.* to distract; to amuse, entertain; **distraerse,** to be absent-minded; to enjoy oneself

distraído, *adj.* absentminded; inattentive

distribuidor, *m.* distributor

distribuir, *va.* to distribute, divide; to sort

distrito, *m.* district

disturbio, *m.* disturbance, interruption

disuadir, *va.* to dissuade

diurno, *adj.* diurnal, by day

diva, *f.* prima donna

divagación, *f.* wandering, digression

diván, *m.* sofa

divergencia, *f.* divergence

diversidad, *f.* diversity; variety of things

diversión, *f.* diversion, pastime, sport

diverso, *adj.* diverse, different; several, sundry

divertido, *adj.* amused; amusing

diverter, *va.* to divert (the attention); to amuse, entertain; **diverterse,** to have an enjoyable time

dividendo, *m.* (math., com.) dividend

dividir, *va., vr.* to divide, separate; to split, break up

divinidad, *f.* god; divinity; woman of exquisite beauty; **la Divinidad,** the Deity

divino, *adj.* divine, heavenly

divisa, *f.* motto, badge

divisar, *vn.* to perceive indistinctly

división, *f.* division; partition; separation; (gram.) hyphen

divociar, *va., vr.* to divorce, separate

divorcio, *m.* divorce

dls., dólares, $ or dol., dollars

dm., decímetro, dm. decimeter

do, *m.* (mus.) do

doblar, *va., vn.* to double, fold; to bend; to toll; **doblarla esquina,** to turn the corner; **doblarse,** to bend, submit

doblez, *m.* crease, fold; *m., f.* duplicity in dealing

doce, *adj., m.* twelve

docena, *f.* dozen

docente, *adj.* teaching; **personal docente,** teaching staff

dócil, *adj.* docile, obedient

docto, *adj.* learned

doctor, *m.* doctor; physician

doctrina, *f.* doctrine

documento, *m.* document

dogma, *m.* dogma

dogmático, *adj.* dogmatic

dólar, *m.* dollar

dolencia *f.* disease, affliction

doler, *vn., vr.* to feel pain; to ache; to be sorry; to repent

doliente, *adj.* suffering; sorrowful; *m.,* mourner

dolor, *m.* pain, aching, ache; grief; regret

doloroso, *adj.* sorrowful; painful

domar, *va.* to tame, subdue, master

domesticar, *va.* to domesticate, tame

doméstico, *adj.* domestic; *n.* domestic, menial

domicilio, *m.* domicile, home, abode

dominación, *f.* domination

dominante, *adj.* dominant, domineering

dominar, *va.* to dominate; to control; to master (a language or a subject); **dominarse,** to control oneself

domingo, *m.* Sunday

dominio, *m.* dominion, domination, power, authority; domain

dominó, *m.* domino (a masquerade garment); game of dominoes

don, *m.* Don, the Spanish title for a gentleman (used only before given name)

don, *m.* gift, quality; **el don de la palabra,** the gift of speech; **don de gentes,** savoir-faire, courteous, pleasant manners

donación, *f.* donation, gift

donaire, *m.* grace, elegance

donativo, *m.* free contribution

doncella, *f.* virgin, maiden; lady's maid

donde, *adv.* where

dondequiera, *adv.* anywhere; wherever

doña, *f.* lady, mistress; title, equivalent to Mrs. or Miss, used only before given name

doquier or **doquiera,** *adv.* anywhere

dorado, *adj.* gilded; *m.* gilding

dorar, *va.* to gild; to palliate

dormido, *adj.* asleep

dormilón, dormilona, *n.* (coll,) sleepyhead; *adj.* fond of sleeping

dormir, *vn.* to sleep; **dormir-se,** to fall asleep

dormitar, *vn.* to doze, to be half asleep

dormitorio, *m.* dormitory, bedroom

dorsal, *adj.* dorsal; **espina dorsal,** spinal column

dorso, *m.* back

dos, *adj., m.* two; **de dos en dos,** by two's, two abreast

doscientos, doscientas, *m., adj.* two hundred

dotar, *va.* to endow, to give a dowry to

dragón, *m.* dragon; dragoon

drama, *m.* drama

dramático, *adj.* dramatic

dramatizar, *va.* to dramatize

drástico, *adj.* drastic

drenaje, *m.* drainage

droga, *f.* drug; (coll.) nuisance

droguería, *f.* drugstore

ducha, *f.* shower bath; douche

duda, *f.* doubt, suspense, hesitation; **poner en duda,** to question; **no cabe duda,** there is no doubt

dudable, *adj.* dubious

dudar, *va., vn.* to doubt, waver

duelo, *m.* duel; grief; mourning

duende, *m.* elf, goblin

dueño, dueña, *n.* owner, master, proprietor; **dueño de sí mismo,** self-controlled

dueto, *m.* duet

dulce, *adj.* sweet; mild, soft, meek; *m.* candy, sweetmeat

dulcería, *f.* confectionery store

dulcificar, *va.* to sweeten

dulzura, *f.* sweetness; gentleness

duodeno, *m.* duodenum

duplicado, *m.* duplicate

duplicar, *va.* to double, duplicate

duque, *m.* duke

durable, *adj.* durable, lasting

duración, *f.* duration, term

duradero, *adj.* lasting, durable

durante, *pres. p.* of **durar,** during

durar, *vn.* to last, endure; to wear well (as clothes)

durazno, *m.* peach; peach tree

dureza, *f.* hardness
durmiente, *adj.* sleeping; *m.* (Sp. Am.) (rail.) cross tie
duro, *adj.* hard, solid; unjust; rigorous, cruel; stubborn; stale (of bread); *m.* peso, dollar
d/v., dias vista, (com.) days' sight

E

e, *conj.* and (used only before words beginning with *i* or *hi*, when not followed by *e*)
ebanista, *m.* cabinetmaker
ébano, *m.* ebony
ebrio, *adj.* inebriated, drunk
eclesiástico, *m.* clergyman, ecclesiastic; *adj.* ecclesiastical
eclipsar, *va.* (ast.) to eclipse; to outshine; **eclipsarse,** to disappear
eclipse, *m.* eclipse
eco, *m.* echo
ecología, *f.* ecology
ecológico *adj.* ecological
economía, *f.* economy
económico, *adj.* economic; economical
economista, *m.* economist
economizar, *va.* to economize
ecuación, *f.* equation
ecuador, *m.* equator
ecuatorial, *adj.* equatorial
ecuestre, *adj.* equestrian
echar, *va.* to cast, throw, dart; to cast away; **echar a perder,** to spoil; **echar de menos,** to miss; **echarse,** to lie, stretch at full length
edad, *f.* age, era, time; **mayor de edad,** of age
Edén, *m.* Eden, paradise
edición, *f.* edition
edificar, *va.* to build
edificio, *m.* building, structure
editor, editora, *n., adj.* publisher; publishing
educación, *f.* education; bringing up
educado, *adj.* educated
educando, educanda, *n.* pupil, scholar
educar, *va.* to educate, instruct
educative, *adj.* educational
EE. UU., E.U., E.U.A. or E.U. de A., Estados Unidos, Estados Unidos de América, U.S., United States, U.S.A., United States of America
efectivamente, *adv.* in effect, truly
efectivo, *adj.* effective, true, certain; *m.* cash; **hacer efectivo,** to cash
efecto, *m.* effect, consequence, purpose; **efectos,** *pl.* merchandise, wares, goods, belongings
efectuar, *va.* to effect, accomplish
efervescencia, *f.* effervescence
eficacia, efficacy
eficaz, *adj.* efficacious, effective
eficiente, *adj.* efficient, effective
efigie, *f.* effigy, image
efímero, *adj.* ephemeral, passing
egipcio, egipcia, *n., adj.* Egyptian
Egipto, *m.* Egypt
egoísmo, *m.* selfishness, egoism
egoísta, *adj.* egoistic, selfish; *m., f.* self-seeker
egreso, *m.* debit, expense
eje, *m.* axle tree, axle, axis, shaft
ejecución, *f.* execution; performance
ejecutante, *m.* performer
ejecutar, *va.* to execute, perform, carry out; to put to death
ejecutivo, *adj., m.* executive
ejemplar, *m.* copy; sample; *adj.* exemplary; excellent
ejemplo, *m.* example; comparison; pattern, copy; **por ejemplo,** for instance
ejercicio, *m.* exercise, practice; (mil.) drill
ejercitar, *va.* to exercise, to put into practice

ejército, *m.* army
ejido, *m.* common land
el, *art. m.* the
él, *pron.* he
elaborar, *va.* to elaborate; to manufacture
elasticidad, *f.* elasticity; resilience
elección, *f.* election; choice
electivo, *adj.* elective
electo, *adj.* elect
elector, *m.* elector
electorado, *m.* electorate
electoral, *adj.* electoral
electricidad, *f.* electricity
electricista, *m.* electrician
eléctrico, *adj.* electric, electrical
electrizar, *va.* to electrify
electrónica, *f.* electronics
electrotipo, in electrotype
elefante, *m.* elephant
elegancia, *f.* elegance
elegible, *adj.* eligible
elegir, *va.* to choose, elect
elemental, *adj.* elemental, elementary
elemento, *m.* element; ingredient; **elementos,** *pl.* elements; rudiments, first principles
elenco, *m.* catalogue, list, index
elevación, *f.* elevation; highness; exaltation, pride; height; (avi.) altitude
elevado, *adj.* elevated, lofty, high
elevador, *m.* elevator, hoist
elevar, *va.* to raise; to elevate; to heave; **elevarse,** to be enraptured; to be puffed up, to rise
eliminación, *f.* elimination
eliminar, *va.* to eliminate
elixir or **elíxir,** *m.* elixir
elocución, *f.* elocution
elocuencia, *f.* eloquence
elocuente, *adj.* eloquent
elogiar, *va.* to praise, eulogize
elogio, *m.* eulogy, praise, compliment
elucidar, *va.* to elucidate, explain
eludir, *va.* to elude

ella, *pron.* she
ello, *neut. pron.* it, that
ellos, ellas, *pron. pl.* they (*masc.* and *fem.*)
emanar, *vn.* to emanate
emancipar, *va.* to emancipate
embajada, *f.* embassy
embajador, *m.* ambassador
embarazada, *adj.* pregnant
embarazo, *m.* embarrassment; obstacle; pregnancy
embarazoso, *adj.* difficult, intricate
embarcación, *f.* embarkation; any vessel or ship
embarcar, *va.* to embark, ship; **embarcarse,** to go on shipboard, embark; (fig.) to engage in any affair
embargar, *va.* to lay an embargo; to impede, restrain
embargo, *m.* embargo on shipping; **sin embargo,** however, nevertheless
embarque, *m.* shipment
embaucar, *va.* to deceive, to trick
embeberse, *vr.* to become absorbed
embelesar, *va., vr.* to amaze, astonish; to charm
embeleso, *m.* rapture, bliss, amazement
embellecer, *va.* to embellish, beautify, adorn
emblanquecer, *va., vr.* to whiten
emblema, *m.* emblem, symbol
embobar, *va.* to amuse, to distract; **embobarse,** to stand gaping
émbolo, *m.* (mech.) wrist pin; piston
emborrachar, *va., vr.* to intoxicate
emboscada, *f.* ambush
embotellar, *va.* to bottle
embragar, *va.* to put in gear
embrague, *m.* clutch, coupling
embriagar, *va., vr.* to intoxicate; to enrapture
embriaguez, *f.* intoxication, drunkenness; rapture
embrollar, *va.* to entangle, embroil

embrollo, *m.* tangle, trickery; embroiling

embromado, *adj.* vexed, annoyed

embrujar, *va.* to bewitch

embrutecer, *va.* to make stupid; **embrutecerse,** to become stupid

embudo, *m.* funnel

embuste, *m.* lie; fraud

embustero, embustera, *n.* impostor, cheat, liar

emergencia, *f.* emergency; emergence

emersión, *f.* emersion

emigración, *f.* emigration

emigrante, *m., f.* emigrant

emigrar, *vn.* to emigrate

eminencia, *f.* eminence

eminente, *adj.* eminent

emisario, *m.* emissary

emisora, *f.* broadcasting station

emocionar, *va., vr.* to touch, move, arouse emotion

empacho, *m.* indigestion; overloading; **sin empacho,** without ceremony; unconcernedly

empalagoso, *adj.* cloying

empalme, *m.* (rail.) junction; (rad.) hookup

empanada, *f.* meat tart

empanizado, *adj.* breaded

empañar, *va.* to dim, blemish; **empañarse,** to become tarnished

empapar, *va.* to soak, drench; **empaparse,** to be soaked; to go deeply into a matter

empapelar, *va.* to paper (a room, etc.)

empaque, *m.* packing

empaquetar, *va.* to make into a package

emparedado, *m.* sandwich

emparejar, *va.* to level; to match, fit; to equalize

empatar, *va.* to equal; to be a tie (in voting, in a game, etc.)

empate, *m.* equality of votes, tie

empeine, *m.* groin; instep; hoof

empellón, *m.* push, heavy blow; **a empellones,** rudely, by dint of blows

empeñar, *va.* to pawn; **empeñarse,** to pledge himself; to persevere

empeño, *m.* obligation; perseverance; pawn

empeorar, *va.* to make worse; *vn.* to grow worse

emperador, *m.* emperor

emperatriz, *f.* empress

empero, *conj.* yet, however

empezar, *va.* to begin

empinar, *va.* to raise, lift; to exalt; **empinarse,** to stand on tiptoe

empleado, empleada, *n.* employee, clerk

emplear, *va.* to hire; to occupy; to use

empleo, *m.* employment, occupation

empobrecer, *va.* to reduce to poverty; *vn.* to become poor

empolvado, *adj.* powdered; dusty

empolvar, *va.* to powder; **empolvarse,** to become dusty

empollar, *va.* to brood, hatch

emprendedor, *adj.* enterprising

emprender, *va.* to undertake

empresa, *f.* enterprise, undertaking; business concern

empresario, *m.* impresario, contractor

empréstito, *m.* loan

empuje, *m.* impulsion, impulse, pushing

empujón, *m.* impulse, push; **a empujones,** pushingly, rudely

empuñar, *va.* to clinch, grip

emular, *va.* to emulate, rival

emulsión, *f.* emulsion

en, *prep.* in; for; on, upon

enagua, *f.,* **enaguas,** *pl.* underskirt, skirt

enaltecer, *va., vr.* to praise, exalt

enamorado, *adj.* in love, enamored, lovesick

enamorar, *va.* to inspire love; to woo; **enamorarse,** to fall in love

enano, *adj.* dwarfish; *n.* dwarf, midget

encabezamiento, *m.* headline; heading

encabezar, *va.* to head a list

encadenar, *va.* to chain, link together; to connect, unite

encajar, *va.* to enchase; to fit in; to push or force in; **encajarse,** to thrust oneself into some narrow place; (coll.) to intrude

encaje, *m.* chasing, inlaid work; lace; socket, groove

encallar, *vn.* (naut.) to run aground

encaminar, *va.* to guide, show the way; **encaminarse,** to take a road, to be on the way

encanecer, *vn.* to grow gray-haired

encantador, *adj.* charming, delightful, enchanting

encantar, *va.* to enchant, charm, delight; to cast a spell

encanto, *m.* enchantment, spell, charm; delightfulness

encapricharse, *vr.* to become stubborn

encaramarse, *vr.* to climb

encarar, *vn.* to face, come face to face

encarcelar, *va.* to imprison

encarecer, *va., vn.* to raise the price; to recommend strongly

encargar, *va.* to charge, commission; **encargarse,** to take upon oneself

encargo, *m.* charge, commission; order, request; responsibility; errand

encariñar, *va.* to inspire affection; **encariñarse con,** to become fond of

encarrilar, *va.,vr.* to place on the right track; to set right

encauzar, *va.* to channel, lead, direct

encendedor, *m.* lighter; cigarette lighter

encender, *va.* to kindle, light, to set on fire; to inflame, incite; **encenderse,** to fly into a rage

encendido, *adj.* inflamed, high-colored; *m.* ignition

encerado, *m.* oilcloth; blackboard

encerrar, *va.* to shut up, confine; to contain; **encerrarse,** to withdraw, go behind closed doors

encía, gum (of the teeth)

enciclopedia, *f.* encyclopedia

enciclopédico, *adj.* encyclopedic

encierro, *m.* confinement, enclosure; cloister; prison

encima, *adv.* above, over; at (the top);over and above, besides

encina, *f.* evergreen oak, live oak

encinta, *adj.* pregnant, expectant (mother)

enclenque, *adj.* feeble, sickly

encoger, *va.* to contract, shorten; to shrink; **encogerse,** to shrink

encogido, *adj.* shrunk; timid

encolerizar, *va., vr.* to provoke, to irritate

encomendar, *va.* to recommend; to instruct; **encomendarse,** to commit oneself to another's protection

encomiar, *va.* to praise

encomiástico, *adj.* complimentary, extolling

encomienda, *f.* commission, charge; message; **encomienda postal,** parcel post

encomio *m.* praise, commendation

encono, *m.* rancor, ill will

encontrar, *va., vn.* to meet, find, encounter; **encontrarse,** to clash; to be of contrary opinions; **encontrarse con,** to meet, come upon

encopetado, *adj.* presumptuous, boastful

encrespar, *va.* to curl, frizzle; **encresparse,** to become rough (as the sea)

encrucijada, *f.* crossroad; street intersection

encuadernador, *m.* book binder

encuadernar, *va.* to bind

books

encuentro, *m.* shock, jostle; encounter, meeting; **salir al encuentro,** to go to encounter; to go to meet a person

encumbrado, *adj.* high, elevated

encumbrar, *va.* to raise, elevate; to mount, ascend

encurtido, *m.* pickle

enchapar, *va.* to veneer, plate

enchilada, *f.* (Mex.) kind of pancake stuffed with various foods and chili

enchufe, *m.* socket joint

endemoniado, *adj.* possessed with the devil; devilish

enderezar, *va.* to rectify; to straighten; **enderezarse,** to stand upright

endiablado, *adj.* devilish, diabolical

endiosar, *va.* to deify; **endiosarse,** to be puffed up with pride

endorso, *m.* endorsement

endosar, *va.* to indorse a bill of exchange

endoso, *m.* endorsement.

endrogarse, *vr.* (Sp. Am.) to get into debt

endulzar, *va.* to sweeten; to soften

endurecer, *va.* to harden; **endurecerse,** to become cruel; to grow hard

endurecido, *adj.* inured, hardened

enemigo, *adj.* hostile, opposed; **enemiga,** *n.* enemy

enemistar, *va.* to make an enemy; *vn.* to become an enemy

energía, *f.* energy, power, vigor; **energía atómica,** atomic energy; **energía nuclear** or **nuclearia,** nuclear or atomic energy

enérgico, *adj.* energetic; expressive

enero, *m.* January

enfadar, *va., vr.* to vex, molest, trouble; to become angry

énfasis, *m.* emphasis,

enfático, *adj.* emphatic

enfermar, *vn.* to fall ill; *va.* to make sick

enfermería, *f.* infirmary

enfermero, enfermera, *n.* nurse; hospital attendant

enfermizo, *adj.* infirm, sickly

enfermo, *adj.* sick, diseased, indisposed; *n.* sick person, patient

enflaquecer, *va.* to make thin; **enflaquecerse,** to lose weight

enfocar, *va.* to focus

enfoque, *m.* focus

enfrenar, *va.* to bridle; to put on the brake; to curb, restrain

enfrentar, *va.* to encounter, face

enfrente, *adv.* opposite, in front

enfriamiento, *m.* refrigeration; cold, chin

enfriar, *va.* to cool, refrigerate; **enfriarse,** to cool down

enfurecer, *va.* to irritate, enrage; **enfurecerse,** to grow furious

engalanar, *va.* to adorn

enganchar, *va.* to hook; to hitch, connect; to ensnare

engañar, *va.* to deceive, cheat; **engañarse,** to be deceived; to make a mistake

engañoso, *adj.* deceitful, misleading

engatusar, *va.* to wheedle, coax

engendrar, *va.* to beget, engender

engordar, *a.* to fatten; to grow fat

engorroso, *adj.* troublesome, cumbrous

engranaje, *m.* gear, gearing

engrandecer, *va.* to augment; to exaggerate; to exalt

engrasar, *va.* to grease, oil

engreimiento, *m.* presumption, vanity; overindulgence

engreír, *va.* to make proud; to spoil, overindulge; **engreírse,** to become vain; to become spoiled or overindulged

enhebrar, *va.* to thread a needle

enhorabuena, *f.* congratulation; felicitation; *adv.* well and good

enhoramala, *adv.* in an evil hour

enigmático, *adj.* enigmatical

enjabonar, *va.* to soap, lather

enjambre, *m.* swarm of bees; crowd

enjaular, *va.* to shut up in a cage; to imprison

enjuagar, *va.* to rinse.

enjuague, *m.* rinsing; rinse

enjuiciar, *va.* to bring a lawsuit to trial; to pass judgment

enlace, *m.* link; kindred, affinity, wedding

enladrillar, *va.* to pave with bricks

enlazar, *va., vr.* to join, unite, connect; to be joined in wedlock

enlodar, *va.* to bemire

enloquecer, *va.* to madden; *vn.* to become insane; **enloquecerse,** to become insane; to become infatuated

enloquecido, *adj.* deranged

enmarañar, *va.* to entangle, involve in difficulties; to puzzle

enmendar, *va.* to correct reform

enmienda, *f.* correction, amendment

enmohecerse, *vr.* to grow moldy or musty; to rust

enmudecer, *vn.* to grow dumb; to become silent

enojado, *adj.* angry, cross

enojar, *va.* to irritate, make angry; to offend; **enojarse,** to become angry

enojo, *m.* peevishness; anger, displeasure

enorgullecer, *va., vr.* to fill with pride; to become proud

enorme, *adj.* enormous, vast, huge

enormidad, *f.* enormity

enredadera, *f.* climbing plant; vine

enredar, *va.* to entangle, ensnare; to puzzle; **enredarse,** to fall in love (unlawful love); to become entangled or involved

enredo, *m.* entanglement; plot of a play

enrejado, *m.* grating; railing (as a fence); trellis-work

enriquecer, *va.* to enrich; *vn.* to grow rich

enrojecer, *va., vr.* to blush

enrollar, *va.* to wind, roll, coil

enronquecer, *va.* to make hoarse; *vn.* to grow hoarse

ensalada, *f.* salad

ensalzar, *va.* to exalt, praise

ensanchar, *va.* to widen, enlarge

ensanche, *m.* widening; gore (in garments); increase

ensangrentar, *va., vr.* to stain with blood

ensayar, *va.* to rehearse; to try

ensenada, *f.* small bay

enseñanza, *f.* teaching, instruction

enseñar, *va.* to teach, instruct; to show

enseres, *m. pl.* chattels; implements, fixtures; household goods

enseriarse, *vr.* (Sp. Am.) to become earnest or serious

ensuciar, *va., vr.* to stain, soil

ensueño, *m.* dream, reverie, illusion

entablar, *va.* to cover with boards; to start (a conversation, debate, etc.)

entapizar, *va.* to cover with tapestry, upholster

entenado, entenada, *n.* stepson, stepdaughter

entender, *va., vn.* to understand, comprehend

entendimiento, *vr.* understanding, knowledge

enterar, *va.* to inform thoroughly; to instruct; to let know. **enterarse (de),** to find out, inform oneself; to be told

entereza, *f.* entireness, integrity; fortitude; uprightness

enternecer, *va.* to soften; to move to compassion; **enternecerse,** to be moved to pity, to be touched

entero, *adj.* whole, entire; perfect, complete; sound

enterrar, *va.* to bury

entidad, *f.* entity, real being; (fig.) consideration, importance

entierro, *m.* burial; interment funeral

entonación, *f.* modulation; intonation, tone, voice

entonar, *va.* to tune, intonate, chant

entonces, *adv.* then, at that time

entorpecer, *va.* to benumb; to stupefy; to hinder

entrada, *f.* entrance, entry, admission; **entradas y gastos,** receipts and expenses

entrañable, *adj.* intimate, affectionate

entrañas, *f. pl.* viscera, intestines; (fig.) heart

entrar, *va., vn.* to enter; to commence

entreacto, *m.* (theat.) intermission

entrecejo, *m.* the space between the eyebrows; frowning, supercilious look

entrega, delivery; surrender; **entrega inmediata,** special delivery

entregar, *va.* to deliver; to restore

entremés, *m.* appetizer

entremeter, *va.* to put one thing between others; **entremeterse,** to intrude

entremetido, entremetida, *n.* meddler, intruder; kibitzer; *adj.* meddling

entrenar, *va.* to train, coach

entrepaño, *m.* panel

entresacar, *va.* to sift, separate; to thin out (hair)

entresuelo, *m.* mezzanine; basement

entretanto, *adv.* meanwhile

entretela, *f.* interlining

entretener, *va.* to amuse; to entertain, divert; **entretenerse,** to amuse oneself

entretenido, *adj.* pleasant,

amusing

entretenimiento, *m.* amusement, entertainment

entretiempo, *m.* season between summer and winter (spring or autumn)

entrevista, *f.* interview

entronque, *m.* crossroads, junction

entumecer, *va.* to benumb; *vn.* to become numb; to swell

entusiasmar, *va.* to arouse enthusiasm, enrapture; **entusiasmarse,** to become enthusiastic

entusiasmo, *m.* enthusiasm

entusiasta, *m., f.* enthusiast; *adj.* enthusiastic

envanecer, *va.* to make vain; to swell with pride; **envanecerse,** to become proud or vain

envasar, *va.* to barrel; to bottle; to can

envase, *m.* packing, bottling; container

envejecer, *va.* to make old; *vn.* to grow old

envenenamiento, *m.* poisoning

envenenar, *va.* to poison

enviado, *m.* envoy, messenger

enviar, *va.* to send, transmit

enviciar, *va.* to corrupt; **enviciarse,** to become strongly addicted (to something)

envidia, *f.* envy; emulation

envidiable, *adj.* enviable

envidiar, *vn.* to envy; to grudge

envidioso, *adj.* envious, jealous

envío, *m.* sending, shipment, remittance

enviudar, *vn.* to become a widower or widow

envoltorio, *m.* bundle of goods

envoltura, *f.* wrapper

envolver, *va.* to involve; to wrap up

enyesar, *va.* to plaster; to put in a cast

epidemia, *f.* epidemic disease

epidermis, *f.* epidermis, cuticle

epigrama, *m.* epigram

epilepsia, *f.* epilepsy

epílogo, *m.* epilogue

episodio, *m.* episode

epistola, *f.* epistle, letter

epitafio, *m.* epitaph

época, *f.* epoch; age, era

epopeya, *f.* epic; epic poem

equidad, equity, honesty

equilátero, *adj.* equilateral

equilibrado, *adj.* balanced

equilibrar, *va.* to balance; to counterbalance

equilibrio, *m.* equilibrium. balance

equinoccio, *m.* equinox

equipaje, *m.* baggage, luggage; equipment

equipar, *va.* to fit out, equip

equipo, *m.* equipment; (sports) team

equitación, *f.* horsemanship

equitativo, *adj.* fair, equitable

equivalente, *adj.* equivalent

equivocación, *f.* error, misunderstanding

equivocar, *va., vr.* to mistake, misconceive, misunderstand

era, *f.* era, age

erigir, *va.* to erect, build

ermitaño, *m.* hermit; hermit crab

erosión, *f.* erosion

erradicación, *f.* extirpation

errante, *adj.* errant, erring, roving

errar, *va. vn.* to err, commit errors

errata, *f.* error in printing

erróneo, *adj.* erroneous

error, *m.* error, mistake

erudito, *adj.* learned, lettered, erudite; *m.* sage, scholar

erupción, *f.* eruption, rash

eructar, erutar, to belch

esbelto, *adj.* svelte

esbozo, *m.* outline, sketch

escabroso, *adj.* rough, uneven; scabrous

escafandra, *f.* diving suit; **escafandra autónoma,** Scuba

escala, *f.* ladder; scale

escalafón, *m.* seniority scale; grade scale

escalar, *va.* to climb, scale

escalera, *f.* stairway; **escalera mecánica,** escalator; **escalera de mano,** stepladder

escalofrío, *m.* (med.) chill

escalón, *m.* step of a stair; degree of dignity; (mil.) echelon

escama, *f.* fish scale

escampar, *vn.* to stop raining

escandalizar, *va., vr.* to scandalize, shock

escándalo, *m.* scandal

escandaloso, *adj.* scandalous

escapada, *f.* escape, flight

escapar, *vn., vr.* to escape, flee

escaparate, *m.* show window, showcase; cupboard, cabinet

escape, *m.* escape, flight; exhaust; **a todo escape,** at full speed

escapulario, *m.* scapulary

escarbadientes, *m.* toothpick

escarbar, *va.* to scratch the earth (as chickens do)

escarcha, *f.* white frost

escardar, *va.* to weed

escarlata, *f.* scarlet color; scarlet cloth

escarlatina, *f.* scarlet fever

escarmentar, *vn.* to profit by experience; to take warning; *va.* to punish severely

escarmiento, *m.* warning, chastisement

escasear, *vn.* to grow less, decrease

escasez, *f.* scantiness, want

escatimar, *va.* to curtail, lessen; to skimp

escena, *f.* stage; scene; incident, episode

escenario, *m.* scenario, stage

escéptico, *adj.* skeptic, skeptical

esclarecer, *va.* to lighten, clear up; to illustrate

esclarecido, *adj.* illustrious, noble

esclavizar, *va., vr.* to enslave

esclavo, esclava, *n.* slave, captive

esclusa, *f.* lock; sluice, floodgate

escoba, *f.* broom

escocés, escoesa, *n., adj.*

Scotsman, Scotswoman; Scotch, Scottish

escoger, *va.* to choose, select

escogido, *adj.* choice, selected

escolar, *m.* scholar, student; *adj.* scholastic

escolástico, *adj.* scholastic

escolta, *f.* (mil.) escort convoy

escollo, *m.* sunken rock, reef; difficulty

escombro, *m.* rubbish, debris; mackerel

esconder, *va., vr.* to hide conceal

escondidas or **escondidillas,** *adv.* in a secret manner

escondido, *adj.* hidden

escopeta, *f.* gun, shotgun

escorbuto, *m.* scurvy

escorial, *m.* dump pile

escorpión, *m.* scorpion

escotado, *adj.* low-necked

escote, *m.* low-cut in a garment

escribano, *m.* notary; clerk

escribiente, *m., f.* amanuensis, clerk

escribir, *va.* to write; **escribir a máquina,** to typewrite

escrito, *m.* writing, manuscript; communication; (law) writ, brief; *p.p.* of **escribir,** written; **por escrito,** in writing

escritor, escritora, *n.* writer, author

escritorio, *m.* writing desk

escritura, *f.* writing; deed; **Escritura,** Scripture

escrúpulo, *m.* doubt, scruple

escrupuloso, *adj.* scrupulous; exact

escrutinio, *m.* scrutiny, inquiry

escuadra, *f.* square; squadron

escuchar, *va.* to listen

escudo, *m.* shield, buckler; coat of arms; scutcheon of a lock; escudo (Sp. coin)

escudriñar, *va.* to search, pry into

escuela, *f.* school; **escuela de párvulos,** kindergarten

escueto, *adj.* devoid of trimmings; unencumbered

esculpir, *va.* to sculpture, carve

escultor, *m.* sculptor, carver

escultura, *f.* sculpture; work of a sculptor

escupidera, *f.* spittoon

escupir, *va.* to spit

escurrir, *va.* to drain to the dregs; *vn.* to drop; to slip, slide; **escurrirse,** to slip away

ESE: estesudeste, ESE or E.S.E., east southeast

ese, esa, *adj.* and **ése, ésa,** *pron.* that; **esos, esas,** *pl.* those

esencia, *f.* essence

esencial, *adj.* essential; principal

esfera, *f.* sphere; globe; dial

esférico, *adj.* spherical

esforzar, *va.* to strengthen; **esforzarse,** to exert oneself, to make an effort

esfuerzo, *m.* effort

esfumarse, *vr.* to disappear, fade away

esgrima, *f.* fencing

eslabón, *m.* link of a chain

esmalte, *m.* enamel; fingernail polish

esmerado, *adj.* painstaking, carefully done

esmerarse, *vr.* to do one's best, to take pains

esmero, *m.* elaborate effort; neatness

eso, *dem. pron. neuter,* that (idea or statement); **por eso,** for that reason, therefore

esófago, *m.* gullet; throat, esophagus

espacial, *adj.* relating to space

espacio, *m.* space, capacity; distance

espacioso, *adj.* spacious

espada, *f.* sword; spade (in cards)

espalda, *f.* back; shoulders; **a espaldas,** behind one's back

espaldar, *m.* back of a seat

espantajo, *m.* scarecrow; bugaboo

espantar, *va.* to frighten, daunt; to chase or drive away

espanto, *m.* fright; menace, threat; wonder, surprise; apparition, spook

España, *f.* Spain

español, española, *n.*, *adj.* Spaniard; Spanish; *m.* Spanish language

esparcimiento, *m.* recreation, relaxation

esparcir, *va.* to scatter; to divulge

espárrago, *m.* asparagus.

espasmo, *m.* spasm

especial, *adj.* special, particular

especialidad, *f.* specialty

especialista, *m.*, *f.* specialist

especializarse, *vr.* to specialize

especie, *f.* species; matter; motive; class, sort, kind

especificación, *f.* specification

especificar, *va.* to specify

específico, *adj.* specific; *m.* patented medicine

espécimen, *m.* specimen, sample

espectáculo, *m.* spectacle, sight; show

espectador, espectadora, *n.* spectator, onlooker

espectro, *m.* specter, phantom, apparition; spectrum

especulación, *f.* speculation

especular, *va.* to speculate

espejismo, *m.* mirage

espejo, *m.* looking glass, mirror

espera, *f.* stay, waiting; (law) adjournment, delay; sala de espera, waiting room

esperanto, *m.* Esperanto

esperanza, *f.* hope, expectation

esperar, *va.* to hope; to expect, to wait for

espesar, *va.*, *vr.* to thicken, condense

espeso, *adj.* thick, dense

espía, *m.*, *f.* spy

espiar, *va.* to spy, lurk

espiga, *f.* ear (of grain)

espina *f.* thorn; thistle; backbone; fishbone; estar en espinas, to be on needles and pins

espinaca, *f.* (bot.) spinach

espinazo, *m.* spine, backbone

espinoso, *adj.* thorny

espiral, *adj.* spiral

espirar, *va.* to exhale; *vn.* to breathe

espiritismo, *m.* spiritualism; spiritism

espíritu, *m.* spirit, soul; genius; ardor; courage; (chem.) spirits; el Espíritu Santo, the Holy Ghost

espiritual, *adj.* spiritual

esplendidez, *f.* splendor, magnificence

espléndido, *adj.* splendid

esplendor, *m.* radiance

esplín, *m.* melancholy

esponjar, *va.* to sponge; esponjarse, to get fluffy; to be puffed up with pride

esponjoso, *adj.* spongy

esponsales, *m. pl.* espousals, betrothal

espontáneo, *adj.* spontaneous

esposa, *f.* wife; esposas, *pl.* handcuffs

esposo, *m.* husband; esposos, *pl.* married couple

espuela, *f.* spur; stimulus; (bot.) larkspur

espumoso, *adj.* frothy, foamy

esputo, *m.* spit, sputum, saliva

esquela, *f.* note, slip of paper

esqueleto, *m.* skeleton

esquema, *m.* diagram, plan

esquiar, *vn.* to ski

esquilar, *va.* to shear

esquina, *f.* corner, angle; doblar la esquina, to turn the corner

esquivar, *va.* to shun, avoid, evade

esquivo, *adj.* shy, reserved

estabilizar, *va.* to stabilize

estable, *adj.* stable

establecer, *va.* to establish, found; to decree

establecimiento, *m.* establishment; founding; household

establo, *m.* stable

estación, *f.* station; position,

situation; season (of the year)

estacionamiento, *m.* parking

estacionar, *va.* to park

estacionario, *adj.* stationary

estadía, *f.* stay, sojourn

estadio, *m.* stadium

estadista, *m.* statesman

estadística, *f.* statistics

estadístico, *adj.* statistical

estado, *m.* state, condition; **estado de cuenta,** statement of an account; **ministro de Estado,** Secretary of State

Estados Unidos de América, *m. pl.* United States of America

estadounidense, *adj.* of the United States of America; *m., f.* person from the U. S. A

estafa, *f.* trick; swindle

estafar, *va.* to deceive, defraud; to swindle

estallar, *vn.* to burst, explode

estallido, *m.* crash; outburst

estambre, *m.* fine wool; stamen of flowers

estampa, *f.* print, stamp

estampar, *va.* to print; to stamp; to imprint

estampido, *m.* report of a gun, etc.; crack, crash; **estampida,** *f.* stampede

estampilla, *f.* signet, rubber stamp; (Sp. Am.) postage stamp

estancia, *f.* stay, sojourn; mansion; (Sp. Am.) cattle ranch; living room

estandarte, *m.* banner, standard

estanque, *m.* pond, pool

estanquillo, *m.* cigar store

estante, *m.* shelf; bookcase

estar, *vn.* to be; to be in a place; **estar de prisa,** to be in a hurry; **estar bien,** to be well; **estar malo,** to be ill

estaroide, *m.* steroid

estatua, *f.* statue

estatura, *f.* stature

estatuto, *m.* statute, law, by-law

este, *m.* east

este, esta, *adj.* and **éste, ésta,** *pron.* this; **estos, estas,** *pl.*

these

estela de vapor, *f.* contrail

estenografía, *f.* stenography, shorthand

estenógrafo, estenógrafa, *n.* stenographer, shorthand writer

estenotipia, *f.* stenotyping

estera, *f.* mat,

estereofónico, estereofónica, *adj.* stereophonic

estereoscopio, *m.* stereoscope

estéril, *adj.* sterile; barren

esterilizar, *va.* to sterilize

esterlina, *adj.* sterling; **libra esterlina,** pound sterling

estero, *m.* estuary, firth; (Arg.) swamp

estética, *f.* aesthetics

estetoscopio, *m.* stethoscope

estiércol, *m.* dung; excrement, manure

estigma, *m.* birthmark; stigma, affront

estilo, *m.* stylus; style; use, custom

estima, *f.* esteem

estimable, *adj.* worthy of esteem

estimar, *va.* to estimate, value; to esteem; to judge

estimular, *va.* to encourage, stimulate

estímulo, *m.* stimulus, encouragement, inducement

estío, *m.* summer

estipular, *va.* to stipulate

estirado, *adj.* forced; taut

estirar, *va.* to dilate, stretch out

estirpe, *f.* race, origin, stock

esto, *pron. neuter* this; **en esto,** at this juncture; **por esto,** for this reason

estoico, *adj.* stoic, indifferent

estómago, *m.* stomach

estorbar, *va.* to hinder, obstruct; to molest

estorbo, *m.* hindrance, impediment

estornudar, *vn.* to sneeze

estornudo, *m.* sneeze

estrangulación, *f.* strangulation; **cuello de estrangulación,** bottleneck

estrategia, *f.* strategy
estratégico, *adj.* strategic
estrechar, *va.* to tighten; to contract, clasp
estrechez, *f.* tightness; narrowness; poverty
estrecho, *m.* strait; *adj.* narrow, close; tight; intimate
estrella, *f.* star
estrellado, *adj.* starry; dashed to pieces; **huevos estrellados,** fried eggs
estrellar, *va.* to dash to pieces; to crash, to hit against; to fry (eggs)
estremecer, *va.* to shake, make tremble; **estremecerse,** to shake; to thrill
estremecimiento, *m.* trembling, shaking, shiver, thrill
estrenar, *va.* to inaugurate; to use for the first time
estreno, *m.* début, first performance, premiere
estreñimiento, *m.* obstruction; constipation
estrépito, *m.* noise, clamor
estribar, *vn.* depend upon (a reason)
estricto, *adj.* strict; severe
estridente, *adj.* strident
estroboscopio, *m.* stroboscope
estrofa, *f.* (poet.) stanza
estropajo, *m.* dishrag; worthless thing
estropear, *va.* to spoil by rough usage
estructura, *f.* structure
estruendo, *m.* clamor, noise
estrujar, *va.* to press, squeeze
estuche, *m.* kit
estudiante, *m.* scholar, student
estudiar, *va.* to study
estudio, *m.* study; studio
estupefacto, *adj.* stupefied
estupendo, *adj.* stupendous
estupidez, *f.* stupidity
etapa, *f.* stage, station, step
etcétera, *f.* et cetera, and so on
éter, *m.* ether
etéreo, *adj.* ethereal
eternidad, *f.* eternity
eterno, *adj.* eternal

ético, *adj.* ethical, moral
etimología, *f.* etymology
etiqueta, *f.* etiquette, formality; label; **de etiqueta,** in formal dress
E.U.A., Estados Unidos de América, U.S.A., United States of America
eucalipto, *m.* eucalyptus
eufonía, euphony
Europa, Europe
europeo, europea, *n.*, *adj.* European
evacuar, *va.* to evacuate, empty
evangelio, *m.* gospel
evaporar, *va.*, *vn.* to evaporate
evasivo, *adj.* evasive, elusive
eventual, *adj.* eventual, fortuitous
evitable, *adj.* avoidable
evocar, *va.* to call out; to invoke
evolución, *f.* evolution; evolvement
exactitud, *f.* exactness
exacto, *adj.* exact; punctual
exageración, *f.* exaggeration
exagerar, *va.* to exaggerate
exaltado, *adj.* hot-headed
exaltar, *va.* to exalt, elevate; to praise; **exaltarse,** to become excited and angry
examen, *m.* examination
exasperar, *va.* to exasperate
excavadora, *f.* excavating machine, steam shovel
excavar, *va.* to excavate
excedente, *adj.* excessive, exceeding; *m.* surplus, excess
exceder, *va.* to exceed
Excelencia, *f.* Excellency (title)
excelencia, *f.* excellence
excelente, *adj.* excellent
excelso, *adj.* elevated, lofty
excentricidad, *f.* eccentricity
excéntrico, *adj.* eccentric
excepción, *f.* exception
excepcional, *adj.* exceptional
excepto, *adv.* excepting
exceptuar, *va.* to except, exempt
excesivo, *adj.* excessive
exceso, *m.* excess

excitar, *va.* to excite, arouse; to urge

exclamación, *f.* exclamation

exclamar, *va.* to exclaim, cry out

excluir, *va.* to exclude

exclusión, *f.* exclusion; preclusion

exclusivo, *adj.* exclusive, select

excomulgar, *va.* to excommunicate

excomunión, *f.* excommunication

excremento, *m.* exerement

excursión, excursion, outing

excusa, *f.* excuse, apology

excusado, *adj.* excused; exempted; *m.* toilet, water closet

excusar, *va.* to excuse, pardon; to exempt; **excusarse,** to decline a request

exento, *adj.* exempt, free

exhausto, *adj.* exhausted

exhibición, *f.* exhibition, exposition

exhibir, *va.* to exhibit, display

exigencia, *f.* exigency, demand

exigente, *adj.* demanding

exigir, *va.* to demand, require

eximir, *va.* to exempt, excuse

existencia, *f.* existence; **en-existencia,** in stock

existir, *vn.* to exist, be

éxito, *m.* outcome; **buen éxito,** success

exorbitante, *adj.* exorbitant

exótico, *adj.* exotic, foreign

expansión, *f.* expansion, extension

expansivo, *adj.* effusive

expedición, *f.* expedition; shipment

expediente, *m.* expedient; pretext; proceedings

expedir, *va.* to expedite, dispatch, forward; to issue

expeler, *va.* to expel, eject

experiencia, *f.* experience

experimentado, *adj.* experienced, expert

experimentar, *va.* to experience; to experiment

experimento, *m.* experiment, trial

experto, *adj.* expert, experienced; **experta,** *n.* expert, old hand

expirar, *vn.* to expire

explayar, *va.* to extend, dilate; **explayarse,** to dwell upon, enlarge upon

explicable, *adj.* explainable

explicación, *f.* explanation

explicar, *va.* to explain, expound; **explicarse,** to explain oneself

explícito, *adj.* explicit

exploración, *f.* exploration

explorador, exploradora, *n.* explorer; scout; *adj.* exploring

explorer, *va.* to explore; to inquire

explosión, *f.* explosion

exponente, *m., f.* exponent; *m.* (math.) exponent

exponer, *va.* to expose; to explain

exportación, *f.* exportation, export

exportador, *adj.* exporting; *m.* exporter

exportar, *va.* to export

expresión, *f.* expression

expresivo, *adj.* expressive

exprimir, *va.* to wring

exprofeso, *adv.* on purpose

expropiar, *va.* to expropriate

expuesto, *adj.* exposed; **lo expuesto,** what has been stated

expulsar, *va.* to expel

exquisito, *adj.* exquisite

éxtasis, *m.* ecstasy, enthusiasm

extender, *va.* to extend, spread; **extenderse,** to spread out

extensión, *f.* extension; extent

extenso, *adj.* extensive, vast

extenuar, *va.* to extenuate

exterior, *adj.* exterior, external; *m.* exterior; abroad

exterminar, *va.* to exterminate

extinguir, *va.* to extinguish

extirpar, *va.* to extirpate

extra, *inseparable prep.* out of, beyond, extra (as a prefix); *adj.* unusually good

extracción, *f.* extraction

extractar, *vn.* to extract. abridge

extracto, *m.* extract

extraer, *va.* to extract

extranjero, *adj.* foreign; **extranjera,** *n.* foreigner, alien; **ir al extranjero,** to go abroad

extrañar, *va.* to miss; **extrañarse,** to be surprised, wonder at

extraordinario, *adj.* extraordinary, uncommon, odd

extrasensorio, extrasensoria, *adj.* extrasensory

extravagancia, *f.* folly, freak

extravagante, *adj.* freakish; eccentric

extraviar, *va.* to mislead; **extraviarse,** to lose one's way

extremidad, *f.* extremity

F

f., franco, (com.) free

f/, fardo, bl. bale; bdl. bundle

f.a.b., franco a bordo, (com.) f.o.b., free on board

fábrica, *f.* factory

fabricación, *f.* manufacture; **fabricación en serie** or **en gran escala,** mass production

fabricante, *m.* manufacturer

fabricar, *va.* to build, construct

facción, *f.* faction; **facciones,** *pl.* features, physiognomy

fácil, *adj.* facile, easy

facilidad, *f.* facility; ability; **facilidades,** *pl.* opportunities; conveniences

factible, *adj.* feasible

factor, *m.* factor, element; (math.) factor

factura, *f.* invoice, bill

facturar, *va.* to invoice; to check (baggage)

facultad, *f.* faculty, authority; ability

facultar, *va.* to authorize

facha, *f.* appearance, aspect

fachada, *f.* facade, face, front

fachendear, *vn.* to brag, boast

faena, *f.* work; fatigue

faisán, *m.* pheasant

faja, *f.* band, belt, sash; girdle

fajar, *va.* to swathe; to girdle

fajina, *f.* toil, chore; bugle call to mess; **hacer fajina,** (coll.) to clean house thoroughly

falsete, *m.* falsetto voice

falso, *adj.* false, untrue

falta, *f.* fault; mistake; want, lack; flaw; **hacer falta,** to be necessary; to be lacking; **sin falta,** without fail; **no faltaba más,** (coll.) that's the last straw

faltar, *vn.* to lack

falto, *adj.* devoid

fallar, *va.* to give sentence, judge; *vn.* to fail, miss

fallecer, *vn.* to die

fallo, *m.* judgment, sentence

familia, *f.* family; species

familiar, *adj.* familiar; colloquial; informal; *m.* member of one's family

familiaridad, *f.* familiarity

familiarizar, *va., vr.* to familiarize

fango, *m.* mire, mud

fantasma, *m.* phantom, ghost

fantástico, *adj.* fantastic; (coll.) superb

farmacéutico, *adj.* pharmaceutical; *m.* pharmacist

farmacia, *f.* pharmacy

faro, *m.* (naut.) lighthouse

farol, *m.* lantern, light

farsa, *f.* farce; sham

farsante, *m.* charlatan; *adj.* boastful; deceitful

fascinador, *adj.* fascinating

fascinar, *va.* to fascinate; to charm

fase, *f.* phase, aspect

fastidiar, *va.* to bore, to annoy

fastidio, *m.* boredom, ennui

fatiga, *f.* fatigue, weariness

fatigar, *va., vr.* to tire, harass

fausto, *adj.* happy, fortunate

favor, *m.* favor

favorable, *adj.* favorable, advantageous, propitious

favorecer, *va.* to favor, protect

favoritismo, *m.* favoritism
favorito, *adj.* favorite, beloved
faz, *f.* face, front
F.C. or f.c., ferrocarril, R.R. or r.r., railway
fe, *f.* faith, belief; testimony; **dar fe,** to certify
Febo or feb.°, febrero, Feb. February
febrero, *m.* February
fecundar, *va.* to fertilize
fecundo, *adj.* fruitful, fertile
fecha, date (of letter, etc.)
fechar, *va.* to date (a letter, document, etc.)
federación, *f.* federation
federal, *adj.* federal
felicidad, *f.* felicity, happiness
felicitar, *va.* to congratulate
feliz, *adj.* happy, fortunate
felpa, *f.* plush
femenino, *adj.* feminine, female
feminista, *m., f.* feminist
fenómeno, *m.* phenomenon
feo, *adj.* ugly; deformed
feraz, *adj.* fertile, fruitful (of vegetation)
feria, *f.* fair, market
feriado, *adj.* suspended (applied to work); **día feriado,** holiday
fermentar, *vn.* to ferment
férreo, *adj.* iron, ferrous; **vía férrea,** railroad
ferretería, *f.* hardware store
ferrocarril, *m.* railroad
ferroviario, *adj.* railroad
fértil, *adj.* fertile, fruitful
fertilizar, *va.* to fertilize
ferviente, *adj.* fervent, ardent
fervor, *m.* fervor, ardor
festejar, *va.* to fete; to celebrate
festejo, *m.* feast, entertainment
festín, *m.* feast, banquet
festivo, *adj.* festive; gay, merry; **día festivo,** holiday
fétido, *adj.* fetid, stinking
feto, *m.* fetus
fiado, *adj.* on trust, on credit
fiador, fiadora, *n.* bondsman, surety (person); *m.* fastener; catch of a lock

fiambre, *m.* cold lunch
fianza, *f.* security, bail
fiar, *va.* to bail; to sell on credit; to commit to another; *vn.* to confide, to trust
fiasco, *m.* failure
ficción, *f.* fiction
ficticio, *adj.* fictitious
ficha, *f.* counter (at games), chip
fidedigno, *adj.* true; **fuente fidedigna,** reliable source
fideos, *m. pl.* vermicelli, spaghetti, noodles
fiebre, *f.* fever; **fiebre aftosa,** hoof-and-mouth disease
fiel, *adj.* faithful, loyal; **fieles,** *m. pl.* the faithful
fieltro, *m.* felt; felt hat
fiera, *f.* wild beast; fiendish person; (coll.) very able or shrewd person
fiero, *adj.* fierce, ferocious
fiesta, *f.* fiesta; feast; festivity, party; **día de fiesta,** holiday
fig., figura, fig. figure
figura, *f.* figure, shape
figurado, *adj.* figurative
figurar, *va.* to shape, fashion; *vn.* to figure, be conspicuous; **figurarse,** to fancy, imagine
figurín, *m.* fashion plate
fijar, *va.* to fix, fasten; to determine; to post; **se prohíbe fijar carteles,** post no bills; **fijarse,** to take notice(of)
fijo, *adj.* fixed, firm
fila, *f.* row, line (of soldiers, etc.)
filantrópico, *adj.* philanthropic
filántropo, *m.* philanthropist
filarmónico, *adj.* philharmonic
filatelia, *f.* philately
filete, *m.* loin, tenderloin
filial, *adj.* filial
filigrana, *f.* filigree
filipino, filipina, *n., adj.* Philippine
filo, *m.* edge (of a knife, etc.)
filosofía, *f.* philosophy
filosófico, *adj.* philosophical
filósofo, *m.* philosopher
filtrar, *va.* to filter, strain

filtro, m. filter

fin, m. end, conclusion; **al fin, por fin**, at last

finado, finada, n., adj. dead, deceased

final, adj. final; m. end, finale

finalidad, f. finality

finalizar, va. to finish, conclude

financiero, adj. financial

finca, f. land or house property; ranch

fineza, f. fineness, perfection; expression of courtesy; delicacy

fingido, adj. feigned, sham

fingir, va., vr. to feign

fino, adj. fine, perfect, pure; delicate; acute, sagacious

firma, f. signature; company, firm

firmar, va. to sign, subscribe

firme, adj. firm, secure; constant, resolute

firmeza, f. firmness

fiscal, m. attorney general, public prosecutor; adj. fiscal

fisco, m. exchequer

física, f. physics

físico, adj. physical; m. physicist; physique; (coll.) face, physiognomy

fisiología, f. physiology

flaco, adj. thin, meager

flamante, adj. flaming, bright; quite new

flautín, m. piccolo, fife

fleco, m. flounce, fringe; bangs (style of haircut)

flecha, f. arrow

flema, f. phlegm

flete, m. (naut.) freight; **flete aéreo**, air freight

flexible, adj. flexible

flojo, adj. loose; lazy

flor, f. flower; **echar flores**, to compliment, flatter

florecer, vn. to blossom, bloom

floreciente, adj. in bloom

florero, m. flower vase

florido, adj. florid, flowery

florista, m., f. florist

flota, f. fleet

flotador, m. float; **flotador de**

hidroavión, pontoon

flotar, vn. to float

flote, m. floating; **a flote**, buoyant, afloat

fluctuar, vn. to fluctuate

fluir, vn. to flow, run (as a liquid)

fluorización, f. fluoridation

fluorizar, va. to fluoridate

focal, adj. focal

foco, m. focus; center; bulb (electric light)

fogoso, adj. fiery, ardent, fervent; impetuous

follaje, m. foliage

folleto, m. pamphlet

fomentar, va. to promote, encourage

fomento, m. promotion, fostering; improvement, development

fonda, f. hotel, inn

fondo, m. depth; bottom; rear; fund(s), capital, stock; essential nature; (art) background; **a fondo**, completely, fully

fonética, f. phonetics

fonógrafo, m. phonograph, gramophone

forastero, adj. strange, exotic; n. stranger, foreigner

forma, form, shape; way

formal, adj. formal; serious

formalidad, f. formality; punctuality; good behavior

formalizar, va. to make official; **formalizarse**, to settle down, become earnest

formar, va. to form, shape

formidable, adj. formidable; terrific

formón, m. chisel; punch

fórmula, f. formula

formular, va. to formulate, draw up

formulario, m. form (for filling in information)

foro, m. court of justice; bar; background of the stage; forum

forrar, va. to line (clothes, etc.); to cover (books, etc.)

fortalecer, va. to fortify, strengthen

fortaleza, f. fortitude,

strength, vigor; (mil. fortress
fortificar, *va.* to fortify
fortuna, *f.* fortune; **por fortuna,** fortunately
forzar, *va.* to force; to ravish
forzoso, *adj.* necessary
fosa, *f.* grave
fosforescente, *adj.* phosphorescent
fósforo, *m.* phosphorus; match
foso, *m.* pit; moat, ditch, fosse; **foso séptico,** septic tank
fotogénico, *adj.* photogenic
fotograbado, *m.* photoengraving, photogravure
fotografía *f.* photograph, picture
fotegrafiar, *va.* to photograph
fotógrafo, *m.* photographer
frac, *m.* evening coat, dress coat
fracasar, *vn.* to fail
fracaso, *m.* failure
fractura, fracture
fragancia, *f.* fragrance, perfume
fragante, *adj.* fragrant; flagrant
fragmento, *m.* fragment
frambuesa, *f.* raspberry
francés, francesa, *adj.* French; *m.* French language; Frenchman; *f.* Frenchwoman
Francia, *f.* France
franco, *adj.* frank, liberal, open, sincere; **franco a bordo,** free on board; **franco de porte,** postpaid; *m.* franc
franja, *f.* fringe; braid, border; stripe
franqueo, *m.* postage
franqueza, *f.* frankness
franquicia, *f.* franchise, grant; **franquicia postal,** free postage
frase, *f.* phrase, sentence
fraternal, *adj.* fraternal, brotherly
fraternidad, *f.* fraternity, brotherhood
fraudulento, *adj.* fraudulent
frazada, *f.* blanket
frecuencia, *f.* frequency; **con frecuencia,** frequently

frecuente, *adj.* frequent
freir, *va.* to fry
fréjol or **frijol,** bean
frenesí, *m.* frenzy
frente, *f.* face; forehead; **frente a frente,** face to face; *m.* (mil.) front line; **en frente,** in front, across the way
fresa,, *f.* strawberry
fresco *adj.* fresh, cool; new; bold; *m.* refreshing air; **tomar el fresco,** to enjoy the cool air
frescura, *f.* freshness, coolness; smart repartee
fresno, *m.* ash tree
frialdad, *f.* coldness; indifference
frijoles, *m. pl.* beans
frío, fría, *adj.* cold; indifferent; *m.* cold; **hacer frío** or **tener frío,** to be cold
frito, *adj.* fried
frivolo, *adj.* frivolous
frondoso, *adj.* leafy
frontera, *f.* frontier, border
frontón, *m.* wall of a handball court; pelota court
frotar, *va.* to rub
fructífero, *adj.* fruitful
frugal, *adj.* frugal, sparing
frugalidad, *f.* frugality
fruncir, *va.* to pleat; to gather, shirr; to pucker; to reduce to a smaller size; **fruncir las cejas,** to knit the eyebrows; **fruncir el ceño,** to frown
fruta, *f.* fruit
frutal, *adj.* fruit-bearing
frutera, *f.* fruit woman; fruit dish
frutería, *f.* fruit store
frutilla, *f.* small fruit; strawberry (in South America)
fruto, *m.* fruit; benefit
fuego, *m.* fire; skin eruption; ardor
fuelle, *m.* bellows, blower
fuente, *f.* fountain; source; issue; spring (of water); platter, dish
fuera, *adv.* outside; **fuera de sí,** frantic, beside oneself; **fuera de alcance,** beyond reach

fuerte, *m.* fortification; fort; *adj.* strong; loud; *adv.* strongly; loudly

fuerza, *f.* force, strength, vigor; violence, coercion; **a fuerza de,** by dint of; **fuerza mayor,** act of God

fuete, *m.* (Sp. Am.) horsewhip

fuga, *f.* flight, escape; leak; (mus.) fugue

fugarse, *vr.* to escape, flee

fugaz, *adj.* fugitive; volatile

fulano, fulana, or **Fulano de Tal,** *n.* John Doe, so-and-so

fulgor, *m.* glow, brilliancy

fulminante, *m.* percussion cap; *adj.* explosive

fumar, *va., vn.* to smoke (cigars ,etc.)

fumigación, *f.* fumigation

funcionamiento, *m.* functioning

funcionar, *vn.* to function; to work, run (as machines)

funcionario, *m.* official, functionary

funda, *f.* case, sheath; slip cover; **funda de almohada,** pillowcase

fundación, *f.* foundation

fundador, fundadora, *n.* founder

fundamental, *adj.* fundamental

fundamento, *m.* foundation, base, groundwork; reason; good behavior

fundar, *va.* to found; to establish

fundir, *va.* to melt metals

fúnebre, *adj.* mournful, sad; funeral

funesto, *adj.* funereal dismal; disastrous

furgón, *m.* baggage, freight,or express car

furor, *m.* fury

fusil, *m.* musket, rifle

fusilar, *va.* to shoot, execute

fusión, *f.* fusion, union

futbol, *m.* football, soccer

futuro, *adj., m.* future

G

g/, gramo, gr. gram

g/, giro, draft

gabardina, *f.* gabardine; raincoat

gabinete, *m.,* cabinet, study

gafas, *f. pl.* spectacles, goggles

galán, *m.* gallant, courtier; lover; actor

galante, *adj.* gallant, courtly; generous, liberal

galantear, *va.* to court, woo

galanteo, *m.* gallantry, courtship

galantería, *f.* gallantry; compliment

galera, *f.* galley

galería, *f.* gallery

galgo, *m.* greyhound

galón, *m.* braid; gallon

galope, *m.* gallop

galvanómetro, *m.* galvanometer

galleta, *f.* cracker; cookie

gallina, *f.* hen; coward

gallinero, *m.* hen coop

gallo, *m.* cock, rooster; **misa de gallo,** midnight mass

gama globulina, *f.* gamma globulin

gana, *f.* appetite; desire, mind; **tener gana,** to be willing; **de buena gana,** voluntarily; **de mala gana,** unwillingly

ganadería, *f.* cattle breeding

ganado, *m.* cattle

ganancia, *f.* gain, profit

ganar, *va.* to gain, win; to beat (in a game); to earn

ganga, *f.* bargain

ganso, gansa, *n.* gander; goose

garage or **garaje,** *m.* garage

garantía, *f.* guarantee, pledge

garantizar, *va.* to guarantee, warrant

garbanzo, *m.* chick-pea

garbo, *m.* gracefulness

garboso, *adj.* graceful

gardenia, *f.* gardenia

garganta, *f.* throat, gullet; gorge

gárgara, *f.* gargle

garrapata, *f.* tick (insect)

garrote, *m.* cudgel, club

gas, *m.* gas

gasolina, *f.* gasoline

gasolinera, *f.* gas station; motor launch

gasómetro, *m.* gas storage tank, gas holder

gastador, *adj.* extravagant

gastar, *va.* to spend; to wear out; to use up

gasto, *m.* expense, cost

gata, *f.* tabby; **a gatas,** on all fours

gatear, *vn.* to creep, crawl

gato, *m.* cat; tomcat; jack

gaucho, *m.* Argentine cowboy

gavilán, *m.* (orn.) hawk

gaviota, *f.* (orn.) gull, sea gull

gazapo, *m.* young rabbit; blunder

gelatina, *f.* gelatine, jelly

gemido, *m.* groan, moan

gemir, *vn.* to groan, moan

gen, *m.* gene

generación, *f.* generation

generador, *m.* generator

general, *m.* general; *adj.* general, usual; **por lo general,** as a rule

generosidad, *f.* generosity

generoso, *adj.* generous

Génesis, *f.* Genesis

genial, *adj.* outstanding

genio, *m.* genius; temper

genital, *adj.* genital

genocidio, *m.* genocide

gente, *f.* people

gentil, *adj.* courteous

gentileza, *f.* gentility; courteous gesture

gentío, *m.* crowd, multitude

gentuza, *f.* rabble, mob

genuino, *adj.* genuine

geografía, *f.* geography.

geográfico, *adj.* geographical

geología, *f.* geology

geólogo, *m.* geologist

geometría, *f.* geometry

gerencia, *f.* management

gerente, *m.* manager

germinar, *vn.* to germinate

gerundio, *m.* (gram.) gerund, present participle

gestión, *f.* action, step

gestionar, *va.* to take steps to obtain something

gesto, *m.* face, aspect; gesture

gigante, *m.* giant; *adj.* gigantic

gigantesco, *adj.* gigantic

gimnasia *f.* gymnastics

gimnasio, *m.* gymnasium

ginebra, *f.* gin

ginecólogo, *m.* gynecologist

girafa, *f.* giraffe

girar, *vn.* to rotate, revolve; (com.) to draw on

girasol, *m.* sunflower

giro, *m.* turn, bend; (com.) draft; **giro a la vista,** sight draft; **giro postal,** money order

gitano, gitana, *n.* gypsy

glacial, *adj.* icy

gladiolo, *m.* (bot.) gladiolus

glicerina, glycerine

glóbulo, *m.* globule

gloria, *f.* glory

glorificar, *va.* to glorify

glorioso, *adj.* glorious

glosario, *m.* glossary

glotón, glotona, *n.*, *adj.* glutton; gluttonous

glucosa, *f.* glucose

gobernación, *f.* government; governor's office or mansion

gobernador, *m.* governor

gobernar, *va.* to govern; to regulate; to direct

gobierno, *m.* government

golfo, *m.* gulf

golondrina, *f.* (orn.) swallow

golosina, *f.* dainty, titbit

goloso, *adj.* gluttonous

golpe, *m.* blow, stroke, hit; knock; **de golpe,** all at once

golpear, *va.*, *vn.* to beat, knock; to bruise; to tap

goma, *f.* gum; rubber; eraser

gordo, *adj.* fat; thick

gordura, *f.* grease; fatness

gorgojo, *m.* grub, weevil

gorila, *m.* (zool.) gorilla

gorra, *f.* cap, bonnet; **de gorra,** (coll.) at others' expense, sponging

gorro, *m.* cap or hood

gota, *f.* drop; gout

gotear, *vn.* to drip

gotera, *f.* leak, leakage

gozar, *va.* to enjoy

gozoso, *adj.* joyful

gr., gramo, gr., gram

grabación, *f.* recording; enraving

grabado, *m.* engraving, illustration; **grabado al agua fuerte,** etching

gracia, *f.* grace; pardon; **gracias,** *pl.* thanks

gracioso, *adj.* graceful; funny, pleasing; *m.* clown, buffoon

grada, *f.* step of a staircase; **gradas,** *pl.* seats of a stadium

grado, *m.* step; degree; grade. .

graduación, *f.* graduation

gradual, *adj.* gradual

graduar, *va., vr.* to graduate; to grade

gráfico, *adj.* graphic; vivid

Gral. General, Gen. General

gramática, *f.* grammar

gramatical, *adj.* grammatical

gramo, *m.* gram

gran, *adj.* contraction of **grande,** great, large, big

granada, *f.* grenade, shell, pomegranate

Gran Bretaña, *f.* Great Britain

grande, *adj.* great; large, big

grandioso, *adj.* grand, magnificent

granero, *m.* granary

granito, *m.* granite

granizo, *m.* hail

granja, *f.* grange, farm

grano, *m.* grain, kernel; pimple; **ir al grano,** to get to the point

grasa, *f.* suet, fat, grease; shoe polish

gratificación, *f.* gratification; gratuity

gratificar, *va.* to gratify, reward

gratitud, *f.* gratitude

grato, *adj.* pleasant, pleasing; **su grata,** your favor (letter)

gratuito, *adj.* free

gravamen, *m.* charge, tax

gravar, *va.* to burden; to tax

grave, *adj.* grave, serious

Grecia, *f.* Greece

gremio, *m.* guild, trade union

griego, *adj.* Greek

grieta, *f.* opening, crack

grillo, *m.* cricket

gringo, gringa, *n.* (Sp. Am.) (coll.) foreigner (especially an Anglo-Saxon)

gripe, *f.* grippe, influenza

gris, *adj.* gray

gritar. *vn.* to scream

grito, *m.* cry, scream

grosería, *f.* insult; coarseness

grosero, *adj.* coarse, rude

grúa, *f.* crane, derrick

gruesa, *f.* gross

grueso, *adj.* thick, coarse

gruñido, *m.* grunt, growl

grupo, *m.* group

gruta, *f.* grotto

gsa., gruesa, gro., gross

gte., gerente, mgr., manager

guacamayo, *m.,* **guacamaya,** *f.* macaw

guante, *m.* glove

guapo, *adj.* courageous; bold; elegant, handsome

guarda, *m., f.* guard, keeper

guardabrisa, *m.* windshield

guardafango, *m.* fender; dashboard

guardar, *va.* to keep; to guard

guardarropa, *m., f.* keeper of a wardrobe; *m.* coatroom

guardia, *f.* guard; watch; *m.* guardsman

guasa, *f.* (coll.) fun, jest

guasón, guasona, *adj.* (coll.) fond of teasing

guatemalteco, guatemalteca, *n., adj.* Guatemalan

guayaba, *f.* guava (fruit); **guayabo,** *m.* guava (tree)

güero, güera, *n., adj.* (Mex.) blond, light-haired. *See* **huero**

guerra, war; **dar guerra,** to be a nuisance (usually a child)

guerrero, *m.* warrior; **guerrera,** *adj.* martial, warlike

guía, *m., f.* guide; guidebook

guiar, *va.* to guide, lead; to drive

Guillermo, William

guillotina, *f.* guillotine

guindar, *va.* to hang

guiñar, *va.* to wink

guión, *m.* hyphen; (rad.) script

guisado, *m.* stew

guisante, *m.* (bot.) pea

guisar, *va.* to cook, stew

guiso, *m.* any edible concoction

guitarra, *f.* guitar

gusano, *m.* maggot, worm

gustar, *va., vn.* to like, be fond of

gusto, *m.* taste; pleasure, delight; choice

gustoso, *adj.* tasty; willing

H

h., habitantes, pop., population

haba, *f.* (bot.) navy bean

Habana, *f.* Havana

habanero, habanera, *n., adj.* native of Havana; of Havana

habano, *m.* Havana cigar

haber, *va.* to have (as an auxiliary verb); to exist; *m.* (com.) credit; **haberes**, *m. pl.* property

habichuela, *f.* kidney bean; **habichuela verde**, string bean

hábil, *adj.* able, skillful

habilidad, *f.* ability, dexterity, aptitude

habilitar, *va.* to qualify, enable; to equip

habitación, *f.* dwelling

habitante, *m., f.* inhabitant

habitar, *va.* to inhabit, reside

hábito, *m.* custom

habituarse, *vr.* to accustom oneself

habla, *f.* speech; language; **sin habla**, speechless

hablador, *adj.* talkative

hablar, *va., vn.* to speak, talk

hacendado, *m.* landholder, farmer

hacendoso, *adj.* industrious, diligent

hacer, *va., vn.* to make, do; to manufacture; **hacer alarde**, to boast; **hacer calor**, to be warm; **hacer frío**, to be cold

hacia, *prep.* toward; about

hacienda, *f.* landed property; farmstead

hada, *f.* fairy

halagar, *va.* to please; to flat-ter

halago, *m.* caress; flattery

halagüeño, *adj.* pleasing; flattering

halcón, *m.* falcon, hawk

haltera, *f.* barbell

hallar, *va.* to find; to discover; to come upon; **hallarse**, to be; **no hallarse**, to be out of sorts

hallazgo, *m.* finding, discovery

hambre, *f.* hunger; famine; **tener hambre**, to be hungry

hambriento, *adj.* hungry; starved

haragán, haragana, *n.* idler; *adj.* lazy

harapo, *m.* rag, tatter

harén, *m.* harem

harina, *f.* flour

harinoso, *adj.* mealy, starchy

harmonía, *f.* harmony

hartar, *va., vr.* to cloy, satiate

harto, *adj.* satiated; sufficient; *adv.* enough

hasta, *prep.* till, until; *conj.* also, even

hazaña, *f.* exploit, feat

hazmerreír, *m.* laughingstock

he, *adv.* behold, look here (generally followed by **aquí** or **allí**); **he aquí**, here it is

hebilla, *f.* buckle

hebra, *f.* thread, filament

hebreo, hebrea, *n.* Hebrew; *m.* Hebrew language; *adj.* Hebraic, Judaical

hecatombe, *f.* massacre, slaughter

hectárea, *f.* hectare

hecho, *adj.* made, done; accustomed; *m.* fact; act, deed

hechura, *f.* making; workmanship

hediondo, *adj.* ill-smelling

helada, *f.* frost; nip

heladería, *f.* ice-cream parlor

helado, *adj.* frozen; icy; *m.* ice cream

helar, *va., vn.* to congeal; to freeze, ice; to astonish, amaze; **helarse**, to be frozen; to congeal

hélice, *f.* propeller

helicóptero, helicopter

hembra, *f.* female; eye of hook; nut of a screw

hemisferio, *m.* hemisphere

hemorragia, *f.* (med.) hemorrhage

hemorroides, *f. pl.* piles, hemorrhoids

heno, *m.* hay

heredar, *va.* to inherit

hereditario, *adj.* hereditary

heredero, heredera, *n.* heir, heiress

hereje, *m., f.* heretic

herencia, *f.* inheritance, heritage; heirship

herida, *f.* wound, hurt

herir, *va.* to wound, to hurt; to offend

hermanastra, *f.* stepsister

hermanastro, *m.* stepbrother

hermano, hermana, *n.* brother, sister; **primo hermano,** or **prima hermana,** first cousin

hermético, *adj.* airtight

hermoso, *adj.* beautiful, handsome

hermosura, *f.* beauty

héroe, *m.* hero

heroico, *adj.* heroic

heroína, *f.* heroine

heroísmo, *m.* heroism

herradura, *f.* horseshoe

herramienta, *f.* tool, implement

herrería, *f.* ironworks

herrero, *m.* blacksmith

hervir, *vn.* to boil

hervor, *m.* boiling; fervor

hidroavión, *m.* seaplane

hidrógeno, *m.* hydrogen

hidropesía, *f.* dropsy

hidroplano, *m.* hydroplane (boat)

hiedra, *f.* ivy

hiel, *f.* gall, bile

hielo, *m.* frost, ice

hiena, *f.* hyena

hierba or **yerba,** *f.* herb; grass; weed

hierbabuena, *f.* (bot.) mint

hierro, *m.* iron; **hierros,** *pl.* fetters

hígado, *m.* liver

higiene, *f.* hygiene

hija, *f.* daughter; child

hijastra, *f.* stepdaughter

hijastro, *m.* stepson

hijo, *m.* son; child

hilar, *va.* to spin

hilera, *f.* row; ridgepole; (mech.) wire drawer

hilo, *m.* thread; linen; wire

hilvanar, *va.* to baste

himno, *m.* hymn; anthem

hincapié, *m.* stress; **hacer hincapié,** to emphasize

hincarse, *vr.* to kneel

hinchado, *adj.* swollen

hinchar, *va., vr.* to swell

hindú, *m., f.* Hindu

hipnotismo, *m.* hypnotism

hipnotizar, *va.* to hypnotize

hipo, *m.* hiccough

hipócrita, *adj., n.* hypocritical; hypocrite

hipopótamo, *m.* hippopotamus

hipoteca, *f.* mortgage

hirviente, *adj.* boiling

hispano, *adj.* Hispanic, Spanish

Hispanoamérica, *f.* Spanish America

hispanoamericano, hispanoamericana, *adj., n.* Spanish-American

histérico, *adj.* hysterical

historia, *f.* history; story

historiador, historiadora, *n.* historian

histórico, *adj.* historical

hocico, *m.* snout, muzzle

hogar, *m.* home; hearth

hoguera, *f.* bonfire; blaze

hoja, *f.* leaf; blade (of knife, sword, etc.); sheet (of paper or metal), **hoja de trébol,** cloverleaf

hohalata, *f.* tin plate

hojear, *va.* to turn the leaves of a book

Holanda, *f.* Holland

holandés, holandésa, *n., adj.* Dutch

holgado, *adj.* loose; in easy circumstances

holgazán, holgazana, *n.* idler

hollín, *m.* soot

hombre, *m.* man, human being

hombro, m. shoulder

homenaje, m. homage, tribute

homicida, m., f. murderer; adj. homicidal

homicidio, m. murder

hondo, adj. profound, deep

hondureño, hondureña, n., adj. Honduran

honesto, adj. honest; modest

hongo, m. mushroom; fungus

honor, m. honor

honorable, adj. honorable

honorario, adj. honorary; m. honorarium, fee

honra, f. honor; chastity (in women); **honras,** pl. funeral honors

honrado, adj. honest, honorable

honrar, va. to honor; **honrarse,** to deem it an honor

hora, f. hour; time

horario, m. hour hand; time table; hours; schedule

horma, f. mold; **horma de zapatos,** shoe last

hormiga, f. ant

hormigón, m. concrete

hormigonera, f. concrete mixer

horno, m. oven; furnace; **alto horno,** blast furnace

horquilla, f. hairpin

horrible, adj. horrible

horror, m. horror, fright

horrorizar, va., vr. to horrify

hortaliza, f. vegetables

hospedaje, m. lodging

hospedar, va., vr. to lodge, board

hospicio, m. orphanage; old peoples home

hospital, m. hospital

hospitalidad, f. hospitality

hospitalización, f. hospitalization

hospitalizar, va. to hospitalize

hostia, f. host; wafer

hotel, m. hotel

hoy, adv. today

hoyo, m. hole, pit

hoz, f. sickle

huelga, f. strike of workmen

huella, f. track, trace

huérfano, huérfana, n., adj. orphan

huero, adj. empty, addle; **huevo huero,** rotten egg

huerta, orchard, vegetable garden

huerto, m. fruit garden

hueso, m. bone; stone, core

huésped, huéspeda, n. guest; boarder

huevo, m. egg

huida, f. flight, escape

huir, vn. to flee, escape

hule, m. rubber; oilcloth .

humanidad, f. humanity, mankind; **humanidades,** pl. humanities, human learning

humanitario, humanitaria, n., adj. humanitarian

humano, adj. human; humane, kind

humedad, f. humidity, moisture, wetness

humedecer, va. to moisten, wet, soak

humedo, adj. humid, wet

humildad, f. humility, humbleness

humilde, adj. humble, meek

humillar, va., vr. to humble; to humiliate

humo, m. smoke; fume

humor, m. humor, disposition

hundir, vn., vr. to submerge; to sink

húngaro, húngara, adj., n. Hungarian

Hungría, f. Hungary

huracán, m. hurricane, storm

hurtar, va. to steal, rob

I

ibérico, adj. Iberian

id., idem, id., same, ditto

ida, f. departure; **idas y venidas,** comings and goings

idea, f. idea; scheme

ideal, m., adj. ideal

idealismo, m. idealism

idealista, n., adj. idealist; idealistic

idealizar, va., vn. to idealize

idear, va. to conceive; to think, to contrive, to plan

idem, item, the same, ditto
idéntico, *adj.* identical
identificar, *va., vr.* to identify
idioma, *m.* language
idiosincrasia, *f.* idiosyncrasy
idiota, *m., f.* idiot; *adj.* idiotic
idolatrar, *va.* to idolize
idolo, *m.* idol
iglesia, *f.* church
ignorancia, *f.* ignorance
ignorante, *adj.* ignorant
ignorar, *va.* to be ignorant of
igual, *adj.* equal, similar
igualar, *va.* to equalize, equal;
  igualarse, to place oneself on
  a level (with)
igualdad, *f.* equality
igualmente, *adv.* equally
ilegal, *adj.* illegal, unlawful
ilegítimo, *adj.* illegitimate
ileso, *adj.* unhurt
iluminación, *f.* illumination,
  lighting
iluminar, *va.* to illumine, illuminate
ilustración, *f.* illustration
ilustrar, *va.* to illustrate; to
  enlighten
ilustre, *adj.* illustrious
imagen, *f.* image
imaginación, *f.* imagination
imaginar, *va., vn.* to imagine
imaginario, *adj.* imaginary,
  fancied
imán, *m.* magnet
imbécil, *m., f.* imbecile, idiot;
  adj. feeble minded
imitación, *f.* imitation
imitar, *va.* to imitate
impaciencia, *f.* impatience
impaciente, *adj.* impatient
impar, *adj.* unequal, odd
imparcial, *adj.* impartial
impartir, *va.* to impart
impávido, *adj.* calm in the
  face of danger
impecable, *adj.* impeccable
impedir, *va.* to impede, prevent
imperar, *vn.* to rule, command; to reign; to prevail
imperativo, *adj.* imperative,
  pressing; *m.* (gram.) imperative (case)
imperdible, *m.* safety pin

imperdonable, *adj.* unpardon-
  able
imperfecto, *adj.* imperfect
imperial, *adj.* imperial
imperialismo, *m.* imperialism
imperio, *m.* empire
imperioso, *adj.* imperious,
  pressing; arrogant
impermeable, *adj.* waterproof;
  m. raincoat
impersonal, *adj.* impersonal
impertinente, *adj.* impertinent; importunate
impertinentes, *m. pl.* lor-
  gnette
ímpetu, *m.* impetus; impetu-
  osity
impetuoso, *adj.* impetuous
implicar, *va., vn.* to impliclite,
  involve
implícito, *adj.* implicit
implorar, *va.* to implore
imponderabilidad, *f.* weightlessness
imponer, *va.* to impose; **impo-
  nerse,** to assert oneself
importador, importadora, *n.*
  importer
importancia, *f.* importance,
  import
importante, *adj.* important
importar, *vn.* to matter; to
  mind; to import
importe, *m.* amount, cost
imposibilidad, *f.* impossibility
imposible, *adj.* impossible
imposición, *f.* imposition
impostor, impostora, *n.* impostor
impotente, *adj.* impotent;
  helpless
impracticable, *adj.* impracticable
imprenta, *f.* printing; printing
  office
imprescindible, *adj.* indis-
  pensible, essential
impresión, *f.* impression; edition; presswork
impresionar, *va.* to impress
impresos, *m. pl.* printed matter
impresor, impresora, *n.*
  printer
imprevisto, *adj.* unforeseen

imprimir *va.* to print

impropio, *adj.* improper, unfit

improvisar, *va.* to improvise

improviso, *adj.* unforeseen; **de improviso,** unexpectedly

impuesto, *m.* tax, impost, duty; **impuesto sobre rentas,** income tax

impulsar, *va.* to further, impel; (mech.) to drive

impulso, *m.* impulse, impulsion, spur

impureza, *f.* impurity

inaccesible, *adj.* inaccessible

inaceptable, *adj.* unacceptable

inagotable, *adj.* inexhaustible

inalámbrico, *adj.* wireless

inaudito, *adj.* unheard of, unusual

inauguración, *f.* inauguration

inaugurar, *va.* to inaugurate

inca, *m.* Inca; Peruvian gold coin

incansable, *adj.* untiring

incapaz., *adj.* incapable, unable

incendiar, *va., vr.* to set on fire

incendio, *m.* fire, conflagration

incentivo, *m.* incentive

incertidumbre, *f.* uncertainty

incidente, *m.* incident

incienso, *m.* incense

incierto, *adj.* uncertain

incitar, *va.* to incite, stir

inclinar, *va., vn.* to incline, slope; **inclinarse por,** to be favorably disposed to

incluir, *va.* to include, comprise; to inclose

inclusive, *adv.* inclusive, including

incluso, inclosed

incógnito, *adj.* unknown

incoherente, *adj.* incoherent

incomodar, *va.* to inconvenience, disturb

incomodidad, *f.* inconvenience, annoyance

incómodo, *adj.* uncomfortable, inconvenient

incomparable, *adj.* incomparable

incompatible, *adj.* incompatible

incompetente, *adj.* incompetent

incompleto, *adj.* incomplete

incomprensible, *adj.* incomprehensible

inconcebible, *adj.* inconceivable

inconsciente, *adj.* unconscious

inconstante, *adj.* inconstant, fickle

inconveniencia, *f.* inconvenience

inconveniente, *adj.* inconvenient; inadvisable; *m.* obstacle; objection

incorporar, *va.* to incorporate; to join; **incorporarse,** to become incorporated; to sit up (in bed)

incorrecto, *adj.* incorrect

incorregible, *adj.* incorrigible

incrédulo, *adj.* incredulous

increíble, *adj.* incredible

incremento, *m.* increment, increase

incubar, *va.* to hatch

inculcar, *va.* to inculcate

incurable, *adj.* incurable

incurrir, *vn.* to incur

indagar, *va.* to investigate

indecente, *adj.* indecent

indeciso, *adj.* undecided

indefinido, *adj.* indefinite

indemnizar, *va.* to indemnify

independencia, *f.* independence

independiente, *adj.* independent

indescriptible, *adj.* indescribable

indicación, *f.* indication

indicar, *va.* to indicate

indicativo, *adj.* indicative; *m., adj.* (gram.) indicative

índice, *m.* mark, sign; hand of a watch or clock; index; forefinger

índico, *adj.* pertaining to the East Indies; **Océano Indico** or **Mar de las Indias,** Indian Ocean

indiferencia, *f.* indifference

indiferente, *adj.* indifferent

indígena, *adj., n.* indigenous, native

indigente, *adj.* indigent,

indigestión, *f.* indigestion

indigesto, *adj.* indigestible

indignación, *f.* indignation, anger

indio, india, *n., adj.* Indian

indirecta, *f.* hint, cue

indirecto, *adj.* indirect

indispensable, *adj.* indispensable

individual, *adj.* individual

individuo, *m.* individual

índole, *f.* disposition, temper; kind; nature

inducir, *va.* to induce

indudable, *adj.* undeniable; evident, certain

indulgencia, *f.* indulgence, forgiveness

industria, *f.* industry

industrial, *adj.* industrial

industrialización, *f.* industrialization

industrializer, *va.* to industrialize

industrioso, *adj.* industrious

inédito, *adj.* not published, unedited

inepto, *adj.* inept, unfit

inercia, *f.* inertia; inactivity

inesperado, *adj.* unexpected

inevitable, *adj.* inevitable

infame, *adj.* infamous, bad; *m., f.* wretch, scoundrel

infancia, *f.* infancy

infante, *m.* infant; any son of the king of Spain, except the heir apparent

infantil, *adj.* infantile

infección, *f.* infection

infectar, *va.* to infect

infeliz, *adj.* unhappy, unfortunate

inferior, *adj.* inferior; lower

inferioridad, *f.* inferiority

inferir, *va.* to infer; to inflict

infiel, *adj.* unfaithful

infierno, *m.* hell

ínfimo, *adj.* lowest

infinidad, *f.* infinity

infinitivo, *m.* (gram.) infinitive

infinito, *adj.* infinite, immense; *adv.* infinitely, immensely; *m.* infinity

inflación, *f.* inflation

inflamable, *adj.* inflammable

intramar, *va.* to inflame; **intramarse,** to catch fire

inflar, *va., vr.* to inflate

influencia, *f.* influence

influenza, *f.* influenza

influir, *va.* to influence

influyente, *adj.* influential

información, *f.* information

informal, *adj.* not punctual; unreliable

informar, *va.* to inform, report

informe, *m.* information; report, account

infortunio, *m.* misfortune

infracción, *f.* violation

infructuoso, *adj.* fruitless

infundado, *adj.* groundless

infundir, *va.* to infuse; to instill

ingeniar, *va.* to conceive; to contrive

ingeniero, *m.* engineer

ingenio, *m.* wit, ingenuity; **ingenio de azúcar,** sugar mill

ingenioso, *adj.* ingenious, witty; resourceful

ingenuidad, *f.* candor, naiveté

ingenuo, *adj.* candid, naive

Inglaterra, *f.* England

inglés, inglesa, *n., adj.* Englishman, Englishwoman; English; *m.* English language

ingratitud, *f.* ingratitude

ingrato, *adj.* ungrateful

ingrediente, *m.* ingredient

ingreso, *m.* (com.) receipts, revenue; entrance

inhumano, *adj.* inhuman

inicial, *f., adj.* initial

iniciar, *va.* to initiate, begin; **iniciarse,** to be initiated

inciativa, *f.* initiative

injusticia, *f.* injustice

inmaculado, *adj.* immaculate

inmediato, *adj.* immediate, next

inmejorable, *adj.* unsurpassable

inmenso, *adj.* immense, infinite

inmersión, immersion, dip

inmigración, *f.* immigration
inmigrar, *vn.* to immigrate
inmoral, *adj.* immoral
inmoralidad, *f.* immorality
inmortal, *adj.* immortal
inmortalidad, *f.* immortality
inmóvil, *adj.* immovable, stable; death-like
inmueble, *adj.* (law) immovable (property); **bienes inmuebles,** real estate
inmundo, *adj.* filthy, dirty
inmune, *adj.* immune
innato, *adj.* inborn, natural
innovación, *f.* innovation
inocencia, *f.* innocence
inocente, *adj.* innocent
inodoro, *m.* water closet
inofensivo, *adj.* harmless
inolvidable, *adj.* unforgettable
inquietud, *f.* restlessness
inquilino, inquilina, *n.* tenant, renter
inquisición, *f.* inquisition
insaciable, *adj.* insatiable
inscribir, *va., vr.* register
inscripción, *f.* inscription
insecto, *m.* insect
inseguro, *adj.* uncertain
inseparable, *adj.* inseparable
inserción, *f.* insertion
insertar, *va.* to insert
inservible, *adj.* useless
insignia, *f.* badge, insignia
insignificante, *adj.* insignificant
insinuación, *f.* insinuation, hint
insinuar, *va.* to insinuate, hint; **insinuarse,** to ingratiate oneself
insistencia, *f.* persistence
insistir, *vn.* to insist
insolente, *adj.* insolent
insomnio, *m.* insomnia
inspección, *f.* inspection
inspector, *m.* inspector
inspiración, *f.* inspiration
inspirar, *va.* to inspire
instalación, *f.* installation
instalar, *va.* to install; **instalarse,** to settle
instantáneo, *adj.* instantaneous; **instantánea,** *f.* snapshot

instigar, *va.* to instigate
instintivo, *adj.* instinctive
instinto, *m.* instinct
institución, *f.* institution
instituto, *m.* institute
institutriz, *f.* governess
instrucción, *f.* instruction; education
instructor, *m.* instructor
instruido, *adj.* well-educated
instruir, *va.* to instruct
instrumento, *m.* instrument; machine
insubordinado, *adj.* insubordinate
insuficiente, *adj.* insufficient
insufrible, *adj.* insufferable
insuperable, *adj.* insurmountable
insurrecto, insurrecta, *n., adj.* insurgent, rebel
intachable, *adj.* blameless; irreproachable
integridad, *f.* integrity, whole
íntegro, *adj.* entire
intelectual, *adj., n.* intellectual
inteligencia, *f.* intelligence; understanding
inteligente, *adj.* intelligent
intemperie, *f.* rough or bad weather; **a la intemperie,** outdoors
intempestivo, *adj.* inopportune
intención, intention
intensidad, intensity
intensificar, *va.* to intensify
intenso, *adj.* intense, ardent
intentar, *va.* to try; to intend
intento, *m.* intent, purpose
intercambio, *m.* interchange
interceder, *vn.* to intercede
interés, *m.* interest
interesante, *adj.* interesting
interesar, *vn., vr.* to be concerned or interested in; *va.* to interest
interino, *adj.* provisional, acting (of an employ or office)
interior, *adj.* interior, internal; **ropa interior,** underwear; *m.* interior
interjección, *f.* (gram.) interjection

intermediar, *va.* to interpose
intermedio, *adj.* intermediate; *m.* intermission; interlude, recess; **por intermedio de**, through, by means of
internacional, *adj.* international
internar, *va.* to intern; to place in a boarding school or asylum; *vn.* to pierce
interno, *adj.* interior, internal, inside; *n.* boarding-school student
interplanetario, interplanetaria, *adj.* interplanetary
interpretación, *f.* interpretation
interpretar, *va.* to interpret, explain; to translate
intérprete, *m.* interpreter
interrogación, *f.* interrogation
interrogar, *va.* to interrogate
interrumpir, *va.* to interrupt
interrupción, *f.* interruption
interruptor, *m.* (elec.) switch
intervalo, *m.* interval
intervención, *f.* intervention
intervenir, *vn.* to intervene, mediate
intestino, *m.* intestine
intimidad, *f.* intimacy
intolerable, *adj.* intolerable
intolerancia, *f.* intolerance
intranquilo, *adj.* restless
intransitive, *adj.* (gram.) intransitive
intriga, *f.* intrigue, plot
intrigante, *adj.* intriguing, scheming
intrínseco, *adj.* intrinsic
introducción, *f.* introduction
introducir, *va.* to introduce; **introducirse**, to gain access (to)
intruso, *adj.* intrusive, obtrusive; *n.* intruder
intuición, *f.* intuition
inundación, *f.* inundation, flood
inundar, *va.* to inundate
inútil, *adj.* useless
invadir, *va.* to invade
inválido, *adj.* invalid, null; *n.* invalid
invariable, *adj.* invariable

invasión, *f.* invasion
invencible, *adj.* invincible
invención, *f.* invention
inventar, *va.* to invent
inventario, *m.* inventory
invento, *m.* invention
invernadero, *m.* (mil). greenhouse
inverosímil, *adj.* unlikely, improbable
inversión, *f.* inversion; investment
invertir, *va.* to invert; (com.) to invest
investigación, *f.* investigation, research
investigar, *va.* to investigate
invierno, *m.* winter
invisible, *adj.* invisible
invitación, *f.* invitation
invitado, invitada, *n.* guest
invitar, *va.* to invite
invocar, *va.* to invoke
involuntario, *adj.* involuntary
inyección, *f.* injection
inyectar, *va.* to inject
ir, *vn.* to go; to walk; to progress; **irse**, to go away, depart
ira, *f.* anger, wrath
iris, *m.* rainbow; iris (of the eye)
Irlanda, *f.* Ireland
irlandés, irlandésa, *n.*, *adj.* Irishman, Irishwoman; Irish
ironía, *f.* irony
irónico, *adj.* ironical
irregular, *adj.* irregular
irremediable, *adj.* irremediable, helpless
irreparable; *adj.* irreparable
irresistible, *adj.* irresistible
irresponsable, *adj.* irresponsible
irrevocable, *adj.* irrevocable
irritación, *f.* irritation; wrath
irritar, *va.* to irritate
isla, *f.* isle,, island
israelita, *n. adj.* Israelite, Jew, Jewish
istmo, *m.* isthmus
Italia, *f.* Italy
italiano, italiana, *n.*, *adj.* Italian; *m.* Italian language
itinerario, *adj.*, *m.* itinerary

izar, *va.* (naut.) to hoist
izquierdo, *adj.* left; left-handed; **izquierda,** *f.* left wing in politics; left, left hand

J

jabalí, *m.* wild boar
jabón, *m.* soap
jacinto, *m.* hyacinth
jactarse, *vr.* to boast
jadeante, *adj.* panting
jai lai, *m.* Basque ball
jaiba, *f.* (Sp. Am.) crab
jalea, *f.* jelly
jamás, *adv.* never
jamón, *m.* ham
Japón, *m.* Japan
japonés, japonesa, *adj., n.* Japanese; *m.* japanese language
jaqueca, *f.* headache
jarabe, *m.* sirup; **jarabe tapatío,** Mexican regional dance
jardín, *m.* garden
jardinero, jardinera, *n.* gardener
jarra, *f.* jug, jar, pitcher
jarro, *m.* pitcher, jug
J.C., Jesucristo, J.C., Jesus Christ
jefatura, *f.* leadership; **jefatura de policía,** police headquarters
jeringa, *f.* syringe
Jesucristo, *m.* Jesus Christ
jesuita, *m., adj.* Jesuit
Jesús, *m.* Jesus; *interj.* goodness!
jinete, *m.* horseman, rider
jira, *f.* strip of cloth; tour; **jira campestre,** picnic
jirafa, *f.* giraffe
jocoso, *adj.* comical
jornada, *f.* one-day march; journey
joroba, *f.* hump
jorobado, *adj.* hunchbacked
jota, *f.* the letter **j**; Spanish dance; **no saber ni jota,** not to know a thing
joven, *adj.* young; *m., f.* young man, young woman
jovial, *adj.* jovial, gay

joya, *f.* jewel
joyería, *f.* jewelry store
joyero, *m.* jeweler
juanete, *m.* bunion
jubilar, *va., vr.* to pension off; to retire
júbilo, *m.* joy
judía, *f.* kidney bean; string bean; Jewess
judicial, *adj.* judicial,juridical
judio, *adj.* Jewish; *m.* Jew
jueves, *m.* Thursday
juez, *m.* judge
jugada, *f.* move (in a game); mean trick
jugar, *va., vn.* to play; to gamble
jugo, *m.* sap, juice
jugoso, *adj.* juicy
juguete, *m.* toy, plaything
juguetón, *adj.* playful
juicio, *m.* judgment, reason; trial
juicioso, *adj.* wise, prudent
julio, *m.* July
junio, *m.* June
junta, *f.* session, meeting; board; **junta directiva,** board of directors
juntar, *va.* to unite; to collect, gather; **juntarse,** to assemble
junto, *adv.* near, close; **junto, junta,** *adj.* united; **juntos,** *pl.* together, side by side
jurado, *m.* jury; juror, juryman
juramento, *m.* oath
jurar, *va., vn.* to swear, make oath; to curse
jurisdicción, *f.* jurisdiction
justicia, *f.* justice; fairness; **la justicia,** the police
justificación, *f.* justification
justificar, *va.* to justify
justo, *adj.* just; fair, upright; tight
juvenil, *adj.* juvenile,youthful
juventud, *f.* youthfulness, youth
juzgado, *m.* tribunal; court
juzgar, *va., vn.* to judge

K

kaki, *m., adj.* khaki

karate, *m.* karate
Kc., **Kilociclo**, kc., kilocycle
Kg. or **kg.**, **kilogramo**, k. or kg., kilogram
kilo, *m.* kilo, kilogram
kilociclo, *m.* kilocycle
kilogramo, *m.* kilogram
kilométrico, **kilométrica**, *adj.* kilometric; (coll.) too long
kilómetro, *m.* kilometer
kilotón, *m.* kiloton
kilovatio, *m.* kilowatt
kiosco, *m.* kiosk, booth
Km. or **km.**, **kilómetro**, km., kilometer
kodak, *m.* kodak
kv. or **k.w.**, **kilovatio**, kw., kilowatt

L

l., **ley**, law; **libro**, bk., book; **litro**, l., liter
L/, **l.ª**, **l.: letra**, bill, draft, letter
£, **libra esterlina**, £, pound sterling
la, *art.* (fem. sing.) the *pron.* (acc. fem. sing.) her, it, as **la vio**, he saw her, **la compré**, I bought it (casa)
laberinto, *m.* labyrinth, maze
labia, *f.* (coll.) gift of gab
labio, *m.* lip; edge of anything
labor, *f.* labor, task; needlework
laborar, *va.*, *vn.* to work; to till
laboratorio, *m.* laboratory
laborioso, *adj.* industrious
labrador, **labradora**, *n.* farmer; peasant
labrar, *va.* to work; to labor, to cultivate the ground
laca, *f.* lac; lacquer
lacio, *adj.* straight (applied to hair)
lacónico, *adj.* laconic
lactancia, *f.* time of suckling
lácteo, *adj.* lacteous, milky
ladino, *adj.* cunning, crafty
lado, *m.* side; party
ladrar, *vn.* to bark
ladrillo, *m.* brick
ladrón, *m.* thief, robber
lagartija, *f.* (zool.) eft, newt

lagarto, *m.* lizard; alligator; (coll.) sly person
lago, *m.* lake
lágrima, *f.* tear
laguna, *f.* lagoon, pond; blank space (as in a text), hiatus; gap
lamentar, *va.* to lament, regret; *vn.*, *vr.* to lament, complain, cry
lamer, *va.* to lick, to lap
lámina, *f.* plate, sheet of metal; copper plate; print, picture
lana, *f.* wool
lanar, *adj.* woolly; **ganado lanar**, sheep
lance, *m.* cast, throw; critical moment; quarrel
lancha, *f.* barge, launch
langosta *f.* locust; lobster
lánguido, *adj.* languid
lanudo. *adj.* woolly, fleecy
lanza, *f.* lance, spear
lanzacohetes, *m.* rocket launcher
lanzar, *va.* to throw, fling; to launch
lapicero, *m.* pencil case
lápida, *f.* tombstone
larga, *f.* delay; **a la larga**, in the long run
largar, *va.* to slacken; to let go; **largarse**, (coll.) to get out, leave
largo, *adj.* long; **larga ejecución (discos)**, long-playing (records); *m.* length
laringe, *f.* larynx
lástima, *f.* pity
lastimar, *va.* to hurt; to wound; **lastimarse**, to be hurt
lata, *f.* tin can; (coll.) nuisance annoyance
latente, *adj.* dormant
lateral, *adj.* lateral
latido, *m.* pant, palpitation; barking
latigazo, *m.* crack of a whip
látigo, *m.* whip
latín, *m.* Latin language
latino, **latina**, *adj.*, *n.* Latin
Latinoamérica, *f.* Latin America

latinoamericano, latinoamericana, *adj.* Latin American
latir, *vn.* to palpitate; to howl (as dogs)
lntitud, *f.* latitude
latón, *m.* brass; brassie
latoso, *adj.* boring; **latosa,** *n.* bore
laurel, *m.* (bot.) laurel; laurel crown
lavado, *m.* washing, wash
lavamanos, *m.* wash bowl
lavandería, *f.* laundry
lavar, *va.* to wash
lavativa, *f.* enema
lavatorio, *m.* lavatory
laxante, *m., adj.* (med.) laxative
lazarillo, *m.* blind man's guide
lazo, *m.* lasso, lariat; tie; bond
lb., libra, lb., pound
Ldo., L.^{do}, or **l.^{do}, Licenciado,** (Sp. Am.) lawyer
le, *pron.* dative case of **él** or **ella**
leal, *adj.* loyal, faithful
lealtad, *f.* loyalty
lección, *f.* lesson
lector, lectora, *n.* reader
leche, *f.* milk
lechería, *f.* dairy
lechero, *m.* milkman, dairyman; *adj.* pertaining to milk
lecho, *m.* bed; litter
lechuga, *f.* lettuce
lechuza, *f.* owl
leer, *va.* to read
legación, *f.* legation, embassy
legal, *adj.* legal, lawful
legalizar, *va.* to legalize
legar, *va.* to depute; to bequeath
legendario. *adj.* legendary
legible, *adj.* legible
legión, *f.* legion
legislación, *f.* legislation
legislativo, *adj.* legislative
legislatura, *f.* legislature
legítimo, *adj.* legitimate
legumbre, *f.* legume; vegetable
leído, *adj.* well-read
lejano, *adj.* distant
lejos, *adv.* far off
lengua, *f.* tongue; language
lenguaje, *m.* language

lente, *m.* or *f.* lens; monocle; **lentes,** *m. pl.* eye glasses; **lentes de contacto,** contact lenses
lenteja, *f.* (bot.) lentil
lentitud, *f.* slowness
lento, *adj.* slow, lazy
leña, *f.* kindling wood
león, *m.* lion
leona, *f.* lioness
leopardo, *m.* leopard
lerdo, *adj.* slow, heavy
lesbiano, *adj.* lesbian
lesion, *f.* wound; injury
letargo, *m.* drowsiness
letra, *f.* letter; handwriting; (com.) draft; words in a song; **al pie de la letra,** literally; **letras,** *pl.* learning, letters
letrado, *adj.* learned, lettered; *m.* lawyer, jurist
letrero, *m.* inscription, label; poster
levadura, *f.* yeast
levantar, *va.* to raise; to impute falsely; **levantarse,** to rise, to get up
leve, *adj.* light; trifling
ley, *f.* law
liberal, *adj.* liberal, generous
libertad, *f.* liberty, freedom
libertinaje, *m.* licentiousness
libra, *f.* pound (weight); **libra esterlina,** pound sterling
librar, *va.* to free, rid
libre, *adj.* free; exempt; *m.* (Mex.) taxicab
librería, *f.* bookstore
librero, *m.* bookseller; bookcase
libreta, *f.* memorandum book
libro, *m.* book
Lic. or **Licdo., licenciado,** (Sp. Am.) lawyer
licencia, *f.* permission, license
licenciado, *m.* licentiate, title given a lawyer
liceo, *m.* lyceum, high school
lícito, *adj.* lawful, licit
licor, *m.* liquor
líder, *m., f.* leader; (labor) instigator, agitator; chief
liebre, *f.* hare
ligar, *va., vr.* to tie, bind; to alloy; to confederate

ligereza, *f.* lightness; levity; swiftness

ligero, *adj.* light, swift

lija, *f.* sandpaper

lima, *f.* file; sweet lime (fruit)

limar, *va.* to file; to polish

limeño, limeña, *n.* native of Lima; *adj.* from Lima

limitación, *f.* limitation

limitar, *va.* to limit

límite, *m.* limit, boundary

limón, *m.* lemon

limonada, *f.* lemonade

limosna, *f.* alms, charity

limosnero, limosnera, *n.* beggar

limpiabotas, *m.* boot-black

limpiar, *va.* to clean

limpieza, *f.* cleanliness

limpio, *adj.* clean

linaza, *f.* linseed

lindo, *adj.* pretty

lino, *m.* flax; linen

linóleo, *m.* linoleum

linotipo, *m.* linotype

linterna, *f.* lantern; **linterna de proyección,** slide projector

lío, *m.* bundle; mess; **armar un lío,** to cause trouble

liquidación, *f.* liquidation, settlement; clearance sale

liquidar, *va.* to liquidate; to settle, clear accounts

líquido, *adj.* liquid, net; *m.* liquid

lira, *f.* lyre

lírico, *adj.* lyrical, lyric

lirio, *m.* iris (flower); lily

Lisboa, *f.* Lisbon

lisiado, *adj.* crippled

liso, *adj.* flat, smooth

lisonja, *f.* flattery

lista, *f.* list; stripe; **pasar lista,** to call the roll

listo, *adj.* ready; alert

literal, *adj.* literal

literario, *adj.* literary

literato, literata, *n.* literary person, writer; *adj.* learned

literatura, *f.* literature

litografía, *f.* lithography

litro, *m.* liter

liviano, *adj.* light; unchaste

lo, *pron.* (acc. case third pers. sing.) him, it; *art.* the (used before an adjective)

lobo, *m.* wolf

local, *adj.* local; *m.* place

localidad, *f.* locality; **localidades,** *pl.* accommodations, tickets, seats

localizar, *va.* to localize

loción, *f.* lotion, wash

loco, loca, *adj., n.* mad, crackbrained

locomotora, *f.* locomotive

locura, *f.* madness, folly; absurdity

locutor, locutora, *n.* (radio) announcer

lodo, *m.* mud, mire

logico, *adj.* logical

lograr, *va.* to gain, obtain

loma, *f.* hillock

lombriz, *f.* earthworm

lomo, *m.* loin

lona, *f.* canvas; sailcloth

Londres, *m.* London

longitud, *f.* length; longitude

loro, *m.* parrot

losa, *f.* flagstone; slab

lote, *m.* lot; share

lotería, *f.* lottery; lotto

loza, *f.* chinaware

Ltda., Sociedad Limitada, (Sp. Am.) Inc., Incorporated

lubricante, *adj., m.* lubricant

lubricar, lubrificar, *va.* to lubricate

luciérnaga, *f.* firefly

lucir, *vn., vr.* to shine, be brilliant; show off

lucrativo, *adj.* lucrative

lucha, *f.* struggle; wrestling

luchar, *vn.* to struggle; to wrestle

luego, *adv.* presently; soon afterwards; **desde luego,** of course; **hasta luego,** good-by

lugar, *m.* place; space; cause, motive

lujo, *m.* luxury; **de lujo,** de luxe

lujoso, *adj.* luxurious

lumbre, *f.* fire; light

lumbrera, *f.* luminary

luna, *f.* moon; glass plate for mirrors; **luna de miel,** honeymoon

lunar, m. mole; blemish

lunes, m. Monday

luneta, f. orchestra seat

lustre, m. luster; splendor

lustroso, adj. bright

luto, m. mourning

luz, f. light; **dar a luz,** to give birth

LL

llaga, f. wound, sore

llama, f. flame; (zool.) llama

llamada, f. call

llamar, va. to call; to invoke; **¿como se llama Ud.?** What is your name?

llamativo, adj. showy

llano, m. field, plain

llanta, f. tire

llanto, m. flood of tears

llanura, f. plain, field

llave, f. key; **llave inglesa,** monkey wrench

llavero, m. key ring

llegada, f. arrival

llegar, vn. to arrive; **llegar a ser,** to become

llenar, va. to fill

lleno, adj. full, replete

llevar, va. to carry, bear, take away; to wear (clothes)

llover, v. imp. to rain

lloviznar, v. imp. to drizzle

lluvia, f. rain

lluvioso, adj. rainy

M

m., masculino, m. masculine; **metro,** m. meter; **milla,** m. mile

maceta, f. flowerpot

macizo, adj. massive, solid

machacar, va. to pound, crush

macho, m. male animal; hook (of hook and eye); adj. masculine, male; vigorous

madrastra, f. stepmother

madre, f. mother

madreperla, f. mother of pearl

madreselva, f. honey-suckle

madrileño, madrileña, n., adj. inhabitant of Madrid; from Madrid

madrina, f. godmother

madrugada, f. dawn

madrugar, vn. to get up early; to anticipate, beforehand

madurar, va., vn. to ripen; to mature

madurez, f. maturity

maduro, adj. ripe; mature

maestra, f. woman teacher

maestría, f. mastership skill

maestro, m. master; expert; teacher; **maestro, maestra,** adj. masterly; **obra maestro,** masterpiece

magia, f. magic

mágico, adj. magical

magnánimo, adj. magnanimous

magnetismo, m. magnetism

magnetófono, m. tape recorder

magnífico, adj. magnificent

magnitud, f. magnitude

maguey, m. (bot.) maguey, century plant

mahometano, mahometana, n., adj. Mohammedan

maíz, m. corn, maize

majar, va. to pound; to mash

majestad, f. majesty

mal, m. evil, hurt, injury; illness; adj. (used only before masculine nouns) bad

malaria, f. malaria

malcriado, adj. ill-bred

maldad, f. wickedness

maldecir, va. to curse

maldición, f. curse

maldito, adj. wicked; damned, cursed

malestar, m. indisposition

maleta, f. suitcase, satchel

malgastar, va. to misspend

malicioso, adj. malicious

maligno, adj. malignant

malnutrido, adj. undernourished

malsano, adj. unhealthful

maltratar, va. to mistreat

mamá, f. mamma

mamar, va., vn. to suck

manada, f. flock, drove

manantial, m. source, spring

manar, vn. to spring from

manco, *adj.* one-handed

mandamiento, *m.* commandment

mandar, *va.* to command; to send; *va., vn.* to govern

mandíbula, *f.* jawbone

mando, *m.* authority, power

mandolina, *f.* mandolin

manecilla, *f.* hand of a clock

manejar, *va.* to manage, handle; to drive (a car, etc.); **manejarse,** to behave

manera, *f.* manner, mode

manga, *f.* sleeve

mango, *m.* handle, heft; mango (a fruit)

manguera, *f.* hose, hose pipe

maní, *m.* (Sp. Am.) peanut

manía, *f.* frenzy, madness

manicero, *m.* peanut vendor

manicomio, *m.* insane asylum

manifestar, *va.* to manifest, show

maniobra, *f.* maneuver

maniquí, *m.* mannikin

manjar, *m.* food; choic morsel

mano, *f.* hand; coat, layer

manómetro, *m.* pressure guage

manosear, *va.* to handle; to muss

mansión, *f.* mansion

manta, *f.* blanket

manteca, *f.* lard

mantel, *m.* tablecloth

mantener, *va., vr.* to maintain, support

mantequilla, *f.* butter

mantilla, *f.* mantilla, headshawl

manual, *adj.* manual, handy; manual

manubrio, *m.* handle bar

manufacturar, *va.* to manufacture

manuscrito, *m.* manuscript; **manuscrito, manuscrita,** *adj.* written by hand

manutención, *f.* maintenance

manzana, *f.* apple; block of houses

manzano, *m.* apple tree

maña, *f.* dexterity; skill, trick; evil habit

mañana, *f.* morning, **pasado**

mañana, day after tomorrow

maoísmo, *m.* Maoism

mapa, *m.* map

maquillaje, *m.* make-up

máquina, *f.* machine, engine; **máquina de escribir,** typewriter

maquinalmente, *adv.* mechanically

maquinaria, *f.* machinery

maquinista, *m.* machinist

mar, *m.* or *f.* sea

maravilla, wonder; **a las mil maravillas,** uncommonly well; exquisitely

maravillarse, *vr.* to wonder, be astonished

maravilloso, *adj.* marvelous

marcar, *va.* to mark

marco, *m.* frame

marcha, *f.* march; **ponerse en marcha,** to proceed, to start off

marchar, *vn.* to march; **marcharse,** to go away, leave

marchitar, *va., vn.* to wither

marchito, *adj.* faded, withered

marea, *f.* tide

marear, *va.* to molest, annoy. **marearse,** to become seasick

mareo, *m.* seasickness

marfil, *m.* ivory

margarita, *f.* daisy

margen, *m.* or *f.* margin; border

mariano, mariana, *adj.* marian, pertaining to the Virgin Mary

marido, *m.* husband

marimba, *f.* marimba

marina, *f.* navy; shipping

marinero, *m.* sailor

marino, *adj.* marine; *m.* seaman, sailor

mariposa, *f.* butterfly; **braza mariposa,** butterfly stroke

mariscal, *m.* marshal

marisco, *m.* shellfish

mármol, *m.* marble

marqués, *m.* marquis

marquesa, *f.* marchioness

marrano, *m.* pig, hog

marta, *f.* marten, marten fur

martes, *m.* Tuesday

martillo. *m.* hammer

marzo, *m.* March
mas, *conj.* but, yet
más, *adv.* more
masa, *f.* dough, paste; mass:
masaje, *m.* massage
máscara, *m.* or *f.* masquerader; *f.* mask
mascota, *f.* mascot
masculino, *adj.* masculine, male
masonería, *f.* freemasonry
masticar, *va.* to chew
mata, *f.* plant, shrub
matadero, *m.* slaughterhouse
matanza, *f.* slaughtering; cattle to be slaughtered; massacre
matar, *va., vr.* to kill
matemática, or **matemáticas,** *f.* mathematics
matemático, *adj.* mathematical; *m.* mathematician
materia, matter, material; subject; matter (pus)
material, *adj.* material; *m.* ingredient; cloth; material
maternal, *adj.* maternal
maternidad, *f.* motherhood
materno, *adj.* maternal, motherly
matiné, *f.* matinée
matiz, *m.* shade of color; shading
matorral, *m.* shrub, thicket
matrícula, *f.* register; license number; roster; entrance fee in a school
matricular, *va., vr.* to matriculate, register
matrimonio, *m.* marriage, matrimony
matriz, *f.* uterus, womb; mold, die; *adj.* main, parent; **casa matriz,** head or main office
matrona, *f.* matron
máxima, *f.* maxim, rule
máxime, *adv.* principally
máximo, *adj.* maximum
mayo, *m.* May
mayonesa, *f., adj.* mayonnaise
mayor, *adj.* greater, larger; elder; **estado mayor,** military staff; *m.* superior; major; **al por mayor,** wholesale
mayordomo, *m.* steward, mayordomo
mayoría, *f.* majority
mayúscula, *f.* capital letter
m/cta., mi cuenta, (com.) my account
m/cte., m/co., moneda corriente, cur., currency
me, *pron.* me (dative case)
mear, *vn.* to urinate
mecánicamente, *adv.* mechanically; automatically
mecánica, *f.* mechanics
mecánico, *adj.* mechanical; *m.* mechanic
mecanismo, *m.* mechanism
mecanografía, *f.* typewriting
mecanógrafo, mecanógrafa, *n.* typist
mecedora, *f.* rocking chair
mecer, *va.* to rock
medalla, *f.* medal
mediados, a mediados de, *adv.* about the middle of
mediano, *adj.* moderate; medium
medianoche, *f.* midnight
mediante, *adv.* by means of, through; **Dios mediante,** God willing
mediar, *vn.* to mediate
medicina, *f.* medicine
médico, *m.* physician; **médica,** *adj.* medical
medida, *f.* measure
medidor, *m.* meter; gauge
medio, *adj.* half, halfway; medium, average; **a medias,** by halves; *m.* way, method; medium; middle; **medios,** *m. pl.* means
mediodía, *m.* noon, midday
medir, *va.* to measure; **medirse,** to be moderate
meditación, *f.* meditation
meditar, *va., vn.* to meditate
Mediterráneo, *m.* Mediterranean
megatón, *m.* megaton
mejicano, mejicana, or **mexicano, mexicana,** *n., adj.* Mexican
mejilla, *f.* cheek
mejor, *adj., adv.* better, best; **a lo mejor,** when least expected

mejora, *f.* improvement

mejorar, *va.* to improve; *vn.,* *vr.* to improve (as to health)

mejoría, *f.* improvement

melancólico, *adj.* melancholy, sad

melocotón, *m.* peach

melodía, *f.* melody

melodioso, *adj.* melodious

melodrama, *m.* melodrama

melón, *m.* melon

mella, *f.* gap; **hacer mella,** to affect

mellizo, melliza, *n., adj.* twin

membrete, *m.* letterhead

membrillo, *m.* quince

memorable, *adj.* rnemorable

memorándum, *m.* memorandum

memoria, *f.* memory; memoir; report (of a conference, etc.)

memorial, *m.* memorial, brief

mencionar, *va.* to mention

mendigo, *m.* beggar

menear, *va.* to stir; **menearse,** (coll.) to wriggle, waddle

menester, *m.* necessity; **ser menester,** to be necessary

menor, *m., f.* minor (one under age); *adj.* less, smaller, minor

menos, *adv.* less; with exception of; **a lo menos,** or **por lo menos,** at least, however; **venir a menos-,** to grow poor; **a menos que,** unless; **echar de menos** to miss

mensaje, *m.* message, errand

mensajero, mensajera, *n.* messenger

menstruación, *f.* menstruation

mensual, *adj.* monthly

mensualidad, *f.* month's allowance; monthly installment

menta, *f.* (bot.) mint

mental, *adj.* mental

mentalidad, *f.* mentality

mentar, *va.* to mention

mente, *f.* mind

mentira, *f.* lie, falsehood; **parecer mentira,** to seem impossible

mentiroso, *adj.* lying, deceit-ful; **mentiroso, mentirosa,** *n.* liar

menú, *m.* bill of fare

menudeo, *m.* retail

menudo, *adj.* small; minute; **a menudo,** repeatedly, often; *m.* small change (money); tripe, entrails

meñique, *m.* little finger

mercado, *m.* market

mercancía, *f.* merchandise

merced, *f.* favor, mercy; will, pleasure

mercenario, *adj.* mercenary

mercurio, *m.* mercury, quicksilver

merendar, *vn.* to lunch

merengue, *m.* meringue

meridiano, *m.* meridian; **pasado meridiano,** afternoon

meridional, *adj.* southern

merienda, *f.* luncheon, light repast

mérito, *m.* merit, desert

merma, *f.* decrease; waste, leakage; shortage

mes, *m.* month

mesa, *f.* table

mesada, *f.* monthly allowance

meseta, *f.* landing (of a staircase); tableland, plateau

Mesías, *m.* Messiah

mestizo, mestiza, *adj., n.* of mixed blood

meta, *f.* goal

metáfora, *f.* metaphor

metal, *m.* metal; voice timbre

metálico, *adj.* metallic, metal

metate, *m.* (Mex.) grinding stone

meter, *va.* to place, put; to introduce, to insert; **meterse,** to meddle, interfere

meticuloso, *adj.* conscientious

metiche, *m., f.* (coll.) prier, meddler

método, *m.* method

métrico, *adj.* metrical

metro, *m.* meter; verse; (Spain, coll.) subway

metrópoli, *f.* metropolis

Mex. or **Mej., Méjico,** Mex., Mexico

m/f., mi favor, my favor

mg., miligramo, mg., milligram

m/g, mi giro, (com.) my draft

mi, *pron.* my; *m.* (mus.) mi

mi, *pron.* me (objective case of the pronoun yo)

microbio, *m.* microbe

micrófono, *m.* microphone

microscopio, *m.* microscope; **microscopio electrónico,** electron microscope

miedo, *m.* fear, dread; **tener miedo,** to be afraid

miel, *f.* honey; **luna de miel,** honeymoon

miembro, *m.* member; limb

mientras, *adv.* in the meantime; while; **mientras tanto,** meanwhile

miércoles, *m.* Wednesday

mierda, *f.* excrement, ordure

miga, *f.* crumb

migaja, *f.* scrap, crumb

mil, *m.* one thousand

milagro, *m.* miracle, wonder

milagroso, *adj.* miraculous

milésimo, *adj.* thousandth

milicia, *f.* militia

miligramo, *m.* milligram

milimetro, *m.* millimeter

militar, *adj.* military

milreis *m.* milreis (Portuguese and Brazilian coin)

milla, *f.* mile

millar, *m.* thousand

millón, *m.* million

millonario, millonaria, *n.* millionaire

mimar, *va.* to flatter, spoil; to fondle, caress

mimbre, *m.* wicker

mimeógrafo, *m.* mimeograph

mina, *f.* mine

mineral, *adj.* mineral

minero, *m.* miner

miniatura, *f.* miniature

mínimo, *adj.* least, smallest

ministerio, *m.* ministry (office), cabinet

ministro, *m.* minister; **Ministro de Estado,** Secretary of State

minoría, minoridad, minority

minucioso, *adj.* meticulous

minúscula, *adj.* small (applied to letters)

minutero, *m.* minute hand

minuto, *m.* minute

mío, mía, *pron.* mine

miope, *n., adj.* nearsighted; near-sighted person

miopía, *f.* nearsightedness

mirada, *f.* glance; gaze

mirar, *va.* to behold, look; to observe; **mirarse,** to look at oneself; to look at one another

mirlo, *m.* blackbird

misa, *f.* mass

misceláneo, *adj.* miscellaneous

miserable, *adj.* miserable, wretched; avaricious

miseria, misery; trifle

misericordia, *f.* mercy

misión, *f.* mission

misionero, *m.* missionary

misterio, *m.* mystery

misterioso, *adj.* mysterious

mitad, *f.* half; middle

mitigar, *va.* to mitigate

mitología, *f.* mythology

mixto, *adj.* mixed, mingled

m/l or m/L, mi letra, my letter, my draft

ml., mililitro, ml., milliliter

mm, milimetro, mm., millimeter

m/n, moneda nacional, national currency

moco, *m.* mucus

mocoso, *adj.* sniveling, mucous; **mocoso, mocosa,** *n.* brat

mochila, *f.* knapsack

moda, *f.* fashion, mode

modales, *m. pl.* manners, breeding

moderación, *f.* moderation

moderado, *adj.* moderate

modernista, *adj.* modernistic

modernizar, *va.* to modernize

moderno, *adj.* modern

modestia, *f.* modesty; humility

modesto, *adj.* modest; unassuming

módico, *adj.* moderate, reasonable (as price)

modo, *m.* mode, manner;

mood; **de ningún modo,** by no means

mofa, f. mockery

mohoso, adj. musty; rusty

mojado, adj. wet

molar, va., vr. to wet, moisten

molde, m. mold; pattern (for a dress, etc.); matrix, cast

moldura, f. molding

mole, m. (Mex.) spicy sauce for fowl and meat

moler, va. to grind

molestar, va. to vex, tease; to trouble

molestia, f. trouble; inconvenience

molino, m. mill; **molino de viento,** windmill

momento, m. moment, while

mona, f. female monkey

monada, f. (coll.) pretty child or thing

monarca, m. monarch

monarquía, f. monarchy

mondongo, m. tripe

moneda, f. money, currency

monja, f. nun

monje, m. monk

monograma, m. monogram

monológo, m. monologue

monopolio, m. monopoly

monosílabo, m. monosyllable

monstruo, m. monster

montaña, f. mountain

montar, vn. to mount (on horseback); to amount to; va. to set (as diamonds)

monto, m. amount, sum

montón, m.heap, pile; **a montones,** abundantly, by heaps

monumento, m. monument

mora, f. blackberry, mulberry

morada, f. abode, residence

morado, adj. violet, purple

moral, f. morals, ethics; adj. moral

moralidad, f. morality, morals

moratorio, f. moratorium

mórbido, adj. morbid

mordaz, adj. sarcastic

morder, va. to bite

moreno, adj. brown, swarthy; brunet

moribundo, adj. dying

morir, vn., vr. to die, expire

moroso, adj. slow, tardy

mortal, adj. mortal; deadly

mosaic, m. tile

mosca, f. fly

mosquitero, m. mosquito net

mosquito, m. mosquito

mostaza, f. mustard

mostrador, m. counter

mostrar, va. to show, exhibit; **mostrarse,** to appear, show oneself

mota, f. powder puff

motín, m. mutiny, riot

motocicleta, f. motorcycle

motor, m. motor, engine

motriz, adj. motor, moving

mover, va. to move; to stir up

móvil, m. motive, incentive

movilizar, va. to mobilize

moza, f. girl, lass; maidservant

mozo, m. youth, lad; waiter

muchacha, f. girl, lass

mucliacho, m. boy, lad

muchedumbre, f. crowd

mucho, adj., adv. much, abundant

mudar, va. to change; to molt; **mudarse,** to change residence

mudo, adj. dumb; silent, mute

mueble, m. piece of furniture; **muebles,** pl. furniture

mueca, grimace

muela, molar tooth

muerte, f. death

muerto, m. corpse; adj. dead

mugre, f. dirt

mujer, f. woman; wife

mula, f. she-mule

mulato, mulata, n., adj. mulatto

muleta, f. crutch

multa, f. fine, penalty

multar, va. to fine

multiplicar, va. to multiply

mundial, adj. world-wide

mundo, m. world

municipal, adj. municipal

muñeca, f. wrist; doll

muralla, f. rampart, wall

murciélago, m. (zool.) bat

murmullo, m. murmur, mutter

murmurar, vn. to murmur; to gossip

muro, m. wall
muscular, adj. muscular
músculo, m. muscle
museo, m. museum
musgo, m. moss:
música, f. music
musical, adj. musical
músico, m. musician
mutación, f. mutation
mutuo, adj. mutual, reciprocal
muy, adv. very; greatly
Mzo. or **mzo., marzo,** Mar., March

N

N., norte, N., No. or no., north
n/, nuestro, our
nabo, m. turnip
Nac., nacional, nat., national
nácar, m. mother of pearl
nacer, vn. to be born
nacido, adj. born; m. tumor, abscess
nacimiento, m. birth; Nativity
nación, f. nation
nacional, adj. national
nacionalidad, f. nationality
nada, f. nothing; **de nada,** don't mention it
nadar, vn. to swim
nadie, pron. nobody, no one
nafta, f. naphtha; (Arg. Urug.) gasoline
naipe, m. playing card
nalga, f. buttock, rump
Nápoles, m. Naples
naranja, f. orange
naranjada, f. orangeade
naranjado, adj. orange-colored
naranjo, m. orange tree
narciso, m. daffodil
narcótico, adj., m. narcotic
nariz, f. nose
narrar, va. to narrate, tell
nasal, adj. nasal
nata, f. film formed on surface of milk when boiled; **la tor y nata,** the cream, the elite
natal, adj. natal, native
natalidad, f. birth rate
natalicio, m. birthday
natilla, f. pl. custard

natividad, f. nativity
nativo, adj. native
natural, adj. natural, native; unaffected
naturaleza, f. nature
naturalmente, adv. naturally
náusea, f. nausea
navaja, f. razor
naval, adj. naval
navegable, adj. navjgable
navegación, f. navigation, shipping
navegar, vn. to navigate
navidad, f. nativity; **Navidad,** Christmas
N.B., Nota Bene, (Latin) N.B., take notice
n/c., or **n/cta. nuestra cuenta,** (com.) our account
NE, nordeste, NE or N.E., northeast
neblina, f. fog; drizzle
nebuloso, adj. foggy, hazy
necedad, f. nonsense
necesario, adj. necessary
necesitar, va., vn. to need
necio, adj. ignorant, silly
néctar, m. nectar
negar, va., vr. to deny, refuse
negativo, adj. negative
negligencia, f. negligence
negociante, m., f. dealer, merchant
negocio, m. business; affair; negotiation; **hombre de negocios,** businessman
negro, adj. black; n. Negro
nene, nena, n. baby
neoyorquino, neoyorquina, n., adj. New Yorker
nervio, m. nerve
neto, adj. net
neumático, m. tire
neumonía, f. pneumonia
neutral, adj. neutral
neutralidad, f. neutrality
neutrino, m. neutrino
neutro, adj. neutral, neuter
nevada, f. snowfall
nevar, vn. imp. to snow
nevera, f. icebox
n/f., nuestro favor, our favor
n/g., nuestro giro, (com.) our draft
niacina, f. niacin

nido, _m._ nest
niebla, _f._ fog, mist
nieta, _f._ granddaughter
nieto, _m._ grandson
nieve, _f._ snow
ninfa, _f._ nymph
ningún, _adj._ (contraction of **ninguno**), no, not any (used only before masculine nouns); **de ningún modo,** in no way, by no means
ninguno, _adj._ none, neither; **en ninguna parte,** no place, nowhere
niña, _f._ little girl; **niña del ojo,** pupil of the eye; **niña de los ojos,** (coll.) apple of one's eye
niñez, _f._ childbood
niño, _adj._ childish; _m._ child, infant
níquel, _m._ nickel
nítido, _adj._ neat; clear
nitrato, _m._ (chem.) nitrate
nitrógeno, _m._ nitrogen
nivel, _m._ level, plane
nivelar, _va._ to level
n/l. or **n/L., nuestra letra,** (com.) our letter, our draft
NNE, nornordeste, NNE or N.N.E., north-northeast
NNO, nornoroeste, NNW or N.N.W., north-north-west
NO, noroeste, NW or N.W., northwest
No. or **N.º, número,** no., number
n/o., nuestra orden, (com.) our order
no, _adv._ no; not
noble, _adj._ noble; illustrious
nobleza, _f._ nobleness, nobility
noción, _f._ notion, idea
nocivo, _adj._ injurious
nocturno, _adj._ nightly; _m._ (mus.) nocturne
noche, _f._ night; **esta noche,** tonight; this evening; **Noche Buena,** Christmas Eve
nombramiento, _m._ nomination; appointment
nombrar, _va._ to name; to nominate; to appoint
nombre, _m._ name; reputation
nominativo, _m._ (gram.) nominative

non, _adj._ odd, uneven
nono, _adj._ ninth
non plus ultra, unexcelled, unsurpassed
nordeste, _m._ northeast
norma, _f._ standard, model, rule
nornoroeste, _m._ northnorth-west
noroeste, _m._ northwest
norte, _m._ north; guide
Norteamérica, _f._ North America
norteamericano, norteamericana, _n., adj._ North America, a native of U. S. A
Noruega, _f._ Norway
noruego, noruega, _n., adj._ Norwegian
nos, _pron._ dative of we
nosotros, nosotras, _pron._ we, ourselves
nostalgia, _f._ homesickess, nostalgia
nota, _f._ note, notice, remark; bill; **nota bene,** N. B. take notice
notable, _adj._ remarkable
notar, _va._ to note, observe, mark
notario, _m._ notary
noticia, _f._ notice; knowledge, information, news; **en espera de sus noticias,** (com.) awaiting your reply
noticiario, _m._ latest news, news report
notificar, _va._ to notify
notorio, _adj._ notorious:
Novbre., nov.ᶜ, noviembre, Nov., November
novecientos, novecientas, _adj., m._ nine hundred
novela, _f._ novel
novelista, _m., f._ novelist
novena, _f._ Novena
noveno, _adj._ ninth
noventa, _m., adj._ ninety
novia, _f._ bride; fiancée
noviembre, _m._ November
novillo, _m._ young bull
novio, _m._ bridegroom; fiancé, sweetheart (male); **viaje de novios,** honeymoon trip
n/r, nuestra remesa, (com.)

our remittance or our shipment

N.S., Nuestro Señor, Our Lord

N.S.J.C., Nuestro Señor Jesucristo, Our Lord Jesus Christ

nuclear, *adj.* nuclear

núcleo, *m.* nucleus, core

nudo, *m.* knot, gnarl

nuera, *f.* daughter-in-law

nuestro, nuestra, *adj., pron.* our, ours

nueva, *f.* news

nueve, *m., adj.* nine

nuez, *f.* walnut; **nuez moscada,** nutmeg

nulidad, *f.* nonentity

nulo, *adj.* null, void

núm., número, no., number

numerar, *va.* to number, numerate

número, *m.* number; cipher

numeroso, *adj.* numerous

nunca, *adv.* never

nupcial, *adj.* nuptial

nupcias, *f., pl.* nuptials, wedding

nutrición, *f.* nutrition, feeding

nutrir, *va.* to nourish

nutritivo, *adj.* nourishing

nylon, *m.* nylon

Ñ

ñame, *m.* (bot.) yam

ñato, ñata, (Sp. Am.) *n., adj.* pug-nosed

O

o, (**ó** when between numbers) *conj.* or

O., oeste, W., West

obedecer, *va.* to obey

obediencia, *f.* obedience

obediente, *adj.* obedient

obertura, *f.* (mus.) overture

obispo, *m.* bishop

objeción, *f.* objection

objetar, *va.* to object, oppose

objetivo, *adj.* objective; *m.* objective, purpose

objeto, *m.* object, thing; purpose

oblicuo, *adj.* oblique

obligación, *f.* obligation

obligado, adj. obliged to; obligated

oblongo, *adj.* oblong

obra, *f.* work, deed

obrar, *va.* to work; to operate, act; *vn.* to act; to ease nature

obrero obrera, *n.* day laborer

obsceno, *adj.* obscene

obsequiar, *va.* to regale; to fete; to make a present of

obsequio, *m.* gift

observación, *f.* observation; remark

observador, observadora, *n.* observer; *adj.* observing

observar, *va.* to observe, watch

obstáculo, *m.* obstacle; **obstáculo sónico,** sonic barrier

obstante, participle of **obstar; no obstante,** notwithstanding, nevertheless

obstar, *va.* to hinder

obstetricia, *f.* obstetrics

obstruir, *va., vr.* to obstruct

ocasión, *f.* occasion, chance; **de ocasión,** used, secondhand

ocasionar, *va.* to cause, occasion

occidental, *adj.* western

occidente, *m.* occident, west

océano, *m.* ocean

ocio, *m.* leisure; idleness

ocioso, *adj.* idle

octava, *f.* octave

octavo, *adj.* eighth

Octbre, oct.ᶜ, octubre, Oct., October

octubre, *m.* October

oculto, *adj.* hidden, concealed

ocupación, *f.* occupation

ocupado, *adj.* busy; occupied

ocupar, *va., vr.* to occupy, be occupied

ocurrencia, *f.* occurrence, event, incident; witty remark

ochenta, *adj., m.* eighty

ocho, *m., adj.* eight

odiar, *va.* to hate; **odiarse,** to hate one another

oeste, *m.* west; west wind

ofender, *va.* to offend; **ofen-**

derse, to take offense
ofensa, *f.* offensive, injury
oferta, *f.* offer; offering; **oferta y demanda,** supply and demand
oficial, *adj.* official; *m.* officer; official
oficiar, *va.* to officiate
oficina, *f.* office, bureau
oficio, *m.* employ, occupation; business; **oficios,** *pl.* divine service
ofrecer, *va.* to offer; **ofrecerse,** to offer one's services; to present itself
ofrecimiento, *m.* offering, promise
oído, *m.* hearing; ear
oír, *va.* to hear; to listen
ojal, *m.* buttonhole
¡ojalá! *interj.* God grant!
ojeada, *f.* glance, look
ojear, *va.* to eye, view; to glance
ojera, *f.* dark circle under the eye
ojo, *m.* eye; sight; eye of a needle
ola, *f.* wave, billow
oler, *va.* to smell, to scent; *vn.* to smell, to smack of
olivo, *m.* olive tree
olor, *m.* odor, scent
oloroso, *adj.* fragrant, odorous
olvidadizo, *adj.* forgetful
olvidar, *va., vr.* to forget
olla, *f.* kettle
ombligo, *m.* navel
omisión, *f.* omission
omitir, *va.* to omit
ómnibus, *m.* omnibus, bus
omnipotente, *adj.* omnipotent
once, *m., adj.* eleven
onceno, *adj.* eleventh
onda, *f.* wave
ondear, *va., vn.* to undu.late, wave
ondulado, *adj.* wavy
O.N.U., Organización de las Naciones Unidas, U.N., United Nations
onz., onza, oz., ounce
onza, *f.* ounce (weight)
opaco, *adj.* opaque, dark
ópalo, *m.* opal

opción, *f.* option, choice
ópera, *f.* opera
operación, *f.* operation; **operación cesarea,** Caesarean operation
operar, *va., vn.* to operate; **operarse,** (med.) to have an operation
opereta, *f.* operetta
opinar, *va., vn.* to give an opinion
opinión, *f.* opinion
opio, *m.* opium
oporto, *m.* port wine
oportunidad, *f.* opportunity
oportuno, *adj.* opportune
oposición, *f.* opposition
optar, *va.* to choose, elect
óptico, *adj.* optic, optical
optimismo, *m.* optimism
optimista, *m., f.* optimist; *adj.* optimistic
opuesto, *adj.* opposite, contrary
opulencia, *f.* wealth, riches
ora, *conj.* whether, either
oración, *f.* oration, speech; prayer; (gram.) sentence
orador, oradora, *n.* orator, speaker
oral, *adj.* oral
orar, *vn.* to pray
oratoria, *f.* oratory
orbe, *m.* earth, globe
orden, *m.* order, arrangement; *f.* order, command; **a sus órdenes,** at your service
ordenar, *va.* to arrange; to order, command
ordeñar, *va.* to milk
ordinario, *adj.* ordinary, usual, common; coarse
oreja, *f.* ear
orejón, *m.* preserved peach
organdí, *m.* organdy
orgánico, *adj.* organic
organismo, *m.* organism
organización, *f.* organization
organizar, *va.* to organize
órgano, *m.* organ
orgullo, *m.* pride, haughtiness
orgulloso, *adj.* proud, haughty
orientación, *f.* orientation; position
oriental, *adj.* oriental, eastern

orientar, *va.* to orient; **orientarse,** to find one's bearings

oriente, *m.* orient, east

original, *adj.* original, primitive; novel, new; *m.* original, first copy

originalidad, *f.* originality

orina, *f.* urine

orines, *m., pl.* urine

orinar, *vn.* to urinate

ornamento, *m.* ornament

ornar, *va.* to trim, adorn

oro, *m.* gold; money

orquesta, *f.* orchestra

orquídea, *f.* orchid

ortografía, *f.* orthography, spelling

ortopédico, *adj.* orthopedic

oruga, *f.* (bot.) rocket; caterpillar

os, *pron.* dative of you, to you

osa, *f.* she-bear; **Osa Mayor,** (ast.) Great Bear, the Dipper

oscurecer, *va., vn., vr.* to darken; to become dark

oscurecimiento, *m.* blackout; darkening

oscuridad, *f.* darkness; obscurity

oscuro, *adj.* obscure, dark; **a oscuras,** in the dark

oso, *m.* bear

ostentar, *va.* to show, display; *vn.* to boast

ostra, *f.* oyster

otoño, *m.* autumn, fall

otro, otra, adj. another, other; **otra vez,** another time, once again

ovación, *f.* ovation

ovalado, *adj.* oval-shaped

ovario, *m.* ovary

oveja, *f.* sheep

oxidar, *va., vr.* to rust

óxido, *m.* (chem.) oxide

oxígeno, *m.* oxygen; **oxígeno líquido,** liquid oxygen

oyente, *m., f.* listener; **oyentes,** audience

P

pabellón, *m.* pavilion; flag

paciencia, *f.* patience

paciente, *adj., m., f.* patient

pacífico, *adj.* pacific, peaceful

pacto, *m.* contract, pact

padecer, *va.* to suffer

padrastro, *m.* stepfather; hangnail

padre, *m.* father; **padres,** *pl.* parents; ancestors

padrenuestro, *m.* the Our Father, the Lord's Prayer

padrino, *m.* godfather; sponsor, protector

paella, *f.* rice, seafood and chicken dish

pagadero, *adj.* payable

pagano, *m.* heathen, pagan

pagaré, *m.* promissory note; I. O. U

página, *f.* page of a book

pago, *m.* pay, payment; (Arg., Urug.) rural home place

paila, *f.* kettle

país, *m.* country, region

paisaje, *m.* landscape

paisano, paisana, *n.* countryman (or woman)

pájaro, *m.* bird

paje, *m.* page

palabra, *f.* word; **de palabra,** by word of mouth; **tener la palabra,** to have the floor

palacio, *m.* palace

paladar, *m.* palate; taste

palco, *m.* box in a theater

pálido, *adj.* pallid, pale

palillo, *m.* toothpick

paliza, *f.* whipping

palma, *f.* palm of the hand

palmera, *f.* palm tree

palmotear, *vn.* to clap hands, applaud

palo, *m.* stick; cudgel; post; blow with a stick

paloma, *f.* dove, pigeon

palomilla, *f.* (Mex.) boys' gang; one's social crowd

palomita, *f.* squab; **palomitas de maíz,** popcorn

palomo, *m.* cock pigeon

palpar, *va.* to feel, touch; to grope

palpitante, *adj.* palpitating; **cuestión palpitante,** important, live issue

palpitar, *vn.* to palpitate, beat, throb

paludismo, *m.* malaria
pampa, *f.* great plain, prairie
pámpano, *m.* pompano (a fish)
pan, *m.* bread
panadería, *f.* bakery
panadero, panadera, *n.* baker
páncreas, *m.* pancreas
pandereta, *f.* tambourine
pandilla, *f.* gang
pando, *adj.* bulging, convex
pánico, *m.* panic, fright
panorama, *m.* panorama
pantalones, *m. pl.* trousers
pantalla, *f.* screen, fire screen; lamp shade
panteón, *m.* cemetery
pantera, *f.* panther
pantorrilla, *f.* calf (of the leg)
pantufla, *f.* slipper, shoe
panza, *f.* belly, paunch
pañal, *m.* diaper
paño, *m.* cloth
pañoleta, *f.* bandanna
pañuelo, *m.* handkerchief
papa, *m.* Pope; *f.* potato; soft food for babies; (coll.) fib, exaggeration
papá, *m.* papa, father
papada, *f.* double chin
papagayo, *m.* parrot
papaya, *f.* papaya
papel, *m.* paper; role, part
papelería, *f.* stationery; stationery store
papeleta, *f.* ballot
paquete, *m.* package, bundle
par, *adj.* par, equal; sin **par,** matchless; *m.* pair; par
para, *prep.* for, to, in order to
parabién, *m.* congratulation, felicitation
parabrisa, *m.* windshield
paracaídas, *m.* parachute
parada, *f.* halt; stop, pause; (mil.) parade
paradero, *m.* whereabouts
parado, *adj.* stopped (as a clock); (Sp. Am.) standing up
paradoja, *f.* paradox
paraguas, *m.* umbrella
paraíso, *m.* paradise
paralelo, *adj., m.* parallel
parálisis, *f.* paralysis
paralizar, *va.* to paralyze; stop, impede; **paralizarse,** to become paralyzed
pararrayo, *m.* lightning rod
parásito, *m.* parasite
parasol, *m.* parasol
parche, *m.* patch; plaster
pardo, *adj.* brown
parecer, *m.* opinion, advice; **al parecer,** apparently; *vn.* to appear, seem; **parecerse,** to resemble
parecido, *m.* resemblance
pared, *f.* wall
pareja, *f.* pair; couple
parentela, *f.* relatives
parentesco, *m.* kingship
pares o nones, *m. pl.* even or odd
pariente, parienta, *n.* kinsman, kinswoman
parir, *va., vn.* to give birth
parisiense, *m., f., adj.* Parisian
parodia, *f.* parody
parpadear, *vn.* to blink
párpado, *m.* eyelid
parque, *m.* park
parra, *f.* grapevine
párrafo, *m.* paragraph
parranda, *f.* spree, revel
parrandear, *vn.* to go on a spree
parrilla, *f.* gridiron, broiler
párroco, *m.* parson
parroquia, *f.* parish
parte, *f.* part; side
partera, *f.* midwife
partición, *f.* partition, division
participación, *f.* participation, share
participar, *va., vn.* to participate, partake; to communicate
participio, *m.* participle
particular, *adj.* particular, special; *m.* civilian; topic
partida, *f.* departure; item, entry; game
partidario, partidaria, *n.* advocate
partido, *m.* party; match; **sacarle partido a,** to take advantage of
partir, *va.* to part, divide; *vn.* to depart; **a partir de,** beginning with
parto, *m.* childbirth

párvulo, *m.* child; **escuela de párvulos,** kindergarten

pasa, *f.* raisin; **ciruela pasa,** prune

pasadero, *adj.* supportable, passable

pasaje, *m.* passage; fare

pasajero, *adj.* transient, transitory; *m.* traveler, passenger

pasaporte, *m.* passport

pasar, *va.* to pass; to suffer; *vn.* to spend (time); *v. imp.* to happen; **pasar por alto,** to overlook; **¿qué pasa?** what is the matter?

pasatiempo, *m.* pastime

Pascua, *f.* Christmas; Easter

pase, *m.* permit

pasear, *va., vn.* to stroll; to ride; **pasearse,** to go out for amusement

paseo, *m.* walk, stroll, ride

pasión, *f.* passion

pasivo, *adj.* passive, inactive; *m.* liabilities of a business house

pasmar, *va.* to benumb; to chill; **pasmarse,** to be astonished

paso, *m.* pace, step; passage

pasta, *f.* paste; dough; binding for books

pastar, *vn.* to pasture

pastel, *m.* pie, cake; cray

pastelero, pastelera, *n.* pastry cook

pasterizar, *va.* to pasteurize

pastilla, *f.* tablet, lozenge

pasto, *m.* pasture

pastor, *m.* shepherd; pastor, minister

pata, *f.* foot and leg of an animal; female duck; **patas arriba,** topsy-turvy

patada, *f.* kick

patán, *m.* yokel, churl

patata, *f.* potato

patear, *va., vn.* to kick, stamp the feet

patente, *adj.* patent, manifest, evident; *f.* patent

paternal, *adj.* paternal

paterno, *adj.* paternal

patético, *adj.* pathetic

patín, *m.* ice skate; **patín de ruedas,** roller skate

patinar, *vn.* to skate; to skid; to spin

patineta, *f.* scooter

patio, *m.* yard, courtyard

pato, pata, *n.* duck

patria, *f.* native country

patriarca. *m.* patriarch

patriota, *m., f.* patriot

patriotismo, *m.* patriotism

patrocinar, *va.* to favor, sponsor

patrón, *m.* patron; employer; pattern

patrulla, *f.* patrol, squad

pausa, *f.* pause

pausar, *vn.* to pause

pauta, *f.* ruler; standard, model; (mus.) ruled staff

pavimentar, *va.* to pave

pavo, *m.* turkey; **pavo real,** peacock

pavor, *m.* fear, terror

payaso, *m.* clown

paz, *f.* peace

p/cta., por cuenta, (com.) on account, for account

P.D., posdata, P. S., postscript

pdo. or p.^{do}, pasado, pt., past

peatón, *m.* pedestrian

peca, *f.* freckle, spot

pecado, *m.* sin

pecador, pecadora, *n.* sinner

pecar, *vn.* to sin

peculiar, *adj.* peculiar

pecuniario, *adj.* financial

pecho, *m.* breast; chest; teat; bosom

pechuga, *f.* breast of a fowl

pedagogía, *f.* pedagogy

pedal, *m.* pedal

pedante, *adj.* pedantic

pedazo, *m.* piece, bit

pedestal, *m.* pedestal

pedido, *m.* request, order

pedigüeño, *adj.* beggary

pedir, *va.* to ask, to beg; to demand;

pedir prestado, to borrow

pedrada, *f.* throw of a stone, blow

pegajoso, *adj.* sticky; contagious

pegar, *va.* to cement, stick, paste; to join, unite; to spank; *vn.* to take root; **pegarse,** to adhere

peinado, *m.* hairdressing, coiffure

peinadora, *f.* hairdresser

peinar, *va., vr.* to comb (the hair)

peine, *m.* comb

pelado, pelada, *n.* (Mex.) person of the lower classes; ignorant peasant; *adj.* coarse, vulgar

pelea, *f.* fight, quarrel

pelear, *vn., vr.* to fight

película, *f.* film

peligro, *m.* danger, peril

peligroso, *adj.* dangerous

pelo, *m.* hair; pile; **tomar el pelo,** to tease

pelota, *f.* pelota, ball; **en pelota,** entirely naked

pelotera, *f.* quarrel, brawl, free-for-all

pelotón, *m.* large ball; crowd; (mil.) platoon

peluquería, *f.* barbershop

peluquero, *m.* barber, hairdresser

pellejo, *m.* skin, hide; pelt

pellizcar, *va.* to pinch

pena, *f.* embarrassment; trouble, affliction; **a duras penas,** with difficulty

penal, *adj.* penal

penalidad, *f.* suffering, trouble; penalty

pendiente, *adj.* pending; **pendiente de pago,** unpaid; *m.* pendant; earring, eardrop; *f.* slope, incline

péndulo, *m.* pendulum

pene, *m.* (anat.) penis

península, *f.* peninsula

penitencia, *f.* penitence, penance

penoso, *adj.* distressing, embarrassing

pensar, *vn.* to think; to intend

pensión, *f.* pension; annuity; price of board and tuition; boarding house

pentagrama, *m.* musical staff

peña, *f.* rock, large stone

peón, *m.* laborer; pawn (in chess)

peor, *adj., adv.* worse

pepino, *m.* cucumber

pepita, *f.* kernel; seed of some fruits; distemper in fowl

pequeño, *adj.* little, small; young

percal, *m.* percale

percance, *m.* misfortune

percepción, *f.* perception

percibir, *va.* to perceive, comprehend

percha, *f.* perch; clothes hanger

perder, *va.* to lose; **echar a perder,** to ruin; to spoil; **perderse,** to go astray

pérdida, *f.* loss, damage

perdiz, *f.* partridge

perdón, *m.* pardon, forgiveness

perdonar, *va.* to pardon, forgive

perecer, *vn.* to perish, die

pereza, *f.* laziness

perezoso, *adj.* lazy, idle

perfección, *f.* perfection

perfecto, *adj.* perfect

perfil, *m.* profile

perforadora, *f.* air drill

perforar, *va.* to perforate

perfumar, *va.* to perfume

perfume, *m.* perfume

pericia, *f.* skill, ability

perifonear, *va.* to broadcast (radio)

perilla, *f.* doorknob; goatee; **de perilla,** to the purpose, in time

periódico, *adj.* periodical; *m.* newspaper

periodismo, *m.* journalism

periodista, *m., f.* journalist

periodo, *m.* period, term

periscopio, *m.* periscope

perito, perita, *n., adj.* expert; skillful, experienced

perjudicar, *va.* to injure, hurt

perjudicial, *adj.* harmful, injurious

perjuicio, *m.* damage

perla, *f.* pearl; **de perlas,** just perfect

permanecer, *vn.* to remain, stay

permanente, *adj.* permanent

permiso, *m.* permission

permitir, *va.* to permit, allow; **permitirse,** to take the liberty; **Dios lo permita,** may God will it

perno, *m.* spike, bolt; (mech.) joint pin

pero, *conj.* but, yet, except; *m.* defect, fault; **poner peros,** to find fault

peróxido, *m.* peroxide

perpendicular, *adj.* perpendicular

perpetuo, *adj.* perpetual

perplejo, *adj.* perplexed

perra, *f.* female dog; bitch

perseguir, *va.* to pursue, persecute

perseverancia, *f.* perseverance, constancy

perseverante, *adj.* persevering

perseverar, *vn.* to persevere

persiana, *f.* venetian blind

persignarse, *vr.* to make the sign of the cross

persistente, *adj.* persistent, tenacious

persistir, *vn.* to persist

persona, *f.* person

personaje, *m.* personage; character (in a play)

personal, *adj.* personal; *m.* personnel, staff

personalidad, *f.* personality

perspectiva, *f.* perspective; prospect; sight, outlook

perspicaz, *adj.* perspicacious, keen

persuadir, *va.* to persuade

pertenecer, *vn.* to belong to

perturbar, *va.* to perturb, disturb

peruano, peruana, *adj., n.* Peruvian

perversidad, *f.* perversity

perverso, *adj.* perverse

pervertir, *va.* to pervert, corrupt

pesadez, *f.* heaviness, fatigue

pesadilla, *f.* nightmare

pesado, *adj.* heavy, weighty

pésame, *m.* message of condolence

pesar, *m.* sorrow, grief; regret, repentance; **a pesar de,** in spite of; *vn.* to weigh; to be heavy; *va.* to weigh

pesca, *f.* fishing, fishery

pescado, *m.* fish (when caught; in the water it is **pez**)

pescador, pescadora, *n.* fisher, fisherman (or woman)

pescar, *va.* to fish

pescuezo, *m.* neck

pesebre, *m.* manger

peseta, *f.* monetary unit of Spain

pesimista, *m., f.* pessimist; *adj.* pessimistic

pésimo, *adj.* very bad

peso, *m.* monetary unit of Sp. Am. countries with sign same as the U. S. dollar; weight, heaviness; balance; load

pestaña, *f.* eyelash

pestañear, *vn.* to wink, move the eyelids

peste, *f.* plague; stench

petaca, *f.* (Sp. Am.) suitcase

petate, *m.* straw sleeping mat

petición, *f.* petition, request, plea

petróleo, *m.* petroleum, oil, mineral oil

petunia, *f.* (bot.) petunia

pez, *m.* fish (in the water); *f.* pitch, tar

piadoso, *adj.* pious, merciful

pianista, *m., f.* pianist

piano, *m.* piano; **piano de cola,** grand piano

picadillo, *m.* mincemeat, hash

picadura, *f.* prick; puncture; bite (of an insect or snake)

picaflor, *m.* hummingbird; fickle person

picante, *adj.* sharp, pricking; hot, highly seasoned; piquant

picaporte, *m.* picklock; catch, bolt; doorlatch

picar, *va.* to prick; to sting; to mince; to itch; **picarse,** to be piqued; to be motheaten; to begin to rot (as fruit)

picardía, *f.* roguery; mischievousness

pícaro, *adj.* roguish; mischievous, malicious; *m.* rogue

picazón, *f.* itching

pico, *m.* beak, bill; peak; pickax; point; odd; a bit over; **cien dólares y pico,** one hundred and odd dollars; **la una y pico,** few minutes past one (o'clock)

picoso, *adj.* (Mex. coll.) hot, highly seasoned:

pichón, *m.* young pigeon; young bird

pie, *m.* foot; base, foundation; **al pie de la letra,** literally; **ponerse de pie,** to stand up

piedad, *f.* mercy, pity

piedra, *f.* stone; gem

pierna, *f.* leg

pieza, *f.* piece; piece of furniture; room

pijamas, *m. pl.* pajamas

pila, *f.* font; pile, battery; heap; holy water basin; **nombre de pila,** Christian name

pilar, *m.* pillar

piloto, *m.* pilot; first mate

pillo, *adj.* roguish; *m.* rogue

pimienta, *f.* pepper

pimpollo, *m.* sprout, bud

pincel, *m.* artist's brush

pinchazo, *m.* puncture; prick

pinta, *f.* spot, blemish; pint

pintar, *va.* to paint, picture; to describe; **pintarse,** to paint one's face

pintor, pintora, *n.* painter, artist

pintoresco, *adj.* picturesque

pintura, *f.* painting; picture

pinzas, *f. pl.* forceps, tweezers

piña, *f.* pineapple; fir cone

piñata, *f.* potful of goodies broken by blindfolded children at games

piojo, *m.* louse

pipa, *f.* wine cask; tobacco pipe

pirámide, *f.* pyramid

pirata, *m.* pirate

piropo, *m.* compliment, flattery

pisada, *f.* footstep; footprint; footfall

pisapapeles, *m.* paperweight

pisar, *va.* to step, tread, trample

piscina, *f.* swimming pool

piso, *m.* floor, story

pisotear, *va.* to trample

pista, *f.* trace, footprint; racetrack

pito, *m.* whistle; **no me importa un pito,** I don't care a straw

pizarrón, *m.* blackboard

pl., plural, *pl.* plural

placa, *f.* plaque; sheet of metal

placer, *m.* pleasure, delight

plan, *m.* plan; design, plot

plancha, *f.* plate; flatiron; slab

planchar, *va.* to iron

planeador, *m.* (avi.) glider

planear, *vn.* to glide

planeta, *m.* planet

piano, *adj.* plane, level; *m.* plane; floorplan; **de piano,** frankly, plainly

planta, *f.* sole of the foot; plant

plantar, *va.* to plant; (coll.) to jilt; **plantarse,** to stand firm

plasma, *m.* plasma

plástico, *adj.* plastic

plata, *f.* silver; money

plataforma, *f.* platform

plátano, *m.* banana; plantain; plane tree

plateado, *adj.* silvery; silver-plated

platero: *m.* silversmith

plática *f.* chat, conversation

platicar, *vn.* to converse, chat

platillo, *m.* saucer; side dish; cymbal

Platino, *m.* platinum

plato, *m.* dish; plate; **lista de platos,** menu; **plato toca discos,** turntable,

playa, *f.* shore, beach

plaza, *f.* square, place; fortified place

plazo, *m.* term, date of payment; **a plazos,** on credit, on time

plegar, *va.* to fold; to pleat

plegaria, *f.* prayer

pleito, *m.* dispute; lawsuit

plenamente, *adv.* fully, completely

pliego, *m.* sheet of paper

plomero, *m.* plumber

plomo, *m.* lead (metal)

pluma, *f.* feather, plume; pen

plumaje, *m.* plumage

P.M. or **p.m., pasado meridiano,** P.M., afternoon

p/o or **P.O., por orden,** (com.) by order

población, *f.* population; town

poblado, *m.* town, village

poblar, *va.* to populate, people

pobre, *adj.* poor, indigent; deficient

pobreza, *f.* poverty

poco, *adj.* little, scanty; *m.* a small part; **pocos,** *pl.* few; **poco,** *adv.* little; **hace poco,** a short time ago

podar, *va.* to prune

poder, *m.* power, authority; command; **en poder de,** in the hands of; **por poder,** by proxy; *vn.* to be able; *v. imp.* to be possible

poderoso, *adj.* powerful

podrir, *vn.* **pudrir**

poema, *m.* poem

poesía, *f.* poetry

poeta, *m.* poet

poético, *adj.* poetic

poetisa, *f.* poetess

polaco, polaca, *n.* Pole; *adj.* Polish; *m.* Polish language

polar, *adj.* polar

Polea, *f.* pulley

policía, *f.* police; *m.* policeman

polígamo, polígama, *n., adj.* polygamist

política, *f.* politics; policy

político, *adj.* political; polite; *m.* politician

póliza, *f.* insurance policy

polo, *m.* pole; polo; **polo acuático,** water polo

Polonia, *f.* Poland

polonio, *m.* polonium

polvera, *f.* compact; vanity case

polvo, *m.* powder; dust

pólvora, *f.* gunpowder

polla, *f.* pullet; pool; (coll.) young girl

pollera, *f.* hen-coop; (Sp. Am.) wide skirt; national costume of Panama

pollo, *m.* young chicken; (coll.) young man

pomo, *m.* small bottle

pompón, *m.* pompon

pómulo, *m.* cheekbone

ponche, *m.* punch (drink)

ponchera, *f.* punchbowl

ponderar, *va.* to ponder, consider, weigh; to exaggerate

poner, *va.* to put, to place; to lay eggs; **poner al corriente,** to acquaint (with), to inform; **ponerse,** to become; to set (as the sun, etc.)

poniente, *m.* west; west wind; *adj.* setting (as sun, etc.)

popa, *f.* (naut.) poop, stern

popular, *adj.* popular

popularidad, *f.* popularity

populoso, *adj.* populous

poquito, *adj.* very little; *m.* a little; **poquito a poquito,** little by little

por, *prep.* for, by, about; through; on account of

porcelana, *f.* porcelain, china

porcentaje, *m.* percentage

porción, *f.* part, portion

pordiosero, pordiosera, *n.* beggar

porfiado, *adj.* obstinate

porfiar, *vn.* to dispute obstinately

pormenor, *m.* detail

poro, *m.* pore

porqué, *m.* cause, reason

¿por qué? *interr.* why?

portada, *f.* title page, frontispiece

portador, portadora, *n.* carrier, bearer

portal, *m.* porch; portico, piazza

portamonedas, *m.* purse, pocketbook

portar, *va.* to carry; to bear (arms, etc.); **portarse,** to behave, comport oneself

portátil, *adj.* portable

porte, *m.* portage, freight, postage; bearing, carriage

portero, portera, *n.* porter, janitor or janitress, concierge

portuario, portuaria, *adj.* relating to a seaport

porvenir, *m.* future

posada, *f.* boardinghouse; inn,

posar 103 prenda

hotel; (Mex.) pre-Christmas party

posar, *vn.* to lodge; to sit down, repose

posdata, *f.* postscript

poseer, *va.* to possess, own

posesión, *f.* possession

posesivo, *adj.* possessive

posibilidad, *f.* possibility

posible, *adj.* possible

posición, *f.* position, place; posture; situation

positivo, *adj.* positive

posponer, *va.* to postpone

postal, *adj.* postal; **paquete postal,** parcel post

poste, *m.* post, pillar

postema, *f.* abscess, tumor

postergar, *va.* to defer, delay

posteridad, *f.* posterity

posterior, *adj.* back, rear

posteriormente, *adv.* later, subsequently

postizo, *adj.* artificial, false

postrarse, *vr.* to prostrate oneself; to kneel down

postre, *adj.* last in order; **a la postre,** at last; *m.* dessert

potasa, *f.* potash

pote, *m.* pot, jar; flowerpot

potencia, power; strength

potente, *adj.* potent, powerful, mighty

pozo, *m.* well; (min.) shaft, pit

P.P., porte pagado, p.p. post-paid

p. p., por poder, (law) by power of attorney or by proxy

ppdo., p.pdo or **p.ºp.ᵈᵒ, próximo pasado,** in the past month

practicante, *m., f.* (med.) intern

practicar, *va.* to practice; to exercise

práctico, *adj.* practical; skillful

precaución, *f.* precaution

precaver, *va.* to prevent, guard against

precedente, *adj.* precedent, foregoing

preceder, *va.* to precede

preciar, *va.* to value, appraise; **preciarse de,** to take pride

in, boast

precio, *m.* price, value

precioso, *adj.* precious; beautiful

precipitación, *f.* inconsiderate haste

precipitar, *va.* to precipitate; **precipitarse,** to run headlong to one's destruction

precisar, *va.* to compel, oblige; to necessitate; to state

precisión, *f.* preciseness; **con toda precisión,** on time, very promptly

preciso, *adj.* necessary, requisite; precise

precoz, *adj.* precocious

precursor, precursora, *n.* forerunner; *adj.* preceding

predicado, *m.* predicate

predicador, *m.* preacher

predicción, *f.* prediction

predilecto, *adj.* favorite

predispuesto, *adj.* biased, predisposed

predominar, *va., vn.* to predominate, prevail

prefacio, *m.* preface

preferencia, *f.* preference; **de preferencia,** preferably

preferente, *adj.* preferred, preferable

preferible, *adj.* preferable

preferir, *va.* to prefer

pregunta, *f.* question, inquiry

preguntar, *va.* to question, inquire

preguntón, preguntona, *n.* inquisitive person; *adj.* inquisitive

prehistórico, *adj.* prehistoric

prejuicio, *m.* prejudice

preliminar, *adj., m.* preliminary

preludio, *m.* prelude

prematuro, *adj.* premature

premeditar, *va.* to premeditate

premiar, *va.* to reward, remunerate

premio, *m.* reward, prize, recompense; (com.) premium; interest

prenda, *f.* pledge, forfeit; pawn; piece of jewelry

prender, *va.* to seize, catch; to imprison; *vn.* to catch or take fire; to take root

prensa, *f.* press, newspapers

preocupar, *va.* to preoccupy; **preocuparse**, to care about, worry

prep., **preposición**, *prep.*, preposition

preparación, *f.* preparation

preparar, *va.*, *vr.* to prepare

preparativo, *m.* preparation

preposición, *f.* (gram.) preposition

prerrogativa, *f.* prerogative, privilege

presa, *f.* capture, seizure; prey; dike, dam

prescribir, *va.* to prescribe

presencia, *f.* presence

presenciar, *va.* to witness, see

presentación, *f.* presentation, introduction

presentar, *va.* to present, introduce; **presentarse**, to appear; to introduce oneself

presente, *adj.* present; *m.* present, gift; instant; **el 20 del presente**, the 20th instant; **hacer presente**, to call attention; **la presente**, the present writing; **tener presente**, to bear in mind

presentimiento, *m.* presentiment, misgiving

presentir, *va.* to have a presentiment

preservación, *f.* preservation

preservar, *va.* to preserve

presidencia, *f.* presidency; chairmanship

presidente, *m.* president; chairman

presidiario, *m.* convict

presidio, *m.* prison

presidir, *va.* to preside

presión, *f.* pressure, pressing; **presión arterial**, blood pressure

préstamo, *m.* loan

presto, *adj.* quick, prompt, ready; *adv.* soon, quickly

presumido, *adj.* presumptuous, arrogant

presupuesto, *m.* estimate; budget

pretender, *va.* to pretend, claim; to try, attempt

pretendiente, *m.* pretender; suitor; candidate, office seeker

pretérito, *adj.* preterit, past

pretexto, *m.* pretext, pretense

prevención, *f.* prevention

prevenir, *va.* to prepare; to foresee; to prevent; to warn; **prevenirse**, to be prepared

preventivo, *adj.* preventive

prever, *va.* to foresee

previo, *adj.* previous

provisión, *f.* foresight

previsor, *adj.* foreseeing, farseeing

prieto, *adj.* brackish, very dark; **prieta**, *n.* very dark person

prima, *f.* (mus.) treble; (com.) premium; female cousin

primario, *adj.* first; **escuela primaria**, elementary school

primavera, *f.* spring (the season)

primeramente, *adv.* in the first place, mainly

primero, *adj.* first, prior, former; **primeros auxilios**, first aid

primitivo, *adj.* primitive, original

primo, **prima**, *n.* cousin

primogénito, **primogénita**, *adj.*, *n.* first-born

primoroso, *adj.* exquisite

princesa, *f.* princess

principal, *adj.* principal, main

príncipe, *m.* prince

principiar, *va.* to begin

principio, *m.* beginning; principle

prioridad, *f.* priority

prisa, *f.* hurry; haste; **a toda prisa**, at full speed; **darse prisa**, to hurry; **tener prisa**, to be in a hurry

prisión, *f.* prison; duress

prisionero, **prisionera**, *n.* prisoner

privado, *adj.* private

privar, *va.*, *vr.* to deprive; to prohibit

privilegiado, *adj.* privileged

pro, *m.* or *f.* profit, benefit, advantage; **en pro de**, in behalf of; **el pro y el contra**, the pro and con

proa, *f.* (naut.) prow, bow

probabilidad, *f.* probability

probable, *adj.* probable, likely

probar, *va.* to try; to prove; to taste; *vn.* to suit, agree; **probarse**, to try on (clothes)

problema, *m.* problem

problemático, *adj.* problematical

procedencia, *f.* origin, source

procedente, *adj.* coming from, proceeding from

proceder, *m.* procedure; *vn.* to proceed, go on; to issue

procesar, *va.* to prosecute; to indict

procesión, *f.* procession

proceso, *m.* process, lawsuit

proclamar, *va.* to proclaim

procurador, *m.* procurer; solicitor; attorney; **procurador publico**, attorney at law; **Procurador General**, Attorney General

prodigar, *va.* to waste, lavish

pródigo *adj.* prodigal

producción, *f.* production

producir, *va.* to produce, yield

productiveo, *adj.* productive, fertile; profitable

producto, *m.* product; amount

prof., **profesor**, prof., professor; **profeta**, prophet

profecía, *f.* prophecy

profesión, *f.* profession

profesor, **profesora**, *n.* professor, teacher

profesorado, *m.* body of teachers, faculty

profeta, *m.* prophet

profundidad, *f.* profoundness; depth; **carga de profundidad**, (mil.) ash can (depth charge)

progenitor, *m.* ancestor, forefather

programa, *m.* program

progresar, *vn.* to progress, to improve

progreso, *m.* progress, advancement

prohibición, *f.* prohibition

prohibir, *va.* to prohibit, forbid

prójimo, *m.* fellow creature; neighbor

prole, *f.* issue, offspring

prólogo, *m.* prologue

promedio, *m.* average

promesa, *f.* promise; pious offering

prometer, *va.* to promise, assure; *vn.* to be promising

prometido, **prometida**, *n.*, *adj.* betrothed

prominente, *adj.* prominent

promoción, *f.* promotion

premover, *va.* to promote, further

pronombre, *m.* pronoun,

pronosticar, *va.* to predict, foretell

prontitud, *f.* promptness

pronto, *adj.* prompt, ready; soon; *adv.* promptly; quickly

pronunciar, *va.* to pronounce; **pronunciarse**, to rebel

propaganda, *f.* propaganda; advertising

propagandista, *m.*, *f.*, *adj.* propagandist

propagar, *va.*, *vr.* to propagate, spread, disseminate

propicio, *adj.* propitious favorable

propiedad, *f.* property; propriety

propietario, *adj.* proprietary; *m.* proprietor; **propietaria**, *f.* proprietress

propina, *f.* tip, gratuity

propio, *adj.* proper; own; characteristic

proponer, *va.* to propose, suggest; **proponerse**, to intend, plan, be determined

proporción, *f.* proportion

proporcionar, *va.* to proportion; to adjust, adapt; to provide, supply

proposición, *f.* proposition

propósito, *m.* purpose; **a propósito**, adequate, fitting; **de propósito**, on purpose; **a propósito de**, apropos of

propuesta, *f.* proposal, offer, proposition; nomination
prorrata, *f.* quota; **a prorrata,** in proportion
prórroga, *f.* extension, renewal
prosa, *f.* prose
prosaico, *adj.* prosaic
proseguir, *va.* to pursue, prosecute; to continue
prosperar, *vn.* to prosper, thrive
prosperidad, *f.* prosperity
próspero, *adj.* prosperous
prostituta, *f.* prostitute
protección, *f.* protection
protector, protectora, *n.* protector
proteger, *va.* to protect
protegido, protegida, *n.* protegé
proteína, *f.* protein
protesta, *f.* protest
protestante, *n., adj.* Protestant
protestar, *va.* to protest
protocolo, *m.* protocol
prototipo, *m.* prototype
protuberancia, *f.* bulge
provecho, *m.* profit, benefit
provechoso, *adj.* beneficial
proveer, *va.* to provide; to provision
proverbio, *m.* proverb
providencia, *f.* providence
provincia, *f.* province
provocar, *va.* to provoke
prox., próximo, next, nearest
próximamente, *adv.* very soon; shortly
próximo, *adj.* next, nearest, following
proyectar, *va.* to project, plan
proyectil, *m.* projectile
proyecto, *m.* project, plan
proyector, *m.* projector; spotlight
prudente, *adj.* prudent, cautious
P. S., posdata, P.S., postscript
psiquiatría, *f.* psychiatry
pte., presente, pres. present
pto., puerto, pt., port; **punto,** pt., point
publicación, *f.* publication
publicar, *va.* to publish, reveal

publicidad, *f.* publicity
público, *adj.* public; *m.* attendance, audience
pudiente, *adj.* rich, opulent
pudín, *m.* pudding
pudor, *m.* modesty, decorum
pudrir, *vn.* to rot
pueblo, *m.* town, village; populace
puente, *m.* bridge; **puente aéreo,** airlift
puerca, *f.* sow
pueril, *adj.* childish
puerta, *f.* door, gateway
pues, *conj.* as, since, because, for; *adv.* then, therefore
puesta, *f.* (ast.) set, setting; **puesta del sol,** sunset
puesto, *m.* place; post; employment; booth; **puesto, puesta,** *adj.* put, set, placed; **puesto que,** since
pujar, *va.* to outbid; to push ahead, push through
pulcro, *adj.* neat, tidy
pulga, *f.* flea
pulgada, *f.* inch
pulmón, *m.* lung; **pulmón de acero,** iron lung
pulmonía, *f.* pneumonia
púlpito, *m.* pulpit
pulsera, *f.* bracelet
pulverizador, *m.* atomizer
pulverizar, *va.* to pulverize, to spray
punta, *f.* point, tip; **punta de combate,** warhead
puntada, *f.* stitch
puntapié, *m.* kick
puntería, *f.* aiming (of firearms); marksmanship
puntiagudo, *adj.* sharppointed
puntilla, *f.* small point; **de puntillas,** on tiptoe
punto, *m.* period; point, end; dot; **estar a punto de,** to be about to; **son las dos en punto,** it is exactly two o'clock
puntual, *adj.* punctual
punzada, *f.* prick, sting; sharp pain
puñado, *m.* handful
puñal, *m.* poniard, dagger

puño, *m.* fist; cuff
pupila, *f.* eyeball, pupil
pupilo, *m.* pupil; scholar; boarder; orphan ward (boy)
pupitre, *m.* writing desk
purga, *f.* physic; purge
purgar, *va.* to purge, purify; to administer a physic; to atone
purgatorio, *m.* purgatory
pus, *m.* pus, matter
puta, *f.* whore
pza.: pieza, pc. piece

Q

q.e.p.d., que en paz descanse, may (he, she) rest in peace
ql. or **q.¹, quintal,** cwt., hundred-weight
qq., quintales, cwts., hundred-weights
que, *relative pron.* that, which, who, whom; **qué,** *interrogative and exclamatory pron.,* what; how; **no hay de que,** don't mention it; *conj.* that; than; whether; because
quebrada, *f.* brook
quebrado, *m.* (math.) fraction; *adj.* broken; bankrupt
quebrar, *va., vr.* to break; *vn.* to fail
quedar, *vn.* to stay, remain; to be left
quedo, *adj.* quiet, still; *adv.* softly, gently
quehacer, *m.* occupation, work; task, chore
queja, *f.* complaint
quejarse, *vr.* to complain of; to moan
quejido, *m.* groan, moan
quemar, *va., vr.* to burn; to kindle; *vn.* to be too hot
querella, *f.* complaint; quarrel
querer, *va.* to wish, desire; to like, love; **querer decir,** to mean, signify; **sin querer,** unwillingly; **Dios quiera,** God grant
querido, *adj.* dear, beloved; *n.* darling, lover
quetzal, *m.* (orn.) quetzal; monetary unit of Guatemala

quiebra, *f.* bankruptcy
quien, *pron.* who, which; **¿quién?** who?
quienquiera, *pron.* whoever
quieto, *adj.* quiet, still
quietud, *f.* quietness, peace
quím., química, chem., chemistry
química, *f.* chemistry
químico, *m.* chemist; *adj.* chemical
quince, *adj., m.* fifteen
quincena, *f.* fortnight; semimonthly pay
quincenal,*adi.*semimonthly
quinientos, quinientas, *adj., m.* five hundred
quinina, quinine
quinta, country house; (mus.) fifth
quintal, *m.* hundredweight
quinto, *m., adj.* fifth
quíntuplo, *adj.* quintuple, fivefold
quirófano, *m.* operating room
quirúrgico, *adj.* surgical
quitar, *va.* to remove, take away
quizá, *adv.* perhaps

R

R., Reverendo, Rev., Reverend; **Respuesta,** reply; **Reprobado,** not passing (in an examination)
rabia, *f.* rage, fury
rabioso, *adj.* rabid; furious
rabo, *m.* tail
racimo, *m.* bunch, cluster (of grapes, etc.)
raciocinio, *m.* reasoning
racional, *adj.* rational; reasonable
radar, *m.* radar
radiación, *f.* radiation
radiador, *m.* radiator
radical, *adj.* radical; *m.* (math.) radical; extremist
radicar, *vn.* to take root; **radicarse,** to take root; to settle, establish oneself
radio, *m.* or *f.* radio, receiver; radio broadcasting station; (math., anat.) radius; (chem.)

radium

radiodifusión, *f.* radio broadcasting

radiodifusora, *f.* broadcasting station

radioescucha, *m., f.* radio listener

radiorreceptor, *m.* radio receiving set

radiotelescopio, *m.* radio telescope

radioyente, *m., f.* radio listener

raja, *f.* splinter, chip of wood; slice (of fruit); fissure, crack

rajar, *va.* to split, chop

ralo, *adj.* thin, sparse

rama, *f.* branch (of a tree, of a family)

ramal, *m.* ramification

ramillete, *m.* bouquet

ramo, *m.* branch (of a tree); branch (of trade, art, etc.); bouquet

rampa, *f.* slope, ramp

rana, *f.* frog

rancio, *adj.* rank, rancid

ranchero, *m.* small farmer

rango, *m.* rank

ranura, *f.* groove

rapidez, *f.* rapidity, speed

rapiña, *f.* rapine, robbery; **ave de rapiña,** bird of prey

rapsodia, *f.* rhapsody

raqueta, *f.* racket; **de raqueta nieve.** snowshoe

raquítico, *adj.* rickety

rascacielos, *m.* skyscraper

rascar, *va.* to scratch, scrape

rasgado, *adj.* torn, open; **boca rasgada,** wide mouth; **ojos rasgados,** large eyes

rasgar, *va.* to tear, rend

rasgo, *m.* dash, stroke; kind gesture; feature, trait

rasguño, *m.* scratch

raso, *m.* satin, sateen; **raso, rasa,** *adj.* plain; flat

raspar, *va.* to scrape, rasp

rastrillo, *m.* hammer of a gun; rake

rastro, *m.* track; sledge; slaughterhouse; sign, token; trail

rata, *f.* (zool.) rat

ratero, *adj.* mean, vile; *m.* pickpocket

ratificar, *va.* to ratify

rato, *m.* while; moment

ratón, *m.* mouse

raya, *f.* stroke; stripe; streak; line; dash (in punctuation)

rayado, *adj.* striped

rayar, *va.* to draw lines, rule; to stripe; **rayar en,** to border on

rayo, *m.* ray, beam of light; flash of lightning; radius; **rayo equis,** X ray

rayón, *m.* rayon

raza, *f.* race, lineage

razón, *f.* reason; cause, motive; ratio, rate; **razón social,** firm name; **dar razón,** to inform, give account; **tener razón,** to be right

rezonable, *adj.* reasonable

razonamiento, *m.* reasoning

reacción, *f.* reaction; **propulsión por reacción,** jet propulsion

reaccionar, *vn.* to react

real, *adj.* real, actual; royal; **pavo real,** peacock

realce, *m.* luster, enhancement; **dar realce,** to highlight, give importance to

realidad, *f.* reality, fact

realismo, *m.* realism

realización, *f.* realization, fulfillment; bargain sale

realizar, *va.* to realize, fulfill

realmente, *adv.* really

realzar, *va.* to raise, elevate; to emboss; to heighten

reanudar, *va.* to renew, resume

rebaja, *f.* deduction; reduction, rebate

rebajar, *va.* to lessen, curtail; to lower (as price); **rebajarse,** to humble oneself

rebanada, *f.* slice

rebaño, *m.* flock of sheep, herd of cattle, drove

rebelarse, *vr.* to rebel

rebelde, *m.* rebel; *adj.* rebellious

rebotar, *va.* to repel; *vn.* to rebound

rebozo, m. woman's shawl

rebuznar, vn. to bray

recado, m. message

recaída, f. relapse

recalcar, va. to emphasize

recámara, f. boudoir, bedroom; chamber of a gun

recapacitar, va. to think over, meditate

recatado, adj. prudent, modest

recelo, m. suspicion, mistrust

recepción, f. reception

receptor, m. radio receiver

receso, m. withdrawal, retirement; recess

receta, f. recipe; prescription

recetar, va. to prescribe

recibir, va. to receive; to let in; to go to meet; **recibirse,** to graduate in a profession

recibo, m. receipt, voucher

recién, adv. recently, lately; **recién casado, recién casada,** newlywed

recio, adj. stout, strong; adv. loudly

recipiente, m. recipient, container

reciprocidad, f. reciprocity

recíproco, adj. reciprocal

recitar, va. to recite

reclamar, va. to claim, demand

recluir, va., vr. to seclude

reclutar, va. to recruit

recobrar, va. to recover

recoger, va. to take back; to gather, pick up; to shelter; **recogerse,** to take shelter or refuge; to retire, to rest

recomendación, f. recommendation

recomendar, va. to recommend

recompensa, f. recompense

reconciliación, f. reconciliation

reconciliar, va., vr. to reconcile

reconocer, va. to examine closely; to acknowledge favors received; to admit; to recognize; (mil.) to reconnoiter

reconocimiento, m. recognition; gratitude; reconnaissance; **reconocimiento médico,** medical examination

reconstituyente, m. (med.) tonic

reconstruir, va. to reconstruct

recopilar, va. to compile; to abridge

recordar, va., vr. to remind; to remember; vn. to call to mind

recorrer, va. to run over, peruse; to travel over

recorrido, m. run, line; expedition

recortar, va. to cut away, trim

recorte, m. cutting; **recorte de periódico,** newspaper clipping

recostar, va. to lean against; **recostarse,** to recline, rest

recrear, va., vr. to amuse, delight, recreate

recreo, m. recreation, pleasure; recess

rectamente, adv. justly, rightly

rectángulo, m. rectangle

rectificar, va. to rectify

recto, adj. straight, direct, right; just

recuerdo, m. remembrance, memory; souvenir; **recuerdos,** pl. regards

recuperar, va. to recover; **recuperarse,** to recover from sickness

recurso, m. recourse; resource; **recursos,** pl. means

rechazar, va. to repel, reject

red, f. net; web; network

redacción, f. editing; editor's office; editorial staff

redactar, va. to edit (a publication); to draw up, draft

redactor, m. editor

redimir, va. to redeem

redondo, adj. around; **a la redonda,** all around

reducción, f. reduction

reducir, va. to reduce

redundante, adj. redundant

reelección, f. re-election

reelegir, va. to re-elect

ref., referencia, ref., reference

refacción, f. repair; **piezas de**

refacción, spare parts

referencia, *f.* reference

referer, *va.* to refer, relate; **referse,** to refer to, relate to

refinamiento, *m.* refinement

refinar, *va.* to refine

reflector, *m.* reflector, search light

reflejar, *va., vr.* to reflect

reflejo, *m.* reflex; reflection, light, glare

reflexionar, *vn.* to reflect, meditate

reforma, *f.* reform

reformar, *va., vr.* to reform, correct

reforzar, *va., vr.* to strengthen, fortify

refrán, *m.* proverb, saying

refrenar, *va.* to refrain, restrain

refrescante, *adj.* refreshing

refrescar, *va.* to refresh; *vn.* to cool; to take the air

refresco, *m.* refreshment; cold drink

refrigerador, *m.* refrigerator

refrigerar, *va.* to refrigerate

refuerzo, *m.* reinforcement

refugiado, refugiada, *n.* refugee

refugiar, *va.* to shelter; **refugiarse,** to take refuge

refuñfuñar, *vn.* to grumble

regadera, *f.* watering pot, sprinkler; (Sp. Am.) **baño de regadera,** shower bath

regalar, *va.* to make a present of

regalo, *m.* present, gift

regañar, *va.* to scold

regar, *va.* to water, irrigate; to spread

regateo, *m.* bargaining, act of haggling

regenerar, *va., vr.* to regenerate

regidor, *m.* governor, prefect

régimen, *m.* regime

regimiento, *m.* regiment

regio, *adj.* royal, kindly

región, *f.* region

regir, *va.* to rule, govern, direct; *vn.* to be in force

registrar, *va.* to register; inspect; to search; to record

registro, *m.* register, registration; record; inspection

regla, *f.* rule, statute, ruler

reglamento, *m.* by-law; regulations

regresar, *vn.* to return, go back

regreso, *m.* return, regression

regular, *va.* to regulate, adjust; *adj.* regular; ordinary

regularidad, *f.* regularity

rehabilitar, *va., vr.* to rehabilitate

rehusar, *va.* to refuse, decline

reina, *f.* queen

reinado, *m.* reign

reinar, *va.* to reign

reino, *m.* kingdom, reign

reintegrar, *va., vr.* to reintegrate, to restore

reir, *vn.* to laugh; **reirse de,** to laugh at

reiterar, *va.* to reiterate, repeat

reja, *f.* lattice; grating; railing

rejuvenecer, *vn.* to be rejuvenated

relación, *f.* relation; report; account; **relaciones,** connections

relacionar, *va.* to relate; to connect; to make acquainted

relámpago, *m.* flash of lightning

relatar, *va.* to relate

relatividad, *f.* relativity

relativo, *adj.* relative, pertaining

relato, *m.* account, narrative

relegar, *va.* to relegate, banish

relevar, *va.* to relieve, substitute

relevo, *m.* (mil.) relief

relieve, *m.* relief (sculpture); **bajo relieve,** bas-relief; **dar relieve,** to emphasize, highlight

religión, *f.* religion

religioso, *adj.* religious

reloj, *m.* clock, watch; **de reloj pulsera,** wrist watch

relojero, *m.* watchmaker

relucir, *vn.* to shine, glitter

rellenar, *va.* to refill; to stuff

remachar, *va.* to rivet

remangar, *va.* to tuck up (sleeves, dress, etc.)

remar, *vn.* to row

remetado, *adj.* utterly ruined; **loco remetado,** stark mad

rematar, *va.* to sell at auction; to finish

remate, *m.* end, conclusion; auction sale; **de remate,** absolutely, hopelessly

remediar, *va.* to remedy; to prevent

remedio, *m.* remedy, reparation; sin **remedio,** inevitable

remendar, *va.* to patch, mend

remesa, *f.* sending of goods; remittance of money

remiendo, *m.* patch, repair

reminiscencia, *f.* reminiscence

remitente, *m., f.* remitter, shipper, sender

remitir, *va.* to send, transmit

remojar, *va.* to soak

remolacha, *f.* beet

remolino, *m.* whirlwind; whirlpool

rémora, *f.* hindrance, cause of delay

remordimiento, *m.* remorse

remoto, *adj.* remote, distant

remunerar, *va.* to remunerate

Renacimiento, *m.* Renaissance

rencor, *m.* rancor, grudge

rendija, *f.* crevice, crack

rendir, *va.* to produce, yield; **rendirse,** to be fatigued; to surrender

renegar, *va.* to deny, disown; *vn.* to curse

renglón, *m.* written or printed line; (com.) part of one's income; items

reno, *m.* reindeer

renombre, *m.* renown

renovar, *va.* to renew, renovate, reform

renta, *f.* rent, income

renuncia, *f.* resignation

reñir, *va., vn.* to wrangle; to quarrel

reo, *m.* offender, criminal

Rep., República, Rep. Repub-lic

reparar, *va.* to repair; to consider, serve

repartir, *va.* to distribute

reparto, *m.* distribution; (theat.) cast of characters

repasar, *va., vn.* to revise, review

repaso, *m.* revision, review

repente, de repente, *adv.* suddenly

repentino, *adj.* sudden

repercusión, *f.* reverberation, repercussion

repetictón, *f.* repetition

repetir, *va.* to repeat

repicar, *va.* to chime

repleto, *adj.* replete

réplica, *f.* reply, answer

replicar, *vn.* to reply, answer; to argue

repollo, *m.* cabbage head

reponer, *va.* to replace; to restore; **reponerse,** to recover lost health

reposo, *m.* rest, repose

representación, *f.* representation; performance

representante, *m., f.* representative

representar, *va.* to represent; to play on the stage

represión, *f.* repression

reprimir, *va.* to repress

reprochar, *va.* to reproach

reproducir, *va.* to reproduce

reptil, *m.* reptile

república, *f.* republic

repuesto, *m.* replacement; **piezas de repuesto,** spare parts

repugnante, *adj.* repugnant

reputación, *f.* reputation

requerir, *va.* to request, demand; to summon; to require

requisito *m.* requisite, requirement

res, *f.* head of cattle; beast; **carne de res,** beef

resaca, *f.* undertow

resaltar, *vn.* to rebound; to stand out; to be evident

resbalar, *vn., vr.* to slip, slide

rescate, *m.* ransom

resentimiento, *m.* resentment

resentirse, *vr.* to resent

reseña, *f.* brief description

reserva, *f.* reserve; reservation; **con** or **bajo la mayor reserva,** in strictest confidence

reservado, *adj.* reserved, cautious

reserver, *va.* to reserve

resfriado, *m.* cold (disease)

resfriarse, *vr.* to catch cold

residencia, *f.* residence

residente, *m., f.* resident

residuo, *m.* residue

resignarse, *vr.* to be resigned

resistencia, *f.* resistance

resistir, *vn., va.* to resist, bear; to oppose

resolución, *f.* resolution

resolver, *va., vr.* to resolve, decide

resollar, *vn.* to breathe

resorte, *m.* spring (elastic body)

respaldar, *va.* to indorse; *m.* back (of seats)

respaldo, *m.* indorsement; back of a seat

respecto, *m.* relation, respect; **a** or **con respecto a,** in regard to

respetable, *adj.* respect

respetar, *va.* to respect

respetuoso, *adj.* respectful

respirar, *vn.* to breathe

resplandor, *m.* splendor, brilliance; light

responder, *va.* to answer

resbonsabilidad, *f.* responsibility

responsable, *adj.* responsible

respuesta, *f.* answer, reply

restante, *m.* rest, remainder

restar, *va.* to subtract; *vn.* to be left, remain

restaurante, *m.* restaurant

restaurar, *va.* to restore

restregar, *va.* to scrub, rub

restricción, *f.* restriction

restringir, *va.* to restrain

resucitar, *va., vn.* to revive

resuello, *m.* breath, breathing

resultado, *m.* result

resultar, *vn.* to result

resumen, *m.* summary

resumir, *va.* to resume

retar, *va.* to challenge

retardar, *va.* to retard, delay

retazo, *m.* remnant

retener, *va.* to retain

retina, *f.* retina

retirar, *va.* to withdraw, retire; **retirarse,** to retire, reretreat

reto, *m.* challenge

retocar, *va.* to retouch (a painting or a photograph)

retoño, *m.* sprout, shoot

retoque, *m.* finishing stroke; retouching

retórica, *f.* rhetoric

retornar, *va. vn.* to return, give back

retorno, *m.* return

retrasar, *va.* to defer, put off; **retrasarse,** to be late; to be backward

retraso, *m.* lateness; delay

retratar, *va.* to draw a portrait of; to photograph

retrato, *m.* portrait, photograph; effigy

retrete, *m.* water closet

retribución, *f.* retribution

reuma, *f.* rheumatism

reunión, *n. f.* meeting

reunir, *va., vr.* to reunite

reventar, *vn.* to burst

reverencia, *f.* reverence, respect; bow, curtsy

reverendo, *adj.* reverend

reverso, *m.* reverse

revés, *m.* reverse, wrong side; misfortune; **al revés,** backwards; inside out

revisar, *va.* to revise, review

revista, *f.* revision, review; magazine

revivir, *vn.* to revive

revolcarse, *vr.* to wallow

revolución, *f.* revolution

revolucionario, *adj., m.* revolutionary

revolver, *va.* to stir

revólver, *m.* revolver

rey, *m.* king

rezagado, *adj.* left behind; **cartas rezagadas,** unclaimed letters

rezar, *va.* to pray

riboflavina, *f.* riboflavin

rico, *adj.* rich, wealthy; delicious

ridiculizar, *va.* to ridicule
ridículo, *adj.* ridiculous
riego, *m.* irrigation, watering
riel, *m.* rail
rienda, *f.* rein of a bridle; **a rienda suelta**, without restraint
riesgo, *m.* risk, jeopardy
rifa, *f.* raffle, lottery
riguroso, *adj.* strict
rimar, *va., vn.* to rhyme
rinoceronte, *m.* rhinoceros,
riñón, *m.* kidney
río, *m.* river, stream
R. I. P., Requiescat In Pace, may (he, she) rest in peace
riqueza, *f.* riches, wealth
risa, *f.* laugh, laughter
risueño, *adj.* smiling, pleasant
ritmo *m.* rhythm; tempo
rito, *m.* rite, ceremony
rival, *m.*rival, competitor
rizo, *m.* curl, frizzle
róbalo or **robalo**, *m.* (zool.) bass
roble, *m.* oak tree
robo, *m.* robbery, theft
roca, *f.* rock, cliff
rociar, *va.* to sprinkle
rocío, *m.* dew
rodar, *vn.* to roll
rodear, *vn.* to encompass
rodilla, *f.* knee
rodillo, *m.* roller, cylinder
rogar, *va.* to entreat, beg; to pray
rojo, *adj.* red; ruddy; **Rojo**, *m.* Red (communist)
rol, *m.* list; roll; catalogue
rollo, *m.* roll; spiral
Roma, *f.* Rome
romance, *adj.* romance; *m.* Romance language; ballad; novel of chivalry
romano, romana, *adj., n.* Roman
romanticismo, *m.* romanticism
romántico, *adj.* romantic; *m.* romanticist
rompecabezas, *m.* riddle, puzzle
ron, *m.* rum
roncar, *vn.* to snore
ronquera, *f.* hoarseness

ropa, *f.* clothing
ropero, *m.* clothes closet
rosa, *f.* rose
rosado, *adj.* flushed; rosy, pink
rosario, *m.* rosary
rosbif, *m.* roast beef
rosca, *f.* screw and nut; rusk, twisted roll
roto, *adj.* broken; ragged; torn
rótula, *f.* kneecap
rotular, *va.* to self-address
rótulo, *m.* inscription, label; sign
rotura, *f.* fracture; breakage
r.p.m., revoluciones por minuto, r.p.m., revolutions per minute
rubí, *m.* ruby; **rubíes**, *pl.* jewels of a watch
rubia, *f.* blonde girl
rubio, *adj.* blond, fair
ruborizarse, *vr.* to blush, flush
rueda, *f.* wheel, circle
ruego, *m.* prayer; plea
ruido, *m.* noise –
ruina, *f.* ruin,,downfall
ruiseñor, *m.* nightingale
rumba, *f.* rumba
rumbo, *m.* course, direction; pomp, ostentation
rumboso, *adj.* magnificent, pompous; liberal
rumor, *m.* rumor, report
ruptura, *f.* rupture, break
rural, *adj.* rural
Rusia, *f.* Russia
ruso, rusa, *n., adj.* Russian
rustico, *adj.* rustic, rural; unbound or in a paper cover (of books)
ruta, *f.* route, road
rutina, *f.* routine, habit

· S

S., San or Santo, St. Saint; **segundo**, second; **sur**, So. or so., south
s., sustantivo, *n.* noun
S.ª, Señora, Mrs. Mistress.
S. A., Sociedad Anónima, Inc. Incorporated; **Su Alteza**, His or Her Highness

sábado, *m.* Saturday
sábana, *f.* bed sheet
sábelotodo, *m.* know-it-all
saber, *va.* to know; to be able to; *vn.* to be very sagacious; **saber a**, to taste of; *m.* learning, knowledge; **a saber**, to wit
sabiduría, *f.* knowledge, wisdom
sabiendas, a sabiendas, *adv.* knowingly, with awareness
sabio, *adj.* sage, wise; *m.* sage, scholar
sabor, *m.* taste, flavor
saborear, *va.* to enjoy, relish
sabroso, *adj.* delicious
sacar, *va.* to draw out; to pull out
sacarina, *f.* saccharine
sacerdote, *m.* priest, clergyman
saciar, *va.* to satiate, quench
saco, *m.* sack, bag; man's coat; jacket
sacramento, *m.* sacrament
sacrificar, *va., vr.* to sacrifice
sacrificio, *m.* sacrifice
sacudir, *va.* to shake, jerk
sagrado, *adj.* sacred
sal, *f.* salt; wit, grace
sala, *f.* hall, parlor
salado, *adj.* salted, salty
salar, *va.* to salt
salario, *m.* salary
salchicha, *f.* sausage
saldar, *va.* to settle, pay
saldo, *m.* balance; **saldo acreedor**, credit balance; **saldo deudor**, debit balance
salero, *m.* saltcellar; (coll.) gracefulness
saleroso, *adj.* graceful
salir *vn.* to go out, leave; to appear; to be issued or published
saliva, *f.* saliva
salón, *m.* parlor, hall, salon; **salón de belleza**, beauty parlor
salsa, *f.* sauce, dressing
saltar, *vn.* to leap, jump
salto, *m.* jump; leap, dive; **salto con pértiga**, pole vault; **salto de altura**, high jump;

salto de longitud, broad jump
salud, *f.* health
saludable, *adj.* healthful
saludar, *va.* to greet
saludo, *m.* salute; greeting.
Salvador, *m.* Saviour
salvadoreño, salvadoreña, *n., adj.* Salvadorian
salvar, *va.* to save, rescue
salvavidas, *m.* life preserver
salvo, *adj.* saved, safe; **sano y salvo**, safe and sound; *adv.* excepting
san, *adj.* saint (before masculine proper names)
sanar, *va., vn.* to heal, recover (health)
sanatoria, *m.* sanitarium, sanatorium
sanción, *f.* sanction
sancionar, *va.* to sanction
sandalia, *f.* sandal
sandía, *f.* watermelon
sangrar, *va., vn.* to bleed
sangre, *f.* blood
sangriento, *adj.* bloody
sanitario, *adj.* sanitary
sano, *adj.* sane; healthy.
Santiago, James
santiguar, *va., vr.* to make the sign of the cross
santo, santa, *adj., m.* saint, holy; sacred
sapo, *m.* toad
S. A. R., Su Alteza Real, His or Her Royal Highness
sarampión, *m.* measles
serape, *m.* serape, shawl
sarcasmo, *m.* sarcasm
sarcástico, *adj.* sarcastic
sardina, *f.* sardine
sargento, *m.* sergeant
sartén, *f.* frying pan
sastre, *m.* tailor
Satanás, *m.* Satan
sátira. *f.* satire
satisfacción, *f.* satisfaction; amends, apology
satisfacer, *va.* to atone; **satisfacerse**, to satisfy oneself
satisfactorio, *adj.* satisfactory
satisfecho, *adj.* satisfied
sauce, *m.* (bot.) willow
saxofón, *m.* saxophone

sazonar, *va.* to season; to mature

Sbre., septiembre, Sept., September.

S. C., su casa, your house, (expresssion of kind hospitality)

s. c. or s/c., su cargo or **su cuenta,** (com.) your account; **su casa,** your house (expression of kind hospitality)

s/cta. or s/c., su cuenta, (com.) your account

SE, sudeste, SE or S.E., southeast

sé, second person imperative singular of **ser,** to be; first person indicative singular of **saber,** to know

se, the reflexive pronoun, possessive to the person or thing that governs the verb. It frequently introduces the passive form of a verb, as **Se dice,** It is said

sebo, *m.* suet; tallow

secante, *m.* blotter

sección, *f.* section

seco, *adj.* dry; arid

secretaría, *f.* secretariat; secretary's office

secretario, secretaria, *n.* secretary

secreto, *adj.* secret; hidden; *m.* secret

secuestrar, *va.* to abduct

secundario, *adj.* secondary; **escuela secundaria,** high school

sed, *f.* thirst; **tener sed,** to be thirsty

seda, *f.* silk

sede, *f.* see, seat of episcopal power

sediento, *adj.* thirsty

sedimento, *m.* sediment

seducir, *va.* to seduce; to attract, charm

seductor, *adj.* attractive, fascinating; *m.* seducer

segregar, *va.* to segregate

seguida, *f.* following; succession; **en seguida,** immediately

seguir, *va.* to follow, pursue

según, *prep.* according to; **según aviso,** as per advice

segundo, *adj.* second; *m.* second (of time)

seguridad, *f.* security; certainty, safety, assurance

seguro, *adj.* secure, safe, sure; firm, constant; *m.* insurance

seis, *adj.* six, sixth (of the month); *m.* six

seiscientos, *adj.* six hundred

selección, *f.* selection

selecto, *adj.* select, choice

selva, *f.* forest

sellar, *va.* to seal, stamp

sello, *m.* seal; stamp; **sello de correo,** postage stamp

semana, *f.* week

semanal, *adj.* weekly

semanario, *adj.* weekly; *m.* weekly publication

sembrar, *va.* to sow, plant

semejante, *adj.* similar, like; *m.* fellow creature

semejanza, *f.* resemblance

semestral, *adj.* semiyearly

semestre, *m.* semester

semi, prefix denoting half

semianual, *adj.* semiannual

semifinal, *adj.* semifinal

senado, *m.* senate

senador, *m.* senator

sencillez, *f.* simplicity; naturalness, candor

sencillo, *adj.* simple; plain

senda, *f.* path, footpath

sendos, *adj. pl.* having one apiece

seno, *m.* breast, bosom; lap; sinus; asylum, refuge

sensación, *f.* sensation, feeling

sensato, *adj.* sensible, wise

sensible, *adj.* sensitive; regrettable; soft-hearted

sentado, *adj.* seated; **dar por sentado,** to take for granted

sentar, *va.* to sit; to seat; **sentarse,** to sit down

sentencia, *f.* sentence, opinion; verdict

sentenciar, *va.* to sentence, pass judgment

sentido, *m.* sense; reason; meaning

sentimental, *adj.* sentimental

sentimiento, *m.* sentiment; grief; feeling; sensation

sentir, *va.* to feel; to regret; to mourn; to think; to foresee; **sentirse,** to be hurt or offended

seña, *f.* sign, mark; password; **señas,** *pl.* address

señal, *f.* sign, signal

señalar, *va.* to mark; to point out

señor, *m.* lord; sir; master; **muy señor mio** or **nuestro,** dear sir; el **Señor,** the Lord

señora, *f.* lady; mistress\

señoría, *f.* lordship

señorita, *f.* young lady,miss

separación, *f.* separation

separado, *adj.* separate, apart; **por separado,** under separate rate cover

separar, *va.* to separate; **separarse,** to separate, to withdraw

sepelio, *m.* burial

septentrional, *adj.* northern

septiembre, *m.* September

séptimo, *adj.* seventh

sepulcro, *m.* sepulcher, grave, tomb

sequía, *f.* dryness; drought

ser, *vn.* to be; to exist; *m.* being, life

serenata, *f.* serenade

serenidad, *f.* serenity, quiet

sereno, *m.* night dampness; night watchman; *adj.* serene, calm; quiet

serie, *f.* series

seriedad, *f.* seriousness

serigrafía, *f.* silkscreen

serio, *adj.* serious, grave

serrucho, *m.* handsaw

servicial, *adj.* diligent

servicio, *m.* service

servidor, *m.* servant, waiter; **su servidor,** at your service; yours truly

servidora, *f.* maidservant; **su servidora,** at your service; yours truly

servil, *adj.* servile, cringing

servilleta, *f.* napkin

servir, *va.* to serve

sesenta, *m., adj.* sixty

sesgo, *m.* bias

sesión, *f.* session, meeting

seso, *m.* brain

setenta, *m., adj.* seventy

severo, *adj.* rigorous

sexagésimo, *adj.* sixtieth

sexismo, *m.* sexism

sexo, *m.* sex

sexto, *adj.* sixth

s/f., su favor, your favor

s/g: su giro, (com.) your draft

si, *conj.* if, whether; *m.* (mus.) si, seventh note of the scale

sí, *adv.* yes; indeed; *pron.* himself; herself; itself; themselves; **volver en sí,** to come to, to recover one's senses

sicoanalizar, *va.* to psychoanalyze

sicología, *f.* psychology

sideral, *adj.* sidereal, astral, space; **viajes siderales,** space travel

siderúrgico, siderúrgica, *adj.* pertaining to iron and steel

siempre, *adv.* always, ever

sien, *f.* temple (of the head)

sierra, *f.* saw; range of mountains

siete, *m., adj.* seven

sífilis, *f.* syphilis

siglo, *m.* century

significado, *m.* meaning

signo, *m.* sign, mark

siguiente, *adj.* following, successive

sílaba, *f.* syllable

silbido, *m.* hiss; whistling

sima, *f.* abyss, gulf

símbolo, *m.* symbol; device

símil, *m.* (rhet.) simile

similar, *adj.* similar

simpatía, *f.* sympathy; charm; **tener simpatía por,** to like someone, to find (someone) pleasant and congenial

simpático *adj.* sympathetic; likable, charming

simpatizar, *vn.* to sympathize; to be congenial

simple, *adj.* simple, silly; insipid

simplificar, *va.* to simplify

simultáneo, *adj.* simultaneous

sin, *prep.* without; **sin embargo,** notwithstanding, nevertheless

sinceridad, *f.* sincerity

sincero, *adj.* sincere, honest

sindicato, *m.* syndicate

sinfonía, *f.* symphony

singular, *adj.* singular; unique

siniestro, *adj.* left (side); sinister; unhappy

sinnúmero, *m.* no end; numberless quantity

sino, *conj.* (after a negative), but; except; besides; only; *m.* destiny, fate.

sinónimo, *m.* synonym; *adj.* synonymous

sintético, *adj.* synthetic

síntoma, *m.* symptom

sinvergüenza, *m.* cad, bounder

siquiatra, *m.* psychiatrist

siquiera, *conj.* at least; though, although; **ni siquiera,** not even

sirena, *f.* foghorn, siren; mermaid

sirviente, sirvienta, *n.* servant

sistema, *m.* system, plan

sistemático, *adj.* systematic

situación, *f.* situation, state, condition

ski, *m.* ski

s/l or **s/L, su letra** (com.) your letter or draft

S. M., Su Majestad, His or Her Majesty

smoking, *m.* Tuxedo coat.

SO, sudoeste, SW or S.W. Southwest

s/o, su orden, (com.) your order

so, *prep.* under; below; **so pena de multa** or **muerte,** under penalty of fine or death

sobaco, *m.* armpit

sobar, *va.* to massage

soberanía, *f.* sovereignty

soberano, soberana, *adj., n.* sovereign

soberbio, *adj.* proud, haughty

soborno, *m.* bribe

sobra, *f.* surplus, excess; remainder; **de sobra,** over and above

sobrante, *m.* residue, surplus

sobrar, *vn.* to have more than is necessary; to be more than enough; to remain

sobre, *prep.* above, over; on, about; *m.* envelope

sobrecama, *f.* bedspread

sobrehumano, *adj.* superhuman

sobrellevar, *va.* to suffer, tolerate

sobremanera, *adv.* exceedingly

sobremesa, *f.* table cover; dessert; **de sobremesa,** immediately after dinner

sobrenombre, *m.* nickname

sobreponerse, *vr.* to master; to show oneself superior to

sobresaliente, *adj.* outstanding, excellent

sobretodo, *m.* overcoat

sobreviviente, *m., f.* survivor

sobrevivir, *vn.* to survive

sobrina, *f.* niece

sobrino, *m.* nephew

sobrio, *adj.* sober, frugal.

Soc., Sociedad, Soc., Society; Co., Company

sociable, *adj.* sociable

social, *adj.* social; **razón social,** firm name

socialista, *m., f.* socialist; *adj.* socialistic

sociedad, *f.* society, company, partnership; **sociedad anónima,** corporation

socio, socia, *n.* associate, partner, member

sociológico, *adj.* sociological

socorrer, *va.* to succor, help, rescue

socorro, *m.* help, aid

sofá, *m.* sofa, couch; **sofá cama,** studio couch

sofocar, *va.* to suffocate; to harass

soga, *f.* rope

sol, *m.* sun; a silver coin of Peru; (mus.) sol

solapa, *f.* lapel

solar, *m.* plot of ground; lot; *adj.* solar; **luz solar,** sun-

shine
solaz, *m.* solace, consolation
soldado, *m.* soldier
soleded, *f.* solitude; lonely place; desert
solicitar, *va.* to solicit; to apply for
solícito, *adj.* solicitous
solicitud, *f.* solicitude, application, petition; **a solicitud,** on request
sólido, *adj.* solid
solitario, a *i.* solitary, lonely
solo, *m.* (mus.) solo; **sola,** *adj.* alone, single
sólo, *adv.* only
soltar, *va.* to untie, loosen, to set at liberty; **soltarse,** to get loose
soltero, *adj.* unmarried; *m.* bachelor; **soltera,** bachelor girl
sollozo, *m.* sob
sombra, *f.* shade, shadow
sombrerera, *f.* hatbox
sombrereria, *f.* hat shop
sombrero, *m.* hat
sombrilla, *f.* parasol
someter, *va.* to submit; to subject
son, *m.* sound, report; Cuban musical rhythm
sonar, *vn.* to sound; to ring; **sonarse,** to blow one's nose
soneto, *m.* sonnet
sonido, *m.* sound
sonoro, *adj.* sonorous
sonreir, *vn., vr.* to smile
sonrisa, *f.* smile
sonrojarse, *vr.* to blush
soñar, *va., vn.* to dream
sopa, *f.* soup
soplar, *va.* to blow; to prompt; **soplarse,** to swell up
sopor, *m.* drowsiness
soporte, *m.* support; brassière
soportar, *va.* to suffer, bear
sorber, *va.* to sip
sordera, *f.* deafness
sordo, *adj.* deaf
sordomudo, sordomuda, *n., adj.* deaf and dumb; mute
sorprendente, *adj.* surprising
sorprender, *va.* to surprise
sorpresa, *f.* surprise

sorteo, *m.* raffle
sortija, *f.* ring; hoop
soso, *adj.* insipid, tasteless
sospecha, *f.* suspicion
sospechar, *va., vn.* to suspect
sospechoso, *adj.* suspicious
sostén, *m.* support
sostenido, *m.* (mus.) sharp (#)
sostenimiento, *m.* sustenance; support
sótano, *m.* cellar, basement
soviet, *m.* soviet
soya, *f.* soybean
s/p, su pagaré, (com.) your promissory note
Sr. or **S.ʳ, Señor,** Mr., Mister
s/r, su remesa, (com.) your remittance or shipment
Sra. or **S.ʳᵃ, Señora,** Mrs., Mistress
Sres. or **S.ʳᵉˢ, Señores,** Messrs., Messieurs
Sría., Secretaría, secretary's office
srio, or **S.ʳⁱᵒ, secretario,** sec., secretary
Srta, or **S.ʳᵗᵃ, Señorita,** Miss
S. S or **s. s., seguro servidor,** devoted servant
S. S., Su Santidad, His Holiness
SS.ᵐᵒ P., Santísimo Padre, Most Holy Father
S.S.S. or **s.s.s., su seguro servidor,** your devoted servant, yours truly
SS. SS. SS. or **ss. ss. ss., sus seguros servidores,** your devoted servants, yours truly
Sto., Santo, St., Saint (masculine)
su, *pron.* his, her, its, one's; **sus,** their
suave, *adj.* smooth, soft
suavizar, *va., vr.* to soften
subasta, *f.* auction
subconsciente, *adj.* subconscious
súbdito, súbdita, *n., adj.* subject (of a king, etc.)
subgerente, *m.* assistant manager
subir, *vn.* to mount, climb; to increase
súbitamente, *adv.* suddenly

subjuntivo, m. (gram.) subjunctive

sublime, adj. sublime, exalted

submarino, m. submarine

subnormal, adj. subnormal

subordinar, va. to subordinate

subrayar, va. to underline

subsecuente, adj. subsequent

subsidio, m. subsidy, aid

subsiguiente, adj. subsequent

subsistir, vn. to subsist, last

subteniente, m. second lieutenant

subterfugio, m. subterfuge

subterráneo, adj. underground; m. subway; cave

suburbano, adj. suburban

suburbio, m. suburb

subvención, f. subsidy

subyugar, va. to subdue

suceder, vn. to succeed, inherit; to happen

sucesión, f. succession; issue, offspring; hereditary succession

sucesivo, adj. successive; **en lo sucesivo**, from now on

suceso, m. outcome, event

sucesor, sucesora, n. successor

sucio, adj. dirty filthy

sucre, m. sucre, monetary unit of Ecuador

Suc.res, **Sucesores**, successors

suculento, adj. succulent

sucumbir, vn. to succumb, perish

sucursal, adj. subsidiary; f. branch, annex

sud, m. south; south wind (used instead of **sur**, when joined to another word)

sudamericano, sudamericana, adj., n. South American

sudar, va., vn. to sweat, perspire

sudeste, m. southeast

sudoeste, m. southwest

sudor, m. sweat, perspiration

Suecia, f. Sweden

sueco, sueca, n., adj. Swedish

suegra, f. mother-in-law

suegro, m. father-in-law

suela, f. sole of the shoe

sueldo, m. salary, pay

suelo, m. floor; ground

suelto, adj. loose; m. change (money); newspaper item

sueño, m. sleep; vision, dream; **tener sueño**, to be sleepy

suero, m. whey; serum (of blood)

suerte, f. chance, lot, fate; **tener suerte**, to be lucky

suficiente, adj. sufficient

sufijo, m. suffix

sufragio, m. vote, suffrage

sufrido, adj. long suffering

sufrimiento, m. sufferance, patience

sufrir, va. to suffer, bear with patience; to undergo

suicidarse, vr. to commit suicide

suicidio, m. suicide

Suiza, f. Switzerland

suizo, suiza, n., adj. Swiss

sujetar, va. to subdue; to subject; to hold; to fasten

sujeto, adj. subject, liable, exposed; m. subject, topic

sultán, m. sultan

suma, f. sum; substance

sumar, va. to add, sum up

sumario, m. summary

suministrar, va. to supply, furnish

suntuoso, adj. sumptuous

superar, va. to surpass, excel

supercarretera, f. superhighway

superhombre, m. superman

superintendente, m. superintendent

superior, adj. superior; upper (in geography); **parte superior**, topside; m. superior

superioridad, f. superiority

superlativo, adj., m. superlative

supermercado, m. supermarket

superstición, f. superstition

super.te, **superintendente**, supt., superintendent

suplente, adj. alternate

súplica, f. petition, request

suplicar, va. to entreat; to

pray, plead

suplir, *va.* to supply; to supplant

supl.ᵗᵉ, suplente, sub., substitute

suponer, *va.* to suppose, surmise

suposición, *f.* supposition, conjecture, basis

supremo, *adj.* supreme:

supresión, *f.* suppression

suprimir, *va.* to suppress; to abolish

supuesto, *m.* supposition; *adj.* supposed, false, assumed; **por supuesto**, of course

sur, *m.* south; south wind

suroeste, *m.* southwest

surtir, *va.* to supply, provide

susceptible, *adj.* susceptible

suscitar, *va.* to excite, stir up

suscribir, *va., vr.* to subscribe; to sign

suscripción, *f.* subscription

suscriptor, suscriptora, *n.* subscriber

susodicho, *adj.* above-mentioned, aforesaid

suspender, *va.* to suspend, stop, cease; to raise up

suspenso, *adj.* suspended, unfinished

suspicaz, *adj.* suspicious, distrustful

suspirar, *vn.* to sigh

suspiro, *m.* sigh

sustancia, *f.* substance

sustancioso, *adj.* substantial, nutritious

sustantivo, *adj., m.* noun

sustento, *m.* sustenance, support

sustitución, *f.* substitution

sustituir, *va.* to substitute

sustituto, sustituta, *adj., n.* substitute

susto, *m.* fright, terror

sustracción, *f.* subtraction

sustraer, *va.* to subtract; **sustraerse**, to retire, withdraw

sutil, *adj.* subtle

sutileza, *f.* subtlety, cunning; finesse; delicacy

suyo, suya, *adj.* his, hers, theirs, one's; his, her, its

own, one's own or their own; **los suyos**, *m. pl.* their own, close friends, relations

T

tabaco, *m.* tobacco

tabla, *f.* board; table; **las tablas**, the stage

tablero, *m.* chessboard; checkerboard; blackboard

tableta, *f.* tablet

tablilla, *f.* tablet, slab; bulletin board

taburete, *m.* stool

tacaño, *adj.* miserly, stingy

taco, *m.* stopper, stopple; wad; billiard cue; (Mex.) sandwich made with a **tortilla**

tacón, *m.* shoe heel

tacto, *m.* touch; tact

tacha, *f.* fault, defect

tachar, *va.* to find fault with; to blot, efface

tafetán, *m.* taffeta

tajada, *f.* slice

tajar, *va.* to cut, chop

tal, *adj.* such; **con tal que**, provided that; **¿qué tal?** how goes it? **tal vez**, perhaps

taladro, *m.* drill

talco, *m.* talc, talcum

talego, *m.* sack

talento, *m.* talent

talón, *m.* heel; (com.) receipt, check; check stub

talonario, *m.* check stubs; **libro talonario**, checkbook; receipt book

talla, *f.* stature, size

tallado, *adj.* cut, carved, engraved

tallar, *va.* to carve in wood

tallarín, *m.* noodle (for soup)

talle, *m.* shape, figure, size; waist

taller, *m.* workshop

tallo, *m.* shoot, sprout, stem

tamal, *m.* tamale

tamaño, *m.* size, shape

tambalear, *vn., vr.* to stagger, waver

también, *adv.* also, too, likewise; as well

tambor, *m.* drum; drummer;

iron cylinder

tamborito, *m.* national folk dance of Panama

tampoco, *adv.* neither, not either (used to enforce a foregoing negative)

tan, *adv.* so, so much, as well, as much; **tan pronto como,** as soon as

tanda, *f.* turn; rotation; shift

Tánger, Tangier

tangible, *adj.* tangible

tango, *m.* tango

tanque, *m.* tank; reservoir, pool

tanto, *m.* certain sum or quantity; *adj.* so much, as much; very great; *adv.* so, in such a manner; a long time; **mientras tanto,** meanwhile; **por lo tanto,** therefore; **tantos,** *pl.* score, points

tapa, *f.* lid, cover

tapacubos, *m.* hub cap

tapar, *va.* to cover; to close; to conceal, hide

tapete, *m.* rug; runner

tapizar, *va.* to upholster

tapón, *m.* cork, plug

taquigrafía, *f.* shorthand, stenography

taquigrafo, taquigrafa, *n.* stenographer

taquilla, *f.* box office

tararear, *va.* to hum (a tune)

tardanza, *f.* tardiness, delay

tardar, *vn., vr.* to delay, put off; **a más tardar,** at the latest

tarde, *f.* afternoon, early evening **buenas tardes,** good afternoon; *adv.* late

tardío, *adj.* slow, tardy

tarea, *f.* task

tarifa, *f.* tariff, charge, rate, fare; price list

tarima, *f.* platform

tarjeta, *f.* card; **tarjeta, postal,** post card

tarro, *m.* jar; mug

tartamudear, *vn.* to stutter, stammer

tasar, *va.* to appraise, value

taxi, *m.* taxicab

taza, *f.* cup; cupful; bowl

te, *pron.* objective and dative cases of **tú** (thou)

té, *m.* tea

teatral, *adj.* theatrical

testro, *m.* theater

tecla, *f.* key of an instrument; key of a typewriter

teclado, *m.* keyboard

técnico, *adj.* technical; **técnica,** *f.* technique; *m.* technician

tecnológico, *adj.* technological

techo, *m.* roof, ceiling; (coll.) dwelling house; **bajo techo,** indoors

tedio, *m.* disgust; boredom

teja, *f.* roof tile

tejer, *va.* to weave, knit

tejido, *m.* texture, web; textile, fabric; (anat.) tissue

telaraña, *f.* cobweb

telef., teléfono, tel., telephone

telefonear, *va., vn.* to telephone

telefonista, *m., f.* telephone operator

teléfono, *m.* telephone

teleg., telegrama, tel., telegram; **telégrafo,** tel. telegraph

telegrafiar, *va., vn.* to telegraph

telégrafo, *m.* telegraph

telegrama, *m.* telegram

telerreceptor, *m.* television set

telescopio, *m.* telescope

televisión, *f.* television

telón, *m.* curtain, backdrop in a theater

tema, *m.* theme; subject

temblor, *m.* trembling, tremor; earthquake

temer, *va., vn.* to fear; to doubt

temeroso, *adj.* timid

temible, *adj.* dreadful, inspiring awe or fear

temor, *m.* dread, fear

témpano, *m.* tympanum; block; iceberg

temperatura, *f.* temperature

tempestad, *f.* tempest; storm

templo, *m.* temple, church

temporada, *f.* period, season

temporal, *adj.* temporary; *m.* tempest, storm

temprano, *adj.* early, anticipated; *adv.* early, prematurely

tenacidad, *f.* tenacity

tenaz, *adj.* tenacious; stubborn

tender, *va.* to spread, expand, extend; to have a tendency

tendón, *m.* tendon, sinew

tenedor, tenedora, *n.* holder; payee (of bill of exchange); **tenedor de libros,** bookkeeper, accountant; *m.* fork

tener, *va.* to take, hold; to possess; to have; **tener cuidado,** to be careful

tenería, *f.* tanyard, tannery

teniente, *m.* lieutenant

tenis, *m.* tennis

tenor, *m.* kind; condition, nature; meaning; (mus.) tenor

tensión, *f.* tension, strain

tentación, *f.* temptation

tentar, *va.* to touch; to grope; to tempt

tentativa, *f.* attempt, trial

ten.te, **teniente,** Lt. or Lieut., Lieutenant

tentempié, *m.* snack, bite

teñir, *va.* to tinge, dye

teoría, *f.* theory

tequila, *m.* tequila (a Mexican liquor)

tercero, *adj.* third; *m.* third person; mediator

tercio, *m., adj.* third

terciopelo, *m.* velvet

terco, *adj.* stubborn

terminante, *adj.* decisive; absolute, strict

terminar, *va.* to finish

término, *m.* term; end; boundary; limit; **término medio,** average

termómetro, *m.* thermometer

termos, *m.* thermos bottle

ternero, ternera, *n.* calf; veal; heifer

terneza, *f.* tenderness

ternura, *f.* tenderness

terquedad, *f.* obstinacy

terraza, *f.* terrace, veranda

terremoto, *m.* earthquake

terreno, *m.* land, ground

terrestre, *adj.* earthly

terrible, *adj.* terrible, dreadful

territorial, *adj.* territorial

territorio, *m.* territory

terror, *m.* terror, dread

terruño, *m.* native land

terso, *adj.* smooth, terse

tertulia, *f.* informal gathering; conversation

tesorería, *f.* treasury

tesorero, tesorera, *n.* treasurer

tesoro, *m.* treasure

testamento, *m.* will, testament

testar, *va., vn.* to make one's will; to bequeath

testarudo, *adj.* obstinate

testículo, *m.* testicle

testigo, *m.* witness

testimonio, *m.* testimony

teta, *f.* dug, teat

tétano, *m.* tetanus, lockjaw

tetera, *f.* teapot, teakettle

textil, *adj., m.* textile

texto, *m.* text

tez. *f.* complexion of the face; hue

ti, *pron.* objective or dative case of **tu**

tía, *f.* aunt

tibio, *adj.* lukewarm

tiburón, *m.* shark

tictac, *m.* ticktock

tiempo, *m.* time, term; season, weather; tempo

tienda, *f.* shop; tent

tierno, *adj.* tender; young; delicate, soft

tierra, *f.* earth; soil; land, ground; native country

tieso, *adj.* stiff, hard, firm; taut

tifoideo, *adj.* typhoid; **tifoidea,** *f.* typhoid fever

tigre, *m.* tiger

tijeras, *f. pl.* scissors

tilde, *f.* tilde, diacritical sign of the letter **ñ**

timbrazo, *n.* sharp bell ring

timbre, *m.* postage stamp; call bell; timbre

timidez, *f.* timidity

tímpano, *m.* kettledrum; eardrum

tina, *f.* tub; **tina de baño**, bathtub

tinaja, *f.* large earthen jar for water

tiniebla, *f.* darkness, obscurity

tino, *m.* good aim; tact; good judgment

tinta, *f.* tint, hue; ink

tinte, *m.* tint, dye

tintero, *m.* inkwell

tintorería, *f.* dry cleaning shop

tío, *m.* uncle

típico, *adj.* typical

tipo, *m.* type, model, pattern; rate, standard; **tipo de cambio**, rate of exchange

tipográfico, *adj.* typographical

tira, *f.* strip

tirabtizón, *m.* corkscrew

tirada, *f.* cast, throw; stroke (golf); edition, issue; presswork

tirador, *m.* doorknob; door knocker

tiranía, *f.* tyranny

tirano, *adj.* tyrannical; **tirana**, *n.* tyrant

tirante, *adj.* taut; **tirantes**, *m. pl.* suspenders

tirar, *va.* to throw, toss, cast; to pull, draw; to shoot; *vn.* to tend, incline

tiritar, *vn.* to shiver

tiro, *m.* cast, throw; shot

tiroides, *adj.*, *f.* (anat.) thyroid (gland)

tirón, *m.* pull, haul, tug; **de un tirón**, all at once, at one stroke

tiroteo, *m.* random shooting, skirmish

tísico, *adj.* tubercular

tisis, *f.* consumption, tuberculosis

titubeo, *m.* hesitation, wavering

tiza, *f.* chalk

tobillera, *f.* anklet; bobbysoxer

tobillo, *m.* ankle

tocador, *m.* dressing table, boudoir

tocar, *va.* to touch; (mus.) to play; to ring a bell; *vn.* to belong; to behoove, fall to one's share

tocayo, tocaya, *n.* namesake

tocino, *m.* bacon, salt pork

todavía, *adv.* yet, still

todopoderoso, *adj.* almighty

tolerante, *adj.* tolerant

tolerar, *vn.* to tolerate

tomar, *va.* to take, seize; to drink

tomate, *m.* tomato

tomo, *m.* tome; volume

tonada, *f.* tune, melody, air

tonelada, *f.* ton

tónico, *m.* tonic

tontería, *f.* nonsense

tonto, *adj.* stupid, foolish; **tonto, tonta**, *n.* fool, dunce

tope, *m.* butt, rub; scuffle; **topes**, *pl.* (rail.) buffers; *adj.* high; **precio tope**, ceiling price

tópico, *m.* topic, subject

toque, *m.* touch; bell ringing; (mil.) call

torbellino, *m.* whirlwind

torcer, *va.* to twist; distort; **torcerse**, to go crooked or astray

torcido, *adj.* twisted

toreo, *m.* bullfighting

torero, *m.* bullfighter

tormenta, *f.* storm, tempest

tormento, *m.* torment

torneo, *m.* tournament

tornillo, *m.* bolt; screw

torno, *m.* lathe; wheel; wheel and axle; dentist's drill

toro, *m.* bull

toronja, *f.* grapefruit

torpe, *adj.* dull, heavy; stupid, awkward

torpeza, *f.* heaviness, stupidity

torrente, *m.* torrent

torso, *m.* trunk, torso

torta, *f.* tart, cake

tortilla, *f.* omelet; (Mex.) kind of pancake

tortuga, *f.* tortoise; turtle

tos, *f.* cough

toser, *vn.* to cough

tostada, *f.* slice of toast; (Mex.)

open-faced meat tart
tostador, *m.* toaster
tostar, *va.* to toast
total, *m.* whole, totality; *adj.* total, entire
totalmente, *adv.* totally
tr., transitive, tr., transitive
traba, *f.* obstacle
trabajar, *va., vn.* to work, labor
trabajo, *m.* work, labor, toil; workmanship; difficulty, trouble
trabajoso, *adj.* laborious
traducción, *f.* translation
traducir, *va.* to translate
traductor, traductora, *n.* translator
traer, *va.* to bring, carry, wear
tráfico, *m.* traffic, trade
tragaluz, *m.* skylight
tragar, *va.* to swallow, glut
trago, *m.* draft of liquor; drink
tragón, *adj.* gluttonous
traición, *f.* treason
traicionar, *va.* to betray
traidor, traidora, *n.* traitor; *adj.* treacherous
traje, *m.* dress, suit, costume; **traje espacial,** space suit
trajinar, *va.* to convey; to bustle about one's work
trama, *f.* plot, conspiracy; weft or woof (of cloth)
tramar, *va.* to weave; to plot
trámite, *m.* requirement; step, passage; (law) procedure
tramo, *m.* flight of stairs; span of a bridge; stretch, section
trampa, *f.* trap, snare; trap door; fraud; **hacer trampa,** to cheat
tramposo, *adj.* deceitful, swindling
trancar, *va.* to barricade
trance, *m.* danger; hypnotic condition; last stage of life; **a todo trance,** at all costs
tranquilidad, *f.* tranquility
tranquilizar, *va., vr.* to soothe, quiet
tranquilo, *adj.* calm, quiet
transacción, *f.* transaction; adjustment
transición, *f.* transition

transigir, *va.* to compromise; *vn.* to give in
tránsito, *m.* passage; road, way; traffic
tranvía, *m.* streetcar
trapo, *m.* rag, tatter
tras, *prep.* after, behind
trasatlántico, *adj., m.* transatlantic
trasbordar, *va.* to transfer, change cars
trascendencia, *f.* transcendency; importance
trascendental, *adj.* transcendental
trascribir, *va.* to transcribe, copy
trascurso, *m.* course (of time)
trasero, *adj.* hind, hinder; **asiento trasero,** back seat; *m.* buttock
trasferir, *va.* to transfer
trasformación, *f.* transformation
trasformar, *va.* to transform
trasfusión, *f.* transfusion
trasladar, *va.* to transport, transfer
trasmisión, *f.* transmission
trasmitir, *va.* to transmit, send
trasnochar, *vn.* to watch, sit up all night
trasparente, *adj.* transparent
traspasar, *va.* to pass over; to trespass; to transfer
trasplantar, *va.* to transplant
trasportar, *va.* to transport, convey; (mus.) to transpose
trasporte, *m.* transportation; transport
trastornado, *adj.* unbalanced, crazy
trastorno, *m.* confusion, upset, overthrow
tratable, *adj.* compliant, pliant; pleasant
tratado, *m.* treaty
tratar, *va.* to treat on a subject; to trade; to treat
trato, *m.* treatment; manner; deal; dealing
travesía, *f.* crossing, voyage; distance
trazar, *va.* to plan out; to pro-

ject; to trace

trébol, *m.* (bot.) clover; **hoja de trébol**, cloverleaf

trece, *m.*, *adj.* thirteen; thirteenth

trecientos, *adj.*, *m.* three hundred

tregua, *f.* truce, recess; **sin tregua**, unceasingly

treinta, *m.*, *adj.* thirty

tremendo, *adj.* tremendous

tren, *m.* train, retinue; (rail.) train

trepar, *vn.* to climb, crawl

tres, *adj.*, *m.* three

trescientos, *adj.*, *m.* three hundred

triangular, *adj.* triangular

triángulo, *m.* triangle

tribu, *f.* tribe

tribuna, *f.* tribune, rostrum

tribunal, *m.* tribunal, court of justice

tributar, *va.* to pay tribute

tributo, *m.* tribute; tax

tricolor, *adj.* tricolored

trigésimo, *adj.* thirtieth

trigueño, *adj.* swarthy, brunet

trimestre, *m.* quarter, space of three months

trinar, *vn.* to trill, quaver

trinchante, *m.* carver; carving knife

trinchera, *f.* trench

trineo, *m.* sleigh, sled

trío, *m.* (mus.) trio

tripa, *f.* gut, entrails, tripe, intestine

triple, *adj.* triple, treble

triplicar, *va.* to treble, triple

tripulación, *f.* crew of a ship

triste, *adj.* sad, mournful

tristeza, *f.* sadness

triunfal, *adj.* triumphal

triunfante, *adj.* triumphant

triunfar, *vn.* to triumph

triunfo, *m.* triumph; trump (in cards)

trivial, *adj.* trivial

triza, *f.* mite; bit, shred

trompa, *f.* trumpet; trunk (of elephants)

trompeta, *f.* trumpet, horn; *m.* trumpeter

trompo, *m.* spinning top

tronco, *m.* tree trunk; log of wood; origin

trono, *m.* throne

tropa, *f.* troop

tropezar, *vn.* to stumble

tropical, *adj.* tropical

trópico, *m.* tropics

tropiezo, *m.* stumble, trip

tropo, *m.* figu speech

trote, *m.* trot; **a trote**, in haste

trovador, **trovadora**, *n.* minstrel

trozo, *m.* piece, fragment

trucha, *f.* trout; crane

trueno, *m.* thunderclap

tu, *adj.* possessive sing. of pronoun **tú**

tú, *pron.* thou, you (*sing.* familiar form)

tuberculosis, *f.* tuberculosis

tubería, *f.* pipe line; tubing; piping

tubo, *m.* tube, pipe, duct

tuerca, *f.* nut (of a screw)

tuerto, *adj.* one-eyed; squint-eyed

tul, *m.* tulle (cloth)

tulipán, *m.* tulip

tullido, *adj.* crippled, maimed

tumba, *f.* tomb, grave

tumbar, *va.*, *vn.* to tumble

tumor, *m.* tumor

túnel, *m.* tunnel

túnica, *f.* tunic

turbante, *m.* turban

turborreactor, *m.* turbojet

turbulento, *adj.* turbid, muddy; stormy, turbulent

turco, **turca**, *n.*, *adj.* Turkish, Turk

turismo, *m.* touring, tourism

turista, *m.*, *f.* tourist

turnar, *vn.* to alternate

turno, *m.* turn; shift

turquesa, *f.* turquoise

turquí, *adj.* turquoise blue

Turquía, *f.* Turkey

turrón, *m.* nougat, candy

tutora, *f.* tutoress

tuyo, **tuya**, *adj.* thine; **los tuyos**, *pl.* thy family, thy people, etc

U

u, *conj.* or (used instead of **o**, when the following word begins with **o** or **ho**)

ubicar, *vn., vr.* to be located

ubre, *f.* dug, teat, udder

Ud., usted, *pron.* you (sing.)

Uds., ustedes, *pron.* you

úlcera, *f.* ulcer

últimamente, *adv.* lately

útimo, *adj.* last, latest; late, latter; remote, final

últ.º, último, ult. last

ultrajar, *va.* to outrage; to abuse

ultramar, *adj., m.* overseas

umbral, *m.* threshold, doorstep; beginning

un, una, *adj.* a, an; one

unánime, *adj.* unanimous

unanimidad, *f.* unanimity

undécimo, *adj.* eleventh

ungüento, *m.* ointment

único, *adj.* unique, only

unidad, *f.* unity; unit

uniforme, *adj., m.* uniform

uniformidad, *f.* uniformity

union, *f.* union

unir, *va.* to join, unite; **unirse**, to associate, get together

universal, *adj.* universal

universidad, *f.* university

universo, *m.* universe

uno, *m.* one; *adj.* one; sole, only

uña, *f.* nail; hoof; claw

urbanidad, *f.* good manners

urbe, *f.* metropolis

urgencia, *f.* urgency, need

urgente, *adj.* urgent

urinario, *adj.* urinary

urraca, *f.* magpie

uruguayo, uruguaya, *n., adj.* Uruguayan

usado, *adj.* used; worn

usar, *va.* to use, make use of; **usarse**, to be in use, be customary

uso, *m.* use, service; custom; mode

usted, *pron.* you (sing.); **ustedes**, you (plural); **usted mismo**, you yourself

útero, *m.* uterus, womb

útil, *adj.* useful, profitable; **útiles**, *m. pl.* utensils, tools

utilidad, *f.* utility; usefulness; profit

utilizar, *va.* to make use of

uva, *f.* grape

V

v., véase, vid., see, refer to; **verbo**, verb

v/, valor, val., value; amt., amount

V. A., Vuestra Alteza, Your Highness. **Versión Autorizada**, A. V., Authorized Version

vaca, *f.* cow

vacaciones, *f. pl.* holidays, vacations

vacante, *adj.* vacant; *f.* vacancy

vaciar, *va.* to empty, clear; to mold; *vn.* to fall, decrease (of waters)

vacilar, *vn.* to hesitate

vacio, *adj.* void, empty; unoccupied; *m.* vacuum; concavity

vacuna, *f.* vaccine

vacunar, *va.* to vaccinate

vacuno, *adj.* bovine

vagón,*m.* car, freight car, coach; **vagón cama**, sleeping car

vahido, *m.* dizziness

vainilla,*f.* vanilla

vaivén,*m.* fluctuation, motion

vajilla, *f.* table service, set of dishes

vale, *m.* promissory note, I.O.U

valenciano, valenciana, *adj., n.* Valencian, from Valencia

valentía, *f.* valor, courage

valer, *vn.* to be valuable, be deserving; to be valid; **valer la pena**, to be worthwhile; **valerse**, to employ; to have recourse to

vilidez, *f.* validity

válido, *adj.* valid; obligatory

valiente, *adj.* brave, courageous

vafija, *f.* valise; mail bag

valioso, *adj.* valuable

valor, *m.* value, price; courage, valor

valorar, *va.* to value

vals, *m.* waltz

valuación, *f.* valuation, appraisal

valle, *m.* valley

¡vamos! *interj.* well let's go! stop!

vanagloriarse, *vr.* to boast

vanidad, *f.* vanity

vanidoso, *adj.* vain, conceited

vano, *adj.* vain; useless; **en vano**, in vain

vapor, *m.* vapor, steam; steamer, steamship

vaquero, *m.* cowherd; herdsman, cowboy; *adj.* pertaining to cowboys

vara, *f.* rod; pole, staff; yard (measure); **vara alta**, sway, high hand

variación, *adj.* variation

variado, varied

variar, *va.* to vary, change; *vn.* to vary

varieded, *f.* variety; diversity

variedades, *f. pl.* variety show

varios, *adj. pl.* some, several

varón, *m.* man, male human being; man of respectability

varonil, *adj.* male, masculine; manful

vaselina, *f.* vaseline, petroleum jelly

vasija, *f.* pot

vaso, *m.* vessel; jar

vástago, *m.* bud, shoot; descendant

vasto, *adj.* vast, huge

¡vaya! *interj.* well, now!

Vd., usted, you (sing.)

vda., viuda, widow

Vds. or VV., ustedes, you (*pl.*)

V.E., Vuestra Excelencia, Your Excellency

véase, see, refer to

vecindad, *f.* neighborhood

vecindario, *m.* neighborhood

vecino, *adj.* neighboring; near; *m.* neighbor; inhabitant

vegetación. *f.* vegetation

vegetal, *adj., m.* vegetable

vegetar, *vn.* to vegetate

vegetariano, vegetariana, *adj., n.* vegetarian

vehículo, *m.* vehicle

veinte, *adj., m.* twenty

veintena, *f.* score, twenty

vejez, *f.* old age

vejiga, *f.* bladder; blister

vela, *f.* watch; watchfulness; candle

velada, *f.* evening entertainment, soiree

velar, *vn.* to watch

velo, *m.* veil; pretext

velocidad, *f.* speed

veloz, *adj.* swift

vello, *m.* down; gossamer; short downy hair

velludo, *adj.* hairy

vena, *f.* vein, blood vessel

venado, *m.* deer; venison

vencer, *va.* to conquer, vanquish; *vn.* to fall due

vencido, *adj.* conquered; due; **darse por vencido**, to give up, yield

venda, *f.* bandage

vendaje, *m.* bandage

vendar, *va.* to bandage

vendedor, vendedora, *n.* seller

vender, *va.* to sell

veneciano, veneciana, *adj., n.* Venetian

veneno, *m.* poison, venom

venenoso, *adj.* poisonous

veneración, *f.* veneration

venerar, *va.* to venerate

venério, *adj.* venereal

vengar, *va.* to revenge, avenge; **vengarse de**, to take revenge on

vengativo, *adj.* revengeful

venia, *f.* pardon; leave, permission; bow

venida, *f.* arrival; return

venidero, *adj.* future, coming, next; **próximo venidero**, the coming month

venir, *vn.* to come, arrive; to follow, succeed; to spring from

venta, *f.* sale; roadside inn

ventaja, *f.* advantage; handicap

ventajoso, *adj.* advantageous

ventana, *f.* window

ventarrón, *m.* violent wind

ventilación, *f.* ventilation

ventilador, *m.* ventilator; fan

ventilar, *va., vr.* to ventilate; to fan; to air; to discuss

ventura, *f.* luck, fortune; **por ventura,** by chance

venturoso, *adj.* lucky, fortunate; happy

ver, *va.* to see, look; to observe; **a ver,** let's see; **hacer ver,** to pretend; *m.* sense of sight, seeing; view; **a mi ver,** in my opinion

veracidad, *f.* veracity

veraneo, *m.* summering; **lugar de veraneo,** *m.* summer resort

verano, *m.* summer

veras, *f. pl.* truth, sincerity; **de veras,** in truth, really

veraz, *adj.* truthful

verbal, *adj.* verbal, oral

verbigracia, *adv.* for example, namely

verbo, *m.* (gram.) verb

verdad, *f.* truth, veracity

verdaderamente, *adv.* truly

verdadero, *adj.* true, real

verde, *m., adj.* green

verdor, *m.* verdure; green

verdulero, verdulera, *n.* vegetable seller

verdura, *f.* verdure; vegetables, garden stuff

vereda, *f.* path, trail

vergel, *m.* flower garden

vergonzoso, *adj.* bashful, shy; shameful

vergüenza, *f.* shame; bashfulness; confusion

verídico, *adj.* truthful

verificar, *va.* to verify, check; **verificarse,** to take place

verja, *f.* grate, lattice

verosímil, *adj.* plausible

verruga, *f.* wart, pimple

versión, *f.* version, interpretation

verso, *m.* verse, stanza

vértebra, *f.* vertebra

vertebrado, vertebrada, *m., adj.* vertebrate

verter, *va., vr.* to pour; *vn.* to flow

vespertino, *adj.* evening

vestíbulo, *m.* vestibule, lobby

vestigio, *m.* vestige, trace

vestir, *va.* to clothe, dress

veterano, *adj.* experienced, long practiced; *m.* veteran, old soldier

vez, *f.* turn, time; **una vez,** once; **a veces, algunas veces,** sometimes; **en vez de,** instead of; **otra vez,** again; **tal vez,** perhaps

vg., v.g., or **v.gr., verbigracia,** e.g., for example

vía, *f.* way, road, route; (rail.) railway, railway line; **vía áerea,** air mail

viaducto, *m.* viaduct; overpass

viajar, *vn.* to travel

viaje, *m.* journey, voyage; **viaje sencillo,** one-way trip; **viaje redondo** or **de ida y vuelta,** round trip

viajero, viajera, *n.* traveler

víbora, *f.* viper

vicecónsul, *m.* vice-consul

vicepresidente, *m.* vice-president vice-chairman

viceversa: *adj.* vice versa

vicio, *m.* vice, folly

víctima, *f.* victim; **víctimas,** *pl.* casualties

victoria, *f.* victory

victorioso, *adj.* victorious

vid, *f.* (bot.) vine

vida, *f.* life

vidriera, *f.* glass case; shop-window

vidrio, *m.* glass

viejo, *adj.* old; ancient

vienés, vienesa, *adj., n.* Viennese

viento, *in.* wind; air

vientre, *m.* belly

viernes, *m.* Friday; **Viernes Santo,** Good Friday

viga, *f.* beam (of timber)

vigente, *adj.* in force

vigésimo, *adj., m.* twentieth

vigilar, *va., vn.* to watch over

vigor, *m.* vigor, strength

vigoroso, *adj.* vigorous

villa, *f.* town

villano, *adj.* rustic, boorish; *m.* villain

vinagre, m. vinegar
vincular, va. to link
vínculo, m. link, bond
vindicar, va. to vindicate; to avenge
vino, m. wine
viña, f. vineyard; grapevine
violación, f. violation
violar, va. to violate; to ravish
violencia, f. violence
violentar, va. to enforce by violent means
violento, adj. violent
violeta, f., adj. violet
violín, m. violin, fiddle
violinista, m., f. violinist
violón, m. bass viol
violonchelo, m. violoncello
virar, va. (naut.) to tack; vn. to turn around
virgen, adj., f. virgin
viril, virile, manly
virología, f. virology
virtud, f. virtue
virtuoso, adj. virtuous
viruela, f. smallpox; **viruelas locas,** chicken pox
visa, f. visa
visita, f. visit; visitor
visitante, m., f. visitor
visitar, va. to visit
víspera, f. evening before; day before; **víspera de Año Nuevo,** New Year's Eve
vistazo, m. glance
visto, adj. obvious; **visto que,** considering that; **por lo visto,** apparently; **visto bueno,** O.K., all right, correct
vistoso, adj. beautiful, showy
vital, adj. vital, essential
vitalicio, adj. during life
vitalidad, f. vitality
vitamina, f. vitamin
vitrina, f. showcase
viuda, f. widow
viudo, m. widower
¡viva! interj. hurrah! hail!
vivacidad, f. vivacity
víveres, m. pl. provisions
viveza, f. liveliness, perspicacity
vividor, vividora, n. sponger
vivienda, f. dwelling house
viviente, adj. alive, living

vivir, vn. to live
vivo, adj. living; lively; ingenious, bright
V. M., Vuestra Majestad, Your Majesty
V.º B.º, visto bueno, O.K., all correct
vocablo, m. word, term
vocabulario, m. vocabulary
vocación, f. vocation, calling
vocal, f. vowel; m. member of a board of directors; adj. vocal, oral
vol., volumen, vol., volume; **voluntad,** will; (com.) good will
volante, m. steering wheel; flier, note, memorandum; ruffle
volcán, m. volcano
volcar, va., vr. to upset
voltear, va. to whirl, over set; vn. to tumble
volumen, m. volume; size
voluminoso, adj. voluminous
voluntario, adj. voluntary; n. volunteer
voluntarioso, adj. willful
volver, va., vn. to return; to turn; **volver en sí,** to recover one's senses
vómito, m. vomiting
voraz, adj. voracious, greedy
vos, pron. you ye
vosotros, vosotroas, pron, pl. you
votación, f. voting
votante, m., f. voter
votar, va., vn. to vote
voto, m. vow; vote; wish; supplication to God; **hacer votos,** tc wish well
voz, f. voice; word, term
V.P., Vicepresidente, Vice Pres., Vice-President
vuelo, m. flight
vuelta, f. turn; circuit; detour; return; **dar la vuelta,** to turn around; to go out for a short walk or ride
vuelto, p. p. of **volver;** m. (sp. Am.) change (money back from a payment)
vuestro, vuestra, pron. your, yours

vulgar, *adj.* vulgar, common, ordinary
vulgaridad, *f.* vulgarity
vulgarismo, *m.* slang
vulgo, *m.* populace, mob
VV or **V.V.**, **ustedes**, you (*pl.*)

W

wáter, *m.* lavatory
whiskey, *m.* whiskey

X

xenón, *m.* xenon
xilófono, *m.* (mus.) xylophone
xilografía, *f.* wood engraving

Y

y, *conj.* and
ya, *adv.* already; presently; immediately; **ya no**, no longer
yanqui, *adj.*, *n.* Yankee
yarda, *f.* yard (measure)
yate, *m.* yacht
yedra, *f.* ivy
yelmo, *m.* helmet
yema, *f.* yolk
yerba or **hierba**, *f.* herb; grass; **yerba buena**, mint; **yerba mate**, Paraguay tea; **yerbas** *pl.* greens, vegetables
yerno, *m.* son-in-law
yeso, *m.* gypsum; plaster, plaster cast
yo, *pron.* I; **yo mismo**, I myself
yodo, *m.* iodine
yuca, *f.* (bot.) yucca
yugo, *m.* yoke
yunque, *m.* anvil
yunta, *f.* couple, yoke
yute, *m.* jute (fiber)

Z

zacate, *m.* (Mex.) hay, grass
zafiro, *m.* sapphire
zafra, *f.* sugar crop
zalamero, **zalamera**, *n.*, *adj.* wheedler, flatterer
zambullirse, *vr.* to plunge into water, dive

zanahoria, *f.* carrot
zancada, *f.* long stride
zanco, *m.* stilt
zancudo, *adj.* long-shanked; wading (bird); *m.* (Sp. Am.) mosquito
zángano, *m.* drone; idler, sponger
zanja, *f.* ditch, trench
zapallo, *m.* (Sp. Am.) squash
zapatear, *va.*, *vn.*, to strike with the shoe; to beat time with the sole of the shoe
zapatería, *f.* shoe store
zapatero, *m.* shoemaker; shoe seller
zapatilla, *f.* pump (shoe), slipper
zapato, *m.* shoe
zar, *m.* czar
zaraza, *f.* chintz; gingham
zarzamora, *f.* brambleberry; blackberry bush
zarzuela, *f.* variety of operetta, musical comedy
zeta, *f.* name of letter z
zigzag, *m.* zigzag
zona, *f.* zone, district
zoología, *f.* zoology
zoológico, *adj.* zoological
zoquete, *m.* block; (coll.) blockhead, numbskull
zorra, *f.* fox; (coll.) prostitute, strumpet
zorrillo, *m.* skunk
zorro, *m.* male fox; cunning fellow
zozobra, *f.* anxiety
zueco, *m.* wooden shoe
zumbar, *vn.* to resound, hum; to buzz; to ring (the ears)
zumbido, *m.* humming, buzzing sound
zumo, *m.* sap, juice
zurdo, *adj.* left; lefthanded
zurrapa, *f.* lees, dregs; trash
zurrar, *va.* to chastise with a whip; **zurrarse**, (coll.) to have an involuntary evacuation of the bowels
zutano, **zutana**, *n.* such a one; **zutano y fulano**, such and such a one, so and so

A

a, *art.* un, uno, una

A. B., Bachelor of Arts, Br. Bachiller

aback, *adv.* detrás, atrás; **to be taken aback,** quedar desconcertado

abandon, *vt.* abandonar

abate, *vt., vi.* minorar, disminuir

abbreviate, *vt.* abreviar

abbreviation, *n.* abreviación, abreviatura, *f.*

abdicate, *vt.* abdicar

abdomen, *n.* abdomen, vientre, *m.*

abduct, *vt.* secuestrar

abhor, *vt.* aborrecer

abide, *vi.* habitar, morar; **to abide by,** cumplir con; atenerse a

ability, *n.* habilidad, aptitud, *f.*

abnormal, *adj.* anormal

aboard, *adj.* abordo

abode, *n.* habitación,

abolish, *vt.* abolir

abominable, *adj.* abominable

abortion, *n.* aborto, *m.*

about, *prep.* cerca de; sobre; acerca; *adv.* aquí y allá; **to be about to,** estar a punto de

above, *prep.* encima, sobre; *adj.* arriba; **above all,** sobre todo, principalmente

aboveboard, *adj.* y *adv.* sincero, al descubierto

abreast, *adj.* de frente

abrupt,*adi.*repentino; rudo

abscess, *n.* absceso, *m.*

absence, *n.* ausencia, *f.*; **leave of absence,** licencia, *f.*

absent, *adj.* ausente

absent-minded, *adj.* distraído

abstain, *vi.* abstenerse

abstract, *vt.* abstraer; compendiar; *adj.* abstracto; *n.* extracto, *m.*

absurd, *adj.* absurdo

abundance, *n.* abundancia, *f.*

abundant, *adj.* abundante

abuse, *vt.* abusar; ultrajar; violar; *n.* abuso, engaño, *m.*

A.C., a.c., alternating current, C.A., corriente alterna

academic, *adj.* académico

academy, *n.* academia, *f.*

accede, *vi.* acceder

accelerator, *n.* acelerador, *m.*

accent, *n.* acento, *m.*; tono, *m.*; *vt.* acentuar

accentuate, *vt.* acentuar

accept, *vt.* aceptar; admitir

acceptance, *n.* aceptación, *f.*

access, *n.* acceso, *m.*; entrada, *f.*

accessory, *adj.* accesorio; *n.* cómplice, *m.* y *f.*

accident, *n.* accidente, *m.*; casualidad, *f.*

accidental, *adj.* accidental, casual

acclaim, *vt.* aclamar, aplaudir

accommodate, *vt.* acomodar, ajustar

accommodating, *adj.* servicial

accompaniment, *n.* (mus.) acompañamiento, *m.*

accompany, *vt.* acompañar

accomplice, *n.* cómplice, *m.* y *f.*

accomplish, *vt.* efectuar, realizar

accord, *n.* acuerdo, convenio, *m.*

accordance, *n.* conformidad, *f.*, acuerdo, *m.*

according, *adj.* conforme; **according to,** según; **accordingly,** *adv.* de conformidad, por consiguiente

account, *n.* cuenta, *f.*; cálculo, *m.*; narración, *f.*; **on account of,** a causa de

accountant, *n.* contador, tenedor de libros, *m.*

accounting, *n.* contabilidad, *f.*

accredited, *adj.* autorizado

accumulate, *vt.* y *vi.* acumular

accurate, *adj.* exacto; atinado

accusation, *n.* acusación, *f.*; cargo, *m.*

accusative, *n.* acusativo, *m.*

accuse, *vt.* acusar; culpar

accustom, *vt.* acostumbrar

ace, *n.* as (de naipe), *m.*; as, aviador sobresaliente, *m.*; *adj.* extraordinario

ache, *n.* dolor, *m.*; *vi.* doler

achieve, *vt.* ejecutar; lograr

achievement, *n.* ejecución, *f.*; hazaña, *f.*

acid, *n.* ácido, *m.*; *adj.* ácido, agrio

acknowledge, *vt.* reconocer; confesar; **acknowledge receipt**, acusar recibo

acoustics, *n.* acústica, *f.*

acquaint, *vt.* enterar, familiarizar; **to be acquainted**, conocer

acquaintance, *n.* conocimiento, *m.*; conocido, *m.*

acquire, *vt.* adquirir

acre, *n.* acre, *m.* (medida)

across, *adv.* al otro lado; *prep.* a través de

acrylic, *adj.* acrílico

act, *vt.* representar; obrar; *vi.* hacer; *n.* acto, hecho, *m.*

ACTH, *n.* (med.) ACTH

acting, *adj.* interino, suplente

action, *n.* acción, operación, *f.*; batalla, *f.*; proceso, *m.*; actividad, *f.*

active, *adj.* activo; eficaz

activity, *n.* actividad, *f.*

actual, *adj.* real; efectivo

acute, *adj.* agudo; ingenioso

A.D.: (in the year of our Lord), D. de J. C. (después de J. C.)

ad, *n.* anuncio, aviso, *m.*

adamant, *adj.* inflexible

adapt, *vt.* adaptar

add, *vt.* sumar; agregar

adding, *n.* suma, *f.*; **adding machine**, calculadora, *f.*

addition, *n.* adición, *f.*

address, *vt.* hablar, dirigir la palabra; *n.* discurso, *m.*; direceión, *f.*

addressee, *n.* destinatario, *m.*

adhere, *vi.* adherir

adhesion, *n.* adherencia, *f.*

adhesive, *adj.* pegajoso, tenaz; **adhesive plaster, adhesive tape**, esparadrapo, *m.*

adjacent, *adj.* adyacente, contiguo

adjective, *n.* adjetivo, *m.*

adjourn, *vt.* y *vi.* clausurar (una reunión, etc.)

adjust, *vt.* ajustar, acomodar

adjustment, *n.* ajuste, arreglo, *m.*

Adm., Admiral, Almte., almirante

administer, *vt.* administrar

administration, *n.* administración

admirable, *adj.* admirable

admiral, *n.* almirante, *m.*

admiration, *n.* admiración, *f.*

admire, *vt.* admirar; contemplar

admirer, *n.* admirador, *m.*; pretendiente, *m.*

admission, *n.* admisión, entrada, *f.*

admit, *vt.* admitir, dar entrada; reconocer

adolescence, *n.* adolescencia, *f.*

adopt,, *vt.* adoptar

adoption, *n.* adopción, *f.*

adrift, *adj.* y *adv.* flotante, al garete

adult, *adj.* y *n.* adulto, adulta

advance, *vt.* avanzar; pagar adelantado; *vi.* progresar; *n.* adelanto, *m.*

advantage, *n.* ventaja, *f.*; provecho, *m.*; **to take advantage of**, aprovecharse de

advantageous, *adj.* ventajoso, útil

adventure, *n.* aventura, *f.*

adventurer, *n.* aventurero, *m.*

adverb. *n.* adverbio, *m.*

adversity, *n.* adversidid, *f.*

advertise, *vt.* avisar, anunciar

advertisement, *n.* aviso, anuncio, *m.*

advice, *n.* consejo, *m.*; parecer, *m.*

advisable, *adj.* prudente, conveniente

advise, *vt.* aconsejar; avisar

adviser, *n.* consejero, *m.*

advisory, *adj.* consultivo

aerial, *adj.* aéreo; *n.* antena, *f.*

aeronautics, *n.* aeronautica, *f.*

aerosol bomb, *n.* bomba de aerosol, *f.*

aerospace, *n.* atmósfera y espacio exterior

affair, *n.* asunto, *m.*

affect, *vt.* conmover; afectar

affected, *adj.* afectado, fingido

affection, *n.* amor, afecto, *m.*

affectionate, *adj.* afectuoso

affiliation, *n.* afiliación, *f.*

affirmative, *adj.* afirmativo

affix, *vt.* anexar, fijar

afflict, *vt.* afligir

afford, *vt.* dar; proveer; tener los medios

afraid, *adj.* miedoso; **to be afraid,** tener miedo

Afro, *adj.* afro

after, *prep.* después de, detrás; *adv.* después

afternoon, *n.* tarde, *f.*

afterward, afterwards, *adv.* después

again, *adv.* otra vez

against, *prep.* contra

age, *n.* edad, *f.*; **of age,** mayor de edad; *vi.* envejecer

agent, *n.* agente, *m.*

aggravate, *vt.* agravar

aggression, *n.* agresión, *f.*

ago, *adv.* pasado, tiempo ha; **long ago,** hace mucho

agony, *n.* agonía, *f.*

agrarian, *adj.* agrario

agree, *vi.* convenir; consentir

agreeable, *adj.* agradable

agreement, *n.* acuerdo, *m.*; conformidad, *f.*

agricultural, *adj.* agrario, agrícola

agriculture, *n.* agricultura, *f.*

aid, *vt.* ayudar, socorrer; *n.* ayuda, *f.*; auxilio, *m.*

ailment, *n.* dolencia, *f.*

aim, *vt.* apuntar; aspirar a; *n.* designio, intento, *m.*; puntería, *f.*

air, *n.* aire, *m.*; tonada, *f.*; **air brush,** aerógrafo, *m.*; **air drill,** perforadora, *f.*; **air freight,** flete aéreo, *m.* **air-conditioned,** *adj.* con aire acondicionado

airlift, *n.* puente aéyeo, *m.*

airplane, *n.* aeroplano, *m.*

airport, *n.* aeropuerto, *m.*

airtight, *adj.* herméticamente cerrado

aisle, *n.* pasillo, *m.*; pasadizo, *m.*

alarm, *n.* alarma, *f.*; **alarm**

clock, reloj despertador, *m.*; *vt.* alarmar

album, *n.* álbum, *m.*

alcoholic, *adj.* alcohólico

alderman, *n.* concejal, *m.*

ale, *n.* varieded de cerveza

alert, *adj.* alerto, vivo

algebra, *n.* álgebra, *f.*

alibi, *n.* (law) coartada, *f.*

alien, *n.* extranjero, extranjera

alike, *adj.* semejante, igual

alive, *adj.* vivo, viviente

all, *adj.* todo; *adv.* enteramente; **all right,** bueno, satisfactorio; *n.* todo, *m.*

allege, *vt.* alegar, declarar

allegiance, *n.* lealtad, *f.*

allegory, *n.* alegoria *f.*

allergen, *n.* alergeno, *m.*

allergic, *adj.* alérgico

alley, *n.* callejón, *m.*

allied, *adj.* aliado

alligator, *n.* lagarto, caimán, *m.*; **alligator pear,** aguacate, *m.*

allot, *vt.* asignar, repartir

allotment, *n.* asignación, *f.*; parte, porción, *f.*

allow, *vt.* conceder; permitir

allowance, *n.* ración, *f.*; mesada, *f.*

allude, *vt.* aludir

alluring, *adj.* seductor

ally, *n.* aliado, asociado, *m.*; *vt.* vincular

almanac, *n.* almanaque, *m.*

almighty, *adj.* omnipotente, todopoderoso

almond, *n.* almendra, *f.*

almost, *adv.* casi, cerca de

alms, *n.* limosna, *f.*

alone, *adj.* solo; *adv.* a solas

along, *adv.* a lo largo; junto con

aloof, *adj.* reservado, apartado

aloud, *adv.* recio; en voz alta

alphabet, *n.* alfabeto, *m.*

Alps, Alpes, *m. pl.*

already, *adv.* ya

also, *adv.* también

alter, *vt.* alterar, modificar

alteration, *n.* alteración, *f.*

alternate, *vt.* alternar, variar; *n.* suplente, *m.* y *f.*

altimeter, *n.* altímetro, *m.*

altitude, *n.* altitud, *f.*
alto, *n.* contralto, *f.*
aluminum, *n.* aluminio, *m.*
always, *adv.* siempre
A.M., Master of Arts, Maestro o Licenciado en Artes
A.M., a.m., before noon, A.M. antemeridiano
am (1ª persona del singular de indicativo del verbo **to be**), soy; estoy
amateur, *n.* aficionado, aficionada
amaze, *vt.* asombrar
amazing, *adj.* asombroso
ambassador, *n.* embajador, *m.*
ambition, *n.* ambición, *f.*
ambitious, *adj.* ambicioso
ambulance, *n.* ambulancia, *f.*
amen, *interj.* amén
amend, *vt., vi.* enmendar
amendment, *n.* enmienda, reforma, *f.*
American, *n.* y *adj.* americano, americana
amiable, *adj.* amable
amid, amidst, *prep.* entre, en medio de
amino acid, *n.* aminoácido, *m.*
ammonia, *n.* amoniaco, *m.*
ammunition, *n.* munición, *f.*
among, amongst, *prep.* entre, en medio de
amount, *n.* suma, *f.; monto, m.; vi.* importar
ample, *adj.* amplio, vasto
amplify, *vt.* ampliar, extender
amputate, *vt.* amputar
amt., amount, v/ valor
amuse, *vt.* divertir
amusement, *n.* diversión, *f.,* pasatiempo, *m.*
amusing, *adj.* divertido
an, *art.* un, uno, una
analysis, *n.* análisis, *m.* y *f.*
analyze, *vt.* analizar
anatomy, *n.* anatomia, *f.*
ancestors, *n. pl.* antepasados, *m. pl.*
ancestry, *n.* linaje, *m.*
anchor, *n.* ancla, áncora, *f.; vi.* echar anclas
ancient, *adj.* antiguo
and, *conj.* y; e (antes de palabras que empiezan con *i* o *hi,* con excepción de *hie*)
Andalusian, *n.* y *adj.* andaluz, andalza
anecdote, *n.* anécdota, *f.*
anesthetic, *adj.* y *n.* anestésico, *m.*
angel, *n.* ángel, *m.*
anger, *n.* ira, cólera, *f.; vt.* enojar, encolerizar
Anglo-Saxon, *n.* y *adj.* anglosajón, anglosajona
angry, *adj.* enojado
anguish, *n.* ansia, angustia, *f.*
animal, *n.* y *adj.* animal, *m.*
animation, *n.* animación, *f.*
ankle, *n.* tobillo, *m.*
anniversary, *n.* aniversario, *m.*
announce, *vt.* anunciar, publicar; notificar, avisar
announcement, *n.* aviso, anuncio, *m.,* notificación, *f.*
announcer, *n.* anunciador, anunciadora; locutor, locutora
annoy, *vt.* molestar; fastidiar
annoyance, *n.* molestia, *f.;* fastidio, *m.;* (coll.) lata,
annual, *adj.* anual
annuity, *n.* pension, anualidad *f.*
annul, *vt.* anular, aniquilar
annulment, *n.* anulación, *f.*
anonymous, *adj.* anónimo
another, *adj.* otro, diferente
answer, *vi.* responder, contestar; *vt.* refutar; contestar; *n.* respuesta, contestación, *f.*
ant, *n.* hormiga, f
antenna, *n.* antena, *f.*
antibiotic, *n.* y *adj.* antibiótico, *m.*
anticipate, *vt.* anticipar, prevenir
antihistamine, *n.* antihistamina, *f.*
antiknock, *n.* antidetonante, *m.*
antimatter, *n.* antimateria, *f.*
antique, *adj.* antiguo; *n.* antigüedad, *f.*
antiseptic, *adj.* antiséptico
antitank gun, *n.* cañón anticarro o antitanque, *m.*
anvil, *n.* yunque, *m.*

anxiety, *n.* ansiedad, *f.*

anxious, *adj.* ansioso

any, *adj.* cualquier, algún

anyhow, *adv.* de cualquier modo; de todos modos

anyone, *pron.* alguno, cualquiera

anything, *pron.* algo

anyway, *adv.* como quiera; de todos modos

apart, *adv.* aparte; separadamente

apartment, *n.* departamento, apartamento, apartamiento

ape, *n.* mono, *m.*; *vt.* imitar

apiece, *adv.* por cabeza, por persona

apologize, *vi.* disculparse

apology, *n.* disculpa, *f.*

apostle, *n.* apóstol, *m.*

apparatus, *n.* aparato, *m.*

apparel, *n.* vestido, *m.*; ropa, *f.*

apparent, *adj.* evidente, aparente

appeal, *vi.* apelar; recurrir; atraer; *n.* súplica, *f.*; (law) apelación, *f.*; simpatía, atracción, *f.*

appear, *vi.* aparecer; ser evidente; salir

appearance, *n.* apariencia, *f.*; aspecto, *m.*

appease, *vt.* apaciguar, aplacar

appendicitis, *n.* apendicitis, *f.*

appendix, *n.* apéndice, *m.*

appetite, *n.* apetito, *m.*

appetizer, *n.* aperitivo, *m.*; entremés, *m.*

applaud, *vt.* aplaudir; aclamar

applause, *n.* aplauso, *m.*

apple, *n.* manzana, *f.*

appliance, *n.* utensilio, aparato, *m.*, herramienta, *f.*

application, *n.* solicitud, *f.*; aplicación, *f.*

apply, *vt.* aplicar; **to apply for,** solicitar; *vi.* dirigirse a, recurrir a

appoint, *vt.* nombrar, designar

appointment, *n.* nombramiento, *m.*; cita, *f.*, compromiso, *m.*

appraise, *vt.* tasar; valuar

appreciate, *vt.* apreciar

apprentice, *n.* aprendiz, *m.*

approach, *vt.* y *vi.* abordar; aproximarse; *n.* acercamiento, *m.*

appropriate, *vt.* apropiar, asignar (una partida); *adj.* apropiado

appropriation, *n.* apropiación, partido, *f.*

approval, *n.* aprobación, *f.*

approve, *vt.* aprobar

approximate, *adj.* aproximado

apricot, *n.* albaricoque, *m.*; (Mex.) chabacano, *m.*

April, *n.* abril, *m.*

apron, *n.* delantal, *m.*

apt, *adj.* apto, idóneo

aptitude, *n.* aptitud, *f.*

aquarium, *n.* acuario, *m.*

aqueduct, *n.* acueducto, *m.*

Arab, Arabian, *n.* y *adj.* árabe, *m.* y *f.*, arábigo, arábiga

arbitrary, *adj.* arbitrario

arbitration, *n.* arbitraje, *m.*

arbor, *n.* enramada, *f.*

arc, *n.* arco, *m.*

arch, *n.* arco (de círculo, de puente, etc.), *m.*

archbishop, *n.* arzobispo, *m.*

archipelago, *n.* archipiélago *m.*

architect, *n.* arquitecto, *m.*

architecture, *n.* arquitectura *f.*

arctic, *adj.* ártico

ardent, *adj.* ardiente, apasionado

ardor, *n.* ardor, *m.*; pasión, *f.*

are, plural y 2ª persona del singular de indicativo del verbo **to be**

area, *n.* área, *f.*; espacio, *m.*; superfide, *f.*

arena, *n.* pista, *f.*

argue, *vi.* disputar, argüir

argument, *n.* argumento, *m.*, controversia, *f.*

arid, *adj.* árido, seco

arise, *vi.* levantarse

aristocracy, *n.* aristocracia, *f.*

aristocrat, *n.* aristócrata, *m.* y *f.*

arithmetic, *n.* aritmética, *f.*

ark, *n.* arca, *f.*

arm, *n.* brazo, *m.*; arma, *f.*

armament, *n.* armamento, *m.*

armistice, *n.* armisticio, *m.*

armor, *n.* armadura, *f.*

armored, *adj.* blindado, acorazado

army, *n.* ejército, *m.*

around, *prep.* en, cerca; *adv.* al rededor

arrange, *vt.* arreglar

arrangement, *n.* arreglo, *m.*

arrest, *n.* arresto, *m.*; detención, *f.*; *vt.* arrestar, prender-

arrival, *n.* arribo, *m.*; llegada, *f.*

arrive, *vi.* arribar; llegar

arrow, *n.* flecha, *f.*; dardo, *m.*

arsenic, *n.* arsénico, *m.*

art, *n.* arte, *m.* y *f.*; ciencia, *f.*; **the fine arts,** las bellas artes

artery, *n.* arteria, *f.*

arthritis, *n.* artritis, *f.*

article, *n.* artículo, *m.*

artillery, *n.* artillería, *f.*

artisan, *n.* artesano, *m.*

artist, *n.* artista, *m.* y *f.*; pintor, pintora

artistic, *adj.* artístico

as, *conj.* y *adv.* como; mientras; pues; visto que, pues que; **as much,** tanto; **as far as,** hasta; **as to,** en cuanto a

ascend, *vi.* ascender, subir

ascent, *n.* subida, *f.*

ash, *n.* (bot.) fresno, *m.*; **ashes,** *pl.* ceniza, *f.*; **ash tray,** cenicero, *m.*

ashamed, *adj.* avergonzado; **to be ashamed,** tener vergüenza

ashore, *adv.* en tierra, a tierra

Asiatic, *n.* y *adj.* asiático, asiática

aside, *adv.* al lado, aparte

ask, *vt.* y *vi.* pedir; interrogar

asleep, *adj.* dormido; **to fall asleep,** dormirse

asparagus, *n.* espárrago, *m.*

aspect, *n.* aspecto, *m.*

aspire, *vi.* aspirar, desear

aspirin, *n.* aspirina, *f.*

ass, *n.* borrico, asno, *m.*

assail, *vt.* asaltar, atacar

assassin, *n.* asesino, *m.*

assassinate, *vt.* asesinar

assault, *n.* asalto, *m.*; *vt.* acometer, asaltar

assemble, *vt.* congregar, convocar; esamblar, armar; *vi.* juntarse

assembly, *n.* asamblea, junta, *f.*; congreso, *m.*; montaje, *m.*; **assembly line,** línea de montaje

assert, *vt.* sostener, mantener; afirmar

assertion, *n.* aserción,

assessment, *n.* impuesto, *m.*; catastro, *m.*

assessor, *n.* asesor, *m.*

asset, *n.* algo de valor; ventaja, *f.*; **assets,** *pl.* (com.) haber, activo, capital, *m.*

assign, *vt.* asignar, destinar

assignment, *n.* asignación, *f.*; tarea escolar, *f.*

assimilate, *vt.* asimilar

assist, *vt.* asistir, ayudar

assistance, *n.* asistencia, *f.*; socorro, *m.*

assistant, *n.* asistente, ayudante, *m.*

associate, *vt.* asociar; acompañar; *adj.* asociado; *n.* socio, compañero, *m.*

association, *n.* asociación, agrupación, *f.*; club, *m.*

assume, *vt.* asumir

assumption, *n.* suposición, *f.*; **Assumption,** *n.* Asuncion, *f.*

assurance, *n.* seguridad, convicción, *f.*

assure, *vt.* asegurar, afirmar

asthma, *n.* asma, *f.*

astonishing, *adj.* asombroso

astounding, *adj.* asombroso

astray, *adj.* y *adv.* extraviado, descaminado; **to lead astray,** desviar, seducir

astringent, *adi.* astringente

astronomy, *n.* astronomía, *f.*

astute, *adj.* astuto; aleve

asylum, *n.* asilo, refugio, *m.*; **insane asylum,** manicomio, *m.*

at, *prep.* a, en; **at once,** al instante; **at last,** al fin, por último

ate, *pretérito* del verbo **eat**

athlete, *n.* atleta, *m.* y *f.*

athletics, *n. pl.* deportes, *m.*

pl.

Atlantic, *n.* y *adj.* Atlántico

atmosphere, *n.* atmósfera, *f.*, ambiente, *m.*

atom, *n.* átomo, *m.*; **atom bomb,** bomba atómica

atomic, *adj.* atómico

atomizer, *n.* pulverizador, *m.*

atone, *vt.* expiar, pagar

attach, *vt.* prender; juntar, adherir; embargar

attachment, *n.* anexo, *m.*

attack, *vt.* atacar; *n.* ataque, *m.*

attain, *vt.* obtener, alcanzar

attempt, *vt.* probar, experimentar; procurar; *n.* tentative, *f.*; prueba, *f.*

attend, *vt.* asistir; *vi.* prestar atención

attendance, *n.* asistencia, *f.*

attention, *n.* atención,

attest, *vt.* atestiguar; dar fe

attire, *n.* atavío, *m.*; *vt.* adornar, ataviar

attitude, *n.* actitud, *f.*

attorney, *n.* abogado, *m.*

attract, *vt.* atraer

attraction, *n.* atracción, *f.*; atractivo, *m.*

attractive, *adj.* atractivo, seductor

attribute, *vt.* atribuir, imputar; *n.* atributo, *m.*

auburn, *adj.* y *n.* castaño rojizo

auction, *n.* subasta, *f.*, remate, *m.*

audacious, *adj.* audaz, temerario

audience, *n.* audiencia, *f.*; auditorio, *m.*; concurrencia, *f.*

audition, *n.* audición, *f.*; *vt.* conceder audición; *vi.* presentar audición

auditor, *n.* contador, *m.*

audio-visual, *adj.* audio-visual

August, *n.* agosto (mes), *m.*

aunt, *n.* tía,

auspices *n. pl.* auspicio, *m.*; protección

austere, *adj.* austero

austerity, *n.* austeridad, crueldad, severidad, *f.*

authentic, *adj.* auténtico

author, *n.* autor, escritor, *m.*

authority, *n.* autoridad, *f.*

authorization, *n.* autorización, *f.*

authorize, *vt.* autorizar

autobiography, *n.* autobiografía, *f.*

auto, *n.* auto, *m.*

autograph, *n.* y *adj.* autógrafo, *m.*

automate, *vt.* automatizar

automatic, *adj.* automático

automobile, *n.* automóvil, *m.*

autumn, *n.* otoño, *m.*

auxiliary, *adj.* auxiliar, asistente

avail, *vt.* aprovechar; *vi.* servir, ser ventajoso; *n.* provecho, *m.*

ave., avenue, av. avenida

avenue, *n.* avenida, *f.*

average, *n.* término medio, promedio, *m.*; *adj.* medio, mediano, común y corriente

aviation, *n.* aviación, *f.*

aviator, *n.* aviador, *m.*

avocado, *n.* aguacate, *m.*

avocation, *n.* diversión, afición, *f.*

avoid, *vt.* evitar, escapar

await, *vt.* aguardar; **awaiting your reply,** en espera de sus noticias

awake, *vt.* y *vi.* despertar; *adj.* despierto

award, *vt.* otorgar, adjudicar; *n.* premio, *m.*, adjudicación, *f.*

aware, *adj.* enterado; consciente

away, *adv.* ausente, fuera

awe, *n.* miedo, pavor, *m.*; temor reverencial, *m.*

awhile, *adv.* por un rato

awkward, *adj.* tosco, torpe

awning, *n.* toldo, *m.*

ax, axe, *n.* segur, *f.*; hacha, *f.*

axis, *n.* eje, *m.*; alianza, *f.*

axle, *n.* eje de una rueda

aye, ay, *adv.* sí

B

B.A., Bachelor of Arts, Br.

Bachiller
babe, n. nene, bebé, m.
baby, n. nene, infante, m.
baby-sit, vi. servir de niñera
bachelor, n. soltero, m.; bachiller, m.
back, n. dorso, m.; espalda, f.; lomo, m.; adj. posterior;vt. sostener, apoyar; adv. atrás, detrás
backbone, n. espinazo, m., espina dorsal f.
background, n. fondo, m.; ambiente, m.; antecedentes, m. pl.; educación, f.
backlash, n. reacción, f.
backup, n. (mil.) apoyo, m.; (com.) acumulación, congestión, f.; adj. suplente
backward, adj. retrógrado; **backwards,** adv. hacia atrás
bacon, n. tocino, m.
bacteria, n. pl. bacterias, f. pl.
badge, n.divisa, f.
baffle, vt. eludir; confundir
bag, n. saco, m.; bolsa, f.
baggage, n. equipaje, m.
bail, n. fianza, f.; fiador, m.; **to go bail for,** salir fiador
bait, vt. cebar; atraer; n. carnada, f.
bake, vt. cocer en horno
baker, n. panadero, m.
bakery, n. panadería,
balance, n. equilibria m.; resto, m.; balance, m.; saldo, m.; vt. equilibrar; saldar; considerar
balcony, n. balcón, m.; galería, f.
bald, adj. calvo
bale, n. bala, f.; paca, f.; vt. embalar
balk, vi. rebelarse (un caballo, etc.)
ball, n. bola, f.; pelota, f.; baile, m.
ballad, n. balada, f.; romance, m.
ballet, n. ballet, m.
ballot, n. balota, papeleta, f.
ballroom, n. salón de baile, m.
balm, n. bálsamo, m.
bamboo, n. bambú, m.
ban, n. edicto, m.; prohibición,

f.; vt. prohibir; excomulgar
banana, n. plátano, m.
band, n. venda, faja, f.; cuadrilla, f.; banda, f.; orquesta, vt. unir, juntar
bandage, n. venda, f.; vendaje, m.; vt. vendar
bandit, n. bandido, bandida
bane, n. veneno, m.; calamidad, f.
banish, vt. desterrar
banister, n. pasamano, m.
bank, n. orilla (de rio), ribera, f.; montón de tierra; banco, m.; **savings bank,** banco de ahorros; vt. poner dinero en un banco
banker, n. banquero, m.
banking, n. banca, f.; adj. bancario
bankrupt, adj. quebrado, en bancarrota
banner, n. bandera, estandarte, m.
banquet, n. banquete, m.
baptism, n. bautismo, bautizo, m.
baptize, vt. bautizar
bar, n. barra, f.; foro, m.; obstáculo, m.; cantina, f.; vt. impedir; excluir; **bars,** rejas, f. pl.
barbaric, adj. bárbaro, cruel, fiero
barbecue, n. barbacoa, f.
barbell, n. haltera, f.
barber, n. barbero, peluquero, m.
barbershop, n. peluquería, barbería, f.
bare, adj. desnudo, descubierto; simple; vt. desnudar, descubrir
barefoot, adj. descalzo
barely, adv. apenas
bargain, n. ganga, f.; vi. regatear
barge, n. chalupa, f.
baritone, n. baritono, m.
bark, n. corteza, f.; ladrido, m.; vi. ladrar
barley, n. cebada, f.
barn, n. granero, establo, m.
barnyard, n. corral, m.
barometer, n. barómetro, m.

barrack, *n.* cuartel, *m.*; barraca, *f.*

barrel, *n.* barril, *m.*; cañón de escopeta, *m.*

barren, *adj.* estéril; seco

barrier, *n.* barrera, *f.*

bartender, *n.* cantinero, *m.*

barter, *vt.* cambiar, trocar

base, *n.* fondo, *m.*; base, *f.*; contrabajo, *m.*; *vt.* apoyar; basar; *adj.* bajo, vil

baseball, *n.* baseball, beisbol, *m.*; pelota de baseball

basement, *n.* sótano, *m.*

bashful, *adj.* vergonzoso

basic, *adj.* fundamental

basis, *n.* base, *f.*

basket, *n.* cesta, canasta, *f.*

basketball, *n.* baloncesto, *m.*; juego de balón, *m.*

bass, *n.* (mus.) contrabajo, *m.*; bajo, *m.*; (zool.) lobina, *f.*, róbalo or robalo, *m.*; *adj.* bajo; **bass viol**, violonchelo, *m.*

bassinet, *n.* cesta-cuna, *f.*

basso, *n.* (mus.) bajo, *m.*

bastard, *n.* y *adj.* bastardo, bastarda

baste, *vt.* pringar la carne; hilvanar

bat, *n.* (baseball) bate, *m.*; murciélago, *m.*

batch, *n.* hornada, *f.*; conjunto, *m.*

bath, *n.* baño, *m.*

bathe, *vt.* y *vi.* bañar, bañarse

bathrobe, *n.* bata de baño, *f.*

bathroom, *n.* cuarto de baño,

bathtub, *n.* bañera, *f.*; tina de baño, *f.*

baton, *n.* batuta, *f.*

battalion, *n.* batallón, *m.*

batter, *n.* pasta culinaria, *f.*; (baseball) bateador, *m.*

battery, *n.* acumulador, *m.*

battle, *n.* batalla, *f.*

bawl, *vi.* gritar, vocear; chillar

bay, *n.* bahía, *f.*

bazaar, *n.* bazar, *m.*

bbl., barrel, brl., barril

B. C., Before Christ, A. de J.C., antes de Jesuscristo

beach, *n.* playa, *f.*

beacon, *n.* faro, *m.*

bead, *n.* cuenta, chaquira, *f.*

beak, *n.* rayo de luz, *m.*; *vi.* brillar

bean, *n.* (bot.) haba, habichuela, *f.*; frijol, *m.*

bear, *n.* oso, *m.*; *vt.* soportar; parir; **to bear in mind**, tener presente

bearer, *n.* portador, portadora

bearing, *n.* comportamiento, *m.*; relación, *f.*

beast, *n.* bestia, *f.*

beastly, *adj.* bestial, brutal

beat, *vt.* golpear; batir; ganar (en un juigo); *vi.* pulsar, palpitar; *n.* pulsación, *f.*; (mus) compás, *m.*

beater, *n.* batidor, m.

beautiful, *adj.* hermoso, hello

beautify, *vt.* embellecer

beauty, *n.* hermosura, belleza, *f.*; beauty parlor, salón de belleza, *m.*

beck, *n.* seña, *f.*; **at one's beck and call**, a la mano, a la disposición

beckon, *vi.* llamar con señas

become, *vt.* sentar, quedar bien; *vi.* hacerse, convertirse; llegar a ser

becoming, *adj.* que sienta o cae bien; decoroso

bed, *n.* cama

bedclothes, *n. pl.* cobertores, *m. pl.*; mantas, colchas, *f. pl.*

bedding, *n.* ropa de cama, *f.*

bedridden, *adj.* postrado en cama

bedroom, *n.* dormitorio, *m.*

bedspread, *n.* sobrecama, *f.*

bee, *n.* abeja, *f.*

beech, *n.* (bot.) haya, *f.*

beef, *n.* carne de res, *f.*

beefsteak, *n.* biftec, bistec, *m.*

beehive, *n.* colmena, *f.*

been, *p. p.* del verbo **be**

beer, *n.* cerveza, *f.*

beet. *n.* remolacha, betarraga, *f.*; (Mex.) betabel, *m.*

beetle, *n.* escarabajo, *m.*

befall, *vi.* sobrevenir

before, *adv.* más adelante; *prep.* antes de, ante; *conj.* antes que

beforehand, *adv.* de antemano

beg, *vt.* mendigar, pedir

began, *pretérito* del verbo **begin**

beggar, *n.* mendigo, mendiga; limosnero, limosnera

begin, *vt.* y *vi.* comenzar, principiar

beginning, *n.* principio, comienzo, *m.*

begun, *p. p.* del verbo begin

behalf, *n.* favor, patrocinio, *m.*; **in behalf of,** en pro de

behave, *vi.* comportarse

behavior, *n.* comportamiento, *m.*

behind,*prep.* detrás; atrás; *adv.*atrás

behold, *vt.* ver, contemplar

beige, *n.* color arena, *m.*

being, *n.* ser, *m.*; existencia, *f.*

belated, *adj.* atrasado

belch, *vi.* eructar (or erutar

Belgium, Bélgica

believe, *vt.* y *vi.* creer; pensar

bell, *n.* campana, *f.*; timbre, m.

bellow, *vi.* bramar; rugir

bellows, *n.* fuelle, *m.*

belly, *n.* vientre, *m.*; panza, barriga, *f.*

belong, *vi.* pertenecer

belongings, *n. pl.* propiedad, *f.*; efectos, *m. pl.*

beloved, *adj.* querido, amado

below, *adv.* y *prep.* debajo, inferior; abajo

belt, *n.* cinturón, *m.*; correa, *f.*

bend, *vt.* doblar, plegar; *vi.* inclinarse

beneath, *adv.* y *prep.* debajo, abajo

benediction, *n.* bendición, *f.*

benefactor, *n.* bienhechor, bienhechora

beneficial, *adj.* beneficioso, útil

beneficiary, *n.* beneficiario, beneficiaria

benefit, *n.* beneficio, *m.*; utilidad, *f.*; provecho, *m.*; *vt.* y *vi.* beneficiar

benevolent, *adj.* benévolo

bequest, *n.* legado, *m.*

bereavement, *n.* luto, duelo, *m.*

beret, *n.* boina, *f.*

berry, *n.* baya, *f.*

berth, *n.* litera, *f.*; camarote, *m.*

beseech, *vt.* suplicar, rogar

beside, besides, *prep.* al lado de; fuera de; *adv.* además

best, *adj. y adv.* mejor; **best man,** padrino de boda

bestow, *vt.* otorgar

bet, *n.* apuesta, *f.*; apostar

betatron, *n.* betatrón

betray, *vt.* traicionar; divulgar (algún secreto)

betrothed, *adj.* comprometido, prometido; *n.* prometido, prometida

better, *adj. y adv.* mejor; *vt.* mejorar; **betters,** *n. pl.* superiores, *m. pl.*

beverage, *n.* bebida, *f.*

bewail, *vt.* y *vi.* lamentar, deplorar

beware, *vi.* tener cuidado

bewilder, *vt., vi.* turbar; confundirse

beyond, *prep.* más allá; fuera de

bias, *n.* parcialidad, *f.*; sesgo, *m.*; **on the bias,** al sesgo; *vt.* inclinar, influir

biased, *adj.* predispuesto

bib, *n.* babero, *m.*

Bible, *n.* Biblia, *f.*

bicker, *vi.* reñir, disputar

bicycle, *n.* bicicleta, *f.*

bid, *vt.* convidar; mandar, ordenar; ofrecer; *n.* licitación, oferta *f.*

bide, *vi.* esperar, aguardar

biennial, *adj.* bienal

big, *adj.* grande

bile, *n.* bilis, *f.*; cólera, *f.*

bilingual, *adj.* bilingüe

bill, *n.* pico de ave, *m.*; cuenta, *f.*; factura, *f.*; **bill of fare,** menú, *m.*; *vt.* facturar; *vi.* arrullar

billfold, *n.* billetera, *f.*

billiards, *n.* billar, *m.*

billion, *n.* billón, *m.*, millón de millones (en España, Inglaterra, y Alemania); mil millones (en Francia y los Estados Unidos)

bimonthly, *adj.* bimestral

bind, *vt.* atar; unir; encuadernar; obligar; *vi.* ser obligatorio

binder, *n.* encuadernador, *m.*

binding, *n.* venda, fala, *f.*; encuadernación, *f.*

binoculars, *n. pl.* gemelos, binóculos, *m. pl.*

bioastronautics, *n. pl.* bioastronáutica, *f.*

biochemical, *adj.* bioquímico

biodegradable, *adj.* biodegradable, hecho de compuestos que se descomponen por bacterias

biography, *n.* biografía, *f.*

biology, *n.* biología, *f.*

biopsy, *n.* biopsia, *f.*

biosphere, *n.* biosfera, *f.*

birch, *n.* (bot.) abedul, *m.*

bird, *n.* ave, *f.*; pájaro, *m.*

birth, *n.* nacimiento, *m.*; origen, *m.*; parto, *m.*; linaje, *m.*; **to give birth,** dar a luz, parir

birthday, *n.* cumpleaños, natalicio, *m.*; **to have a birthday,** cumplir años

birthmark, *n.* lunar, *m.*

birthplace, *n.* lugar de nacimiento, *m.*

biscuit, *n.* galleta

bishop, *n.* obispo, *m.*; alfil (en el ajedrez), *m.*

bit, *n.* pedacito, *m.*; **two bits** (coll. E.U.A.), 25¢ (moneda de E.U.A.); *pretérito* del verbo **bite**

bite, *vt.* morder; *n.* mordida, *f.*; tentempié, *m.*

bitten, *p. p.* del verbo **bite**

bitter, *adj.* amargo

bitterness, *n.* amargor, *m.*; amargura, *f.*

biweekly, *adj.* quincenal; *adv.* quincenalmente

B/L, b.l., bill of lading, conto., conocimiento de embarque

blab, *vt.*, *vi.* charlar, divulgar; chismear

black, *adj.* negro; oscuro; *n.* negro, *m.*

blackberry, *n.* zarzamora, mora, *f.*

blackboard, *n.* pizarra, *f.*; encerado, pizarrón, tablero, *m.*

blacksmith, *n.* herrero, *m.*

bladder, *n.* vejiga, *f.*

blade, *n.* brizna, hoja, *f.*

blame, *vt.* culpar

blameless, *adj.* inocente, intachable

bland, *adj.* blando, suave

blank, *adj.* en blanco; **blank form,** blanco, esqueleto, *m.*; *n.* blanco, espacio en blanco, *m.*

blanket, *n.* frazada, manta, *f.*; *adj.* general

blasé, *adj.* abúlico

blast, *n.* explosión, *f.*; chorro, *m.*; **blast furnace,** alto horno, *m.*

blaze, *n.* fuerg *m.*; incendio, *m.*; hoguera, *f.*; *vi.* resplandecer

bleach, *vt.*, *vi.* blanquear

bleat, *n.* balido, *m.*; *vi.* balar

bled, *pretérito* y *p. p.* del verbo **bleed**

bleed, *vt.*, *vi.* sangrar

blemish, *vt.* manchar; infamar; *n.* tacha, *f.*; infamia, *f.*; lunar, *m.*

blend, *vt.* mezclar, combinar; *vi.* armonizar; *n.* mezcla, *f.*; ammonía, *f.*

bless, *vt.* bendecir, santiguar

blessing, *n.* bendición, *f.*

blind, *adj.* ciego; oculto; *vt.* cegar; deslumbrar; *n.* subterfugio, *m.*; **Venetian blinds,** persianas

blindfold, *vt.* vendar los ojos

bink, *vi.* guiñar, parpadear

bliss, *n.* felicidad, *f.*; embeleso, *m.*

blister, *n.* vejiga, ampolla, *f.*; *vi.* ampollarse

bloat, *vi.* abotagarse

bloc, *n.* bloque, *m.*

block, *n.* bloque, *m.*; obstáculo, *m.*; manzana (de una calle), *f.*; *vi.* bloquear

blond, blonde, *n.* y *adj.* rubio, bia; (Mex.) güero, güera

blood, *n.* sangre, *f.*

blood bank, *n.* banco de sangre, *m.*

bloody, *adj.* sangriento

bloom, n. flor, f.; florecimiento, m.; vi. florecer

blossom, n. flor, f.; capullo, botón, m.; vi. florecer

blot, vt. manchar (lo escrito); cancelar; n. mancha, f.

blotter, n. papel secante, m.

blouse n. blusa, f.

blow, n. golpe, m.; vi. soplar, sonar; vt. soplar; inflar

blowout, n. reventazón, f.; (auto.) ruptura de neumático o llanta

blue, adj. azul, celeste

bluebird, n. (orn.) azulejo, m.

blues, n. pl. (coll.) melancolía, f.; tipo de jazz melancólico

bluff. n. risco escarpado, morro, m.; fanfarronada, f.; vi. engañar, hacer alarde

bluing, blueing, n. añil, m.

blunder, n. desatino, disparate, m.; vt. y vi. desatinar, equivocarse

blur, n. mancha, f.; vt. manchar; infamar

blvd., boulevard, bulevar, m.

boar, n. verraco, m.; **wild boar,** jabalí, m.

board, n. tabla, f.; mesa, f.; (naut.) bordo, m.; **board of directors,** directorio, m., junta directiva, f.;vt.abordar; entablar; vi. residir en casa de huéspedes; recibir huéspedes

boardinghouse, n. casa de huéspedes, pensión, f.

boast, n. jactancia, ostentación, f.; vi. presumir; jactarse

boastful. adj. iactancioso

boat, n. barco, m., embarcación, f.; barca, f.

bob, vi. menearse

bobby pin, n. horquilla, f.

bode, vt. y vi. presagiar

bodily, adj. y adv. corpóreo; en peso

body, n. cuerpo, m.; individuo, m.; gremio, m.

bodyguard, n. (mil.) guardaespaldas, m.

boil, vi. hervir, bullir; vt. cocer; n. (med.) nacido, m.

boiler, n. caldera, f.

boisterous, adj. ruidoso

bold, adj. audaz

bolt, n. tornillo, m.; cerrojo, m.

bom n. bomba, f.

bond, n. vínculo, lazo, m.; (com.) bono, m.

bone, n. hueso, m.; vt. deshuesar

boneless, adj. sin huesos, deshuesado

bonfire, n. hoguera, fogata, f.

bonnet, n. gorra, f.; bonete, m.

bony, adj. huesudo

boob, booby, n. tonto, tonta

book, n. libro, m.; vt. asentar en un libro, inscribir

bookcase, n. librero, m.

bookkeeper, n. tenedor de libros, m.

booklet, n. folleto, m.

bookstore, n. librería, f.

boom, n. estampido, m.; auge industrial, m.

boon, n. favor, m.

boost, vt. levantar; vi. aprobar con entusiasmo; n. ayuda, f., empuje, m.

boot, n. bota, f.; **to boot,** además, por añadidura

bootblack, n. limpiabotas, m.

booth, n. puesto, m.; cabina, f.; reservado, m.

bootlegger, n. contrabandista (usualmente de licores), m.

booty, n. botín, m.; presa, f.; saqueo, m.

border, n. orilla, f.; borde, m.; frontera, f.; vi. confinar; bordear

borderline, n. límite, m., orilla, f.; adj. incierto

boric, adj. bórico; **boric acid,** ácido bórico

boring, adj. fastidioso, latoso

born, adj. nacido; destinado; **to be born,** nacer

borne, p. p. del verbo **bear**

borrow, vt. pedir prestado

bosom, n. seno, pecho, m.

botanical, adj. botátnico

botany, n. botánica, f.

both, pron. y adj. ambos, ambas

bother, vt. molestar; incomodar; n. estorbo, m.; molestia, f.

bottle, *n.* botella, *f.*; *vt.* embotellar

bottleneck, *n.* cuello de botella, *m.*; cuello de estrangulación, *m.*

bottom, *n.* fondo, *m.*

bottomless, *adj.* insondable; sin fondo

boudoir, *n.* tocador, *m.*, recámara, *f.*

bough, *n.* rama (de un árbol), *f.*

bought, *pretérito y p. p.* del verbo **buy**

bouillon, *n.* caldo, *m.*

boulevard, *n.* paseo, bulevar, *m.*

bounce, *vi.* arremeter, brincar

bouncing, *adj.* fuerte, robusto

bound, *n.* límite, *m.*; salto, *m.*; *vt.* confinar, limitar; *vi.* brincar; *pretérito y p. p.* del verbo **bind**; *adj.* destinado; **bound for,** con rumbo

boundary, *n.* límite, *m.*; frontera, *f.*

boundless, *adj.* ilimitado, infinito

bouquet, *n.* ramillete de flores, ramo, *m.*

bout, *n.* encuentro, combate, *m.*

bow, *vi.* encorvarse; hacer reverencia; *n.* reverencia, inclinación, *f.*

bow, *n.* arco, *m.*; lazo (de cinta, etc.), *m.*; (naut.) proa, *f.*

bowels, *n. pl.* intestinos, *m. pl.*; entrañas, *f. pl.*

bowl, *n.* taza, *f.*; **wash bowl,** lavamanos, *m.*; *vi.* jugar boliche o bolos

bowlegged, *adj.* patizambo

box, *n.* caja, *f.*; cofre, *m.*; **box office,** taquilla, *f.*; *vi.* boxear

boxer, *n.* boxeador, pugilista, *m.*

boxing, *n.* boxeo, pugilato, *m.*

boy, *n.* muchacho, *m.*; niño, *m.*; **boy scout,** muchacho explorador, *m.*

boycott, *n.* boicot, boicoteo, *m.*

boyhood, *n.* niñez (varones), *f.*

boyish, *adj.* pueril, propio de un niño varón

bra, *n.* brassière, *m.*, soporte (para senos), *m.*

bracelet, *n.* brazalete, *m.*, pulsera, *f.*

bracket, *n.* ménsula, *f.*; (fig.) categoría, *f.*; **brackets,** *pl.* (print.) corchetes, *m. pl.*

brag, *n.* jactancia, *f.*; *vi.* jactarse

brain, *n.* cerebro, *m.*

brake, *n.* freno, *m.*

branch, *n.* rama (de árbol), *f.*

brand, *n.* marca, *f.*; nota de infamia, *f.*; marca de fábrica, *f.*; *vt.* herrar (ganado); infamar

brandy, aguardiente, *m.*; coñac, *m.*

brass, *n.* latión, bronce, *m.*

brave, *adj.* valiente

brawl, *n.* pelotera, *f.*

bray, *vi.* rebuznar; *n.* rebuzno (del asno), *m.*

breach, *n.* rotura, brecha, *f.*; violación, *f.*

bread, *n.* pan, *m.*

break, *vt. y vi.* quebrar; violar; *n.* rotura, *f.*; intrrrupción, *f.*

break-even point, *n.* punto en que un negocio empieza a cubrir los gastos que ocasiona

breakfast, *n.* almuerzo, desayuno, *m.*

breast, *n.* pecho, seno, *m.*; tetas, *f. pl.*

breath, *n.* aliento, *m.*, respiración, *f.*; soplo (de aire), *m.*

breathe, *vt. y vi.* respirar; resollar

breathing, *n.* respiración, *f.*

breathless, *adj.* falto de aliento

bred, *pretérito y p. p.* del verbo **breed; well bred,** bien educado, de buenos modales

breech, *n.* trasero, *m.*

breeches, *n. pl.* calzones, *m. pl.*

breed, *n.* casta, raza, *f.*; *vt.* procrear, engendrar; educar

breeder reactor, *n.* reactor reproductor, *m.*

breeding, *n.* crianza, *f.*; moda-

les, *m. pl.*
breeze, *n.* brisa, *f.*
brewery, *n.* cervecería, *f.*
bribe, *n.* cohecho, soborno, *m.*; *vt.* sobornar
brick, *n.* ladrillo, *m.*
bricklayer, *n.* albañil, *m.*
bridal, *adj.* nupcial
bride, *n.* novia, desposada, *f.*
bridegroom, *n.* novio, desposado, *m.*
bridesmaid, *n.* madrina de boda, *f.*
bridge, *n.* puente, *m.*
bridgework, *n.* puente dental, *m.*
bridle, *n.* brida, *f.*, freno, *m.*; *vt.* embridar; reprimir, refrenar
brief, *adj.* breve, sucinto; *n.* compendio *m.*; (law) escrito, *m.*; **brief case,** portapapeles, *m.*
brig, *n.* bergantín, *m.*
bright, *adj.* claro, brillante; vivo
brighten, *vt.* pulir, dar lustre; *vi.* aclarar
brightness, *n.* esplendor, *m.*, brillantez, *f.*
brilliance, brilliancy, *n.* brillantez, *f.*, brillo, esplendor, *m.*
brilliant, *adj.* brillante; luminoso; resplandeciente; *n.* brillante, *m.*
brim, *n.* borde, extremo *m.*; orilla, *f.*; ala (de sombrero), *f.*
bring, *vt.* llevar, traer; **to bring about,** efectuar; **to bring up,** educar
brink, *n.* orilla, *f.*; margen, *m.* y *f.*, borde, *m.*
broad, *adj.* ancho; **broad jump,** salto de longitud, *m.*
broadcast, *n.* radiodifusión, *f.*; *vt.* radiodifundir, perifonear
broaden, *vi.* ensancharse
broad-minded, *adj.* tolerante
broil, *vt.* asar (carne, etc.)
broiler, *n.* parrilla, *f.*
broke, *pretérito* del verbo **break;** *adj.* (coll.) en bancarrota; sin dinero
broken, *adj.* roto, quebrado

broker, *n.* corredor, agente, *m.*
bronchitis, *n.* bronquitis, *f.*
brooch, *n.* broche, *m.*
brood, *n.* cría, nidada, *f.*
brook, *n.* arroyo, *m.*, quebrada, *f.*
broom, *n.* escoba, *f.*
broth, *n.* caldo, *m.*
brother, *n.* hermano, *m.*
brotherhood, *n.* hermandad; fraternidad, *f.*
brother-in-law, *n.* cuñado, *m.*
brotherly, *adj.* fraternal
brought, *pretérito* y *p. p.* del verbo **bring**
brow, *n.* ceja , *f.*; frente, *f.*
brown, *adj.* castaño, pardo; *vt.* dorar, tostar
bruise, *vt.* magullar; *n.* magulladura, contusión, *f.*
brunet, brunette, *n., adj.* trigueño, trigueña, moreno, morena
brush, *n.* escobilla, *f.*; brocha, *f.*; cepillo, *m.*; *vt.* acepillar
brutal, *adj.* brutal, bruto
brute, *n.* bruto, *m.*; *adj.* feroz, bestial
B.S., Bachelor of Science, Br. en C., Bachiller en Ciencias
bu., bushel, medida de áridos (Ingl. 36.37 litros; E.U. 35.28 litros)
bubble, *n.* burbuja, *f.*; *vi.* bullir; **bubble over,** borbotar; hervir
buckle, *n.* hebilla, *f.*; *vt.* afianzar
bud, *n.* pimpollo, botón, *m.*; capullo, *m.*
buddy, *n.* hermano, compañero, muchachito, *m.*
budget, *n.* presupuesto, *m.*
buffalo, *n.* búfalo, *m.*
buffers, *n. pl.* (rail.) parachoques, *m. pl.*
buffet, *n.* aparador, *m.*; ambigú, *m.*
bug, *n.* insecto, *m.*
bugle, *n.* clarín, *m.*; corneta, *f.*
bugler, *n.* corneta, trompetero, *m.*
build, *vt.* edificar; construir
builder, *n.* arquitecto, constructor, *m.*

building, *n.* edificio, *m.*; construcción, *f.*

bulb, *n.* bulbo, *m.*; **electric light bulb,** foco o bombilla de luz eléctrica

bulge, *vi.* combarse

bulk, *n.* masa, *f.*; bulto, volumen, *m.*; **in bulk,** a granel

bull, *n.* toro, *m.*

bulldog, *n.* bulldog, *m.*

bulldoze, *vt.* intimidar

bullet, *n.* bala, *f.*

bulletin, *n.* boletín, *m.*; **bulletin board,** tablilla para noticias, *f.*

bulletproof, *adj.* a prueba de bala

bullfight, *n.* corrida de toros, *f.*

bullfighter, *n.* torero, toreador, *m.*

bully, *n.* valentón, *m.*; rufián, *m.*; *vi.* fanfarronear

bulwark, *n.* baluarte, *m.*; *vt.* fortificar

bum, *n.* hombre vago, *m.*

bumblebee, *n.* abejón, abejorro, zángano, *m.*

bump, *n.* hinchazón, *f.*; golpe, *m.*; *vt.* y *vi.* chocar contra

bumper, *n.* amortiguador de golpes, *m.*; (auto) defensa, *f.*

bunch, *n.* ramo, racimo, *m.*

bundle, *n.* haz (de leña, etc.), *m.*; bulto, *m.*; *vt.* atar, hacer un lío o un bulto; **bundle up,** envolver; abrigarse

bunion, *n.* juanete, *m.*

bunk, *n.* (coll.) cama, *f.*; patraña, *f.*

buoy, *n.* boya, *f.*

burden, *n.* carga, *f.*, cargo, *m.*; *vt.* cargar; gravar

bureau, *n.* armario, *m.*; tocador, *m.*, cómoda, *f.*, oficina, *f.*; departamento, *m.*

burglar, *n.* ladrón, *m.*

burial, *n.* entierro, *m.*

burlap, *n.* arpillera, *f.*

burlesque, *adj.* burlesco; *vt.* y *vi.* burlarse; parodiar

burn, *vt.* quemar, incendiar; *vi.* arder; *n.* quemadura, *f.*

burst, *vi.* reventar; abrirse; *n.* reventón, *m.*

bury, *vt.* enterrar, sepultar

bus, *n.* ómnibus, camión, *m.*

bushel, *n.* medida de áridos (Ingl. 36.37 litros; E.U. 35.28 litros)

business, *n.* negocio, *m.*, ocupación, *f.*

businessman, *n.* comerciante, *m.*

businesswoman, *n.* mujer de negocios

bust, *n.* busto, *m.*

bustle, *n.* confusión, *f.*; ruido, *m.*

busy, *adj.* ocupado; atareado

busybody, *n.* entremetido, entremetida

but, *prep.* excepto; *conj.* y *adv.* menos; pero; solamente

butcher, *n.* carnicero, *m.*; *vt.* matar atrozmente

butt, *n.* cabezada (golpe de la cabeza), *f.*; colilla (de cigarro), *f.*

butter, *n.* mantequilla, manteca, *f.*

butterfly, *n.* mariposa, *f.*

buttermilk, *n.* suero de mantequilla, *m.*; (Mex,) jocoqui, *m.*

butterscotch, *n.* especie de dulce de azúcar y mantequilla

buttock, *n.* nalga, *f.*; anca, *f.*

button, *n.* botón, *m.*; *vt.* abotonar

buttonhole, *n.* ojal, *m.*

buxom, *adj.* robusto y rollizo

buy, *vt.* comprar

buzz, *n.* susurro, soplo, *m.*; *vi.* zumbar, cuchichear

buzzer, *n.* zumbador, *m.*

by, *prep.* por; a, en; de, con; al lado de, cerca de; *adv.* cerca, al lado de

bygone, *adj.* pasado

bylaws, *n. pl.* estatutos, *m. pl.*, reglamento, *m.*

by-pass, *n.* desviación, *f.*; *vt.* evadir, eludir

by-product, *n.* derivado, *m.*

C

C., centigrade, C., centigrado;

current, corrte., cte., corriente

C.A., Central America, C.A. Centro América

cab, n. coche de plaza, coche de alquiler, m.

cabdriver, n. cochero, m.; (auto.) taxista, m. y f.

cabana, n. cabaña, f.

cabaret, n. cabaret, m.

cabbage, n. repollo, m.; berza, col, f.

cabin, n. cabaña, cabina, barraca, f.; camarote, m.

cabinet, n. gabinete, m.; ministerio, m.

cabinetmaker, n. ebanista, m.

cable, n. cable, cablegrama, m.

cablegram, n. cablegrama, m.

cackle, vi. cacarear, graznar; n. cacareo, m.; charla, f.

cactus, n. (bot.) cacto, m.

cad, n. sinverguenza, m.

cadence, n. cadencia, f.

cadet, n. cadete, m.

café, n. café, restaurante, m.

cafeteria, n. restaurante en donde se sirve uno mismo

cake, n. bollo, m.; torta, f.; bizcocho, pastel, m.; vi. endurecerse; coagularse

calamity, n. calamidad, miseria f.

calcimine, n. lechada, f.

calcium, n. calcio, m.

calculate, vt. calcular, contar

calendar, n. calendario, m.

calf, n. ternero, ternera; cuero de ternero; **calf of the leg**, pantorrilla, f.

calfskin, n. piel de ternera, f.; becerro, m.

caliber, n. calibre, m.

calisthentics, n. pl. calisténica, gimnasia

call, vt. llamar nombrar; convocar, citar; n. llamada, f.; vocación, profesión, f.

calling, n. profesión, vocación, f.

callous, adj. calloso, endurecido; insensible

calm, n. calma, tranquilidad, f.; vt. calmar; aplacar; **to calm down**, serenar, sere-

narse

camera, n. cámara, f.

camouflage, n. (mil.) camuflage, m., simulación, f., engaño, m.

camp, n. campamento, campo, m.; vi. acampar

campaign, n. campaña, f.

campfire, n. hoguera en el campo

camphor, n. alcanfor, m.

campus, n. patio o terrenos de una universidad, etc

can, vi. poder, saber; vt. envasar en latas; n. lata, f., bote de lata; **can opener**, abrelatas, m.

Canada, Canadá, m.

Canadian, n. y adj. canadiense

canal, n. canal, m.

Canal Zone, Zona del Canal, f.

Canaries, Canary Islands, Las Canarias, Islas Canarias, f. pl.

canary, n. canario, m.

canasta, n. canasta, f. (juego de naipes)

cancel, vt. cancelar, borrar; anular

cancer, n. cáncer, m.

candid, adj. cándido, ingenuo

candidate, n. candidato, candidata, aspirante (a un puesto, cargo, etc.), m. y f.

candied, adj. garapiñado, en almíbar

candle, n. vela, bujía, f.

candlestick, n. candelero, m.

candy, n. confite, bombón, dulce, m.

cane, n. caña, f.; bastón, m.

cannibal, n. caníbal, m., antropófago, antropófaga

cannon, n. cañón, m.

canoe, n. canoa, f.; bote, m.; (Mex.) chalupa, f.; piragua, f.

canonize, vt. canonizar

cantaloupe, n. melón de verano, m.

canteen, n. (mil.) cantina, f., especie de tienda de provisiones para soldados; cantimplora, f.

canvas, n. lona

canvass, *vi.* solicitar votos, etc

canyon, *n.* desfiladero, cañon, *m.*

cap, *n.* gofia, *f.*, cachucha, *f.*; **cap and gown**, traje académico o toga y birrete

cap., **capital letter**, may., letra mayúscula

capable, *adj.* capaz

capacity, *n.* capacidad, *f.*; inteligencia, habilidad, *f.*; **seating capacity**, cabida, *f.*, cupo, *m.*

cape, *n.* cabo, *m.*; capa, *f.*; capota, *f.*; capote, *m.*

Cape Horn, Cabo de Hornos, *m.*

Cape of Good Hope, Cabo de Buena Esperanza, *m.*

caper, *n.* travesura, *f.*; alcaparra, *f.*

capital, *adj.* capital, excelente; principal; **capital punishment**, pena de muerte; *n.* (arch.) capitel, *m.*; capital (la ciudad principal), *f.*; capital, fondo, *m.*; mayuscula, *f.*

capitalist, *n.* capitalista, *m.* y *f.*

captain, *n.* capitán, *m.*

capricious, *adj.* caprichoso

capsize, *vt.*, *vr.* volcar, volcarse

capt., **Captain**, cap., capitán

captain, *n.* capitán, *m.*

captivate, *vt.* cautivar

captive, *n.* cautivo, va, esclavo, esclava

capture, *n.* captura, *f.*; toma, *f.*; *vt.* apresar; capturar

car, *n.* carreta, *f.*; carro, *m.*; coche, *m.*

caravan, *n.* caravana, *f.*

carbon, *n.* carbón, *m.*; **carbon paper**, papel carbón

carburetor, *n.* carburador, *m.*

carcass, *n.* animal muerto, *m.*; casco, *m.*; armazón, *m.*

card, *n.* naipe, *m.*, carta, *f.*; tarjeta, *f.*

cardinal, *adj.* cardinal, principal; rojo, purpurado; *n.* cardenal, *m.*; (orn.) cardenal, *m.*

care, *n.* cuidado, *m.*; cargo, *m.*; vigilancia, *f.*; *vi.* cuidar, tener cuidado

career, *n.* carrera, profesión, *f.*

carefree, *adj.* sin cuidados

careful, *adj.* cuidadoso, solícito

careless, *adj.* descuidado

caress, *n.* caricia, *f.*; *vt.* acariciar, halagar

caretaker, *n.* velador, *m.*

carfare, *n.* pasaje (de tranvía), *m.*

carnation, *n.* (bot.) clavel, *m.*

carnival, *n.* carnaval, *m.*

carol, *n.* villancico, *m.*

carpenter, *n.* carpintero, *m.*

carpet, *n.* tapiz, *m.*; **carpet sweeper**, barredor de alfombra, *m.*

carport, *n.* cobertizo para auto

carriage, *n.* porte, talante, *m.*; coche, carruaje, *m.*; cureña de cañón, *f.*

carrier, *n.* portador, carretero, *m.*; **aircraft carrier**, porta aviones, *m.*; **carrier pigeon**, paloma mensajera, *f.*

carrot, *n.* zanahoria,

carry, *vt.* llevar, conducir; portar; cargar; **to carry on**, continuar; **to carry out**, llevar a cabo, realizar

cart, *n.* carro, *m.*; carreta, *f.*; carretón, *m.*; *vt.* y *vi.* acarrear

cartload, *n.* carretada,

cartoon, *n.* caricatura, *f.*

cartridge, *n.* cartucho, *m.*; **cartridge shell**, cápsula, *f.*

carve, *vt.* cincelar; trinchar, tajar; grabar; *vi.* esculpir

case, *n.* estado, *m.*; situación, *f.*; caso, *m.*; estuche, *m.*, caja, *f.*; (gram.) caso, *m.*

cash, *n.* dinero contante o efectivo; *vt.* cobrar o hacer effectivo (un cheque, etc.)

cashier, *n.* cajero, cajera

cashmere, *n.* casimir (tela), *m.*

cask, *n.* barril, tonel, *m.*

casket, *n.* ataúd, *m.*

casserole, *n.* cacerola, *f.*

cast, *vt.* tirar, lanzar; echar; modelar; *n.* tiro, golpe, *m.*; (theat.) reparto, *m.*; *adj.* fundido, **cast iron**, hierro colado; **cast steel**, acero fundido

castanets, *n. pl.* castañuelas, *f. pl.*

Castile, Castilla, *f.*

Castilian, *n.* y *adj.* castellano, castellana

castle, *n.* castillo, *m.*

castor, *adj.* descartado

castor, *n.* castor, *m.*; sombrero castor; **castor oil,** aceite de ricino, *m.*

casual, *adj.* casual, fortuito

casualty, *n.* casualidad, *f.*; acaso, accidente, *m.*; caso, *m.*; **casualties,** *n. pl.* victimas de accidentes o de guerra, etc

cat, *n.* gato, *m.*, gata, **to let the cat out of the bag,** revelar un secreto

cat., catalog, catálogo; **catechism,** catecismo

catalogue, *n.* catálogo, *m.*

Catatonia, Cataluña, *f.*

Catalonian, *n.* y *adj.* catalán, catalana

cataract, *n.* cascada, catarata, *f.*; (med.) catarata, *f.*

catarrh, *n.* catarro, *m.*

catastrophe, *n.* catástrofe, *f.*

catch, *vt.* coger, agarrar; atrapar; *vi.* pegarse, ser contagioso; **to catch cold,** resfriarse; *n.* botín, *m.*, presa, *f.*; captura, *f.*; trampa, *f.*

catcher, *n.* (baseball) parador de la pelota, *m.*

catching, *adj.* contagioso

catchy, *adj.* atrayente, pegajoso

catechism, *n.* catecismo, *m.*

category, *n.* categoría, *f.*

caterpillar, *n.* oruga, *f.*

cathartic, *adj.* (med.) catártico; *n.* purgante, laxante, *m.*

cathedral, *n.* catedral, *f.*

catholic, *n.* y *adj.* católico, católica

catholicism, catolicismo, *m.*

catsup, *n.* salsa de tomate, *f.*

cattle, *n.* ganado, *m.*

caught, *pretérito* y *p. p.* del verbo **catch**

cauliflower, *n.* coliflor, *f.*

cause, *n.* causa, *f.*; razón, *f.*; motivo, *m.*; *vt.* motivar, causar

caution, *n.* prudencia, precaución, *f.*; aviso, *m.*; *vt.* advertir

cautious, *adj.* prudente, cauto

cavalier, *n.* caballero, *m.*

cavalry, *n.* caballería,

cave, *n.* caverna, *f.*

cc., c.c., cubic centimeter, centímetro cúbico

C.E., Civil Engineer, Ing. Civil, Ingeniero Civil

cede, *vt.* ceder, trasferir

ceiling, *n.* techo o cielo raso, *m.*; (avi.) cielo máximo; *adj.* máximo

celebrate, *vt.* celebrar

celebration, *n.* celebración, *f.*

celebrity, *n.* celebridad, fama, *f.*; persona célebre

celestial, *adj.* celestial

cell, *n.* celda, *f.*; célula, *f.*

cellar, *n.* sótano, *m.*, bodega, *f.*

cello, *n.* violonchelo, *m.*

cement, *n.* cemento, *m.*; *vt.* cimentar

cemetery, *n.* cementerio, *m.*

cen., cent., central, cent. central

censor, *n.* censor, *m.*; crítico, *m.*

censorship, *n.* censura, *f.*

censure, *n.* censura, reprensión, *f.*; *vt.* censurar, criticar

census, *n.* censo, encabezamiento, *m.*

cent, *n.* centavo, *m.*; céntimo, *m.*; per por ciento

cent., centigrade, C. centígrado; **century,** siglo

centennial, *n.* y *adj.* centenario, *m.*

center, *n.* centro, *m.*; *vt.* centrar; reconcentrar; *vi.* colocarse en el centro, reconcentrarse

centigrade, *adj.* centígrado

centigram, *n.* centigramo, *m.*

centimeter, *n.* centímetro, *m.*

centipede, *n.* ciempiés, *m.*

central, *adj.* central; céntrico

Central America, América Central, *f.*

centralize, *vt.* centralizar

century, *n.* centuria, *f.*; siglo, *m.*

ceramics, n. cerámica, f.
cereal, n. cereal, m.
cerebral, adj. cerebral
ceremony, n. ceremonia.
certain, adj. cierto, evidente
certainty, n. certeza, seguridad, f.; certidumbre, f.
certificate, n. certificado, m.; (com.) bono, m.; certificación, f.
certified, adj. certificado
certify, vt. certificar, afirmar; dar fe
chagrin, n. mortificación, f.; disgusto, m.
chain, n. cadena, f.; serie, sucesión, f.; vt. encadenar
chair, n. silla
chairman, n. presidente (de una reunión o junta) m.
chalk, n. greda, f.; tiza, f.; yeso, m.
challenge, n. desafío, m.; vt. desafiar; retar
chamber, n. cámara, f.; aposento, m.
champagne, n. vino de Champaña, champaña, m.
champion, n. campeón, campeona
championship, n. campeonato, m.
chance, n. ventura, suerte, oportunidad, casualidad, f., acaso, m.; riesgo, m.; **by chance,** si acaso; vi. acaecer, acontecer; adj. fortuito, casual
change, vt. cambiar; variar; vi. variar, alterarse; n. cambio, m.
channel, n. canal, m.; conducto, m.
chaos, n. caos, m.
chapel, n. capilla, f.
chaperon, n. dueña, f.; acompañante de respeto
chaplain, n. capellán, m.
chapter, n. capítulo, m.
character, n. carácter, m.; letra, f.; calidad, f.; (theat.) papel, m.; personaje, m.
characteristic, adj. característico; típico; n. rasgo, m. peculiaridad, f.

charge, vt. encargar, comisionar; cobrar; cargar; acusar, imputar; n. cargo, cuidado, m.; acusación, f.; costo, m.; ataque, m.
charity, n. caridad, beneficencia, f.
charm, n. encanto, m.; atractivo, m.; vt. encantar; seducir
charming, adj. seductor; simpático, encantador
charter, n. carta constitucional, f.; vt. fletar (un barco, etc.); estatuir; **charter member,** miembro o socio fundador, m.
chase, vt. cazar; perseguir; n. caza, f.
chaste, adj. casto; puro
chastise, vt. castigar
chastity, n. castidad, f.
chat, vi. charlar, platicar; n. plática, charla, conversación, f.
chauffeur, n. chofer, m.
cheap, adj. barato
cheapen, vt. abaratar; denigrar
cheat, vt. engañar, hacer trampa; n. trampista, trápala, m. y f.
check, vt. reprimir, refrenar; verificar, comprobar; n. cheque, m.; restricción, f.; freno, m.
checkers, n. juego de damas, m.
checkroom, n. guardarropa, m.
cheek, n. cachete, carrillo, m., mejilla, f.
cheer, n. alegría, f.; vt. animar, alentar; vi. regocijarse
cheerful, adj. alegre, jovial
chef, n. cocinero, m.
chemical, adj. químico; n. sustancia química.
chemist, n. químico, química
chemistry, n. química, f.
cherish, vt. estimar
cherry, n. cereza, f.; adj. bermejo, rojo cereza
chess, n. juego de ajedrez, m.
chest, n. pecho, m.; cofre, m.; **chest of drawers,** cómoda, f.

chestnut, n. castaña, adj. castaño

chewing gum, n. chicle, m.

chick, n. pollito, polluelo, m.

chicken, n. pollo, m.; (fig.) joven, m. y f.; **chicken pox,** viruelas locas, varicela, f.

chief, adj. principal, capital; n. jefe, m.

child, n. niño, niña

childbirth, n. parto, alumbramiento, m.

childhood, n. infancia, niñez, f.

childish, adj. frívolo, pueril

children, n. pl. niños, m. pl.; hijos, m. pl.

Chilean, n. y adj. chileno, chilena

chill, adj. frío; n. frío, m.; escalofrío, m.; vt. enfriar; helar

chimney, n. chimenea, f.

chin, n. barba, f.

china, chinaware, n. porcelana, loza, f.

chintz, n. zaraza,

chip, vt. astillarse; n. astilla, f.; raspadura, f.

chirp, m. chirriar, gorjear; gorjeo, chirrido, m.

chisel, n. cincel, m.; vt. cincelar, grabar; (coll.) estafar, engañar

chivalrous, chivalric, adj. caballeroso

chivalry, n. caballería, f.; hazaña, f.

chives, n. cebolleta, f.

chlorine, n. cloro, m.

chloroform, n. cloroformo, m.

chocolate, n. chocolate, m.

choice, n. selección, f.; preferencia, f.; adj. selecto, escogido

choir, n. coro, m.

choose, vt. escoger, elegir

chop, vt. tajar, cortar; picar; n. chuleta, f.

choral, adj. coral

chord, n. (mus.) acorde, m.; cuerda, f.

chore, n. quehacer, m.; **chores,** n. pl. quehaceres de la casa, m. pl.

chorus, n. coro, m.

chose, pretérito del verbo **choose**

Christ, n. Jesucristo, Cristo, m.

christening, n. bautismo, bautizo, m.

Christian, n. y adj. cristiano, cristiana; **Christian name,** nombre de pila, m.

Christianity, m. cristianismo, m.

Christmas, n. Navidad, Pascua, f.; **Christmas gift,** aguinaldo, m.; **Christmas Eve,** Nochebuena, f.

chromium, n. cromo, m.

chronic, adj. crónico

chronicle, n. crónica, f., informe, m.

chubby, adj. gordo, rechoncho

chuckle, vi. reirse entre dientes

chum, n. camarada, m. y f. compañero, compañera

church, n. iglesia, f.; templo, m.

C.I.F., c.i.f., cost, insurance and freight, c.s.f., costo, seguro y flete

cigar, n. cigarro, puro, m.

cigarette, n. cigarrillo, cigarro, m.

cinema, n. cinematógrafo, m.

CIO, C.I.O., Congress of Industrial Organizations, C.I.O., Congreso de Organizaciones Industriales (de E.U.A.)

cipher, n. cifra, f., número, m.; cero, m.

circle, n. círculo, m.; rueda, f.; vt. circundar; cercar

circuit, n. circuito, m.

circular, adj. circular, redondo; n. carta circular, f.

circulate, vi. circular

circulation, n. circulación, f.

circumference, n. circunferencia, f.

circumstance, n. circunstancia, condición, f.; incidente, m.

circus, n. circo, m.

cite, vt. citar (a juicio); citar, referirse a

citizen, *n.* ciudadano, ciudadana

citizenship, *n.* ciudadanía, *f.*; nacionalidad, *f.*

citric, *adj.* cítrico

city, *n.* ciudad, *f.*; **city hall,** ayuntamiento, palacio municipal, *m.*

civic, *adj.* cívico; civics, *n.* instrucción cívica, *f.*

civil, *adj.* civil, cortés

civilian, *n.* particular, *m.*

civilization, *n.* civilización, *f.*

civilize, *vt.* civilizar

clad, *adj.* vestido, cubierto

claim, *vt.* reclamar; *n.* pretensión, *f.*; derecho, *m.*; reclamo, *m.*

clam, *n.* almeja, *f.*

clamorous, *adj.* clamoroso, estrepitoso

clamp, *n.* grapa, laña, *f.*; sujetador, *m.*; *vt.* sujetar, afianzar

clan, *n.* familia, tribu, *f.*

clandestine, *adj.* clandestino

clap, *vi.* palmotear, aplaudir

clapping, *n.* aplauso, palmoteo, *m.*

clarify, *vt.* y *vi.* clarificar, aclarar

clarinet, *n.* clarinete, *m.*

clash, *vi.* encontrarse; chocar; *n.* estrépito, *m.*; disputa, *f.*; choque, *m.*

clasp, *n.* broche, *m.*; hebilla, *f.*; sujetador, *m.*; abrazo, *m.*; *vt.* abrochar; abrazar

class, *n.* clase, *f.*; género, *m.*; categoría, *f.*

classic, *adj.* clásico; *n.* autor clásico; obra clásica

classical, *adj.* clásico

classify, *vt.* clasificar, graduar

classmate, *n.* condiscípulo, la

classroom, *n.* sala de clase, *f.*

clean, *adj.* limpio; casto; *vt.* limpiar

cleaning, *n.* limpieza, *f.*

cleanliness, *n.* limpieza, *f.*; aseo *m.*

clear: *adj.* claro, lúcido; neto; *vt.* clarificar, aclarar; absolver; *vi.* aclararse

clef, *n.* (mtís.) clave, *f.*

clemency, *n.* clemencia, *f.*

clergy, *n.* clero, *m.*

clergyman, *n.* eclesiástico, *m.*

clerical, *adj.* clerical, eclesiástico; **clerica work,** trabajo de oficina

clerk, *n.* escribiente, *m.*; dependiente, *m.*

clever, *adj.* hábil; inteligente

cliff, *n.* precipicio, *m.*, barranca, *f.*

climate, *n.* clima, *m.*,

climax, *n.* culminación, *f.*

climb, *vt.* escalar, trepar; *vi.* subir

cling, *vi.* adherirse, pegarse

clinic, *adj.* clínico; *n.* clínica, *f.*; consultorio, *m.*

clip, *vt.* cortar a raíz; *n.* tijeretada, *f.*; grapa, *f.*, gancho, *m.*

clipper, *n.* (avi.) clíper, *m.*; trasquilador, *m.*; **clippers,** *n. pl.* tijeras podadoras, *f. pl.*

clipping, *n.* recorte, *m.*

cloak, *n.* capa, *f.*; capote, *m.*

cloakroom, *n.* guardarropa, *m.*

clock, *n.* reloj, *m.*; **alarm clock,** despertador, *m.*

clog, *n.* obstáculo, *m.*; *vt.* obstruir; *vi.* coagularse

close, *vt.* cerrar, tapar; *vi.* cerrarse; *adj.* avaro; *adv.* cerca

closet, *n.* ropero, *m.*

close-up, *n.* fotografía de cerca, *f.*

clot, *n.* coagulación, *f.*; *vi.* cuajarse, coagularse

cloth, *n.* paño, *m.*; mantel, *m.*; lienzo, *m.*; material, *m.*

clothe, *vt.* vestir, cubrir.

clothes, *n. pl.* vestidura, *f.*; ropaje, *m.*; **clothes closet,** ropero, *m.*

clothespin, *n.* gancho para tender la ropa, *m.*

clothing, *n.* ropa, *f.*

clove, *n.* (bot.) clavo, *m.*

clover, *n.* trébol, *m.*

cloverleaf, *n.* hoja de trébol, *f.*; **cloverleaf (highway crossing),** *n.* hoja de triébol, *f.*

clown, *n.* payaso, payasa

club, *n.* club, *m.*, agrupación, *f.*; garrote, *m.*

clue, *n.* seña, *f.*; indicio, *m.*

clutch, *n.* (auto.) embrague,

m.; *vt.* embragar; agarrar

clutter, *vt.* poner en desorden; *vi.* atroparse

Co., co., company, Cía., Comp., Compania; **county,** condado

coach, *n.* coche, *m.*; carroza, *f.*; vagón, *m.*; entrenador (en un deporte), *m.*; *vt.* entrenar, preparar

coarse, *adj.* basto; ordinario; rústico

coast, *n.* costa, *f.*

coat, *n.* saco, *m.*, casaca, *f.*; abrigo, *m.*

cobbler, *n.* remendón, *m.*

cobweb, *n.* telaraña,

cock, *n.* gallo, *m.*

cockroach, *n.* cucaracha, *f.*

cocktail, *n.* cocktail, coctel, *m.*

cocoa, *n.* cacao, *m.*; chocolate

coconut, *n.* coco, *m.*

cocoon, *n.* capullo, *m.*

cod, *n.* bacalao, *m.*

C.O.D., c.o.d., cash on delivery, collect on delivery, C.A.E., cóbrese al entregar

code, *n.* código, *m.*; clave, *f.*

codfish, *n.* bacalao, *m.*

cod-liver oil, *n.* aceite de hígado de bacalao, *m.*

coeducational, *adj.* coeducativo

coffee, *n.* café, *m.*

coffeepot, *n.* cafetera,

cog, *n.* diente (de rueda), *m.*

cogwheel, *n.* rueda dentada, *f.*

coherence, *n.* coherencia, *f.*

cohesion, *n.* coherencia, cohesión, *f.*

coiffure, *n.* peinado, tocado, *m.*

coil, *vt.* recoger; enrollar; *n.* (elec.) carrete, *m.*; bobina, *f.*

coin, *n.* cuña, *f.*; moneda acuñada; dinero, *m.*; *vt.* inventar

coincide, *vi.* coincidir

coincidence, *n.* coincidencia, *f.*; casualidad, *f.*

Col., Colonel, Cnel. Coronel

colander, *n.* coladera, colador, *m.*

cold, *adj.* frío; **to be cold,** hacer frío; tener frío; *n.* frío, *m.*; frialdad, *f.*; (med.) resfriado, *m.*

coleslaw, *n.* ensalada de col cruda y picada

collaborate, *vt.* colaborar

collapse, *vi.* desplomarse; desmayarse; *n.* colapso, *m.*; derrumbe, desplome, *m.*

collapsible, *adj.* plegadizo

collar, *n.* collar, *m.*; cuello, *m.*

collarbone, *n.* clavícula,

collect, *vt.* recoger; cobrar

collection, *n.* colección, *f.*; colecta, *f.*; cobro, *m.*

collective, *adj.* colectivo

collectivization, *n.* colectivización, *f.*

collectivize, *vt.* colectivizar

collector, *n.* colector, *m.*; agente de cobros, *m.*

college, *n.* colegio, *m.*; escuela superior, universidad, *f.*

collie, *n.* perro de pastor, *m.*

collision, *n.* colisión, choque, *m.*

colon, *n.* colon, *m.*; dos puntos (signo de puntuación)

colonel, *n.* coronel, *m.*

colonial, *adj.* colonial

colony, *n.* colonia, *f.*

color, *n.* color, *m.*

colored, *adj.* colorado, pintado, teñido; de raza negra; con prejuicio

colorful, *adj.* pintoresco

coloring, *n.* colorido, *m.*; colorante, *m.*

colorless, *adj.* descolorido

colossal, *adj.* colosal

Columbus, Colón

column, *n.* columna, *f.*

columnist, *n.* diarista, *m.* y *f.*, periodista encargado de una sección especial

Com., Commander, jefe

coma, *n.* (med.) coma, *f.*; letargo, *m.*

comb, *n.* peine, *m.*; *vt.* peinar; cardar (la lana)

combat, *n.* combate, *m.*; batalla, *f.*; *vt.* y *vi.* combatir; resistir

combine, *vt.* combinar; *vi.* unirse

combustible, *adj.* y *n.* combustible, *m.*

combustion, n. combustión, f.

Comdr., Commander, jefe

come, vi. venir, acontecer; originar

comedian, n. comediante, m. y f., cómico, cómca

comedy, n. comedia, f.

comfort, n. consuelo, m.; comodidad, f.; vt. confortar; consolar

comfortable, adj. cómodo

comforter, n. colcha, f.

comforting, adj. consolador

comical, adj. chistoso, gracioso, bufo

coming, n. venida, llegada, f.; adj. venidero, entrante

comma , n. (gram.) coma, f.

command, vt. ordenar; mandar; n. orden, f.

commander, n. jefe, m., comandante, m.

commandment, n. mandamiento, m.

commemorate, vt. conmemorar; celebrar

comment, n. comentario, m.; vt. comentar

commentator, n. comentador, comentadora; (rad.) locutor, m.

commerce, n. comercio, m.

commercial, adj. comercial; n. (rad.) anuncio comercial, m.

commission, n. comisión, f.; vt. comisionar; encargar

commissioner, n. comisionado, delegado, m.

commit, vt. cometer; encargar; **to commit to memory**, aprender de memoria

committee, n. comité, m., comisión, junta, f.

commodity, n. mercancías, f. pl.

common, adj. común, público, general; ordinario

Common Market, n. Mereado Común, m.

commonwealth, n. república, f.; estado, m.; nación, f.

communicate, vt. comunicar, participar; vi. comunicarse

communication, n. comunicación, f.; **communications**

satellite, satélite de radiodifusión;

communion, n. comunion, f.; **to take communion**, comulgar

communism, n. comunismo, m.

communist, n. comunista, m. y f.

community, n. comunidad, f.; colectividad, f.; adj. comunal

commute, vt. conmutar; vi. viajar diariamente de un lugar a otro

compact, adj. compacto; sólido; n. polvera, f.; (auto.) coche o carro compacto

companion, n. companero, companera; acompañante, m. y f.

companionship, n. camaradería, f., compañerismo m.

company, n. compañía, f.; sociedad, f.

compare, vt. comparar; confrontar

compartment, n. compartimiento, compartimento, m.

compass, n. compás, m. piedad, f.

compel, vt. obligar

compensate, vt. y vi. compensar

compensation, n. compensación

competent, adj. competente, capaz

competition, n. competencia, f.

competitor, n. competidor, competidora; rival, m. y f.

compile, vt. compilar

complain, vi. quejarse, lamentarse

complaint, n. queja, f.

complement, n. complemento, m.

complete, adj. completo; vt. completar, acabar

complex, adj. complejo, compuesto; n. complejo m.

compliance, n. condescendencia, f.; consentimiento, m.; **in compliance with**, de acuerdo con, aocediendo (a sus deseos, etc.)

complicate, *vt.* complicar

compliment, *n.* lisonja, *f.*; piropo, requiebro, *m.*

comply, *vi.* cumplir; condescender

compose, *vt.* componer; sosegar; **to compose oneself,** serenarse

composed, *adj.* sosegado, moderado; **to be composed of,** componerse de

composer, *n.* autor, autora; compositor, compositora

composite, *n.* compuesto, *m.*; mezcla, *f.*

composure, *n.* calma, tranquilidad, *f.*

compound, *vt.* combinar; *adj.* compuesto; *n.* compuesto, *m.*

comprehend, *vt.* comprender; contener

comprehension, *n.* comprensión, *f.*

compress, *vt.* comprimir, estrechar; *n.* (med.) fomento, *m.*

comprise, *vt.* comprender, incluir

compromise, *n.* compromiso, convenio, *m.*; *vt.* transigir

compulsory, *adj.* obligatorio, compulsivo

compute, *vt.* computar, calcular

computer, (electronic) *n.* calculador electrónico, *m.*

comrade, *n.* camarada, *m.* y *f.*; compañero, compañera

con., against, contra; **conclusion,** conclusión

concede, *vt.* conceder, admitir

conceit, *n.* presunción, *f.*

conceive, *vt.* concebir

concentrate, *vt.* y *vi.* concentrar

concentration, *n.* concentración, *f.*

concept, *n.* concepto, *m.*

conception, *n.* concepción, *f.*; concepto, *m.*

concern, *vt.* concernir, importar; pertenecer; *n.* negocio, *m.*; interés, *m.*

concerned, *adj.* interesado; mortificado

concerning, *prep.* tocante a, respecto a

concession, *n.* concesión, cesión, *f.*

conciliation, *n.* conciliación, *f.*

concise, *adj.* conciso, sucinto

conclude, *vt.* concluir

concord, *n.* concordia, armonía, *f.*

concrete, *adj.* concreto; *n.* hormigón, cemento, *m.*; **concrete mixer,** hormigonera, *f.*

concussion, *n.* concusión, *f.*

condemn, *vt.* condenar

condense, *vt.* condensar; comprimir

condescend, *vi.* condescender; consentir

condescending, *adj.* complaciente, afable

condition, *n.* condición, *f.*; requisto, *m.*; estado, *m.*

condolence, *n.* pésame, *m.*, condolencia, *f.*

condominium, *n.* condominio, *m.*, propiedad horizontal

conduct, *n.* conducta, *f.*; conducción (de tropas), *f.*; **safe conduct,** salvoconducto, *m.*

conduct, *vt.* conducir, guiar

conductor, *n.* conductor, *m.*; guía, director, *m.*

confection, *n.* confitura, *f.*; confección, *f.*; confite, *m.*

confederate, *vi.* confederarse; *adj.* confederado; *n.* confederado, *m.*

confederation, *n.* federación, confederación, *f.*

confer, *vi.* conferenciar; consultarse; *vt.* otorgar

conference, *n.* conferencia, *f.*; sesión, junta, *f.*

confess, *vt.* y *vi.* confesar, confesarse

confession, *n.* confesión,

confide, *vt.* y *vi.* confiar; fiarse

confidence, *n.* confianza, seguridad, *f.*

confident, *adj.* cierto; seguro; confiado

confidential, *adj.* confidencial

confine, *vt.* limitar; aprisionar; *vi.* confinar

confinement, *n.* prisión, *f.*; encierro, *m.*; parto, *m.*

confirm, *vt.* confirmar; ratificar

confirmation, *n.* confirmación, *f.*; ratificación, *f.*

confiscate, *vt.* confiscar, decomisar

conflict, *n.* conflicto, *m.*; *vt.* estar en conflicto

conform, *vt.* y *vi.* conformar

conformity, *n.* conformidad, *f.*

confound, *vt.* confundir; **confound it!** *interj.* ¡caracoles!

confront, *vt.* confrontar, comparar

comfrontation, *n.* enfrentamiento, *m.*; careo, *m.*

confuse, *vt.* confundir; desordenar

confused, *adj.* confuso, desorientado

confusion, *n.* confusión, *f.*

congeal, *vt.* y *vi.* congelar

congenial, *adj.* congenial, compatible; **to be congenial,** simpatizar

congratulate, *vt.* felicitar

congregate, *vt.* congregar, reunir

congregation, *n.* congregación, reunión, *f.*

congress, *n.* congreso, *m.*

conjecture, *n.* conjetura, suposición, *f.*; *vt.* conjeturar; pronosticar

conjugate, *vt.* conjugar

conjunction, *n.* conjunción, *f.*

connect, *vt.* juntar, enlazar; relacionar

connection, *n.* conexión, *f.*; **connections,** *n. pl.* relaciones, *f. pl.*

connoisseur, *n.* perito, perita, conocedor, conocedora

conquer, *vt.* conquistar; vencer

conqueror *n.* vencedor, conquistador, *m.*

conquest, *n.* conquista, *f.*

conscience, *n.* conciencia, *f.*; escrúpulo, *m.*

conscientious, *adj.* concienzudo

conscious, *adj.* consciente;

consciously, *adv.* a sabiendas

consciousness, *n.* conocimiento, sentido, *m.*

conscription, *n.* reclutamiento obligatorio, *m.*

consecrate, *vt.* consagrar; dedicar

consecutive, *adj.* consecutivo

consent, *n.* consentimiento, *m.*; aprobación, *f.*; *vt.* consentir; aprobar

consequence, *n.* consecuencia, *f.*; importancia, *f.*

consequent, *adj.* consecutivo; consiguiente

conservation, *n.* conservación, *f.*

conservative, *adj.* conservador

conservatory, *n.* conservatorio, *m.*; invernadero, *m.*

conserve, *vt.* conservar, cuidar; hacer conservas

consider, *vt.* considerar, examinar; *vi.* pensar, deliberar; reflexionar

considerable, *adj.* considerable; importante; bastante

considerate, *adj.* considetado, prudente

consideration, *n.* consideración, *f.*; deliberación, *f.*

considering, *prep.* en vista de

consign, *vt.* consignar

consignee, *n.* consignatario, consignataria

consist, *vi.* consistir

consistent, *adj.* consistente; congruente

consolation, *n.* consuelo, *m.*

console, *vt.* consolar

consolidate, *vt.* y *vi.* consolidar, consolidarse

consort, *n.* consorte, *m.* y *f.*; esposo, esposa

conspicuous, *adj.* conspicuo, llamativo

conspiracy, *n.* conspiración, *f.*; trama, *f.*; complot, *m.*

conspire, *vt.* y *vi.* conspirar, maquinar

constant, *adj.* constante; fiel

consternation, *n.* consternación, *f.*

constipation, *n.* estreñimiento, *m.*

constitute, *vt.* constituir

constitution, *n.* constitución, *f.*

constitutional, *adj.* constitucional, legal

constrain, *vt.* constreñir; restringir

construct, *vt.* construir

construction, *n.* construcción, *f.*

construe, *vt.* interpretar

consul, *n.* cónsul, *m.*

consulate, *n.* consulado, *m.*

consult, *vt.* y *vi.* consultar

consultation, *n.* consulta, deliberación, *f.*

consume, *vt.* y *vi.* consumir

consumer, *n.* consumidor, consumidora

consumption, *n.* consumo, *m.*; consunción, tisis, *f.*

contact, *n.* contacto, *m.*; **contact lenses,** lentes de contacto; *vt.* y *vi.* tocar; poner en contacto

contagious, *adj.* contagioso

contain, *vt.* contener, comprender; caber; reprimir

container, *n.* envase, *m.*; recipiente, *m.*

contaminate, *vt.* contaminar

contemplate, *vt.* contemplar; *vi.* meditar, pensar

contempt, *n.* desprecio, desdén, *m.*

contend, *vi.* contender, disputar, afirmar

content, *adj.* contento, satisfecho; *vt.* contentar; *n.* contento, *m.*; satisfacción, *f.*

content, *n.* contenido, *m.*; contenido, *m.*; **contents,** *pl.* contenido, *m.*

contention, *n.* contención, *f.*

contentment, *n.* contentamiento, placer, *m.*

contest, *vt.* disputar, litigar; *n.* concurso, *m.*; competencia, *f.*

contestant, *n.* contendiente, litigante, *m.* y *f.*; concursante, *m.* y *f.*

continent, *n.* continente, *m.*

continental, *adj.* continental

contingent, *n.* contingente, *m.*; cuota, *f.*

continuation, *n.* continuación, *f.*; serie, *f.*

continue, *vt.* continuar; *vi.* durar, perseverar, persistir

continuity, *n.* continuidad, *f.*

continuous, *adj.* continuo

contour, *n.* contorno, *m.*

contract, *vt.* contraer; abreviar; contratar; *vi.* contraerse; *n.* contrato, pacto, *m.*

contraction, *n.* contracción, *f.*; abreviatura, *f.*

contradict, *vt.* contradecir

contradiction, *n.* contradicción, oposición, *f.*

contrail, *n.* estela de vapor, *f.*

contralto, *n.* contralto (voz), *m.*; contralto (persona), *m.* y *f.*

contrary, *adj.* contrario, opuesto; **on the contrary,** al contrario

contrast, *n.* contraste, *m.*; oposición, *f.*; *vt.* contrastar, oponer

contribute, *vt.* contribuir, ayudar

contributor, *n.* contribudador, contribudadora, contribuyente, *m.* y *f.*

contrite, *adj.* contrito, arrepentido

contrive, *vt.* inventar, maquinar

control, *n.* inspección, *f.*; control, *m.*; gobierno, *m.*; *vt.* restringir; gobernar; **to control oneself,** contenerse

convalescence, *n.* convalecencia, *f.*

convalescent, *adj.* convaleciente

convene, *vt.* convocar; *vi.* juntarse

convenience, *n.* conveniencia, comodidad, *f.*

convenient, *adj.* conveniente, cómodo

convent, *n.* convento, monasterio, *m.*

convention, *n.* convención, *f.*

conventional, *adj.* convencional; tradicional

conversation, *n.* conversación, plática, *f.*

converse, *vi.* conversar, platicar

convert, *vt.* convertir, reducir; *vi.* convertirse; *n.* converso, convertido , *m.*

convey, *vt.* trasportar; trasmitir; conducir

convict, *n.* reo, convicto, presidiario, *m.*

conviction, *n.* convicción,

convince, *vt.* convencer

convincing, *adj.* convincente

convulsion, *n.* convulsión, *f.*

cook, *n.* cocinero, cocinera; *vt., vi.* cocinar, guisar, cocer

cookbook, *n.* libro de cocina, *m.*

cooking, *n.* cocina, *f.*; arte de cocinar, *m.*

cool, *adj.* fresco; indiferente; *vt.* enfriar, refrescar

coop, *n.* gallinero, *m.*; *vt.* enjaular, encarcelar

cooperate, *vi.* cooperar

cooperation, *n.* cooperación *f.*

co-ordinate, *vt.* coordinar

co-ordination, *n.* coordinación, *f.*

cop, *n.* (coll.) policía, gendarme, *m.*

copper, *n.* cobre, *m.*; cobre (color), *m.*

copy, *n.* copia, *f.*; original, *m.*; ejemplar de algún libro; *vt.* copiar; imitar

copyright, *n.* propiedad de una obra literaria; derechos de autor, *m. pl.*; patente, *f.*

coquette, *n.* coqueta, *f.*

coral, *n.* coral, *m.*; *adj.* de coral

cord, *n.* cuerda, *f.*; cordel, *m.*; cordón, pasamano, *m.*

cordial, *adj.* cordial, amistoso; *n.* cordial (licor), *m.*

core, *n.* cuesco, *m.*; interior, corazón, *m.*; núcleo, *m.*

cork, *n.* corcho, *m.*

corkscrew, *n.* tirabuzón, *m.*

corn, *n.* maíz, *m.*; callo, *m.*

corncob, *n.* mazorca, *f.*

corned beef, *n.* cecina, *f.*, carne de vaca en salmuera

corner, *n.* ángulo, *m.*; rincón, *m.*; esquina, *f.*

cornstalk, *n.* tallo de maíz

cornstarch, *n.* almidón de maíz, *m.*

Corp., corp., corporal, cabo; **corporation,** S.A. sociedad anónima

corporal, *n.* (mil.) cabo, *m.*; *adj.* corpóreo, corporal; material, físico

corporate, *adj.* colectivo

corporation, *n.* corporación, *f.*; gremio, *m.*; sociedad anónima, *f.*

corps, *n.* regimiento, *m.*; cuerpo, *m.*; **air corps,** cuerpo de aviación, *m.*

correct, *vt.* corregir, castigar; rectificar; *adj.* correcto, cierto

correction, *n.* corrección, *f.*

correspond, *vi.* corresponder; sostener correspondencia

correspondence, *n.* correspondencia, *f.*; reciprocidad, *f.*

correspondent, *n.* corresponsal, *m.*

corrugated, *adj.* corrugado

corrupt, *vt.* y *vi.* corromper; sobornar; *adj.* corrompido

corruption, *n.* corrupción, *f.*

cosmetic, *adj.* y *n.* cosmético, *m.*

cosmopolitan, cosmopolite, *n.* y *adj.* cosmopolita, *m.* y *f.*

cost, *n.* coste, costo, precio, *m.*; expensas, *f. pl.*; *vi.* costar

costly, *adj.* costoso, caro

costume, *n.* traje, *m.*; ropa, *f.*; disfraz, *m.*

cottage, *n.* cabaña, choza, *f.*; **cottage cheese,** requesón, *m.*

cotton, *n.* algodón, *m.*

couch, *n.* canapé, sofá, *m.*

cough, *n.* tos, *f.*; *vi.* toser

council, *n.* concilio, concejo, *m.*

counsel, *n.* consejo, aviso, *m.*; abogado, *m.*

counselor, counsellor, *n.* consejero, abogado, *m.*

count, *vt.* contar, numerar;

calcular; **to count on,** confiar, depender de; *n.* cuenta, *f.*; cálculo, *m.*; conde (título), *m.*

countdown, *n.* conteo, *m.*

counter, *n.* mostrador, *m.*

counteract, *vt.* contrarrestar

counterfeit, *adj.* falsificado

countless, *adj.* innumerable

country, *n.* país, *m.*; campo, *m.*; patria, *f.*; *adj.* campestre, rural

countryman, *n.* paisano, paisana, compatriota, *m. y f.*

county, *n.* condado, *m.*

couple, *n.* par, *m.*; *vt.* unir, parear, casar; *vi.* juntarse

coupon, *n.* cupón, talón, *m.*

courage, *n.* valor, *m.*

courageous, *adj.* valiente

course, *n.* curso, *m.*; carrera, *f.*; ruta, *f.*; rumbo, *m.*; plato, *m.*; **of course,** por supuesto

court, *n.* corte, *f.*; juzgado, tribunal, *m.*; palacio, *m.*; patio, *m.*; cortejo, *m.*; *vt.* cortejar

courteous, *adj.* cortés

courtesy, *n.* cortesía, *f.*

courtship, *n.* cortejo, *m.*; galantería, *f.*

cousin, *n.* primo, ma; **first cousin,** primo hermano, prima hermana

cover, *n.* cubierta, *f.*; *vt.* cubrir; tapar; ocultar

cow, *n.* vaca, *f.*

coward, *n.* cobarde, *m. y f.*

cowardice, *n.* cobardía,

cowardly, *adj.* cobarde

cowboy, *n.* vaquero, *m.*

cowhide, *n.* cuero, *m.*

co-worker, *n.* colaborador, colaboradora, compañero o compañera de trabajo

cozy, *adj.* cómodo y agradable

C.P.A., Certified Public Accountant, C.P.T., Contador Público Titulado

crab, *n.* cangrejo, *m.*; (Sp. Am.) jaiba, *f.*; **crab apple,** manzana silvestre, *f.*

crack, *n.* crujido, *m.*; hendedura, raja, *f.*; *vt.* hender, rajar; romper; *vi.* agrietarse

cracked, *adj.* quebrado, rajado; (coll.) demente

cracker, *n.* galleta, *f.*

cradle, *n.* cuna, *f.*

craft, *n.* arte, *m.*; artificio, *m.*; astucia, *f.*

crafty, *adj.* astuto

cramp, *n.* calambre, *m.*

crane, *n.* (orn.) grulla, *f.*; (mech.) grúa, *f.*

cranium, *n.* craneo, *m.*

crank, *n.* manivela, *f.*; manija, *f.*; (coll.) maniático, maniática

crash, *vi.* estallar, rechinar; estrellar; *n.* estallido, choque, *m.*

crazy, *adj.* loco

cream, *n.* crema, *f.*; nata, *f.*

creamy, *adj.* cremoso

crease, *n.* pliegue, *m.*; *vt.* plegar

create, *vt.* crear; causar

creation, *n.* creación, *f.*

creative, *adj.* creador

creator, *n.* criador, criadora; **the Creator,** el Criador

credit, *n.* crédito, *m.*; **credit card,** tarjeta de crédito, *f.*; *vt.* creer, fiar, acreditar

creditor, *n.* acreedor, acreedora

creep, *vi.* arrastrar; gatear

cremate, *vt.* incinerar cadáveres

cretonne, *n.* cretona, *f.*

crevice, *n.* raja, hendidura, *f.*

crew, *n.* (naut.) tripulación, *f.*

crime, *n.* crimen, delito, *m.*

criminal, *adj.* criminal, reo; *n.* reo convicto, criminal, *m. y f.*

crimson, *adj.* carmesí, bermejo

crinoline, *n.* crinolina, *f.*

cripple, *n.* lisiado, lisiada; *vt.* tullir

crisis, *n.* crisis, *f.*

crisp, *adj.* crespo; fresco, terso (aplicase, a la lechuga, el apio, etc.)

crisscross, *adj.* entrelazado

criterion, *n.* criterio, *m.*

critic, *n.* crítico, *m.*

critical, *adj.* crítico; delicado

criticism, *n.* crítica, *f.*; censura, *f.*

criticize, *vt.* criticar, censurar

crochet, *n.* labor con aguja de gancho; *vt.* tejer con aguja de gancho

crocodile, *n.* cocodrilo, *m.*

crony, *n.* amigo (o conocido) antiguo

crook, *n.* gancho, *m.*; curva, *f.*; ladrón, ladrona

crooked, *adj.* torcido; perverso; tortuoso

crop, *n.* cosecha, *f.*; cabello cortado corto

cross, *n.* cruz, *f.*; *adj.* enojado; mal humorado; *vt.* atravesar, cruzar

crossing, *n.* (rail.) cruce, *m.*

crossword puzzle, *n.* crucigrama, rompecabezas, *m.*

crow, *n.* (orn.) cuervo, *m.*; canto del gallo; *vi.* cantar el gallo; alardear

crowd, *n.* multitud, *f.*; *vt.* amontonar

crowded, *adj.* concurrido, lleno de gente

crown, *n.* corona, *f.*; *vt.* coronar; recompensar

crown prince, *n.* príncipe heredero, *m.*

crucifix, *n.* crucifijo, *m.*

crucify, *vt.* crucificar; atormentar

crude, *adj.* crudo, tosco; **crude (ore, oil, etc.)** (mineral, petróleo, etc.) bruto

cruel, *adj.* cruel, inhumano

cruelty, *n.* crueldad, *f.*

cruise, *n.* travesía marítima; excursión, *f.*; *vi.* navegar; cruzar (el mar o el país)

crumb *n.* miga, *f.*

crumble, *vt.* desmigajar, desmenuzar; *vi.* desmoronarse

crumple, *vt.* arrugar, ajar

crunch, *vi.* crujir

crusade, *n.* cruzada, *f.*

crush, *vt.* apretar, oprimir; machacar

crust, *n.* costra, *f.*; corteza, *f.*

crutch, *n.* muleta, *f.*

cry, *vt.* y *vi.* gritar; exclamar; llorar; *n.* grito, *m.*; lianto, *m.*

crystal, *n.* cristal, *m.*

C.S.T., **Central Standard Time**, hora normal del centro (de E.U.A.)

cub, *n.* cachorro, *m.*

Cuban, *n.* y *adj.* cubano, cubana

cubbyhole, *n.* casilla, *f.*

cube, *n.* cubo, *m.*

cubic, cubical, *adj.* cúbico

cucumber, *n.* pepino, *m.*

cuddle, *vt.* y *vi.* abrazar; acariciarse

cue, *n.* rabo, *m.*, coleta, *f.*; apunte de comedia, *m.*; taco (de billar), *m.*

cuff, *n.* puño de camisa o de vestido, *m.*; **cuff links**, gemelos, *m. pl.*; (Sp. Am.) mancuernillas, *f. pl.*

culinary, *adj.* culinario

culminate, *vi.* culminar

culprit, *n.* delincuente, criminal, *m.*

cult, *n.* culto, *m.*

cultivate, *vt.* cultivar

cultivation, *n.* cultivo, *m.*

cultural, *adj.* cultural

culture, *n.* cultura, civilización, *f.*

cumbersome, *adj.* engorroso

cunning, *adj.* astuto; intrigante; *n.* astucia, sutileza, *f.*

cup, *n.* taza, *f.*

cupboard, *n.* armario, aparador, *m.*, alacena, *f.*

cupful, *n.* taza (medida), *f.*

cupola, *n.* cúpula, *f.*

curb, *n.* freno, *m.*; restricción, *f.*; orilla de la acera, *f.*; *vt.* refrenar

curdle, *vt.* y *vi.* cuajar, coagular

cure, *n.* remedio, *m.*; *vt.* curar, sanar

cure-all, *n.* panacea, *f.*

curiosity, *n.* curiosidad, *f.*; rareza, *f.*

curious, *adj.* curioso

curl, *n.* rizo, *m.*; *vt.* rizar (el cabello); *vi.* rizarse, encresparse

currency, circulación, *f.*; moneda corriente, *f.*, dinero *m.*

current, *adj.* corriente, del día; *n.* corriente, *f.*

curse, *vt.* maldecir; *n.* maldición, f.

curtain, n. cortina, f., telón (en los teatros), m.

curve, vt. encorvar; n. curva, combadura, f.

cushion, n. cojín, m., almohada, f.

custody, n. custodia, f.; cuidado, m.

custom, n. costumbre, f.; uso, m.; **customs,** n. pl. aduana, f.

customary, adj. usual, acostumbrado

customer, n. cliente, m. y f.

customhouse, n. aduana, f.

cut, vt. cortar; herir; **to cut short,** interrumpir; n. cortadura, f.; herida, f.; (print.) grabado, m.

cute, adj. gracioso, chistoso

cutlery, n. cuchillería, f.

cutlet, n. costilla, chuleta, f.

cutting, adj. cortante; sarcástico

cwt., hundredweight, ql., quintal

cycle, n. ciclo, m.

cyclone, n. ciclón, m.

cyclotron, n. ciclotrón, m.

cylinder, n. cilindro, m.

cypher, cipher, n. cifra, cero, m.

cyst, n. quiste, m.; lobanillo, m.

C. Z., Canal Zone, Z. del C. Zona del Canal

czar, n. zar, m.

D

d., date, fha., fecha; **daughter,** hija; **day,** día; **diameter,** diámetro; **died,** murió

D.A., District Attorney, fiscal

d/a, days after acceptance, d/v, días vista

dad, daddy, n. papá, m.

daffodil, n. (bot.) narciso, m.

dagger, n. daga, f., puñal, m.

dahlia, n. (bot.) dalia, f.

daily, adj. diario, cotidiano; adv. diariamente

dainty, adj. delicado; meticuloso, refinado

dairy, n. lechería, f.

daisy, n, margarita, f.

dam, n. dique, m.; presa, f.; represa, f.; vt. represar; tapar

damage, n. daño, detrimento, m.; perjuicio, m.; **damages,** n. pl. daños y perjuicios, m. pl.; vt. dañar

damask, n. damasco, m.

dame, n. dama, señora, f.

damn, vt. condenar; maldecir; **damn!, damn it!** interj. ¡maldito sea!

damp, adj. húmedo

dampen, vt. humedecer; desanimar

dampness, n. humedad, f.

dance, n. danza, f.; baile, m.; vi. bailar

dancer, n. danzarín, danzarina, bailarín, bailarina

dandelion, n. diente de león, amargón, m.

dandy, n. petimetre, m.; adj. (coll.) excelente

danger, n. peligro, riesgo, m.

dangerous, adj. peligroso

Danish, n. y adj. danés, danesa, dinamarqués, dinamarquesa

D.A.R., Daughters of the American Revolution, Organización "Hijas de la Revolución Norteamericana."

dare, vi. atreverse, arriesgarse; vt. desafiar, provocar; n. reto, m.

daredevil, n. temerario, temeraria; calavera, m.

daring, n. osadía, f.; adj. temerario; emprendedor

dark, adj. oscuro, opaco; moreno, trigueño; n. oscuridad, f.; ignorancia, f.

darken, vt. y vi. oscurecer

darkness, n. oscuridad, f.; tinieblas, f. pl.

darling, n. predilecto, predilecta, favorito, favorita; adj. querido, amado

dash, n. arranque, m.; acometida, f.; (gram.) raya, f.; vt. arrojar, tirar; chocar, estrellar

data, n. pl. datos, m. pl.; **data**

processing, proceso de datos, proceso de información por computadoras

date, *n.* fecha, *f.*; cita, *f.*; (bot.) dátil, *m.*

dated, *adj.* fechado

daughter, *n.* hija, *f.*; **daughter-in-law,** nuera, *f.*

daunt, *vt.* intimidar

dauntless, *adj.* intrépido, afrojado

davenport, *n.* sofá, *m.*

dawn, *n.* alba, *f.*; madrugada *f.*; *vi.* amanecer

day, *n.* día, *m.*; **day after tomorrow,** pasado mañana

daylight, *n.* día, *m.*, luz del día, luz natural, *f.*

daze, *vt.* atolondrar

dazzle, *vt.* deslumbrar

D.C., District of Columbia, D.C., Distrito de Columbia, E.U.A.

d.c., direct current, C.D. corriente directa; C.C. corriente continua

DDT, DDT (insecticida), *m.*

dead, *adj.* muerto; marchito; **dead letter,** carta no reclamada

deaden, *vt.* amortecer

deadlock, *n.* paro, *m.*; desacuerdo, *m.*

deadly, *adj.* mortal

deaf, *adj.* sordo

deaf-mute, *n.* sordomudo, sordomuda

deafness, *n.* sordera, *f.*

deal, *n.* negocio, convenio, *m.*; (com.) trato, *m.*; mano (en el juego de naipes), *f.*; *vt.* tratar; dar (las cartas)

dealer, *n.* comerciante, *m.*

dealing, *n.* trato, *m.*; comercio, *m.*; **dealings,** *n. pl.* transacciones, *f. pl.*; relaciones, *f. pl.*

dean, *n.* deán, decano, *m.*

dear, *adj.* querido; costoso, caro

death, *n.* muerte.

debate, *n.* debate, *m.*; *vt.* y *vi.* deliberar; disputar

debit, *n.* debe, cargo, *m.*; *vt.* adeudar

debris, *n.* despojos, escom-

bros, *m. pl.*

debt, *n.* deuda, *f.*; débito, *m.*

debtor, *n.* deudor, deudora

debut, *n.* estreno, debut, *m.*

debutante, *n.* debutante, *f.*

Dec., December, dic., diciembre

decade, *n.* década, *f.*

decay, *vi.* decaer, declinar; degenerar; *n.* decadencia, *f.*; (dent.) caries, *f.*

deceased, *n.* y *adj.* muerto, muerta, difunto, difunta

deceit, *n.* engaño, fraude, *m.*

deceitful, *adj.* fraudulento, engañoso

December, *n.* diciembre, *m.*

decency, *n.* decencia, *f.*; modestia, *f.*

decent, *adj.* decente, razonable

decimal, *adj.* decimal

decipher, *vt.* descifrar

decision, *n.* decisión, determinación, resolución, *f.*

decisive, *adj.* decisivo

deck, *n.* (naut.) bordo, *m.*, cubierta, *f.*; baraja de naipes, *f.*; *vt.* adornar

declare, *vt.* declarar, manifestar

decline, *vt.* (gram.) declinar; rehusar; *vi.* decaer; *n.* declinación, *f.*; decadencia, *f.*; declive, *m.*

decorate, *vt.* decorar, adornar; condecorar

decoy, *vt.* atraer (algún pájaro); embaucar, engañar

decrease, *vt.* y *vi.* disminuir, reducir

decree, *n.* decreto, edicto, *m.*; *vt.* decretar, ordenar

dedicate, *vt.* dedicar; consagrar

dedication, *n.* dedicación, *f.*; dedicatoria, *f.*

deduct, *vt.* deducir, sustraer

deduction, *n.* deducción, rebaja, *f.*; descuento, *m.*

deed, *n.* hecho, *m.*; hazaña, *f.*; (com.) escritura, *f.*

deem, *vi.* juzgar, estimar

deep, *adj.* profundo; subido (aplícase al color); intenso

deepen, *vt.* profundizar

deepfreeze, *n.* congeladora, *f.*

deer, *n. sing. y pl.* ciervo, ciervos, venado, venados, *m.*

deface, *vt.* desfigurar

defame, *vt.* difamar; calumniar

default, *n.* defecto, *m.*, falta, *f.*; *vt. y vi.* faltar, delinquir

defeat, *n.* derrota, *f.*; *vt.* derrotar; frustrar

defend, *vt.* defender; proteger

defendant, *n.* (law) demandado, demandada, acusado, acusada

defender, *n.* defensor, abogado, *m.*

defer, *vt.* diferir, posponer

deference, *n.* deferencia, *f.*; respeto, *m.*

defiance, *n.* desafío, *m.*

deficiency, *n.* deficiencia, *f.*

deficit, *n.* déficit, *m.*

define, *vt.* definir; determinar

definite, *adj.* definido; concreto

definition, *n.* definición, *f.*

deform, *vt.* deformar, desfigurar

deformity, *n.* deformidad, *f.*

defraud, *vt.* defraudar; frustrar

defray, *vt.* costear; sufragar

defrost, *vt.* descongelar, deshelar

defy *vt.* desafiar, retar

degrade, *vt.* degradar; deshonrar

degree, *n.* grado, *m.*; rango, *m.*; **by degrees,** gradualmente

deject, *vt.* abatir, desanimar

del., delegate, delegado; **delete,** suprímase

delay, *vt.* retardar; *vi.* demorar; *n.* demora, *f.*

delegate, *vt.* delegar, diputar; *n.* delegado, delegada, diputado, diputada

delegation, *n.* delegación, *f.*

delete, *vt.* suprimir

deliberate, *vt.* deliberar, considerar; *adj.* premeditado

deliberation, *n.* delibera ción, *f.*

delicacy, *n.* delicadeza, *f.*; manjar, *m.*

delicate, *adj.* delicado

delicious, *adj.* delicioso

delight, *n.* delicia, *f.*; deleite, *m.*; *vt. y vi.* deleitar

delightful, *adj.* delicioso; deleitable

delinquency, *n.* delincuencia,

delinquent, *n. y adj.* delincuente, *m. y f.*

deliver, *vt.* entregar; libertar; relatar; partear

delivery, *n.* entrega, *f.*; liberación, *f.*; parto, *m.*

deluxe, *adj.* de lujo

demand, *n.* demanda, *f.*; *vt.* pedir, exigir

demented, *adj.* demente, loco

demitasse, *n.* tacita (de café), *f.*

democracy, *n.* democracia, *f.*

democrat, *n.* demócrata, *m. y f.*

demolish, *vt.* demoler, arrasar

demon, *n.* demonio, diablo, *m.*

demonstrate, *vt.* demostrar

demonstration, *n.* demostración, *f.*

demonstrative, *adj.* demostrativo, expresivo

demotion, *n.* (mil.) degradación, *f.*; descenso de rango

den, *n.* caverna, *f.*; cuarto de lectura o de estudio, *m.*

denim, *n.* mezclilla, tela gruesa de algodón, *f.*

Denmark, Dinamarca

denomination, *n.* denominación, *f.*

denominational, *adj.* sectario

denominator, *n.* (math.) denominador, *m.*

denote, *vt.* denotar, indicar

denounce, *vt.* denunciar

dense, *adj.* denso, espeso; estúpido

dent, *n.* abolladura, *f.*; mella, *f.*; *vt.* abollar

dental, *adj.* dental

dentifrice, *adj. y n.* dentífrico, *m.*

dentist, *n.* dentista, *m.*

denture, *n.* dentadura postiza, *f.*

deodorant, *adj.,* *m.* desodorante

depart, *vi.* partir; irse, salir; morir

department, *n.* departamento, *m.*

departure, *n.* partida, salida, *f.*; desviación, *f.*

depend, *vi.* depender

dependable, *adj.* digno de confianza

dependent, *n.* dependiente, *m.*

depict, *vt.* pintar, retratar; describir

deplete, *vt.* agotar, vaciar

deplorable, *adj.* deplorable

deplore, *vt.* deplorar, lamentar

deport, *vt.* deportar

deportment, *n.* conducta, *f.*

deposit, *vt.* depositar; *n.* depósito, *m.*

depot, *n.* (rail.) estación, *f.*

depressed, *adj.* deprimido

depression, *n.* depresión, *f.*

deprive, *vt.* privar, despojar

dept., department, dep., depto., departamento

depth, *n.* profundidad, *f.*; abismo, *m.*

deputy, *n.* diputado, delegado, *m.*

derail, *vt.* descarrilar

derivation, *n.* derivación, *f.*

derive, *vt.* y *vi.* derivar; proceder

descend, *vi.* descender

descendant, *n.* descendiente, *m.* y *f.*

describe, *vt.* describir

description, *n.* descripción, *f.*

desert, *n.* desierto, *m.*; merecimiento, *m.*; *vt.* abandonar; *vi.* (mil.) desertar

desertion, *n.* deserción, *f.*

design, *vt.* designar, proyectar; diseñar; *n.* diseño, plan, *m.*

designate, *vt.* designar, señalar

designer, *n.* dibujante, proyectista, *m.* y *f.*

desire, *n.* deseo, *m.*; *vt.* desear

desk, *n.* escritorio, pupitre, *m.*

desolation, *n.* desolación, destrucción, *f.*

despair, *n.* desesperación, *f.*; *vi.* desesperar

desperate, *adj.* desesperado; furioso

desperation, *n.* desesperación, *f.*

despise, *vt.* despreciar; desdeñar

despite, *n.* despecho, *m.*; *prep.* a despecho de

despondent, *adj.* abatido, desalentado

despot, *n.* déspota, *m.* y *f.*

dessert, *n.* postre, *m.*

destination, *n.* destino, *m.*

destine, *vt.* destinar, dedicar

destiny, *n.* destino, hado, *m.*; suerte, *f.*

destitute, *adj.* carente; necesitado

destroy, *vt.* destruir

destruction, *n.* destrucción, ruina, *f.*

detach, *vt.* separar, desprender

detail, *n.* detalle, *m.*; particularidad, *f.*; (mil.) destacamento, *m.*; **in detail,** al por menor; detalladamente; *vt.* detallar

detect, *vt.* descubrir; discernir

detective, *n.* detective, *m.*

détente, *n.* relajación en la tensión, distensión, *f.*

deter, *vt.* disuadir

deteriorate, *vt.* deteriorar

determination, *n.* determinación, *f.*

determine, *vt.* determinar, decidir; **to be determined,** proponerse

detest, *vt.* detestar, aborrecer

detract, *vt.* disminuir; *vi.* denigrar

detriment, *n.* detrimento, perjuicio *m.*

develop, *vt.* desarrollar; revelar (una fotografía)

development, *n.* desarrollo, *m.*

deviate, *vi.* desviarse

device, *n.* invento, *m.*; aparato, mecanismo, *m.*

devil, *n.* diablo, demonio, *m.*

devise, *vt.* inventar; idear

devoid, *adj.* vacío; carente

devote, *vt.* dedicar; consagrar

devotion, *n.* devoción, *f.*; dedicación, *f.*

devout, *adj.* devoto, piadoso

dew, *n.* rocío, *m.*

diabetes, *n.* diabetes, *f.*

diabolic, diabolical, *adj.* diabólico

diagnose, *vt.* diagnosticar

diagnosis, *n.* diagnosis, *f.*

diagonal, *n.* y *adj.* diagonal, *f.*

diagram, *n.* diagrama, *m.*

dial, *n.* esfera de reloj, *f.*; cuadrante, *m.*; **dial telephone,** teléfono automático, *m.*

dialect, *n.* dialecto, *m.*

diameter, *n.* diámetro, *m.*

diamond, *n.* diamante, *m.*; brillante, *m.*; oros (de baraja), *m. pl.*

diaper, *n.* pañal, *m.*

diarrhea, *n.* diarrea, *f.*

diary, *n.* diario, *m.*

dictate, *vt.* dietar

dictation, *n.* dictado, *m.*

dictator, *n.* dictador, *m.*

dictatorship, *n.* dictadura, *f.*

diction, *n.* dicción, *f.*

dictionary, *n.* diccionario, *m.*

did, *pretérito* del verbo **do**

die, *vi.* morir, expirar; marchitarse; *n.* dado, *m.*; molde, *m.*, matriz, *f.*

diet, *n.* dieta, *f.*; régimen, *m.*; *vi.* estar a dieta

differ, *vi.* diferenciarse; contradecir

difference, *n.* diferencia, *f.*

different, *adj.* diferente

difficult, *adj.* difícil

difficulty, *n.* dificultad, *f.*

digest, *vt.* digerir, clasificar; *vi.* digerir; *n.* extracto, compendio, *m.*

digestion, *n.* digestión, *f.*

dignified, *adj.* serio, grave

dignity, *n.* dignidad, *f.*

dike, *n.* dique, canal, *m.*

dilate, *vt.* y *vi.* dilatar, extender

diligent, *adj.* diligente, aplicado

dim, *adj.* turbio de vista; oscuro; *vt.* oscurecer

dime, *n.* moneda de plata de diez centavos en E. U. A.

dimension, *n.* dimensión, *f.*

diminish, *vt.* y *vi.* disminuir

diminutive, *adj.* y *n.* diminutivo, *m.*

dine, *vi.* comer, cenar

diner, *n.* coche comedor, *m.*

dining, *adj.* comedor; **dining car,** coche comedor; **dining room,** comedor, *m.*

dinner, *n.* comida, cena, *f.*

dip, *vt.* remojar, sumergir; *vi.* sumergirse; inclinarse; *n.* inmersión, *f.*

diphtheria, *n.* difteria, *f.*

diploma, *n.* diploma, *m.*

diplomacy, *n.* diplomacia, *f.*

diplomat, *n.* diplomático, *m.*

diplomatic, *adj.* diplomático

direct, *adj.* directo, derecho, recto; *vt.* dirigir

direction, *n.* dirección, manejo, *m.*; rumbo, *m.*

director, *n.* director, *m.*

directory, *n.* directorio, *m.*; *f.* guía,

dirt, *n.* suciedad, mugre, *f.*

dirty, *adj.* sucio; vil, bajo; *vt.* ensuciar

disadvantage, *n.* desventaja, *f.*

disagree, *vi.* discordar, estar en desacuerdo; hacer daño (el alimento)

disagreeable, *adj.* desagradable

disagreement, *n.* desacuerdo, *m.*

disappear, *vi.* desaparecer

disappearance, *n.* desaparición, *f.*

disappoint, *vt.* decepcionar

disappointment, *n.* decepción, *f.*

disapproval, *n.* desaprobación, censura, *f.*

disapprove, *vt.* desaprobar

disarmament, *n.* desarme, *m.*

disaster, *n.* desastre, *m.*

disastrous, *adj.* desastroso

disbursement, *n.* desembolso, *m.*

discard, *vt.* descartar; *n.* descarte (en el juego de naipes), *m.*

discharge, *vt.* descargar, pagar (una deuda, etc.); despedir; *n.* descarga, *f.*; descargo, *m.*

disciple, *n.* discípulo, *m.*

discipline, *n.* disciplina, *f.*; *vt.* disciplinar

disclose, *vt.* descubrir, revelar

discomfort, *n.* incomodidad, *f.*

disconnect, *vt.* desunir, separar

discontent, *n.* descontento, *m.*; *adj.* malcontento

discontinue, *vt.* descontinuar

discotheque, *n.* discoteca, *f.*

discount, *n.* descuento, *m.*; rebaja, *f.*; *vt.* descontar

discourage, *vt.* desalentar, desanimar

discouragement, *n.* desaliento, *m.*

discover, *vt.* descubrir

discovery, *n.* descubrimiento, *m.*

discretion, *n.* discreción, *f.*

discriminate, *vt.* distinguir

discrimination, *n.* discriminación, *f.*

discuss, *vt.* discutir

discussion, *n.* discusión, *f.*

disease, *n.* mal, *m.*; enfermedad, *f.*

diseased, *adj.* enfermo

disfigure, *vt.* desfigurar, afear

disgrace, *n.* deshonra, *f.*; desgracia, *f.*; *vt.* des honrar

disgraceful, *adj.* deshonroso, vergonzoso

disguise, *vt.* disfrazar; simular; *n.* disfraz, *m.*; máscara, *f.*

disgust, *n.* disgusto, *m.*; aversión, *f.*; *vt.* disgustar, repugnar

dish, *n.* fuente, *f.*, plato, *m.*

dishearten, *vt.* desalentar, descorazonar

disillusion, *n.* desengaño, *m.*, desilusión, *f.*; *vt.* desengañar

disinfect, *vt.* desinfectar

disinfectant, *n.* desinfectante, *m.*

disloyal, *adj.* desleal; infiel

disloyalty, *n.* deslealtad, *f.*

disobedient, *adj.* desobediente

disobey, *vt.* desobedecer

disorder, *n.* desorden, *m.*

disorderly, *adj.* desarreglado, confuso

dispatch, *n.* despacho, *m.*; embarque, *m.*; *vt.* despachar; embarcar; remitir

dispel, *vt.* disipar, dispersar

dispensary, *n.* dispensario, *m.*

dispensation, *n.* dispensa, *f.*

dispense, *vt.* dispensar; distribuir

displaced, *adj.* desplazado, dislocado

display, *vt.* desplegar; exponer; ostentar; *n.* exhibición, *f.*; ostentación, *f.*

displease, *vt.* disgustar; ofender; desagradar

dispose, *vt.* disponer; dar; *vi.* vender; trasferir

disposition, *n.* disposición, *f.*; indole, *f.*; carácter, *m.*

dispute, *n.* disputa, controversia, *f.*; *vt.* y *vi.* disputar

disqualify, *vi.* inhabilitar

disregard, *vt.* desatender, desdeñar; *n.* desatención, *f.*

disreputable, *adj.* despreciable

disrupt, *vt.* y *vi.* desbaratar, hacer pedazos; desorganizar

dissatisfaction, *n.* descontento, disgusto, *m.*

disseminate, *vt.* diseminar, propagar

dissension, *n.* disensión, discordia, *f.*

dissipation, *n.* disipación, *f.*; libertinaje, *m.*

dissolve, *vt.* y *vi.* disolver

dissuade, *vt.* disuadir

distance, *n.* distancia, *f.*

distant, *adj.* distante, lejano; esquivo

distasteful, *adj.* desagradable

distinct, *adj.* distinto, diferente; claro, sin confusión

distinction, *n.* distinción, diferencia, *f.*

distinguish, *vt.* distinguir; discerner; **distinguished,** *adj.* distinguido, eminente

distress, *n.* aflicción, *f.*; *vt.* angustiar, acongojar

distribute, *vt.* distribuir, repartir

distributor, *n.* distribuidor, distribuidora

district, *n.* distrito, *m.*

distrust, *vt.* desconfiar; *n.* desconfianza, *f.*

disturb, *vt.* perturbar, estorbar

ditch, *n.* zanja, *f.*

dive, *vi.* sumergirse, zambullirse; bucear; *n.* zambullidura, *f.*; (Mex.) clavado, *m.*

diver, *n.* buzo, *m.*

diversion, *n.* diversión, *f.*; pasatiempo, *m.*

diversity, *n.* diversidad, *f.*

divert, *vt.* desviar; divertir

divide, *vt.* dividir; repartir; desunir; *vi.* dividirse

dividend, *n.* dividendo, *m.*

divine, *adj.* divino; sublime

diving, *n.* buceo, *m.*; **diving suit,** escafandra, *f.*

divinity, *n.* divinidad, *f.*

division, *n.* división, *f.*

divorce, *n.* divorcio, *m.*; *vt.* y *vi.* divorciar, divorciarse

DNA, deoxyribonucleic acid, ácido ribonucleico

do, *vt.* hacer, ejecutar; *vi.* obrar

docile, *adj.* dócil, apacible

doctor, *n.* doctor, médico, *m.*

doctrine, *n.* doctrina, *f.*

document, *n.* documento, *m.*

dodge, *vt.* evadir, esquivar

does, tercera persona del singular del verbo **do**

dog, *n.* perro, *m.*

doghouse, *n.* perrera, *f.*, casa de perro; (coll.) **to be in the doghouse,** estar castigado, estar en desgracia

dolly, *n.* pañito de adorno, *m.*

doings, *n. pl.* hechos, *m. pl.*

doll, *n.* muñeca, *f.*

dollar, *n.* dólar, peso (moneda de E.U.A.), *m.*

dome, *n.* cúpula, *f.*

domestic, *adj.* doméstico

domesticate, *vt.* domesticar

dominate, *vt.* y *vi.* dominar

domination, *n.* dominación, *f.*

domineering, *adj.* tiránico

Dominican Republic, República Dominicana, *f.*

domino, *n.* dominó, *m.*

donate, *vt.* donar, contribuir

donation, *n.* contribución, donación, *f.*

done, *adj.* hecho; cocido, asado; *p. p.* del verbo **do**

donkey, *n.* burro, asno, *m.*

doom, *n.* condena, *f.*; suerte, *f.*; *vt.* sentenciar, condenar

door, *n.* puerta, *f.*

doorbell, *n.* timbre de llamada, *m.*

doorknob, *n.* tirador, *m.* perilla, *f.*

doorman, *n.* portero, *m.*

doorstep, *n.* umbral, *m.*

doorway, *n.* puerta de entrada, *f.*

dope, *n.* narcótico, *m.*, droga heroica; (coll.) información, *f.*

dormitory, *n.* dormitorio, *m.*

dot, *n.* punto, *m.*

doubt, *n.* duda, sospecha, *f.*; *vt.* y *vi.* dudar

doubtful, *adj.* dudoso

doubtless, *adj.* indudable

dough, *n.* masa, pasta, *f.*

doughnut, *n.* rosquilla, *f.*, especie de buñuelo

dove, *n.* paloma, *f.*

dowdy, *adj.* desaliñado

down, *n.* plumón, *m.*; bozo, vello, *m.*; **ups and downs,** vaivenes, *m. pl.*; *adv.* abajo

downcast, *adj.* cabizbajo

downfall, *n.* ruina, decadencia, *f.*

downpour, *n.* aguacero, *m.*

downstairs, *adv.* abajo; *n.* piso inferior, *m.*

downtown, *n.* centro, *m.*, parte céntrica de una ciudad

doze, *vi.* dormitar

dozen, *n.* docena, *f.*

D.P., displaced person, persona desplazada

Dr., Doctor, Dr., Doctor

draft, *n.* dibujo, *m.*; (com.) giro, *m.*; corriente de aire; (mil.) conscripción, *f.*; **rough draft,** borrador, *m.*; *vt.* dibujar; redactar

draftsman, *n.* dibujante, *m.*

drag, *vt.* arrastrar; *vi.* arrastrarse; *n.* rémora, *f.*; (coll.) influencia, *f.*

dragon, *n.* dragón, *m.*

dragonfly, *n.* libélula, *f.*

drain, *vt.* desaguar; colar; *n.* desaguadero, *m.*

drainage, *n.* desagüe, *m.*; saneamiento, *m.*

drake, *n.* ánade macho, *m.*

drama, *n.* drama, *m.*

dramatic, dramatical, *adj.* dramático

dramatics, *n.* arte dramático; deciamación, *f.*

drank, *pretérito* del verbo **drink**

drape, *n.* cortina, *f.*; *vt.* vestir, colgar decorativamente

drapery, *n.* cortinaje, *m.*

draw, *vt.* tirar, traer; atraer; dibujar; girar, librar una letra de cambio

drawback, *n.* desventaja, *f.*

drawer, *n.* gaveta, *f.*; **drawers,** *n. pl.* calzones, *m. pl.*; calzoncillos, *m. pl.*

drawing, *n.* dibujo, *m.*; rifa, *f.*; **drawing room,** sala de recibo, *f.*

dread, *n.* miedo, terror, *m.*; *vt.* y *vi.* temer

dreadful, *adj.* terrible, espantoso

dream, *n.* suero, *m.*; fantasia, *f.*; *vi.* soñar; imaginarse

dreary, *adj.* espantoso, triste

dregs, *n. pl.* heces, *f. pl.*; escoria, *f.*

drench, *vt.* empapar, molar

dress, *n.* vestido, *m.*; traje, *m.*; *vt.* vestir, ataviar; curar (las heridas); *vi.* vestirse

dresser, *n.* tocador, *m.*

dressing, *n.* curación, *f.*; salsa, *f.*

dressy, *adj.* (coll.) vistoso; te, de vestir

drift, *n.* significado, *m.*; (naut.) deriva, *f.*

drill, *n.* taladro, *m.*, barrena, *f.*; (mil.) instrucción de reclutas; *vt.* taladrar; (mil.) disciplinar reclutas

drink, *vt.* y *vi.* beber; embriagarse; *n.* bebida, *f.*

drip, *vt.* y *vi.* gotear, destilar; *n.* gotera, *f.*

drive, *n.* paseo, *m.*; pulso, *m.*; *vt.* y *vi.* impeler; guiar, manejar, conducir; (mech.) impulsar; andar en coche

drive-in, *n.* restaurante o cine para automovilistas

driven, *p. p.* del verbo **drive**

driver, *n.* cochero, *m.*; carretero, *m.*; conductor, *m.*; chofer, *m.*

driving, *adj.* motriz; conductor; impulsor; **driving school,** autoescuela, *f.*, escuela de manejo

drizzle, *vi.* lloviznar; *n.* llovizna, *f.*

drone, *n.* zangano de colmena, *m.*; haragán, *m.*

droop, *vi.* inclinarse, colgar; desanimarse

drop, *n.* gota, *f.*; **letter drop,** buzón, *m.*; *vt.* soltar; cesar; dejar caer

dropsy, *n.* hidropesia,

drove, *n.* manada, *f.*; rebaño, *m.*; *pretérito* del verbo **drive**

drown, *vt.* y *vi.* sumergir; anegar

drudgery, *n.* trabajo arduo y monótono

drug, *n.* droga, *f.*, medicamento, *m.*; *vt.* narcotizar

druggist, *n.* farmacéutico, boticario, *m.*

drugstore, *n.* botica, *f.*

drum, *n.* tambor, *m.*; tímpano (del oído), *m.*

drumstick, *n.* palillo de tambor; pata (de ave cocida), *f.*

drunk, *adj.* borracho, ebrio, embriagado; *p. p.* del verbo **drink**

drunkard, *n.* borrachón, *m.*

dry, *adj.* árido, seco; aburrido; **dry cleaning,** lavado en seco; *vt.* y *vi.* secar; enjugar

D.S.T., Daylight Saving Time, hora oficial (aprovechamiento de luz del día)

duck, *n.* ánade, *m.* y *f.*, pato, pata; *vt.* zambullir; *vi.* zambullirse; agacharse

due, *adj.* debido, adecuado; **to**

become due, (com.) vencerse (una deuda, un plazo, etc.); **dues,** *n. pl.* cuota, *f.*

dumb, *adj.* mudo; (coll.) estúpido

dump, *n.* vaciadero, depósito, *m.*; **dumps,** *n. pl.* abatimiento, *m.*, murria, *f.*

dumpling, *n.* empanada, *f.*

dunce, *n.* tonto, tonta

dungeon, *n.* calabozo, *m.*

dupe, *n.* bobo, boba; victima, *f.*; *vt.* engañar, embaucar

duplicate, *n.* duplicado, *m.*; copia, *f.*; *vt.* duplicar

durable, *adj.* durable, duradero

duration, *n.* duración, *f.*

during, *prep.* durante

dusk, *n.* crepúsculo, *m.*

dusky, *adj.* oscuro

dust, *n.* polvo, *m.*

duster, *n.* plumero, *m.*; bata corta de mujer

dusty, *adj.* polvoriento; empolvado

Dutch, *adj.* holandés, holandesa

duty, *n.* deber, *m.*; obligación, *f.*; **custom duties,** derechos de aduana

dwarf, *n.* enano, enana

dwell, *vi.* habitar, morar

dwelling, *n.* habitación, residencia, *f.*

dye, *vt.* teñir, colorar; *n.* tinte, colorante, *m.*

dying, *adj.* agonizante, moribundo

dynamic, *adj.* dinámico, enérgico

dynamite, *n.* dinamita, *f.*

dynasty, *n.* dinastía, *f.*

dysentery, *n.* disenteria, *f.*

E

E., east, E., este, oriente

ea., each, c/u., cada uno

each, *adj.* cada; *pron.* cada uno, cada una, cada cual

eager, *adj.* deseoso, ansioso

eagle, *n.* águila, *f.*

ear, *n.* oreja, *f.*; oído, *m.*; (bot.) espiga *f.*

earache, *n.* dolor de oído, *m.*

eardrum, *n.* tímpano, *m.*

early, *adj.* y *adv.* temprano

earmuff, *n.* orejera, *f.*

earn, *vt.* ganar, obtener

earnest, *adj.* fervoroso; serio

earnings, *n. pl.* ingresos, *m. pl.*, ganancias, *f. pl.*

earphone, *n.* audífono, auricular, *m.*

earth, *n.* tierra, *f.*

earthly, *adj.* terrestre, mundano

earthquake, *n.* terremoto, *m.*

ease, *n.* facilidad, *f.*; **at ease,** sosegado; *vt.* aliviar

easel, *n.* caballete, *m.*

easily, *adv.* fácilmente

east, *n.* oriente, este, *m.*

Easter, *n.* Pascua de Resurrección, *f.*

easterly, eastern, *adj.* oriental, del este

easy, *adj.* fácil

eat, *vt.* comer

ebony, *n.* ébano, *m.*

eccentric, *adj.* excéntrico

ecclesiastic, *adj.* y *n.* eclesiástico, *m.*

echo, *n.* eco, *m.*; *vi.* resonar, repercutir (la voz)

eclipse, *n.* eclipse, *m.*; *vt.* eclipsar

ecological, *adj.* ecológico

ecology, *n.* ecología, *f.*

economic, economical, *adj.* económico

economics, *n.* economía, *f.*

economize, *vt.* y *vi.* economizar

economy, *n.* economía, *f.*; frugalidad, *f.*

edit, *vt.* redactar; dirigir (una publicación); revisar o corregir (un artículo, etc.)

edition, *n.* edición, *f.*; publicación, *f.*; impresión, *f.*; tirada, *f.*

editor, *n.* director, redactor (de una publicación), *m.*

editorial, *n.* editorial, *m.*

educate, *vt.* educar; enseñar

educated, *adj.* educado, instruido

education, *n.* educación, *f.*;

crianza, f.

educational, adj. educativo

eel, n. anguila, f.

efface, vt. borrar, destruir

effect, n. efecto, m.; realidad, f.; **effects,** n. pl. efectos, bienes, m. pl.; vt. efectuar, ejecutar

effective, adj. eficaz; efectivo; real

effervescent, adj. efervescente,

efficiency, n. eficiencia, f.

efficient, adj. eficaz; eficiente

effort n. esfuerzo, empeño, m.

effusive, adj. efusivo, expansivo

e.g., for example, p.ej., por ejemplo, vg. verbigracia

egg, n. huevo, m.

eggplant, n. (bot.) berenjena, f.

eggshell, n. cáscara o cascarón de huevo

egg-yolk, n. yema de huevo, f.

ego, n. ego, yo, m.

egoism, egotism, n. egoísmo, m.

Egypt, Egipto

Egyptian, n. y adj. egipcio, egipcia

eight, adj. y n. ocho, m.

eighteen, adj. y n. dieciocho, m.

eighteenth, adj. y n. décimoctavo, m.

eighth, adj. y n. octavo, m.

eighty, adj. y n. ochenta, m.

either, pron. y adj. cualquiera, uno de dos; conj. o, sea, ya, ora

elaborate, vt. elaborar; adj. elaborado, trabajado, primoroso

elapse, vi. pasar, trascurrir (el tiempo)

elated, adj. exaltado, animoso

elder, adj. que tiene más edad, mayor; n. anciano, antepasado, m.; eclesiástico, m.; (bot.) saúco, m.

elderly, adj. de edad madura

eldest, adj. el mayor, el más anciano

elect, vt. elegir

election, n. elección, f.; **elections,** elecciones, f. pl.

electoral, adj. electoral

electric, electrical, adj. eléctrico

electrician, n. electricista, m.

electricity, n. electricidad, f.

electrocute, vt. electrocutar

electronics, n. electrónica, f.

elegance, n. elegancia, f.

elegant, adj. elegante

element, n. elemento, m.; principio, m.

elemental, adj. elemental

elementary, adj. simple

elephant, n. elefante, m.

elevate, vt. elevar, alzar

elevation, n. elevación, f.; altura, f.

elevator, n. ascensor, elevador, m.

eleven, n. y adj. once, m.

eleventh, n. y adj. onceno, undécimo, m.

eligible, adj. elegible; deseable

eliminate, vt. eliminar, descartar

elope, vi. fugarse con un amante

elopement, n. fuga, huida (con un amante), f.

eloquence, n. elocuencia,

eloquent, adj. elocuente

else, adj. otro; adv. en lugar distinto; en forma distinta; **nothing else,** nada más; conj. de otro modo; si no

elsewhere, adv. en otra parte

elude, vt. eludir, evadir

elusive, adj. evasivo

emanate, vi. emanar

emancipation, n. emancipación, f.

embankment, n. dique, m., presa, f.; terraplén, m.

embargo, n. embargo, m.; vt. embargar

embark, vt. y vi. embarcar; embarcarse

embarrass, vt. avergonzar, desconcertar

embarrassing, adj. penoso

embarrassment, n. vergüenza, pena, f.

embassy, n. embajada, f.

embezzle, vt. desfalcar
emblem, n. emblema, m.
embrace, vt. abrazar; contener; n. abrazo, m.
embroider, vt. bordar
emerge, vi. salir, surgir
emergency, n. emergencia, f.
emigrate, vi. emigrar
eminence, n. eminencia, excelencia, f.
eminent, adj. eminente
emotion, n. emoción, f.
emperor, n. emperador, m.
emphasis, n. énfasis, m.
emphasize, vt. recalcar
emphatic, adj. enfático
empire, n. imperio, m.
employ, vt. emplear, ocupar; n. empleo, m.
employee, n. empleado, empleada
employer, n. amo, patrón, m.
employment, n. empleo, m.; ocupación, f.
empress, n. emperatriz, f.
empty, adj. vacío; vano; vt. vaciar, verter
enable, vt. habilitar; facilitar
enamel, n. esmalte, charol, m.
enchanting, adj. encantador
encircle, vt. circundar
enclose, vt. cercar, circundar; incluir
enclosure, n. cercado, m.; anexo (en una carta), m.
encounter, n. encuentro, m.; duelo, m.; pelea, f.; vi. encontrarse
encourage, vt. animar, alentar
encouragement, n. estímulo, aliento, m.
encouraging, adj. alentador
encyclopedia, n. enciclopedia, f.
end, n. fin, m.; término, m.; propósito, intento, m.; vt. matar, concluir; terminar; vi. acabarse
endeavor, vi. esforzarse; intentar; n. esfuerzo, m.
ending, n. conclusión, f.; muerte, f.
endless, adj. infinito, perpetuo, sin fin
endorse, vt. endosar (una letra

de cambio)
endorsement, n. endorso o endoso, m.
endurance, n. duración, f.; paciencia, resistencia, f.
endure, vt. sufrir, aguantar, soportar; vi. durar
ENE, E.N.E., east-north-east, ENE, estenordeste
energetic, adj. enérgico, vigoroso
enforce, vt. poner en vigor
enforcement, n. compulsión, f.; cumplimiento (de una ley), m.
engage, vt. empeñar, obligar; ocupar; vt. comprometerse
engaged, adj. comprometido
engagement, n. noviazgo, compromiso, m.; cita, f.
engine, n. máquina, f.; locomotora, f.
engineer, n. ingeniero, m.; maquinista, m.
engineering, n. ingeniería, f.
England, Inglaterra, f.
English, n. y adj. inglés, m.; **English Channel,** Canal de la Mancha
Englishman, n. inglés, m.
Englishwoman, n. inglesa, f.
enjoy, vt. gozar; disfrutar de
enjoyable, adj. agradable
enjoyment, n. goce, disfrute, m.; placer, m.
enlarge, vt. ampliar; vi. extenderse, dilatarse
enlargement, n. aumento, m.; ampliación, f.
enlist, vt. alistar, reclutar; vi. inscribirse como recluta, engancharse
enliven, vt. animar; avivar
enormous, adj. enorme
enough, adj. bastante, suficiente; adv. suficientemente
enroll, vt. registrar, inscribir
ensemble, n. conjunto, m.
entangle, vt. enmarañar, embrollar
enter, vt. entrar, admitir; vi. entrar
enterprise, n. empresa, f.
enterprising, adj. emprendedor

entertain, *vt.* entretener; agasajar; divertir

entertaining, *adj.* divertido, chistoso

entertainment, *n.* festejo, *m.*; diversión, *f.*, entretenimiento, *m.*

enthusiasm, *n.* entusiasmo, *m.*

enthusiastic, *adj.* entusiasmado, entusiasta

entire, *adj.* entero

entrance, *n.* entrada, *f.*; admisión, *f.* ingreso, *m.*

entreat, *vt.* rogar, suplicar,

entrust, *vt.* confiar

entry, *n.* entrada, *f.*; (com.) partida, *f.*

envious, *adj.* envioso

environment, *n.* ambiente, *m.*

environmental, *adj.* ambiental

envy, *n.* envidia, *f.*; *vt.* envidiar

epic, *adj.* épico; *n.* epopeya, *f.*

epidemic, *adj.* epidémico; *n.* epidemia, *f.*

epileptic, *adj.* y *n.* epiléptico, *m.*

episode, *n.* episodio, *m.*

epoch, *n.* época, era, *f.*

equal, *adj.* igual; semejante; *n.* igual, *m.*; *vt.* igualar

equality, *n.* igualdad, *f.*

equator, *n.* ecuador, *m.*

equilibrium, *n.* equilibrio, *m.*

equipment, *n.* equipo, *m.*

equitable, *adj.* equitativo

equivalent, *n.* y *adj.* equivalente, *m.*

era, *n.* edad, época, era, *f.*

erase, *vt.* borrár

eraser, *n.* goma de borrar, *f.*, borrador, *m.*

erect, *vt.* erigir; establecer; *adj.* derecho, erguido

erosion, *n.* erosión, *f.*

err, *vi.* errar; desviarse

errand, *n.* recado, mensaje, *m.*

erroneous, *adj.* erróneo; falso

error, *n.* error, yerro, *m.*

eruption, *n.* erupción, *f.*

escalate, *vi.* crecer

escalator, *n.* escalera mecánica, *f.*

escapade, *n.* travesura, *f.*

escape, *vt.* evitar; escapar; *vi.* evadirse, salvarse; *n.* escapada, huida, fuga, *f.*

escort, *n.* escolta, *f.*; acompañant *m.*; *vt.* escoltar, acompañar

especial, *adj.* especial, excepcional; **especially,** *adv.* particularmente; sobre todo

essay, *n.* ensayo literario, *m.*

essence, *n.* esencia, *f.*

essential, *adj.* esencial

E.S.T., Eastern Standard Time, hora normal de la region oriental de E.U.A

establish, *vt.* establecer

establishment, *n.* establecimiento, *m.*

estate, *n.* patrimonio, *m.*; bienes, *m. pl.*; predio, *m.*

esteem, *vt.* estimar; *n.* consideración, *f.*

esthetic, *adj.* estético; **esthetics,** *n.* estética, *f.*

estimate, *vt.* estimar, apreciar, tasar; *n.* cálculo, *m.*; presupuesto, *m.*

estrogen, *n.* estrogeno, *m.*

etching, *n.* aguafuerte, *f.*

eternal, *adj.* eterno

eternity, *n.* eternidad, *f.*

ether, *n.* éter, *m.*

etiquette, *n.* etiqueta, *f.*

Europe, Europa *f.*

European, *n.* y *adj.* europeo, europea

evacuate, *vt.* evacuar

evacuation, *n.* evacuación, *f.*

evaluate, *vt.* avaluar, evaluar

evaporate, *vi.* evaporarse; **evaporated milk,** leche evaporada

even, *adj.* llano, igual; *adv.* aun, aun cuando; *vt.* igualar, allanar

evening, *adj.* vespertino; *n.* tarde, noche, *f.*

event, *n.* evento, acontecimiento, *m.*

eventful, *adj.* memorable

eventual, *adj.* eventual, fortuito; **eventually,** *adv.* finalmente, con el tiempo

ever, *adj.* siempre; **ever since,**

desde que

everlasting, *adj.* eterno

every, *adj.* todo, cada; **every day**, todos los días

everybody, *pron.* cada uno, cada una; todo el mundo

everyday, *adj.* ordinario, rutinario

everything, *n.* todo, *m.*

everywhere, *adv.* en todas partes

evil, *adj.* malo; *n.* malidad, *f.*; daño, *m.*; mal, *m.*

evoke, *vt.* evocar

evolution, *n.* evolución, desarrollo, *m.*

exact, *adj.* exacto, puntual; *vt.* exigir

exacting, *adj.* exigente

exaggerate, *vt.* exagerar

exaggeration, *n.* exageración, *f.*

examination, *n.* examen, *m.*

examine, *vt.* examinar

exasperation, *n.* exasperación, irritación, *f.*

excavate, *vt.* excavar

excavation, *n.* excavación, *f.*; cavidad, *f.*

exceed, *vt.* exceder

exceedingly, *adv.* altamente

excel, *vt.* sobresalir, superar

excellent, *adj.* excelente; sobresaliente

except, *vt.* exceptuar, excluir

exception, *n.* excepción, exclusión, *f.*

exceptional, *adj.* excepcional

excerpt, *vt.* extraer; extractar; *n.* extracto, *m.*

excess, *n.* exceso, *m.*

exchange, *vt.* cambiar; *n.* cambio, *m.*; bolsa, lonja, *f.*

excite, *vt.* excitar; estimular

excitement, *n.* excitación, *f.*, comoción, *f.*

exclaim, *vi.* exclamar

exclamation, *n.* exclamación, *f.*; **exclamation mark, exclamation point**, punto de admiraión

exclude, *vt.* excluir

exclusion, *n.* exclusión, exclusiva, *f.*; excepción, *f.*

exclusive, *adj.* exclusivo

excrement, *n.* excremento, *m.*

excursion, *n.* excursión, expedición, *f.*

excuse, *vt.* excusar; perdonar; *n.* excusa, *f.*

execute, *vt.* ejecutar; llevar a cabo, cumplir

execution, n, ejecución, *f.*

executioner, *n.* verdugo, *m.*

executive, *adj.* y *n.* ejecutivo, *m.*

exemplify, *vt.* ejemplificar

exempt, *adj.* exento; *vt.* eximir, exentar

exemption, *n.* exención, franquicia, *f.*

exercise, *n.* ejercicio, *m.*; ensayo, *m.*; práctica, *f.*; *vi.* hacer ejercicio; *vt.* ejercer

exhaust, *n.* (auto., avi.) escape, *m.*; *vt.* agotar, consumir

exhausting, *adj.* agotador

exhibit, *vt.* exhibir; mostrar; *n.* exhibición, *f.*

exhibition, *n.* exhibición, presentación, *f.*; espectáculo, *m.*

exile, *n.* destierro, *m.*; desterrado, *m.*; *vt.* desterrar, deportar

exist, *vi.* existir

existence. *n.* existencia, *f.*

existing, *adj.* actual, presente

exit, *n.* salida, *f.*

exorbitant, *adj.* exorbitante, excesivo

exotic, *adj.* exótico, extranjero

expand, *vt.* extender, dilatar

expansion, *n.* expansión, *f.*

expect, *vt.* esperar

expectant, *adj.* que espera; encinta, embarazada

expedite, *vt.* acelerar; expedir

expel, *vt.* expeler, expulsar

expenditure, *n.* gasto, desembolso, *m.*

expense, *n.* gasto, *m.*

expensive, *adj.* caro, costoso

experience, *n.* experiencia, *f.*; práctica, *f.*; *vt.* experimentar; saber

experienced, *adj.* experimentado; versado, perito

experiment, *n.* experimento, *m.*; prueba, *f.*; *vt.* experimentar

expert, *adj.* experto, diestro; perito; *n.* maestro, maestra; conocedor, conocedora; perito, perita

expiration, *n.* expiración, *f.*; muerte, *f.*; vencimiento (de una letra o pagaré, etc.), *m.*

expire, *vi.* expirar, morir

explain, *vt.* explicar

explanation, *n.* explicación, aclaración, *f.*

explode, *vt.* y *vi.* volar, estallar, hacer explosión

explore, *vt.* explorar

explorer, *n.* explorador, *m.*

explosion, *n.* explosión, *f.*

export, *vt.* exportar

export, exportation, *n.* exportación, *f.*

expose, *vt.* exponer; mostrar; descubrir

exposition, *n.* exposición, exhibición, *f.*

express, *vt.* expresar, exteriorizar; *adj.* expreso, claro, a propósito; *n.* expreso, correo expreso, *m.*

expression, *n.* expresión, *f.*

expressive, *adj.* expresivo

expressway, *n.* autopista, *f.*

expropriate, *vt.* expropiar, confiscar

exquisite, *adj.* exquisito

extemporaneous, *adj.* extemporáneo, improviso

extend, *vt.* extender; **to extend (time),** prorrogar (un plazo)

extension, *n.* extensión, *f.*; prórroga, *f.*

extensive, *adj.* extenso; amplio

extent, *n.* extensión, *f.*; grado, *m.*

exterior, *n.* y *adj.* exterior, *m.*

exterminate, *vt.* exterminar

external, *adj.* externo, exterior

extinguish, *vt.* extinguir; suprimir

extra, *adj.* extraordinario, adicional; *n.* suplemento extraordinario de un periódico

extract, *vt.* extraer; extractar; *n.* extracto, *m.*; compendio, *m.*

extraction, *n.* extracción, *f.*

extraordinary, *adj.* extraordinario

extrasensory, *adj.* extrasensorio, extrasensoria

extravagance, *n.* extravagancia, *f.*; derroche, *m.*

extravagant, *adj.* extravagante, singular, excesivo; derrochador

extreme, *adj.* extremo; último; *n.* extremo, *m.*

extremity, *n.* extremidad, *f.*

exuberance, *n.* exuberancia, *f.*

exult, *vi.* regocijarse

eye, *n.* ojo, *m.*, vista, *f.*

eyeball, *n.* niña del ojo, *f.*

eyebrow, *n.* ceja, *f.*

eyeglass, *n.* anteojo, *m.*

eyelash, *n.* pestaña, *f.*

eyelid, *n.* párpado, *m.*

eyesight, *n.* vista, *f.*

eyestrain, *n.* cansancio o tensión de los ojos

F

F., Fellow, miembro de una sociedad científica o académica; **Fahrenheit,** Fahrenheit; **Friday,** vier., viernes

f., following, sig.^{te}, siguiente; **feminine,** *f.*, femenino; **folio,** fol., folio

fabricate, *vt.* fabricar, edificar; inventar (una leyen da, una mentira, etc.)

face, *n.* cara, faz, *f.*; fachada, *f.*; frente, *f.*; **to lose face,** sufrir pérdida de prestigio; **face value,** valor nominal o aparente; *vt.* encararse; hacer frente

facilitate, *vt.* facilitar

fact, *n.* hecho, *m.*; realidad, *f.*; **in fact,** en efecto, verdaderamente

factor, *n.* factor, *m.*; agente, *m.*

factory, *n.* fábrica, *f.*, taller, *m.*

faculty, *n.* facultad, *f.*; profesorado, *m.*

fade, *vi.* marchitarse; desteñirse

fail, *vt.* abandonar; decepcionar; reprobar (a un estudiante); *vi.* fallar, fracasar; *n.* falta, *f.*

failure, *n.* fracaso, *m.*; quiebra, bancarrota,

faint, *vi.* desmayarse

fair, *adj.* hermoso, bello; blanco; rubio; justo; *n.* feria, exposición, *f.*

fairly, *adv.* claramente; bastante; **fairly well,** bastante bien

fairness, *n.* hermosura, *f.*; equidad, *f.*

fairy, *n.* hada, *f.*, duende, *m.*; **fairy tale,** cuento de hadas, *m.*

faith, *n.* fe, *f.*

faithful, *adj.* fiel, leal

faithless, *adj.* infiel

fake, *adj.* (coll.) falso, fraudulento; *vt.* (coll.) engañar; imitar

faker, *n.* farsante, *m.* y *f.*

fall, *vi.* caer, caerse; *n.* caída, *f.*; otoño, *m.*

false, *adj.* falso, pérfido; postizo

falsehood, *n.* falseded, *f.*; mentira, *f.*

familiar, *adj.* familiar, casero, conocido

familiarity, *n.* familiaridad, *f.*

family, *n.* familia, *f.*; linaje, *m.*; clase, especie, *f.*

famine, *n.* hambre, *f.*; carestía, *f.*

fan, *n.* abanico, *m.*; ventilador, *m.*; aficionado, aficionada; *vt.* abanicar

fancy, *n.* fantasía, imaginación, *f.*; capricho, *m.*; *adj.* de fantasía; *vt.* y *vi.* imaginar; gustar de; suponer

far, *adv.* lejos; *adj.* lejano, distante, remoto

faraway, *adj.* lejano

fare, *n.* alimento, *m.*, comida, *f.*; pasaje, *m.*, tarifa, *f.*

farewell, *n.* despedida, *f.*

farfetched, *adj.* forzado, traído de los cabellos

farm, *n.* hacienda, granja, *f.*

farmer, *n.* labrador, labradora; hacendado, hacendada; agricultor, agricultora

farming, *n.* agricultura, cultivo, *m.*

far-off, *adj.* remoto, distante

far-reaching, *adj.* de gran alcance, trascendental

farsighted, *adj.* présbita, présbite; (fig.) precavido

farther, *adj.* y *adv.* mas lejos; más adelante

farthest, *adj.* más distante, más remoto; *adv.* a la mayor distancia

fascinate, *vt.* fascinar, encantar

fascinating, *adj.* fascinador, seductor

fashion, *n.* moda, *f.*; uso, *m.*, costumbre, *f.*; *vt.* formar, amoldar

fashionable, *adj.* en boga, de moda; elegante

fast, *vi.* ayunar; *n.* ayuno, *m.*; *adj.* firme, estable; veloz; *adv.* de prisa

fasten, *vt.* afirmar, fijar

fat, *adj.* gordo; **to get fat,** engordar; *n.* gordo, *m.*, gordura, *f.*; grasa, manteca, *f.*; sebo, *m.*

fate, *n.* hado, destino, *m.*

fateful, *adj.* funesto

father, *n.* padre, *m.*

father-in-law, *n.* suegro, *m.*

fatherland, *n.* patria *f.*

fatherless, *adj.* huérfano de padre

fatherly, *adj.* paternal

fatigue, *n.* fatiga, *f.*, cansancio, *m.*

fatten, *vt.* cebar, engordar

faucet, *n.* grifo *m.*; **water faucet,** toma, llave, *f.*, caño de agua, *m.*

favor, *n.* favor, beneficio, *m.*; **your favor,** su grata (carta); *vt.* favorecer, proteger, apoyar

favorable, *adj.* favorable, propicio; provechoso

favorite, *n.* y *adj.* favorito, favorita

FBI, Federal Bureau of Investigation, Departamento Federal de Investigación

fear, *vt.* y *vi.* temer, tener miedo; *n.* miedo, terror, pavor, *m.*

fearful, *adj.* temeroso; tímido

fearless, *adj.* intrépido

feasible, *adj.* factible, práctico

feast, *n.* banquete, festín, *m.*; fiesta, *f.*; *vt.* festejar; *vi.* comer opíparamente

feat, *n.* hecho, *m.*; acción, hazaña, *f.*

feather, *n.* pluma (de ave) *f.*

featherweight, *n.* peso pluma, *m.*

feature, *n.* facción del rostro; rasgo, *m.*; atracción principal; **double feature,** función de dos películas, *f.*; **features,** *n. pl.* facciones, *f. pl.*, fisonomía, *f.*

February, febrero, *m.*

federal, *adj.* federal

federation, *n.* confedera,ción, federación, *f.*

fee, *n.* paga, gratificación, *f.*; honorarios, derechos, *m. pl.*

feeble, *adj.* flaco, débil

feeble-minded, *adj.* retardado mentalmente

feed, *vt.* pacer; nutrir; alimentar; *n.* alimento, *m.*; pasto, *m.*

feeding, *n.* nutrición, alimento, *m.*

feel, *vt.* sentir; palpar

feeling, *n.* tacto, *m.*; sensibilidad, *f.*; sentimiento, *m.*

feet, *n. pl.* de **foot,** pies, *m. pl.*

feign, *vt.* y *vi.* inventar, fingir; simular

felicitation, *n.* felicitación, *f.*

fellow, *n.* compañero, camarada, *m.*; sujeto, *m.*; becario, *m.*

fellowship, *n.* beca (en una universidad), *f.*; camaradería, *f.*

female, *n.* hembra, *f.*; *adj.* femenino

feminine, *adj.* femenino

fence, *n.* cerca, valla, *f.*; *vt.* cercar; *vi.* esgrimir

fencing, *n.* esgrima, *f.*

fender, *n.* guardafango, *m.*

fertile, *adj.* fértil, fecundo

fertilizer, *n.* abono, *m.*

fervent, *adj.* ferviente; fervoroso

fervor, *n.* fervor, ardor, *m.*

festival, *n.* fiesta, *f.*

festive, *adj.* festivo, alegre

festivity, *n.* festividad, *f.*

fever, *n.* fiebre, *f.*

fiancé, *n.* novio, *m.*

fiancée, *n.* novia, *f.*

fickle, *adj.* voluble, inconstante

fiction, *n.* ficción, *f.*; invención, *f.*

fictitious, *adj.* ficticio; fingido

fiddle, *n.* violín, *m.*

fiddler, *n.* violinista, *m. y f.*

field, *n.* campo, *m.*; *adj.* campal

fierce, *adj.* fiero, feroz

fiery, *adj.* fogoso

fifteen, *n. y adj.* quince, *m.*

fifteenth, *n. y adj.* décimoquinto, *m.*

fifth, *n. y adj.* quinto, *m.*; quinto de galón (medida de vinos y licores)

fiftieth, *n. y adj.* quincuagésimo, *m.*

fifty, *n. y adj.* cincuenta, *m.*

fifty-fifty, *adj. y adv.* mitad y mitad

fight, *vi.* pelear; reñir; luchar; *n.* pelea, *f.*

fighter, *n.* luchador, luchadora; **fighter plane,** caza, *m.*

figure, *n.* figura, *f.*; cifra, *f.*; *vt.* figurar

file, *n.* archivo, *m.*; (mil.) fila, hilera, *f.*; lima, *f.*; *vt.* archivar; limar

filial, *adj.* filial

fill, *vt.* y *vi.* llenar, henchir; hartar; **to fill out,** llenar (un cuestionario, etc.)

filling, *n.* relleno, *m.*; orificación (de un diente), *f.*; **filling station,** estación de gasolina, *f.*

filly, *n.* potranca, *f.*

film, *n.* película, *f.*; membrana, *f.*

filter, *n.* filtro, *m.*; **filter-tip,** *adj.* de boquilla-filtro; *vt.* filtrar

filthy, *adj.* sucio, puerco

final, *adj.* final, útimo; definitivo; **finally,** *adv.* finalmente, por útimo; **finals,** último examen, juego, etc.

finality, *n.* finalidad, *f.*

finance, *n.* finaiizas, *f. pl.*

financial, *adj.* financiero

find, *vt.* hallar, descubrir; *n.* hallazgo, descubrimiento, *m.*

fine, *adj.* fino; bueno; **the fine arts,** las bellas artes; *n.* multa, *f.; vt.* multar

finesse, *n.* sutileza, *f.*

finger, *n.* dedo, *m.*

fingernail, *n.* uña, *f.*

fingerprints, *n. pl.* impresiones digitales, *f. pl.*

finish, *vt.* acabar, terminar; *n.* conclusión, *f.*, final, *m.*

fire, *n.* fuego, *m.*; candela, *f.*; incendio, *m.; vi.* (mil.) tirar, hacer fuego

firearms, *n. pl.* armas de fuego, *f. pl.*

firefly, *n.* luciérnaga, *f.*, cocuyo, cucuyo, *m.*

fireman, *n.* bombero, *m.*; (rail.) fogonero, *m.*

fireplace, *n.* hogar, *m.*, chimenea, *f.*

fireplug, *n.* boca de incendios, toma de agua, *f.*

fireproof, *adj.* a prueba de fuego, refractario

fireside, *n.*sitio cerca a la chimenea u hogar; vida de hogar

fireworks, *n. pl.* fuegos artificiales, *m. pl.*

firm, *adj.* firme, estable; *n.* (com.) empresa, razón social, *f.*

firmament, *n.* firmamento, *m.*

first, *adj.* primero; primario; delantero; **first aid,** primeros auxilios; *adv.* primeramente

first-class, *adj.* de primera clase

firsthand, *adj.* directo, de primera mano

fiscal, *adj.* fiscal, del fisco

fish, *n.* pez, *m.*; pescado, *m.*; *vt.* y *vi.* pescar

fisherman, *n.* pescador, *m.*

fishing, *n.* pesca, *f.*

fist, *n.* puño, *m.*

fit, *adj.* apto, idóneo, capaz; *n.* convulsión, *f.*; ataque, *m.; vt.* ajustar, acomodar, adaptar;

sentar, quedar bien

five, *n.* y *adj.* cinco, *m.*

fix, *vt.* fijar, establecer; componer

fixtures, *n. pl.* enseres, *m. pl.*; instalación (eléctrica), *f.*

flag, *n.* bandera, *f.*; pabellon, *m.*

flagpole, *n.* asta de bandera, *f.*

flamingo, *n.* (orn.) flamenco, *m.*

flap, *n.* bragueta, *f.*; solapa, *f.*; aleta, *f.; vt.* y *vi.* aletear; sacudir

flash, *n.* relámpago, *m.*; llamarada, *f.*; destello, *m.; vi.* relampaguear; brillar

flashback, *n.* interrupción de la continuidad de un relato

flashlight, *n.* linterna, linterna eléctrica de bolsillo, *f.*

flat, *adj.* plano; insípido; **flat tire,** llanta desinflada, neumático desinflado; *n.* (mus.) bemol, *m.*; apartamiento, apartamento, *m.*

flatten, *vt.* allanar; aplastar

flatter, *vt.* adular

flavor, *n.* sabor, gusto, *m.*

flavoring, *n.* condimento, *m.*

flaw, *n.* falta, tacha,

flawless, *adj.* sin tacha

flax, *n.* lino, *m.*

flaxseed, *n.* semill de lino, *f.*

flea, *n.* pulga, *f.*

flee, *vi.* escapar; huir

fleecy, *adj.* lanudo

fleeting, *adj.* pasajero, fugitivo

flesh, *n.* carne, *f.*

flew, *pretérito* del verbo **fly**

flexible, *adj.* flexible

flicker, *vi.* aletear, fluctuar; *n.* aleteo, *m.*; **flicker of an eyelash,** pestañeo, *m.*

flier, *n.* aviador, aviadora; tren muy rápido

flight, *n.* buida, fuga, *f.*; vuelo, *m.*

fling, *vt.* lanzar, echar; *vi.* lanzarse con violencia; *n.* tiro, *m.*; tentativa, *f.*

flirt, *vi.* coquetear; *n.* coqueta, *f.*

flirtation, *n.* coqueteria, *f.*

float, *vi.* flotar; *n.* carro alegórico, *m.*; flotador, *m.*

flock, *n.* manada, *f.*; rebaño, *m.*; gentío, *m.*; *vi.* congregarse

flood, *n.* diluvio, *m.*; inundación, *f.*; *vt.* inundar

floor, *n.* suelo, piso, *m.*

flounder, *n.* (pez) rodaballo, *m.*

flour, *n.* harina, *f.*

flourish, *vi.* prosperar; *n.* floreo de palabras; rasgo (de una pluma), *m.*; lozanía, *f.*

flow, *vi.* fluir, manar; *n.* flujo, *m.*, corriente, *f.*

flower, *n.* flor, *f.*

flowery, *adj.* florido

flu, *n.* (coll.) influenza, gripe, *f.*, trancazo, *m.*

fluent, *adj.* fluido; fluente, fácil; **fluently,** *adv.* con fluidez

fluorescent, *adj.* fluorescente; **fluorescent lighting,** aluminado fluorescente, *m.*

fluoridate, *vt.* fluorizar

fluoridation, *n.* fluoruración, *f.*

flush, *vt.* limpiar con un chorro de agua (por ej., un inodoro); *vi.* sonrojarse, ruborizarse; *n.* rubor, *m.*

fluster, *vt.* confundir, atropellar; *vi.* confundirse

flutter, *vt.* turbar, desordenar; *vi.* revolotear; flamear

fly, *vt.* y *vi.* volar; huir; *n.* mosca, *f.*; volante, *m.*

flying, *n.* vuelo, *m.*; aviación, *f.*; *adj.* volante, volador; de pasada

F.M. or **f.m., frequency modulation,** (rad.) modulación de frecuencia

f.o.b. or **F.O.B., free on board,** L.A.B., libre a bordo o f.a.b. franco a bordo

focus, *n.* foco, *m.*, punto céntrico; enfoque, *m.*; *vt.* enfocar

foe, *n.* adversario, adversaria, enemigo, enemiga

fog, *n.* niebla, *f.*

foil, *vt.* vencer; frustrar

fold, *n.* redil, *m.*; plegadura, *f.*, doblez, *m.*; *vt.* plegar, doblar

folder, *n.* folleto, *m.*; papelera, *f.*

foliage, *n.* follaje, *m.*

folk, *n.* gente, *f.*; **folk music,** música tradicional, *f.*; **folk song,** romance, *m.*, copla, *f.*

folklore, *n.* folklore, *m.*, tradiciones populares, *f. pl.*

follow, *vt.* seguir; *vi.* seguirse, resultar, provenir

following, *n.* séquito, cortejo, *m.*; profesión, *f.*; *adj.* próximo, siguiente

follow-up, *adj.* que sigue

fond, *adj.* afectuoso; aficionado; **to be fond of,** aficionarse, tener simpatía por

fondle, *vt.* mimar, acariciar

fondness, *n.* debilidad, *f.*; afición, *f.*

food, *n.* alimento, *m.*; comida, *f.*

fool, *n.* loco, loca, tonto, tonta, bobo, boba; *vt.* engañar; *vi.* tontear

foolish, *adj.* bobo, tonto, majadero

foolproof, *adj.* muy evidente, fácil hasta para un tonto

foot, *n.* pie, *m.*

football, *n.* futbol americano, *m.*; pelota de futbol, *f.*

footlights, *n. pl.* luces del proscenio; (fig.) el teatro, las tablas

footmark, *n.* huella, *f.*

footnote, *n.* anotación, glosa, *f.*; nota, *f.*

footprint, *n.* huella, pisada, *f.*

footstep, *n.* paso, *m.*; pisada, *f.*

footwear, *n.* calzado, *m.*

for, *prep.* para; por; *conj.* porque, pues; **what for?** ¿para qué?

forbear, *vt.* y *vi.* cesar, detenerse; abstenerse

forbearance, *n.* paciencia, *f.*

forbid, *vt.* prohibir; **God forbid!** Dios no quiera!

forbidden, *adj.* prohibido

force, *n.* fuerza, *f.*; poder, vigor, *m.*; valor, *m.*; **forces,** tropas, *f. pl.*; *vt.* forzar, violentar; obligar

forceful, *adj.* fuerte, poderoso; dominante

forceps, *n. pl.* pinzas, *f. pl.*

forearm, *n.* antebrazo, *m.*

forebear, *n.* antepasado, *m.*

foreboding, *n.* corazonada, *f.*

forecast, *vt.* y *vi.* proyectar, prever; *n.* previsión, *f.*; profecía *f.*; **weather forecast,** pronóstico del tiempo, *m.*

foreclosure, *n.* juicio hipotecario, *m.*

forefather, *n.* abuelo, antepasado, *m.*

forefinger, *n.* índice, *m.*

foregoing, *adj.* anterior, precedente

foreground, *n.* delantera, *f.*; primer plano, *m.*

foreign, *adj.* extranjero

foreigner, *n.* extranjero, extranjera, forastero, forastera

foreman, *n.* capataz, *m.*

forenoon, *n.* la mañana, las horas antes del mediodía

forerunner, *n.* precursor, precursora; predecesor, predecesora

foresee, *vt.* prever

foresight, *n.* previsión, *f.*

forest, *n.* bosque, *m.*; selva, *f.*

foreword, *n.* prefacio, prólogo, preámbulo, *m.*

forfeit, *n.* multa, *f.*; prenda, *f.*; *vt.* decomisar; perder

forget, *vt.* olvidar; descuidar

forgetful, *adj.* olvidadizo

forget-me-not, *n.* (bot.) nomeolvides, *f.*

forgive, *vt.* perdonar

forgiveness, *n.* perdón, *m.*

forgot, *pretérito* del verbo **forget**

forlorn, *adj.* abandonado, perdido

form, *n.* forma, *f.*; esqueleto, modelo, *m.*; modo, *m.*; **form letter,** carta circular, *f.*; *vt.* formar; concebir; *vi.* formarse

formal, *adj.* formal, metódico ceremonioso

formality, *n.* formalidad, *f.*

formation, *n.* formación, *f.*

former, *adj.* precedente; previo; **formerly,** *adv.* antiguamente, en tiempos pasados

formidable, *adj.* formidable, terrible

forsaken, *adj.* desamparado

fort, *n.* fortaleza, *f.*, fuerte, *m.*

forth, *adv.* en adelante; afuera; **and so forth,** y así sucesivamente, et cétera

forthcoming, *adj.* próximo

fortieth, *n.* y *adj.* cuadragésimo, *m.*

fortify, *vt.* fortificar

fortnight, *n.* quincena, *f.*, quince días; dos semanas

fortress, *n.* (mfl.) fortaleza, *f.*

fortunate, *adj.* afortunado, dichoso; **fortunately,** *adv.* felizmente, por fortuna

fortune, *n.* fortune, *f.*; suerte, *f.*

forty, *n.* y *adj.* cuarenta, *m.*

forum, *n.* foro, tribunal, *m.*

forward, *adj.* delantero; precoz; atrevido; *adv.* adelante, más allá; *vt.* expedir, trasmitir

forwards, *adv.* adelante

foul, *adj.* sucio, detestable; **foul ball,** pelota *foul* (que cae fuera del primer o tercer ángulo del rombal de baseball); **foul play,** conducta falsa y pérfida; jugada sucia, *f.*

found, *vt.* fundar, establecer; basar

foundation, *n.* fundación, *f.*; fundamento, *m.*, pie, *m.*; fondo, *m.*

founder, *n.* fundador, fundadora

fountain, *n.* fuente, *f.*; manantial, *m.*; **fountain pen,** plumafuente, estilográfica, *f.*

four, *n.* y *adj.* cuatro, *m.*

fourteen, *n.* y *adj.* catorce, *m.*

fourteenth, *n.* y *adj.* décimocuarto, *m.*

fourth, *n.* y *adj.* cuarto, *m.*

fox, *n.* zorra, *f.*, zorro, *m.*

foxy, *adj.* astuto

fracture, *n.* fractura, *f.*; *vt.* fracturar, romper

fragment, *n.* fragmento, trozo, *m.*

fragrance, *n.* fragancia, *f.*

fragrant, *adj.* fragante, oloroso

frame, *n.* marco, *m.*; bastidor,

m.; armazón, *f.*
France, Francia
franchise, *n.* franquicia, inmunidad, *f.*
frank, *adj.* franco, sincero; **frankly,** *adv.* francamente
frankfurter, *n.* salchicha, *f.*
fraternal, *adj.* fraternal
fraternity, *n.* fraternidad, *f.*
freak, *n.* monstruosidad, *f.*
freakish, *adj.* estrambótico
freckle, *n.* peca, *f.*
free, *adj.* libre; liberal; gratuito, gratis; *vt.* libertar; librar; eximir
freedom, *n.* libertad, *f.*
freethinker, *n.* librepensador, librepensadora
freeze, *vi.* helar, helarse; *vt.* helar, congelar
freezer, *n.* congelador, *m.*; **deep freezer,** congeladora, *f.*, congelador, *m.*
freezing, *n.* congelación, *f.*
freight, *n.* carga, *f.*; flete, *m.*; porte, *m.*
French, *adj.* francés, francesa
Frenchman, *n.* francés, *m.*
frenzy, *n.* frenesí, *m.*; locura, *f.*
frequency, *n.* frecuencia, *f.*
frequent, *adj.* frecuente; **frequently,** *adv.* con frecuencia
fresh, *adj.* fresco; nuevo; atrevido
freshen, *vt.* refrescar
freshman, *n.* estudiante de primer año; novicio, novicia
fretful, *adj.* enojadizo
Friday, *n.* viernes, *m.*; **Good Friday,** Viernes Santo
fried, *adj.* frito
friend, *n.* amigo, amiga
friendless, *adj.* sin amigos
friendly, *adj.* amigable, amistoso
friendship, *n.* amistad, *f.*
fright, *n.* susto, terror, *m.*
frighten, *vt.* espantar
frightful, *adj.* espantoso
frivolous, *adj.* frívolo, vano
frolic, *n.* alegría, *f.*; travesura, *f.*; *vi.* retozar, juguetear
from, *prep.* de; desde; **from now on,** en lo sucesivo

front, *n.* frente, *m.*
frontier, *n.* frontera, *f.*
frontispiece, *n.* frontispicio, *m.*; portada, *f.*
frost, *n.* helada, *f.*
frosting, *n.* confitura o betún (para pasteles)
froth, *n.* espuma (de algún líquido), *f.*
frown, *vi.* fruncir el entrecejo; *n.* ceño, *m.*; mala cara, *f.*
froze, *pretérito* del verbo **freeze**
frozen, *adj.* helado; congelado
fruit, *n.* fruto, fruta; producto, *m.*
fruitcake, *n.* torta o pastel de frutas
fruitful, *adj.* fructífero, fértil
fruitless, *adj.* estéril; inútil
frustration, *n.* contratiempo, chasco, *m.*
fry, *vt.* freír
frying pan, *n.* sartén, *f.*
fudge, *n.* variedad de dulce de chocolate
fulfil, *vt.* cumplir, realizar
full, *adj.* lleno, repleto
full-grown, *adj.* desarrollado, crecido, maduro
fumigate, *vt.* fumigar
fun, *n.* chanza, burla, *f.*; diversión, *f.*; **to make fun of,** burlarse de; **to have fun,** divertirse
fund, *n.* fondo, (dinero), *m.*
fundamental, *adj.* fundamental, básico
funnel, *n.* embudo, *m.*
funny, *adj.* cómico
furlough, *n.* (mil.) licencia, *f.*; permiso, *m.*
furnace, *n.* horno, *m.*; caldera, *f.*
furnish, *vt.* proveer; equipar
furnished, *adj.* amueblado
furniture, *n.* mobiliario, *m.*, muebles, *m. pl.*
furor, *n.* rabia, *f.*; entusiasmo, *m.*
further, *adj.* ulterior, más distante; *adv.* más lejos, más allá; aun; *vt.* adelantar, promover
furthermore, *adv.* además

furthest, *adj.* y *adv.* más lejos, más remoto

fuss, *n.* (coll.) alboroto, *m.;* *vi.* preocuparse por pequeñeces

fussy, *adj.* melindroso; exigente

future, *adj.* futuro, venidero; *n.* lo futuro, porvenir, *m.*

G

gain, *n.* ganancia, *f.;* interés, beneficio, *m.;* *vt.* ganar; conseguir

gall, *n.* hiel, *f.;* rencor, odio, *m.;* **gall bladder,** vesícula biliar, *f.*

gallant, *adj.* galante; *n.* galán, *m.*

gallantry, *n.* galantería, *f.*

gallery, *n.* galería,

galley, *n.* (naut.) galera, *f.;* **galley roof,** (print.) galerada, *f.,* primera prueba

gallon, *n.* galón, *m.*

gallop, *n.* galope, *m.;* *vi.* galopar

gallstone, *n.* cálculo biliario, *m.*

galvanometer, *n.* galvanómetro, *m.*

gamble, *vi.* jugar por dinero; aventurar

gambling, *n.* juego por dinero, *m.*

game, *n.* juego, *m.*

gamma globulin, *n.* gama globulina, *f.*

gang, *n.* cuadrilla, banda, pandilla, *f.*

gangster, *n.* rufián, *m.*

gap, *n.* boquete, *m.;* brecha, *f.;* laguna, *f.*

gape, *vi.* bostezar, boquear

garage, *n.* garaje, garage, *m.* cochera, *f.*

garb, *n.* vestidura, *f.*

garbage, *n.* basura, *f.*

garden, *n.* huerto, *m.;* jardín, *m.*

gardener, *n.* jardinero, jardinera

gardenia, *n.* gardenia, *f.*

gargle, *vt.* y *vi.* hacer gárgaras; *n.* gárgara, *f.*

garlic, *n.* (bot.) ajo, *m.*

garment, *n.* vestidura, *f.*

garrison, *n.* (mil.) guarnición, *f.;* fortaleza, *f.*

gas, *n.* gas, *m.;* **gas station,** gasolinera, *f.*

gasoline, *n.* gasolina, *f.*

gas-storage tank, *n.* gasómetro, *m.*

gate, *n.* puerta, *f.*

gateway, *n.* entrada, *f.*

gather, *vt.* recoger, amontonar, reunir; inferir; *vi.* juntarse

gathering, *n.* reunión, *f.*

gaze, *vi.* contemplar

gear, *n.* engranaje, *m.;* **to put in gear,** embragar

geese, *n.* *pl.* de **goose,** gansos, *m.* *pl.*

gelatine, *n.* gelatina, *f.*

gem, *n.* joya, *f.*

Gen., General, Gral., General

gender, *n.* género, *m.*

gene, *n.* gen, *m.*

general, *adj.* general, común, usual; *n.* general, *m.;* **in general,** por lo común

generation, *n.* generación, *f.*

generator, *n.* generador, *m.*

generosity, *n.* generosidad, *f.*

generous, *adj.* generoso

genetics, *n.* genética, *f.*

genius, *n.* genio, *m.*

genocide, *n.* genocidio, *m.*

genteel, *adj.* gentil, elegante

Gentile, *n.* gentil, *m.* y *f.*

gentle, *adj.* suave, dócil

gentleman, *n.* caballero, *m.*

gentleness, *n.* gentileza, *f.*

genuine, *adj.* genuino, puro

geographic, geographical, *adj.* geográfico

geography, *n.* geografía, *f.*

geology, *n.* geología, *f.*

geometric, geometrical, *adj.* geométrico

geometry, *n.* geometría, *f.;* **solid geometry,** geometría del espacio

German, *n.* y *adj.* alemán, alemana

Germany, Alemania, *f.*

gesture, *n.* gesto, movimiento, *m.*

get, *vt.* obtener, conseguir; *vi.* llegar; ponerse

ghastly, *adj.* pálido, cadavérico

ghost, *n.* espectro, *m.*; fantasma, *m.*

giant, *n.* gigante, *m.*

gift, *n.* don, *m.*; presente, obsequio, *m.*

gifted, *adj.* hábil, talentoso

gigantic, *adv.* gigantesco

gin, *n.* ginebra, *f.*

ginger, *n.* jengibre, *m.*

gingerly, *adv.* cautelosamente; *adj.* cauteloso

gingham, *n.* zaraza, *f.*

giraffe, *n.* jirafa, *f.*

girdle, *n.* faja, cinturón, *m.*

girl, *n.* muchacha, niña, *f.*

girlhood, *n.* niñez, *f.*, juventud femenina

give, *vt.* y *vi.* dar, conceder; **to give birth,** dar a luz; **to give up,** rendirse, darse por vencido

given, *p. p.* del verbo **give**

gladiolus, *n.* gladiolo, *m.*

gladness, *n.* alegría, *f.*, regocijo, placer, *m.*

glamor, glamour, *n.* encanto, hechizo, *m.*, elegancia, *f.*

glamorous, *adj.* fascinador, encantador

glance, *n.* vistazo, *m.*; ojeada, *f.*; **at first glance,** a primera vista; *vt.* verligeramente

glare, *n.* deslumbramiento, *m.*; reflejo, *m.*; mirada penetrante; *vi.* relumbrar, brillar; echar miradas de indignación

glaring, *adj.* deslumbrante; penetrante

glass, *n.* vidrio, *m.*; vaso para beber; espejo, *m.*; **glasses,** *n. pl.* anteojos, *m. pl.*; *adj.* de vidrio

glassful, *n.* vaso, *m.*, vaso lleno

glassware, *n.* cristalería, *f.*

glee, *n.* alegría, *f.*; gozo, *m.*; **glee club,** coro, *m.*

glide, *vi.* deslizarse; planear

glider, *n.* (avi.) planeador, *m.*

glint, *n.* lustre, brillo, *m.*

glisten, *vi.* centellear

glitter, *vi.* destellar; *n.* destello

globe, *n.* globo, *m.*; esfera, *f.*; orbe, *m.*

gloom, *n.* oscuridad, melancolía, tristeza, *f.*

gloomy, *adj.* sombrio oscuro; triste, melancólico

glorify, *vt.* glorificar, celebrar

glorious, *adj.* glorioso

glory, *n.* gloria, fama, *f.*

glossy, *adj.* lustroso, brillante

glove, *n.* guante, *m.*

glow, *vi.* arder; relucir

glowworm, *n.* luciérnaga, *f.*

glue, *n.* cola, *f.*, sustancia glutinosa; *vt.* encolar, pegar

glutton, *n.* glotón, glotona

gm., gram, *g.*, gramo

G-Man, *n.* (E. U. A.) miembro de la policía secreta

go, *vi.* ir, irse, andar, caminar; partir; huir; to awa marcharse, salir; **to go away,** marcharse, salir; **to go back,** regresar; *n.* (coll.) energía, *f.*; **on the go,** en plena actividad

goal, *n.*meta, *f.*; fin, *m.*

goat, *n.* cabra, chiva, *f.*

gobbler, *n.* pavo, *m.*; glotón, glotona

goblet, *n.* copa, *f.*; cáliz, *m.*

goblin, *n.* duende, *m.*

God, *n.*; Dios, *m.*; **God willing,** Dios mediante

god, *n.* dios *m.*

godchild, *n.* ahijado, ahijada

godess, *n.* diosa, *f.*

godfather, *n.* padrino, *m.*

godmother, *n.* madrina, *f.*

godsend, *n.* bendición, cosa llovida del cielo

Godspeed, *n.* bienandanza, *f.*

goes, 3ª persona del singular del verbo **go**

gold, *n.* oro, *m.*

golden, *ddj.* de oro; excelente

goldenrod, (bot.) vara de San José, vara de oro, *f.*

goldfish, *n.* carpa dorada, *f.*

goldsmith, *n.* orfebre, *m.*

good, *adj.* bueno; bondadoso; apto; perito

good-bye, *n.* adiós, *m.*

good-looking, *adj.* bien pare-

cido, guapo
goodness, *n.* bondad, *f.*
goose, *n.* ganso, *m.*
gorge, *n.* barranco, *m.*
gorgeous, *adj.* primoroso
gorilla, *n.* (zool.) gorila,
gospel, *n.* evangelio, *m.*
gout, *n.* (med.) gota, *f.*
govern, *vt.* y *vi.* gobernar
governess, *n.* institutriz, *f.*
government, *n.* gobierno, *m.*
governor, *n.* gobernador, *m.*;
    gobernante, *m.*
grace, *n.* gracia, *f.*; favor, *m.*;
    to say grace, bendecir la me-
    sa; *vt.* agraciar
graceful, *adj.* agraciado
gracious, *adj.* gentil, afable
grade, *n.* grado, *m.*; pendiente,
    f.; nivel, *m.*; calidad, *f.*; **grade**
    school, escuela premaria, *f.*
gradual, *adj.* gradual
graduate, *vt.* y *vi.* graduar,
    graduarse, recibirse; *n.* gra-
    duado, graduada
graduation, *n.* graduación, *f.*
grain, *n.* grano, *m.*; semilla, *f.*
gram, *n.* gramo (peso), *m.*
grammar, *n.* gramática, *f.*;
    grammar school, escuela
    primaria o elemental, *f.*
grammatical, *adj.* gramatical
grand, *adj.* grande, ilustre; es-
    pléndido; **grand piano,** piano
    de cola, *m.*
grandchild, *n.* nieto, nieta
granddaughter, *n.* nieta, *f.*
grandeur, *n.* pompa, *f.*
grandfather, *n.* abuelo, *m.*
grandmother, *n.* abuela, *f.*
grandparent, *n.* abuelo, abue-
    la
grandson, *n.* nieto, *m.*
granite, *n.* granito, *m.*
grant, *vt.* conceder; conferir;
    granting that, supuesto que;
    to take for granted, dar por
    sentado; *n.* subvención, *f.*
grape, *n.* uva, *f.*
grapefruit, *n.* toronja, *f.*
graph, *n.* diagrama, *m.*; gráfi-
    co, *m.*
graphic, *adj.* gráfico; pintores-
    co
grasp, *vt.* empuñar, agarrar;

comprender; *n.* puño, puña-
    do, *m.*; dominio, *m.*
grasping, *adj.* codicioso
grass, *n.* hierba, *f.*; yerba, *f.*,
    césped, *m.*
grasshopper, *n.* saltamontes,
    m.
grate, *n.* reja, verja, rejilla, *f.*;
    vt. rallar; irritar
grateful, *adj.* agradecido
gratify, *vt.* gratificar
gratis, *adj.* gratuito, gratis;
    adv. gratis, de balde
gratitude, *n.* gratitud, *f.*
grave, *n.* sepultura, *f.*; tumba,
    fosa, *f.*; *adj.* grave, serio
graveyard, *n.* cementerio, *m.*
gravity, *n.* graveded, *f.*; serie-
    dad, *f.*
gravy, *n.* jugo de la carne, *m.*,
    salsa, *f.*
graze, *vt.* pastorear; tocar lige-
    ramente; *vi.* rozar; pacer
grease, *n.* grasa, *f.*; *vt.* engra-
    sar, lubricar
greasy, *adj.* grasiento
great, *adj.* gran, grande; ilus-
    tre; **greatly,** *adv.* grandemen-
    te, muy, mucho
Great Britain, Gran Bretaña,
    f.
great-grandchild, *n.* biznieto,
    biznieta
great-grandparent, *n.* bisa-
    buelo, bisabuela
Grecian, *n.* y *adj.* griego, grie-
    ga
Greece, Grecia, *f.*
greed, greediness, *n.* voraci-
    dad, *f.*; codicia, *f.*
greedy, *adj.* voraz, goloso; co-
    dicioso
Greek, *n. adj.* griego, griega
green, *adj.* verde, fresco; no
    maduro; *n.* verde, *m.*, verdor,
    m.; **greens,** *n. pl.* verduras,
    hortalizas, *f. pl.*
Greenland, Groenlandia, *f.*
greet, *vt.* saludar
greeting, *n.* saludo, *m.*
grew, *pretérito* del verbo **grow**
greyhound, *n.* galgo, lebrel, *m.*
grief, *n.* dolor, *m.*, aflicción, *f.*
grieve, *vt.* agraviar, afligir; *vi.*
    afligirse, llorar

grill, vt. asar en parrillas; n. parrilla, f.

grim, adj. feo; austero

grimace, n. mueca, f.

grime, n. suciedad,

grimy, adj. sucio

grin, n. risa franca, f.; vi. reirse francamente

grind, vt. moler; afilar

grinder, n. molinillo, m.; amolador, m.

grip, vt. agarrar, empuñar; n. maleta, f.

grippe, n. gripe, f.; influenza, f.

gripping, adj. emocionante

gristle, n. cartílago, m.

gritty, adj. arenoso

groan, vi. gemir; n. gemido, quejido, m.

grocer, n. abacero, m.; (Sp. Am.) abarrotero, m.

grocery, n. abacería, f.; **grocery store,** tienda de comestibles, f.; (Sp. Am.) tienda de abarrotes, f.

groom, n. criado, m.; mozo de caballos; novio, m.

gross, n. gruesa, f.; todo, m.

ground, n. tierra, f.; país, m.; terreno, suelo, m.

groundless, adj. infundado

group, n. grupo, m.

grow, vt. cultivar; vi. crecer

grown, p. p. del verbo **grow**

grown-up, adj. mayor de edad, maduro; n. persona mayor de edad

growth, n. crecimiento, m.; nacencia, f., tumor, m.

grudge, n. rencor, odio, m.; envidia

grudgingly, adv. con repugnancia, de mala gana

gruff, adj. ceñudo, brusco

grumble, vi. gruñir; murmurar

grumpy, adj. regañón, quejoso

guarantee, vt. garantizar

guaranty, n. garante, m.; garantía, f.

guard, n. guarda, guardia, f., centinela, m. y f.; vigilante, m.; vt. defender; custodiar; vi. guardarse; prevenirse; velar

guardian, n. tutor, m.; guardián, m.

guess, vt. y vi. conjeturar; adivinar; n. conjetura, f.

guest, n. huésped, huéspeda, invitado, invitada, convidado, convidada

guide, vt. guiar, dirigir; n. guía, m. y f.

guilt, n. delito, m.; culpa, f.

guilty, adj. culpable

guitar, n. guitarra, f.

gulf, n. golfo, m.; abismo , m.

Gulf Stream, n. corriente del Golfo de México, f.

gum, n. gorna, f.; encía, f.; **chewing gum,** chicle, m., goma de mascar, f.

gumbo, n. (bot.) quimbombó, m.

gumption, n. (coll.) iniciativa, inventiva, f.

gun, n. arma de fuego; fusil, m.; escopeta, f.; pistola, f., revólver, m.

gunpowder, n. pólvora, f.

gust, n. soplo de aire, m.; ráfaga, f.

gusto, n. gusto, placer, m.

gut, n. intestino, m., cuerda de tripa, f.; **guts,** n. pl. (coll.) valor, m., valentía, f.

gutter, n. zanja, f.; caño, m.

guy, n. tipo, sujeto, m.

gymnasium, n. gimnasio, m.

gypsy, n. y adj. gitano, gitana

H

habit, n. hábito, vestido, m.; costumbre, f.

habitation, n. habitación, f.; domicilio, m.

habitual, adj. habitual

had, pretérito y p. p. del verbo **have**

haddock, n. (pez) merluza, f.

Hades, n. pl. los infiernos, m. pl.

hag, n. bruja, hechicera, f.

haggard, adj. ojeroso, trasnochado

hail, n. granizo, m.; saludo, m.; vt. saludar; vi. granizar; **hail!** interj. ¡viva!

hair, *n.* cabello pelo, *m.*

hairbrush, *n.* cepillo para el cabello, *m.*

hair-do, *n.* (coll.) peinado, *m.*

hairdresser, *n.* peluquero, *m.*; peinador, peinadora

hairpin, *n.* horquilla, *f.*

hairy, *adj.* peludo

hale, *adj.* sano, vigoroso

half, *n.* mitad, *f.*; *adj.* medio

half-breed, *n.* y *adj.* mestizo, mestiza

halfhearted, *adj.* indiferente, sin entusiasmo

half-hour, *n.* media hora, *f.*

halfway, *adv.* a medio camino, a medias

hall, *n.* vestíbulo, *m.*, sala, *f.*; salón, colegio, *m.*; sala, *f.*; cámara, *f.*

hallow, *vt.* consagrar, santificar

Halloween, *n.* víspera de Todos los Santos, *f.*

hallway, *n.* vestíbulo, atrio, *m.*

halo, *n.* halo, nimbo, *m.*, corona, *f.*

halves, *n. pl.* de **half,** mitades, *f. pl.*, **by halves,** a medias

ham, *n.* jamón, *m.*

hamburger, *n.* carne picada de res; emparedado de carne molida

hammer, *n.* martillo, *m.*; *vt.* martillar

hamper, *n.* cesto grande (para ropa, etc.); *vt.* estorbar, impedir

hand, *n.* mano, *f.*; obrero, *m.*; mano o manecilla (de un reloj), *f.*; **at hand,** a la mano, *vt.* alargar; entregar

handbag, *n.* bolsa, *f.*; maletilla, *f.*

handcuff, *n.* manilla, *f.*; esposas, *f. pl.*

handful, *n.* puñado, *m.*

handicap, *n.* obstáculo, *m.*; ventaja, *f.* (en juegos)

handiwork, *n.* obra manual, *f.*

handkerchief, *n.* pañuelo, *m.*

handle, *n.* mango, *m.*, asa, manigueta, *f.*; *vt.* manejar; tratar

handmade, *adj.* hecho a mano

handshake, *n.* apretón de manos, *m.*

handsome, *adj.* hermoso, bello

handwork, *n.* trabajo a mano, *m.*

handwriting, *n.* escritura, *f.*; caligrafía, *f.*; letra, *f.*

handy, *adj.* manual; diestro, hábil

hang, *vt.* colgar, suspender; ahorcar; *vi.* colgar; ser ahorcado; pegarse

hangnail, *n.* uñero, padrastro, *m.*

haphazard, *adj.* casual, descuidado

happen, *vi.* acontecer, suceder

happening, *n.* suceso, acontecimiento, *m.*

happily, *adv.* felizmente

happiness, *n.* felicidad, dicha, *f.*

happy, *adj.* feliz

hard, *adj.* duro, firme; difícil; severo, rígido

hard-boiled, *adj.* cocido hasta endurecerse; **hard-boiled eggs,** huevos duros, *m. pl.*

harden, *vt.* y *vi.* endurecer, endurecerse

hardly, *adv.* apenas

hardship, *n.* injusticia, *f.*; trabajo, *m.*

hardtop, *n.* toldo rígido; *adj.* con toldo rígido

hardware, *n.* ferretería, *f.*

hardy, *adj.* fuerte, robusto

hare, *n.* liebre, *f.*

harem, *n.* harén, *m.*

harm, *n.* mal, daño, *m.*; perjuicio, *m.*; *vt.* dañar, injuriar

harmful, *adj.* perjudicial

harmless, *adj.* inofensivo

harmonize, *vt.* y *vi.* armonizar

harmony, *n.* armonía, *f.*

harp, *n.* arpa, *f.*

harsh, *adj.* áspero, austero

harvest, *n.* cosecha, *f.*

has, 3ª persona del singular del verbo **have**

hash, *n.* jigote, picadillo, *m.*

hassock, *n.* cojín para los pies, *m.*

haste, *n.* prisa, *f.*

hasten, *vt.* y *vi.* acelerar, apresurar

hastily, *adv.* precipitadamente

hasty, *adj.* apresurado

hat, *n.* sombrero, *m.*

hatch, *vt.* criar pollos; empollar

hate, *n.* odio, *m.;* *vt.* odiar, detestar

hateful, *adj.* odioso, detestable

haul, *vt.* tirar, halar; acarrear

haunt, *vt.* frecuentar, rondar; perseguir; *n.* guarida, *f.*

haunted, *adj.* encantado, frecuentado por espantos

Havana, Habana

haven, *n.* puerto, *m.;* abrigo, asilo, *m.*

Hawaiian Islands, Islas Hawaianas, *f. pl.*

hawk, *n.* (orn.) halcón, gavilán, *m.*

hay, *n.* heno, *m.;* **hay fever,** romadizo, *m.*, fiebre del heno, *f.*

hazard, *n.* acaso, accidente, *m.;* riesgo, *m.;* *vt.* arriesgar; aventurar

haze, *n.* niebla, bruma, *f.*

hazel, *n.* avellano, *m.;* *adj.* castaño

hazelnut, *n.* avellano, *f.*

hazy, *adj.* anieblado, oscuro

H-Bomb, *n.* bomba H, *m.*

he, *pron.* él

head, *n.* cabeza, *f.;* jefe, *m.;* *vt.* gobernar, dirigir

headache, *n.* dolor de cabeza, *m.;* jaqueca, *f.*

headfirst, *adv.* de cabeza

headgear, *n.* tocado, *m.*

heading, *n.* título, membrete, *m.*

headline, *n.* encabezamiento, título (de un periódico, etc.), *m.*

headquarters, *n.* (mil.) cuartel general, *m.;* jefatura, administración, *f.*

headstrong, *adj.* testarudo, cabezudo

heal, *vt.* y *vi.* curar, sanar, cicatrizar

health, *n.* salud, sanidad, *f.*

healthy, *adj.* sano; saludable

heap, *n.* montón, *m.;* *vt.* amontonar, acumular

hear, *vt.* y *vi.* oir; escuchar

hearing, *n.* oído, *m.*, oreja, *f.;* audiencia, *f.*

hearsay, *n.* rumor, *m.*

hearse, *n.* carroza fúnebre, *f.*

heart, *n.* corazón, *m.;* alma, *f.;* interior, centro, *m.;* animo, valor, *m.;* **by heart,** de memoria; **heart attack,** ataque al corazón; **heart transplant,** trasplante de corazón, trasplante cardíaco

heartbroken, *adj.* transido de dolor

heartburn, *n.* acedía, *f.*

heartfelt, *adj.* expresivo, sentido, sincero

hearth, *n.* hogar, fogón, *m.*, chimenea, *f.*

heartless, *adj.* inhumano, cruel

heart-to-heart, *adj.* sincero, abierto; confidencial

hearty, *adj.* cordial

heat, *n.* calor, *m.;* ardor, *m.;* *vt.* calentar

heater, *n.* calorífero, *m.;* **hot-air heater,** calorífero de aire caliente

heathen, *n.* gentil, *m.* y *f.*, pagano, pagana

heating, *n.* calefacción, *f.*

heave, *vt.* alzar; elevar; (naut.) virar para proa; *vi.* palpitar

heaven, *n.* cielo, *m.*

heavenly, *adj.* celeste, divino

heaviness, *n.* pesadez, *f.*

heavy, *adj.* pesado

heavyweight, *n.* boxeador de peso mayor, *m.*

hectic, *adj.* inquieto, agitado

heed, *vt.* atender, observar; *n.* cuidado, *m.;* atención, precaución, *f.*

heel, *n.* talón, carcañal, calcañar, *m.;* tacón, *m.;* (coll.) canalla, *m.*

height, *n.* altura, elevación, *f.*

heighten, *vt.* realzar

heir, *n.* heredero, *m.*

heiress, *n.* heredera, *f.*

heirloom, *n.* reliquia de familia, *f.*

helicopter, *n.* helicóptero, *m.*

hell, *n.* infierno, *m.*

hello, *interj.* ¡qué hay! ¡qué hubo! (expresión de saludo)

helmet, *n.* yelmo, casco, *m.*

help, *vt.* y *vi.* ayudar, socorrer; aliviar, remediar; evitar; *n.* ayuda, *f.*; socorro, remedio, *m.*

helpful, *adj.* util, provechoso

helpless, *adj.* irremediable

hem, *n.* bastilla, *f.*; *vt.* bastillar

hemisphere, *n.* hemisferio, *m.*

hemoglobin, *n.* (med.) hemoglobina, *f.*

hemorrhage, *n.* hemorragia, *f.*

hemorrhoids, *n. pl.* hemorroides, almorranas, *f. pl.*

hemp, *n.* ciñamo, *m.*

hemstitch, *n.* (costura) vainica, *f.*; *vt.* (costura) hacer una vainica

hen, *n.* gallina, *f.*

henceforth, *adv.* de aquí en adelante; en lo sucesivo

hencoop, *n.* gallinero, *m.*

her, *pron.* su, ella, de ella, a ella

herald, *n.* heraldo, *m.*

herb, *n.* yerba, hierba, *f.*

herd, *n.* hato, rebaño, *m.*; manada, *f.*

here, *adv.* aquí, acá

hereabouts, *adv.* aquí al rededor

hereafter, *adv.* en lo futuro; *n.* estado venidero, el futuro, *m.*

hereditary, *adj.* hereditario

heredity, *n.* derecho de su cesión, *m.*; herencia, *f.*

heretofore, *adv.* antes, en tiempos pasados; hasta ahora

heritage, *n.* herencia, *f.*

hermetic, *adj.* hermético

hermit, *n.* ermitaño, *m.*

hero, *n.* héroe, *m.*

heroic, *adj.* heroico; **heroics,** *n. pl.* expresión o acto extravagantes

heroine, *n.* heroína, *f.*

heroism, *n.* heroísmo, *m.*

heron, *n.* garza, *f.*

herring, *n.* arenque, *m.*

hers, *pron.* suyo, de ella

herself, *pron.* si, ella misma

hesitate, *vi.* vacilar, titubear

hesitation, *n.* duda, *f.*, titubeo, *m.*

hiccough, *n.* hipo, *m.*; *vi.* tener hipo

hid, *pretérito* del verbo **hide**

hidden, *adj.* escondido; secreto

hide, *vt.* esconder; *vi.* esconderse; *n.* cuero, *m.*; piel, *f.*

hide-and-seek, *n.* escondite, *m.*

hideous, *adj.* horripilante

high, *adj.* alto, elevado; **high jump,** salto de altura, *m.*

highball, *n.* highball, *m.*, bebida compuesta de aguardiente con soda

high-grade, *adj.* de alta calidad, excelente

highland, *n.* tierra montañosa

Highness, *n.* Alteza, *f.*

highness, *n.* altura, *f.*

high-strung, *adj.* nervioso, excitable

highway, *n.* carretera, *f.*

hike, *n.* paseo a pie, *m.*

hilarious, *adj.* alegre y bullicioso

him, *pron.* le, a él

himself, *pron.* sí, él mismo

hinder, *vt.* impedir, estorbar

hindrance, *n.* impedimento, obstáculo, *m.*; rémora, *f.*

hint, *n.* seña, *f.*; sugestión, insinuación, *f.*; *vt.* insinuar; sugerir; hacer señas

hip, *n.* cadera, *f.*

hippopotamus, *n.* hipopótamo, *m.*

hippie, hippy, *n.* hippie, *m.* y *f.*

hire, *vt.* alquilar; arrendar; *n.* alquiler, *m.*; salario, *m.*

his, *pron.* su, suyo, de él

historian, *n.* historiador, *m.*

historic, historical, *adj.* histórico

history, *n.* historia, *f.*

hit, *vt.* golpear; atinar; *n.* golpe, *m.*; (coll.) éxito, *m.*

hive, *n.* colmena, *f.*

hives, *n.* (med.) urticaria, *f.*, ronchas, *f. pl.*

hoard, *n.* montón, *m.*; tesoro escondido, *m.*; *vt.* atesorar, acumular

hoax, *n.* burla, *f.*; petardo, *m.*; *vt.* engañar, burlar

hobby, *n.* afición, *f.*

hockey, *n.* hockey, *m.* juego de patinadores sobre el hielo

hog, *n.* cerdo, puerco, *m.*

hoist, *vt.* alzar; (naut.) izar; *n.* grúa, *f.*; cabria, *f.*; montacargas, *m.*

hold, *vt.* tener, asir; detener; sostener; contener; sujetar; *pl.* mantenerse

holdup, *n.* asalto, robo, *m.*

hole, *n.* agujero, *m.*; hoyo, *m.*; hueco, *m.*

holiday, *n.* día de fiesta, día festivo, *m.*; **holidays**, *n. pl.* vacaciones, *f. pl.*

Holland, Holanda

holly, *n.* (bot.) acebo, *m.*

holster, *n.* funda de pistola

holy, *adj.* santo

homage, *n.* homenaje, culto, *m.*

home, *n.* casa, morada, *f.*, hogar, *m.*; *adj.* doméstico

homeland, *n.* patria, *f.*

homeless, *adj.* sin hogar

homely, *adj.* feo

homemade, *adj.* hecho en casa; casero

homemaker, *n.* ama de casa, *f.*

homesick, *adj.* nostálgico

homesickness, *n.* nostalgia. *f.*

homework, *n.* tarea, *f.*

homicide, *n.* homicidio, *m.*; homicida, *m.* y *f.*

honest, *adj.* honesto, probo; honrado; justo

honesty, *n.* honestidad, justicia, probidad, *f.*; honradez, *f.*

honey, *n.* miel, *f.*; dulzura, *f.*

honeybee, *n.* abeja obrera

honeycomb, *n.* panal, *m.*

honeysuckle, *n.* (bot.) madreselva, *f.*

honor, *n.* honra, *f.*, honor, lauro, *m.*; *vt.* honrar; **to honor (a draft)**, (com.) aceptar

(un giro o letra de cambio)

honorable, *adj.* honorable; ilustre; respatable

honorary, *adj.* honorario

hood, *n.* caperuza, *f.*; gorro, *m.*; (auto.) cubierta del motor

hoodlum, *n.* (coll.) pillo, tunante, *m.*

hook, *n.* gancho, *m.*; anzuelo, *m.*; *vt.* enganchar

hop, *n.* salto *m.*; **hops**, (bot.) lúpulo, *m.*; *vi.* saltar, brincar

hope, *n.* esperanza, *f.*; *vi.* esperar

hopeless, *adj.* desesperado; sin remedio

hormone, *n.* hormón, *m.*, hormona, *f.*

horn, *n.* cuerno, *m.*; corneta, *f.*; trompeta, *f.*; bocina, *f.*; klaxon, *m.*

hornet, *n.* abejón, *m.*

horoscope, *n.* horóscopo *m.*

horrible, *adj.* horrible

horrid, *adj.* horroroso

horrify, *va.* horrorizar

horror, *n.* horror, terror, *m.*

hors d'oeuvre, *n. pl.* entremés, *m.*

horse, *n.* caballo, *m.*

horseback, *n.* espinazo del caballo; **on horseback**, a caballo

horseman, *n.* jinete, *m.*

horsepower, *n.* caballo de fuerza o potencia, *m.*

horseshoe, *n.* herradura de caballo, *f.*

horticulture, *n.* horticultura, jardinería, *f.*

hose, *n.* medias, *f. pl.*; manguera, *f.*; tubo flexible, *m.*

hosiery, *n.* medias, *f. pl.*; calcetines, *m. pl.*

hospitable, *adj.* hospitalario

hospital, *n.* hospital, *m.*

hospitality, *n.* hospitalidad, *f.*

hospitalization, *n.* hospitalización, *f.*

hospitalize, *vt.* hospitalizar

host, *n.* anfitrión, *m.*; huésped, *m.*; hostia, *f.*

hostel, *n.* posada, hostería, *f.*, hotel, *m.*

hostess, *n.* anfitriona, *f.*

hot, *adj.* caliente, cálido; ardiente; picante; (coll.) excitante agitado, violento; **hot line,** línea de emergencia

hotel, *n.* posada, fonda, *f.*, hotel, *m.*

hot-tempered, *adj.* colérico

hound, *n.* sabueso, *m.*

hour, *n.* hora, *f.*

hourly, *adv.* a cada hora; frecuentemente; *adj.* por hora, frecuente

house, *n.* casa, *f.*; linaje, *m.*; cámara (del parlamento), *f.*; **House of Representatives,** Cámara de Representantes; **to keep house,** ser ama de casa; *vt.* y *vi.* albergar, residir

housecoat, *n.* bata de casa

household, *n.* familia, *f.*; casa, *f.*; establecimiento, *m.*; **household management,** manejo doméstico, *m.*

housekeeper, *n.* ama de casa, jefe de familia, *f.*; ama de llaves, *f.*

housewife, *n.* ama de casa, *f.*

housework, *n.* quehaceres domésticos, *m. pl.*

housing, *n.* alojamiento, *m.*

how, *adv.* cómo, cuán; cuánto

however, *adv.* como quiera, como quiera que sea; sin embargo, no obstante

hub, *n.* cubo, *m.*; centro, *m.*; **hub cap,** tapacubos, *m.*

hubbub, *n.* alboroto, tumulto, *m.*

hue, *n.* color, *m.*; tez del rostro, *f.*; matiz, *m.*

hug, *vt.* abrazar, acariciar; *n.* abrazo, *m.*

huge, *adj.* vasto, enorme

hull, *n.* cáscara, *f.*; (naut.) casco (de un buque), *m.*; *vt.* descortezar, pelar

hullabaloo, *n.* tumulto, al boroto, *m.*

hum, *vi.* zumbar, susurrar, murmurar; *vt.* tararear (una canción, etc.); *n.* zumbido, *m.*

human, *n.* y *adj.* humano, humana

humane, *adj.* humano

humanitarian, *n.* filántropo, filántropa; *adj.* humanitario

humanity, *n.* humanidad *f.*

humankind, *n.* el género o linaje humano *m.*

humble, *adj.* humilde, modesto; *vt.* humillar; **to humble oneself,** humillarse

humid, *adj.* húmedo

humidity, *n.* humedad, *f.*

humiliate, *vt.* humillar

humiliation, *n.* humillación, mortificación, *f.*

humility, *n.* humildad, *f.*

humor, *n.* humor, *m.*; *vt.* complacer, dar gusto

humorist, *n.* humorista, *m.* y *f.*

humorous, *adj.* chistoso, jocoso

hump, *n.* giba, joroba, *f.*

hunch, *n.* giba, *f.*; (coll.) idea, *f.*

hunchback, *n.* joroba, *f.*; jorobado, jorobada

hundred, *adj.* cien, ciento; *n.* centenar, *m.*

hundredth, *n.* y *adj.* centésimo, *m.*

hundredweight, *n.* quintal, *m.*

hung, *pretérito* y *p.p.* del verbo **hang**

Hungary, Hungría

hunger, *n.* hambre, *f.*

hungry, *adj.* hambriento; **to be hungry,** tener hambre

hunk, *n.* pedazo grande, *m.*

hunt, *vt.* cazar; perseguir; buscar; *n.* caza, *f.*

hunter, *n.* cazador, *m.*; perro de monte, perro de caza, *m.*

hunting, *n.* montería, caza, *f.*

hurdle, *n.* valla, *f.*; obstáculo; **hurdles,** *pl.* carrera de vallas, *f.*

hurrah! *interj.* ¡viva!

hurricane, *n.* huracán, *m.*

hurry, *vt.* acelerar, apresurar, precipitar; *vi.* atropellarse, apresurarse; *n.* precipitación, *f.* ; urgencia, *f.*

hurt, *vt.* dañar, hacer daño, herir; ofender; *n.* mal, daño, perjuicio, *m.*; herida, *f.*; *adj.* sentido; lastimado; perjudicado

husband, n. marido, esposo, m.

husky, adj. fuerte; robusto

hustle, vt. y vi. bullir; apurar (un trabajo); apurarse, andar de prisa

hut, n. cabaña, choza, f.

hydraulic, adj. hidráulico

hydrofoil, n. aereodeslizador, hidrofoil, m.

hydrogen, n. (chem.) hidrógeno, m.; **hydrogen bomb,** bomba de hidrógeno

hydroplane, n. (naut.) hidroplano, m.; (avi.) hidroavión, m.

hygiene, n. higiene, f.

hygienic, adj. higiénico

hymn, n. himno, m.

hyphen, n. guión, m.

hypnotic, adj. hipnótico

hypnotize, vt. hipnotizar

hypocrite, n. hipócrita, m. y f.

hypocritical, adj. hipócrita, disimulado

hypodermic, adj. hipodérmico

hysteria, n. histeria, f., histerismo, m.

hysteric, hysterical, adj. histérico

hysterics, n. pl. paroxismo histérico, m.

I

I, pron. yo

ICBM, I.C.B.M., **intercontinental ballistic missile,** cohete balístico intercontinental

ice, n. hielo, m.; **ice skate,** patín de hielo, m.; **ice water,** agua helada

iceberg, n. témpano de hielo, m.

icebox, n. refrigerador, m., nevera, f.

ice cream, n. helado, mantecado, m., nieve, f.

iceman, n. repartidor de hielo, m.

icicle, n. carámbano, m.

icing, n., betún o confitura (para pasteles)

icy, adj. helado; frío; (fig.) indiferente

idea, n. idea, f.; concepto, m.

ideal, adj. ideal

idealism, n. idealismo, m.

idealistic, adj. idealista

identical, adj. idéntico

identification, n. identificación, f.

identify, vt. identificar

idiomatic, idiomatical, adj. idiomático

idiot, n. idiota, m. y f.

idiotic, adj. tonto, bobo

idle, adj. ocioso, perezoso

idleness, n. ociosidad, pereza, f.

idol, n. idolo, m.; imagen, f.

idolize, vt. idolatrar

idyl, n. idilio, m.

i.e., that is, i.e., es decir, esto es

if, conj. si; aunque, supuesto que

ignorance, n. ignorancia, f.

ignorant, adj. ignorante, inculto

ignore, vt. pasar por alto, desconocer

ill, adj. malo, enfermo; adv. mal, malament

ill-bred, adj. malcriado, descortés

illegal, adj. ilegal

illegible, adj. ilegible

illegitimate, adj. ilegítimo

ill-gotten, adj. mal habido

ill-humored, adj. malhumorado

illiterate, adj. analfabeto

ill-mannered, adj. malcriado, descortés

illuminate, vt. iluminar

illumination, n. iluminación, f.; alumbrado, m.

illumine, vt. iluminar

illustrate, vt. ilustrar; explicar

illustrated, adj. ilustrado, de grabados

illustration, n. ilustración, f.; ejemplo, m.; grabado, m.

illustrious, adj. ilustre, célebre

image, n. imagen, estatua, f.

imaginary, adj. imaginario

imagination, n. imaginación, f.

imagine, vt. imaginar; idear, inventar

imbecile, n. y adj. imbécil, m. y f.

imitate, vt. imitar, copiar

imitation, n. imitación, copia, f.

imitator, n. imitador, imitadora

immaculate, adj. inmaculado, puro

immature, adj. inmaturo

immediate, adj. inmediato; **immediately,** adv. en seguida

immense, adj. inmenso

immensity, n. inmensidad, f.

immerse, vt. sumergir

immersion, n. inmersión,

immigrant, n. inmigrante, m. y f.

immigrate, vi. inmigrar

immigration, n. inmigración, f.

imminent, adj. inminente

immobile, adj. inmóvil

immoral, adj. immoral, depravado

immorality, n. inmoralidad f.

immortal, adj. immortal

immune, adj. inmune, exento

immunity, n. inmunidad, franquicia, f.

immunize, vt. inmunizar

impair, vt. deteriorar; disminuir

impart, vt. comunicar

impartial, adj. imparcial

impartiality, n. imparcialidad, f.

impassable, adj. intransitable

impassive, adj. impasible

impatience, n. impaciencia, f.

impatient, adj. impaciente

impediment, n. impedimento, obstáculo, m.

impel, vt. impeler, impulsar

imperative, adj. imperativo, imprescindible

imperfect, adj. imperfecto, defectuoso; n. (gram.) pretérito imperfecto

imperfection, n. imperfección, f., defecto, m.

impersonate, vt. personificar; representar

impersonation, n. personificación, f.; (theat.) representación, f.

impertinence, n. impertinencia, f.; descaro, m.

impertinent, adj. impertinente

impetuous, adj. impetuoso

implement, n. herramienta, f.; utensilio, m.; vt. ejecutar, completar

implicate, vt. implicar, envolver

implicit, adj. implícito

implied, adj. implícito

implore, vt. implorar, suplicar

imply, vt. implicar

impolite, adj. descortés

import, vt. importar; significar; n. importancia, f.; importe, m.; sentido, m.; **import duties,** derechos de importación, m. pl.

importance, n. importancia, f.

important, adj. importante

importing, adj. importador; n. importación, f.

impose, vt. imponer

imposing, adj. imponente

imposition, n. imposición, carga, f.

impossibility, n. imposibilidad, f.

impossible, adj. imposible

impostor, n. impostor, impostora

impotent, adj. impotente; incapaz

impress, vt. imprimir, estampar

impression, n. impresión, f.

impressive, adj. imponente

imprint, vt. imprimir; estampar; n. impresión, f.; huella, f.

imprisonment, n. prisión, f., encierro, m.

improbable, adj. inverosímil

impromptu, adj. extemporáneo

improper, adj. impropio, indecente

improve, vt. y vi. mejorar, perfeccionar; vi. progresar

improvement, *n.* mejoramiento, perfeccionamiento, *m.*
improvise, *vt.* improvisar
impulse, *n.* impulso, *m.*; ímpetu, *m.*
in., inch, pulgada; *pl.* das **inches,** plgs., pulgadas
inability, *n.* incapacidad, *f.*
inaccurate, *adj.* inexacto
inactive, *adj.* inanimado
inaugurate, *vt.* inaugurar
inauguration, *n.* inauguración, *f.*
Inc., Incorporated, (Sp. Am.) S.A., Sociedad Anónima, Ltda., Sociedad Limitada
incapable, *adj.* incapaz
incense, *n.* incienso, *m.*; *vt.* exasperar, provocar
incentive, *n.* incentivo, estímulo, *m.*
inch, *n.* pulgada, *f.*
incident, *n.* incidente *m.*
incidental, *adj.* accidental, casual
incite, *vt.* incitar, estimular
inclination, *n.* inclinación, propensión, *f.*; declive, *m.*
incline, *vt.* inclinar; *vi.* inclinarse; *n.* pendiente, *f.*
include, *vt.* incluir
inclusion, *n.* inclusión, *f.*
inclusive, *adj.* inclusivo
incognito, *adj.* y *adv.* de incógnito
incoherent, *adj.* incoherente
income, *n.* renta, *f.*, entradas, *f. pl.*; **income tax,** impuesto sobre rentas
incomparable, *adj.* incomparable
incompatible, *adj.* incompatible
incompetent, *adj.* incompetente
incomplete, *adj.* incompleto
inconceivable, *adj.* inconcebible
inconvenience, *n.* incomodidad, *vt.* incomodar
inconvenient, *adj.* inconveniente
incorporate, *vt.* y *vi.* incorporar
incorporation, *n.* incorporación, *f.*

incorrect, *adj.* incorrecto
incorrigible, *adj.* incorregible
increase, *vt.* aumentar; *vi.* crecer, aumentarse; *n.* aumento, *m.*
incredible, *adj.* increíble
incubator, *n.* incubadora, *f.*
incur, *vt.* incurrir; ocurrir
incurable, *adj.* incurable
indebted, *adj.* endeudado, obligado,
indebtedness, *n.* deuda, obligación, *f.*
indecent, *adj.* indecente
indecision, *n.* indecisión, *f.*
indeed, *adv.* verdaderamente, de veras; sí
indefinite, *adj.* indefinido
indelible, *adj.* indeleble
indentation, *n.* margen, *m.*
independence, *n.* independencia ,
independent, *adj.* independiente
indescribable, *adj.* indesriptible
indestructible, *adj.* indestructible
index, *n.* índice, elenco, *m.*
India, *n.* India, *f.*
Indian, *n.* y *adj.* indiano, indiana; indio, india
indicate, *vt.* indicar
indication, *n.* indicación, *f.*; indicio, *m.*; señal, *f.*
indicative, *n.* (gram.) indicativo, *m.*; *adj.* indicativo
indict, *vt.* procesar
indictment, *n.* denuncia, *f.*
indifference, *n.* indiferencia, apatía, *f.*
indigenous, *adj.* indígena
indigent, *adj.* indigente, pobre
indigestion, *n.* indigestión, *f.*
indignation, *n.* indignación, *f.*
indignity, *n.* indignidad, *f.*
indirect, *adj.* indirecto
indiscreet, *adj.* indiscreto
indiscretion, *n.* indiscreción, imprudencia, *f.*
indispensable, *adj.* indispensable
indisposed, *adj.* indispuesto, achacoso

indistinct, *adj.* confuse; borroso

individual, *adj.* individual; *n.* individuo, *m.*

induce, *vt.* inducir, persuadir

inducement, *n.* motivo, móvil, aliciente, *m.*

indulgence, *n.* indulgencia, *f.*, mimo, *m.*

indulgent, *adj.* indulgente

industrial, *adj.* industrial

industrialization, *n.* industrialización, *f.*

industrialize, *vt.* industrializar

industrious, *adj.* hacendoso; trabajador

industry, *n.* industria, *f.*

inefficiency, *n.* ineficacia, *f.*

inefficient, *adj.* ineficaz

inept, *adj.* inepto

inescapable, *adj.* ineludible

inevitable, *adj.* inevitable

inexcusable, *adj.* inexcusable

inexhaustible, *adj.* inagotable

inexpensive, *adj.* barato

inexperienced, *adj.* inexperto, sin experiencia

infallible, *adj.* infalible

infamy, *n.* infamia, *f.*

infancy, *n.* infancia, *f.*

infant, *n.* infante, m; niño, niña

infantile, *adj.* pueril, infantil; **infantile paralysis,** parálisis infantil, *f.*

infantry, *n.* infantería,

infect, *vt.* infectar

infection, *n.* infección,

infer, *vt.* inferer, deducir

inferior, *adj.* inferior

inferiority, *n.* inferioridad, *f.*; **inferiority complex,** complejo de inferioridad, *m.*

infinite, *adj.* infinito; **infinitely,** *adv.* infinitamente

infinitive, *n.* infinitivo, *m.*

infinity, *n.* infinidad, eternidad,. *f.*

infirmary, *n.* enfermería,

inflame, *vt.* y *vi.* inflamar

inflammable, *adj.* inflamable

inflation, *n.* inflación, *f.*

inflection, *n.* inflexión, modulación de la voz, *f.*

inflict, *vt.* castigar; infligir (penas corporales, etc.)

influence, *n.* influencia, *f.*; *vt.* influir

influential, *adj.* influyente

influenza, *n.* (med.) influenza, gripe, *f.*, trancazo, *m.*

inform, *vt.* informar

informal, *adj.* íntimo, sin formulismos

information, *n.* información, instrucción, *f.*; informe, *m.*; aviso, *m.*

ingenious, *adj.* ingenioso

ingenuity, *n.* ingeniosidad, inventiva, *f.*

ingratitude, *n.* ingratitud, *f.*

ingredient, *n.* ingrediente, *m.*

ingrown, *adj.* crecido hacia dentro; **ingrown nail,** uñero, *m.*

inhabit, *vt.* habitar

inhabitant, *n.* habitante, residente, *m.* y *f.*

inherent, *adj.* inherente

inherit, *vt.* heredar

inheritance, *n.* herencia, *f.*; patrimonio, *m.*

inhibition, *n.* inhibición, *f.*

inhuman, *adj.* inhumano

initial, *n.* y *adj.* inicial, *f.*

initiation, *n.* iniciación, *f.*

initiative, *n.* iniciativa, *f.*

inject, *vt.* inyectar

injection, *n.* inyección, *f.*

injure, *vt.* injuriar, ofender; hacer daño

injurious, *adj.* perjudicial, nocivo

injury, *n.* perjuicio, *m.*; daño, *m.*

injustice, *n.* injusticia, *f.*

ink, *n.* tinta, *f.*

inkling, *n.* insinuación, noción vaga, *f.*

inkstand, *n.* tintero, *m.*

inmate, *n.* inquilino, inquilina; preso, presa

inn, *n.* posada, *f.*

inner, *adj.* interior

innocence, *n.* inocencia, *f.*

innocent, *adj.* inocente

innovation, *n.* innovación, *f.*

inoculate, *vt.* inocular; inyectar

inoffensive, *adj.* inofensivo

input, *n.* (elec.) entrada, *f.*; (fig.) gasto, *f.*

inquest, *n.* indagación, *f.*

inquire, *vt.* preguntar (alguna cosa); *vi.* inquirir, examinar

inquiry, *n.* pregunta, *f.*; investigación *f.*

inquisition, *n.* inquisición *f.*

inquisitive, *adj.* curioso, preguntón

insane, *adj.* loco, demente

insanity, *n.* locura, *f.*

inscription, *n.* inscripción, letra, leyenda, *f.*; letrero, *m.*; dedicatoria, *f.*

insect, *n.* insecto, bicho, *m.*

insecurity, *n.* inseguridad, *f.*

inseparable, *adj.* inseparable

insert, *vt.* insertar, meter

insertion, *n.* inserción, *f.*

inside, *n.* y *adj.* interior, *m.*; insides, (coll.) entrañas, *f. pl.*; on the inside, por dentro; *adv.* adentro, dentro; inside out, al revés

insignia, *n. pl.* insignias, *f. pl.*; estandartes, *m. pl.*

insignificant, *adj.* insignificante; trivial

insincere, *adj.* insincero

insincerity, *n.* insinceridad, *f.*

insinuate, *vt.* insinuar; *vi.* congraciarse

insinuation, *n.* insinuación, *f.*

insist, *vi.* insistir, persistir

insistence, *n.* insistencia, *f.*

insistent, *adj.* insistente, persistente

insolent, *adj.* insolente

insomnia, *n.* insomnio, *m.*

inspect, *vt.* inspeccionar

inspection, *n.* inspección, *f.*

inspector, *n.* inspector, *m.*

inspiration, *n.* inspiración, *f.*

inspire, *vt.* inspirar

installation, *n.* instalación *f.*

installment, instalment, *n.*; plazo, *m.*; monthly installment, mensualidad, *f.*

instant, *adj.* instante, urgente; presents; the 20th instant, el 20 del presente; instantly, *adv.* un instante; *n.* instante, momento, *m.*

instead, *adv.* en lugar de, en vez de

instigate, *vt.*, instigar

instinct, *n.* instinto, *m.*

instinctive, *adj.* instintivo

institute, *vt.* instituir, establecer; *n.* instituto, *m.*

institution, *n.* institución, *f.*

instruct, *vt.* instruir, enseñar

instruction, *n.* instrucción, enseñanza, *f.*

instructor, *n.* instructor, *m.*

instrument, *n.* instrumento, *m.*

insufferable, *adj.* insufrible, insoportable

insufficient, *adj.* insuficiente

insulating, *adj.* (elec.) aislante

insurance, *n.* seguro, *m.*; life insurance, seguro de vida, *m.*

integration, *n.* integración, *f.*

integrity, *n.* integridad, *f.*

intellect, *n.* intelecto, *m.*

intellectual, *n.* intelectual, *m.* y *f.*; *adj.* intelectual, mental

intelligence, *n.* inteligencia, *f.*

intelligent, *adj.* inteligente

intend, *vt.* intentar; *vi.* proponerse

intense, *adj.* intenso; vehemente

intensify, *vt.* intensificar

intensive, *adj.* completo, concentrado

intent, *adj.* atento, cuidadoso; *n.* intento, designio, *m.*

intention, *n.* intención, *f.*; designio, *m.*; (fig.) mira, *f.*

intentional, *adj.* intencional

intercede, *vi.* interceder, mediar

interest, *vt.* interesar; empeñar; *n.* interés, provecho, *m.*

interesting, *adj.* interesante, atractivo

interfere, *vi.* intervenir

interference, *n.* mediación, ingerencia, *f.*

interjection, *n.* (gram.) interjección, *f.*

interlining, *n.* entretela, *f.*

interlude, *n.* intermedio, *m.*

intermediary, *adj.* y *n.* intermediario, intermediaria

interment, *n.* entierro, *m.*; sepultura, *f.*

interminable, *adj.* interminable

intermission, *n.* intermedio, *m.*

intern, *vt.* internar; encerrar; *n.* (med.) practicante, *m.*; médico interno (en un hospital), *m.*

international, *adj.* internacional

interpret, *vt.* interpretar

interpretation, *n.* interpretación, *f.*; versión, *f.*

interpreter, *n.* intérprete, *m.* y *f.*

interrogate, *vt.* interrogar, examinar

interrogation, *n.* interrogación, pregunta, *f.*

interrupt, *vt.* interrumpir

interruption, *n.* interrupción, *f.*

intersection, *n.* intersección, *f.*; bocacalle, *f.*

interval, *n.* intervalo, *m.*

intervene, *vi.* intervenir

intervention, *n.* intervención, *f.*

interview, *n.* entrevista, *f.*; *vt.* entrevistar

intestinal, *adj.* intestinal

intestine, *adj.* intestino; **intestines,** *n. pl.* intestinos, *m. pl.*

intimacy, *n.* intimidad, confianza, *f.*; familiaridad, *f.*

intimate, *adj.* íntimo, familiar; *vt.* insinuar, dar a entender

intolerable, *adj.* intolerable

intolerance, *n.* intolerancia, *f.*

intolerant, *adj.* intolerante

intoxicant, *n.* bebida alcohólica, *f.*

intoxicated, *adj.* ebrio, borracho

intoxicating, *adj.* embriagante

intoxication, *n.* embriaguez, *f.*; intoxicación, *f.*

intransitive, *adj.* (gram.) intransitivo

intrepid, *adj.* arrojado, intrépido

intricate, *adj.* complicado; complejo

intrigue, *n.* intriga, *f.*

introduce, *vt.* introducir, meter; **to introduce (a person),** presentar (a una persona)

introduction, *n.* introducción, *f.*; presentación, *f.*; prólogo, preámbulo, *m.*

intrude, *vi.* entremeterse, introducirse

intuition, *n.* intuición,

inundate, *vt.* inundar

inundation, *n.* inundación, *f.*

invade, *vt.* invadir

invalid, *adj.* inválido; nulo; *n.* inválido, inválida

invaluable, *adj.* inapreciable

invariable, *adj.* invariable

invasion, *n.* invasion, *f.*

inveigle, *vt.* persuadir

invent, *vt.* inventar

invention, *n.* invención, *f.*; invento, *m.*

inventor, *n.* inventor, *m.*

inventory, *n.* inventario, *m.*

invert, *vt.* invertir

invest, *vt.* investir; invertir

investigate, *vt.* investigar

investigation, *n.* investigación,

investment *n.* inversión, *f.*

invisible, *adj.* invisible

invitation, *n.* invitación, *f.*

invite, *vt.* convidar, invitar

invoice, *n.* factura, *f.*; *vt.* facturar

invoke, *vt.* invocar

involuntary, *adj.* involuntario

involve, *vt.* envolver, implicar

iodine, *n.* yodo, *m.*

I.O.U., IOU, I owe you, pagaré, vale

Ireland, Irlanda, *f.*

iris, *n.* arco iris, *m.*; (anat.) iris, *m.*; (bot.) flor de lis, *f.*

Irish, *n.* y *adj.* irlandés, irlandesa

iron, *n.* hierro, *m.*; *vt.* planchar

ironical, *adj.* irónico

ironing, *n.* planchado, *m.*

irony, *n.* ironía, *f.*

irradiate, *vt.* y *vi.* irradiar, brillar

irregular, *adj.* irregular

irrelevant, *adj.* no aplicable

irreproachable, *adj.* irreprochable

irresistible, *adj.* irresistible

irresponsible, *adj.* irresponsable

irrigation, *n.* riego, *m.*; irrigación, *f.*

irritate, *vt.* irritar, exasperar

is, 3ª persona del singular del verbo **be**

island, *n.* isla, *f.*

isolate, *vt.* aislar, apartar

isolation, *n.* aislamiento, *m.*

isthmus, *n.* istmo, *m.*

it, *pron.* él, ella, ello, lo, la le

italic, *n.* bastardilla, *f.*

Italy, Italia, *f.*

itch, *n.* picazón, *f.*; *vi.* picar

item, *n.* artículo, suelto, *m.*; (com.) renglón, *m.*

itinerary, *n.* itinerario, *m.*

its, *pron.* su, suyo

itself, *pron.* el mismo, la misma, lo mismo; si; **by itself,** de por sí

ivory, *n.* marfil, *m.*

ivy, *n.* hiedra, *f.*

J

jack, *n.* (mech.) gato, *m.*; sota, *f.*; **jack pot,** premio grande, *m.*

jackass, *n.* burro, asno, *m.*

jacket, *n.* chaqueta, *f.*, saco, *m.*; envoltura, *f.*

jail, *n.* cárcel , *f.*

jam, *n.* compotá, conserva, *f.*; apretadura, *f.*; aprieto, *m.*; *vt.* apiñar, apretar

janitor, *n.* portero, conserje, *m.*

January, *n.* enero, *m.*

Japan, japón, *m.*

Japanese, *n.* y *adj.* japonés, japonesa, nipón, nipóna

jar, *vi.* chocar; discordar; *n.* jarro, *m.*

jct., junction emp. empalme, *m.*; confluencia, *f.*

jealous, celoso

jealousy, *n.* celos, *m. pl.*

jeans, *n. pl.* pantalones ajustados de dril, generalmente azules

jelly, *n.* jalea, gelatina, *f.*

jest, *n.* chanza, burla, *f.*; *vi.* chancear

Jesuit, *n.* jesuita, *m.*

Jesus Christ, Jesucristo

jet, *n.* (min.) azabache, *m.*; (mech.) mechero, *m.*; boquilla, *f.*; **jet plane,** avión de retropropulsión, *m.*; **jet propulsion,** propulsión por reacción, *f.*

Jew, *n.* judío, judía

jewel, *n.* joya, alhaja, *f.*; rubi (de un reloj), *m.*

jeweler, *n.* joyero, *m.*

jewelry, *n.* joyería, *f.*

Jewish, *adj.* judío

jiffy, *n.* (coll.) tris, momentito, *m.*

jilt, *vt.* dar calabazas, plantar

jingle, *vi.* retiñir, resonar; *n.* retintín, *m.*

job, *n.* empleo, *m.*; (Mex. coll.) chamba, *f.*

jockey, *n.* jinete, *m.*

join, *vt.* y *vi.* juntar, unir

joint, *n.* coyuntura, articulación, *f.*; *adj.* unido; participante; **jointly,** *adv.* conjuntamente, en común,

joke, *n.* chanza, chiste, *m.*; *vi.* chancear, bromear

jolly, *adj.* alegre, jovial

jolt, *vt.* y *vi.* sacudir; *n.* sacudida, *f.*

journal, *n.* diario, periódico, *m.*

journalism, *n.* periodismo, *m.*

journalist, *n.* periodista, *m.* y *f.*

journey, *n.* jornada, *f.*; viaje, *m.*; *vi.* viajar

jowl, *n.* quijada, *f.*

joy, *n.* alegría, *f.*; júbilo, *m.*

joyful, joyous, *adj.* alegre

judge, *n.* juez *m.*; *vi.* juzgar; inferir

judgment, judgement, *n.* juicio, *m.*; opinión, *f.*

judicial, *adj.* judicial

jug, *n.* jarro, *m.*

juice, *n.* zumo, jugo, *m.*

juicy, *adj.* jugoso

jukebox, *n.* sinfonola, *f.*

July, n. (mes) julio, m.
jumble, n. mezcla, confusión, f.
jump, vi. saltar, brincar; n. salto, m.
junction, n. empalme, m.; bifurcación, f.
June, n. (mes) junio, m.
jungle, n. matorral, m.
junior, adj. más joven; n. estudiante de tercer año
junk, n. chatarra, f., hierro viejo, m.; baratijas, f. pl.
jury, n. jurado, m.
just, adj. justo; adv. sólo
justice, n. justicia, f., derecho, m.; juez, m.
justify, vt. justificar
juvenile, adj. juvenil

K

karate, n. karate, m.
kc., kilocycle, kc., kilociclo
keen, adj. agudo; penetrante, sutil, vivo
keep, vt. mantener, retener; guardar; **to keep accounts,** llevar cuentas; n. manutención, f.
keepsake, n. recuerdo, m.
kettle, n. caldera, olla, f.
key, n. llave, f.; (mus.) clave, f.; tecla, f.
keyboard, n. teclado, m.
keyhole, n. agujero de la llave, m.
kg., kilogram, kg., kilogramo
kick, vt. patear, acocear; vi. patear; (coll.) reclamar, objetar; n. puntapié, m., patada, f.; (coll.) efecto estimulador, m.
kid, n. cabrito, m.; (coll.) muchacho, muchacha
kidnap, vt. secuestrar
kidney, n. riñón, m., **kidney bean,** variedad de frijol
kill, vt. matar, asesinar
kilocycle, n. kilociclo, m.
kilogram, n. kilogramo, m.
kilometer, n. kilómetro, m.
kiloton, n. kilotón. m.
kilowatt, n. kilovatio, m.
kin, n. parentesco, m.; afini-

dad, f.
kind, adj. benévolo, bondadoso; n. género, m.; clase, f.
kindergarten, n. escuela de párvulos, f., jardín de la infancia, m.
kindness, n. benevolencia, f.
king, n. rey, m.
kingdom, n. reino, m.
kinky, adj. grifo; ensortijado
kinsfolk, n. parientes, m. pl.
kiss, n. beso, m.; vt. besar
kitchen. n. cocina. f.
kite, n. cometa, birlocha, f.
kitten, n. gatito, gatita
km., kilometer, km., kilómetro
knack, n. maña, destreza, f.
knee, n. rodilla, f.
kneecap, n. rótula,
kneel, vi. arrodillarse
knew, pretérito del verbo **know**
knife, n. cuchillo, m.
knight, n. caballero, m.
knit, vt. y vi. enlazar; tejer
knitting, n. tejido con agujas, m.
knives, n. pl. de **knife,** cuchillos, m. pl.
knock, vt. y vi. tocar; pegar; n. golpe, m.; llamada, f.
knockout, n. golpe decisivo, (en el boxeo), m.
knot, n. nudo, m.; lazo, m.; vt. anudar
know, vt. y vi. conocer, saber
know-how, n. conocimiento práctico, m.
knowledge, n. conocimiento, saber, m.
knuckle, n. coyuntura, f.

L

£, pound, £, libra esterlina, f.
label, n. marbete, m., etiqueta, f.; rótulo, m.; vt. rotular
labor, n. trabajo, m.; labor, f.; **to be in labor,** estar de parto; vt. y vi. trabajar; afanarse
laboratory, n. laboratorio, m.
laborer, n. trabajador, obrero, m.
lace, n. lazo, cordón, m.; enca-

je, *m.*; *vt.* amarrar (los cordones de los zapatos, etc.)

lack, *vt.* y *vi.* carecer; faltar algo; *n.* falta, carencia, *f.*

lacquer, *n.* laca, *f.*

lad, *n.* mozo, muchacho, *m.*

ladder, *n.* escalera portátil, *f.*

ladle, *n.* cucharón, cazo, *m.*

lady, *n.* señora, senorita, dama, *f.*

lagoon, *n.* laguna, *f.*

laid, *pretérito* y *p.p.* del verbo **lay**

lain, *p.p.* del verbo **lie**

lake, *n.* lago, *m.*

lamb, *n.* cordero, *m.*

lament, *vt.* y *vi.* lamentar; *n.* lamento, *m.*

land, *n.* país, *m.*; región, *f.*; territorio, *m.*; tierra, *f.*; *vt.* y *vi.* desembarcar; saltar en tierra

landlady, *n.* affendadora, *f.*

landlord, *n.* propietario, casero, *m.*

landmark, *n.* señal, marca, *f.*; hecho o acontecimiento importante, *m.*

landslide, *n.* derrumbe, *m.*; (pol.) mayoría de votos abrumadora, *f.*

language, *n.* lengua, *f.*; lenguaje, idioma, *m.*

lantern, *n.* linterna, *f.*; farol, *m.*

lapel, *n.* solapa, *f.*

lapse, *n.* lapso, *m.*; *vi.* caducar (un plazo, etc.)

large, *adj.* grande, amplio

lark, *n.* (orn.) alondra, *f.*

larynx, *n.* laringe, *f.*

laser, *n.* rayo laser

last, *n.* doncella, moza, *f.*

last, *adj.* último; **at last,** al fin, por último; *vi.* durar; subsistir; *n.* horma de zapato, *f.*

late, *adj.* tardo, lento; difunto; *adv.* tarde; **lately,** *adv.* recientemente

later, *adj.* posterior; *adv.* más tarde

lateral, *adj.* lateral

latest, *adj.* último; más reciente; **at the latest,** a mis tardar

Latin, *n.* latín (lenguaje), *m.*; *n.* y *adj.* latino, latina

Latin American, *n.* latinoamericano, latinoamericana

latitude, *n.* latitud, *f.*

latter, *adj.* posterior, último

laugh, *vi.* reir; *n.* risa, risotada, *f.*

laughter, *n.* risa, *f.*

laundress, *n.* lavandera, *f.*

laundry, *n.* lavandería, *f.*

lavatory, *n.* lavabo, lavatorio, *m.*

lavish, *adj.* pródigo; gastador; *vt.* disipar, prodigar

law, *n.* ley, *f.*; derecho, *m.*

lawful, *adj.* legal; legitimo

lawn, *n.* prado, césped, *m.*

lawsuit, *n.* pleito, *m.*, demanda, *f.*

lawyer, *n.* abogado, *m.*

laxative, *n.* y *adj.* purgante, laxante, *m.*

lay, *vt.* poner, colocar; poner (un huevo)

lay, *adj.* laico, secular, seglar; *pretérito* del verbo **lie**

layer, *n.* capa, *f.*, estrato, *m.*

lazy, *adj.* perezoso

lb., pound, lb. libra

lead, *vt.* conducir, guiar; *vi.* mandar, tener el mando; sobresalir, ser el primero; *n.* delantera, *f.*

lead, *n.* plomo, *m.*; **lead pencil,** lápiz, *m.*

leader, *n.* líder, guia, *m.*

leadership, *n.* capacidad dirigente, *f.*

leading, *adj.* principal

leaf, *n.* hoja (de una planta), *f.*; hoja (de un libro), *f.*

leafy, *adj.* frondoso

league, *n.* liga, alianza, *f.*; legua, *f.*

leak, *n.* fuga, *f.*, goteo, *m.*; *vi.* gotear, salirse o escaparse (el agua, gas, etc.)

lean, *vt.* y *vi.* inclinar, apoyarse

leap, *vi.* saltar, brincar; *n.* salto, *m.*; **leap year,** año bisiesto, *m.*

learn, *vt.* y *vi.* aprender, conocer; saber

learning, *n.* erudición, *f.*; saber, *m.*

lease, *n.* contrato, arrendamiento, *m.*; *vt.* arrendar

least, *adj.* mínimo; *adv.* en el grado mínimo

leave, *n.* licencia, *f.*, permiso, *m.*; despedida, *f.*; *vt. y vi.* dejar, abandonar; salir

leaves, *n. pl.* de **leaf,** hojas, *f. pl.*

left, *adj.* izquierdo; *n.* izquierda, *f.*

leg, *n.* pierna, *f.*

legacy, *n.* legado, *m.*

legal, *adj.* legal, legítimo

legation, *n.* legación, embajada, *f.*

legislation, *n.* legislación *f.*

legislature, *n.* legislatura, *f.*

legitimate, *adj.* legítimo

leisure, *n.* ocio, *m.*; comodidad, *f.*; **at leisure,** cómodamente, con sosiego; **leisure hours,** horas o ratos libres

lemon, *n.* limón, *m.*

lemonade, *n.* limonada, *f.*

length, *n.* longitud, *f.*; duración, *f.*; distancia, *f.*

lengthen, *vt. y vi.* alargar

lengthy, *adj.* largo

Lent, *n.* cuaresma, *f.*

leopard, *n.* leopardo, *m.*

leprosy, *n.* lepra, *f.*

lesbian, *adj.* lesbiano

lesion, *n.* lesión, *f.*

less, *adj.* inferior, menos; *adv.* menos

lessen, *vt. y vi.* disminuir

lesson, *n.* lección, *f.*

let, *vt.* dejar, permitir; arrendar

letter, *n.* letra, *f.*; carta, *f.*

letterhead, *n.* membrete, *m.*

lettering, *n.* inscripción, leyenda, *f.*

lettuce, *n.* lechuga, *f.*

level, *adj.* llano, plano; *vt.* allanar; nivelar

liability, *n.* responsabilidad, *f.*; **liabilities,** (com.) pasivo, *m.*, créditos pasivos

liable, *adj.* sujeto, expuesto a; responsable; capaz

liar, *n.* mentiroso, mentirosa

liberal, *adj.* liberal; generoso

liberate, *vt.* libertar

liberty, *n.* libertad, *f.*

librarian, *n.* bibliotecario, bibliotecaria

library, *n.* biblioteca,. *f.*

license, licence, *n.* licencia, *f.*; permiso, *m.*

lick, *vt.* lamer, chupar; (coll.) golpear; derrotar (en una pelea, etc.)

lid, *n.* tapa, *f.*, tapadera, *f.*

lie, *n.* mentira, *f.*; *vi.* mentir, acostarse; descansar

lieutenant, *n.* teniente, *m.*

life, *n.* vida, *f.*; ser, *m.*

lifeboat, *n.* bote de salvamento, *m.*

lifeguard, *n.* vigilante, *m.*

lifeless, *adj.* muerto, inanimado

lift, *vt.* alzar, elevar

lift-off, *n.* despegue, lanzamiento, *m.*

light, *n.* luz, *f.*; claridad, *f.*; *adj.* ligero, liviano; claro; blondo; *vt.* encender; alumbrar

lighten, *vt.* iluminar; aligerar; aclarar

lighthouse, *n.* faro, *m.*

lighting, *n.* iluminación, *f.*

lightning, *n.* relámpago, *m.*

likable, *adj.* simpático. agradable

like, *adj.* semejante; igual; *adv.* como; *vt. y vi.* querer; gustar, agradar alguna cosa

likely , *adj.* probable

likeness, *n.* semejanza,. *f.*

lily, *n.* lirio, *m.*

limb, *n.* miembro (del cuerpo), *m.*; pierna, *f.*; rama (de un árbol), *f.*

lime, *n.* cal, *f.*; limón mexicano, *m.*

limelight, *n.* centro de atención pública

limit, *n.* límite, término, *m.*; *vt.* restringir

limited, *adj.* limitado

limp, *vi.* cojear; *n.* cojera, *f.*; *adj.* flojo, blando

linen, *n.* lienzo, lino, *m.*; tela de hilo; ropa blanca

linger, *vi.* demorarse

lingerie, *n.* ropa intima, *f.*

link, *n.* eslabón, *m.*; vínculo, *m.*; *vt.* y *vi.* unir, vincular

linkup, *n.* acoplamiento, enlace, *m.*, unión, *f.*

lion, *n.* león, *m.*

lip, *n.* labio borde, *m.*

lipstick, *n.* lápiz para los labios, lápiz labial, *m.*

liquid, *adj.*y *n.* líquido, *m.*

liquor, *n.* licor, *m.*

Lisbon, Lisboa

lisp, *vi.* cecear

list, *n.* lista, *f.*, elenco, *m.*; catálogo, *m.*; *vt.* poner en lista; registrar

listen, *vi.* escuchar

liter, *n.* litro, *m.*

literal, *adj.* literal

literary, *adj.* literario

literature, *n.* literatura, *f.*

little, *adj.* pequeño; poco; chico; *n.* poco, *m.*

live, *vi.* vivir

live, *adj.* vivo

lively, *adj.* vivo, aiegre

liver, *n.* hígado, *m.*

lives, *n. pl.* de **life,** vidas, *f. pl.*

livestock, *n.* ganado, *m.*; ganadería, *f.*

living, *n.* subsistencia, *f.*

lid, *n.* lagarto, *m.*, lagartija, *f.*

llama, *n.* (zool.) llama, *f.*

L.L.D., Doctor of Laws, Doctor en Derecho

load, *vt.* cargar; *n.* carga, *f.*

loaf, *n.* pan, *m.*; *vi.* holgazanear

loan, *n.* préstamo, *m.*; *vt.* prestar

loathe, *vt.* aborrecer, detestar

loaves, *n. pl.* de **loaf,** panes, *m. pl.*

lobby, *n.* vestíbulo, *m.*

lobster, *n.* langosta, *f.*

local, *adj.* local

locality, *n.* localidad, *f.*

locate, *vt.* ubicar, colocar

location, *n.* ubicación, *f.*

lock, *n.* cerradura, cerraja, *f.*; compuerta, *f.*; *vt.* y *vi.* cerrar con llave

locker, *n.* armario, *m.*; gaveta, *f.*

locket, *n.* medallón, guardape-

lo, *m.*

lockjaw, *n.* tétano, *m.*

locksmith, *n.* cerrajero, *m.* ·

locomotive, *n.* locomotora, *f.*

lodge, *n.* casita en el bosque, *f.*; logia, *f.*; *vt.* alojar; fijar en la memoria; *vi.* residir

lodging, *n.* hospedaje, *m.*

lofty,*adj.* alto, sublime

logic, *n.* lógica, *f.*

logical, *adj.* lógico

loin, *n.* ijada, *f.*, ijar, *m.*; **loins,** *n. pl.* lomos, *m. pl.*

loiter, *vi.* holgazanear

London, Londres

lone, *adj.* solitario

loneliness, *n.* soledad, *f.*

lonely, *adj.* **lonesome**

lonesome, *adj.* solitario, triste

long, *adj.* largo, prolongado; *adv.* durante mucho tiempo

longing, *n.* anhelo, *m.*

long-playing (records), *adj.* (discos) de larga ejecución

look, *vt.* y *vi.* mirar; parecer; buscar; *n.* aspecto, *m.*; mirada, *f.*

loom, *n.* telar, *m.*

loose, *adj.* suelto, desatado

loosen, *vt.* aflojar, desatar

loot, *n.* pillaje, botín, *m.*

lord, *n.* señor *m.*; amo, dueño, *m.*; lord (título de nobleza inglés), *m.*

lose, *vt.* y *vi.* perder, perderse

loss, *n.* pérdida, *f.*; **to be at a loss,** estar perplejo

lot, *n.* suerte, *f.*; lote, *m.*

lotion, *n.* loción *f.*

lottery, *n.* lotería, rifa, *f.*

loud, *adj.* ruidoso; fuerte, recio, alto; chillón

loudspeaker, *n.* altoparlante, altavoz, *m.*

lounge, *n.* sofá, canapé, *m.*; salón social, *m.*

louse, *n.* (*pl.* **lice**), piojo, *m.*

lovable, *adj.* digno de ser querido

love, *n.* amor, cariño, *m.*; *vt.* amar; querer

lovely, *adj.* bello

lover, *n.* amante, galán, *m.*

low, *adj.* bajo, pequeño; abatido; vil ; *adv.* a precio bajo; en posición baja

lower, *adj.* más bajo; *vt.* bajar; disminuir

lowly, *adj.* humilde

lox, (liquid oxygen) *n.* oxígeno líquido, *m.*

loyal, *adj.* leal, fiel

loyalty, *n.* lealtad, *f.*

L.P., long-playing, L.E., larga ejecución (discos)

lubricant, *n.* y *adj.* lubricante, *m.*

luck, *n.* suerte, *f.*

luckily, *adv.* afortunadamente

lucky, *adj.* afortunado

lukewarm, *adj.* tibio

lullaby, *n.* canción de cuna

lumber, *n.* madera de construcción, *f.*

lump, *n.* protuberancia, *f.*; **lump of sugar**, terrón de azúcar, *m.*; *vi.* aterronarse; agrumarse

lunatic, *adj.* y *n.* loco, loca

lunch, *n.* merienda, *f.*, almuerzo, *m.*; *vi.* almorzar, merendar

luncheon, *n.* almuerzo, *m.*

lung, *n.* pulmón, *m.*

lure, *n.* señuelo, cebo, *m.*; *vt.* atraer, seducir

lurk, *vi.* espiar

luscious, *adj.* delicioso, atractivo

luster, lustre, *n.* lustre, *m.*, brillantez, *f.*

luxuriant, *adj.* exuberante

luxurious, *adj.* lujoso

luxury, *n.* lujo, *m.*

lyric, lyrical, *adj.* lírico

M

macaroni, *n.* macarrones, *m. pl.*

machine, *n.* máquina, *f.*; **machine gun**, ametralladora, *f.*

machinery, *n.* maquinaria, *f.*

machinist, *n.* maquinista, mecánico , *m.*

mackerel, *n.* (pez) escombro, *m.*, caballa, *f.*

mad, *adj.* loco, furioso

madam, madame, *n.* madama, señora, *f.*

made, *adj.* hecho, fabricado

made-to-order, *adj.* hecho a la medida o a la orden

made-up, *adj.* ficticio; pintado

madness, *n.* locura, *f.*

magazine, *n.* revista, *f.*

magic, *n.* magia, *f.*; *adj.* mágico

magician, *n.* mago, nigromante, *m.*

magistrate, *n.* magistrado, *m.*

magnanimous, *adj.* magnánimo

magnesia, *n.* magnesia, *f.*

magnet, *n.* imán, *m.*

magnetism, *n.* magnetismo, *m.*

magnificent, *adj.* magnífico

magnify, *vt.* magnificar

magnitude, *n.* magnitud. *f.*

magnolia, *n.* magnolia, *f.*

magpie, *n.* urraca, *f.*

mahogany, *n.* caoba, *f.*

maid, maiden, *n.* doncella, joven, *f.*; moza, criada, *f.*

maiden, *adj.* virgen, virginal; **maiden name**, nombre de soltera; *n.* doncella, joven, *f.*

mail, *n.* correo, *m.*; correspondencia, *f.*

mailbox, *n.* buzón, *m.*

mailman, *n.* cartero, *m.*

main, *adj.* principal; esencial; **main office**, casa matriz; **mainly**, *adv.* principalmente

maintain, *vt.* y *vi.* mantener, sostener; conservar

maintenance, *n.* mantenimiento *m.*

maize, *n.* maíz, *m.*

majestic, majestical, *adj.* majestuoso

majesty, *n.* majestad, *f.*

major, *adj.* mayor; *n.* (mil.) mayor, *m.*

majority, *n.* mayoría, *f.*; pluralidad, *f.*

make, *vt.* hacer, fabricar; obligar, forzar; *n.* hechura, *f.*

make-up, *n.* maquillaje, *m.*

malaria, *n.* paludismo, *m.*

male, *adj.* masculino; *n.* macho, *m.*

malice, *n.* malicia, *f.*

malicious, *adj.* malicioso

malignant, *adj.* maligno
malt, *n.* malta, *f.*
maltreat, *vt.* maltratar
mamma, mama, *n.* mamá, *f.*
mammal, *n.* mamífero, *m.*
man, *n.* hombre, *m.*; marido, *m.*
manage, *vt.* y *vi.* manejar, administrar
management, *n.* manejo. *m.*, administración, dirección, *f.*; gerencia, *f.*
manager, *n.* administrador, director, *m.*; gerente, *m.*
mandolin, *n.* mandolina, *f.*
maneuver, *n.* maniobra, *f.*; *vt.* y *vi.* manjobrar
manger, *n.* pesebre, *m.*
mangle, *n.* planchadora mecánica, *f.*; *vt.* mutilar
manhood, *n.* virilidad, *f.*; edad viril, hombría, *f.*
manicure, *n.* manicuro, manicura; arte de arreglar las uñas; *vt.* arreglar las uñas
manifest, *adj.* manifiesto, patente
manikin, *n.* maniquí, *m.*
mankind, *n.* género humano, *m.*, humanidad, *f.*
manly, *adj.* varonil
manner, *n.* manera, *f.*, modo, *m.*; forma, *f.*; método, *m.*; **manners**, *n. pl.*, modales, *m. pl.*
mansion, *n.* mansión, residencia, *f.*
manual, *n.* manual, *m.*; *adj.* manual; **manual training**, instrucción en artes y oficios
manufacture, *n.* manufactura, fabricación, *f.*; *vt.* fabricar, manufacturar
manuscript, *n.* manuscrito, escrito, *m.*; original, *m.*
many, *adj.* muchos. muchas
Maoism, *n.* maoismo, *m.*
map, *n.* mapa, *m.*
maple, *n.* arce, *m.*
marble, *n.* mármol, *m.*; canica, bola, *f.*
March, *n.* marzo, *m.*
march, *n.* marcha, *f.*; *vi.* marchar, caminar
margin, *n.* margen, *m.* y *f.*;

borde, *m.*
marimba, *n.* marimba, *f.*
marina, *n.* estación de gasolina para los botes
marine, *n.* marina, *f.*; soldado de marina, *m.*; *adj.* marino
mariner, *n.* marinero, *m.*
marionette, *n.* títere, *m.*
maritime, *adj.* maritimo
mark, *n.* marca, *f.*; señal, nota, *f.*; seña, *f.*; calificación, *vt.* marcar; advertir
market, *n.* mercado, *m.*
marquis, *n.* marqués, *m.*
marriage, *n.* matrimonio, casamiento, *m.*
marry, *vt.* y *vi.* casar, casarse
marshal, *n.* mariscal, *m.*
martial, *adj.* marcial, guerrero
marvel, *n.* maravilla, *f.*, prodigio, *m.*; *vi.* maravillarse
marvelous, *adj.* maravilloso
mascot, *n.* mascota, *f.*
masculine, *adj.* masculino; varonil
mash, *vt.* majar
mask, *n.* máscara, *f.*; *vt.* enmascarar; disimular
mason, *n.* albañil, *m.*; masón, *m.*
masquerade, *n.* mascarada, *f.*
mass, *n.* misa, *f.*; masa, *f.*, bulto, *m.*; **masses**, *n. pl.* las masas, *f. pl*
massage, *n.* masaje, *m.*, soba, *f.*; *vt.* sobar
massive, *adj.* macizo, sólido
master, *n.* amo, dueño. *m.*; maestro, *m.*; señor, *m.*; señorito, *m.*; patrón, *m.*; *vt.* domar, dominar
mat, *n.* estera, esterilla, *f.*
match, *n.* fósforo, *m.*; cerilla, *f.*, cerillo, *m.*; partido, *m.*; contrincante. *m.*, casamiento, *m.*; *vt.* igualar; aparear
mate, *n.* consorte, *m.* o *f.*; compañero, compañera; piloto, *m.*; *vt.* desposar; igualar
material, *adj.* material, fisico; *n.* material, *m.*, tela, *f.*
maternal, *adj.* maternal, materno
maternity, *n.* maternidad, *f.*
mathematical, *adj.* matemáti-

co

mathematics, *n. pl.* matemáticas, *f. pl.*

matinee, *n.* matiné, *f.*

matriculate, *vt.* matricular

matrimony, *n.* matrimonio, *m.*

matter, *n.* materia, sustancia, *f.*; asunto, objeto, *m.*; **what is the matter?** ¿de qué se trata?; *vi.* importar, ser importante

maximum, *adj.* máximo

May, *n.* mayo, *m.*

may, *vi.* poder; ser posible

maybe, *adv.* quizás, tal vez

mayonnaise, *n.* mayonesa, *f.*

mayor, *n.* corregidor, alcalde, *m.*

maze, *n.* laberinto, *m.*

M.C., Master of Ceremonies, Maestro de Ceremonias

M.D., Doctor of Medicine, Doctor en Medicina

me, *pron.* mí; me

meadow, *n.* prado, *m.*

meal, *n.* comida, *f.*; harina, *f.*

mean, *adj.* bajo, vil, despreciable; **means,** *n. pl.* medios, recursos, *m. pl.*; **by all means,** sin falta; **by no means,** de ningún modo; *vt. y vi.* significar; querer decir

meaning, *n.* significado, *m.*

meantime, *adv.* mientras tanto

meanwhile, *adv.* entretanto, mientras tanto

measles, *n. pl.* sarampión, *m.*; rubeola, *f.*

measure, *n.* medida, *f.*; (mus.) compás, *m.*; *vt.* medir

measurement, *n.* medición, *f.*; medida, *f.*

meat, *n.* carne, *f.*

mechanic, *n.* mecánico, *m.*

mechanical, *adj.* mecánico; rutinario

mechanics, *n. pl.* mecánica, *f.*

mechanism, *n.* mecanismo, *m.*

medal, *n.* medalla, *f.*

mediate, *vi.* mediar

medical, *adj.* médico

medicare, *n.* asistencia médica estatal para personas mayores de 65 años

medicine, *n.* medicina, *f.*

mediocre, *adj.* mediocre

meditation, *n.* meditación, *f.*

medium, *n.* medio, *m.*; *adj.* mediano

meet, *vt. y vi.* encontrar, convocar, reunir

meeting, *n.* sesión, reunión, *f.*

melancholy, *n.* melancolía, *f.*

melodious, *adj.* melodioso

melodrama, *n.* melodrama, *m.*

melody, *n.* melodía, *f.*

melon, *n.* melón, *m.*

member, *n.* miembro, socio, *m.*

membership, *n.* personal de socios, *m.*

memo., memorandum, memorándum, *m.*

memorable, *adj.* memorable

memorandum, *n.* memorándum, volante, *m.*

memorial, *n.* memoria, *f.*; memorial, *m.*; *adj.* conmemorativo

Memorial Day, *n.* Día de los soldados muertos en la guerra (30 de mayo)

memorize, *vt.* memorizar, aprender de memoria

memory, *n.* memoria, *f.*; recuerdo, *m.*; retentiva, *f.*

men, *n. pl.* de **man,** hombres, *m. pl*

menstruation, *n.* menstruación, *f.*

mentality, *n.* mentalidad, *f.*

mention, *n.* mención, *f.*; *vt.* mencionar; **don't mention it,** no hay de qué

menu, *n.* menú, *m.*

merchandise, *n.* mercancía, *f.*

merchant, *n.* comerciante, *m.*

merciful, *adj.* misericordioso

merciless, *adj.* inhumano

mercury, *n.* mercurio, *m.*

mercy, *n.* misericordia,

merge, *vt.* unir, combinar; *vi.* absorberse, fundirse, converger

meridian, *n.* meridiano, *m.*

meringue, *n.* merengue, *m.*

merit, *n.* mérito, *m.*; merecimiento, *m.*; *vt.* merecer

merry, *adj.* alegre, jovial
merry-go-round, *n.* caballitos, *m. pl.*, tiovivo, *m.*
mess, *n.* (mil.) comida, *f.*; confusión, *f.*; aprieto, lío, *m.*; suciedad, *f.*
message, *n.* mensaje, *m.*
messenger, *n.* mensajero, mensajera
metal, *n.* metal,. *m.*; **metal shears,** cizalla, *f.*
meter, *n.* medidor, contador, *m.*; metro, *m.*
method, *n.* método, *m.*
methodical. *adj.* metódico
meticulous, *adj.* metictiloso
metric, *adj.* métrico
metropolis, *n.* metrópoli, capital, *f.*
Mexico, Méjico
mezzanine, *n.* (theat.) entresuelo, *m.*, mezanina, *f.*
mfg., manufacturing, manuf., manufactura
mfr., manufacturer, fab. fabricante
mg., milligram, mg. miligramo
mice, *n. pl.* de **mouse,** ratones, *m. pl.*
microbe, *n.* microbio, *m.*
microphone, *n.* micrófono, *m.*
microscope, *n.* microscopio, *m.*
midday, *n.* mediodía, *m.*
middle, *n.* medio, centro, *m.*, mitad, *f.*
middle-aged, *adj.* entrado en años, de edad madura
middle class, *n.* clase media, *f.*
midnight, *n.* media noche, *f.*
midwife, *n.* partera, *f.*
might, *n.* poder, *m.*, fuerza, *f.*; *pretérito* del verbo **may**
mighty, *adj.* fuerte, potente
migraine, *n.* jaqueca, *f.*
migrate, *vi.* emigrar
mild, *adj.* apacible, suave
mile, *n.* milla , *f.*
mileage, *n.* kilometraje, *m.*
military, *adj.* militar
milk, *n.* leche, *f.*; *vt.* ordeñar
milkman, *n.* lechero, *m.*
milky, *adj.* lácteo; lechoso; lechero

Milky Way, *n.* Vía Láctea, *f.*
mill, *n.* molino, *m.*
milligram, *n.* miligramo, *m.*
millimeter, *n.* milimetro, *m.*
millinery, *n.* confección de sombreros para señora
million, *n.* millón, *m.*
millionaire, *n.* y *adj.* millonario, millonaria
mind, *n.* mente, *f.*; intención, *f.*; opinión, *f.*; ánimo, *m.*; *vt.* importar; obedecer; *vi.* tener cuidado; preocuparse;
mine, *pron.* mío, mía, míos, mías; *n.* mina, *f.*
miner, *n.* minero, *m.*
mineral, *adj.* y *n.* mineral, *m.*
miniature, *n.* miniatura, *f.*
minimum, *n.* mínimum, mínimo, *m.*; *adj.* mínimo:
mining, *n.* minería, *f.*
minister, *n.* ministro, pastor, *m.*
ministry, *n.* ministerio, *m.*
minnow, *n.* varieded de pez pequeño
minor, *adj.* menor, pequeño; (mus.) menor; *n.* menor (de edad), *m.* y *f.*
minority, *n.* minoridad, *f.*; minoría, *f.*
mint, *n.* (bot.) menta, *f.*; casa de moneda, *f.*; *vt.* acuñar
minuet, *n.* minué, *m.*
minus, *prep.* menos; *adj.* negativo; *n.* (math.) el signo menos
minute, *adj.* menudo, pequeño
minute, *n.* minuto, *m.*
miracle, *n.* milagro, *m.*; maravilla, *f.*
miraculous, *adj.* milagroso
mirror, *n.* espejo, *m.*
misbehave, *vi.* portarse mal
miscarriage, *n.* aborto, malparto, *m.*
miscellaneous, *adj.* misceláneo, mezclado
mischief, *n.* travesura, *f.*
mischievous, *adj.* travieso, pícaro
misdeed, *n.* delito, *m.*
miser, *n.* avaro, avara

miserable, *adj.* miserable, infeliz

miserly, *adj.* tacaño

misery, *n.* miseria, *f.*; infortunio, *m.*

misfortune, *n.* infortunio, *m.*; calamidad, *f.*

misgiving, *n.* recelo, *m.*; presentimiento, *m.*

mishap, *n.* desventura, *f.*; contratiempo, *m.*

misleading, *adj.* engañoso, desorientador

miss, *n.* señorita, *f.*; pérdida, falta, *f.*; *vt.* errar; echar de menos

missile, *n.* proyectil, *m.*

missing, *adj.* que falta; perdido

mission, *n.* misión, comisión, *f.*; cometido, m.

missionary, *n.* misionero, *m.*

missive, *n.* carta, misiva, *f.*

misspell, *vt.* deletrear mal, escribir con mala ortografía

mistake, *n.* equivocación, *f.*, error, *m.*; *vt.* equivocar; *vi.* equivocarse, engañarse

Mister, *n.* Señor (título), *m.*

mistress, *n.* ama, *f.*; señora, *f.*; concubina, *f.*

misunderstand, *vt.* entender mal una cosa

misunderstanding, *n.* mal entendimiento, *m.*

mm., millimeter, mm., milímetro

moan, *n.* lamento, gemido, *m.*; *vi.* afligirse,quejarse

mob, *n.* populacho, *m.*

mobile, *adj.* movedizo, móvil

mobilize, *vt.* movilizar

mock, *vt.* mofar, burlar; *n.* mofa, burla, *f.*; *adj.* ficticio, falso

mockingbird, *n.* (orn.) sinsonte, arrendajo, *m.*

mode, *n.* modo, *m.*; forma, *f.*; manera, *f.*

moderate, *adj.* moderado; módico

moderation, *n.* moderación, *f.*

modern, *adj.* moderno

modernistic, *adj.* modernista

modest, *adj.* modesto

modesty, *n.* modestia, decencia, *f.*, pudor, *m.*

modify, *vt.* modificar

moist, *adj.* húmedo, mojado

moisten, *vt.* humedecer

moisture, *n.* humedad, *f.*; jugosidad, *f.*

molar, *adj.* molar; **molar teeth,** muelas, *f. pl.*

molasses, *n.* melaza, *f.*

mold, *n.* moho, *m.*; molde, *m.*; matriz, *f.*; *vt.* enmohecer, moldar; formar; *vi.* enmohecerse

molding, *n.* molduras, *f. pl.*

moldy, *adj.* mohoso

mole, *n.* topo, *m.*; lunar, *m.*

molt, *vi.* mudar, estar de muda las aves

moment, *n.* momento, rato, *m.*

momentary, *adj.* momentáneo

momentous, *adj.* importante

monarch, *n.* monarca, *m.*

monarchy, *n.* monarquía, *f.*

monastery, *n.* monasterio, *m.*

Monday, *n.* lunes, *m.*

monetary, *adj.* monetario

money, *n.* moneda, *f.*; dinero, *m.*; plata, *f.*; **paper money,** papel moneda

monk, *n.* monje, *m.*

monkey, *n.* mono, mona; simio, mia; **monkey wrench,** llave inglesa, *f.*

monogram, *n.* monograma, *m.*

monologue, *n.* monólogo, *m.*

monopolize, *vt.* monopolizar, acaparar

monopoly, *n.* monopolio, *m.*

monster, *n.* monstruo, *m.*

month, *n.* mes, *m.*

monthly, *adj.* mensual

monument, *n.* monumento, *m.*

mood, *n.* humor, talante, *m.*

moody, *adj.* caprichoso, veleidoso

moon, *n.* luna, *f.*

moonlight, *n.* luz de la luna *f.*

moose, *n.* (zool.) alce, *m.*

mop, *n.* (Sp. Am.) trapeador, *m.*; *vt.* (Sp. Am.) trapear

moral, *adj.* moral, ético; *n.* moraleja, *f.*; **morals,** *n. pl.* moralidad, conducta, *f.*

morale, *n.* moralidad, *f.*; animación, *f.*

morality, *n.* ética, moralidad, *f.*

moratorium, *n.* moratoria, *f.*

more, *adj.* más, adicional; *adv.* más, en mayor grado

moreover, *adv.* además

morning, *n.* mañana, *f.*; **good morning,** buenos días; *adj.* matutino

morphine, *n.* morfina, *f.*

mortal, *adj.* mortal; humano; *n.* mortal, *m.*

mortgage, *n.* hipoteca, *f.*; *vt.* hipotecar

mosquito, *n.* mosquito, *m.*

most, *adj.* más; *adv.* sumamente, en sumo grado; *n.* los más; mayor número; mayo valor; **mostly,** *adv.* por lo común; principalmente

motel, *n.* hotel para automovilistas, *m.*

mother, *n.* madre, *f.*

motherhood, *n.* maternidad, *f.*

mother-in-law, *n.* suegra, *f.*

motherless, *adj.* huérfana de madre

motif, *n.* motivo, tema, *m.*

motion, *n.* movimiento, *m.*, moción, *f.*; **motion picture,** cinema, cinematógrafo, *m.*; *vt.* proponer

motionless, *adj.* inmóvil

motor, *n.* motor, *m.*

motorcade, *n.* procesión o desfile de automóviles

motorcar, *n.* automóvil, *m.*

motorcycle, *n.* motocicleta, *f.*

motorist, *n.* automovilista, motorista, *m.* y *f.*

motorman, *n.* motorista, *m.*

mountain, *n.* montaña, sierra, *f.*, monte, *m.*

mountainous, *adj.* montañoso

mourn, *vt.* deplorar; *vi.* lamentar; llevar luto

mourning, *n.* luto, *m.*

mouse, *n.* ratón, *m.*

mouth, *n.* boca, *f.*

mouthful, *n.* bocado, *m.*

mouthpiece, *n.* boquilla, *f.*

move, *vt.* mover; proponer; emocionar; *vt.* moverse, me-

nearse; *n.* movimiento

movement, *n.* movimiento, *m.*; moción, *f.*

movie, *n.* **movies,** *n. pl.* (coll.) cine, cinema, cinematógrafo, *m.*

moving, *adj.* conmovedor; **moving picture,** cine, cinema, cinematógrafo, *m.*

mow, *vt.* guadañar, segar

mph, m.p.h., miles per hour, m.p.h. millas por hora

much, *adj.* y *adv.* mucho

mucous, *adj.* mocoso, viscoso

mud, *n.* lodo, *m.*

muddle, *vt.* enturbiar; confundir

muffin, *n.* bizcochuelo, *m.*

muffler, *n.* (auto.) silenciador, *m.*, sordina, *f.*; desconectador, *m.*

mule, *n.* mula, *f.*

multimillionaire, *n.* multimillonario, multimillonaria

multiplication, *n.* multiplicación, *f.*

multiply, *vt.* y *vi.* multiplicar

mumble, *vt.* y *vi.* gruñir; murmurar

municipal, *adj.* municipal

munition, *n.* municiones, *f. pl.*

murder, *n.* asesinato, homicidio, *m.*; *vt.* asesinar

murderer, *n.* asesino, asesinar

murmur, *n.* murmullo, *m.*; cuchicheo, *m.*; *vi.* murmurar

muscle, *n.* músculo, *m.*

muscular, *adj.* muscular

museum, *n.* museo, *m.*

mushroom, *n.* hongo, *m.*

music, *n.* música, *f.*

musical, *adj.* musical

musician, *n.* músico, *m.*

mustard, *n.* mostaza, *f.*

mute, *adj.* mudo, silencioso

mutilate, *vt.* mutilar

mutiny, *n.* motín, tumulto, *m.*

mutter, *vt.* y *vt.* murmurar, hablar entre dientes

mutton, *n.* carnero, *m.*

mutual, *adj.* mutuo, recíproco

my, *pron.* mi, mis

myself, *pron.* yo mismo

mysterious, *adj.* misterioso

mystery, *n.* misterio, *m.*

myth, *n.* fábula, *f.*, mito, *m.*
mythology, *n.* mitología,

N

nab, *vt.* atrapar, prender
nag, *n.* jaca, *f.*, jaco, *m.*; *vt. y vi.* regañar, sermonear
nail, *n.* uña, *f.*; garra, *f.*; clavo, *m.*; *vt.* clavar
naked, *adj.* desnudo
name, *n.* nombre, *m.*; fama, reputación, *f.*
nameless, *adj.* sin nombre
namely, *adv.* a saber
namesake, *n.* tocayo, tocaya
nap, *n.* siesta, *f.*; pelo (de una tela), *m.*
napkin, *n.* servilleta,
narcotic, *adj.* narcótico
narrate, *vt.* narrar, relatar
narrative, *n.* relato, *m.*
narrow, *adj.* angosto, estrecho
narrowminded, *adj.* intolerante
NASA, National Aeronautics and Space Administration, Administración Nacional de Aeronáɾtica y del Espacio
nasal, *adj.* nasal
nasty, *adj.* sucio, puerco; desagradable
natal, *adj.* nativo; natal
nation, *n.* nación, *f.*
national, *adj.* nacional
nationality, *n.* nacionalidad, *f.*
native, *adj.* nativo; *n.* natural, *m. y f.*
NATO, North Atlantic Treaty Organization, OTAN, Organización del Tratado del Atlántico Norte
natural, *adj.* natural; sencillo; *n.* (mus.) becuadro, *m.*
nature, *n.* naturaleza, *f.*; indole, *f.*; **good nature,** buen humor, *m.*
naught, *n.* nada, *f.*; cero, *m.*
naughty, *adj.* travieso, pícaro
nausea, *n.* náusea, basca, *f.*
naval, *adj.* náutico, naval
navel, *n.* ombligo, *m.*
navigable, *adj.* navegable
navigate, *vt. y vi.* navegar
navigation, *n.* navegación, *f.*

navy, *n.* marina, *f.*
NE, N.E., n.e., northeast, N.E., nordeste
near, *prep.* cerca de, junto a; *adv.* casi; cerca, cerca de; *adj.* cercano
nearby, *adj.* cercano, próximo; *adv.* cerca, a la mano
neat, *adj.* pulido; ordenado
necessary, *adj.* necesario
necessity, *n.* necesidad, *f.*
neck, *n.* cuello, *m.*
necklace, *n.* collar, *m.*
necktie, *n.* corbata, *f.*
nectar, *n.* néctar, *m.*
negative, *adj.* negativo; *n.* negativa, *f.*
neglect, *vt.* descuidar, desatender; *n.* negligencia, *f.*
negligee, *n.* bata de casa, *f.*
negligence, *n.* negligencia, *f.*
negotiation, *n.* negociación, *f.*
negro, *n.* negro, negra
neighbor, *n.* vecino, vecina
neighborhood, *n.* vecindad, *f.*; vecindario, *m.*; inmediación, cercanía, *f.*
neither, *conj.* ni; *adj.* ninguno; *pron.* ninguno, ni uno ni otro
nephew, *n.* sobrino, *m.*
nerve, *n.* nervio, *m.*; (coll.) descaro, *m.*
nest, *n.* nido, *m.*
net, *n.* red, *f.*; malla, *f.*; *adj.* neto, líquido
Netherlands, Países Bajos, *m. pl.*
network, *n.* red radiodifusora o televisora, *f.*
neuralgia, *n.* neuralgia, *f.*
neutral, *adj.* neutral
neutrality, *n.* neutralidad, *f.*
neutron bomb, *n.* bomba de neutrón
never, *adv.* nunca, jamas; **never mind,** no importa
nevertheless, *adv.* no obstante
new, *adj.* nuevo
newcomer, *n.* recién llegado, recién llegada
newlywed, *n.* recién casado, recién casada
news, *n. pl.* novedad, *f.*, nuevas, noticias, *f. pl.*

newsboy, *n.* vendedor de periódicos, *m.*

newspaper, *n.* gaceta, *f.*; periódico, *m.*; diario, *m.*

next, *adj.* próximo; entrante, venidero; *adv.* inmediatamente después

niacin, *n.* niacina, *f.*

nice, *adj.* fino; elegante

nickel, *n.* níquel, *m.*

nickel-plated, *adj.* niquelado

nickname, *n.* apodo, *m.*

niece, *n.* sobrina, *f.*

night, *n.* noche, *f.*; **good night,** buenas noches

nightgown, *n.* camisón, *m.*, camisa de dormir, *f.*

nightingale, *n.* ruiseñor, *m.*

nightmare, *n.* pesadilla, *f.*

nimble, *adj.* ligero, ágil

nine, *n.* y *adj.* nueve, *m.*

nineteen, *n.* y *adj.* diez y nueve, diecinueve, *m.*

nineteenth, *n.* y *adj.* décimonono, *m.*

ninety, *n.* y *adj.* noventa, *m.*

ninth, *n.* y *adj.* nono, noveno, *m.*

nitrogen, *n.* nitrógeno, *m.*

no, *adv.* no; *adj.* ningún, ninguno; **by no means, in no way,** de ningún modo

No., north, N., norte

nobility, *n.* nobleza, *f.*

noble, *n.* y *adj.* noble, *m.* y *f.*

nobody, *pron.* nadie, ninguno, ninguna; *n.* persona insignificante, *f.*

noise, *n.* ruido, *m.*

noiseless, *adj.* sin ruido

noisy, *adj.* ruidoso

nominate, *vt.* nombrar, proponer (a alguien para un pueso, cargo, etc.)

nominative, *n.* (gram.) nominativo, *m.*

none, *pron.* nadie, ninguno

nonsense, *n.* tontería, *f.*; disparate, absurdo, *m.*

nonsensical, *adj.* absurdo; tonto

nonstop, *adj.* directo, sin parar

noodle, *n.* tallarín, fideo, *m.*

noon, *n.* mediodía, *m.*

noonday, *n.* mediodía, *m.*

north, *n.* norte, *m.*; *adj.* septentrional

northeast, *n.* nordeste, *m.*

northerly, northern, *adj.* septentrional

North Pole, *n.* Polo Artico, Polo Norte, *m.*

northward, northwards, *adv.* hacia el norte

northwest, *n.* noroeste, *m.*

Norway, Noruega

nose, *n.* nariz, *f.*; olfato, *m.*

not, *adv.* no

notary, notario, *m.*

note, *n.* nota, *f.*; billete, *m.*; consecuencia, *f.*; comentario, *m.*; (mus.) nota, *f.*; *vt.* notar, observar

notebook, *n.* librito de apuntes, *m.*

noted, *adj.* afamado, célebre

noteworthy, *adj.* notable

nothing, *n.* nada, *f.*

notice, *n.* noticia, *f.*; aviso, *m.*; nota, *f.*; *vt.* observar

noticeable, *adj.* notable, reparable

notify, *vt.* notificar

notion, *n.* noción, *f.*; opinion, *f.*; idea, *f.*; **notions,** *n. pl.* mercería, *f.*

notorious, *adj.* notorio

notwithstanding, *conj.* no obstante, aunque

noun, *n.* sustantivo, *m.*

nourish, *vt.* nutrir, alimentar

nourishing, *adj.* nutritivo

novel, *n.* novela, *f.*; *adj.* novedoso, original

novelist, *n.* novelista, *m.* y *f.*

novice, *n.* novicio, novicia

nowadays, *adv.* hoy día

nowhere, *adv.* en ninguna parte

nucleus, *n.* núcleo, *m.*

nude, *adj.* desnudo

nuisance, *n.* estorbo, *m.*; (coll.) lata, *f.*

null, *adj.* nulo, inválido

numb, *adj.* entumecido; *vt.* entumecer

number, *n.* número, *m.*; cantidad, *f.*; cifra, *f.*; *vt.* numerar

numeral, *adj.* numeral; *n.* número, *m.*, cifra, *f.*

numerator, *n.* (math.) numerador, *m.*

numerical, *adj.* numérico

nun, *n.* monja, *f.*

nuptial, *adj.* nupcial; **nuptials,** *n. pl.* nupcias, *f. pl.*

nurse, *n.* enfermera, *f.*; miñera, *f.*; **wet nurse,** nodriza, nutriz, *f.*; *vt.* criar, amamantar; cuidar (un enfermo)

nursery, *n.* cuarto de los niños, *m.*; criadero, *m.*

nursemaid, *n.* niñera, aya, *f.*; (Sp. Am.) nana, *f.*

nut, *n.* nuez, *f.*; tuerca, *f.*

nutmeg, *n.* nuez moscada, *f.*

nutrition, *n.* nutrición, *f.*

nutritious, nutritive, *adj.* nutritivo, alimenticio

NW, N.W., n.w., north-west, NO, noroeste

nylon, *n.* nylon, *m.*

nymph, *n.* ninfa, *f.*

O

oak, *n.* roble, *m.*, encina, *f.*

oasis, *n.* oasis, *m.*

oath, *n.* juramento, *m.*; blasfemia, *f.*

obedience, *n.* obediencia, *f.*

obedient, *adj.* obediente

obey, *vt.* obedecer

object, *n.* objeto, *m.*; punto, *m.*; (gram.) complemento, *m.*; *vt.* objetar

objection, *n.* objeción, *f.*

objective, *n.* meta, *f.*; objetivo, *m.*

obligation, *n.* obligación, *f.*; compromiso, *m.*

oblige, *vt.* obligar; complacer, favorecer

obliging, *adj.* servicial; condescendiente

obscene, *adj.* obsceno

obscure, *adj.* oscuro

obscurity, *n.* oscuridad, *f.*

observation, *n.* observación, *f.*

observatory, *n.* observatorio, *m.*

observe, *vt.* observer, mirar; notar; guarder (una fiesta, etc.)

obsession, *n.* obsesión, *f.*

obsolete, *adj.* anticuado

obstacle, *n.* obstáculo, *m.*

obstetrician, *n.* partera, *m.*

obstinate, *adj.* terco, porfiado

obstruction, *n.* obstrucción,

occasion, *n.* ocasión, *vt.* ocasionar causar

occasional, *adj.* ocasional, casual

occident, *n.* occidente, *m.*

occupation, *n.* ocupación, *f.*; empleo, *m.*; quehacer, *m.*

occupy, *vt.* ocupar, emplear

ocean, *n.* océano, *m.*

o'clock, del reloj; por el reloj; **at two o'clock,** a las dos

October, *n.* octubre, *m.*

odds, *n. pl.* differencia, disparidad, *f.*; **odds and ends,** trozos o fragmentos sobrantes

odor, odour, *n.* olor, *m.*; fragancia, *f.*

off, *adj.* y *adv.* lejos, a distancia; **hands off,** no tocar

offend, *vt.* ofender, irritar

offense, *n.* ofensa, *f.*; crimen, delito, *m.*

offensive, *adj.* ofensivo; *n.* (mil.) ofensiva, *f.*

offer, *vt.* ofrecer; *vi.* ofrecerse; *n.* oferta, propuesta, *f.*

office, *n.* oficina, *f.*; cargo, *m.*

officer, *n.* oficial, *m.*; funcionario, *m.*; agente de policía, *m.*

official, *adj.* oficial; *n.* oficial, funcionario, *m.*; **officially,** *adv.* oficialmente

offset, *vt.* balancear, compensar

offspring, *n.* prole, *f.*; descendencia, *f.*

oft, often, oftentimes, *adv.* muchas veces, frecuentemente, a menudo

ogre, *n.* ogro, *m.*

oil, *n.* aceite, *m.*; petróleo, *m.*; *vt.* aceitar, engrasar

oilcloth, *n.* encerado, hule, *m.*

oily, *adj.* aceitoso

ointment, *n.* ungüento, *m.*

O. K., all correct, correcto, V.º B.º, visto bueno

okay, *adj.* y *adv.* bueno, está

bien; *vt.* aprobar; dar el visto bueno; *n.* aprobación, *f.*, visto bueno

okra, *n.* (bot.) quimbombó, *m.*

old, *adj.* viejo; antiguo

old-fashioned, *adj.* anticuado, fuera de moda

olive, *n.* olivo, *m.*; oliva, aceituna, *f.*; **olive oil**, aceite de oliva

omelet, omelette, *n.* tortilla de huevos, *f.*

omen, *n.* agüero, *m.*

omission, *n.* omisión, *f.*; descuido, *m.*

omit, *vt.* omitir

omnibus, *n.* ómnibus, *m.*

on, *prep.* sobre, encima, en; de; a; *adv.* adelante, sin cesar

once, *adv.* una vez; **at once**, en seguida

one, *adj.* un, uno

oneself, *pron.* sí mismo

one-sided, *adj.* unilateral, parcial

one-way, *adj.* en una sola dirección

onion, *n.* cebolla, *f.*

only, *adj.* único, solo; mero; *adv.*; solamente

opal, *n.* ópalo, *m.*

open, *adj.* abierto; sincero, franco; cándido; *vt.* abrir; descubrir; *vi.* abrirse

opening, *n.* abertura

open-minded, *adj.* liberal; imparcial

opera, ópera, *f.*

operate, *vi.* obrar; operar

operating room, *n.* quirófano, *m.*

operation, *n.* operación, *f.*; funcionamiento, *m.*

opponent, *n.* antagonista, *m.* y *f.*; contendiente, *m.* y *f.*

opportune, *adj.* oportuno

opposite, *adj.* opuesto; contrario; frente; *n.* antagonista, *m.* y *f.*, adversario, adversaria

opposition, *n.* oposición

optic, optical, *adj.* óptico

optimism, *n.* optimismo, *m.*

optimistic, *adj.* optimista

or, *conj.* o; ó (entre números); u (antes de o y ho)

oral, *adj.* oral, vocal; **orally**, *adv.* oralmente, de palabra

orange, *n.* naranja, *f.*

orangeade, *n.* naranjada, *f.*

oration, *n.* oración, *f.*, discurso, *m.*

orator, *n.* orador, oradora

orchestra, *n.* orquesta, *f.*

orchid, *n.* orquídea, *f.*

order, *n.* orden, *m.* y *f.*; mandato, *m.*; encargo, *m.*; (com.) pedido, *m.*; **out of order**, descompuesto; *vt.* ordenar, arreglar; hacer un pedido

ordinary, *adj.* ordinario

organ, *n.* órgano, *m.*

organdy, *n.* organdí, *m.*

organ-grinder, *n.* organillero, *m.*

organic, *adj.* orgánico

organism, *n.* organismo, *m.*

organist, *n.* organista, *m.* y *f.*

organization, *n.* organización,

organize, *vt.* organizar

orient, *n.* oriente, *m.*

oriental, *adj.* oriental

origin, *n.* origen, principio, *m.*

original, *adj.* original

originality, *n.* originalidad, *f.*

originate, *vt.* y *vi.* originar; provenir

ornament, *n.* adorno, *m.*

orphan, *n.* y *adj.* huérfano, huérfana

orphanage, *n.* orfanato, *m.*

ostrich, *n.* avestruz, *m.*

other, *pron.* y *adj.* otro

otherwise, *adv.* de otra manera, por otra parte

ounce, *n.* onza, *f.*

our, ours, *pron.* nuestro, nuestra, nuestros, nuestras

ourselves, *pron. pl.* nosotros mismos

out, *adv.* fuera, afuera; *adj.* de fuera; **out!** *interj.* ¡fuera!

outcome, *n.* consecuencia, *f.* resultado, *m.*

outdoor, *adj.* al aire libre, fuera de casa

outdoors, *adv.* al aire libre, a la intemperie

outer, *adj.* exterior

outfit, *n.* vestido, *m.*, vestimenta, *f.*; *vt.* equipar, ataviar

outgoing, *adj.* saliente, de salida

outgrow, *vt.* quedar chico (vestido, calzado, etc.)

outing, *n.* excursión campestre,*f.*

outlaw, *n.* bandido, *m.*

outlet,*n.* salida, *f.*; desagüe, *m.*; sangrador, tomadero, *m.*

outline, *n.* contorno, *m.*; bosquejo, *m.*; silueta, *f.*; *vt.* esbozar

outlook, *n.* perspectiva, *f.*

out-of-date, *adj.* anticuado

outrage, *n.* ultraje, *m.*

outrageous, *adj.* atroz

outside, *n.* superficie, *f.*; exterior, *m.*; *adv.* afuera

outskirts, *n. pl.* suburbios, *m. pl.*; afueras, *f. pl.*

outstanding, *adj.* sobresaliente, notable

oval, *n.* óvalo, *m.*; *adj.* oval, ovalado

ovary, *n.* ovario, *m.*

oven, *n.* horno, *m.*

over, *prep.* sobre, encima; **all over**, por todos lados; **over and over**, repetidas veces

overboard, *adv.* (naut.) al agua, al mar

overcoat, *n.* abrigo, *m.*

overcome, *vt.* vencer; superar; salvar (obstáculos)

overeat, *vi.* hartarse, comer demasiado

overflow, *vi.* rebosar; desbordar; *n.* superabundancia, *f.*

overkill, *n.* capacidad destructiva superior a la necesaria

overlook, *vt.* pasar por alto, tolerar; descuidar

overnight, *adv.* durante o toda la noche; *adj.* de una noche

overpass, *n.* paso superior, *m.*

overpower, *vt.* predominar

oversea, **overseas**, *adv.* ultramar; *adj.* de ultramar

oversight, *n.* equivocación, *f.*; olvido, *m.*

overthrow, *vt.* derribar, derrocar; *n.* derrocamiento, *m.*

overtime, *n.* trabajo en exceso

de las horas regulares

overture, *n.* (mus.) obertura, *f.*

overweight, *n.* exceso de peso

overwhelming, *adj.* abrumador

overwork, *vt.* hacer trabajar demasiado; *vi.* trabajar demasiado

owe, *vt.* deber, tener deudas; estar obligado

owl, **owlet**, *n.* lechuza, *f.*

own, *adj.* propio; **my own**, mío, mía; *vt.* poseer; **to own up**, confesar

owner, *n.* dueño, dueña, propietario, propietaria

ox, *n.* buey, *m.*

oxygen, *n.* oxígeno, *m.*

oyster, *n.* ostra, *f.*, ostión, *m.*

oz., **ounce**, **ounces**, onz., onza, onzas

P

pace, *n.* paso, *m.*, marcha, *f.*; *vi.* pasear

pacemaker, *n.* (med.) aparato cardiocinético, *m.*, marcador de paso, marcapasos, *m.*

Pacific, *n.* Pacífico, *m.*

package, *n.* bulto, *m.*; paquete, *m.*

packing, *n.* envase, *m.*; empaque, *m.*; relleno, *m.*

pad, *n.* cojincillo, *m.*, almohadilla, *f.*, relleno, *m.*; **pad (of paper)**, bloc (de papel), *m.*; *vt.* rellenar

paddle, *vi.* remar; *n.* canalete (especie de remo), *m.*; pala (para remar), *f.*

page, *n.* página, *f.*; paje, *m.*

pageant, *n.* espectáculo público, *m.*, procesión, *f.*

pail, *n.* cubo, *m.*

pain, *n.* dolor, *m.*

painful, *adj.* doloroso; penoso

painstaking, *adj.* laborioso

paint, *vt.* y *vi.* pintar; *n.* pintura, *f.*

painter, *n.* pintor, pintora

painting, *n.* pintura, *f.*

pair, *n.* par, *m.*; *vt.* parear; *vi.* aparearse

pajamas, *n. pl.* pijamas, *m. pl.*

pal, n. compañero, compañera, gran amigo, gran amiga

palace, n. palacio, m.

palate, n. paladar, m.

pale, adj. pálido

paleness, n. palidez, f.

palm, n. (bot.) palma, f.; palma (de la mano), f.

Palm Sunday, n. domingo de Ramos, m.

pamper, vt. mimar

pamphlet, n. folleto, libreto, m.

Panama, Panama

Panamanian, n. y adj. panameño, panameña

pancake, n. especie de tortilla de masa que se cuece en una plancha metálica

pant, vi. palpitar; jadear; n. jadeo, m.; **pants,** n. pl. pantalones, m. pl.

panther, n. pantera, f.

panties, n. pl. pantalones (de mujer), m. pl.

pantry, n. despensa, f.

pants, n. pl. pantalones, m. pl.

paper, n. papel, m.; periódico, m.; vt. empapelar

paprika, n. pimentón, m.

par, n. equivalencia, f.; igualdad, f.; **at par,** a la par

parade, n. desfile, m.

paradise, n. paraíso, m.

paragraph, n. párrafo, m.

parallel, n. línea paralela, f.; adj. paralelo; vt. parangonar; ser paralelo a

paralysis, n. parálisis, f.

paralytic, paralytical, adj. paralítico

paralyze, vt. paralizar

paramount, adj. supremo, superior

parasite, n. parásito, m.

parcel, n. paquete, m.; bulto, m.; **parcel post,** paquete postal, m.

pardon, n. perdón, m., gracia, f.; vt. perdonar

parent, n. padre, m.; madre, f.; **parents,** n. pl. padres, m. pl.

parental, adj. paternal; maternal

parish, n. parroquia, f.

park, n. parque, m.; vt. estacionar (vehículos)

parking, n. estacionamiento (de automóviles), m.

parlor, n. sala, f.

parochial, adj. parroquial

parole, n. libertad condicional que se da a un prisionero; vt. y vi. libertar bajo palabra

parrot, n. papagayo, loro, m.

parson, n. párroco, m.

part, n. parte, f.; papel (de un actor), m.; obligación, f.; **in part,** parcialmente; vt. partir, separar, desunir; vi. separarse

participate, vt. participar

participle, n. (gram.) participio, m.

particular, adj. particular, singular

parting, n. separación, partida, f.; raya (en el cabello), f.

partition, n. partición, separación, f.; tabique, m.

party, n. partido, m.; fiesta, tertulia, f.

pass, vt. pasar; traspasar; vi. pasar, ocurrir, trascurrir; n. paso, camino, m.; pase, m.

passage, n. pasaje, m.; travesía, f.; pasadizo, m.

passenger, n. pasajero, pasajera

passing, adj. pasajero, transitorio; n. paso, m.; **in passing,** al pasar

passion, n. pasión, f.

passive, adj. pasivo

passport, n. pasaporte, m.

password, n. contraseña, f.

past, adj. pasado; **past tense,** (gram.) pretérito, m.; n. pasado, m.; prep. más allá de

paste, n. pasta, f.; engrudo, m.; vt. pegar (con engrudo)

pasteurize, vt. pasterizar

pastime, n. pasatiempo, m.

pastry, n. pastelería, f.

pasture, n. pasto, m.; vt. y vi. pastar, pacer

patch, n. remiendo, parche, m.; vt. remendar

patent, n. patente, f., vt. patentar

paternal, *adj.* paternal
path, *n.* senda, *f.*, sendero, *m.*
patient, *adj.* paciente, sufrido; *n.* enfermo, enferma; paciente, doliente, *m.* y *f.*
patriot, *n.* patriota, *m.*
patriotic, *adj.* patriótico
patriotism, *n.* patriotismo, *m.*
patrol, *n.* patrulla, *f.*
patron, *n.* patrón, protector, *m.*; **patron saint**, santo patrón, *m.*
patronize, *vt.* patrocinar
pattern, modelo, *m.*; patrón, *m.*; muestra, *f.*
pauper, *n.* pobre, *m.* y *f.*, limosnero, limosnera
pause, *n.* pausa, *f.*; *vi.* pausar; deliberar
paw, *n.* garra, *f.*
pawn, *n.* prenda, *f.*; peón (de ajedrez), *m.*; *vt.* empeñar
pawnshop, *n.* casa de empeño, *f.*
pay, *vt.* pagar; saldar; *n.* paga, *f.*, pago, *m.*
payable, *adj.* pagadero
payload, *n.* carga útil, *f.*
payment, *n.* pago, *m.*; paga, *f.*; recompensa, *f.*
payola, *n.* cohecho, soborno *m.*
pea, *n.* guisante, *m.*; (Mex.) chícharo, *m.*
peace, *n.* paz, *f.*; **Peace Corps**, Cuerpo de Paz
peaceful, *adj.* pacífico, apacible
peach, *n.* melocotón, durazno, *m.*
peacock, *n.* pavo real, *m.*
peanut, *n.* cacahuate, cacahuete, maní, *m.*
peasant, *n.* campesino, campesina
pebble, *n.* guijarro, *m.*, piedrecilla, *f.*
peculiar, *adj.* peculiar, singular
pedal, *n.* pedal, *m.*
peddler, *n.* buhonero, *m.*
pedestal, *n.* pedestal, *m.*
pedestrian, *n.* peatón, peatona
pediatrician, *n.* (med.) pedia-

tra, *m.* y *f.*
pedigreed, *adj.* de casta escogida
peel, *vt.* descortezar, pelar; *n.* corteza, *f.*
peerless, *adj.* sin par
pen, *n.* pluma, *f.*; corral, *m.*
penalty, *n.* pena, *f.*; castigo, *m.*; multa, *f.*
pencil, *n.* pince, *m.*; lápiz, *m.*
pending, *adj.* pendiente
penetrate, *vt.* y *vi.* penetrar
penicillin, *n.* penicilina, *f.*
peninsula, *n.* península, *f.*
penitence, *n.* penitencia,
penitentiary, *n.* penitenciaría, *f.*
penknife, *n.* cortaplumas, *m.*
penmanship, *n.* caligrafía, *f.*
penniless, *adj.* indigente
penny, *n.* centavo, *m.*
pension, *n.* pensión, *f.*; *vt.* pensionar
people, *n.* gente, *f.*; pueblo, *m.*; nación, *f.*
pep, *n.* (coll.) energía, *f.*, entusiasmo, *m.*
pepper, *n.* pimienta, *f.*
peppermint, *n.* menta, *f.*
per, *prep.* por; **per capita**, por persona, por cabeza; **per cent**, por ciento (%)
perceive, *vt.* percibir, comprender
percentage, *n.* porcentaje, *m.*
perception, *n.* percepción, *f.*
percussion, *n.* percussión *f.*; **percussion section**, (mus.) batería, *f.*
perfect, *adj.* perfecto; *vt.* perfeccionar
perfection, *n.* perfección, *f.*
perforate, *vt.* perforar
perforation, *n.* perforación, *f.*
perform, *vt.* ejecutar; efectuar; realizer; *vi.* (theat.) representar
performance, *n.* ejecución, *f.*; cumplimiento, *m.*; actuación, *f.*; representación teatral, funcion, *f.*
perfume, *n.* perfume, *m.*
perhaps, *adv.* quizá, tal vez
peril, *n.* peligro, riesgo, *m.*
period, *n.* periodo, *m.*; época,

f.; punto, *m.*
periodic, *adj.* periódico
periodical, *n.* periódico, *m.*; *adj.* periodico
perish, *vi.* perecer
permanent, *adj.* permanente; **permanent wave,** ondulado permanente, *m.*
permission, *n.* permiso, *m.*, licencia, *f.*
permit, *vt.* permitir; *n.* permiso, *m.*
peroxide, *n.* peróxido, *m.*
perpendicular, *adj.* perpendicular
perpetual, *adj.* perpetuo
persecute, *vt.* perseguir
persecution, *n.* persecución, *f.*
perseverance, *n.* perseverancia, *f.*
persist, *vi.* persistir
persistent, *adj.* persistente
person, *n.* persona, *f.*
personal, *adj.* personal
personality, *n.* personalidad, *f.*
personnel, *n.* personal, *m.*
perspective, *n.* perspectiva, *f.*
perspiration, *n.* traspiración, *f.*, sudor, *m.*
perspire, *vi.* traspirar, sudar
persuade, *vt.* persuadir
pertain, *vi.* relacionar, tocar
perturb, *vt.* perturbar
perverse, *adj.* perverso
perversion *n.* perversión, *f.*
perversity, *n.* perversidad, *f.*
pervert, *vt.* perverter, corromper
pessimist, *n.* pesimista, *m.* y *f.*
pessimistic, *adj.* pesimista
pest, *n.* reste, pestilencia, *f.*
pet, *n.* favorito, favorita; *vt.* mimar
petition, *n.* petición, súplica, *f.*; *vt.* suplicar, pedir
pew, *n.* banco de iglesia, *m.*
phantom, *n.* espectro, fantasma, *m.*
pharmacist, *n.* boticario, farmacéutico, *m.*
pharmacy, *n.* farmacia, botica, *f.*
phase, *n.* fase, *f.*, aspecto, *m.*
philanthropic, philanthropi-

cal, *adj.* filantrópico
philately, *n.* filatelia, *f.*
Philippines, Filipinas
philosopher, *n.* filósofo *m.*
philosophy, *n.* filosofia *f.*
phone, *n.* (coll.) teléfono, *m.*; *vt.* (coll.) telefonear
phonetics, *n. pl.* fonética, *f.*
photo, *n.* (coll.) **photograph**
photogenic, *adj.* fotogénico
photograph, *n.* fotografia, *f.*; retrato, *m.*; *vt.* fotograflar, retratar
photographer, *n.* fotógrafo, *m.*
physic, *n.* purgante, *m.*, purga, *f.*; **physics,** *n. pl.* fisica, *f.*; *vt.* purgar, dar un purgante
physical, *adj.* fisico
physician, *n.* médico, *m.*
physics, *n.* fisica, *f.*
physiology, *n.* fisiología, *f.*
physique, *n.* fisico, *m.*
pianist, *n.* pianista, *m.* y *f.*
piano, *n.* piano, *m.*
pickle, *n.* encurtido, *m.*
pickpocket, *n.* ratero, ratera, ladrón, ladrona
picnic, *n.* merienda campestre, *f.*; día de campo, *m.*
picture, *n.* retrato, *m.*; fotografia, *f.*; cuadro, *m.*; **motion picture,** película, *f.*
picturesque, *adj.* pintoresco
pie, *n.* pastel, *m.*
piece, *n.* pedazo, *m.*; pieza, obra, *f.*
pier, *n.* muelle, *m.*
pig, *n.* cerdo, *m.*, puerco, puerca
pigeon, *n.* palomo, *m.*, paloma, *f.*
pile, *n.* pila, *f.*; montón, *m.*; **piles,** *n. pl.* hemorroides, almorranas, *f. pl.*; *vt.* amontonar, apilar
pill, *n.* píldora, *f.*
pillar, *n.* pilar, poste, *m.*, columna, *f.*
pillow, *n.* almohada, *f.*, cojín, *m.*
pillowcase, pillowslip, *n.* funda, *f.*
pilot, *n.* piloto, *m.*
pimento, *n.* pimiento, *m.*
pimple, *n.* grano, barro, *m.*

pin, *n.* alfiler, *m.*, prendedor, *m.*; **safety pin**, imperdible, alfiler de gancho; *vt.* asegurar con alfileres; fijar con clavija

pinafore, *n.* delantal de niña, *m.*

pinch, *vt.* pellizcar; *vi.* escatimar gastos; *n.* pellizco, *m.*; aprieto, *m.*

pineapple, *n.* piña, *f.*; ananá, ananás, *f.*

pink, *n.* (bot.) clavel, *m.*; *adj.* rosado, sonrosado

pint, *n.* pinta (medida de líquidos), *f.*

pious, *adj.* piadoso

pipe, *n.* tubo, conducto, caño, *m.*; pipa para fumar, *f.*

pirate, *n.* pirata, *m.*

pit, *n.* hoyo, *m.*

pitcher, *n.* cántaro, *m.*; (baseball) lanzador de pelota

pitiful, *adj.* lastimoso

pity, *n.* piedad, compasión, *f.*; *vt.* compadecer

pkg., package, bto., bulto, paquete

place, *n.* lugar, sitio, *m.*; local, *m.*; **to take place**, verificarse; *vt.* colocar; poner

plague, *n.* peste, plaga, *f.*; *vt.* atormentar

plain, *adj.* sencillo; simple; evidente; *n.* llano, *m.*

plan, *n.* plan, *m.*; *vt.* planear, proyectar

plane, *n.* (avi.) avión, *m.*; plano; *m.*; cepillo, *m.*

planet, *n.* planeta, *m.*

plant, *n.* planta, *f.*

plasma, *n.* plasma, *m.*

plastic, *adj.* plástico

plate, *n.* placa, *f.*; clisé, *m.*; plato, *m.*

platform, *n.* plataforma, tarima, *f.*

platter, *n.* fuente, *f.*, plato grande, *m.*

play, *n.* juego, *m.*; recreo, *m.*; comedia, *f.*; *vt.* y *vi.* jugar; (mus.) tocar

playback, *n.* reproducción en magnetófono

playboy, *n.* muchacho travieso, hombre de mundo, cala-

vera, *m.*

playful, *adj.* juguetón, travieso

playground, *n.* campo de deportes o de juegos, *m.*

playmate, *n.* compañero o compañera de juego

plaything, *n.* juguete, *m.*

plea, *n.* ruego, *m.*; súplica, *f.*; petición, *f.*

plead, *vt.* alegar; suplicar

please, *vt.* agradar, complacer

pleasing, *adj.* agradable, grato

pleasure, *n.* placer, *m.*

plot, *n.* pedazo pequeño de terreno; trama, *f.*; complot, *m.*; *vt.* y *vi.* conspirar, tramar

plug, n: tapón, *m.*; (elec.) clavija, *f.*; *vt.* tapar; (elec.) conectar

plumber, *n.* plomero, *m.*

plunge, *vt.* y *vi.* sumergir, precipitarse

plus, *prep.* más

p.m., afternoon, p.m., pasado meridiano, tarde

pneumonia, *n.* neumonía, pulmonía, *f.*

pocket, *n.* bolsillo, *m.*

pocketbook, *n.* portamonedas, *m.*, cartera, *f.*; (fig.) dinero, *m.*

pocketknife, *n.* cortaplumas, *m.*

poem, *n.* poema, *m.*

poet, *n.* poeta, *m.*

poetic, poetical, *adj.* poético

poetry, *n.* poesía, *f.*

point, *n.* punta, *f.*; punto, *m.*; **point of view**, punto de vista; *vt.* apuntar; **to point out**, señalar

poison, *n.* veneno, *m.*; *vt.* envenenar

poker, *n.* hurgón, *m.*; póker (juego de naipes), *m.*

Poland, Polonia

polar, *adj.* polar; **polar bear**, oso blanco, *m.*

Pole, *n.* polaco, polaca

pole, *n.* polo, *m.*; palo, *m.*; **pole vault**, salto con pértiga, *m.*

police, *n.* policía, *f.*

policeman, *n.* policía, *m.*

policewoman, *n.* mujer policía, *f.*

policy, *n.* póliza, *f.*; política, *f.*: sistema, *m.*

polite, *adj.* cortés

politeness, *n.* cortesía, *f.*

political, *adj.* político

politician, *n.* político, *m.*

politics, *n. pl.* política, *f.*

pond, *n.* charca, *f.*

ponder, *vt.* y *vi.* ponderar

pontoon, *n.* (avi.) flotador de hidroavión, *m.*

pony, *n.* caballito, *m.*

pool, *n.* charco. *m.*

poor, *adj.* pobre; deficiente

popcorn, *n.* palomitas de maíz, *f. pl.*

Pope, *n.* papa, *m.*

poplar, *n.* álamo temblón, *m.*

poppy, *n.* amapola, *f.*

popular, *adj.* popular

popularity, *n.* popularidad, *f.*

population, *n.* población, *f.*, número de habitantes, *m.*

populous, *adj.* populoso

porcelain, *n.* porcelana, *f.*

porch, *n.* pórtico, vestíbulo, *m.*

pork, *n.* carne de puerco, *f.*

port, *n.* puerto, *m.*; vino de Oporto, *m.*

portable, *adj.* portátil

porter, *n.* portero, *m.*; mozo, *m.*

portion, *n.* porción, ración, *f.*

portrait, *n.* retrato, *m.*

Portuguese, *n.* y *adj.* portugués, portuguesa

pose, *n.* postura, actitud

position, *n.* posición, situación, *f.*

positive, *adj.* positive, real

possess, *vt.* poseer

possession, *n.* posesión, *f.*

possessive, *adj.* posesivo

possibility, *n.* posibilidad, *f.*

possible, *adj.* posible

post, *n.* correo, *m.*; puesto, *m.*; empleo, *m.*; poste, *m.*; *vt.* fijar; **post no bills,** se prohibe fijar carteles

postage, *n.* franqueo, *m.*

postal, *adj.* postal; **postal card,** tarjeta postal, *f.*

poster, *n.* cartel, cartelón, *m.*

posterity, *n.* posteridad, *f.*

postman, *n.* cartero, *m.*

postmark, *n.* sello o marca de la oficina de correos

post office, *n.* correo, *m.*, oficina postal, *f.*

postpaid, *adj.* franco; con porte pagado

postpone, *vt.* posponer

postscript, *n.* posdata, *f.*

postwar, *n.* postguerra, *f.*

pot, *n.* olla, *f.*

potato, *n.* patata, papa, *f.*

potent, *adj.* potente

pouch, *n.* buche, *m.*; bolsa, *f.*

poultry, *n.* aves de corral, *f. pl.*

pound, *n.* libra, *f.*; **pound sterling,** libra esterlina, *f.*; *vt.* machacar

pour, *vt.* verter; *vi.* fluir con rapidez; llover a cántaros

poverty, *n.* pobreza, *f.*

POW, (prisoner of war), *n.* prisionero de guerra, *m.*

powder, *n.* polvo, *m.*; pólvora, *f.*; **powder puff,** borla o mota de empolvarse; *vt.* pulverizar; empolvar

power, *n.* poder, *m.*; potencia, *f.*

powerful, *adj.* poderoso

powerless, *adj.* impotente

pp., pages, págs., páginas; **past participle,** p. pdo., participio pasado

practice, *n.* práctica, *f.*; costumbre, *f.*; *vt.* y *vi.* practicar, ejercer; ensayar

praise, *n.* alabanza, *f.*; *vt.* alabar, ensalzar

pray, *vt.* y *vi.* rezar, rogar

prayer, *n.* oración, súplica, *f.*; **the Lord's Prayer,** el Padre Nuestro, *m.*

preach, *vt.* y *vi.* predicar

preacher, *n.* predicador, *m.*

preamble, *n.* preámbulo, *m.*

precaution, *n.* precaución, *f.*

precede, *vt.* preceder

precedent, *adj.* y *n.* precedente, *m.*

preceding, *adj.* precursor

precious, *adj.* precioso; valioso

precipitation, *n.* precipitación, *f.*

precise, *adj.* preciso, exacto

predecessor, n. predecesor, predecesora, antecesor, antecesora

predict, vt. predecir

predominate, vt. predominar

preface, n. prefacio, m.

prefer, vt. preferir

preferable, adj. preferible

preference, n. preferencia, f.

pregnant, adj. encinta

prejudice, n. prejuicio, m.

preliminary, adj. preliminar

premature, adj. prematuro

premier, n. primer ministro, m.

premiere, n. estreno, m.

premium, n. premio, m.; prima, f.

premonition, n. presentimiento, m.

preparation, n. preparación, f.; preparativo, m.

prepare, vt. preparar; vi. prepararse

preposition, n. preposición, f.

prescribe, vt. y vi. prescribir; recetar

prescription, n. receta medicinal, f.

presence, n. presencia, f.; **presence of mind,** serenidad de ánimo, f.

present, n. presente, regalo, m.; adj. presente; vt. presentar, regalar

presentable, adj. presentable, decente

preserve, vt. preserver, conservar; n. conserva, confitura, f.

preside, vi. presidir

presidency, n. presidencia, f.

president, n. presidente, m.

press, vt. planchar; oprimir, compeler; n. prensa, f.; imprenta, f.

pressing, urgente

pressure, n. presión, f.; **pressure gauge,** manómetro, m.

pretend, vt. simular, fingir

pretense, pretence, n. pretexto, m.; pretensión, f.

pretext, n. pretexto, m.

pretty, adj. bonito

prevent, vt. prevenir

prevention, n. prevención, f.

preventive, adj. y n. preventivo, m.

preview, n. exhibición preliminar, f.

previous, adj. previo

price, n. precio, valor, m.

priceless, adj. inapreciable

priest, n. sacerdote, cura, m.

primary, adj. primario

primitive, adj. primitivo

princess, n. princesa, f.

principal, adj. principal; n. principal, jefe, m.; rector, director (de un colegio), m.; capital (dinero empleado), m.

principle, n. principio, fundamento, m.

print, vt. estampar, imprimir; n. impresión, estampa, f.

printed, adj. impreso; **printed matter,** impresos, m. pl.

printer, n. impresor, m.

prison, n. prisión, cárcel, f.

prisoner, n. prisionero, prisionera

private, adj. privado; secreto; particular; **private enterprise,** empresa particular, f.; n. soldado raso, m.

prize, n. premio, m.

prizefighter, n. pugilista, boxeador, m.

pro, prep. para, pro; adj. en el lado afirmativo (de un debate, etc.); **the pros and cons,** el pro y el contra

probability, n. probabilidad, f.

probable, adj. probable

probation, n. prueba, f.; libertad condicional, f.

problem, n. problema, m.

proceed, vi. proceder; **proceeds,** n. pl. producto, rédito, m.

process, n. proceso, m.

procession, n. procesión, f.

produce, vt. producir; rendir

product, n. producto, m.

production, n. producción, f.

Prof., prof., professor, Prof., profesor

profit, n. ganancia, f.; provecho, m.; vt. y vi. aprovechar

profitable, adj. provechoso,

productivo

program, *n.* programa, *m.*; *vt.* programar

progress, *vt.* progreso, *m.*; adelanto, *m.*; *vi.* progresar

prohibit, *vt.* prohibir

prohibition, *n.* prohibición, *f.*

project, *vt.* proyectar, trazar; *n.* proyecto, *m.*

prominent, *adj.* prominente

promise, *n.* promesa, *f.*; *vt.* prometer

promising, *adj.* prometedor

promote, *vt.* promover

promotion, *n.* promoción, *f.*

prompt, *adj.* pronto, listo; **promptly,** *adv.* pronto; *vt.* apuntar (en el teatro)

pronoun, *n.* pronombre, *m.*

pronounce, *vt.* pronunciar

pronunciation, *n.* pronunciación, *f.*

proof, *n.* prueba, *f.*

proofread, *vt.* corregir pruebas

propaganda, *n.* propaganda, *f.*

propagandist, *adj.* y *n.* propagandista, propagador, *m.*

proper, *adj.* propio; debido

property, *n.* propiedad, *f.*

prophecy, *n.* profecía, *f.*

prophet, *n.* profeta, *m.*

proportion, *n.* proporción, *f.*

proposal, *n.* propuesta, proposición, *f.*; oferta, *f.*

propose, *vt.* proponer

proposition, *n.* proposición, propuesta, *f.*

proprietor, *n.* propietario, propietaria, dueño, dueña

prose, *n.* prosa, *f.*

prosecutor, *n.* acusador, *m.*

prospect, *n.* perspectiva, *f.*

prosper, *vt.* y *vi.* prosperar

prosperity, *n.* prosperidad, *f.*

prosperous, *adj.* próspero

prostitution, *n.* prostitución, *f.*

prostrate, *adj.* decaído, postrado

protect, *vt.* proteger, amparar

protection, *n.* protección,

protector, *n.* protector, protectora

protein, *n.* proteína, *f.*

protest, *vt.* y *vi.* protestar; *n.*

protesta, *f.*

Protestant, *n.* y *adj.* protestante, *m.* y *f.*

prove, *vt.* probar

proverb, *n.* proverbio, *m.*

provide, *vt.* proveer, surtir

provided, *adj.* provisto; **provided that,** con tal que

providence, *n.* providencia, *f.* ; economía, *f.*

province, *n.* provincia, *f.*; jurisdicción, *f.*

provision, *n.* provisión, *f.*; **provisions,** *n. pl.* comestibles, *m. pl.*

provisional, *adj.* provisional

proxy, *n.* apoderado, apoderada; **by proxy,** por poder

P.S., postscript, P.D., posdata

psalm, *n.* salmo, *m.*

psychiatry, *n.* siquiatría, *f.*

psychoanalyze, *vt.* sicoanalizar

psychology, *n.* sicología, *f.*

P. T. A.: Parent-Teacher Association, Asociación de Padres y Maestros

public, *adj.* y *n.* público, *m.*

publication, *n.* publicación, *f.*

publicity, *n.* publicidad, *f.*

publish, *vt.* publicar

puff, *n.* bufido, soplo, *m.*; bocanada, *f.*; **powder puff,** mota o borla para polvos, *f.*; *vt.* y *vi.* hinchar; soplar

puffy, *adj.* hinchado

pull, *vt.* tirar, halar.; *n.* tirón, *m.*. influencia. *f.*

pulpit, *n.* púlpito, *m.*

pump, *n.* bomba, *f.*; zapatilla, *f.*; *vt.* sondear; sonsacar

pumpkin, *n.* calabaza, *f.*

pun, *n.* equívoco, chiste, *m.*; juego de palabras, *m.*

punch, *n.* puñetazo, *m.*; ponche, *m.*

punctual, *adj.* puntual

punctuation, *n.* puntuación, *f.*

puncture, *n.* pinchazo, *m.*

punish, *vt.* castigar

punishment, *n.* castigo, *m.*

pupil, *n.* (anat.) pupila, *f.*; pupilo, *m.*; discípulo, discípula; **pupil of the eye,** niña del ojo, *f.*

puppy, *n.* perrillo, cachorro, *m.*

purgatory, *n.* purgatorio, *m.*

purple, *adj.* morado

purpose, *n.* intención, *f.*; **on purpose,** de propósito

purse, *n.* bolsa, *f.*, portamonedas, *m.*

pursue, *vt.* y *vi.* perseguir; seguir

pursuit, *n.* persecución, *f.*

puss, pussy, *n.* micho, gato, *m.*

put, *vt.* poner, colocar

puzzle, *n.* rompecabezas, *m.*; *vt.* y *vi.* confundir

pyramid, *n.* pirámide,

Q

qt., quantity, cantidad; **quart,** cuarto de galón.

quail, *n.* codorniz, *f.*

quake, *vi.* temblar, tiritar; *n.* temblor, *m.*

Quaker, *n.* y *adj.* cuáquero, cuáquera

qualification, *n.* aptitud, *f.*; requisito, *m.*

quantity, *n.* cantidad, *f.*

quarantine, *n.* cuarentena, *f.*

quarrel, *n.* riña, pelea, *f.*; *vi.* reñir, disputar

quart, *n.* un cuarto de galón, *m.*

quarter, *n.* cuarto, *m.*; cuarta parte; cuartel, *m.*; moneda de E.U.A. de 25 centavos de dólar

quarterly, *adj.* trimestral

quartet, *n.* cuarteto, *m.*

queen, *n.* reina, *f.*; dama (en el juego de ajedrez), *f.*

queenly, *adj.* majestuoso, como una reina

question, *n.* cuestión, *f.*; asunto, *m.*; duda, *f.*; pregunta, *f.*; *vi.* preguntar; *vt.* desconfiar, poner en duda

questionable, *adj.* dudoso

questionnaire, *n.* cuestionario, *m.*

quick, *adj.* veloz; ligero, pronto; **quickly,** *adv.* rápidamente

quiet, *adj.* quieto, tranquilo, callado; *n.* calma, serenidad, *f.*; *vt.* tranquilizar

quinine, *n.* quinina, *f.*

quiz, *vt.* examinar; *n.* examen *m.*

quorum, *n.* quórum, *m.*

quota, *n.* cuota, *f.*

quotation, *n.* cotización, cita, *f.*; **quotation marks,** comillas, *f. pl.*

quote, *vt.* citar; **to quote (a price),** cotizar (precio)

quotient, *n.* cuociente o cociente, *m.*

R

rabbit, *n.* conejo, *m.*

race, *n.* raza, *f.*; carrera, corrida, *f.*; *vi.* correr

rack, *n.* (mech.) cremallera, *f.*

racket, *n.* raqueta, *f.*

radar, *n.* radar, *m.*

radiance, *n.* esplendor, *m.*

radiator, *n.* calentador, *m.*; (auto.) radiador, *m.*

radio, *n.* radio. *m.* y *f.*

radio telescope, *n.* radiotelescopio *m.*

radius, *n.* (math., anat.) radio, *m.*

rage, *n.* rabia, *f.*; furor, *m.*, cólera, *f.*; *vi.* rabiar, encolerizarse

rail, *n.* balaustrada, *f.*; (rail.) carril, riel, *m.*; **by rail,** por ferrocarril

railing, *n.* baranda, *f.*, barandal *m.*; carril, *m.*

railroad, *n.* ferrocarril, *m.*

railway, *n.* ferrocarril, *m.*

rain, *n.* lluvia, *f.*; *vi.* llover

rainbow, *n.* arco iris, *m.*

raincoat, *n.* impermeable, *m.*

raindrop, *n.* gota de lluvia, *f.*

rainy, *adj.* lluvioso

raise, *vt.* levantar, alzar

raisin, *n.* pasa, *f.*

ran, *pretérito* del verbo **run**

ranch, *n.* hacienda, *f.*; rancho, *m.*

random, *n.* ventura, casualidad, *f.*; **at random,** al azar

rang, *pretérito* del verbo **ring**

range, *vt.* clasificar; *vi.* fluctuar; alcance, *m.*; cocina económica, estufa, *f.*

rank, *n.* fila, hilera, *f.*; clase, *f.*; grado, rango, *m.*

ransom, *vt.* rescatar; *n.* rescate, *m.*

rape, *n.* fuerza, *f.*; estupro, *m.*; *vt.* estuprar

rash, *adj.* precipitado, temerario; *n.* roncha, *f.*; erupción, *f.*; sarpullido, *m.*

raspberry, *n.* frambuesa, *f.*

rat, *n.* rata, *f.*

rate, *n.* tipo, *m.*, tasa, *f.*; precio, valor, *m.*; **at the rate of,** a razón de; *vt.* tasar, apreciar; calcular, calificar

rather, *adv.* más bien; bastante; mejor dicho

ratify, *vt.* ratificar

rattle, *vt.* y *vi.* hacer ruido; **to become rattled,** confundirse; *n.* sonajero, *m.*; matraca, *f.*

rattlesnake, *n.* culebra de cascabel, *f.*

raw, *adj.* crudo; en bruto; **raw materials,** primeras materias, *f. pl.*

ray, *n.* rayo (de luz), *m.*

rayon, *n.* rayón, *m.*

razor, *n.* navaja de afeitar, *f.*

rd., road, camino; **rod,** pértica

reach, *vt.* alcanzar; *vi.* extenderse, llegar

read, *vt.* leer; interpretar

reader, *n.* lector, lectora

readily, *adv.* prontamente; de buena gana

reading, *n.* lectura, *f.*

real, *adj.* real, verdado, efectivo; **real estate,** bienes raíces o inmuebles, *m. pl.*

realistic, *adj.* realista; natural

reality, *n.* realidad, *f.*

realize, *vt.* realizer; darse cuenta de

really, *adv.* realmente

reap, *vt.* segar

rear, *n.* retaguardia, *f.*; parte posterior, *f.*; *adj.* posterior; *vt.* criar, educar

reason, *n.* razón, *f.*; motivo, *m.*; *vt.* razonar, raciocinar

reasonable, *adj.* razonable

reassure, *vt.* volver a asegurar

rebate, *n.* rebaja, *f.*

rebel, *n.* rebelde, *m.* y *f.*; *adj.* insurrecto; *vi.* rebelarse; insubordinarse

rebirth, *n.* renacimiento, *m.*

rebuild, *vt.* reconstruir

receipt, *n.* recibo, *m.*; receta, *f.*

receive, *vt.* recibir; admitir

receiver, *n.* receptor, *m.*; recipiente, *m.*; audífono, *m.*

reception, *n.* recepción, *f.*

receptionist, *n.* recepcionista, *m.* y *f.*, recibidor, m

recess, *n.* receso, recreo, *m.*

recipe, *n.* receta de cocina, *f.*

recipient, *n.* receptor, receptora

reciprocal, *adj.* recíproco

reciprocate, *vi.* corresponder

recital, *n.* recitación, *f.*; concierto, *m.*

recitation, *n.* recitación,

recite, *vt.* recitar; declamar

recognition, *n.* reconocimiento, *m.*; agradecimiento, *m.*

recognize, *vt.* reconocer

recommend, *vt.* recomendar

recommendation, *n.* recomendación, *f.*

recompense, *n.* recompensa, *f.*; *vt.* recompensar

reconciliation, *n.* reconciliación, *f.*

record, *vt.* registrar; grabar; *n.* registro, archivo, *m.*; disco, *m.*; *adj.* sin precedente; **off-the-record,** confidencial, extraoficial

recover, *vt.* recobrar; *vi.* restablecerse

recovery, *n.* restablecimiento, *m.*

recruit, *vt.* reclutar; *n.* (mil.) recluta, *m.*

rectangle, *n.* rectángulo, *m.*

rectangular, *adj.* rectangular

rectify, *vt.* rectificar

recuperate, *vi.* restablecerse; *vt.* recobrar, recuperar

red, *adj.* rojo; colorado; **Red, (communist),** *n.*, *adj.* rojo (communista)

redbreast, *n.* petirrojo, pechirrojo, *m.*

redden, *vi.* enrojecer

redeem, *vt.* redimir

redeemer, *n.* redentor, redentora, salvador, salvadora; the **Redeemer**, el Redentor

red-haired, *adj.* pelirrojo

reduce, *vt.* reducir

reduction, *n.* reducción, rebaja, *f.*

refer, *vt.* y *vi.* referir, dirigir

referee, *n.* árbitro, *m.*

reference, *n.* referencia, *f.*

refill, *vt.* rellenar; *n.* relleno, *m.*

refine, *vt.* y *vi.* refinar, purificar

refinement, *n.* refinamiento, *m.*

reflect, *vt.* y *vi.* rerejar; reflexionar

reflection, *n.* reflexión, meditación, *f.*; reflejo, *m.*

reflex, *adj.* reflejo

reform, *vt.* y *vi.* reformar; *n.* reforma, *f.*

reformatory, *n.* reformatorio *m.*

refrain, *vi.* abstenerse; *n.* estribillo, *m.*

refresh, *vt.* refrescar

refreshment, *n.* refresco, refrigerio, *m.*

refrigerate, *vt.* refrigerar

refrigeration, *n.* refrigeración, *f.*

refrigerator, *n.* refrigerador, *m.*

refuge, *n.* refugio, asilo, *m.*

refugee, *n.* refugiado, refugiada

refuse, *vt.* rehusar, repulsar; *n.* desecho, *m.*, sobra, *f.*

regard, *vt.* estimar; considerar; *n.* consideración, *f.*; respeto, *m.*; **regards**, *m. pl.*, recuerdos, *m. pl.*, memorias, *f. pl.*; **in regard to**, en cuanto a, respecto a, con respecto a; **in this regard**, a este respecto

regime, *n.* régimen. *m.*

regiment, *n.* regimiento, *m.*

region, *n.* región, *f.*

regional, *adj.* regional

register, *n.* registro, *m.*; **cash register**, caja registradora, *f.*; *vt.* registrar; certificar (una carta); *vi.* matricularse, registrarse

regret, *n.* arrepentimiento, *m.*; pesar, *m.*; *vt.* lamentar, deplorar

regrettable, *adj.* lamentable, depiorable

regular, *adj.* regular; ordinario

regularity, *n.* regularidad, *f.*

rehabilitation, *n.* rehabilitación, *f.*

rehearsal, *n.* (theat.) ensayo, *m.*

rehearse, *vt.* (theat.) ensayar

reign, *n.* reinado, reino, *m.*; *vi.* reinar, prevalecer, imperar

reimburse, *vt.* rembolsar

rein, *n.* rienda, *f.*

reindeer, *n. sing.* y *pl.*. reno(s) rangífero(s), *m.*

reinforced, *adj.* reforzado

relate, *vt.* referir

related, *adj.* emparentado

relation, *n.* relación, *f.*; parentesco, *m.*

relative, *adj.* relativo; *n.* pariente, *m.* y *f.*

relax, *vt.* aflojar; *vi.* descansar, reposar

relaxation, *n.* reposo, descanso, *m.*

relay, *n.* trasmisión, *f.*; **relay race**, carrera de relevos, *f.*

release, *vt.* soltar, libertar; dar al público

relentless, *adj.* inflexible

relevant, *adj.* pertinente; concerniente

reliable, *adj.* digno de confianza, responsable

relief, *n.* alivio, consuelo, *m.*

relieve, *vt.* aliviar; relevar

religion, *n.* religión, *f.* ; culto, *m.*

religious, *adj.* religioso

relish, *n.* sabor, *m.*; gusto, deleite, *m.*; condimento, *m.*

relocate, *vt.* establecer de nuevo

remain, *vi.* quedar, restar, permanecer

remark, *n.* observación, nota,

f., comentario, *m.*

remarkable, *adj.* notable, interesante

remedy, *n.* remedio, medicamento, *m.*; *vt.* remediar

remember, *vt.* recordar, tener presente; dar memorias; *vi.* acordarse

remit, *vt.* y *vi.* remitir

remittance, *n.* remesa, *f.*; remisión, *f.*

remorse, *n.* remordimiento, *m.*

remote, *adj.* remoto, lejano

remove, *vt.* remover, alejar; quitar

render, *vt.* rendir

rendezvous, *n.* cita (particularmente amorosa), *f.*

renew, *vt.* renovar

renewal, *n.* prórroga,

rent, *n.* renta, *f.*, alquiler, *m.*; *vt.* arrendar, alquilar

repair, *vt.* reparar; *n.* remiendo, *m.*, reparación, compostura, *f.*

repeal, *vt.* abrogar, revocar; *n.* revocación, *f.*

repeat, *vt.* repetir

repent, *vi.* arrepentirse

repentance, *n.* arrepentimiento, *m.*

repertoire, *n.* repertorio, *m.*

repetition, *n.* repetición, *f.*

reply, *vt.* replicar, contestar, responder; *n.* respuesta, contestación, *f.*

report, *vt.* informar; dar cuenta; *n.* rumor, *m.*; informe, *m.*

reporter, *n.* reportero, *m.*; periodista, *m.* y *f.*

represent, *vt.* representar

representation, *n.* representación, *f.*

representative, *adj.* representativo; *n.* representante, *m.* y *f.*; **House of Representatives,** Cámara de Representantes

reprint, *n.* reimpresión, *f.*

reproduce, *vt.* reproducir

reptile, *n.* reptil, *m.*

republic, *n.* república,

reputation, *n.* reputación, *f.*

request, *n.* solicitud, súplica, *f.*; *vt.* suplicar; pedir, solicitar

require, *vt.* requerir, demandar

requirement, *n.* requisito, *m.*

rescue, *n.* rescate, *m.*; *vt.* socorrer; salvar

research, *n.* investigación, *f.*

resemblance, *n.* semejanza, *f.*

resemble, *vi.* parecerse a

resent, *vt.* resentir

resentment, *n.* resentimiento, *m.*

reservation, *n.* reservación, *f.*

reserve, *vt.* reservar; *n.* reserva, *f.*

residence, *n.* residencia, *f.*

resident, *n.* y *adj.* residente, *m.* y *f.*

residential, *adj.* residencial

resign, *vt.* y *vi.* resignar, renunciar, ceder; conformarse

resignation, *n.* resignación, *f.*; renuncia, *f.*

resist, *vt.* y *vi.* resistir; oponerse

resistance, *n.* resistencia, *f.*

resolution, *n.* resolución, *f.*

resolve, *vt.* resolver; decretar; *vi.* resolverse

resort, *vi.* recurrir; *n.* recurso; **summer resort,** lugar de veraneo, *m.*

resource, *n.* recurso, *m.*

resourceful, *adj.* ingenioso, hábil

respect, *n.* respecto, *m.*; respeto, *m.*; *vt.* apreciar; respetar

respectable, *adj.* respetable; decente

respectful, *adj.* respetuoso; **respectfully,** *adv.* respetuosamente

respond, *vt.* responder

response, *n.* respuesta, réplica, *f.*

responsibility, *n.* responsabilidad, *f.*

responsible, *adj.* responsable

rest, *n.* reposo, *m.*; resto, restante, *m.*; **rest room,** sala de descanso, *f.*; *vt.* poner a descansar; apoyar; *vi.* resposar, recostar

restaurant, *n.* restaurante, *m.* fonda, *f.*

restless, *adj.* inquieto

restore, *vt.* restaurar, restituir

restrain, vt, restringir

restrict, *vt.* restringir, limitar

result, *n.* resultado, *m.*; consecuencia, *f.*; *vi.* resultar

resurrect, *vt.* resucitar

retail, *n.* venta al por menor *f.*, menudeo, *m.*

retain, *vt.* retener, guardar

retire, *vt.* retirar; *vi.* retirarse, sustraerse

return, *vt.* devolver; *n.* retorno, *m.*; vuelta, *f.*

reunion, *n.* reunión, *f.*

Rev., Reverend, R., Reverendo

revelation, *n.* revelación, *f.*

reverend, *adj.* reverendo; venerable; *n.* sacerdote, *m.*

reverse, *n.* reverso (de una moneda), *m.*; revés, *m.*; *adj.* inverso; contrario

review, *n.* revista, *f.*; reseña, *f.*; repaso, *m.*; *vt.* (mil.) revistar; repasar

revise, *vt.* revisar

revoke, *vt.* revocar, anular

revolt, *vi.* rebelarse; *n.* rebelión, *f.*

revolting, *adj.* repugnante

revolution, *n.* revolución, *f.*

revolutionary, *n.* y *adj.* revolucionario, revolucionaria

revolve, *vi.* girar

revolver, *n.* revólver, *m.*, pistola, *f.*

reward, *n.* recompensa, *f.*; *vt.* recompensar

RFD, r.f.d., rural free delivery, distribución gratuita del correo en regiones rurales

rhinoceros, *n.* rinoceronte, *m.*

rhyme, *n.* rima, *f.*; *vi.* rimar

rhythm, *n.* ritmo, *m.*

rib, *n.* costilla, *f.*

riboflavin, *n.* riboflavina, *f.*

rice, *n.* arroz, *m.*

rich, *adj.* rico; opulento

riches, *n. pl.* riqueza, *f.*; bienes, *m. pl.*

rid, *vt.* librar, desembarazar

riddle, *n.* enigma, rompecabezas, *m.*

ride, *vi.* cabalgar; andar en coche; *n.* paseo a caballo o en coche

ridge, *n.* espinazo, lomo, *m.*; cordillera, *f.*

ridiculous, *adj.* ridículo

riding, *n.* paseo a caballo o en coche; *adj.* relativo a la equitación

rifle, *n.* fusil, *m.*

right, *adj.* derecho, recto; justo; *adv.* rectamente; **to be right,** tener razón; *n.* justicia, *f.*; derecho, *m.*; mano derecha, *f.*; (pol.) derecha, *f.*

ring, *n.* círculo, cerco, *m.*; anillo, *m.*; campaneo, *m.*; *vt.* sonar; **to ring the bell,** tocar la campanilla, tocar el timbre; *vi.* resonar

rinse, *vt.* enjuagar

riot, *n.* pelotera, *f.*; motín, *m.*

ripe, *adj.* maduro, sazonado

ripen, *vt.* y *vi.* madurar

rise, *vi.* levantarse; nacer, salir (los astros); rebelarse; ascender; *n.* levantamiento, *m.*; subida, *f.*; salida (del sol), *f.*

risen, *p. p.* del verbo **rise**

risk, *n.* riesgo, peligro, *m.*; *vt.* arriesgar

risky, *adj.* peligroso

rival, *n.* rival, *m.* y *f.*

river, *n.* río, *m.*

R.N., registered nurse, enfermera titulada, *f.*

RNA, ribonucleic acid, *n.* ácido ribonucleico

roach, *n.* cucaracha, *f.*

road, *n.* camino, *m.*

roar, *vi.* rugir; bramar; *n.* rugido, *m.*

roast, *vt.* asar

rob, *vt.* robar, hurtar

robber, *n.* ladrón, ladrona

robbery, *n.* robo, *m.*

robe, *n.* manto, *m.*; toga, *f.*

robin, *n.* (orn.) petirrojo, pechirrojo, pechicolorado, *m.*

rock, *n.* roca, *f.*; *vt.* mecer; arrullar; *vi.* balancearse

rock n' roll, rock-and-roll, *n.* música y baile popular, rock, *m.*

rocket, *n.* cohete, *m.*; **rocket launcher,** lanzacohetes, *m.*

rocky, *adj.* peñascoso, rocoso. roqueño

rode, *pretérito* del verbo ride

role, *n.* papel, *m.*, parte, *f.*

roll, *vt.* rodar; arrollar, enrollar; *vi.* rodar; girar; *n.* rollo, *m.*; lista, *f.*; panecillo, *m.*

Roman, *adj.* romano; manesco; *n.* y *adj.* romano, romana

romance, *n.* romance, cuento, *m.*; idilio, *m.*; aventura romántica, *f.*

romantic, *adj.* romántico; sentimental

roof, *n.* tejado, techo, *m.*; azotea, *f.*; paladar, *m.*

room, *n.* cuarto, *m.*, habitación, cámara, *f.*; lugar, espacio, *m.*

roommate, *n.* compañero o compañera de cuarto

roomy, *adj.* espacioso

rooster, *n.* gallo, *m.*

rope, *n.* cuerda, *f.*

rosary, *n.* rosario, *m.*

rose, *n.* (bot.) rosa, *f.*; color de rosa; *pretérito* del verbo rise

rotary engine, *n.* máquina rotativa, máquina alternativa

rotate, *vt.* y *vi.* girar, alternarse

rotten, *adj.* podrido, corrompido

rough, *adj.* áspero; brusco

round, *adj.* redondo

rout, *vt.* derrotar

route, *n.* ruta, vía, *f.*

routine, *n.* rutina, *f.*

row, *n.* riña, pelea, *f.*

row, *n.* hilera, fila, *f.*; *vt.* y *vi.* remar, bogar

rowboat, *n.* bote de remos *m.*

royal, *adj.* real; regio

royalty, *n.* realeza, *f.*; royalties, *n. pl.* regalías, *f. pl.*

R.R., railroad, f.c., ferrocarril; Right Reverend, Reverendísimo

R.S.V.P., please answer, sírvase enviar respuesta

rub, *vt.* frotar, restregar,

rubber, *n.* goma, *f.*, caucho, *m.*; rubbers, *n. pl.* chanclos, zapatos de goma, *m. pl.*; *adj.* de goma, de caucho

rubbish, *n.* basura, *f.*; desechos, *m. pl.*

ruby, *n.* rubí, *m.*

rude, *adj.* rudo, grosero

rug, *n.* alfombra, *f.*

ruin, *n.* ruina, *f.*; perdición, *f.*; *vt.* arruinar; echar a perder

rule, *n.* mando, *m.*; regla, *f.*; norma, *f.*; *vt.* y *vi.* gobernar; dirigir

ruler, *n.* gobernante, *m.*; regla, *f.*

Rumanian, *n.* y *adj.* rumano, rumana

rumba, *n.* rumba, *f.*

rumor, *n.* rumor, runrún, *m.*

run, *vi.* correr; fluir, manar

rural, *adj.* rural, rústico

rush, *n.* prisa, *f.*; *vi.* ir de prisa, apresurarse

Russia, Rusia

Russian, *n.* y *adj.* ruso, rusa

rusty, *adj.* mohoso, enmohecido

rut, *n.* rutina, *f.*; brama, *f.*

ruthless, *adj.* cruel

rye, *n.* centeno, *m.*

S

S.A., Salvation Army, Ejército de Salvación; South America, S.A., Sud América; South Africa, Sud Africa

sabotage, *n.* sabotaje, *m.*

saccharine, *n.* sacarina, *f.*

sack, *n.* saco, talego, *m.*

sacrament, *n.* sacramento, *m.*

sacred, *adj.* sagrado

sacrifice, *n.* sacrificio, *m.*; *vt.* y *vi.* sacrificar

sad, *adj.* triste

sadness, *n.* tristeza, *f.*

safe, *adj.* seguro; salvo; *n.* caja fuerte, *f.*

safeguard, *vt.* proteger

safety, *n.* seguridad, *f.*; safety pin, alfiler de gancho, imperdible, *m.*

sage, *n.* y *adj.* sabio, *m.*

sail, *n.* vela, *f.*; *vi.* navegar

sailboat, *n.* buque de vela, *m.*

sailor, *n.* marinero, *m.*

saint, *n.* santo, santa

sake, *n.* causa, razón, *f.*; amor,

m., consideración, *f.*

salad, *n.* ensalada, *f.*

salary, *n.* salario, sueldo, *m.*

sale, *n.* venta, *f.*; barata, *f.*

salesman, *n.* vendedor, *m.*

saliva, *n.* saliva, *f.*

saloon, *n.* cantina, taberna, *f.*

salt, *n.* sal, *f.*

salty, *adj.* salado

salute, *vt.* saludar; *n.* saludo, *m.*

salvation, *n.* salvación, *f.*

salve, *n.* ungüento, *m.*, pomada *f.*

sanatorium, *n.* sanatorio, *m.*

sanction, *n.* sanción, *vt.* sancionar

sandal, *n.* sandalia, *f.*

sandwich, *n.* sandwich, emparedado, *m.*

sane, *adj.* sano, sensato

sanetarium, *n.* sanatorio, *m.*

sanitary, *adj.* sanitario

sanity, *n.* cordura, *f.*

sap, *n.* savia, *f.*

sapphire, *n.* zafiro, *m.*

sarcasm, *n.* sarcasmo, *m.*

sarcastic, *adj.* sarcástico

sardine, *n.* sardina, *f.*

sat, *pretérito* y *p. p.* del verbo **sit**

Sat., Saturday, sáb. sábado

Satan, *n.* Satanás, *m.*

satin, *n.* raso, *m.*

satisfaction, *n.* satisfacción, *f.*

satisfactory, *adj.* satisfactorio

satisfy, *vt.* satisfacer

Saturday, *n.* sábado, *m.*

sauce, *n.* salsa, *f.*

sausage, *n.* salchicha, *f.*

save, *vt.* salvar; economizar

saving, *adj.* económico; **savings,** *n. pl.* ahorros, *m. pl.*

Saviour, *n.* Redentor, *m.*

saw, *n.* sierra, *f.*; *vt.* serrar; *pretérito* del verbo **see**

scaffold, *n.* andamio, *m.*

scald, *vt.* escaldar

scale, *n.* balanza, *f.*; báscula, *f.*; escala, *f.*; escama, *f.*; *vt.* escalar

scalp, *n.* cuero cabelludo, *m.*

scandal, *n.* escándalo, *m.*

Scandinavia, Escandinavia

scant, scanty, *adj.* escaso,

parco

scarce, *adj.* raro; **scarcely,** *adv.* apenas, escasamente

scare, *n.* susto, *m.*; *vt.* espantar

scarf, *n.* bufanda, *f.*

scarlet, *n.* y *adj.* escarlata, *f.*; **scarlet fever,** escarlatina, *f.*

scatter, *vt.* y *vi.* esparcir, derramarse

scene, *n.* escena, *f.*

scenery, *n.* vista, *f.*; (theat.) decoración, *f.*

schedule, *n.* plan, programa, *m.*

scheme, *n.* proyecto, plan, *m.*

scholar, *n.* estudiante, *m.* y *f.*; erudito, erudita

scholarly, *adj.* erudito

scholarship, *n.* beca, *f.*

school, *n.* escuela, *f.*; **high school,** escuela secundaria, *f.*

schoolteacher, *n.* maestro o maestra de escuela

science, *n.* ciencia, *f.*

scientific, *adj.* científico

scissors, *n. pl.* tijeras, *f. pl.*

scoff, *vi.* mofarse

scold, *vt.* y *vi.* regañar

scooter, *n.* patineta, *f.*

scope, *n.* alcance, *m.*

scorched, *adj.* chamuscado

score, *n.* veintena, *f.*; (mus.) partitura, *f.*; tanteo, *m.*; *vt.* tantear; calificar; *vi.* hacer tantos

scorn, *vt.* y *vi.* despreciar; *n.* desdén, menosprecio, *m.*

Scotland, Escocia

scoundrel, *n.* infame, *m.* y *f.*

scout, *n.* (mil.) centinela avanzada; **boy scout,** niño explorador; **girl scout,** niña exploradora; *vi.* (mil.) explorar

scrap, *n.* migaja, *f.*

scrapbook, *n.* álbum de recortes, *m.*

scrape, *vt.* y *vi.* raspar; arañar; *n.* dificultad, *f.*, lío, *m.*

scratch, *vt.* rascar, raspar; borrar

scream, *vi.* chillar; *n.* chillido, grito, *m.*

screen, *n.* tamiz, *m.*; biombo,

m.; pantalla, f.; vt. tamizar

screw, n. tomillo, m.; clavo de rosca, m.; **screw driver,** destornillador, m.; **to screw in,** atornillar

Scripture, n. Escritura Sagrada, f.

scuba, n. escafandra autónoma, f.

sculptor, n. escultor, m.

sculptress, n. escultora, f.

sculpture, n. escultura, f.

sea, n. mar, m. y f.; **sea plane,** hidroavión, m.

seal, n. sello, m.; (zool.) foca, f.; vt. sellar

seam, n. costura, f.

seamstress, n. costurera, f.

search, vt. examinar, registrar; escudriñar; busca, f.

seasick, adj. mareado

season, n. estación, f.; tiempo, m.; vt. sazonar

seasoning, n. condimento, m.

seat, n. silla, f.; localidad, f.

seat belt, n. cinturón de seguridad, cinturón de asiento

second, adj. segundo; n. segundo, m.; vt. apoyar

secondary, adj. secundario

secondhand, adj. de ocasión; de segunda mano

secrecy, n. secreto, m.

secret, n. secreto, m.; adj. privado

secretariat, n. secretaría, f.

secretary, n. secretario, secretaria

sect, n. secta, f.

section, n. sección, f.

secure, adj. seguro; salvo; vt. asegurar; conseguir

security, n. seguridad, f.; defensa, f.; fianza, f.

sedative, n. y adj. sedante, calmante, m.

seduce, vt. seducir

see, vt. y vi. ver, observar

seem, vi. parecer

seen, p. p. del verbo **see**

seep, vi. colarse, escurrirse

segregation, n. segregación, f.

seize, vt. agarrar, prender

seldom, adv. rara vez

select, vt. elegir, escoger; adj. selecto, escogido

selection, n. selección, f.

self, adj. propio, mismo

self-controlled, adj. dueño de sí mismo

self-defense, n. defensa propia, f.

self-denial, n. abnegación, f.

selfish, adj. egoísta

semester, n. semestre, m.

semicolon, n. punto y coma, m.

semifinal, adj. semifinal

semimonthly, adj. quincenal

seminary, n. seminario, m.

Sen., sen., Senate, senado; **Senator,** senador; **senior,** padre; socio más antiguo o más caracterizado

senate, n. senado, m.

senator, n. senador, m.

send, vt. enviar, mandar

senior, adj. mayor; n. estudiante de cuarto año, m.

seniority, n. antigüedad, f.

sense, n. sensatez, f.; **common sense,** sentido común, m.

sensible, adj. juicioso

sensitive, adj. sensible; sensitivo

sentence, n. sentencia, f.; (gram.) oración, f.; vt. sentenciar, condenar

sentiment, n. sentimiento, m.; opinión, f.

sentimental, adj. sentimental

separate, vt. y vi. separar; adj. separado

separation, n. separación, f.

September, n. septiembre, m.

serenade, n. serenata, f.; (Mex.) gallo, m.

serene, adj. sereno

serenity, n. serenidad, f.

series, n. serie, cadena, f.

serious, adj. serio, grave

sermon, n. sermon, m.

serpent, n. serpiente, f.

servant, n. criado, criada; sirviente, sirvienta

serve, vt. y vi. servir

service, n. servicio, m.; servidumbre, f.

session, n. sesión, f.

set, *vt.* poner, colocar, fijar; *vi.* ponerse (el sol o los astros); cuajarse; *n.* juego, *m.*, colección, *f.*

settle, *vt.* arreglar; calmar; solventar (deudas); *vi.* establecerse, radicarse; sosegarse

settlement, *n.* establecimiento, *m.*; liquidación, *f.*

seven, *n.* y *adj.* siete, *m.*

seventeen, *adj.* y *n.* diez y siete, diecisiete, *m.*

seventeenth, *adj.* décimoséptimo

seventh, *adj.* séptimo

seventy, *n.* y *adj.* setenta, *m.*

several, *adj.* diversos, varios

severe, *adj.* severo

sew, *vt.* y *vi.* coser

sewage, *n.* inmundicias, *f. pl.*; **sewage system**, alcantarillado, *m.*

sewer, *n.* cloaca, alcantarilla, *f.*; caño, *m.*

sewing, *n.* costura, *f.*; **sewing machine**, máquina de coser, *f.*

sex, *n.* sexo, *m.*

sexual, *adj.* sexual

shabby, *adj.* destartalado

shack, *n.* choza, cabaña, *f.*

shade, *n.* sombra, *f.*; matiz, *m.*

shadow, *n.* sombra, *f.*

shady, *adj.* opaco; sospechoso

shake, *vt.* sacudir; agitar; *vi.* temblar; **to shake hands**, darse las manos; *n.* sacudida, *f.*

shape, *vt.* y *vi.* formar; *n.* forma, figura, *f.*

share, *n.* parte, cuota, *f.*; (com.) acción, *f.*; participación, *f.*; *vt.* y *vi.* compartir

shark, *n.* tiburón, *m.*

sharp, *adj.* agudo, astuto; afilado; *n.* (mus.) sostenido, *m.*; **two o'clock sharp**, las dos en punto

sharpener, *n.* afilador, amolador, *m.*; **pencil sharpener**, tajalápices, *m.*

shatter, *vt.* y *vi.* destrozar, estrellar

shawl, *n.* chal, mantón, *m.*

she, *pron.* ella

sheep, *n. sing.* y *pl.* oveja(s), *f.*; carnero, *m.*

sheepish, *adj.* timido, cortado

sheet, *n.* pliego (de papel), *m.*; **bed sheet**, sábana, *f.*

shell, *n.* cáscara, *f.*; concha, *f.*; *vt.* descascarar, descortezar

shelter, *n.* asilo, refugio, *m.*

shepherd, *n.* pastor, *m.*

sheriff, *n.* alguacil, *m.*, funcionario administrativo de un condado

sherry, *n.* jerez, *m.*

shield, *n.* escudo, *m.*; *vt.* defender; amparar

shift, *vt.* y *vt.* cambiarse; ingeniarse; *n.* tanda, *f.*

shin, *n.* espinilla, *f.*

shine, *vi.* lucir, brillar; *vt.* dar lustre (a los zapatos , etc.); *n.* brillo, *m.*

shining, *adj.* reluciente

shiny, *adj.* brillante

ship, *n.* buque, barco, *m.*; *vt.* embarcar; expedir

shipment, *n.* embarque, *m.*, remesa, *f.*

shirk, *vt.* esquivar, evitar

shirt, *n.* camisa, *f.*

shock, *n.* choque, *m.*; conmoción, *f.*; *vt.* chocar; sacudir; conmover; **shock absorber**, amortiguador, *m.*

shocking, *adj.* ofensivo

shoe, *n.* zapato, *m.*

shoemaker, *n.* zapatero, *m.*

shone, *pretérito* y *p. p.* del verbo **shine**

shop, *n.* tienda, *f.*; *vt.* hacer compras

shopping, *n.* compras, *f. pl.*

short, *adj.* corto; conciso

shorten, *vt.* acortar; abreviar

shortening, *n.* acortamiento, *m.*; manteca o grasa vegetal, *f.*

shorthand, *n.* taquigrafia, *f.*

shorts, *n. pl.* calzoncillos, *m. pl.*; pantalones cortos, *m. pl.*

shortsighted, *adj.* miope

shot, *n.* tiro, *m.*

shotgun, *n.* escopeta, *f.*

should, *subj.* y *condicional* de **shall**; usase como auxiliar de otros verbos

shoulder, *n.* hombro, *m.*
shout, *vi.* aclamar; gritar
shovel, *n.* pala, *f.*
show, *vt.* mostrar, enseñar, probar; *n.* espectáculo, *m.* función, *f.*
shower, *n.* aguacero, *m.*; *vi.* llover; *vt.* derramar profusamente
shrank, *pretérito* del verbo **shrink**
shred, *n.* triza, *f.*; jirón, *m.*; *vt.* picar, rallar
shrimp, *n.* camarón, *m.*
shrink, *vi.* encogerse
shrunk, *p. p.* del verbo **shrink**
shudder, *vi.* estremecerse
shut, *vt.* cerrar, encerrar
shy, *adj.* tímido
sick *adj.* malo, enfermo
sickly, *adj.* enfermizo
sickness, *n.* enfermedad, *f.*
side, *n.* lado, *m.*; costado, *m.*; facción, *f.*; partido, *m.*; *adj.* lateral
sidewalk, *n.* banqueta, acera, *f.*
sideways, *adv.* de lado
sift, *vt.* cerner; cribar
sigh, *vi.* suspirar, gemir; *n.* suspiro, *m.*
sign, *n.* señal, *f.*, indigo, *m.*; signo, *m.*; letrero, *m.*; *vt.* y *vi.* firmar
signal, *n.* señal, seña, *f.*
signature, *n.* firma, *f.*
significance, *n.* importancia, significación, *f.*
silence, *n.* silencio, *m.*
silent, *adj.* silencioso
silk, *n.* seda, *f.*
silkscreen, *n.* serigrafía, *f.*
silky, *adj.* sedoso
sill, *n.* alfeiza, *f.*
silly, *adj.* tonto, bobo
silver, *n.* plata, *f.*
silvery, *adj.* plateado
similar, *adj.* similar
simple, *adj.* simple
simplicity, *n.* simplicidad, *f.*
simplify, *vt.* simplificar
simply, *adv.* simplemente
simultaneous, *adj.* simultáneo
sin, *n.* pecado, *m.*, culpa, *f.*; *vi.*

pecar, faltar
since, *adv.* desde entonces; *conj.* puesto que; *prep.* desde, después
sincere, *adj.* sincere, franco
sincerity, *n.* sinceridad, *f.*
sinew, *n.* tendón, *m.*
sinful, *adj.* pecaminoso
sing, *vt.* y *vi.* cantar
singe, *vt.* chamuscar
singer, *n.* cantante, *m.* y *f.*
singing, *n.* canto, *m.*
single, *adj.* solo; soltero, soltera
sink, *vt.* y *vi.* hundir; *n.* fregadero, *m.*
sinner, *n.* pecador, pecadora
sinus, *n.* seno (cavidad) *m.*
sip, *vt.* y *vi.* sorber; *n.* sorbo, *m.*
sir, *n.* señor, *m.*
siren, *n.* sirena, *f.*
sister, *n.* hermana, *f.*
sister-in-law, *n.* cuñada, *f.*
sit, *vi.* sentarse
situation, *n.* situación, *f.*
six, *n.* y *adj.* seis, *m.*
sixteen, *n.* y *adj.* diez y seis, dieciseis
sixteenth, *adj.* y *n.* décimosexto, *m.*
sixth, *n.* y *adj.* sexto, *m.*
sixty, *n.* y *adj.* sesenta, *m.*
size, *n.* tamaño, *m.*, talla, *f.*
sizzle, *vi.* chamuscar
skate, *n.* patín, *m.*; **ice skate,** patín de hielo, *m.*; **roller skate,** patín de ruedas, *m.*; *vi.* patinar
skeleton, *n.* esqueleto, *m.*; **skeleton key,** llave maestra, *f.*
sketch, *n.* esbozo, *m.*; bosquejo, *m.*; *vt.* bosquejar, esbozar
skill, *n.* destreza, pericia, *f.*
skillet, *n.* cazuela, sartén, *f.*
skillful, skilful, *adj.* práctico, diestro
skin, *n.* cutis, *m.*; piel, *f.*
skinny, *adj.* flaco
skip, *vi.* saltar, brincar; *vt.* pasar, omitir; *n.* salto, brinco, *m.*
skunk, *n.* zorrillo, zorrino, *m.*
sky, *n.* cielo, *m.*

skylight, n. claraboya, f.

skyscraper, n. rascacielos, m.

slander, vt. calumniar, infamar; n. calumnia, f.

slang, n. vulgarismo, m.

slap, n. manotada, f.; **slap on the face**, bofetada, f.; vt. dar una bofetada

slave, n. esclavo, esclava

slavery, n. esclavitud, f.

slay, vt. matar

slayer, n. asesino, m.

sleep, vi. dormir; n. sueño, m.

sleepless, adj. desvelado

sleepy, adj. soñoliento

sleet, n. cellisca, aguanieve, f.

sleeve, n. manga, f.

sleeveless, adj. sin mangas

slender, adj. delgado

slice, n. rebanada, f.; vt. rebanar, tajar

slide, vt. correr; vi. deslizarse; n. diapositiva, f.; **slide projector**, linterna de proyección, f.

slight, adj. leve; n. desaire, m.; vt. desairar

slim, adj. delgado, sutil

sling, n. honda, f.

slip, n. resbalón, m.; enagua, f.; vi. resbalar

slipper, n. zapatilla, f.

sloppy, adj. desaliñado

slot, n. hendedura, f.

slow, adj. tardío, lento; adv. despacio

slums, n. pl. barrios bajos, m. pl.; viviendas escuálidas, f. pl.

slumber, vi. dormitar; n. sueño ligero

slush, n. lodo, cieno, m.

sly, adj. astuto; furtivo

small, adj. pequenño, chico

smallpox, n. viruelas, f. pl.

smart, adj. inteligente; elegante

smear, vt. manchar; calumniari,

smell, vt. y vi. oler; olfatear; n. olfato, m.; olor, m.; hediondez, f.

smile, vi. sonreir, sonreirse; n. sonrisa, f.

smoke, n. humo, m.; vt. y vi. ahumar; fumar (tabaco)

smooth, adj. liso, pulido

smother, vt. sofocar

smuggling, n. contrabando, m.

snake, n. culebra, f.

snap, vt. y vi. romper; chasquear

snappy, adj. vivaz, animado

snapshot, n. instantánea, fotografía, f.

snare, n. trampa, f.

snarl, vi. enredar

snatch, vt. arrebatar

sneeze, vi. estornudar; n. estornudo, m.

sniff, vt. olfatear

snoop, vi. espiar, acechar

snooze, vi. dormitar

snore, vi. roncar

snow, n. nieve, f.; vi. nevar

snowfall, n. nevada, f.

snowflake, n. copo de nieve, m.

snowmobile, n. vehículo automotor para marchar sobre la nieve

snowshoe, n. raqueta de nieve, f.

so, adv. asi; tal

So., South, S., Sur

soak, vt. y vi. remojar

soap, n. jabón, m.

soar, vi. remontarse

sob, n. sollozo, m.; vi. sollozar

sober, adj. sobrio; serio

soccer, n. futbol, m.

sociable, adj. sociable

social, adj. social; sociable; **social worker**, asistente social

socialism, n. socialismo, m.

socialize, vt. socializar; **socialized medicine**, medicina estatal

society, n. sociedad, f.; compañía, f.

sociology, n. sociología, f.

sock, n. calcetín, m.

socket, n. enchufe, m.; cuenca (del ojo), f.

sod, n. césped, m.; tierra, f.

soda, n. sosa, soda, f.; **baking soda**, bicarbonato de sosa o de soda

sofa, n. sofá, m.

soft, *adj.* blando, suave

soft-boiled, *adj.* pasado por agua

soften, *vt.* ablandar

soggy, *adj.* empapado

soil, *vt.* ensuciar, emporcar; *n.* tierra, *f.*

solar, *adj.* solar; **solar battery,** batería solar; **solar energy,** energía solar

sold, *p. p.* vendido

soldier, *n.* soldado, *m.*

sole, *n.* planta, *f.*; suela, *f.*; *adj.* único, solo

solicit, *vt.* solicitar; pedir

solid, *adj.* sólido, compacto; entero; *n.* sólido, *m.*

solid-fuel space rocket, *n.* cohete especial de combustible sólido, *m.*

solitary, *adj.* solitario

solitude, *n.* soledad, *f.*

solo, *n.* y *adj.* solo, *m.*

solve, *vt.* resolver, solucionar

some, *adj.* algún; cierto; algo de

somebody, *pron.* alguno, alguna

somehow, *adv.* de algún modo

something, *n.* alguna cosa; algo, *m.*; **something else,** alguna otra cosa

sometimes, *adv.* a veces

somewhere, *adv.* en alguna parte

son, *n.* hijo, *m.*

sonic barrier, *n.* obstáculo sonic *m.*

sonic boom, *n.* trueno sónico, estrépito sónico, *m.*

son-in-law, *n.* yerno, *m.*

soothe, *vt.* calmar, sosegar

sophisticated, *adj.* refinado; complicado

soprano, *n.* soprano, tiple, *m.* y *f.*

sore, *n.* llaga, úlcera, *f.*; *adj.* doloroso penoso; (coll.) enojado, resentido

sorority, *n.* hermandad de mujeres, *f.*

sorry, *adj.* triste; afligido

soul, *n.* alma, *f.*; esencia, *f.*

sound, *adj.* sano; entero; *n.* sonido, *m.*; *vt.* sondar; *vi.* so-

nar, resonar

soup, *n.* sopa, *f.*

sour, *adj.* agrio, ácido; *vt.* y *vi.* agriar, agriarse

south, *n.* sur, sud, *m.*

southeast, *n.* sureste, sudeste, *m.*

southern, *adj.* meridional

southwest, *n.* sudoeste, *m.*

souvenir, *n.* recuerdo, *m.*

sovereign, *n.* y *adj.* soberano, soberana

soviet, *n.* soviet, *m.*

sow, *n.* puerca, marrana, *f.*

sow, *vt.* sembrar, sementar

soybean, *n.* soya, *f.*

space, *n.* espacio, *m.*; lugar, *m.*; **space capsule,** cabina espacial; **space travel,** viajes espaciales o siderales

spaceship, *n.* astronave, *f.*

spacious, *adj.* espacioso

spade, *n.* azadón, *m.*; espada (naipe),

Spain, España, *f.*

span, *n.* espacio, trecho, *m.*

Spaniard, *n.* y *adj.* español, española

Spanish, *adj.* español

spank, *vt.* pegar, dar nalgadas

spare, *vt.* y *vi.* ahorrar, evitar; *adj.* de reserva; **spare time,** tiempo desocupado; **spare tire,** neumático o llanta de repuesto

spark, *n.* chispa, *f.*

spat, *n.* riña, *f.*; *vi.* reñir

spats, *n. pl.* polainas, *f. pl.*

speak, *vt.* y *vi.* hablar

speaker, *n.* orador, oradora

spear, *n.* lanza, *f.*; pica, *f.*

spearmint, *n.* hierbabuena, *f.*

special, *adj.* especial

specialize, *vt.* y *vi.* especializar

specimen, *n.* muestra, *f.*

spectacle, *n.* espectáculo, *m.*; **spectacles,** *n. pl.* anteojos, espejuelos, *m. pl.*

spectacular, *adj.* espectacular

spectator, *n.* espectador, espectadora

speculate, *vi.* especular

speech, *n.* habla, *f.*; discurso, *m.*

speechless, *adj.* sin habla

speed, *n.* rapidez, *f.*; *vt.* apresurar; *vi.* darse prisa

speedy, *adj.* veloz

spell, *n.* hechizo, encanto, *m.*; *vt.* y *vi.* deletrear

spelling, *n.* ortografía, *f.*; deletreo, *m.*

spend, *vt.* gastar; consumir

spendihrift, *n.* botarate, *m.* y *f.*

sphere, *n.* esfera, *f.*

spider, *n.* araña, *f.*

spill, *vt.* derramar, verter

spin, *vt.* hilar; *vt.* y *vi.* girar; *n.* vuelta, *f.*; paseo, *m.*

spinach, *n.* espinaca, *f.*

spinal, *adj.* espinal; **spinal column,** columna vertebral, espina dorsal, *f.*

spine, *n.* espina, *f.*

spiral, *adj.* espiral

spirit, *n.* espíritu, *m.*; ánimo, valor, *m.*; fantasma, *m.*

spirited, *adj.* vivo, brioso

spiritual, *adj.* espiritual

spit, *vt.* y *vi.* escupir

spite, *n.* rencor, *m.*; **in spite of,** a pesar de

spiteful, *adj.* rencoroso

splash, *vt.* salpicar

splendid, *adj.* espléndido

splint, *n.* astilla, *f.*; **splints,** *n. pl.* tablillas para entablillar

splinter, *n.* astilla, *f.*

split, *vt.* y *vi.* hender, rajar; *n.* hendidura, raja, *f.*

spleen, *n.* bazo, *m.*; esplín, *m.*

spoil, *vt.* y *vi.* dañar; pudrir; mimar demasiado; **spoils,** *n. pl.* despojo, botín, *m.*

spoke, *n.* rayo de rueda, *m.*; *pretérito* del verbo **speak**

sponsor, *n.* fiador, *m.*; padrino, *m.*; garante, *m.* y *f.*; anunciante (de un programa de radio, etc.), *m.*

spontaneous, *adj.* espontáneo

spool, *n.* bobina, carrete, carretel, *m.*

spoon, *n.* cuchara, *f.*

spoonful, *n.* cucharada, *f.*

sport, *n.* recreo, pasatiempo, *m.*; deporte, *m.*

sportsman, *n.* deportista, *m.*

spot, *n.* mancha, *f.*; sitio, lugar, *m.*; *vt.* manchar

spotless, *adj.* sin mancha

spotlight, *n.* proyector, *m.*

spouse, *n.* esposo, esposa

sprain, *vt.* dislocar; *n.* torcedura, *f.*

sprang, *pretérito* del verbo **spring**

spray, *vt.* rociar, pulverizar

spread, *vt.* y *vi.* extender; *n.* sobrecama, colcha, *f.*

spring, *vi.* brotar; provenir; saltar, brincar; *n.* primavera, *f.*; elasticidad, *f.*; muelle, resorte, *m.*

sprinkle, *vt.* rociar; salpicar; *vi.* lloviznar

spur, *n.* espuela, *f.*; **on the spur of the moment,** en un impulso repentino; *vt.* estimular

sputnik, *n.* sputnik, *m.*, satélite artificial

spy, *n.* espía, *m.* y *f.*; *vt.* y *vi.* espiar

sq., square, cuadrado, *m.*; plaza, *f.*

squabble, *vi.* reñir; *n.* riña, *f.*

squander, *vt.* malgastar

square, *adj.* cuadrado; equitativo; *n.* cuadro, *m.*; plaza, *f.*; *vt.* cuadrar; ajustar

squaw, *n.* mujer india de E.U.A

squeal, *vi.* gritar; delatar

squeeze, *vt.* apretar, estrechar; *n.* abrazo, *m.*; apretón, *m.*

squirrel, *n.* ardilla, *f.*

S.S., steamship, v., vapor; **Sunday School,** escuela dominical

St., Saint, Sto., San, Santo; Sta., Santa; **Strait,** Estrecho; **Street,** Calle

stable, *n.* establo, *m.*; *adj.* estable

stadium, *n.* estadio, *m.*

staff, *n.* báculo, palo, *m.*; personal, *m.*

stag, *n.* ciervo, *m.*; **stag party,** tertulia para hombres, *f.*

stage, *n.* escenario, *m.*; teatro, *m.*, las tablas, *f. pl.*; *vt.* poner en escena

stagecoach, n. diligencia, f.

stagger, vi. vacilar, titubear; vt. escalonar, alternar

stainless, adj. limpio, inmaculado; inoxidable

stair, n. escalón, m.; **stairs,** n. pl. escalera, f.

stairway, n. escalera, f.

stake, n. estaca, f.; vt. apostar; arriesgar

stale, adj. viejo, rancio

stamina, n. resistencia, f.

stamp, vt. patear, dar golpes (con los pies); estampar, imprimir, sellar; n. sello, m.; estampa, f.; timbre, m.; **postage stamp,** sello de correo, m.

stand, vi. estar en pie o derecho; sostenerse; resistir; pararse; n. puesto, sitio, m.; tarima, f.

standard, n. norma, f.; **standard of living,** nivel o norma de vida; adj. normal

starch, n. almidón, m.; vt. almidonar

stare, vt. clavar la vista; n. mirada fija, f.

start, vi. sobrecogerse, estremecerse; vt. comenzar; n. sobresalto, m.; principio, m.

starter, n. iniciador, iniciadora; (auto.) arranque, m.

starve, vi. perecer de hambre

state, n. estado, m.; condición, f.; vt. declarar

statement, n. estado de cuenta, m.; declaración, f.

stateroom, n. camarote, m.; compartimiento, m.

statesman, n. estadista, m.

station, n. estación, **station wagon,** camioneta, f.

stationary, adj. estacionario, fijo

stationery, n. papel de escribir, m.

statistics, n. pl. estadística, f.

statue, n. estatua, f.

staunch, adj. firme; fiel

stay, n. permanencia, f.; vi. quedarse, permanecer

steady, adj. firme, fijo

steak, n. bistec, m.

steam, n. vapor, m.; **steamroller,** apisonadora, f.

steamship, n. vapor, m.

steep, adj. empinado

steeple, n. campanario, m.

steer, n. novillo, m.; vt. guiar, dirigir

stenographer, n. taquígrafo, taquígrafa, estenógrafo, estenógrafa; mecanógrafo, mecanógrafa

stenography, n. taquigrafía, estenografía,

step, n. paso, escalón, m.; trámite, m.; gestión, f.; vi. dar un paso; andar; vt. pisar

stepbrother, n. medio hermano, hermanastro, m.

stepdaughter, n. hijastra, f.

stepfather, n. padrastro, m.

stepladder, n. escalera de mano, f.

stepmother, n. madrastra, f.

stepson, n. hijastro, m.

stereophonic, adj. estereofónico, estereofónica

sterling, adj. genuino, verdadero; **sterling silver,** plata esterlina,

stern, adj. austero, severo; n. (naut.) popa, f.

stew, vt. guisar; n. guisado, guiso, m.

streward, n. mayordomo, m.

stewardess, n. (avi.) azafata, aeromoza, f.

stick, palo, bastón, m.; vi. pegarse

sticky, adj. pegajoso

stiff, adj. tieso; rígido

stifle, vt. sofocar

still, vt. aquietar, aplacar; destilar; adj. silencioso, tranquilo; adv. todavía; no obstante

stilt, n. zanco, m.

stimulate, vt. estimular

stimulation, n. estímulo, m.

sting, vt. picar o morder (un insecto); n. aguijón m.

stingy, adj. tacaño, avaro

stipulate, vt. y vi. estipular

stir, vt. agitar; revolver; incitar

stirring, adj. emocionante

stitch, vt. coser; n. puntada,

f.; punto, *m.*

stock, *n.* linaje, *m.*; (com.) capital, principal, *m.*; (com.) acción, *f.*; ganado, *m.*; proveer, abastecer

stockholder, *n.* accionista, *m.* y *f.*

stole, *n.* estola, *f.*; *pretérito* del verbo **steal**

stomach, *n.* estómago, *m.*

stone, *n.* piedra, *f.*; hueso de fruta, *m.*; *vt.* apedrear; deshuesar

stood, *pretérito* y *p. p.* del verbo **stand**

stool, *n.* banquillo, *m.*; evacuación, *f.*

stop, *vt.* cesar, suspender, *vi.* pararse, hacer alto; *n.* parada, *f.*

store, *n.* almacén, *m.*; *vt.* proveer, abastecer

storeroom, *n.* deposito, *m.*

stork, *n.* cigüeña,

storm, *n.* tempestad, *f.*; *vi.* haber tormenta

stormy, *adj.* tempestuoso

story, *n.* cuento, *m.*; piso de una casa, *m.*

straight, *adj.* derecho, recto; *adv.* directamente, en línea recta

straighten, *vt.* enderezar

strain, *vt.* colar, filtrar; *vi.* esforzarse; *n.* tensión, tirantez, *f.*

strainer, *n.* colador, *m.*

strange, *adj.* extraño; raro

stranger, *n.* extranjero, extranjera

strap, *n.* correa, *f.*

strategy, *n.* estrategia, *f.*

strawberry, *n.* fresa; (Sp. Am.) frutilla, *f.*

stray, *vi.* extraviarse

stream, *n.* arroyo, *m.*; corriente, *f.*

streamline, *vt.* simplificar

street, *n.* calle, *f.*

streetcar, *n.* tranvía, *m.*

strength, *n.* fuerza, *f.*

strengthen, *vt.* reforzar

strenuous, *adj.* estrenuo

stress, *n.* fuerza, *f.*; acento, *m.*; tensión *f.*; *vt.* acentuar, dar

énfasis

stretch, *vt.* y *vi.* tirar; extenderse

stretcher, *n.* estirador, *m.*; camilla, *f.*

strict, *adj.* estricto, riguroso

stride, *n.* tranco, *m.*; adelanto, avance, *m.*; *vt.* cruzar, pasar por encima; *vi.* andar a pasos largos

strike, *vt.* y *vi.* golpear; declararse en huelga

striking, *adj.* llamativo

string, *n.* cordón, *m.*; cuerda, *f.*; hilera, *f.*; **string bean,** habichuela verde, judía, *f.*, (Mex.) ejote, *m.*

strip, *n.* tira, faja, *f.*; *vt.* desnudar, despojar

stripe, *n.* raya, lista, *f.*

striped, *adj.* rayado

stroboscope, *n.* estroboscopio, *m.*

stroke, *n.* golpe, *m.*; caricia, *f.*; *vt.* acariciar

stroll, *vi.* vagar, pasearse, *m.*

strong, *adj.* fuerte

structure, *n.* edificio, *m.*

struggle, *n.* lucha, *f.*; *vi.* luchar

stubborn, *adj.* testarudo

student, *n.* estudiante, estudianta, alumno, alumna

studio couch, *n.* sofá cama

study, *n.* estudio, *m.*; gabinete, *m.*; *vt.* estudiar

stuff, *n.* materia, *f.*; *vt.* llenar; rellenar; *vi.* abracarse; tragar

stuffing, *n.* relleno, *m.*

stumble, *vt.* tropezar

stupendous, *adj.* estupendo

stupid, *adj.* estúpido

stupidity, *n.* estupidez, *f.*

sturdy, *adj.* fuerte, robusto

style, *n.* estilo, *m.*; moda, *f.*

stylish, *adj.* elegante, de moda

subconscious, *adj.* subconsciente

subject, *n.* tema, tópico, *m.*; asignatura, *f.*; *adj.* sujeto, sometido a; *vt.* sujetar, someter

submarine, *n.* y *adj.* submarino, *m.*

submerge, *vt.* sumergir

submission, *n.* sumisión, *f.*

submit, *vt.* someter, rendir

subordinate, *n.* y *adj.* subalterno, *m.*; *vt.* subordinar

subscribe, *vt.* y *vi.* suscribir

subscriber, *n.* suscriptor, suscriptora, abonado, abonada

subscription, *n.* suscripción, *f.*, abono, *m.*

subsequent, *adj.* subsiguiente, subsecuente

subsist, *vi.* subsistir; existir

substance, *n.* sustancia, *f.*

substantive, *n.* sustantivo, *m.*

substitute, *vt.* sustituir; *n.* suplente, *m.*

substitution, *n.* sustitución, *f.*

subtle, *adj.* sutil

subtract, *vt.* sustraer; restar

subtraction, *n.* sustracción, *f.*; resta, *f.*

suburb, *n.* suburbio, *m.*

suburban, *adj.* suburbano

subway, *n.* túnel, *m.*; ferrocarril subterráneo, *m.*

sucaryl, *n.* nombre comercial de un compuesto ezucarado parecido a la sacarina

succeed, *vt.* y *vi.* lograr, tener éxito; seguir

success, *n.* buen éxito, *m.*

successful, *adj.* próspero, dichoso; **to be successful,** tener buen éxito

succession, sucesión, *f.*; herencia, *f.*

successor, *n.* sucesor, sucesora

such, *adj.* y *pron.* tal, semejante

sudden, *adj.* repentino; **suddenly,** *adv.* de repente

sue, *vt.* y *vi.* demandar, poner pleito

suffer, *vt.* y *vi.* sufrir

suffice, *vt.* y *vi.* bastar

sufficient, *adj.* suficiente

suffocate, *vt.* y *vi.* sofocar

sufrage, *n.* sufragio, voto, *m.*

sugar, *n.* azúcar, *m.* y *f.*

suicide, *n.* suicidio, *m.*; suicida, *m.* y *f.*

suit, *n.* vestido, *m.*; traje, *m.*; pleito, *m.*; *vt.* y *vi.* adaptar; ajustarse; *vt.* sentar, caer bien

suitable, *adj.* adecuado

suitcase, *n.* maleta, *f.*

sulky, *adj.* malhumorado

sulphur, *n.* azufre, *m.*

sum, *n.* suma, *f.*

summary, *n.* sumario, *m.*

summer, *n.* verano, *m.*

summertime, *n.* verano, *m.*

summit, *n.* cumbre, *f.*

summon, *vt.* citar, convocar

sun, *n.* sol, *m.*

sunbeam, *n.* rayo de sol, *m.*

Sunday, *n.* domingo, *m.*

sunflower, *n.* girasol, *m.*

sung, *p. p.* del verbo **sing**

sunken, del verbo **sink**

sunlight, *n.* luz del sol, *f.*

sunny, *adj.* asoleado; alegre

sunrise, *n.* salida del sol, *f.*

sunset, *n.* ocaso, *m.*

sunshine, *n.* luz del sol, *f.*

sunstroke, *n.* insolación, *f.*

superb, *adj.* excelente

superhighway, *n.* supercarretera, *f.*

superhuman, *adj.* sobrehumano

superintendent, *n.* superintendente, mayordomo, *m.*

superior, *n.* y *adj.* superior, *m.*

superiority, *n.* superioridad, *f.*

superlative, *adj.* y *n.* superlativo, *m.*

superman, *n.* superhombre, *m.*

supermarket, *n.* supermercado, *m.*

supernatural, *adj.* sobrenatural

superpower, *n.* superpotencia, *f.*

superstitious, *adj.* supersticioso

supervise, *vt.* inspeccionar

supervision, *n.* dirección, inspección, *f.*

supervisor, *n.* superintendente, *m.* y *f.*; inspector, inspectora

supper, *n.* cena, *f.*

supply, *vt.* suplir, proporcionar; *n.* surtido, *m.*; provisión, *f.*; **supply and demand,** oferta y demanda

support, *vt.* sostener; soportar; basar; *n.* sustento, *m.*; apoyo, *m.*

suppose, *vt.* suponer

supposition, *n.* suposición, *f.*, supuesto, *m.*

suppress, *vt.* suprimir; reprimir

supremacy, *n.* supremacia, *f.*

supreme, *adj.* supremo

Supt., supt., superintendent, super.^{te}, superintendente

sure, *adj.* seguro, cierto; **surely,** *adv.* sin duda

surgeon, *n.* cirujano, *m.*

surgery, *n.* cirugía, *f.*

surgical, *adj.* quirúrgico

surname, *n.* apellido, *m.*

surplus, *n.* sobrante, *m.*

surprise, *vt.* sorprender; *n.* sorpresa, *f.*

surprising, *adj.* sorprendente

surrender, *vt.* y *vi.* rendir; renunciar; *n.* rendición, *f.*

surround, *vt.* circundar, rodear

surroundings, *n. pl.* cercanías, *f. pl.*; ambiente, *m.*

survey, *vt.* inspeccionar, examinar; *n.* inspección, *f.*; apeo (de tierras), *m.*

surveying, *n.* agrimensura, *f.*

survive, *vi.* sobrevivir

survivor, *n.* sobreviviente, *m.* y *f.*

susceptible, *adj.* susceptible

suspect, *vt.* y *vi* sospechar

suspend, *vt.* suspender, colgar

suspenders, *n. pl.* tirantes, *m. pl.*

suspense, *n.* incertidumbre, *f.*

suspicion, *n.* sospecha, *f.*

suspicious, *adj.* sospechoso

sustain, *vt.* sostener, sustentar

sustenance, *n.* sostenimiento, sustento, *m.*

SW, S.W., s.w., southwest, SO., Sudoeste

swallow, *n.* golondrina, *f.*; bocado, *m.*; *vt.* tragar

swam, *pretérito* del verbo **swim**

swan, *n.* cisne, *m.*

swap, *vt.* y *vi.* (coll.) cambalachear, cambiar

swarm, *n.* enjambre, *m.*; gentío, *m.*

swear, *vt.* y *vi.* jurar; juramentar

sweat, *n.* sudor, *m.*; *vt.* sudar; trasudar

sweater, *n.* suéter, *m.*

Sweden, Suecia

sweet, *adj.* dulce; grato

sweeten, *vt.* endulzar

sweetheart, *n.* novio, novia

sweetness, *n.* dulzura, *f.*

swell, *vi.* hincharse; *adj.* (coll.) espléndido

swelling, *n.* hinchazón, *f.*

swelter, *vi.* ahogarse de calor

swim, *vi.* nadar

swimming, *n.* natación, *f.*

swindle, *vt.* estafar; *n.* estafa, *f.*, petardo, *m.*

swing, *vi.* balancear, oscilar; mecerse; columpio, *m.*

switch, *n.* (elec.) interruptor, conmutador, *m.*; *vt.* desviar

switchboard, *n.* conmutador telefónico, *m.*

Switzerland, Suiza

swivel, *vt.* y *vi.* girar

swollen, *adj.* hinchado, inflado

sword, *n.* espada, *f.*

swordfish, *n.* pez espada, *m.*

swore, *pretérito* del verbo **swear**

sworn, *p. p.* del verbo **swear**

syllable, *n.* sílaba, *f.*

symbol, *n.* símbolo, *m.*

symbolic, *adj.* simbólico

sympathize, *vi.* simpatizar

sympathy, *n.* compasión, condolencia, *f.*; simpatía, *f.*

symphony, *n.* sinfonía, *f.*

symptom, *n.* síntoma, *m.*

syndicate, *n.* sindicato, *m.*

synonym, *n.* sinónimo, *m.*

synopsis, *n.* sinopsis, *f.*

synthesis, *n.* síntesis,

synthetic, *adj.* sintético

syrup, *n.* jarabe, *m.*

system, *n.* sistema, *m.*

T

table, *n.* mesa, *f.*

tablecloth, *n.* mantel, *m.*

tablespoon, *n.* cuchara, *f.*

tablespoonful, *n.* cucharada, *f.*

tablet, *n.* tableta, *f.*; pastilla, *f.*; (med.) oblea, *f.*

taboo, tabu, *n.* tabú, *m.*: *adj.* prohibido

tact, *n.* tacto, *m.*

tactful, *adj.* prudente

tactics, *n. pl.* táctica, *f.*

tactless, *adj.* sin tacto

taffeta, *n.* tafetán, *m.*

tail, *n.* cola, *f.*, rabo, *m.*

tailor, *n.* sastre, *m.*

take, *vt.* tomar, coger, asir

talcum, *n.* talco, *m.*

tale, *n.* cuento, *m.*

talent, *n.* talento, *m.*; ingenio, *m.*; capacidad, *f.*

talk, *vi.* hablar, conversar; *n.* plática, charla, *f.*

tall, *adj.* alto, elevado

tallow, *n.* sebo, *m.*

tambourine, *n.* pandereta, *f.*

tame, *adj.* domesticado; manso; *vt.* domesticar

tang, *n.* sabor, *m.*

tangerine, *n.* mandarina *f.*

tangle, *vt.* y *vi.* enredar, embrollar

tango, *n.* tango, *m.*

tank, *n.* (mil) tanque, *m.*

tantalizing, *adj.* atormentador

tap, *vt.* tocar o golpear ligeramente; *n.* palmada suave, *f.*; **tap dance**, baile zapateado (de E. U. A.)

tape, *n.* cinta, *f.*; *vt.* vendar; grabar; **tape recorder**, magnetófono, *m.*

tar, *n.* alquitrán, *m.*

tardiness, *n.* tardanza, *f.*

tardy, *adj.* tardío; lento

target, *n.* blanco, *m.*; meta, *f.*

tariff, *n.* tarifa, *f.*

taste, *n.* gusto, *m.*; sabor, *m.*; *vt.* y *vi.* probar; tener sabor

tasteful, *adj.* de buen gusto

tasteless, *adj.* insípido

tasty, *adj.* gustoso

tattered, *adj.* andrajoso

tattletale, *n.* chismoso, chismosa

tavern, *n.* taberna, *f.*

tax, *n.* impuesto, *m.*, contribu-

ción, *f.*; **income tax**, impuesto de rentas; *vt.* imponer tributos

taxi, *n.* taxímetro, *m.*

taxicab, *n.* taxímetro, automóvil de alquiler, *m.*; (Mex.) libre, *m.*

tea, *n.* té, *m.*

teach, *vt.* enseñar, instruir

teacher, *n.* maestro, maestra, profesor, profesora

teaching, *n.* enseñanza,

teacup, *n.* taza para té, *f.*

teakettle, *n.* tetera, *f.*

team, *n.* tiro de caballos, *m.*; (deportes) equipo, *m.*

teapot, *n.* tetera, *f.*

tear, *vt.* despedazar; *n.* rasgón, jirón, *m.*

tear, *n.* lágrima, *f.*

tearoom, *n.* salón de té, *m.*

teaspoon, *n.* cucharita, *f.*

teat, *n.* ubre, *f.*; teta, *f.*

technical, *adj.* técnico

technician, *n.* técnico, *m.*

technique, *n.* técnica, *f.*

tedious, *adj.* fastidioso

teen-ager, *n.* adolescente, *m.* y *f.*

teens, *n. pl.* números y años desde 13 hasta 20; periodo de trece a diecinueve años de edad

teeth, *n. pl.* de **tooth**, dientes, *m. pl.*

telecast, *vt.* y *vi.* televisar; *n.* teledifusión, *f.*

telegram, *n.* telegrama, *m.*

telegraph, *n.* telégrafo, *m.*; *vi.* telegrafiar

telepathy, *n.* telepatía, *f.*

telephone, *n.* teléfono, *m.*; **dial telephone**, teléfono automático, *m.*; *vt.* y *vi.* telefonear

teleprompter, *n.* apuntador electrónico, *m.*

telescope, *n.* telescopio, *m.*

television, *n.* televisión *f.*; **television set**, telerreceptor, aparto de televisión

temper, *n.* temperamento, *m.*; humor, genio, *m.*

temperament, *n.* temperamento, *m.*; carácter, genio, *m.*

temperate, *adj.* templado, moderado, sobrio

temperature, *n.* temperatura, *f.*

tempest, *n.* tempested, *f.*

temple, *n.* templo, *m.*; sien, *f.*

temporarily, *adj.* temporalmente

tempt, *vt.* tentar; provocar

temptation, *n.* tentación, *f.*

tempting, *adj.* tentador

ten, *n.* y *adj.* diez, *m.*

tenant, *n.* inquilino, inquilina

tendency, *n.* tendencia, *f.*

tender, *adj.* tierno, delicado

tenderloin, *n.* filete, solomillo, *m.*

tenderness, *n.* terneza, *f.*

tennis, *n.* tenis, *m.*

tenor, *n.* (mus.) tenor, *m.*

tense, *adj.* tieso; tenso; *n.* (gram.) tiempo, *m.*

tension, *n.* tensión, *f.*

tent, *n.* tienda de campaña, *f.*

tentative, *adj.* tentativo

tenth, *n.* y *adj.* décimo, *m.*

tepid, *adj.* tibio

term, *n.* plazo, *m.*; tiempo, periodo, *m.*; **terms of payment,** condiciones de pago, *f. pl.*

terminate, *vt.* y *vi.* terminar

terrace, *n.* terraza, *f.*

terrestrial, *adj.* terrestre

terrible, *adj.* terrible

terrify, *vt.* espantar, llenar de terror

territory, *n.* territorio, *m.*

terror, *n.* terror, *m.*

test, *n.* ensayo, *m.*, prueba, *f.*; examen, *m.*; *vt.* ensayar, probar; examinar

Testament, *n.* Testamento, *m.*

testament, *n.* testamento, *m.*

testify, *vt.* testificar, atestiguar

testimony, *n.* testimonio, *m.*

text, *n.* texto, *m.*; tema, *m.*

textbook, *n.* libro de texto, *m.*

texture, *n.* textura, *f.*

than, *conj.* que o de (en sentido comparativo)

thank, *vt.* dar gracias; **thanks,** *n. pl.* gracias, *f. pl.*

thankful, *adj.* agradecido

Thanksgiving, Thanksgiving

Day, *n.* dia de dar gracias (en Estados Unidos)

that, *dem. pron.* ése, ésa, eso; aquél, aquélla, aquello; *rel. pron.* que, quien, el cual, la cual, lo cual; *conj.* que, por que, para que; *adj.* ese, esa, aquel, aquella

the, *art.* el, la, lo; los, las

theater, *n.* teatro, *m.*

theatrical, *adj.* teatral

thee, *pron.* (acusativo de **thou**) ti, a ti

theft, *n.* hurto, robo, *m.*

their, *adj.* su, suyo, soya; sus, suyos, suyas; **theirs,** *pron.* el suyo, la suya, los suyos, las suyas

them, *pron.* (*acusativo y dativo de they*) los, las, les; ellos, ellas

theme, *n.* tema, asunto, *m.*; (mus.) motivo, *m.*

themselves, *pron. pl.* ellos mismos, ellas mismas; sí mismos

then, *adv.* entonces, después; **now and then,** de cuando en cuando

theology, *n.* teologia, *f.*

there, *adv.* allí, allá

thereafter, *adv.* después; subsiguientemente

thereby, *adv.* por medio de eso

therefore, *adv.* por lo tanto

thermometer, *n.* termómetro, *m.*

these, *pron. pl.* éstos, éstas; *adj.* estos, estas

thick, *adj.* espeso, grueso

thicken, *vt.* y *vi.* espesar

thief, *n.* ladrón, ladrona

thin, *adj.* delgado, flaco

thing, *n.* cosa, *f.*

think, *vt.* y *vi.* pensar; creer

thinking, *n.* pensamiento, *m.*; opinión, *f.*

third, *n.* y *adj.* tercero, *m.*

thirst, *n.* sed, *f.*

thirsty, *adj.* sediento; **to be thirsty,** tener sed

thirteen, *n.* y *adj.* trece, *m.*

thirteenth, *n.* y *adj.* décimotercio, *m.*

thirtieth, *n.* y *adj.* treintavo, *m.*; *adj.* trigésimo

thirty, *n.* y *adj.* treinta. *m.*

this, *adj.* este, esta; esto; *pron.* éste, ésta

thorn, *n.* espina, *f.*

those, *adj. pl.* de **that,** aquellos, aquellas; esos, esas; *pron.* aquéllos, aquéllas; ésos, ésas

though, *conj.* aunque; *adv.* (coll.) sin embargo

thought, *n.* pensamiento, *m.*; concepto, *m.*; *pretérito* y *p. p.* del verbo **think**

thoughtful, *adj.* pensativo; considerado

thoughtless, *adj.* inconsiderado

thousand, *n.* mil, *m.*; millar, *m.*

thousandth, *n.* y *adj.* milésimo, *m.*

threader, *n.* (mech.) terraja, *f.*

threat, *n.* amenaza,

threaten, *vt.* amenazar

three, *n.* y *adj.* tres, *m.*

thresh, *vt.* trillar

threshold, *n.* umbral, *m.*

threw, *pretérito* del verbo **throw**

thrice, *adv.* tres veces

thrift, *n.* frugalidad, *f.*

thrifty, *adj.* ahorrativo, frugal

thrill, *vt.* emocionar; *vi.* estremecerse; *n.* emoción, *f.*

thrilling, *adj.* emocionante

thrive, *vi.* prosperar

throat, *n.* garganta, *f.*

throb, *vi.* palpitar, vibrar

throne. *n.* trono, *m.*

throng, *n.* gentío, *m.*

throttle, *n.* válvula reguladora, *f.*; acelerador, *m.*

through, *prep.* a través, por medio de; por

throw, *vt.* echar, arrojar; *n.* tiro, *m.*, tirada *f.*

thrown, *p. p.* del verbo **throw**

thumbtack, *n.* chinche, tachuela, *f.*

thunder, *n.* trueno, *m.*; estrépito, *m.*; *vt.* y *vi.* tronar

Thursday, *n.* jueves, *m.*

thwart, *vt.* frustrar

ticket, *n.* billete, *m.*; (Sp. Am.) boleto, *m.*, boleta, *f.*

tickle, *vt.* hacer cosquillas a alguno; *vi.* tener cosquillas

tide, *n.* marea, *f.*

tidings, *n. pl.* noticias, *f. pl.*

tidy, *adj.* pulcro

tie, *vt.* atar; enlazer; *n.* nudo, *m.*; corbata, *f.*

tiger, *n.* tigre, *m.*

tight, *adj.* tieso; apretado; (coll.) tacaño

tighten, *vt.* estirar; apretar

tigress, *n.* tigire hembra

tile, *n.* teja, *f.*; azulejo, *m.*

till, *prep.* y *conj.* hasta que, hasta; *vt.* cultivar, labrar

time, *n.* tiempo, *m.*; (mus.) compás, *m.*; edad, época, *f.*; hora, *f.*; vez, *f.*

timely, *adj.* oportuno

timetable, *n.* itinerario, *m.*

timid, *adj.* tímido

tin, *n.* estaño, *m.*; hojalata, *f.*; **tin can,** lata, *f.*

tingle, *vi.* latir, punzar

tint, *n.* tinte, *m.*; *vt.* teñir, colorar

tiny, *adj.* pequeño, chico

tip, *n.* punta, extremidad, *f.*; gratificación, propina, *f.*; información oportuna; *vt.* dar propina; ladear; volcar

tiptoe, *n.* punta del pie, *f.*; **on tiptoe,** de puntillas

tire, *n.* llanta, goma, *f.*; neumático, *m.* ; *vt.* cansar, fatigar; *vi.* cansarse

tired, *adj.* cansado

tissue, *n.* (anat.) tejido, *m.*; **tissue paper,** papel de seda, *m.*

title, *n.* título, *m.*

to, *prep.* a. para; por; de; hasta; en; con; que; *adv.* hacia determinado objeto; **he came to,** volvió en sí

toad, *n.* sapo, *m.*

toast, *vt.* tostar; brindar; *n.* tostada, *f.*, pan tostado, *m.*; brindis, *m.*

toaster, *n.* tostador, *m.*

toastmaster, *n.* maestro de ceremonias, *m.*

tobacco, *n.* tabaco , *m.*

today, *n.* y *adv.* hoy *m.*

toddle, *vi.* tambalearse

toe, *n.* dedo del pie, *m.*

toenail, *n.* uña del dedo del pie, *f.*

together, *adv.* juntamente

toil, *vi.* afanarse; *n.* fatiga, *f.*; afán, *m.*

toilet, *n.* tocado, *m.*; excusado, retrete, *m.*

token, *n.* símbolo, *m.*; recuerdo, *m.*

told, *pretérito* del verbo **tell**

tolerence, *n.* tolerancia, *f.*

tolerate, *vt.* tolerar

toll, *n.* peaje, portazgo, *m.*; tañido, *m.*; **toll call,** llamada telefónica de larga distancia; *vi.* sonar las campanas

tomato, *n.* tomate, *m.*

tomb, *n.* tumba, *f.*

tomorrow, *n.* y *adv.* mañana, *f.*

ton, *n.* tonelada, *f.*

tongue, *n.* lengua, *f.*

tonic, *n.* tónico, reconstituyente, *m.*; (mus.) tónica, *f.*

tonight, *n.* y *adv.* esta noche

tonsil, *n.* amígdala, *f.*

too, *adv.* demasiado; también

took, *pretérito* del verbo **take**

tool, *n.* herramienta, *f.*

toot, *vt.* y *vi.* sonar una bocina

tooth, *n.* diente, *m.*

toothache, *n.* dolor de muelas, *m.*

toothbrush, *n.* cepillo de dientes, *m.*

toothpaste, *n.* pasta dentífrica, *f.*

toothpick, *n.* escarbadientes, palillo de dientes, *m.*

top, *n.* cima, cumbre, *f.*; trompo, *m.*

topaz, *n.* topacio, *m.*

topcoat, *n.* sobretodo, abrigo, *m.*

topic, *n.* tópico, asunto, *m.*

topsy-turvy, *adv.* patas arriba, desordenadamente

torch, *n.* antorcha, *f.*

tore, *pretérito* del verbo **tear**

toreador, *n.* torero, *m.*

torment, *n.* tormento, *m.*; *vt.* atormentar

torn, *adj.* destrozado; descosido; *p. p.* del verbo **tear**

torpedo, *n.* torpedo, *m.*

tortoise-shell, *adj.* de carey

torture, *n.* tortura, *f.*, martirio, *m.*; *vt.* atormentar, torturar

toss, *vt.* tirar, lanzar, arrojar; agitar, sacudir; *vi.* agitarse; menearse

tot, *n.* niñito, niñita

total, *n.* total, *m.*; *adj.* entero, completo

totter, *vi.* tambalear

touch, *vt.* tocar, palpar; emocionar, conmover; *n.* tacto, *m.*; toque, contacto, *m.*

touching, *adj.* conmovedor

tough, *adj.* tosco; correoso; fuerte, vigoroso

toughen, *vi.* endurecerse; *vt.* endurecer

touring, *n.* turismo, *m.*

tourist, *n.* turista, *m.* y *f.*; viajero, viajera; **tourist court,** posada para turistas, *f.*

tournament, *n.* torneo, concurso, *m.*

toward, towards, *prep.* hacia, con dirección a

town, *n.* pueblo, *m.*, población, *f.*

trace, *n.* huella, pisada, *f.*; vestigio, *m.*; *vt.* delinear, trazar

track, *n.* vestigio, *m.*; huella, pista, *f.*; vía *f.*

trade, *n.* comercio, tráfico, *m.*; negocio, trato, *m.*; *vt.* comerciar, negociar

trade-mark, *n.* marca de fábrica, *f.*

traffic, *n.* tráfico, *m.*

trail, *vt.* y *vi.* rastrear; arrastrar; *n.* rastro, *m.*; pisada, *f.*; sendero, *m.*

trailer, *n.* carro de remolque, *m.*

train, *vt.* enseñar, adiestrar; entrenar; *n.* tren, *m.*; cola (de vestido), *f.*

training, *n.* educación, disciplina, *f.*; entrenamiento, *m.*

traitor, *n.* traidor, *m.*

transact, *vt.* negociar, transigir

transaction, *n.* transacción, *f.*

transatlantic, *adj.* trasatlántico

transfer, *vt.* trasferir; *n.* traspaso, *m.*; trastado, *m.*

transform, *vt.* y *vi.* trasformar

transfusion, *n.* trasfusión, *f.*

transient, *adj.* pasajero, transitorio

transit, *n.* transito, *m.*

transition, *n.* transición, *f.*

transitive, *adj.* transitivo

translate, *vt.* traducir

translation, *n.* traducción, *f.*

translator, *n.* traductor, traductora

transmission, *n.* (mech.) caja de cambios, *f.*

transmit, *vt.* trasmitir

transom, *n.* travesaño, *m.*

transparent, *adj.* trasparente

transport, *vt.* trasportar

transportation, *n.* trasportación, *f.*, trasporte, *m.*

trap, *n.* trampa, *f.*; *vt.* atrapar

trapeze, *n.* trapecio, *m.*

trash, *adj.* despreciable

travel, *vt.* y *vi.* viajar

traveler, *n.* viajero, viajera

tray, *n.* bandeja, *f.*; (Mex.) charola, *f.*

treacherous, *adj.* traidor

treachery, *n.* traición, *f.*

tread, *vt.* y *vi.* pisar, hollar; *n.* pisada, *f.*

treason, *n.* traición, *f.*

treasure, *n.* tesoro, *m.*; *vt.* atesorar; apreciar

treasurer, *n.* tesorero, tesorera

treasury, *n.* tesorería, *f.*

treat, *vt.* y *vi.* tratar; regalar; *n.* convite, *m.*

treatment, *n.* trato, *m.*; tratamiento, *m.*

treaty, *n.* tratado, *m.*

tree, *n.* árbol, *m.*

tremble, *vi.* temblar

tremendous, *adj.* tremendo; inmenso

trench, *n.* trinchera, *f.*

trespass, *vt.* traspasar, violar

trial, *n.* prueba, *f.*; ensayo, *m.*; (law) juicio, *m.*

triangle, *n.* triángulo, *m.*

triangular, *adj.* triangular

tribe, *n.* tribu, *f.*

tribulation, *n.* tribulación, *f.*

tribunal, *n.* tribunal, *m.*

tribute, *n.* tributo, *m.*

tricycle, *n.* triciclo, velocípedo, *m.*

trill, *n.* trino, *m.*

trillion, *n.* trillón, *m.*, la tercera potencia de un millón, o 1,000,000,000,000,000,000 (en la América Ibera, España Inglaterra, y Alemania); un millón de millones, o 1,000,000,000,000 (en Francia y los Estados Unidos)

trim, *adj.* bien ataviado; *n.* adorno, *m.*; *vt.* adornar, ornar; recortar

trinket, *n.* joya, alhaja, *f.*

trio, *n.* terceto, trío, *m.*

trip, *vt.* saltar, brincar; hacer tropezar; *vi.* tropezar; *n.* viaje, *m.*

triple, *adj.* triple

triplicate, *vt.* triplicar; *adj.* triplicado

trite, *adj.* trivial, banal

triumph, *n.* triunfo, *m.*; *vi.* triunfar; vencer

triumphant, *adj.* triunfante

trivial, *adj.* trivial, vulgar

trolley, *n.* tranvía, *m.*

trombone, *n.* trombón, *m.*

troop, *n.* tropa, *f.*

tropics, *n. pl.* trópico, *m.*

tropical, *adj.* tropical

troubadour, *n.* trovador, *m.*

trouble, *vt.* incomodar, molestar; *vi.* incomodarse; *n.* pena, *f.*; molestia, *f.*; trabajo, *m.*

troubled, *adj.* afligido

troublesome, *adj.* molesto, fastidioso

trousers, *n. pl.* calzones, pantalones, *m. pl.*

trousseau, *n.* ajuar de novia, *m.*

trout, *n.* trucha, *f.*

truce, *n.* tregua, *f.*

truck, *n.* camión, *m.*

true, *adj.* verdadero, cierto

truly, *adv.* en verdad

trumpet, *n.* trompeta, trompa, *f.*

trunk, *n.* tronco, *m.*; baúl, cofre, *m.*; **trunk (of an elephant),** trompa, *f.*

trunks, *n. pl.* calzones, *m. pl.*

trust, *n.* confianza, *f.*; crédito,
m.; *vt.* y *vi.* confiar

trustee, *n.* fideicomisario, de-
positario, *m.*

trustworthy, *adj.* digno de
confianza

truth, *n.* verdad, *f.*

truthful, *adj.* verídico, veraz

truthfulness, *n.* veracidad, *f.*

try, *vt.* y *vi.* probar; experimentar; intentar

trying, *adj.* cruel, penoso

tub, *n.* tina, *f.*

tube, *n.* tubo, caño, *m.*

tuberculosis, *n.* tuberculosis,
tisis, *f.*

tug, *vt.* tirar con fuerza; arrancar

tugboat, *n.* remolcador, *m.*

tuition, *n.* instrucción, enseñanza, *f.*

tumble, *vi.* caer, voltear; *n.*
caída, *f.*

tumor, *n.* tumor, *m.*

tuna, *n.* (bot.) tuna, *f.*; **tuna
fish,** atún, *m.*

tune, *n.* tono, *m.*; tonada, *f.*;
vt. afinar (un instrumento
musical)

tunic, *n.* túnica, *f.*

tunnel, *n.* túnel, *m.*

turban, *n.* turbante, *m.*

turbojet, *n.* turborreactor, *m.*

turf, *n.* césped, *m.*

turkey, *n.* pavo, *m.*

Turkey, *n.* Turquía, *f.*

Turkish, *adj.* turco

turmoil, *n.* confusión, *f.*

turn, *vt.* volver, trocar; *vi.* volver, girar, voltear; *n.* vuelta,
f.; giro, *m.*; turno, *m.*

turnip, *n.* (bot.) nabo, *m.*

turquoise, *n.* turquesa, *f.*

turtle, *n.* tortuga, *f.*

turtledove, *n.* tórtola, f

tuxedo, *n.* smoking, *m.*

tweezers, *n. pl.* pinzas, *f. pl.*;
tenacillas, *f. pl.*

twelfth, *n.* y *adj.* duodécimo,
m.

twelve, *n.* y *adj.* doce, *m.*

twentieth, *n.* y *adj.* vigésimo,
m.

twenty, *n.* y *adj.* veinte, *m.*

twice, *adv.* dos veces

twig, *n.* varita, varilla, *f.*

twilight, *n.* crepúsculo, *m.*

twine, *vt.* torcer, enroscar; *vi.*
entrelazarse

twinge, *n.* punzada, *f.*; *vi.* arder; sufrir dolor (de una punzada, etc.)

twinkle, *vi.* parpadear; *n.* pestañeo, *m.*

twinkling, *n.* pestañeo, *m.*;
momento, *m.*

twirl, *vt.* voltear; hacer girar

twist, *vt.* y *vi.* torcer

two, *n.* y *adj.* dos , *m.*

type, *n.* tipo, *m.*; clase, *f.*; *vt.* y
vi. escribir en máquina

typewrite, *vt.* escribir a máquina

typewriter, *n.* máquina de escribir, *f.*

typhoid, *adj.* tifoideo; **typhoid
fever,** fiebre tifoidea, *f.*

typical, *adj.* típico

typing, *n.* mecanografía, *f.*

typist, *n.* mecanógrafo, mecanógrafa

typographical, *adj.* tipográfico

tyranny, *n.* tiranía, *f.*

tyrant, *n.* tirano, *m.*

U

U., University, Universidad

udder, *n.* ubre, *f.*

ugliness, *n.* fealdad, *f.*

ugly, *adj.* feo

ulcer , *n.* úlcera, *f.*

ultimatum, *n.* ultimátum, *m.*

ultra, *adj.* extremo, excesivo

ultrasonic, *adj.* ultrasónico

umbrella, *n.* paraguas, *m.*

umpire, *n.* árbitro, *m.*; *vt.* arbitrar

UN, United Nations, N.U., Naciones Unidas

unable, *adj.* incapaz

unanimity, *n.* unanimidad, *f.*

unanimous, *adj.* unánime

unarmed, *adj.* desarmado

unassuming, *adj.* sin preten-
siones

unattached, *adj.* separado; disponible
unattainable, *adj.* inasequible
unavoidable, *adj.* inevitable
unawares, *adv.* inadvertidamente
unbalanced, *adj.* trastornado
unbearable, *adj.* intolerable
unbiased, *adj.* imparcial
unbutton, *vt.* desabotonar
uncertain, *adj.* inseguro
uncertainty, *n.* incertidumbre, *f.*
uncle, *n.* tío, *m.*
uncomfortable, *adj.* incómodo
unconcerned, *adj.* indiferente
unconditional, *adj.* incondicional
unconscious, *adj.* inconsciente
undecided, *adj.* indeciso
under, *prep.* debajo de, bajo; *adv.* abajo
underage, *adj.* menor de edad
underclothing, *n.* ropa interior, *f.*
undergo, *vt.* sufrir; sostener
underground, *adj.* subterráneo
underhanded, *adj.* clandestino
underline, *vt.* subrayar
underneath, *adv.* debajo
underprivileged, *adj.* desvalido, necesitado
underscore, *vt.* subrayar
undershirt, *n.* camiseta, *f.*
undersigned, *n.* y *adj.* suscrito, suscrita
underskirt, *n.* enagua, *f.*; fondo, *m.*
understand, *vt.* entender, comprender
understanding, *n.* entendimiento, *m.*; *adj.* comprensivo
undertake, vt. y *vi.* emprender
undertaker, *n.* empresario o director de pompas fúnebres
undertaking, *n.* empresa, obra, *f.*
undertow, *n.* resaca, *f.*
underwear, *n.* ropa interior, *f.*
underweight, *adj.* de bajo peso
undesirable, *adj.* nocivo

undivided, *adj.* entero
undress, *vt.* desvestir; desnudar
unearth, *vt.* desenterrar; reveler, divulgar
unemployed, *adj.* desocupado
unending, *adj.* sin fin
unequal, *adj.* desigual
uneven, *adj.* desigual
unexpected, *adj.* inesperado
unfailing, *adj.* infalible
unfair, *adj.* injusto
unfamiliar, *adj.* desconocido
unfavorable, *adj.* desfavorable
unfit, *adj.* inepto, incapaz; indigno
unfold, *vt.* desplegar
unforeseen, *adj.* imprevisto
unforgettable, *adj.* inolvidable
unfortunate, *adj.* desafortunado, infeliz
unfounded, *adj.* infundado
unfurl, *vt.* desplegar
ungrounded, *adj.* infundado
unhappy, *adj.* infeliz
unharmed, *adj.* ileso, incólume
unhealthy, *adj.* malsano
unheard (of), *adj.* inaudito
unhurt, *adj.* ileso
uniform, *n.* y *adj.* uniforme, *m.*
uniformity, *n.* uniformidad, *f.*
union, *n.* unión, *f.*
unique, *adj.* único; singular
unison, *n.* concordancia, *f.*; **in unison,** al unisono
unit, *n.* unidad, *f.*
unite, *vt.* y *vi.* unir, juntarse
united, *adj.* unido, junto
United States of America, Estados Unidos de América
unity, *n.* unidad, *f.*; unión, *f.*
universal, *adj.* universal; **universal joint,** cardán, *m.*
universe, *n.* universo, *m.*
university, *n.* universidad, *f.*
unkind, *adj.* cruel
unknowingly, *adv.* sin saberlo
unknown, *adj.* desconocido
unlike, *adj.* desemejante
unlikely, *adj.* improbable
unlimited, *adj.* ilimitado
unlock, *vt.* abrir alguna cerradura

unlucky, *adj.* desafortunado
unmarried, *adj.* soltero, soltera
unnatural, *adj.* artificial
unnecessary, *adj.* innecesario
unofficial, *adj.* extraoficial
unpack, *vt.* desempacar
unpaid, *adj.* sin pagar, pendiente de pago
unpopular, *adj.* impopular
unprincipled, *adj.* sin escrúpulos
unravel, *vt.* desenredar; resolver
unreal, *adj.* fantástico, ilusorio
unreserved, *adj.* franco, abierto
unscrew, *vt.* destornillar
unscrupulous, *adj.* sin escrúpulos
unseemly, *adj.* indecoroso
unseen, *adj.* no visto
unselfish, *adj.* desinteresado
unsettled, *adj.* incierto, indeciso; **unsettled accounts,** cuentas por pagar
unsightly, *adj.* feo
unskilled, *adj.* inexperto
unsound, *adj.* inestable; falso
unsuitable, *adj.* inadecuado
untangle, *vt.* desenredar
untie, *vt.* soltar, desamrrar
until, *prep.* y *conj.* hasta, hasta que
untimely, *adj.* intempestivo
untold, *adj.* no relatado
unusual, *adj.* inusitado, poco común
unveil, *vt.* y *vi.* descubrir; revelar; estrenar
unwilling, *adj.* sin deseos; **unwillingly,** *adv.* de mala gana
unwind, *vt.* desenrollar
unwise, *adj.* imprudente
unworthy, *adj.* indigno, vil
unwritten, *adj.* verbal, no escrito
up, *adv.* arriba, en lo alto; *prep.* hasta; **to make up,** hacer las paces; inventar; compensar; maquillarse; **to bring up,** criar, educar; **to call up,** telefonear
upbringing, *n.* educación,

crianza, *f.*
upholster, *vt.* entapizar
upkeep, *n.* mantenimiento, *m.*
upon, *prep.* sobre encima
upper, *adj.* superior; más elevado
upright, *adj.* derecho, recto
uproar, *n.* tumulto, alboroto, *m.*
upset, *vt.* y *vi.* volcar, trastornar; *adj.* mortificado
upside-down, *adj.* al revés; de arriba abajo
upstairs, *adv.* arriba
up-to-date, *adj.* moderno, de ultima moda, reciente
upward, *adv.* hacia arriba
uranium, *n.* uranio, *m.*
urban, *adj.* urbano
urge, *vt.* y *vi.* incitar, instar
urgent, *adj.* urgente
urinate, *vi.* orinar, mear
urine, *n.* orina, *f.*, orines, *m. pl.*
U.S.A., United States of America, E.U.A. Estados Unidos de América
usable, *adj.* utilizable
usage, *n.* uso, *m.*
use, *n.* uso, *m.*, servicio, *m.*; *vt.* y *vi.* usar, emplear; acostumbrar
used, *adj.* gastado, usado
useful, *adj.* útil
usefulness, *n.* utilidad, *f.*
useless, *adj.* inútil
usher, *n.* acomodador, *m.*
usual, *adj.* común, ordinario; **usually,** *adv.* de costumbre
utensil, *n.* utensilio, *m.*
utility, *n.* utilidad, *f.*; **public utilities,** servicios públicos *m. pl.*

V

vacancy, *n.* vacante, *f.*
vacant, *adj.* vacío, vacante
vacation, *n.* vacación, *f.*
vaccinate, *vt.* vacunar
vaccination, *n.* vacuna, *f.*; vacunación, *f.*
vaccine, *n.* vacuna, *f.*
vacuum, *n.* vacío, *m.*; **vacuum cleaner,** aspiradora, *f.*, barre-

dor al vacio, *m.*

vain, *adj.* vano, inútil; vanidoso, presentuoso

valet, *n.* criado, camarero, *m.*

valid, *adj.* válido

valley, *n.* valle, *m.*

valuable, *adj.* valioso; **valuables,** *n. pl.* tesoros, *m. pl.*, joyas, *f. pl.*

value, *n.* valor, precio, importe, *m.*; *vt.* valuar, apreciar

vanilla, *n.* vainilla, *f.*

vanish, *vi.* desaparecer

vanity, *n.* vanidad, *f.*; **vanity case,** polvera, *f.*

variety, *n.* variedad, *f.*

various, *adj.* diferentes

varnish, *n.* barniz, *m.*; *vt.* barnizer; charolar

vary, *vt.* y *vi.* variar

vase, *n.* jarrón, florero, *m.*

vast, *adj.* vasto; inmenso

vault, *n.* bóveda, *f.*

veal, *n.* ternera, *f.*; **veal cutlet,** chuleta de ternera, *f.*

vegetable, *adj.* vegetal; *n.* vegetal, *m.*; **vegetables,** *n. pl.* verduras, hortalizas, *f. pl.*

vegetation, *n.* vegetación, *f.*

vehicle, *n.* vehículo, *m.*

veil, *n.* velo, *m.*; *vt.* encubrir, ocultar

vein, *n.* vena, *f.*

velocity, *n.* velocidad, *f.*

velvet, *n.* terciopelo, *m.*

velveteen, *n.* pana, *f.*

venerate, *vt.* venerar, honrar

veneration, *n.* veneración, *f.*

Venetian, *n.* y *adj.* veneciano, veneciana

Venezuelan, *n.* y *adj.* venezolano, venezolana

vengeance, *n.* venganza, *f.*

Venice, Venecia

venison, *n.* carne de venado, *f.*

ventilate, *vt.* ventilar

ventilation, *n.* ventilación, *f.*

veracity, *n.* veracidad, *f.*

veranda, *n.* terraza, *f.*

verb, *n.* (gram.) verbo, *m.*

verbal, *adj.* verbal, literal; **verbally,** *adv.* oralmente, de palabra

verbatim, *adv.* palabra por palabra

verdict, n (law) veredicto, *m.*; sentencia, *f.*, dictamen, *m.*

verify, *vt.* verificar

versatile, *adj.* hábil para muchas cosas

verse, *n.* verso, *m.*

version, *n.* versión, traducción, *f.*

vessel, *n.* vasija, *f.*, vaso, *m.*; buque, *m.*

vest, *n.* chaleco, *m.*

vestibule, *n.* zaguán, *m.*

vestige, *n.* vestigio, *m.*

vest-pocket, *adj.* propio para el bolsillo del chaleco; pequeño; **vest-pocket edition,** edición en miniatura, *f.*

veteran, *n.* y *adj.* veterano, veterana

vex, *vt.* contrariar; **vexed,** *adj.* molesto, contrariado

via, *prep.* por la vía de; por; **via airmail,** por via aérea

viaduct, *n.* viaducto, *m.*

vice, *n.* vicio, *m.*

vice-consul, *n.* vicecónsul, *m.*

vice-president, *n.* vice-presidente, *m.*

vicinity, *n.* vecindad, proximidad, *f.*

victim, *n.* víctima, *f.*

victorious, *adj.* victorioso

victory, *n.* victoria, *f.*

video, *n.* televisión, *f.*

Vienna, Viena, *f.*

Viennese, *n.* y *adj.* vienés, vienesa

view, *n.* vista, *f.*; paisaje, *m.*; *vt.* mirar, ver

viewpoint, *n.* punto de vista, *m.*

vigor, *n.* vigor, *m.*

vigorous, *adj.* vigoroso

villa, *n.* quinta, *f.*

village, *n.* aldea, *f.*

villain, *n.* malvado, *m.*

vim, *n.* energía, *f.*, vigor, *m.*

vindicate, *vt.* vindicar, defender

vine, *n.* vid, *f.*

vinegar, *n.* vinagre, *m.*

vineyard, *n.* viña, *f.*, viñedo, *m.*

viol, *n.* (mus.) violón, *m.*

viola, *n.* (mus.) viola, *f.*

violate, *vt.* violar
violation, *n.* violación, *f.*
violence, *n.* violencia, *f.*
violent, *adj.* violento
violet, *n.* (bot.) violeta, *f.*
violin, *n.* violín, *m.*
violinist, *n.* violinista, *m.* y *f.*
virgin, *n.* virgen, *f.*; *adj.* virginal; virgen
virology, *n.* virología, *f.*
virtue, *n.* virtud, *f.*
virtuous, *adj.* virtuoso
virus, *n.* (med.) virus, *m.*
visa, *n.* visa, *f.*
viscount, *n.* vizconde, *m.*
vision, *n.* visión, *f.*
visit, *vt.* y *vi.* visitar; *n.* visita, *f.*
visitor, *n.* visitante, *m.* y *f.*
visualize, *vt.* vislumbrar
vital, *adj.* vital; **vital statistics,** estadística demográfica, *f.*
vitality, *n.* vitalidad, *f.*
vitamin, *n.* vitamina, *f.*
vivacious, *adj.* vivaz
vivacity, *n.* vivacidad, *f.*
vivid, *adj.* vivo, vivaz; gráfico
viz., *adv.* a saber, esto es
vocabulary, *n.* vocabulario, *m.*
vocal, *adj.* vocal
vocalist, *n.* cantante, *m.* y *f.*
vocation, *n.* vocación, carrera, profesión, *f.*; oficio, *m.*
vocational, *adj.* práctico, profesional; **vocational school,** escuela de artes y oficios, escuela práctica, *f.*
vogue, *n.* moda, *f.*; boga, *f.*
voice, *n.* voz, *f.*
void, *n.* y *adj.* vacío, *m.*; *vt.* anular
volcano, *n.* volcán, *m.*
volleyball, *n.* balonvolea, *m.*
volume, *n.* volumen, *m.*
voluntarily, *adv.* voluntariamente
volunteer, *n.* voluntario, *m.*
vote, *n.* voto, sufragio, *m.*; *vt.* votar
voter, *n.* votante, *m.* y *f.*
voucher, *n.* comprobante, recibo, *m.*
vow, *n.* voto, *m.*; *vt.* y *vi.* dedicar, consagrar; hacer votos; jurar
vowel, *n.* vocal, *f.*
voyage, *n.* viaje marítimo, *m.*
v.t., transitive verb, v.tr., verbo transitivo
vulgar, *adj.* vulgar, cursi
vulgarity, *n.* vulgaridad, *f.*

W

w., week, semana; **west,** O., oeste; **width,** ancho; **wife,** esposa
wafer, *n.* hostia, *f.*; oblea, *f.*; galletica, *f.*
wag, *vt.* mover ligeramente; **to wag the tail,** menear la cola; *n.* meneo, *m.*
wage, *vt.* apostar; emprender; **wages,** *n. pl.* sueldo, salario, *m.*
wager, *n.* apuesta, *f.*; *vt.* apostar
wagon, *n.* carreta, *f.*; vagón, *m.*
wail, *vi.* lamentarse
waist, *n.* cintura, *f.*
waistline, *n.* cintura, *f.*
wait, *vi.* esperar, aguardar
waiter, *n.* sirviente, mozo, *m.*
waitress, *n.* camarera, criada, mesera, *f.*
wake, *vi.* velar; despertarse; *vt.* despertar; *n.* vigilia, *f.*; velorio *m.*
walk, *vt.* y *vi.* pasear, andar, caminar; *n.* paseo, *m.*, caminata, *f.*
wallet, *n.* cartera, *f.*
walnut, *n.* nogal, *m.*; nuez, *f.*
wand, *n.* vara, varita, *f.*; batuta, *f.*
wander, *vi.* vagar, rodar; extraviarse
wanderer, *n.* peregrino, *m.*
want, *vt.* y *vi.* desear, querer, anhelar; faltar; *vi.* estar necesitado; *n.* falta, carencia, *f.*
war, *n.* guerra, *f.*
warden, *n.* custodio, guardián, *m.* alcalde, *m.*
wardrobe, *n.* guardarropa, *f.*, ropero, *m.*; vestuario, *m.*
warehouse, *n.* almacén, depósito, *m.*, bodega, *f.*
warhead, *n.* punta de comba-

te, *f.*

warm, *adj.* caliente; abrigador; cordial, caluroso; **to be warm,** hacer calor; tener calor; *vt.* calentar

warmth, *n.* calor, *m.;* ardor, fervor, *m.*

warn, *vt.* avisar; advertir

warrant, *vt.* autorizar; garantizar; *n.* decreto de prisión, *m.;* autorización, *f.*

warship, *n.* barco de guerra, *m.*

wart, *n.* verruga, *f.*

wartime, *n.* época de guerra, *f.*

was, 1ª y 3ª persona del singular del pretérito del verbo **be**

wash, *vt.* y *vi.* lavar; *n.* loción, ablución, *f.;* lavado, *m.*

washable, *adj.* lavable

washer, *n.* máquina lavadora, *f.;* (mech.) arandela, *f.*

washing, *n.* lavado, *m.;* ropa para lavar; **washing machine,** máquina de lavar, lavadora, *f.*

wasp, *n.* avispa, *f.*

waste, *vt.* desperdiciar; malgastar; *vi.* gastarse; *n.* desperdicio, *m.;* despilfarro, *m.*

wastebasket, *n.* cesta para papeles

wasteful, *adj.* despilfarrador

wastepaper, *n.* papel de desecho, *m.*

watch, *n.* vigilia, vela, *f.;* centinela, *f.;* reloj de bolsillo, *m.;* **wrist watch,** reloj de pulsera, *m.;vt.* observar; *vi.* velar, custodiar

water, *n.* agua, *f.;* **running water,** agua corriente, *f.;* **water closet,** retrete, *m.;* **water color,** acuarela, *f.;* **water meter,** contador de agua, *m.;* **water polo,** polo acuático, *m.;* **water skiing,** esquí náutico o acuático, *m.;* *vt.* irrigar, regar

watermelon, *n.* sandía, *f.*

waterproof, *adj.* a prueba de agua; impermeable

watery, *adj.* aguado

watt, *n.* vatio, *m.*

wattmeter, *n.* vatímetro, *m.*

wave, *n.* ola, onda, *f.;* *vt.* agitar, menear; *vi.* ondear; saludar

wavy, *adj.* ondeado, ondulado

wax, *n.* cera, **wax paper,** papel encerado, *m.;* *vt.* encerar

way, *n.* camino, *m.,* senda, ruta, *f.;* modo, *m.,* forma, *f.;* medio, *m.;* **by the way,** a propósito

we, *pron.* nosotros, nosotras

weak, *adj.* débil

weaken, *vt.* y *vi.* debilitar

wealth, *n.* riqueza, *f.;* bienes, *m. pl.*

wealthy, *adj.* rico, adinerado

weapon, *n.* arma, *f.*

wear, *vt.* gastar, consumir; llevar puesto, traer; *vi.* gastarse; *n.* uso, *m.*

weariness, *n.* cansancio, *m.*

weather, *n.* tiempo, *m.,* temperatura, *f.*

weave, *vt.* tejer; trenzar

web, *n.* red, *f.*

wed, *vt.* y *vi.* casar, casarse

wedding, *n.* boda, *f.,* casamiento, matrimonio, *m.*

wedge, *n.* cuña, *f.;* *vt.* acuñar; apretar

Wednesday, *n.* miércoles, *m.*

wee, *adj.* pequeñito

weed, *n.* mala hierba, *f.*

week, *n.* semana, *f.*

weekday, *n.* día de trabajo, *m.*

week-end, *adj.* de fin de semana

weekly, *adj.* semanal, semanario; *adv.* semanalmente

weigh, *vt.* y *vi.* pesar; considerar

weight, *n.* peso, *m.;* pesadez, *f.*

weightlessness, *n.* imponderabilidad, *f.*

weird, *adj.* extraño, sobrenatural, misterioso

welcome, *adj.* bienvenido; *n.* bienvenida, *f.;* *vt.* dar la bienvenida

weld, *vt.* soldar

welfare *n.* bienestar, *m.*

well, *n.* pozo, *m.;* *adj.* bueno, sano; *adv.* bien

well-being, *n.* felicidad, prosperidad, *f.*

well-bred, *adj.* bien educado, de buenos modales

well-done, *adj.* bien hecho; bien cocido

well-timed, *adj.* oportuno

well-to-do, *adj.* acomodado, rico

wench, *n.* mozuela, *f.*

went, *pretérto* del verbo **go**

were, 2ª persona del singular y plural del *pretérto* del verbo **be**

west, *n.* poniente, occidente oeste, *m.*

westerly, western, *adj.* occidental

West Indies, Antillas, *f. pl.*

wet, *adj.* húmedo, mojado; *vt.* molar, humedecer

whale, *n.* ballena, *f.*

wharf, *n.* muelle, *m.*

what, *pron.* qué; lo que, aquello que; **what is the matter?** ¿qué pasa?

whatever, *pron.* y *adj.* cualquier cosa, lo que sea

wheat, *n.* trigo, *m.*

wheel, *n.* rueda, *f.*

wheelbarrow, *n.* carretilla, *f.*

when, *adv.* cuando; cuándo

whence, *adv.* de donde; de quien

whenever, *adv.* siempre que

where, *adv.* donde; dónde

whereabouts, *n.* paradero, *m.*; *adv.* por donde, hacia donde

whereas, *conj.* por cuanto, mientras que; considerando

whereby, *adv.* con lo cual

wherein, *adv.* en lo cual

whereof, *adv.* de lo cual

whereon, *adv.* sobre lo cual

whereupon, *adv.* entonces, en consecuencia de lo cual

wherever, *adv.* dondequiera que

whet, *vt.* afilar, amolar; exciter

whether, *conj.* que; si; ora

whey, *n.* suero, *m.*

which, *pron.* que, el cual, la cual, los cuales, las cuales; cuál

whichever, *pron.* y *adj.* cualquiera que

whiff, *n.* bocanada de humo,

fumada, *f.*

while, *n.* rato, *m.*; vez, *f.*; momento, *m.*; **to be worth while,** valer la pena; *conj.* mientras, durante

whim, *n.* antojo, capricho, *m.*

whimsical, *adj.* caprichoso, fantástico

whip, *n.* azote, látigo, *m.*; *vt.* azotar

whipped cream, *n.* crema batida, *f.*

whirl, *vt.* y *vi.* girar; hacer girar; moverse rápidamente; *n.* remolino, *m.*; vuelta, *f.*

whirlwind, *n.* torbellino, remolino, *m.*

whisker, *m.* patilla, *f.*

whiskey, whisky, *n.* whiskey, *m.*

whisper, *vi.* cuchichear; *n.* cuchicheo, secreto, *m.*

whistle, *vt.* y *vi.* silbar; chiflar; *n.* silbido, *m.*; pito, *m.*

white, *adj.* blanco, pálido; cano, canoso; puro; *n.* color blanco; clara (de huevo)

white-haired, *adj.* canoso

whiten, *vt.* y *vi.* blanquear; blanquearse

who, *pron.* quien, que; quién

whoever, *pron.* quienquiera

whole, *adj.* todo, total; entero; *n.* todo, total, *m.*; **the whole,** conjunto, *m.*

wholehearted, *adj.* sincero, cordial

wholesale, *n.* venta al por mayor, *f.*

wholesome, *adj.* sano, saludable

whole-wheat, *adj.* de trigo entero

wholly, *adv.* totalmente

whom, *pron.* acusativo de **who** (quien)

whooping cough, *n.* tosferina, *f.*

whore, *n.* puta, *f.*

whose, *pron.* (genitivo de **who** y **which**) cuyo, cuya, cuyos, cuyas, de quien de quienes

why, *adv.* ¿por qué?

wicked, *adj.* malvado, perverso

wide, *adj.* ancho, extenso; **widely**, *adv.* ampliamente

wide-awake, *adj.* despierto, alerta

widen, *vt.* ensanchar, ampliar

widespread, *adj.* diseminado

widow, *n.* viuda, *f.*

widower, *n.* viudo, *m.*

width, *n.* anchura, *f.*

wield, *vt.* manejar, empuñar

wife, *n.* esposa, mujer, *f.*

wild, *adj.* silvestre; salvaje

wilderness, *n.* desierto, *m.*, selva, *f.*

wilful, *adj.* voluntarioso

will, *n.* voluntad, *f.*; capricho, *m.*; testamento, *m.*; *vt.* legar, dejar en testamento; verbo auxiliar que indica futuro

willing, *adj.* deseoso, listo; **willingly**, *adv.* de buena gana

willow, *n.* (bot.) sauce, *m.*

win, *vt.* y *vi.* ganar, obtener

wind, *n.* viento, *m.*; pedo, *m.*

wind, *vt.* enrollar; dar cuerda (a un reloj, etc.); torcer; envolver; *vi.* serpentear

winded, *adj.* sin fuerzas

window, *n.* ventana, *f.*

windpipe, *n.* (anat.) tráquea, *f.*

windshield, *n.* parabrisas, *m.*

wine, *n.* vino, *m.*

wing, *n.* ala, *f.*; lado, costado, *m.*; **wings**, *pl.* (theat.) bastidores, *m. pl.*

wink, *vt.* y *vi.* guiñar, pestañear

winner, *n.* vencedor, vencedora

winning, *adj.* atractivo; **winnings**, *n. pl.* ganancias, *f. pl.*

winsome, *adj.* simpático

winter, *n.* invierno, *m.*

winterize, *vt.* acondicionar para uso invernal

wipe, *vt.* secar, limpiar; borrar; **to wipe out**, obliterar; arruinar

wire, *n.* alambre, *m.*; *vt.* alambrar; *vi.* (coll.) telegrafiar, cablegrafiar

wireless, *n.* telegrafía inalámbrica, *f.*

wisdom, *n.* sabiduría, *f.*; juicio, *m.*

wisdom tooth, *n.* muela del juicio, muela cordal, *f.*

wise, *adj.* sabio, juicioso, prudente

wish, *vt.* desear, querer; *n.* anhelo, deseo, *m.*

wishful, *adj.* deseoso; **wishful thinking**, ilusiones, *f. pl.*

wisp, *n.* fragmento, *m.*; pizca, *f.*

wit, *n.* ingenio, *m.*, agudeza, sal, *f.*; **to wit**, a saber

witch, *n.* bruja, hechicera, *f.*

with, *prep.* con; por; de; a

withdraw, *vt.* quitar; retirar; *vi.* retirarse, apartarse

wither, *vi.* marchitarse

withhold, *vt.* detener, retener

within, *prep.* dentro, adentro

without, *prep.* sin; fuera, afuera; *adv.* exteriormente

withstand, *vt.* oponer, resistir

witness, *n.* testimonio, *m.*; testigo, *m.*; *vt.* atestiguar, testificar; *vi.* servir de testigo; presenciar

witty, *adj.* ingenioso

wives, *n. pl.* de **wife**, esposas, mujeres, *f. pl.*

wizard, *n.* hechicero, mago, *m.*

wobble, *vt.* bambolear

woe, *n.* dolor, *m.*, aflicción, *f.*

wolf, *n.* lobo, *m.*

wolves, *n. pl.* de **wolf**, lobos, *m. pl.*

woman, *n.* mujer, *f.*

womanhood, *n.* la mujer en general

womanly, *adj.* femenino

womb, *n.* útero, *m.*, matriz, *f.*

women, *n. pl.* de **woman**, mujeres, *f. pl.*

wonder, *n.* milagro, *m.*; prodigio, *m.*; maravilla, *f.*; *vi.* maravillarse (de)

wonderful, *adj.* maravilloso

won't, contracción de **will not**

woo, *vt.* cortejar

wood, *n.* madera, *f.*; leña, *f.*; **woods**, *pl.* bosque, *m.*

woodchuck, *n.* (zool.) marmota, *f.*

woodcutter, *n.* leñador, *m.*

wooded, *adj.* arbolado

wooden, *adj.* de madera

woodland, *n.* bosque, *m.*, selva, *f.*

woodman, *n.* cazador, *m.*; guardabosque, *m.*

woodpecker, *n.* (orn.) picamaderos, *m.*

wool, *n.* lana, *f.*

woolen, *adj.* de lana

word, *n.* palabra, voz, *f.*; *vt.* expresar

wore, *pretérito* del verbo **wear**

work, *vi.* trabajar; funcionar; *vt.* trabajar; *n.* trabajo, *m.*

worker, *n.* trabajador, obrero, *m.*

workingman, *n.* obrero, *m.*

workroom, *n.* taller, *m.*

works, *n.* fábrica, *f.*, taller, *m.*

workshop, *n.* taller, *m.*

world, *n.* mundo, *m.*

worldly, *adj.* mundano

world-wide, *adj.* mundial

worm, *n.* gusano, *m.*

worn, *p. p.* del verbo **wear**

worn-out, *adj.* rendido, gastado

worry, *n.* cuidado, *m.*; preocupación, ansia, *f.*; *vt.* molestar, atormentar; *vi.* preocuparse

worse, *adj.* y *adv.* peor

worship, *n.* culto, *m.*; adoración, *f.*; *vt.* adorar, venerar

worst, *adj.* pésimo, malísimo; *n.* lo peor, lo más malo

worth, *n.* valor, precio, *m.*; mérito, *m.*, valía, *f.*; *adj.* meritorio, digno; **to be worth while,** merecer o valer la pensa

worthless, *adj.* inservible, sin valor

would, *pret.* y *subj.* de **will,** para expresar deseo, condición, acción

wound, *n.* herida, llaga, *f.*; *vt.* herir

wove, *pretérito* del verbo **weave**

woven, *p. p.* del verbo **weave**

wrangle, *vi.* reñir, discutir

wrap, *vt.* arrollar; envolver; *n.* abrigo, *m.*

wrapping, *n.* envoltura, *f.*

wrath, *n.* ira, cólera, *f.*

wreath, *n.* corona, guirnalda *f.*

wreck, *n.* naufragio, *m.*; destrucción, *f.*; colisión, *f.*, *vt.* arruinar; destruir

wren, *n.* (orn.) reyezuelo, *m.*

wrench, *vt.* arrancar; torcer; *n.* torcedura (del pie, etc.); destornillador, *m.*; **monkey wrench,** llave inglesa, *f.*

wrest, *vt.* arrancar, quitar a fuerza

wrestle, *vi.* luchar a brazo partido; *n.* lucha, *f.*

wrestling, *n.* lucha, *f.*

wretch, *n.* infeliz, *m.*; infame, *m.*

wretched, *adj.* infeliz, mísero

wriggle, *vi.* retorcerse; menearse

wring, *vt.* exprimir, torcer

wringer, *n.* torcedor, *m.*

wrinkle, *n.* arruga, *f.*; *vt.* arrugar

wrist, *n.* muñeca (de la mano), *f.*; **wrist watch,** reloj de pulsera, *m.*

write, *vt.* escribir

writer, *n.* escritor, escritora, autor, autora; novelista, *m.* y *f.*

writhe, *vt.* torcer; *vi.* contorcerse,

written, *p. p.* del verbo **write**

wrong, *n.* perjuicio, *m.*; injusticia, *f.*; error, *m.*; *adj.* incorrecto, erróneo; injusto; falso; *vt.* hacer un mal, injuriar; agraviar; **wrongly,** *adv.* mal, injustamente; al revés

wrote, *pretérito* del verbo **write**

wt., weight, P. peso

X

Xmas, Christmas, Navidad, Pascua de Navidad

X ray, *n.* rayo X o Roentgen; **X-ray picture,** radiografía, *f.*; *vt.* examinar con rayos X, radiografiar

Y

yacht, *n.* (naut.) yate, *m.*

yam, n. (bot.) batata, f.; (Sp. Am.) camote, m.

yank, vt. (coll.) sacudir, tirar de golpe; n. abreviatura de **yankee**

yankee, n. y adj. yanqui, m. y f.

yard, n. corral, m.; patio, m.; yarda (medida), f.

yardstick, n. yarda de medir, f.

yarn, n. estambre, m.; (coll.) cuento exagerado, m.

yawn, vi. bostezar; n. bostezo, m.

yd., yard, yd., yarda

year, n. año, m.

yearly, adj. anual; adv. anualmente

yearn, vi. anhelar

yearning, n. anhelo, m.

yeast, n. levadura, f.

yell, vi. aullar, gritar; n. grito, aullido, m.

yellow, adj., n. amarllo, m.

yelp, vi. latir, ladrar; n. aullido, latido, m.

yes, adv. sí

yesterday, adv. ayer; **day before yesterday,** anteayer

yet, adv. todavía, aún; conj. sin embargo

yield, vt. y vi. producir, rendir

yoke, n. yugo, m.; yunta, f.

yolk, n. yema (de huevo) f.

you, pron. tú, usted; vosotros, vosotras, ustedes

young, adj. joven; **young man,** joven, m.; **young woman,** joven, señorita, f.

youngster, n. jovencito, jovencita, chiquillo, chiquilla, muchacho , muchacha

your, yours, pron. tu, su, vuestro, de ustedes, de vosotros

yourself, pron. usted mismo; **yourselves,** ustedes mismos

youth, n. juventud, adolescencia, f.; joven, m.

youthful, adj. juvenil

Z

zeal, n. celo, ardor, ahinco , m.

zebra, n. cebra, f.

zero, n. cero, m.

zest, n. gusto, fervor, m.

zigzag, n. zigzag, m.

zinc, n. (chem.) cinc, zinc, m.; **zinc chloride,** cloruro de cinc, m.

zipper, n. cremallera, f.; cierre automático, m.

zone, n. zona, f.

zoo, n. jardín zoológico, m.

zoological, adj. zoológico

zoology, n. zoología, f.

A Taste of Spain

Spain offers a variety of food and that echoes throughout the western world. In the Americas, the Spanish style is reflected in the traditional dishes of Central and South America, as well as those of the Caribbean. We thought you might enjoy a sampling, some familiar and some not so familiar, but all guaranteed to be delicious.

Chili con Queso

---

  2 tablespoons olive oil
  ½ cup onion, finely chopped
  1 tablespoon flour
  2 cups canned tomatoes, finely chopped, with liquid
  ½ cup green chilies, finely chopped
  1 teaspoon chili powder
  3 cups Monterey Jack cheese, shredded

---

1. Heat olive oil in a heavy skillet and sauté the onion until tender. Stir in flour and continue cooking for 2 minutes.
2. Stir in tomatoes, chilies, and chili powder. Simmer, stirring often, for 15 minutes or until the mixture has thickened somewhat.
3. Reduce the heat and add the cheese, stirring until melted. Serve warmed with fresh vegetables, tortilla chips, or bread for dipping.

Refried Beans

---

  4 tablespoons bacon fat
  2 tablespoons onions, finely chopped
  2 cups kidney or pinto beans, cooked & drained
  Salt

---

1. Heat the fat in a heavy skillet and sauté the onion just until soft.
2. Add beans to the pan and cook while mashing with a fork until all of the fat is absorbed and the beans are fairly dry.
3. Salt to taste.

NOTES: Flavor the beans with a bit of tomato paste, hot chili powder, or salsa.

—Spread refried beans over tortillas, or thin with a bit of broth to serve as a dip.

Party Quesadillas

*This simplified version of the traditional Mexican preparation,
sort of a cross between a quesadilla and a tostada, is a great
way to add variety to a buffet or snack table.*

½ cup mayonnaise
¼ cup salsa
2½ cups cheese, shredded
8 10-inch flour tortillas
Olive oil

---

1. Combine mayonnaise, salsa, and cheese.
2. Spread cheese mixture over 4 tortillas and cover with
   remaining 4 tortillas.
3. Brush tops with olive oil and brown under the broiler for
   about 1 minute. Turn, brush with olive oil, and brown the
   other side.
4. Cut into wedges and serve.

NOTES: Use any cheese that melts well such as Jack,
Muenster, or cheddar.

For variety, garnish each serving with a thin avocado slice
or spread with guacamole.

—Spread a thin layer of refried beans over the second
tortilla before putting the sandwich together.

Easy Salsa

---

1 cup canned tomatoes, diced or crushed
¼ cup onions, finely chopped
1 small hot red or green pepper, minced
½ teaspoon coriander
1 clove garlic, minced
Pinch of cloves
Salt & pepper

Combine all measured ingredients well. Season with salt and
pepper to taste. Refrigerate 1 to 2 hours to blend flavors.
Serve with chips for dipping or over cold meat, poultry, or
fish.

Chicken with Salsa

Serves 4

1 or 2 large chicken breasts, about 2 pounds
2 bay leaves
Pinch of thyme
¼ cup parsley, chopped

1. Place chicken breasts in a skillet with about ½ inch of water containing 1 bay leaf and a pinch of thyme. Bring water to a boil; reduce heat and simmer covered for 20 to 30 minutes or until cooked through. Set aside to cool.
2. While chicken cooks, prepare *Easy Salsa*.
3. Remove skin from chicken and carefully cut the flesh into ¼-inch-thick slices. Overlap slices on a serving platter or on individual plates and spread salsa over. Sprinkle with parsley. Serve cold.

For variety, green olives may be added to the sauce.

Spanish Chicken

Serves 4

2 tablespoons olive oil
2½ to 3 pound chicken, cut into serving pieces
1½ cups onions, sliced
¾ cup green peppers, cut into strips
½ cup lean smoked ham, finely chopped
1 teaspoon garlic, minced
4 cups tomatoes, fresh or canned, peeled, seeded, & finely chopped
Salt & pepper
12 each black & green olives, sliced

1. Heat 1 tablespoon olive oil in a heavy skillet and brown chicken lightly on all sides, adding more oil if needed. Remove chicken from the pan and set aside.
2. Add onion, pepper, ham, and garlic to the pan and sauté until the vegetables are barely soft.
3. Add tomatoes to the pan and bring to a boil.
4. Return chicken to the pan, turning to coat with sauce. Cook for 30 minutes, or until chicken is cooked through.
5. Remove chicken from the pan and boil until the sauce has thickened. Season to taste with salt and pepper. Stir in the olives, and serve.

Chicken with Green Chilies

¼ cup canned green chili peppers
1 cup onion, chopped
1 teaspoon garlic, crushed
¾ cup chicken broth
1 tablespoon vinegar
1 teaspoon sugar
½ teaspoon coriander seeds, finely ground
¼ teaspoon cinnamon, finely ground
¼ teaspoon cloves, finely ground
1 cup tomatoes, crushed or diced, drained
2 tablespoons olive oil
1 chicken, about 3 pounds, cut into serving pieces
Salt & pepper

1. In a blender, purée the chili peppers, onion, and garlic with the chicken broth or force the ingredients through a food mill and a strainer.
2. In a large bowl, combine purée with the vinegar, sugar, coriander, cinnamon, cloves and tomatoes; set aside.
3. Have ready a baking dish large enough to hold the chicken in one layer. In a heavy skillet, heat the olive oil and sauté the chicken a few pieces at a time, turning to brown well on all sides. As chicken pieces are ready, dip them in the bowl to coat with sauce and place them in the baking dish.
4. Pour remaining sauce over the chicken and bake at 350° for about 1 hour, or until chicken is cooked through. About 45 minutes into the baking, baste chicken parts with the sauce or turn them over.
5. When chicken is done, remove to a serving platter. Skim off fat and boil liquid in a sauce pan to reduce it. Serve over the chicken.

Skimming fat from pan juices is easier if the liquid is poured into a heatproof container and placed in the freezer. After a few minutes, fat will rise to the top. If time permits, chill for about 30 minutes and the fat will solidify.

Paella
A classic Spanish dish.

Serves 8

¼ cup olive oil
1 frying chicken, cut up, or about 3 pounds of chicken parts
½ cup onion, sliced or chopped
2 cloves garlic, minced
½ pound tomatoes, peeled, fresh or canned
2 cups rice, uncooked
1 teaspoon saffron dissolved in 4 cups water
Salt & pepper
1 cup peas, fresh or frozen
1 sweet red pepper, cut into strips
¼ pound medium shrimp, shelled
8 each clams and mussels in the shell

---

1. In a large skillet or kettle, heat the olive oil and brown the chicken on all sides.

2. Add the onion and continue to cook while stirring until the onion is transparent.

3. Add garlic, tomatoes, rice, saffron, and water. Stir to combine. Add salt and pepper to taste. Cover and cook for 15 minutes over low heat.

4. Stir the pot from top to bottom to prevent rice from browning. Arrange peas and red pepper strips over the top of the rice and cook for 10 more minutes.
    Note: If canned peas are used, add them with the seafood.

5. Arrange shrimp, clams, and mussels on top of the rice. Cover and cook for 5 to 10 minutes, or until the shellfish open. Serve in the skillet or kettle and enjoy!
    Note: Check the rice to be sure that it does not overcook. If the rice is already tender, steam the seafood in a separate pot with a small amount of water. If rice is very firm, cook for about 5 minutes longer before adding seafood.

NOTE: The traditional paella pan is a large covered skillet with metal handles on two sides, somewhat like a heavy wok with a flat bottom, although an iron kettle also serves very well.

Cocido (Spanish Stew)

Another classic, not so well known as paella, but one that qualifies as our all-time favorite. Don't let the long list of ingredients daunt you. Works great in a crock pot as well, using canned chick peas—merely combine all the ingredients and cook on low for several hours.

Serves 4

1 pound dried chick peas
1 pound lean beef, cut into 1-inch cubes
1 cup onion, chopped
1 cup fresh tomato, diced
¼ cup green pepper, chopped
1 clove garlic, minced
¼ pound Canadian bacon, diced
½ pound pumpkin, cut into 1-inch cubes
½ cup carrots, sliced thick
2 Spanish or Italian sausages, sliced thick
1 pound potatoes, peeled & cubed
½ pound green beans, cut in 1-inch pieces
½ teaspoon cumin
Salt & pepper

1. Soak chick peas overnight or boil for 2 minutes, then cover and allow to rest for 1 hour.

2. Add the beef, onion, tomatoes, green pepper, garlic, and Canadian bacon to the pot with the beans. Pour in sufficient water to cover and simmer with the pot covered, until the chick peas are tender, about 1 hour. If necessary, add more water as the beans cook.

3. Stir in the pumpkin, carrots, sausage, potatoes, green beans, and cumin. Cook for an additional 30 minutes, or until vegetables are tender.

4. Correct the seasoning and serve.

Tex-Mex Chili

---

3 thin strips bacon
1½ pounds lean beef, chuck or round, diced; or 1½
   pounds lean ground beef
1 cup onion, minced
2 cups tomatoes, canned, crushed or diced, with juice
1 bay leaf
½ teaspoon each cinnamon & salt
1 tablespoon cumin
3 tablespoons chili powder, or to taste

---

1. Over low heat in a large skillet, fry bacon until crisp and set aside.

2. In fat remaining in the pan, sauté beef, shaking the pan to brown on all sides. Add onion and continue cooking until lightly colored.

3. Crumble the bacon and return to the pan with tomato, bay leaf, cinnamon, salt, cumin, and chili powder. Cover and simmer for 1 hour.

4. Correct seasoning and serve with tortillas or crackers, chopped onion, and shredded cheese.

NOTES: If ground meat is used, brown in a small amount of oil, then pour off the rendered fat before combining with bacon fat and sautéed onions.

—**Serve** chili over beans, spaghetti, or rice.

—**Beans can be cooked with the chili**—add 3 to 4 cups of cooked kidney, navy, or pinto beans for the final 30 minutes of cooking.

—**For a spicier dish,** add chopped jalapeños or pepper sauce.

—**If chili is too thick,** stir in a little water and cook for 5 to 10 minutes to blend flavors.

HEALTH NOTE: 2 tablespoons olive oil can be substituted for the bacon and bacon fat.

For variety, use a mixture of beef and pork.

—Minced green peppers can be sautéed with the onions.

—A clove of garlic, minced, can be added to the pan with the tomatoes and beans.

Arroz con Pollo (Chicken with Rice)

¼ cup olive oil
2½ to 3 pound chicken, cut into serving pieces
1 cup rice, uncooked
¼ cup onion, finely chopped
1 clove garlic, minced
2 cups canned tomatoes, diced, with liquid
½ teaspoon oregano
Dash of hot sauce
Salt & pepper
1 cup canned peas or frozen & cooked peas

1. Heat olive oil in a large, heavy skillet and brown chicken pieces on all sides. Remove chicken and set aside.

2. In the same pan, heat rice, onion, and garlic, stirring until onion is softened and the rice takes on a bit of color.

3. Return the chicken to the pan with tomatoes, oregano, hot sauce, and 1 cup water. Cover and simmer gently for 20 minutes or just until rice is soft, chicken is cooked through and most of the liquid has been absorbed.

4. Season with salt and pepper to taste and carefully mix in the peas. Continue cooking just to heat through.

Turkey Española

Serves 4

½ pound loose sausage, preferable Spanish
1 cup rice, uncooked
1 cup tomatoes, crushed or diced
¼ teaspoon saffron
2 cups chicken broth
1½ cups cooked turkey, diced
½ cup green peppers, cut into thin strips
¼ cup onion, finely chopped
½ teaspoon ground cumin
1 clove garlic, minced
2 tablespoons pimientos, chopped

more...

1. Brown the sausage in a large heavy skillet.
2. Add rice and cook until the rice takes on a bit of color.
3. Add tomatoes and cook for 5 minutes.
4. Dissolve saffron in the then add to the pan with turkey, peppers, onion, cumin, and garlic. Cook, covered, over low heat for 40 minutes or until rice is tender. Stir in pimientos and continue cooking just to heat through.

Pork Mexicaine

Serves 4

1 cup flat beer
2 tablespoons soy sauce
2 tablespoons brown sugar
1 tablespoon dry mustard
2 cloves garlic, minced
Hot pepper sauce or chili peppers
Salt & pepper
1½ pounds lean pork, sliced or cubed
1 fresh lime

1. Combine the beer, soy sauce, sugar, mustard, garlic, and hot sauce or peppers to taste in a saucepan. Heat briefly and stir just to combine flavors. Season with salt and pepper to taste. Set aside to cool.
2. Cover meat with the marinade and refrigerate overnight, stirring occasionally.
3. Thread meat on skewers or place loose in a broiler pan. Broil about 4 inches from the heat, basting often with the marinade, for 15 minutes or until the meat is cooked through.
4. Sprinkle with lime juice and serve.

NOTE: If wooden skewer are used, soak them in water for at least an hour ahead of time.

Chili Bake

1 pound lean ground beef
2 thin strips bacon
½ cup onion, minced
¼ cup green pepper, minced
¾ cup tomatoes, canned, crushed, with juice
¼ teaspoon each cinnamon, allspice, & salt
2 teaspoons chili powder, or to taste
Tortilla chips, about 5 ounces
½ cup cheddar cheese, shredded

1. In a large skillet, brown beef using a little oil if necessary. Drain off oil and set beef aside.

2. Over low heat in the same skillet, fry bacon until crisp and set aside.

3. Sauté onion and pepper in bacon grease, just until soft. Crumble bacon and return to pan with meat, tomato, cinnamon, allspice, salt, and chili powder. Simmer for about 1 hour covered.

4. In an oven dish, place alternating layers of chips and chili, beginning with chips and ending with chili. Cover with cheese and bake at 350° for 20 to 30 minutes.

Black Bean Soup

1 pound black beans
1 small onion, finely chopped
¼ cup celery, finely chopped
4 whole cloves
¼ pound pork or ham, finely chopped
2 tablespoons sherry
4 teaspoons lemon juice
1 teaspoon Worcestershire sauce
Pinch of sugar
Salt & pepper

1. Rinse beans in several changes of water until liquid runs clear. Cover with fresh water, boil for 2 minutes, and allow to stand, covered, for 2 hours. Add onion, celery, cloves, and meat. Cook for 2 hours, or until beans are soft, adding more water from time to time, if necessary.

more...

2. Press through a sieve or food processor, then add sherry, lemon juice, Worcestershire, and sugar.

3. Heat through and correct seasoning with salt and pepper.

4. Serve garnished with thinly sliced lemon, chopped hard cooked eggs, or fresh chopped onion.

Easy Mexican Skillet

1 pound bulk sausage
¼ cup onion, finely chopped
½ cup pepper, finely chopped
1 cup uncooked macaroni
2 tablespoons sugar
1 teaspoon salt
1 teaspoon chili powder
1 pound can tomatoes
8 ounce can tomato sauce
½ cup sour cream
Parmesan cheese

1. In a heavy skillet, lightly brown sausage, adding a little oil if necessary.

2. Pour off excess fat; add onion and pepper. Cook slowly until vegetables are tender.

3. Add uncooked macaroni, sugar, salt, chili powder, tomatoes with liquid, and tomato sauce. Cover and simmer 20 to 30 minutes. Add water, a little at a time, if needed.

4. Stir in sour cream. Heat through, taking care not to boil the mixture after adding sour cream. Serve sprinkled with Parmesan cheese.

Tex-Mex Loaf

1 tablespoon olive oil
2 tablespoons onion, chopped
2 tablespoons green pepper, chopped
1 pound ground beef
1 egg, lightly beaten with ¼ cup milk
1 cup cracker crumbs
2 tablespoons jalapeño peppers, chopped
1 teaspoon salt
¼ teaspoon pepper

1. Heat oil in a heavy skillet. Lightly sauté the onion and green pepper. Drain well.

2. Lightly mix the sautéed onion and pepper with ground beef, egg mixture, cracker crumbs, jalapeños, salt, and pepper.

3. Form the mixture into a loaf and place in a lightly greased baking pan. Bake for about 40 minutes in a 350° oven.

4. If loaf becomes dry, baste with a bit of broth, or add a little water to the bottom of the pan and cover with foil.

5. Serve sliced with *Picante Sauce* (recipe follows).

NOTES: The heat from jalapeño peppers varies somewhat based on age, where they were grown, etc. Adjust the quantity in the recipe depending on their strength and your personal taste. Or substitute other hot peppers for the jalapeños.

—The loaf can be brushed with a bit of ketchup, chili sauce, barbecue sauce, or tomato sauce about 10 minutes before baking is finished.

For variety, add finely chopped celery to the mixture.

—Include tomato in the mixture, fresh or canned, roughly chopped and well-drained.

—Prepared mustard, horseradish, or Worcestershire sauce may be added to the meat.

—Whole stuffed green olives will add flavor and color to the loaf as well.

Picante Sauce

1 tablespoon olive oil
¼ cup onion, finely chopped
¼ cup green pepper, finely chopped
2 cloves garlic, minced
½ teaspoon chili powder
1 tablespoon vinegar
1 cup canned tomato pieces
Salt & pepper to taste

1. Heat olive oil in a small saucepan and lightly sauté onion and green pepper.

2. Add remaining ingredients, bring to a boil, and allow to simmer for about 20 minutes or until the sauce has thickened a bit.

3. This sauce is best if allowed to rest for a few hours or overnight in the refrigerator.

NOTE: Adjust the amount of garlic, chili powder, and vinegar to suit your personal taste.

—*Picante Sauce* is suitable for serving hot or cold with meat, poultry, or fish.

Cuban Style Black Beans & Rice

Serves 4 to 6

1½ cups black beans
4 slices bacon, finely chopped & fried
1 clove garlic, crushed
1 small onion, finely chopped
1 teaspoon chili powder
Salt
Cayenne pepper
Meat stock or broth
2 cups cooked rice

1. Wash beans, cover with 5 cups water. Soak overnight (or bring to boil, boil 2 minutes, cover and let stand 1 hour). Boil beans in salted water until tender. Drain. Add bacon, garlic and onion. Season with chili powder, salt, cayenne. Add broth to cover beans and simmer until beans fall apart.

2. A little and make thick sauce. Pour over rice.

Arroz Doce (Sweet Rice)

Serves 4

1 cup cooked rice
¼ cup milk
8 ounces sweetened condensed milk
¼ cup sugar

1. Place cooked rice and milk in a small saucepan and warm over low heat.

2. In a small skillet carmelize the sugar by heating it over low heat while stirring constantly until golden brown. Pour the caramel over the rice and mix well. Serve warm.